ATTITUDES
AND
OPINIONS

ATTITUDES AND OPINIONS

Third Edition

By

Stuart Oskamp
Claremont Graduate University

P. Wesley Schultz
California State University, San Marcos

Psychology Press
Taylor & Francis Group

NEW YORK AND LONDON

First published 2005 by Lawrence Erlbaum Associates, Inc.

Published 2014 by Psychology Press
711 Third Avenue, New York, NY 10017

and by Psychology Press
27 Church Road, Hove, East Sussex, BN3 2FA

First issued in paperback 2014

Psychology Press is an imprint of the Taylor & Francis Group, an informa business

Copyright © 2005 by Lawrence Erlbaum Associates, Inc.

Library of Congress Cataloging-in-Publication Data

Oskamp, Stuart.
    Attitudes and opinions / by Stuart Oskamp, P. Wesley Schultz.—3rd ed.
        p.   cm.
    Includes bibliographical references and index.
    ISBN 978-0-8058-4769-7 (casebound : alk. paper)
        1. Public opinion.   2. Attitude (Psychology)   3.Public opinion polls.   I. Schultz, P. Wesley.
    II. Title.

    HM261.O75   2004
    303.3'8—dc22   2004018654

    ISBN-13:978-0-8058-4769-7 (hbk)
    ISBN-13:978-1-138-00391-0 (pbk)

We dedicate this book, with gratitude, to the mentors who have especially influenced our lives. Among many others, they include Lee Winder, Bill Stone, Bernard McGrane, Jack Hilgard, Charles Haner, Lew Goldberg, Leon Festinger, Dale Berger, and Al Bandura.

Contents

Preface

These are exciting times for attitude researchers, for recent years have seen notable advances in both topics and methods involved in studying attitudes. New measurement approaches have emerged, new models for the structure and organization of attitudes have been proposed, and new research findings about attitude formation, attitude change, and attitude-behavior relationships have re-invigorated the field. The widespread availability of desktop computing technology, the rise of the Internet, and increasingly sophisticated approaches to sampling and polling have stimulated a new generation of attitude scholars. Public opinion measures have become widely used by both public and private organizations, and new polls on a wide range of topics appear daily in the mass media.

Attitudes and opinions are crucial aspects of people's lives, and they influence the affairs of groups, organizations, and nations. They are the general area that has been most studied by social psychologists over the years, and yet they often receive skimpy coverage in psychology textbooks. Attitudes and opinions are also central to the concerns of other academic disciplines, including sociologists, political scientists, communications researchers, and many other social scientists. Methodologically, they have been studied by descriptive researchers, measurement specialists, public opinion pollers, theorists, and experimentalists.

The first main goal of this book is *breadth of coverage*, which includes the key contributions and concerns of all these fields and approaches, and thus helps to bridge the gaps between them. We have tried to avoid the one-sided emphasis of many texts, which may concentrate solely on the area of attitude change, or attitude theories, or attitude measurement. The book covers those topics in some depth, but it also includes major sections on the structure and functions of attitudes, the nature of public opinion, public opinion polling, attitude formation, communication of attitudes and opinions, attitude-behavior relationships, and the content of public opinion on the most socially important topics. Among the key themes of the volume are the usefulness of attitudes in our everyday lives, persuasion processes that lead to attitude change, and the social impact and policy implications of attitudes and opinions.

A second major aim of this book is *relevance to people's lives* and key concerns. It stresses principles and research findings on topics that are salient and recurrent to citizens today. In particular, Part Two of the volume covers many important contemporary social issues, including political attitudes and voting behavior, international attitudes and terrorism, racism and prejudice, sexism and gender roles, and attitudes about environmental issues.

Throughout the text we have taken a broad and interdisciplinary perspective. Although the book is intended primarily for upper-division or graduate-level psychology courses in Attitudes, it is also appropriate for courses in Survey Research, Public Opinion, Persuasion, or similar courses in political science, sociology, or communication departments. We have tried to write a scholarly, yet engaging, text. To aid understanding, we have included a number of learning aids, such as a clear organizational structure indicated by topic headings, summaries at the end of each chapter, and important terms being highlighted in bold face throughout. We have also aimed to meet the needs of advanced students for a scholarly reference work by including a very large number of references to the research literature (more than 2,000). Our goal was to be rigorous in approach, but also interesting in both content and style.

In writing the third edition of this book, we have tried to capture some of the excitement and energy of modern attitude research, while at the same time maintaining scientific objectivity. We have sought to integrate many of the new, cutting-edge findings with the tried-and-true methods and theories that have emerged from nearly 100 years of psychological research. New ideas and approaches are taking attitude research in new directions. As social science research attempts to build on the cognitive revolution, and to link cognition and affect, the construct of *attitude* stands at the interface.

All the chapters in the book have been completely revised, and we have added two entirely new chapters, covering implicit attitudes and environmental attitudes. All public opinion poll data have been updated with the most recent findings, and time trends in attitudes about many issues have been extended. We have expanded and updated the section on international attitudes to reflect the terrorist attacks of September 11, 2001, and the subsequent invasions of Afghanistan and Iraq.

ACKNOWLEDGMENTS

The revision of this book reflects the contributions (both direct and indirect) of many individuals. Our academic homes, Claremont Graduate University, and California State University, San Marcos, have provided intellectually stimulating environments in which to work. Discussions and presentations by colleagues at professional meetings have proven invaluable in identifying many in-press or in-progress studies. These meetings include those of the Society for the Psychological Study of Social Issues (SPSSI), the Society for Experimental Social Psychology (SESP), and the Society for Personality and Social Psychology (SPSP). Our appreciation goes to the many colleagues who read and commented on chapters as they were being revised: Chris Aberson, Riley Dunlap, Tony Greenwald, Florian Kaiser, and Cees Midden. A great many students helped in identifying materials, preparing and organizing materials, and assisting in all stages of manuscript preparation—particularly Christine Jarvis, Dulce Contreras, and Jessica Nolan. We are grateful to the reviewers of this edition, and of previous editions, whose suggestions and criticisms helped to make this a better book. They include: Icek Aizen, University of Massachusetts; Dolores Albarracin, University of Florida; Eugene Borgida, University of Minnesota; Blair Johnson, University of Connecticut; and James Olson, University of Western Ontario. We also thank Debra Riegert and her staff at Lawrence Erlbaum Associates for their direction and coordination of the project.

And most importantly, we thank our wives and children, for inspiring us to write and for enabling us to do so.

—*Stuart Oskamp*
Claremont, California
—*P. Wesley Schultz*
San Marcos, California

ATTITUDES
AND
OPINIONS

Approaches to Studying
Attitudes and Opinions

1

Background: History and Concepts

Attitude. It's the current buzzword. It's also one of the most important factors of success, according to more than 1,000 top- and middle-level executives of 13 major American corporations....Your attitude can make or break your career.
—Allan Cox, 1983.

What are laws but the expressions of the opinion of some class, which has power over the rest of the community? By what was the world ever governed but by the opinion of some person or persons? By what else can it ever be governed?
—Thomas B. Macaulay, 1830.

As these quotations illustrate, attitudes and opinions are important. They can help people, they can hurt people, they have influenced the course of history. Novelists and poets describe them, historians weigh and assess them, average citizens explain people's behavior in terms of their attitudes, politicians attempt to understand and shape public opinion. Consequently social psychologists, too, have long had a great interest in attitudes and opinions and have devised many ways of studying them. This book describes these research methods, summarizes the important findings on major aspects of attitudes and opinions, and tries to clarify the many current theories and controversies in the field.

WHY STUDY ATTITUDES?

One long-standing controversy has been whether to study attitudes or behavior. This debate goes back to the early years of social psychology, when it was just beginning to be differentiated from other areas of psychology and sociology. For instance, the well-known sociologist Read Bain (1928, p. 940) wrote, "The development of sociology as a natural science has been hindered by ... too much attention to subjective factors, such as ... attitudes." Behaviorists, following the lead of psychologists such as B. F. Skinner (1957), have generally tried to avoid use of "mentalistic concepts" like attitude, and to study observable behavior instead.

However, the majority view among social psychologists was best expressed in a landmark handbook chapter by Gordon Allport, one of the founders of the field (see Box 1–1). Writing in 1935, he stressed the central importance of attitudes:

The concept of attitude is probably the most distinctive and indispensable concept in contemporary American social psychology.... This useful, one might almost say peaceful, concept has been so widely adopted that it has virtually established itself as the keystone in the edifice of American social psychology. (p. 798)

3

*Photograph courtesy of
Harvard University News Office.
Reprinted by permission.*

Box 1–1 GORDON ALLPORT, *Champion of Attitudes*

Gordon Allport (1897–1967) was one of the most famous and beloved social psychologists of his day. He received his B.A., M.A., and Ph.D. from Harvard and taught there continuously from 1930 until his death. He served as chairman of Harvard's psychology department, president of the American Psychological Association, editor of the major journal in social psychology for 12 years, and was a member of numerous national and international committees.

Allport's interests within social psychology were broad. He wrote several major textbooks on personality, as well as The Psychology of Rumor, The Nature of Prejudice, The Psychology of Radio, *books on religion, expressive movement, and research methods, and also over 200 articles. An authority on attitudes, he wrote classic chapters covering that topic in three successive editions of the* Handbook of Social Psychology *(1935, 1954, 1968), and his final chapter was reprinted in the 1985* Handbook.

Although there have been some periods since then when research in other areas of social psychology, such as small-group dynamics, has somewhat overshadowed the amount of work on attitudes, by and large the study of attitudes and related topics has remained dominant (McGuire, 1985). In their research review, Petty and Wegener (1998) declared, "Although it has become cliche to say that the attitude construct is the most indispensable construct in contemporary social psychology, this statement appears as true today as when G. W. Allport (1935) initially wrote it" (p. 323). Other reviews of the field agree that the high interest in attitude research seems likely to continue in the foreseeable future (Tesser & Shaffer, 1990; Eagly & Chaiken, 1993, 1998; Olson & Zanna, 1993; Petty, Wegener, & Fabrigar, 1997; Ajzen, 2001).

The word *attitude* is widely used in everyday speech to describe a person or explain behavior; for instance, "She has a very good attitude toward her work." People often speak of someone's attitude as the cause of his or her actions toward another person or an object; for example, "Her hostile attitude was shown in everything she did." Similarly, in his 1935 review, Allport concluded that the concept of attitudes was "bearing most of the descriptive and explanatory burdens of social psychology" (p. 804).

Why is attitude such a popular and useful concept'? We can point to several reasons:

1. "Attitude" is a *shorthand* term. A single attitude (e.g., love for one's family) can summarize many different behaviors (spending time with them, kissing them, comforting them, agreeing with them, doing things for them).

2. An attitude can be considered the *cause* of a person's behavior toward another person or an object.

3. The concept of attitude helps to explain the *consistency* of a person's behavior, for a single attitude may underlie many different actions. (In turn, Allport said, the consistency of individual behavior helps to explain the stability of society.)

4. Attitudes are *important in their own right*, regardless of their relation to a person's behavior. Your attitudes toward various individuals, institutions, and social issues (e.g., a political party, the church, capital punishment, the President of the United States) reflect the way you perceive the world around you, and they are worth studying for their own sake.

5. The concept of attitude is relatively *neutral and acceptable* to many theoretical schools of thought. For instance, it bridges the controversy between heredity and environment, for both instinct and learning can be involved in the formation of attitudes. It is broad enough to include the operation of unconscious determinants and the dynamic interplay of conflicting motives, which have been stressed by Freud and other psychoanalysts. At the same time it provides a topic of common interest to theorists as diverse as phenomenologists, behaviorists, and cognitive psychologists.

6. Attitude is an *interdisciplinary* concept. Not just psychologists but also sociologists, political scientists, communication researchers, and anthropologists all study attitudes. In particular, the subarea of public opinion—the shared attitudes of many members of a society—is of great interest to students of politics, public affairs, and communication.

Five Ways of Studying Attitudes

Given the usefulness of the term *attitudes*, it is not surprising that it has attracted a great deal of research attention. Five different ways of studying attitudes and opinions have typified most of the research studies in the area. Surprisingly, there has been very little overlap or interaction between the adherents of these five approaches, so that in most cases their work has been carried on with little cross-fertilization from the methods or findings of the other groups of researchers. The five different approaches are as follows:

Description.   Attitude describers typically study the views held by a single interesting group of people (for instance, recent immigrants, or state legislators). Or they may compare the opinions of two or more groups (for example, the attitudes of white-collar workers versus those of blue-collar workers on the topic of labor unions). To some extent they may overlap with the next two groups of researchers (the measurers and the pollers), but the describers are usually less concerned with sophisticated quantification than are the measurers and less concerned with representative sampling than are the pollers. They are also less interested in understanding and explaining the underlying bases for attitudes than are the theorists and experimenters.

Measurement.   Attitude measurers have developed many highly sophisticated methods for quantifying and scaling attitudes. The best-known methods of building attitude scales are discussed in Chapter 3. It is surprising, but true, that public opinion pollers and attitude experimenters have made very little use of these sophisticated measurement methods, and attitude describers have made only a little more use of them.

Polls.   Public opinion pollers are generally concerned with the attitudes on important social issues held by very large groups of people (for instance, the voting intentions of all registered voters of a state, or the opinions about crime and punishment held by adult citizens). The procedures and problems of public opinion polling are discussed in Chapter 6. At their best, polls are careful to *sample* systematically or randomly (rather than haphazardly) from the total population so that their results will be *representative* of the opinions of the total population.

Theories.   Attitude theorists are primarily concerned with explaining the basic nature of attitudes, how attitudes are formed, and how they can be changed. In most cases they have not been concerned with the precise measurement of attitudes nor with their content, socially important or not. However, because they need to demonstrate the correctness of their theories through experimental evidence, there has been more overlap and interaction between the theorists and the experimenters than between any of the other groups. Chapters 10 and 11 discuss both theories and research on attitude change.

Experiments.   By definition, experiments involve manipulating a situation so as to create two or more different levels of the independent variable (for instance, two different kinds of persuasive message) and observing their effect on the dependent variable. Attitude experimenters have concentrated on investigating the factors that can produce attitude *change* and on testing the hypotheses of the attitude theorists. They have usually been relatively unconcerned with sophisticated measurement methods, and they generally choose to experiment on attitude topics of little importance or relevance to their subjects, for such attitudes can more easily be changed in a short-term laboratory situation. However, there have also been a number of experiments done on topics of greater social importance, such as basic personal values, racial attitudes, or health-care practices.

Themes of This Book

There are a number of general themes that recur throughout this book and help to organize the information in the various content areas. The major ones are these:

- Social cognitive processes. **Social cognition** refers to our thought processes about people and social situations. It includes the ways we gather social information, organize it, and interpret it. Thus social cognition processes are important in determining the way our attitudes and opinions are formed, strengthened, and changed over the course of time.
- Functions of attitudes and opinions. Our attitudes and opinions are *useful* to us. They are convenient aids to our thinking, decision-making, and actions in innumerable social situations. They summarize and organize our thoughts and reactions to other people, situations, objects, and ideas.
- Attitude measurement and research methods. Many specialized ways of measuring attitudes and opinions have been developed, and distinctive research methods have also been established, particularly in the areas of survey research and attitude change.
- Different types of attitudes. Explicitly stated attitudes have been the type most often studied. However, in recent years, much research has been focused on implicit attitudes, which can be inferred from individuals' response times or physiological responses when they are presented with crucial stimuli.
- Attitude formation and transmission. The processes by which attitudes and opinions are formed are important topics in many sections of this volume, as are the ways that attitudes and opinions are communicated, both through the mass media and through personal communication.
- Persuasion and attitude change. This is one of the areas most heavily studied by social psychologists, so portions of the immense research literature are discussed at many points in the text.
- Attitude–behavior relationships. As mentioned earlier, the choice of attitudes versus behavior as a major focus of study has long been a controversy in social psychology, and the question of how closely people's attitudes and behavior are related is a key

issue in the field—one that is crucial in attempts to predict, understand, or change people's behavior.

- Social impact and policy implications of attitudes and opinions. This theme shows up at many points, in discussions of the structure of public opinion and of how (if at all) public opinion influences public policy or is influenced by it.

DEFINITIONS OF "ATTITUDE"

So far we have been using the term "attitude" without defining it. Because it is a common term in the English language, every reader will probably have a notion of its meaning. Unfortunately, however, there may be relatively little overlap between your notion and that of other readers. Indeed, there has sometimes been little overlap between the definitions of attitude suggested by different social scientists.

At the outset, we must emphasize that scientific usage of the term attitude is different from some current colloquial or slang meanings of the word. Social scientists would agree that everyone has many attitudes, on many different topics. Therefore, they do not use the phrase "having an attitude" with the current slang meaning of being pugnacious or sullenly deviant. Nor do they use the term to refer to broader personality characteristics, such as those implied in the colloquial phrase "a bad attitude" (Eagly & Chaiken, 1993, p. 9).

Originally the term "attitude" referred to a person's bodily position or posture, and it is still sometimes used in this way—for instance, "He sat slumped in an attitude of dejection." There is a marvelous example in Gilbert and Sullivan's operetta *H.M.S. Pinafore*, in which the proper stance for a British tar is described (Gilbert, 1932, p. 31—see Figure 1–1):

His foot should stamp and his throat should growl,
His hair should twirl and his face should scowl;
His eyes should flash and his breast protrude,
And this should be his customary attitude.

FIGURE 1–1   A British tar.

Box 1–2 Sample Definitions of "Attitude"

COMPREHENSIVE—An attitude is a mental or neural state of readiness, organized through experience, exerting a directive or dynamic influence upon the individual's response to all objects and situations with which it is related. (G. Allport, 1935, p. 810)
SIMPLE—Attitudes are likes and dislikes. (Bem, 1970, p. 14)
EMPHASIS ON EVALUATION—Attitude is a psychological tendency that is expressed by evaluating a particular entity with some degree of favor or disfavor. (Eagly & Chaiken, 1993, p. 1)
EMPHASIS ON LEARNING AND CONSISTENCY—An attitude is a learned predisposition to respond in a consistently favorable or unfavorable manner with respect to a given object. (Fishbein & Ajzen, 1975, p. 6)

In social science, however, the term has come to mean a "posture of the mind," rather than of the body. In his careful review, Allport (1935) cited many definitions with varying emphases and concluded with a comprehensive definition of his own. The aspects stressed in various early definitions include attitude as a mental set or disposition, attitude as a readiness to respond, the physiological basis of attitudes, their permanence, their learned nature, and their evaluative character. Since Allport's time, most definitions have followed his lead and have become rather similar in their main emphases, though differing in some details. Box 1–2 presents Allport's comprehensive definition together with a representative selection of more recent delineations of the concept of attitude. Although Allport's definition may seem unduly complex, careful thought will show that each of its phrases makes a specific and important contribution to understanding the concept, as McGuire (1969, pp. 142–149) explained in detail.

The central feature of most definitions of attitude, according to Allport, is the idea of **readiness for response**. That is, an attitude is not behavior, not something that a person does; rather it is a preparation for behavior, a predisposition to respond in a particular way to the attitude object. The term **attitude object** is used to include things, people, places, ideas, actions, or situations, either singular or plural. For instance, it could be a group of people (e.g., teenagers), an inanimate object (e.g., the city park), an action (e.g., drinking beer), an abstract concept (e.g., civil rights), or an idea linking several concepts (e.g., rights of teenagers to drink beer in the city park).

Another point stressed by Allport is the **motivating** or driving force of attitudes. That is, attitudes are not just a passive result of past experience. Instead they have two active functions, described by Allport as "exerting a directive or dynamic influence." "Dynamic" indicates that they impel or motivate behavior—that is, they can be what behaviorists or psychoanalysts call "drives." "Directive" indicates that attitudes guide the form and manner of behavior into particular channels, encouraging some actions and deterring others.

An important aspect of many attitudes is their **relatively enduring** nature, though that does not hold true for all attitudes. This stability was illustrated by a study of attitudes toward nuclear power following the 1986 nuclear reactor meltdown at Chernobyl in the U.S.S.R. On five occasions, from 1986 to 1988, Midden and Verplanken (1990) measured a variety of attitudes and beliefs about nuclear power in a sample of Dutch respondents. Results across that 3-year period showed a modest level of stability in individual attitudes, with general attitudes toward nuclear power showing more stability than beliefs about specific issues. In other research, even over periods as long as *20 years*, people's values and vocational interests have been shown to have a high degree of stability (Kelly, 1955).

However, other kinds of attitudes that are unimportant to people are apt to display greater fluctuations, and newly formed attitudes may be quite changeable.

In recent years the **evaluative** aspect of attitudes has been increasingly stressed. That is, an attitude is now generally seen as a disposition to respond *in a favorable or unfavorable manner* to given objects. For example, Olson and Maio (2003) define attitudes as "tendencies to evaluate objects favorably or unfavorably" (p. 299). In many studies the evaluative dimension of Osgood's Semantic Differential (Osgood, Suci, & Tannenbaum, 1957) is used *alone*, without other dimensions, as the sole measure of attitudes. This emphasis is clearly shown in Bem's simple definition: "Attitudes are likes and dislikes" (1970, p. 14). Although this statement is an oversimplification, it emphasizes the central importance of the evaluative aspect of attitudes.

Most theorists agree that attitudes are **represented in memory** as a part of a person's knowledge structures. That is, they consist of associated networks of interconnected beliefs and evaluations (Olson & Zanna, 1993). However, as we discuss in the next section, there is an alternative viewpoint that attitudes are largely *constructed* at any given point in time, based on other information (e.g., past experiences, current mood, surroundings) that is currently salient and thus is easily called to mind.

The **learned** nature of attitudes is stressed in many definitions, as in that of Fishbein and Ajzen in Box 1–2. However, Eagly and Chaiken (1993) have omitted that aspect because they note that, at least occasionally, attitudes may originate in part from a biological or genetic source (McGuire, 1985).

Summarizing the above considerations, we will use the following definition of **attitude** in this book: *An attitude is a predisposition to respond in a favorable or unfavorable manner with respect to a given attitude object.*

THEORETICAL VIEWS ABOUT ATTITUDES

Tri-Componential Viewpoint

There are several main theoretical viewpoints about the essential nature of attitudes (cf. Olson & Maio, 2003). An older one, called the **tri-componential viewpoint**, holds that an attitude is a single entity but that it has three aspects or components: affective, behavioral, and cognitive—the ABCs of attitudes (see Figure 1–2). To illustrate, let's consider a person's attitudes about riding a motorcycle.

A. An **affective (emotional)** component. This refers to the feelings and emotions one has toward the object. For instance,
   "Riding a motorcycle is fun."
   "Riding a motorcycle is exciting."
B. A **behavioral** component, consisting of one's action tendencies toward the object. For example,
   "I ride motorcycles every chance I get."
   "If I had the money, I would buy a motorcycle."
C. A **cognitive** component, consisting of the ideas and beliefs that one has about the attitude object. For example,
   "Motorcycles are fast."
   "Riding a motorcycle instead of a car saves gas."

This conceptual distinction among thoughts, feelings, and actions as separate but interrelated parts of an attitude has a long history in philosophy. The term "attitude" was

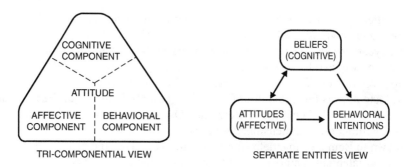

FIGURE 1–2 Two viewpoints on components of attitudes.

first used by Herbert Spencer in 1862 (Allport, 1985), but the thought–emotion–behavior distinction is essentially identical with one made by Plato, who used the terminology of cognition, affection, and conation.

However, honored as this tripartite division is in tradition, and clear as it seems conceptually, there is still an important question about its *empirical* validity and usefulness. The view of attitudes as having separate cognitive, affective, and behavioral components raises the question of consistency among these components. This view requires a relatively high (but not perfect) degree of consistency. If there is little or no consistency among them, there is no reason to consider the three components as aspects of the same concept (attitude); instead they would have to be viewed as entirely independent entities. On the other hand, if they are perfectly correlated, they cannot be separate components; in this case they would merely be different names for the same thing.

McGuire (1969, p. 157) concluded, after surveying the literature, that the three components have proved to be so highly intercorrelated that "theorists who insist on distinguishing them should bear the burden of proving that the distinction is worthwhile." However, an opposite conclusion was reached by Krech, Crutchfield, and Ballachey (1962), who favored the tripartite view. On the basis of their review of the literature, they stated that there are only "moderately high" relationships among the three components (typically, correlation coefficients of about $+0.5$); and they even cited evidence from one study showing a relationship as low as $r = +0.2$ or $+0.3$ between the cognitive and the behavioral components. Later studies have confirmed the view that there usually are moderately strong relationships among the three components (Bagozzi, Tybout, Craig, & Sternthal, 1979; Breckler, 1984; Eagly, Mladinic, & Otto, 1994; Huskinson & Haddock, 2004).

A final issue for the tri-componential viewpoint is the question of whether every attitude must have all three components. Research findings suggest that some attitudes do not have these three distinguishable aspects. For instance, some emotional reactions toward an attitude object, such as spiders, may not have any cognitive knowledge base (Zajonc, 1980), whereas attitudes about a social issue like capital punishment may be entirely cognitive (cf. Olson & Maio, 2003). Similarly, there are individual differences in attitude structure: Some people hold attitudes with consistent affective and cognitive components, whereas others tend to give more weight to either the cognitive or the affective elements (Huskinson & Haddock, 2004). Therefore the tri-componential viewpoint, though it is heuristically useful in pointing out common aspects of attitudes, seems too strong as a formal model (Eagly & Chaiken, 1993).

Separate Entities Viewpoint

A newer theoretical view of attitudes is that the three components described above are distinct, **separate entities**, which may or may not be related, depending on the particular situation (see Figure 1–2). This viewpoint has been strongly advocated by Fishbein and Ajzen (1975). In their theory, the term attitude is reserved solely for the affective dimension, indicating evaluation or favorability toward an object. The cognitive dimension they label as **beliefs**, is defined as indicating a person's subjective probability that an object has a particular characteristic (for example, how sure the person feels that "This book is interesting," or that "Smoking marijuana is no more dangerous than drinking alcohol"). The behavioral dimension they refer to as **behavioral intentions** is defined as indicating a person's subjective probability that he or she will perform a particular behavior toward an object (e.g., "I intend to read this book," or "I am going to write my congressperson about legalization of marijuana").

Fishbein and Ajzen point out that a person usually has various beliefs about the same object and that these beliefs are not necessarily related. For instance, if someone believes "This book is interesting," that person may or may not also believe "This book is attractively printed" or "This book is inexpensive." The same situation also holds true for behavioral intentions. "I intend to read this book" does not imply "I am going to buy this book" nor even "I am going to study this book carefully." By contrast, these authors say, all measures of a person's *affect* toward a particular object should be highly related: "I like this book" *does* imply "I enjoy reading it," and such responses should be quite consistent with the same person's answers to an attitude scale evaluating the book.

A final point about the separate entities viewpoint is that there is no necessary congruence among beliefs, attitudes, and behavioral intentions, which the tri-componential viewpoint would consider all aspects of the same attitude. "I like this book" (attitude) does *not* necessarily imply "This book is inexpensive" (belief), nor does it imply "I am going to buy this book" (behavioral intention). Thus, these distinctions provide a justification for treating the three concepts as entirely separate entities. This viewpoint can be seen as having both theoretical and empirical advantages over the older tripartite view of attitude components.

The conflicting findings mentioned above about the varying degrees of relationship among the three supposed attitude "components" in different studies give support to the separate entities viewpoint because this view does not require a necessary connection among these concepts but does allow for a strong relationship under certain specified conditions. Fishbein and Ajzen (1972) pointed out that most attitude scales are made up of several items stating various beliefs or intentions about the attitude object. However, many beliefs or intentions will not make satisfactory items for such a scale. Examples include beliefs that are so widely agreed on that they are not held differentially by people with different attitudes ("President Bush is a Republican"); or statements whose evaluative significance is ambiguous (e.g., "As a national leader, President Bush's performance is about average"— disagreement here might indicate either a high or a low evaluation of Bush). Thus it is only when an "attitude scale" has been carefully constructed from several well-chosen belief or intention items that we should expect it to correlate highly with other standard attitude measures. In any case there will always be many possible items about particular beliefs or behavioral intentions that will not correlate highly with such a scale (e.g., "I believe President Bush is the Messiah," or "I am going to write President Bush a letter").

Latent Process Viewpoint

A third theoretical view of attitudes that emphasizes some different aspects has been called a **latent process** viewpoint (DeFleur & Westie, 1963). This approach postulates a hidden process occurring within the individual, which we call an attitude; and it uses this attitude as an explanation of the relationship between stimulus events and the individual's responses.

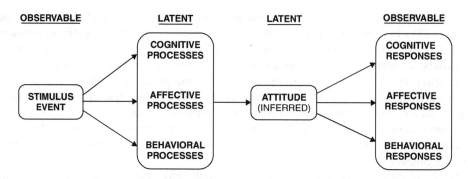

FIGURE 1–3 The latent process viewpoint.

In this conception, an attitude has the status of an **intervening variable**—a theoretical construct that is not observable in itself, but which mediates or helps to explain the relationship between certain observable stimulus events (the environmental situation) and certain behavioral responses. For instance, the concept that a man has a prejudiced attitude can help to explain the relationship between such an antecedent event as his being seated next to a black person and such responses as an increase in his galvanic skin response (GSR) measure, or his getting up and moving to a different chair. Similarly, a woman's political attitudes can help to explain why she would go to hear and cheer a speech by one political candidate, but turn off the TV when a different candidate was on the air.

A diagram of this view of attitudes is shown in Figure 1–3. It indicates that stimulus events can arouse a person's cognitive, affective, and/or behavioral processes, many of which are nonobservable. Together or separately, these processes can produce an attitude toward objects involved in the stimulus situation, and this attitude is a nonobservable or latent construct. However, the presence of an attitude will give rise to, and can be measured in terms of, observable responses, which may be cognitive, affective, and/or behavioral reactions to the attitude object. This model is basically similar to that advocated by Eagly and Chaiken (1993).

This approach has some important advantages over the previous two viewpoints. Like the tri-componential view, it avoids the possible oversimplicity of the separate entities view, which equates attitude solely with affective or emotional responses, thus ruling out cognitions or behaviors as part of the attitude concept. It is superior to the tri-componential view in that it avoids the requirement that the three supposed "components" of an attitude should show a moderately high degree of congruence. Instead, it clarifies that any given attitude may arise from one, two, or all three of the types of processes (cognitive, affective, or behavioral) set off by particular stimulus events (Zanna & Rempel, 1988), and similarly it specifies that the attitude may be shown in one, two, or three of the corresponding types of observable responses (Breckler, 1984).

Attitudes Are Inferred

A point on which almost all theorists are agreed is that attitudes are inferred constructs. Although they may be defined as constituting a readiness for response, we stated that they are not behavior per se. Thus it follows that they cannot be directly observed, as habits or other responses can be. How then can we reach conclusions about them? Only through a process of inference, based on the study of responses which *are* observable. Allport (1935) phrased the situation clearly:

How does one know that [attitudes] exist at all? Only by necessary inference. There *must* be something to account for the consistency of conduct. It is the meaningful resemblances between activities and their congruence with one another that leads the psychologist inescapably to postulate some such generalized forms of readiness as the term "attitude" denotes. (p. 836)

Attitudes May Be Constructed "On the Spot"

Attitude construction is the process by which a person comes to *express* an attitude. Strongly held attitudes are usually quite stable across time, and they can easily be retrieved from memory and stated. Weaker attitudes may include various partially inconsistent beliefs and feelings, and stating them may involve selecting which aspect to express, based on the surrounding situation and which particular beliefs or feelings are called to mind. There are also instances in which a person may not have an existing attitude about a particular topic, but when asked can easily construct one (Nayakankuppam & Priester, 2003).

When individuals construct an attitude, they may draw from a large database of information, including their past behaviors, their mood, their surroundings, the context in which the question was asked, and a range of beliefs about the attitude object (Wilson & Hodges, 1992). Tesser (1978) has gone so far as to propose that all attitudes may involve this process of construction:

An attitude at a particular point in time is the result of a constructive process. . . . *there is not a single attitude toward an object* but, rather, any number of attitudes depending on the number of schemas available for thinking about the object. (pp. 297–298)

RELATED CONCEPTS

Having defined "attitude," we now need to present brief definitions of several other terms that are related to the concept of attitude, or are sometimes even used synonymously with it. You should keep in mind that each of these terms has been used and defined in various ways and that there is never complete agreement with any given usage. However, these definitions will help to clarify the distinctions between each of these terms and the concept of attitude.

Belief

Many theorists would agree with Fishbein and Ajzen's (1975) definition that **beliefs** are statements indicating a person's subjective probability that an object has a particular characteristic. Other ways of putting this are that they assert the truth or falsity of propositions about the object, or that they state a relationship between the object and some characteristic—for instance, "This book is informative," "Einstein's theory of relativity is important," "My boss is easygoing." Within the separate entities viewpoint, this definition is advantageous in that it distinguishes clearly between beliefs and attitudes: In that framework, beliefs are cognitive—thoughts and ideas; whereas attitudes are affective—feelings and emotions.

This approach raises a question, however, about how to treat an intermediate category, which we may call **evaluative beliefs**—that is, beliefs that state a value judgment about an object. Examples are "My boss is a nice guy," or "Freedom of the press is a good thing." Clearly, evaluative beliefs are closely linked to attitudes of liking or disliking, and sometimes they are almost indistinguishable from them. For instance, consider "My boss is a nice guy" (evaluative belief) and "I like my boss" (attitude). A good resolution of this issue is to consider that a person's attitude toward an object summarizes his or her evaluative beliefs about the object.

This definitional issue does not arise within the latent process viewpoint as we have described it. There, an attitude can be shown by cognitive responses that show evaluation, such as evaluative belief statements, and equally as well by affective responses of liking or disliking, or by behavioral responses (e.g., actions of approach or avoidance). Thus an attitude might be conceptualized as *a summary of all of a person's evaluative beliefs about, affective reactions toward, and behavioral responses to an attitude object.*

Opinion

As the title of this book indicates, **opinion** is an important concept and one closely related to the concept of attitude. Sometimes the two terms have been used synonymously, leading McGuire (1969, p. 152) to characterize the situation as "names in search of a distinction, rather than a distinction in search of a terminology." However, more often, distinctions have been made between attitudes and opinions, though there are many different views as to what the nature of the distinction should be.

The viewpoint that we prefer is that *opinions are equivalent to beliefs*—quite often, they are evaluative beliefs. That is, they are usually narrower in content or scope than attitudes, and they are often primarily cognitive. However, in many cases they are evaluative, and thus they are specific parts of the general evaluative orientation which we call an attitude. Another way of putting this is that opinions involve a person's judgments about the likelihood of events or relationships regarding some object, and they also may involve evaluations of an event or object on specific dimensions. Thus, in this view, the statement "My dog Rex is a faithful companion" is an opinion, whereas the broader declaration "I love old Rex" is an attitude statement. Similarly, "Recycling used cans and bottles saves natural resources" is an opinion, whereas "It's a good thing to recycle used cans and bottles" is an attitude.

McGuire (1985) warned about definitional distinctions such as the ones we have been considering, emphasizing that in order to be useful they must have clear-cut empirical consequences. He questioned the value of distinguishing between attitudes and opinions:

> Distinctions deserve to be made only insofar as they make a difference such that the distinguished variables relate differently to third variables of interest. (p. 241)

In our conceptual view, opinions are beliefs. Because there are now extensive research findings showing differential relationships of beliefs and attitudes to other concepts (e.g., Fishbein & Ajzen, 1975), it is important to make a distinction between attitudes and opinions.

Nevertheless, the term "opinion" continues to be used synonymously with "attitude," particularly in the area of survey research and polling. There the phrase **public opinion** is the commonly accepted term to designate the shared attitudes *and* beliefs of large segments of a society. We discuss public opinion further in the next major section of this chapter.

Value

There is more general agreement about the relationship of values to attitudes than about the previous terms. The most common view is that a **value** is an important life-goal or societal condition desired by a person (Rokeach, 1968; Schwartz, 1992; Rohan, 2000). Values are usually broad abstract concepts, such as freedom, justice, beauty, happiness, or service to others, though sometimes they are more concrete, such as money or material possessions. Values are ends rather than means—the goals people strive to reach rather than the methods that they use to get there. A recent summary of theories and empirical research on values has been presented by Seligman, Olson, and Zanna (1996).

Because values are a person's goals or standards in life, it is clear that individuals will have strong positive attitudes toward the values they hold. Thus values can be viewed as very special attitude objects—they involve strong favorable attitudes being directed toward abstract concepts concerned with one's major goals for oneself or for the world. In addition, values are very important and central in a person's whole system of attitudes and beliefs—that is, they are resistant to change, and they influence many other beliefs and attitudes (Rokeach, 1979; Kahle, 1983; Tetlock, 1986). For instance, if you have a key value of piety, it will influence your views about many religious concepts and issues, as well as your attitudes toward national leaders, friends, activities, and so on. On the other hand, if patriotism is your main value, you will favor different activities and leaders: You will wave the flag, go to Fourth of July parades, and applaud patriotic speeches, rather than spending your time in religious services, prayer, or listening to broadcast evangelists.

Habit

Habits can be easily distinguished from attitudes. They are frequently-repeated patterns of behavior, whereas attitudes are not behavior per se, though they may be shown in behavioral responses (Ajzen, 2002). Habits are usually quite automatic and standardized in their manner of performance, but they require the presence of the appropriate stimulus object in order to occur (e.g., saying "sir" to a superior officer in the armed forces). By contrast, attitudes may be expressed in many different ways, and even in the absence of the stimulus object (e.g., I like to watch snow falling even though, as a Southern Californian, I haven't seen any close up in several years). Like most attitudes, habits are learned through experience; but, unlike them, they are frequently nonevaluative in nature. For instance, a habit of scratching one's head or of saying "you know" frequently in conversation does not necessarily imply a favorable attitude toward these activities.

Trait

Personality traits are also quite distinct from attitudes. First, traits are not generally evaluative, whereas all attitudes involve evaluation. Second, traits are broader behavioral patterns, both on the stimulus side and on the response side (Eagly & Chaiken, 1993). That is, personality traits are apt to entail many different behaviors and to be directed toward many attitude objects, whereas each attitude has a single attitude object (though it may be as broad as a group of people or things, or it may be an abstract concept). For instance, a trait of helpfulness would be shown toward many different stimulus individuals (family members, friends, even casual acquaintances) and in many different actions (e.g., supporting, advising, assisting them, etc.). By contrast, a pro-American attitude would be demonstrated in a variety of favorable responses, but only ones that are directed toward American institutions or groups.

WHAT IS PUBLIC OPINION?

You are undoubtedly familiar with public opinion polls such as those of George Gallup and Louis Harris, and you know that they involve asking questions of large groups of

---

Box 1–3 Differing Definitions of "Public Opinion"

Many varied definitions of the concept of "public opinion" have been suggested by different authors over the years, emphasizing the following specific aspects:

> *RATIONALLY FORMED—Public opinion is the social judgment of a self-conscious community on a question of general import after rational public discussion. (Young, 1923)*
> *WELL-INFORMED (ELITE GROUP)—Public opinion may be said to be that sentiment on any given subject which is entertained by the best informed, most intelligent, and most moral persons in the community. (MacKinnon, 1828)*
> *IMPORTANT TOPIC—The attitudes, feelings, or ideas of the large body of the people about important public issues. (Minar, 1960)*
> *EXTENT OF AGREEMENT—. . . a majority is not enough, and unanimity is not required, but the opinion must be such that while the majority may not share it, they feel bound, by conviction, not by fear, to accept it. (Lowell, 1913)*
> *INTENSITY—. . . public opinion is more than a matter of numbers. The intensity of the opinions is quite as important. Public opinion is a composite of numbers and intensity. (Munro, 1931)*
> *EFFECTIVE INFLUENCE—Public opinion in this discussion may simply be taken to mean those opinions held by private persons which governments find it prudent to heed. (Key, 1961)*
> *GENERAL DEFINITION—The study of public opinion is, therefore, the study of collections of individual opinions wherever they may be found. (Childs, 1965)*

Source: Extracts from pp. 13–24 of *Public Opinion: Nature, Formation, and Role* by H. L. Childs. © 1965 by Litton Educational Publishing, Inc. Reprinted by permission of Wadsworth, Inc. Childs' volume fully references the sources of all these definition.

---

people. However, you might be surprised to learn that the term "public opinion" is one that has led to just as many difficulties in definition as the term "attitude" (Bennett, 1980).

In general, **public opinion** refers to the shared opinions and attitudes of large groups of people (sometimes called "publics") who have particular characteristics in common— for example, all registered voters in Illinois, or all small-business owners in a particular city. However, there are some aspects of more complete definitions that have provoked debate for more than 200 years. Box 1–3 contains a sample of specific definitions of "public opinion," presented both for their great variety and for their historical interest. Harwood Childs (1965) reviewed the definitional debates in detail and concluded that it is unwisely restrictive to include many specifications in defining public opinion, such as the particular public involved, the subject matter of the opinions, or the extent of consensus, and so forth. Child's general definition is recommended as the most useful one for our purposes because of its breadth and lack of restrictions. A modern discussion of the complications in defining public opinion has been offered by Kinder (1998).

Historically, the first mention of public opinion polls being used to get indications of the strength of political candidates was in 1824. In that year newspapers reported two straw votes, one in Delaware and one in North Carolina, where select groups of citizens were asked whom they preferred for U.S. President. Interestingly enough, Andrew Jackson won both of these "polls," though it was not until 1828 that he gained wide enough support to be elected president (Roll & Cantril, 1980).

We will take up the characteristics of modern public opinion polls, as well as issues and problems involved in such polling, at length in Chapter 6. Building on that background, Chapter 7 describes the structure of public opinion, and Chapter 12 discusses the relationship of public opinion to public policy.

APPROACHES TO ATTITUDE AND OPINION RESEARCH

Different disciplines have typically approached the study of attitudes and opinions in rather different ways. The four major disciplines that treat attitudes and opinions as part of their subject matter are sociology, communication research, political science, and psychology. In each field there have been many scientists who have done excellent, highly regarded work on attitudes and opinions, utilizing a variety of approaches. Although we should avoid overgeneralizing, some of the five ways of studying attitudes mentioned early in this chapter are more common in each field than are others.

In sociology, the most frequently used method of attitude research has been *description* of various social groups. Quite often the choice of which groups to study has been based on variables such as social class or position in an organization (e.g., blue-collar workers, or supervisors). To a lesser extent, such research also usually involves some emphasis on attitude *measurement* through written questionnaires or interviews.

In communication research, the typical approach has also involved *description* as well as *measurement*, but the subject matter is usually written or spoken messages. Here the method of study is generally **content analysis**, a careful systematic method of describing the manifest and/or latent content of written or oral communications (cf. Neuendorf, 2002).

In political science, the most common approach has been *polling*, though again some workers have used other methods, particularly *description*. A predominant interest in political science has been the study of public opinion, and the most common way of determining public opinion has been to use a face-to-face interview, asking many detailed questions of a large sample of people from the relevant classification (e.g., voters, PTA members, or business executives).

In psychology, the most common way of studying attitudes has been *experimentation*, though each of the other approaches has had its adherents. Usually the focus of experiments has been on attempts to change an attitude by manipulating one or more situational factors, or on measuring individual differences (such as personality dimensions) which are related to attitude change. Very often the attitude chosen for changing was one that was unimportant or even completely new to the participants, so that it could be influenced more easily; and generally only immediate or short-term attitude change has been studied.

We will see many of these research features and the approaches typical of each discipline illustrated in the ensuing chapters.

SUMMARY

The concept of attitude was a very important one in social psychology's formative years and still remains so today. Although many varied definitions have been offered, in general an attitude can be defined as a predisposition to respond in a favorable or unfavorable manner to a particular object or class of objects. Attitudes have been studied with five relatively independent approaches: description, measurement, polls, theories, and experiments.

One traditional view of attitudes is that they have three interrelated components: cognitive, affective, and behavioral. A later approach is to consider these three aspects as separate and distinct entities, calling them beliefs, attitudes, and behavioral intentions. A third viewpoint, called a latent process approach, is favored in this text. It considers attitudes as unobservable intervening variables, which must be inferred from observable responses. It holds that attitudes can arise from stimulus events through cognitive, affective, and/or behavioral processes, and that they can be demonstrated by any or all of these three types of responses.

Beliefs, opinions, values, habits, and traits are concepts that are related to the concept of attitude, but are not synonymous with it. Whereas an attitude is a general evaluative orientation toward an object, a belief or an opinion is narrower in scope and generally more cognitive in nature. "Public opinion" refers to the shared opinions and attitudes of many members of a society. It is an important topic in many disciplines, being studied by sociologists, communication researchers, political scientists, and psychologists. Because attitudes and opinions are important in so many different fields of study, this text adopts an interdisciplinary approach to its subject matter.

2

Social Perception and Social Cognition

The human understanding when it has once adopted an opinion draws all things else to support and agree with it.—Francis Bacon, 1620.

Thinking is the hardest work there is, which is the probable reason why so few engage in it.—Henry Ford.

Imagine meeting someone for the first time. When you first set eyes on her, you would recognize her as being a person and a woman, and you would note certain facts about her—perhaps her height, build, and hair color, or the type of clothes she is wearing. You may also infer other facts about her—estimate her age and activities from her behavior, or guess where she grew up from her accent. In addition, you will probably make other, more subjective judgments about her—her personality, interests, attractiveness, intelligence, friendliness, and so on. Some of your judgments may be influenced by stereotypes that you already hold about different categories of people—about Southerners, overweight people, athletic types, or socialites. Even though you have only just met her, you will already have developed a set of expectations and opinions about her.

All of these types of perception and judgment fall in the realm of social cognition. **Social cognition** refers to our thought processes about other people, ourselves, and social situations—that is, how we understand and make sense of social stimuli. Social cognition includes the ways in which people gather social information, organize it, and interpret it (Kunda, 1999). It is intimately related to the topic of attitudes, for social perceptions, beliefs, and attributions comprise the cognitive components on which attitudes are based.

As a research area, social cognition experienced an explosion of activity starting about 1975 (Higgins & Bargh, 1987; Wyer & Srull, 1994), including the publication of new journals, handbooks, and influential textbooks; and by 1990 it had become the most heavily studied area in social psychology (Hamilton, Devine, & Ostrom, 1994). In her 1998 review chapter, Taylor stated, "Although the numbers are waning now, at one time, social cognition was believed to account for more than 85 percent of the submissions [to the leading social psychology journal]" (p. 72).

CHARACTERISTICS OF PERCEPTION

The first stage of social cognition is perception, the reception and organization of sensory information about people or social situations. Social perception, like our perception of any object or situation, has a number of important characteristics (Schneider, Hastorf, & Ellsworth, 1979). We can illustrate these characteristics by considering a concrete situation: You have just entered an office and you see another person seated behind a desk.

19

1. Perception is *immediate*. As you first glance into the room, you are immediately aware of the person there. There is no apparent delay in this process of awareness.

2. Perception is *selective*. Your attention focuses on only a few objects out of the multitude that are within your sensory range. For instance, you may note the person and the desk but ignore the walls, the floor covering, pictures, and other objects in the room, even though they impinge on your sense organs just as much or even more than the person or the desk. Thus perception is an *active* process, not just a passive receptive process.

3. Perception is *structured*. Although your eyes merely receive light waves of various frequencies and degrees of brightness, you organize that complex stimulation into a pattern of shapes, colors, and sizes. The separate groups of stimuli—hair, face, clothes, hands, and so forth—are integrated into a structured whole: You perceive a person.

4. Perception is *stable*. This is best illustrated by our experience of **constancies** in perception: The apparent size, shape, and color of objects remain constant even though we view them from different distances and angles and in different amounts of light. For example, as you approach the person and the desk, their images on your retina increase in size, but you do not perceive these objects as growing taller or wider.

5. Perception is *meaningful*. In interpreting a pattern of stimuli as a person, you have already imparted meaning to the sensory experience, but you don't stop there. You immediately integrate aspects of his or her facial features, body build, clothing, hairstyle, and so on, and you perceive the person as male or female, young or old, tall or short, stout or thin. Similarly, animals are perceived as being cats or dogs, birds or reptiles, and objects are understood as boxes, bricks, or houses. Thus our perceptual experience is organized into meaningful categories.

Social Perception

There are also some ways in which perception of people is *unlike* perception of objects (Schneider et al., 1979). We perceive people (and sometimes animals, but not inanimate objects) as causal agents. They do certain things, and they have various intentions and personal traits, whereas objects are not perceived as having intrinsic causal efficacy, intentions, or traits. (The issues of causality, intentions, and personal characteristics are central to the topic of attribution, which is discussed later in this chapter.) Second, we perceive personal interactions as being dynamic. That is, unlike objects, other people adjust their behavior in response to us, and vice versa. Third, because we expect other people to have basic human characteristics like our own, we typically perceive them as having specific emotions and attitudes that are not directly observable.

Our perception of the world around us is usually quite accurate, or **veridical**. If it were not, our lives and welfare would constantly be endangered by our mistakes in judging the height of curbs, the speed of approaching cars, the heat of stoves, and so on. However, we know that sometimes our senses can be fooled, as they are in the misleading perceptual situations that we call **illusions**. Similarly, the visual cues that we all normally rely on can sometimes mislead us. For instance, the clarity of outlines helps us determine the nearness of objects; but when visibility is poor, as in foggy weather, the distance of objects is often overestimated because their outlines are blurred, and as a result our chances of crashing into the car ahead of us are increased. On the other hand, when visibility is unusually good, the contours of objects are seen very sharply, and consequently the objects seem much closer than they really are, like mountains in clear desert air (Tversky & Kahneman, 1974).

Although physical perception is occasionally mistaken, *social* perception is much more likely to be inaccurate, for it suffers from numerous sources of subjectivity and unreliability. We turn now to a discussion of some of the main sources of potential error.

COMMON THOUGHT PROCESSES

There are many thought processes that people use to simplify and give order to their everyday decisions and interactions with others. These processes of social cognition have been much studied by both cognitive psychologists (Tversky & Kahneman, 1974) and social psychologists (Ross, 1977). We will discuss two aspects of such thought processes: heuristics and biases.

Heuristics

The adjective *heuristic* means "helpful in discovering things." As described by Tversky and Kahneman (1974), **heuristics** are convenient, informal guides that people find helpful and often follow in making decisions or predictions. Among the most important and frequently used ones are the availability, adjustment, and representativeness heuristics.

The Availability Heuristic. This is the use of readily available (salient) information about events, such as instances that are easily remembered or imagined. This heuristic is often used in making estimates of the frequency or probability of events. For example, if you were asked what percentage of people have serious automobile accidents each year, an easy and convenient basis for making your estimate would be to think of how many accidents you could remember among your friends or relatives. If you could easily recall several serious crashes, you would probably give a higher estimate than if you could remember no auto accidents occurring to these individuals (MacLeod & Campbell, 1992; Garcia-Marques, Maddox, & Hamilton, 2002).

In general, use of the availability heuristic aids people in making accurate estimates (Hogarth, 1981), for when examples of some kind of event (e.g., thunder showers) can be remembered easily, that type of event may have been quite frequent. However, the availability heuristic can and often does lead people to incorrect judgments as well. For instance, hearing news reports of a violent crime—a dramatically available, salient bit of information—leads people to increase their estimates of the frequency of such crimes, and as a consequence they often substantially overestimate the occurrence of crimes (Doob, 1982; Wolfgang & Weiner, 1982). The selective emphasis of media coverage often contributes to such erroneous estimates. Careful studies have shown that people underestimate the frequency of fatal diseases, which are relatively rarely reported in U.S. newspapers, and overestimate the frequency of accidents, fires, tornadoes, murders, and other violent causes of death, which are much more often reported in the media. Thus, media coverage of such events contributes to their salience in people's awareness, and subjective judgments of their frequency are correlated as much as 0.70 or more with the amount of media coverage (Slovic, Fischhoff, & Lichtenstein, 1980).

Availability also enters into the estimation of risks involved in possible future courses of action. Use of one's imagination to construct scenarios of possible future events has been termed the **simulation heuristic** (Kahneman & Tversky, 1982—see Box 2–1). A typical example can be seen in the following analysis of the disastrous terrorist attack on New York City's World Trade Center in 2001.

The World Trade Center building itself had previously been attacked and damaged in 1993 by a truck packed with explosives, and similar attacks had killed U.S. personnel in military barracks in Saudi Arabia and destroyed U.S. embassies in Kenya and Tanzania. Consequently, planning to prevent such attacks had focused largely on deterring the use of truck bombs. Extending their consideration of the type of vehicles that could be used, government safety experts even analyzed the possibility of a small plane being flown into a

Photograph courtesy of
Daniel Kahneman.
Reprinted by permission.

Photograph courtesy
of Amos Tversky.
Reprinted by
permission.

Box 2–1   DANIEL KAHNEMAN and AMOS TVERSKY, *Analysts of Judgment and
Decision Making*

*Daniel Kahneman and Amos Tversky are unique in being the first team of unrelated
psychologists to be jointly honored with the American Psychological Association's Distinguished Scientific Contribution Award. In their collaboration, they originated the
concept of heuristics as aids in people's judgments about uncertain events, and they
developed "prospect theory" as an alternative to the classical rational theory of choice
among risky options. Their partnership began at the Hebrew University in Jerusalem in
1969 and continued in North America, resulting in two joint books and more than 25 joint
articles and chapters before Tversky died in 1996.*

*Both Kahneman and Tversky were born in Israel in the 1930s, attended Hebrew Uni-
versity, spent a period in military service, earned their Ph.D.s in the United States in the
1960s, and soon returned to teach at Hebrew University. Kahneman's doctorate was from
Berkeley, Tversky's from the University of Michigan, but both specialized in mathematical
and statistical aspects of psychology. Both spent separate periods as fellows at Harvard's
Center for Cognitive Studies and a joint period at the Oregon Research Institute. In the
late 1970s, Tversky moved to Stanford, while Kahneman moved to the University of British
Columbia, later to Berkeley, and in 1993 to Princeton, where his work continues.*

*Each of them also maintained independent research programs and published numer-
ous other books and many articles—Kahneman on the topics of attention and perception,
Tversky on mathematical psychology and measurement. Although an early colleague predicted that their collaboration wouldn't last long "because of differences in temperament
and style," they found that they greatly enjoyed their tenacious arguments about the best
way to express their ideas, and they marveled at their good fortune in finding "that serious
work could be so much fun." In 2002, Kahneman won the Nobel Prize in economics for
his collaborative work with Tversky in integrating psychological research into economics,
and he said "Certainly we would have gotten this [award] together."*

skyscraper, concluding that its effects would be relatively limited. But they failed to imagine the use of a commercial jet liner, fully loaded with fuel, which could ignite fires so hot
that they would melt the steel structure of the skyscraper and cause its top floors to cas-
cade down and crush all of the lower floors. Janis (1985) referred to this kind of cognitive
problem as the "unsqueaky wheel trap," because the unsqueaky wheel gets little attention.

The Adjustment Heuristic.   This approach involves making estimates or predictions by starting with some salient initial value (an **anchor**) and "adjusting" it upward

or downward. However, the adjustments that people make are usually too small, and the result is an **anchoring effect**, in which the initial value overinfluences the subsequent predictions (e.g., Peake & Cervone, 1989; Mussweiler & Strack, 2000). A common situation where this heuristic is displayed is in people's predictions of the future range of some index, such as the Dow-Jones stock market average's range during the coming year. Most people apparently start with the current level as their initial value, and they frequently underadjust, thus predicting a range that is narrower than the values that actually occur.

Similarly, we frequently use our own norms or habits as the anchor when we are estimating the behavior of other people. We may know intellectually that many other people do not feel or act as we do, and yet we are still unlikely to adjust our estimates of their behavior far enough away from the anchor provided by our own standards. In a clever demonstration of this phenomenon, students were asked if they would be willing to walk around their college campus for 30 minutes wearing a large advertising placard saying "Eat at Joe's." Some students agreed to do so, whereas others were unwilling. Then they were asked to estimate what percentage of their classmates would have made the same decision they did. Those who had agreed to wear the sandwich board estimated that 62% of other students would also agree, whereas those who refused estimated that only 33% of students would agree to the task (Ross, Greene, & House, 1977).

Other experiments have established the important finding that anchoring effects can positively or negatively influence estimates of one's own abilities, and those estimates in turn can affect one's later behavioral persistence in a task, becoming "self-fulfilling prophecies" (Cervone & Peake, 1986). Such effects may be one of the sources of "learned helplessness"—clarifying, for instance, why children from deprived backgrounds become discouraged from trying to go on to higher education.

The Representativeness Heuristic.   This is a method of making judgments or predictions about probability by relying on bits of information that you consider representative (typical) features of a group or category. For instance, you might believe that librarians are typically neat and tidy people. Then, if you were asked to guess whether various individuals were librarians or not, you might look for evidence about whether they were neat and tidy. While using these limited cues, people commonly ignore other useful data such as the amount of evidence available, the reliability and/or validity of the evidence, the likelihood of statistical regression effects, and **base-rates** of the behavior being predicted (i.e., its probability in the population at large, or "prior probability"; Tversky & Kahneman, 1974, 1982).

To take an example, suppose you were told that Joe Garrigo had been a star Little League ballplayer, and you were then asked to predict whether he was now a professional baseball player or a business executive. Because being a star athlete as a child is a common or representative characteristic of later professional athletes, you might rely on that cue and predict that Joe became a pro player. However, such a procedure would overlook the scantiness of the single predictor cue, the fact that *many* star Little Leaguers do not go on to big league sports, and the base-rate information that there are many more business executives than professional baseball players. Thus being a star youth athlete is not a very valid predictor of later professional status, and the base-rate probabilities strongly suggest that many more youthful stars become business executives than become pro athletes.

Biases

Biases in people's thought processes often result from or are combined with the preceding heuristics, and they can produce many errors in judgment. Among the important biases are the so-called fundamental attribution error, underestimation of role-related be-havior, the false consensus bias, overlooking nonoccurrences, reliance on vivid or concrete evidence, ignoring base-rates, making overly extreme predictions, and the persistence of initial impressions (Ross, 1977; Nisbett & Ross, 1980). Note that we are dealing here with purely cognitive sources of bias, not *motivational* ones such as the phenomenon of wishful thinking—that is, increased belief in the likelihood of something desirable because we *want* it to be true (Tversky & Kahneman, 1974).

The Fundamental Attribution Error.   The so-called fundamental attribution error is the widespread human tendency to overestimate the importance of personal character-istics as the cause of other people's behavior and to underestimate the importance of situational influences. For instance, if you observe one person hurting another, you are more likely to explain it in terms of the first person's having a hostile or sadistic personality than to attribute it to situational conditions that forced the first person's actions. This was demonstrated experimentally in Bierbrauer's (1973) reenactment of the classic Milgram (1963) study in which participants thought they were delivering strong shocks to a victim. In the reenactment, even participants who had taken the role of the person giving the shock overlooked the strength of the situational forces compelling that behavior and dramatically underestimated the percentage of people who would yield to those situational forces.

Underestimation of Role-Related Aspects of Behavior.   This is a common tendency that is closely related to the fundamental attribution error. Holding a social role such as teacher, boss, or member of the upper class confers considerable control over one's personal interactions, and thus it offers many opportunities to display one's strengths and conceal one's weaknesses. The cognitive tendency to overlook the extent of role-related behavior adds to our overestimation of the importance of personal characteristics. For instance, a teacher can appear very knowledgeable by confining class discussions to topics that he or she knows a lot about and avoiding other topics. An experimental demonstration of this principle required one participant to think up questions on any esoteric informational topic, which another person had to try to answer. In this situation, both the answerers and uninvolved observers typically overestimated the difference in the two individuals' knowledge, saying that the questioner was much more knowledgeable than the answerer. Thus they overlooked the impact of the participants' roles in the situation (Ross, Amabile, & Steinmetz, 1977).

The False Consensus Bias.   This is one result of the availability heuristic previ-ously discussed. It is displayed in the fact that most people overestimate the frequency of other people's acting or thinking the same way as themselves (Fields & Schuman, 1976; Ross, Greene, & House, 1977). For instance, if you have recently fed pigeons in the park, learned to ski, gone to an art exhibit, or taken some other distinctive action, you will usually remember having done so and consequently will tend to overestimate how often other people do the same things. In addition to the availability of such memories, there are several other cognitive tendencies that all tend to push people's judgments in the direction of the false consensus effect (Zuckerman, Mann, & Bernieri, 1982; Deutsch, 1989). For a review of research in this area, see Marks and Miller (1987).

Overlooking Nonoccurrences.   Also related to the availability heuristic is peo-ple's tendency to overlook nonoccurrences because they are less salient—less easily clas-sified and remembered—than occurrences. For instance, you meet a new acquaintance briefly and afterward you try to decide whether she liked you. The things she said and did may be easily remembered and interpreted, but the equally informative things she did *not* do and say are apt to be too little noticed to be weighted properly in your judgments. Examples would include if she did *not* prolong the encounter, nor listen attentively to you, nor smile at you frequently, and so on. This typical cognitive tendency was illustrated in a Sherlock Holmes story by Dr. Watson's comment that nothing unusual had happened during the night. However, Holmes overcame this cognitive set, noticed the fact that a particular dog did *not* bark at the nighttime intruder, and used this insight to help solve one of his cases (Ross, 1977).

Reliance on Vivid or Concrete Information.   Another common human characteristic, which is also related to the availability heuristic, is too much reliance on vivid or concrete information, such as that provided by a specific instance. For example, suppose you are trying to decide what college courses to take or what kind of car to buy. If you are like most people, you will tend to be strongly influenced by vivid bits of specific information from a friend or acquaintance—for instance, that they took a particular course and thought it was terrific, or they bought a particular make of car and got a lemon. People typically pay much more attention to such information than to general, but abstract, information such as the ratings of courses in university-wide student handbooks or the repair records of cars published by *Consumer Reports*—which of course have much more general validity (Borgida & Nisbett, 1977; Nisbett & Ross, 1980).

Ignoring Base-Rate Information.   The reverse side of that cognitive bias is the widespread pattern of ignoring **base-rate** information (relevant data on large groups of cases), which is almost always presented in abstract or "pallid" form. However, summaries of base-rate probabilities, such as frequency-of-repair records for thousands of cars, usually provide the best predictor information available as to how any one car will perform. Nevertheless, in their passion for vivid, concrete information, most people largely or entirely disregard the much more useful base-rate information (Hamill, Wilson, & Nisbett, 1980).

Making Overly Extreme Predictions.   Another important type of cognitive error is making overly extreme predictions. For instance, suppose you were given individual students' mathematical aptitude test scores and were asked to predict the same students' verbal aptitude test scores. There are two biases that operate here, both of which foster overly extreme predictions. First, most people assume a stronger relation between the two variables (in this case, math and verbal aptitude) than actually exists. Second, utilizing the adjustment heuristic, most people make predictions on the dependent variable that are nearly as extreme as the scores on the predictor variable (e.g., if Joe is at the 90th percentile in math, they predict that he will be close to the 90th percentile in verbal aptitude). This procedure is contradicted by the phenomenon of **statistical regression**—the fact that on any imperfectly correlated dimensions, most people's scores will be much closer to the mean on the second variable than they are on the first one. However, even students and professionals who are familiar with the concept of regression tend to ignore it and make predictions that are too extreme. As a result, Ross (1977, p. 203) concluded,

> It is difficult to resist the blunt summary that, when it comes to predictions, a little knowledge (i.e., knowledge of a weakly related predictor variable) is a dangerous thing.

Persistence of Initial Impressions.   This is the final cognitive bias that we discuss here. Even though initial impressions are subject to all of the sources of error we have discussed, nevertheless people tend to cling to them much too fervently. That is, when presented with additional information that should change their initial judgments, people tend to make grossly insufficient adjustments. Like the bias involved in making extreme predictions, this is an example of the adjustment heuristic and the anchoring effect, for our initial impression provides an anchor that prevents our later judgments from shifting as far as the evidence warrants. This phenomenon has been shown in many types of social psychological situations and tasks, going back as far as Asch's (1946) classic study of first impressions. It is apt to occur even in controlled experiments in which the initial information is later completely discredited (Anderson, Lepper, & Ross, 1980). More-over, *ambiguous* new information is often interpreted by recipients as credible support, which strengthens their original beliefs (Lord, Ross, & Lepper, 1979). Thus this cognitive tendency may help to explain the persistence of laypeople's beliefs and also of scientists' theories, even in the face of seemingly contradictory evidence.

Conclusion

The preceding discussion has illustrated the large number of heuristic methods and cognitive biases that researchers have found to operate in people's thinking and decision making. These heuristics and biases in social perception are analogous to the perceptual illusions that can occur in people's observation of the physical world. However, just as people's physical perception is usually quite accurate despite the occasional occurrence of illusions, research reviews have concluded that social perception is also usually "good enough" for the needs of the perceiver. That is, in the light of their usual purposes and contexts, as well as their goals in a given interaction, people tend to "construct the meaning of their social environment well enough to enable effective action" (Fiske, 1993, p. 182). A further hopeful conclusion concerns the performance of experts in a given area of knowledge. Although they are also subject to the same heuristics and biases as laypeople, knowledgeable decision makers who are performing realistic and familiar tasks within their area of expertise are generally less influenced by these sources of error (e.g., Smith & Kida, 1991).

STEREOTYPES AND SCHEMAS

Continuing our discussion of people's use of convenient shortcuts in their thoughts and decisions, we note that one of the most common of these shortcuts is the use of stereotypes. This term originally referred to a metal printer's plate, which could faithfully print thousands of copies of a picture, all exactly alike. Later the word was borrowed by Walter Lippmann (1922), the famous author and commentator on public affairs. He used it to mean "pictures in our heads" about various racial, national, or social groups—that is, perceptions of members of a given group as all being identical copies of each other, all having the same characteristics and traits.

Although the term **stereotype** has become widely used, various social scientists have defined it in somewhat different ways. We will define it simply as *a mental image or generalized set of beliefs that a person holds about most members of a particular social group*. Of necessity, such beliefs are highly simplified, and they may be strongly evaluative and rigidly resistant to change (e.g., "most dogs are vicious," "women are irrational").

Note that this definition does not specify that stereotypes must be inaccurate, as some authors do. The reason for this omission will become clear in the following paragraphs. Note also that the definition does not specify that stereotypes must be shared beliefs—an individual can have his or her own idiosyncratic stereotype of another group of people (e.g., "women are highly logical"), though when we speak of *social* stereotypes, we mean ones that are shared by many individuals. People often develop stereotypes about their own groups as well as about outgroups that they do not belong to (e.g., Prentice & Miller, 2002).

Stereotypes develop and persist because they are *useful* (Hilton & von Hippel, 1996). They reduce the tremendous complexity of the world around us into a few simple guidelines, which we can use in our everyday thoughts and decisions. If we "know" that "all politicians are crooked," we can dismiss government scandals without having to think very hard about what should be done to prevent or control them. Similarly, if we believe that "women are irrational," we won't hire one to be our lawyer. Unfortunately, however, the simpler and more convenient the stereotype, the more likely it is to be inaccurate, at least in part.

The inaccuracy of stereotypes has been much emphasized, particularly in the field of racial attitudes, where the terms "stereotype" and "prejudice" have taken on derogatory connotations. In one classic study, the stereotype shared by citizens of Fresno, California, about the local Armenian minority group was shown not only to be false, but to be opposite to reality on many characteristics—e.g., Armenians were actually more law abiding than average rather than less so (LaPiere, 1936). However, several authors have pointed out that many stereotypes (though not necessarily all) have a *kernel of truth* in them (e.g., Triandis, 1977; Judd & Park, 1993). Campbell (1967) has convincingly presented the reasons for a possible kernel of truth, stressing that the traits that are most important to a perceiving group and the traits on which it differs most from another group will be likely to enter into its stereotype of the other group. To take one example, because cleanliness is an important characteristic to most Americans, and relatively unimportant to many primitive societies, it is more apt to enter into Americans' stereotypes of primitive societies than into those societies' stereotypes of Americans. Thus, paradoxically, a stereotype is *determined largely by the nature of the perceiving group*, and relatively little by the nature of the group that it ostensibly describes.

Although many stereotypes may contain a kernel of truth, a key feature of stereotypes is that they are *overgeneralized*. That is, the characteristics attributed to the group (e.g., women are emotional) are believed to apply to all members of the group. When generalized in this way, the stereotype is very likely to be inaccurate—clearly, not all women are emotional.

Formation of Stereotypes

Much of the research on stereotypes treats them as a result of people's normal cognitive and motivational processes of learning and adapting to the world around them (Hamilton, 1981a; Hilton & von Hippel, 1996). It should be emphasized that, like other beliefs and attitudes, a person's stereotypes are often not the product of personal experience with the group in question. They may also derive largely, or entirely, from one or more of the following four sources:

1. Explicit teaching. Particularly when children are young, they are frequently given explicit stereotypic information by their parents as they are taught about life ("kitties are nice," "damn politicians," "dirty commies," "honest cops," or "police brutality"). Later on, peers and teachers may also pass on stereotypes directly. However, this explicit transmission of stereotypes is augmented by three other processes, which occur with much less conscious awareness.

2. Incidental learning, particularly from the mass media. This is typically a process of associative learning, in which members of a social group are repeatedly paired with particular personal characteristics. For instance, time after time, images in old movies have shown blacks as lazy or stupid, American Indians as bloodthirsty or treacherous, women as subservient housewives, and so on. Although more recent movies and TV shows have included a wider range of behaviors for these groups, there are still subtle forms of racism in their portrayal of African Americans and other ethnic minority groups. First, all minority groups have been presented on television in far lower proportions than their share of the national population. Second, when they are presented, minorities such as foreigners and Latinos are especially likely to be depicted in lower-status occupations and criminal activities (Rothman, Lichter, & Lichter, 1992; Gerbner, 1993). On children's TV programs, more than half of the villains have accents, typically German or Russian (Mendelson & Young, 1972). The repeated portrayal of such characteristics as being typical of particular social groups is a potent source of stereotypes among the mass media audience.

3. Illusory correlation. In contrast with the preceding two processes, in which stereotypic information is actually presented in different degrees of association with various social groups, in the process of **illusory correlation** people come to perceive a correlation of particular traits with a given social group, even in cases where they have not been differentially associated. Experiments on social cognition have shown that this illogical process often occurs in situations where subjects are presented with instances in which two groups of different size (a numerical majority group and minority group) are paired with two or more kinds of traits or behaviors having different frequencies (a common one such as honesty and a rare one, such as being a criminal). In this situation, even when there is no differential association of any trait with any group, subjects nevertheless typically tend to see an association of the *small* group with the *rare* trait (Hamilton 1981b; Mullen & Johnson, 1990), though there are some conditions where this effect is not found (e.g., Hamilton, Stroessner, & Mackie, 1993). In a real-life situation, this phenomenon would mean that individuals would generally form a stereotype associating a minority group (or any outgroup that was seldom contacted) with various uncommon traits or behaviors. Some of these traits could be favorable ones, but because negative traits like criminality are generally quite rare, stereotypes are usually composed mostly of negative traits.

Illusory correlation can be seen as an example of the availability heuristic at work. The rare, extreme behavior is apt to be more memorable than more common traits. When it is paired with members of a majority group, the perceiver has plenty of contrary examples to counteract the association, but when it is occasionally paired with a member of a rarely encountered outgroup, the association of two rare categories is salient and its frequency tends to be exaggerated by the perceiver. This process can be seen, not only in the formation of stereotypes, but also in maintaining and strengthening them once they are formed. That is, even in sets of data where there is no differential association of an outgroup with one of its established stereotypic traits, perceivers tend to see one as being present (Hamilton & Rose, 1980). And once such a perceived association is formed, people tend to maintain it and strengthen it, even in the absence of any supporting evidence (Hilton & von Hippel, 1996).

Other studies show that stereotypes serve as hypotheses about new acquaintances, but that people test them out in a biased manner by looking solely for confirmatory information, and thus they rarely ever learn about instances in which the stereotypes are false (Darley & Gross, 1983). In such cases, instead of "seeing is believing," people's behavior indicates that "believing is seeing" (Hamilton, 1981b).

4. Self-fulfilling prophecies. A fourth way in which stereotypes may be formed and strengthened is when people's expectations about another person cause them to behave in ways that elicit the behavior that they expected. As an example, in one illustrative experiment pairs of college students held phone conversations. When one of the students was led to believe that his partner was physically attractive, his conversational approach led her to exhibit more sociable behavior than occurred in the control condition where students were not given that expectation (Snyder, Tanke, & Berscheid, 1977).

Social Schemas

In addition to stereotypes, social schemas are another type of shortcut device that people use to help them operate efficiently in their social interactions. A **schema** is an abstract, general expectation about how some part of the world operates, built up on the basis of our own past experience with specific examples. Social schemas (also called schemata) provide patterns of expectations that help us to function in social situations on the basis of typical, expected interaction patterns without thinking in detail about the characteristics of the particular individuals or occasions that we are dealing with. In using schemas, perceivers actively create their own versions of reality. Research has shown that schemas "influence the encoding of new information, memory for old information, and inferences where information is missing" (Fiske & Taylor, 1991, p. 121).

There are five general types of social schemas, as follows. **Role schemas** describe the norms and behavior expected of people in various social categories based on age, sex, race, occupation, and so on (e.g., grandmothers, or missionaries). Stereotypes can be viewed as a particularly important subcategory of role schemas. **Person schemas** summarize your actual or vicarious experience concerning the characteristics of broad types of people or of specific individuals (e.g., extroverts, or your roommate). **Self-schemas** are simplified conceptions that people hold about their own key traits, goals, feelings, and behavior. Different individuals' self-schemas stress different dimensions (e.g., their weight or their sense of humor) and omit many other dimensions.

Event schemas comprise knowledge about the normal sequence of events in familiar social situations, such as baseball games, buying groceries, or asking for a date. Event schemas are also called **scripts** and, like actors' scripts in the theater, they include props, roles, typical actions, and rules for the sequence of events (Abelson, 1981). Finally, **procedural social schemas** are relatively content-free rules for how pertinent information is to be sought and linked together. The most-studied types are causal schemas (ways of explaining the causes of events), which are discussed later in this chapter as an aspect of attribution theory. The use of any of these types of schemas can make learning, memory, and inference faster and easier, but it often also makes them less accurate.

Schema research has cast important light on the process of stereotyping. For instance, studies have shown that role schemas can influence the earliest stages of perception, and thus it is possible for someone's very first impressions of an outgroup member to be mistaken and to omit many of the person's true characteristics (Klatzky, Martin, & Kane, 1982). In general, people perceive any **outgroup** (i.e., a group or classificatory category to which they do not belong) as being more homogeneous and less variable than their own membership groups (Mullen & Hu, 1989; Amidon & Boldry, 2002). This is called the **outgroup homogeneity effect**, and it applies especially strongly to numerical minority groups (Bartsch & Judd, 1993). People also consistently evaluate their own ingroups as being *better* on many different dimensions (Hilton & von Hippel, 1996). This is true not only for racial, occupational, and gender groups, but also for such trivial characteristics as eye color or alphabetical position of one's name, and even for arbitrary assignments to groups such as children's teams (Wilder & Cooper, 1981; Park & Rothbart, 1982). These biases in making evaluative and variability judgments about outgroups are magnified when there is competition between the groups (Weber, 1994).

As a result of these tendencies, people are often willing to make rash inferences about outgroups concerning whom they have very little knowledge—sometimes even on the basis of a single item of information. Similarly, people who are busy with multiple tasks tend to remember information about individuals better when it confirms their stereotype of the group (Macrae, Hewstone, & Griffiths, 1993), and the same is true of prejudiced people who have strong stereotypes (von Hippel, Sekaquaptewa, & Vargas, 1995).

Although schemas can change over time, there are several different cognitive and motivational processes that contribute to their continuation (Hilton & von Hippel, 1996). Thus, one of their main features is their perseverance—sometimes even when the evidence that produced them is completely discredited (Anderson, Lepper, & Ross, 1980). When discrepant information is encountered, a schema about an individual is more likely to change than is a stereotype about a whole social group (Wyer & Gordon, 1982). One kind of change that fairly often occurs in a group stereotype is the *formation of a subtype* to contain the discrepant individual (e.g., a brilliant janitor), with no change in the schema for the group as a whole (Kunda & Oleson, 1995).

Automatic Social Cognition

Recent research findings on many topics have demonstrated that "a surprising amount of social cognition and perception happens automatically" (Fiske, 1993, p. 182). One example is the topic of mistaken first impressions, mentioned earlier in this chapter. Other examples come from research on priming effects and mood induction, in which an initial stimulus word or phrase or a mood-inducing experience typically has an effect on a person's judgments or attitudinal responses, but without the individual's being aware of the effects (for a thorough review, see Wegner & Bargh, 1998). In these kinds of research, people are generally aware of the stimulus but not of the resulting process, but in some situations, such as **subliminal perception**, people are unaware of both the stimulus and the resulting cognitive process (Bargh, 1989). An important example of these kinds of automatic responses is discussed at length in Chapter 4, on implicit attitudes.

ATTRIBUTION PROCESSES

Our next topic, attribution processes, has been one of the most studied aspects of social cognition in recent years. It was so prominent in the 1970s and 1980s that various reviewers termed it "the single most pervasive influence upon social psychology in the past decade" (Cialdini, Petty, & Cacioppo, 1981, p. 389) and "the leading theoretical concern and dominant empirical topic of the field" (Fiske & Taylor, 1984, p. 20). The number of scientific articles on attribution that were published each year tripled from 1974 to 1984 and continued to increase into the 1990s (Smith, 1994).

What do we mean by **attribution**? Essentially, it refers to our process of making inferences about the unobservable characteristics of other people, objects, events, or ourselves. By far the predominant aspect of attribution processes that has been studied is the topic of perceived causality: that is, how we decide about the causes of behavior or events. Another important aspect is the attribution of responsibility: that is, our judgments about whether people are responsible for particular events, and how we assign praise or blame for their actions. In addition to these central topics, attributional concepts and principles have been applied to many different social psychological topics, such as perceptions of freedom, physical attractiveness, success or failure in achievement, close relationships, mental and physical health, and even issues in international foreign policy. Interested readers may want to consult one of the longer discussions of attribution theory and research (e.g., Jaspars, Fincham, & Hewstone, 1983; Weary, Stanley, & Harvey, 1989; Fiske & Taylor, 1991).

Heider's Theory of Naive Psychology

There is not just one attribution theory, but several parallel and partly overlapping approaches. In origin, they all stem from Fritz Heider's (1944) early paper on phenomenal causality, that is, on how people make inferences or attributions about the causes of events. Later Heider (1958) expanded his attribution principles in his book on interpersonal relations, which is also the source of many of the central principles of consistency theory (see Box 2–2).

Heider proposed to build a theory of causal inference from studying people's "naive psychology"—that is, their everyday ways of thinking about events and making sense out of the world. He felt that individuals necessarily developed some causal notions about events and behavior because such notions were crucial in their attempts to understand, predict, and control the world around them. In contrast to the previously discussed emphasis on heuristics and biases, Heider and the other early attribution theorists tended to see people as making their judgments and inferences in a relatively logical and rational manner—as "intuitive scientists."

Photograph courtesy of Fritz Heider.
Reprinted by permission.

Box 2–2   FRITZ HEIDER, *Father of Attribution Theory*

Fritz Heider's career was greatly influenced by the school of Gestalt psychology. Born in Vienna, Austria, in 1896, he took a Ph.D. in psychology at the University of Graz in 1920. Later he attended lectures by Lewin, Köhler, and Wertheimer at the University of Berlin, translated one of Lewin's books, and wrote about Gestalt theory and Lewinian theory. After three years of teaching at the University of Hamburg, he came to America in 1930 to do research and teach with Koffka at Smith College. He remained there, doing much of his research on problems of deafness, until moving to the University of Kansas in 1947.

Heider is famous for his development of both attribution theory and consistency theory. His major work, The Psychology of Interpersonal Relations *(1958), has much in common with Lewin's field theory, and the following year he was honored with the Lewin Memorial Award by the Society for the Psychological Study of Social Issues. Among his other honors is the American Psychological Association's Distinguished Scientific Contribution Award for his work on social perception. Retired in 1967, he lived in Lawrence, Kansas, until his death in 1988.*

Heider was interested primarily in the conditions under which attributions about the stable dispositions of people (e.g., their friendliness, honesty, likes and dislikes, etc.) would be made, based on information about their actions. This is a question that we all try to answer for ourselves many times every day (e.g., "I wonder why she smiled at me"), so it has great practical as well as scientific interest. Depending on the situation, attribution processes may result in attitude formation, attitude change, or support for one's existing attitudes.

Heider (1958) distinguished between internal attribution and external attribution. **Internal attribution** concludes that the cause of an individual's actions is a personal disposition—for example, "she smiled because she is friendly." **External attribution** concludes that the cause of a person's actions is a factor outside the person—for example, "He succeeded because of good luck," or "because the task was easy." Thus we may attribute the cause of a person's actions to his or her own characteristics, to situational factors, or to a combination of both. How do we arrive at this conclusion in any given instance? Heider says that we consider three factors: the person's *ability, intention*, and *exertion*. We evaluate ability in relation to the difficulty of the task, and we evaluate exertion by observation of the person's apparent effort. Intention is the hardest factor to evaluate because many actions have both intended and unintended consequences; therefore, it is difficult to determine the person's intentions from observing the consequences of his or her actions. Nevertheless, Heider concluded that only when we perceive the person as intending the action's consequences do we infer **personal causality** and make internal attributions about the person's dispositions or traits.

Heider also discussed the perception of people's responsibility for social outcomes. This is often the next question raised after the determination of causality—first, what caused an event? and then, who was responsible? For instance, suppose your car hit a parked car; who was responsible for the accident? Heider posited five different levels or aspects of responsibility that are considered in a sequential fashion in order to determine a person's accountability for such an event. First, **association** is mere linkage in time and space. If you were in the car, whether or not you were driving, you would be associated with the accident, and at a primitive level you might be considered at least partially responsible. Second, **commission** means that you carried out or caused the action. It would be present if you were the driver. Third, **foreseeability** concerns whether or not you could foresee the outcome. If you had just come over the crest of a hill and found the other car parked right ahead of you in the middle of the road, foreseeability would be absent, and you would be held less responsible. Fourth, **intentionality** may be present or absent even when you could foresee the outcome. If a pothole in the pavement made you swerve and hit the other car, the crash would be an unintentional one. Finally, **justification** may sometimes be present even where the action was intentional. For instance, you would be justified (and therefore less responsible legally or morally) if you intentionally chose to hit the car rather than to run over a child who dashed out in front of you. As these examples suggest, not only do people consider such factors in their personal judgments about responsibility, but they are also built into our society's moral codes and legal procedures—e.g., the various gradations of homicide, from murder through negligent manslaughter to justified self-defense.

Jones and Davis' Theory of Correspondent Inferences

Heider's discussion of attribution principles has been extended in many directions by several groups of theorists, of whom the most influential have been Jones and Davis (1965) and Kelley (1967). Jones and Davis focused on the process of making *internal* attributions about personal causality, whereas Kelley concentrated largely on *external* attributions about impersonal situational causes.

Jones and Davis (1965) hold that, when people act, the causal sequence is that their dispositions (long-term, stable personal characteristics) lead to their intentions, which in turn produce their actions. That is,

CAUSATION: dispositions → intentions → actions.

However, in making *inferences* about personal causation, this process is reversed, as follows:

CAUSAL INFERENCE: observed actions → intentions → dispositions.

Thus, Jones and Davis propose that people first observe another person's actions and the effects of those actions, then use that information to infer the person's intentions, and finally make attributions about the person's traits or dispositions on the basis of the inferred intentions. This is called the **theory of correspondent inferences** because the perceiver is trying to form an inference that the person's behavior and intentions *correspond* to an underlying, stable personality characteristic. This inference process is a tricky one because the evidence is often unclear or incomplete, and the perceiver has to act like a detective or a scientist in puzzling out the true causal factors behind events.

Jones and Davis' theory suggests four factors that help to increase the correspondence of inferences (that is, the strength and confidence of people's causal attributions): lack of social desirability, noncommon effects, hedonic relevance, and personalism.

1. The **social desirability** of another person's actions decreases the strength of our attributions about them, whereas socially undesirable actions give us more confidence in our attributions (Skowronski & Carlston, 1989). This is true because most people follow social norms and act in socially desirable ways most of the time, and thus it is unclear whether such behavior reflects their real dispositions or merely their understanding of what is expected of them. If a wife gives her husband a peck on the cheek in public, this in-role behavior doesn't tell us much about her true feelings, but if she hits him in public, her behavior is much more informative.

2. The **noncommon effects** resulting from a chosen and an unchosen action are also informative about the chooser's motives and dispositions, whereas the effects that the two actions have in common don't help us make such attributions. Suppose a friend of yours is trying to decide between two summer jobs. If both would require him to live in a city, both involve desk work, and both are well paid, these common effects don't help you to understand his motives. However, if one is near his girlfriend's home whereas the other is far away, and he chooses the nearby job, that noncommon effect of the chosen and unchosen alternatives strengthens the inference that being near his girlfriend is important to him. If the two choices have more than one noncommon effect (for instance, one job also requires mathematical skills and the other doesn't), then your attribution about the real reason for his choice will be less clear and less confident.

It is also possible to observe a person's successive actions over a period of time and make inferences about their underlying dispositions (Jones & McGillis, 1976). The flip side of the noncommon effects principle is that, when a person has taken *both* of two actions, their *common effects* are informative about the person's motives, whereas their noncommon effects are irrelevant. If your friend had held several very different jobs in turn, and the only thing that they had in common was that they all paid very well, that common effect would be a factor allowing you to make confident attributions about your friend's goals in life.

3. The **hedonic relevance** of a person's actions means the degree to which they are beneficial or harmful to the perceiver. In general, greater hedonic relevance produces stronger and more confident attributions. If I borrow your car and have an accident with it, you will be more inclined to view me as a reckless scoundrel than if the accident had occurred in someone else's car.

4. The **personalism** of a person's actions means the degree to which they are viewed as being aimed specifically at the perceiver. Personalism is roughly equivalent to intentionality, and it also increases the strength of attributions. If I not only had an accident in your car, but in addition you believe that I wrecked it intentionally to harass you, your conclusion about my wickedness will be even stronger.

Jones and his colleagues have suggested a few other factors that influence the attribution process. One key requirement for making correspondent inferences is the presence of some freedom of *choice* in the actor's behavior. In contrast, it is not safe to make dispositional attributions if the person's actions are situationally constrained in some way, such as being required by law or performed under the shadow of threats. Another factor that prevents confident attributions is behavior that is part of a *social role*. As previously suggested regarding social desirability, in-role behavior is not a good basis for dispositional attributions, but out-of-role behavior or role-inconsistent behavior is. Finally, our *prior*

Photograph courtesy of Edward E. Jones.
Reprinted by permission.

Box 2–3 EDWARD E. JONES, *Researcher on Attribution and Self-Presentation*

Edward E. (Ned) Jones was born in Buffalo, New York, in 1926 and studied history at Swarthmore and social psychology at Harvard, where he also earned his Ph.D. following some postwar military service in Japan. In 1953 he took his first faculty position at Duke University, where he spent 24 happy years and developed a strong social psychology program. In 1977 he moved to Princeton to accept an endowed professorship and won the American Psychology Association's Award for Distinguished Scientific Contributions.

Jones was an early convert to the experimental side of social psychology, and his dissertation was an experimental study of authoritarianism as a determinant of first-impression formation. He was coauthor of a noted social psychology textbook and wrote a prize-winning research monograph on ingratiation in self-presentation. His central contributions to attribution theory included classic papers with Keith Davis on correspondent inferences and with Richard Nisbett on actor–observer differences. In subsequent years he coauthored or authored books on social stigma, minority-group mental health, and interpersonal perception, remaining active in research until his death in 1993.

expectations about a person are attributions that develop as a result of our past experiences with that person, and later behavior that departs from them can give us a basis for refining these dispositional attributions (Jones & McGillis, 1976). For instance, if your normally unflappable roommate got very excited when running for a student office, you might conclude that the social approval involved in winning the election was one of her most highly valued goals. However, if a person's behavior departs too much from your expectations, *skepticism* is likely to be aroused—if your roommate got too hyper, you might suspect that she was really putting on an act.

In conclusion, it can be seen that Jones and Davis' attribution theory presents a rational cognitive model of how people make causal inferences about people and events around them, and it largely ignores affective and motivational bases of the perceiver's judgments. It focuses mainly on the logical, rational processes that people *should* use in making attributions, as Kelley's parallel theory likewise does, and for this reason these theories have been termed **normative models** or guidelines for how social cognition should proceed (Fiske & Taylor, 1991). However, as we have seen earlier in this chapter, there are many pervasive biases and sources of error that cause people's inferences to depart in certain ways from the normative models specified by these theories.

Kelley's Theory of Covariation

Harold Kelley's (1967) covariation theory of attribution is complementary to Jones and Davis' approach. Whereas Jones and Davis focused on internal attributions about personal causality, Kelley's theory dealt mainly with *external* attributions about objects and stimuli in the environment; however, it can also be applied to self-perception and to internal causal inferences about other people's behavior. It concerns situations in which one has *repeated observations* of behavior or events, whereas Jones and Davis' original formulation was limited to inferences about single actions.

Kelley (1967) proposed that people make causal inferences by using the principle of covariation in much the same way that scientists use analysis of variance (ANOVA) to determine which of several possible independent variables actually affects a set of repeated observations. The **covariation principle** posits that an effect will be attributed to a causal factor that is present when the effect is present and absent when the effect is absent. For instance, if my wife rarely ever complains about my clothes, but protests every time I wear my old threadbare jacket, there is a covariation between my wearing the jacket and her complaints, and it is likely that something about the jacket causes the complaints. By contrast, if her protests occur approximately equally whether I am wearing my old jacket or my new one, it is unlikely that the old jacket is the cause of the complaints.

According to Kelley's theory, there are three kinds of possible causes for such social effects: persons, entities (environmental objects), and times (occasions or situations). How can people know whether they have correctly attributed a given effect to a particular cause? Kelley suggests that, in assessing covariation, they consider three key dimensions of information about the possible causes—distinctiveness, consistency, and consensus information. To see how this works, imagine that your friend Steve has told you he loved the movie *Vampire's Castle*. This effect could be due to the movie's excellence (an external attribution) or to Steve's poor taste regarding movies (an internal attribution). An external attribution that the movie was a good one would be strengthened by information on these three key dimensions:

1. **Distinctiveness**—Was Steve's reaction to this movie distinctively different from his feeling about other movies, or does he love almost any movie he sees?

2. **Consistency**—Was Steve's response to the movie similar when he saw it at other times and under other conditions (e.g., with and without his girlfriend)?
3. **Consensus**—Did Steve's reaction resemble the consensus of other people who saw the movie?

If your analysis found high distinctiveness, high consistency, and high consensus, you would be very confident in concluding that the movie was a good one (an external or entity attribution). Another pattern that would be clearly interpretable is low distinctiveness, high consistency, and low consensus, leading to a person attribution—that is, Steve enjoys any old movie at any time, but others don't agree with him, so he must be undiscriminating (McArthur, 1972). Other patterns of information can lead to an attribution of joint responsibility for the effect (e.g., it's a good movie, but Steve is a poor judge of movies), or to ambiguous causal conclusions.

As you might expect from the section earlier in this chapter on ignoring base-rate information, research has shown that people's attributions often rely relatively little on consensus information (Kassin, 1979; Borgida & Brekke, 1981); but cues of distinctiveness and consistency are quite generally utilized (Kelley & Michela, 1980). However, people frequently make attributions in situations where they have no time to collect repeated observations, or when they want to understand a single event and thus they have no evidence about distinctiveness, consistency, or consensus. For such situations, a later paper by Kelley (1972a) described two attributional principles that are often used: discounting and augmentation.

Discounting.   The **discounting principle** posits that the importance of any given cause in producing a particular effect will be discounted in a situation where there are other plausible causes. For instance, if a college classmate gave you an unexpected compliment, you would ordinarily be tempted to believe it; but you would be much more inclined to discount its sincerity if you discovered that the classmate was hoping to get on your good side and borrow your car for the weekend. The discounting principle is similar to Jones and Davis' notion of noncommon effects, for each noncommon effect between two actions constitutes a plausible cause for the chosen action, and strength of inference is greater whenever the number of plausible causes (and thus, noncommon effects) is small. Research studies have generally supported both the discounting and noncommon effects principles (Kelley & Michela, 1980).

Augmentation.   In a situation where there are multiple plausible causes for a given effect, some possible causes might facilitate the effect whereas others might inhibit it (make it less likely). In such cases the **augmentation principle**, which is roughly opposite to the discounting principle, may be applied. It holds that if an effect occurs in the presence of a plausible inhibitory cause, people will attribute more strength to the facilitative cause than if it were operating in the absence of an inhibitory cause. In other words, the facilitative cause is seen as having to be stronger in order to overcome the opposite effect of the inhibitory cause. For example, if your friend buys tickets to a rock concert despite their very high price, you would conclude that he really liked the musicians, whereas if he went to a low-priced concert, you'd be less sure of his degree of enthusiasm for those performers. There is also research support for this augmentation process (Ginzel, Jones, & Swann, 1987).

Causal Schemas

In another later paper, Kelley (1972b) departed from his earlier emphasis on people as being logical and rational, proposing that much of our causal attribution is not done in

Photograph courtesy of Harold H. Kelley. Reprinted by permission.

Box 2–4 HAROLD H. KELLEY, *Analyst of Attribution and Personal Relationships*

Harold Kelley began life in 1921 in Idaho, grew up in California's central valley, and earned a B.A. and M.A. in psychology at Berkeley. During World War II he served in the Aviation Psychology program, and following the war he earned his Ph.D. in Kurt Lewin's newly formed Research Center for Group Dynamics at MIT. When the Center moved to the University of Michigan in 1948 following Lewin's untimely death, Kelley took his first faculty position there. In 1950 he became an assistant professor at Yale, where he did research in Carl Hovland's Attitude Change Program and was coauthor (with Hovland and Janis) of the classic volume Communication and Persuasion. *In 1955 he moved to the University of Minnesota and in 1961 to UCLA, where he remained active until his death in 2003.*

Kelley's early interest in social perception led to his dissertation on first impressions. Later he worked closely with John Thibaut on small-group and interpersonal phenomena, jointly authoring The Psychology of Groups *(1959) and* Interpersonal Relations: A Theory of Interdependence *(1978). Coauthor of 10 books and over 100 articles, Kelley was perhaps best known for his contributions to attribution theory, detailed in this chapter. Subsequently he wrote several books analyzing the structure and processes of close personal relationships. He was honored with the American Psychological Association's Distinguished Scientific Contribution Award and elected a member of the National Academy of Sciences and the American Academy of Arts and Sciences.*

the careful, full-scale manner described in his covariation or ANOVA model. Oftentimes there is not enough information available, or we do not have the time or interest to do a complete causal analysis. In such situations we may use causal schemas as a shortcut to make causal inferences. Kelley identified two main types of causal schemas: (1) The **multiple necessary causes schema** applies to tasks that are very difficult, such as winning an Olympic gold medal. Here many causes are necessary for success (ability, training, effort, etc.), so success tells us that all of these causes were present, but failure would not tell us which was missing. (2) The **multiple sufficient causes schema** applies to tasks that are very easy, such as winning a game against a small child. Here any one of several causes might be sufficient for success (ability, effort, and experience in the game), so failure tells us that none of them were present; however, success would not tell us which one(s) was (were) missing, and so we would tend to use the discounting principle in assessing them (Fiske & Taylor, 1991). It is also sometimes possible to use the strength of effects (e.g., how close the contest was) to infer how strong some of the causal factors were (e.g., how much ability or effort the winner displayed).

Bem's Self-Perception Theory

A fourth theorist who has made important contributions, particularly in the area of self-attributions, is Daryl Bem (1967, 1972). Bem stated that his self-perception theory derived from a radical behaviorist position, based on B. F. Skinner's (1957) operant behavioral analysis of human verbal behavior. He originally presented his ideas as a critique of and an alternative to cognitive dissonance theory (a controversy that we discuss later in Chapter 11). However, because of his focus on the previously neglected area of how people make inferences about *their own* intentions, goals, and traits, his work has been acknowledged as an important addition to the field of attribution theory.

Bem holds that people are not nearly as aware of, nor as clear about, their own internal feelings and beliefs as they think they are. Bem's **self-perception principle** states that

> Individuals come to "know" their own attitudes, emotions, and other internal states partially by inferring them from observations of their own overt behavior and/or the circumstances in which this behavior occurs. Thus, to the extent that internal cues are weak, ambiguous, or uninterpretable, the individual is functionally in the same position as an outside observer, an observer who must necessarily rely upon those same external cues to infer the individual's inner states. (1972, p. 2)

In the beginning, Bem says, every child learns about his or her external environment through discrimination training by adults and other children around him or her. By verbal labeling and corroboration or correction, children learn to distinguish between dogs and cats, for instance, and between anger and happiness in other people. In the same way, says Bem, through self-perception we also learn to label our own inner feelings of hunger, anger, anxiety, or liking. To use his favorite example, we decide that we like brown bread by observing the fact that we eat a lot of it. The other factor that is important in determining our self-attributions is whether the external circumstances constrain our behavior. If we realize that the only bread our mother serves us is brown bread, we will be less likely to conclude that our eating it indicates great fondness for it.

In his first theoretical papers, Bem (1967) stated even more strongly the dramatic and unorthodox claim that people do not really know their attitudes and beliefs until they act, that they can infer these internal states only from their behavior, and that they even may be unable to remember any internal states that are discrepant from their behavior (Bem & McConnell, 1970). Later he retreated from this extreme position and claimed only that individuals use *partially* the same external evidence as outside observers do, as previously quoted. However, his theory does not tell us how to determine whether a person's internal cues are "weak, ambiguous, or uninterpretable" in a given situation (though he suggests that that is very often true), so there is no clear way to determine how much the person has to rely on external cues. Also, his theory does not contain any motivational principles about why or when people will make attributions. Nevertheless, Bem's focus on inferences about the self and his emphasis on one's own behavior as an important inferential cue have stimulated much important attributional research.

Bem has also applied his theory to attitude change, positing that it occurs in reaction to self-observed behaviors *combined with* observation of external cues, which indicate whether or not the behavior is apt to be valid or truthful. For instance, if an actor in a TV commercial says "I like Busy Bakers' brown bread," but we know that he was paid to make the commercial, we may doubt whether that is his true attitude. In a contrary example, if a person is subtly induced to say something opposed to his former opinion under conditions that suggest truthfulness, he is apt to decide that he really believes the statement that he has made.

As a real-life instance of this process, Bem (1970) has asserted that police station interrogation conditions constitute a truth-telling situation for most people, and that in such situations certain wily interrogation procedures can induce prisoners to make *and to believe in* false confessions about crimes, which they have not really committed. This is a particularly surprising and dramatic example of attitude change, and Bem has backed up his claims with clear-cut evidence from a laboratory experiment, which showed exactly this process at work. However, it should be noted that other investigators have had difficulty in replicating these results (Kiesler & Munson, 1975).

In comparison with Kelley's or Jones and Davis' attribution theories, Bem's theory is a very simple one, and it proposes that people normally do very little cognitive work in making their attributions. In its emphasis on the simple, shortcut nature of social cognition, Bem's theory is consistent with the work on heuristics and biases described earlier in this chapter. Thus it anticipated the subsequently developed **cognitive miser** view of social cognition—the conclusion that people's attributions generally do not follow the normative models of rational inference processes, but rather take shortcuts that require as little time and effort in information processing as possible (Fiske & Taylor, 1984).

A Later Conclusion. In more recent research, the pendulum has swung back to a compromise between normative models of rational inference and the cognitive miser view that emphasizes shortcuts and heuristic processes in attribution. Experimental findings have suggested that the shortcut processing generally occurs in situations where the consequences for the social perceiver are minimal, but that in more important situations more time and information is often used in determining one's attributions and attitudes (Taylor, 1975). This balancing act was termed the **motivated tactician** approach by Fiske and Taylor (1991), who noted that it reintroduced motivational and emotional factors into models of social cognition. The motivated tactician is neither consistently stingy with cognitive attention nor consistently thorough in making inferences (Taylor, 1998):

> The motivated tactician is viewed as having multiple information processing strategies available, selecting among them on the basis of goals, motives, needs, and forces in the environment. (p. 75)

Actor–Observer Differences

In the vast research literature on attribution, one of the most important topics is actor–observer differences. Here the term *actor* means a participant who has taken part in some social interaction, whereas an *observer* is an uninvolved individual who has merely watched the interaction. Jones and Nisbett (1972) proposed that actors tend to attribute their actions to situational factors, whereas observers of the same actions tend to attribute them to stable personal dispositions of the actor, including abilities, traits, and attitudes (the fundamental attribution error again). There is a large body of support for this principle, though some exceptions have also been found (Watson, 1982). The difference has been summed up provocatively in Triandis' (1977) comment that actors seem to believe Skinnerian theory, whereas observers appear to prefer Allport's trait theory.

What might be the reasons for this pervasive finding? One factor is the amount of knowledge that each person has about the actor's past behavior: The observer, who has seen the actor in only one situation, may assume that his or her behavior in other situations is consistent and so make a dispositional attribution, whereas the actor is aware of much variability in his or her own past behavior, depending on the situation that he or she was in (see Figure 2–1). Research has confirmed this difference and shown that, as we know a person

FIGURE 2–1
An example of actor–observer differences. Observers often attribute behavior to internal characteristics of the actor, whereas the actor often attributes it to situational pressures.

longer, we tend to make fewer trait attributions and give more situational explanations for his or her behavior (Goldberg, 1981; White & Younger, 1988).

Another factor is visual salience or focus of attention, which is due to the differing visual perspectives of the actor and the observer. In the typical experimental situation the observer is watching the actor's behavior while the actor is attending to incoming situational stimuli related to his task. In an experiment that made a clever use of videotape feedback, Storms (1973) showed that, when these visual perspectives were reversed, the types of attributions made by the actor and observer were also reversed. When the actor who had just completed a short conversation saw a replay of his behavior from the visual perspective of the observer, his attributions became less situational; and when the observer saw a replay of the discussion made from the actor's visual perspective, his attributions became *more* situational than the actor's revised ones. Another study showed that observers' attributions can also be made more situational by instructing the observers to empathize with the actor (Regan & Totten, 1975).

Motivational factors may also enter into this phenomenon (Johnson et al., 1985). One motivation that has been suggested for observers' tendencies to use trait attributions is the need for personal control: If they think that other people's behavior is consistent (such as a personal trait), they will have a better chance of predicting it and perhaps also of influencing it in the future (Miller, Norman, & Wright, 1978).

Certain exceptions to the actor–observer pattern also seem to stem from motivational factors. In line with a self-esteem or egotism hypothesis, it has been found that actors give more internal attributions for their own positive behaviors and less internal explanations for their negative behaviors, such as harmful actions or failures (Taylor & Koivumaki, 1976; Schlenker, Hallam, & McCown, 1983). Contrariwise, observers give more internal attributions for actors' harmful actions than for their beneficial ones. In competitive games it has been found that winners tend to give dispositional explanations for their success, but losers (who are also actors) attribute the outcome more to external factors, particularly luck (Lau & Russell, 1980).

The general pattern of actor–observer differences in attribution is well-established, and these latter findings show how research has turned toward investigating when and why it occurs and its resulting effects. This is a very important area of research, with many practical implications for relationships between managers and workers, husbands and wives, and parents and children (Weary, Stanley, & Harvey, 1989). For example, extending the actor–observer relationship by analogy to ingroups and outgroups in the area of intergroup prejudice, Aboud and Taylor (1971) found that people typically explain the behavior of members of their ingroup by using role (external) attributions, whereas they use (internal) ethnic personality traits to explain the behavior of outgroup members. Furthermore, as in the egotistically motivated differential attribution patterns mentioned in the preceding paragraph, people have been found to attribute their own ethnic group's desirable behavior to internal factors and its undesirable behavior to external causes, whereas they do just the opposite in explaining *outgroups'* desirable and undesirable behavior (Taylor & Jaggi, 1974; Hewstone, 1989). Pettigrew (1979) named this pattern the **ultimate attribution error**.

Self-Attributions, Self-Esteem, and Self-Presentation

In addition to the research previously described on actors' attributions about their own behavior, there has been considerable other work on self-attributions. Bem's self-perception theory, which was discussed earlier, was modified by Nisbett and Valins (1972) to indicate that people infer their beliefs and attitudes from their behavior *only if* they perceive the behavior to have resulted from their true feelings toward the attitude object, but not if they perceive their behavior to have been constrained by some other aspect of the situation (for instance, norms, roles, or instructions). Because the actor–observer literature shows that people frequently see their own behavior as being determined by some aspect of the situation, it follows that Bem's self-perception theory will not apply in those circumstances.

In this area of research, we deal with *motivational* aspects of attribution, as opposed to strictly cognitive (informational) processes. That is, people's motivation to maintain or enhance their self-esteem can influence the attributions they make. In general, people usually take more causal responsibility for their favorable outcomes than for their unfavorable ones—that is, they make internal attributions for their own success and external ones for their failure. This pattern of taking credit for one's successes and denying blame for one's failures has been termed a **self-serving bias** or ego-defensive bias (Greenwald, 1980; Weary, 1980).

Self-serving attributive biases have been found to occur when subjects' outcomes and attributions are entirely private, so they cannot be due solely to attempts to impress others (Riess et al., 1981; Greenberg, Pyszczynski, & Solomon, 1982). People usually display self-serving biases on tasks that are stereotypically expected of their sex, but not on tasks expected of the opposite sex (Mirels, 1980). Real-world demonstrations of self-serving biases have been shown in coaches' and athletes' attributions for athletic performance (Lau & Russell, 1980; Mullen & Riordan, 1988), in premed students' attributions for their admission or rejection by medical schools (Smith & Manard, 1980), and in corporation officers' reports to their stockholders (Bettman & Weitz, 1983). Similar self-serving effects have been found in a variety of cultures (Fletcher & Ward, 1988). Thus people clearly do slant their attributions to make themselves feel good. However, further research has shown that self-enhancing attributions for success are more common and larger than self-protective attributions that deny responsibility for failure (Miller & Ross, 1975). Also, people are less likely to make self-serving attributions on dimensions where their own positions are objectively clear (e.g., income—Marks & Miller, 1988).

A related form of attributional bias is aimed at making a favorable *self-presentation* to others, not just to oneself. This is an aspect of **impression-management theory** (Schlenker, 1980; Jones & Pittman, 1982). A typical research design in this area compares attributions under relatively private conditions with those made under identical but public conditions (e.g., Schlenker, Weigold, & Hallam, 1990). When college students make attributions in front of student peers, they typically further embellish their private self-serving attributions (Weary, 1980). However, individuals who are high in social anxiety and those who expect their behavior to be reviewed by prestigious or expert evaluators are likely to reverse the self-promotional approach and accept more responsibility for failure than for success (Arkin, Appelman, & Burger, 1980; Weary et al., 1982; Miller & Schlenker, 1985). This modesty effect, though it underplays one's accomplishments, may ultimately gain more approval from others than boastfulness would.

Evaluation of Attribution Theory

Attribution theory was first proposed in the 1950s, became the most prolific research area in social psychology in the 1970s and 1980s, and still maintains its position as a central topic in the heavily studied field of social cognition. A number of important attributional theories have been proposed, which apply similar principles to various different situations and phenomena. Many research areas have been identified and explored, and attribution concepts have been applied to a host of social issues such as helping behavior, romantic attraction, and treatment of various clinical problems (e.g., Weary et al., 1989; Graham & Folkes, 1990). Yet there is still much that we don't know about attributions.

One danger of the many fascinating offshoots of attribution theory is that concentration on them will distract researchers and prevent them from ever constructing a firm and unified framework for the theory. Some of the important topics that need further study are how attributions are used in building people's self-identity concepts, the variety of individual differences in attributional styles, the nature of linkages between attributions and behavior, the consequences of attributions in close relationships, and extending attribution theory to analyze the accounts and narrative explanations that people give for events in their lives (Weary et al., 1989).

In some areas there have been encouraging linkups of attributional concepts with other theoretical viewpoints, such as learned helplessness (Abramson & Martin, 1981) and symbolic interactionism from sociology (Crittenden, 1983). Despite its problems and unfilled gaps, attribution theory has clarified many cognitive processes as well as common biases in thinking, helping us to understand how people interpret events and assign meanings to their life situations.

SUMMARY

Social cognition is the process by which we understand people and social situations, and it forms the cognitive basis of our attitudes. It begins with perception, which selects stimuli and imparts meaning to them; but, particularly in the social realm, perception can also introduce error into our thinking. In their usual thought processes, people often use convenient, shortcut guides for making decisions or predictions, such as the availability, adjustment, and representativeness heuristics. These heuristics often result in, or are combined with, various cognitive biases, and the result is many errors of human judgment.

Stereotypes are images or beliefs that a person holds about most members of a particular social group. Although useful in simplifying our everyday thoughts and decisions, they are overly simple, evaluative, and resistant to change. Also, they are very often inaccurate, though they may contain a "kernel of truth." We may form stereotypes from explicit teaching, from incidental learning such as we gain from the mass media, by incorrectly perceiving illusory correlations in events, or by inducing the behavior we expect from another person through our own actions (a process termed self-fulfilling prophecy).

Attribution is the process of making inferences about the unobservable characteristics of people, social objects, or events—especially the perception of causality in events or behavior. Attribution theory was initiated by Fritz Heider, whose approach has been extended by Jones and Davis' theory of correspondent inferences, Kelley's covariation theory and causal schema concepts, Bem's self-perception theory, and others—each being a particular version of attribution theory with its own set of principles. Although there is still no single, unified attribution theory, various attribution concepts have spurred extensive research in many areas, and attribution ideas have been applied to a wide variety of real-world social issues.

3

Explicit Measures of Attitudes

That guy Arnold sure is hot!

Auto dealers are just out to make a quick buck, and they'll rip off their customers every time they get a chance.

School vouchers are a bad idea because they will take money away from public schools.

These are all expressions of attitudes. They describe a person's feelings toward another person, a group, a situation, or an idea. Attitudes can be expressed in many ways—with different words, different tonal inflections, and different degrees of intensity. Some of the color and richness of the ways in which attitudes and opinions are often expressed is captured in the quotations from actual public opinion interviews shown in Box 3–1.

How can statements like these be studied scientifically? To compare them in any systematic way, we have to classify them into two or more categories (e.g., pro or anti concerning some group or idea) or, preferably, measure them on a quantitative scale (e.g., indicating *degree* of favorability or unfavorability). Furthermore, the classification or measurement must be **reliable**, that is, consistent. Reliability means (a) that two different raters agree on their classification of the statements to a high degree, and also (b) that on two different occasions the respondents' statements are largely consistent. Reliability and validity of measurement are discussed later in this chapter.

In this chapter, we examine ways of measuring **explicit attitudes**—evaluations that a person is consciously aware of and can express. In the next chapter, we examine **implicit attitudes**—evaluations that are automatic and function without a person's awareness or ability to control them (Greenwald & Banaji, 1995; Dovidio, Kawakami, & Gaertner, 2002).

TYPES OF ATTITUDE QUESTIONS

All measures of explicit attitudes rely on self-report. There are two basic types of questions that are used to obtain statements of attitudes and opinions. Some of the interview questions quoted in Box 3–1 are **open-ended** questions—ones that give the respondent a free choice of how to answer and what to mention (e.g., "What do you think was the main cause of these disturbances?"). Other questions are **closed-ended**—that is, ones that present two or more alternative answers for the respondent to choose between (e.g., "Have the disturbances helped or hurt the cause of Negro rights?"). Often an interview will use both types of questions because they have complementary advantages and disadvantages.

44

Box 3–1 Examples of Opinion Interview Responses

The following responses are selected quotations from public opinion interviews conducted in 1968 by the Survey Research Center at the University of Michigan on the subject of white attitudes toward blacks, and particularly toward the urban riots of the preceding year. Here are some quotes from one respondent:

Q. What do you think was the main cause of these disturbances?

A. Nigger agitators. Martin Luther King and Rap Brown and that black bastard Carmichael.

Q. Have the disturbances helped or hurt the cause of Negro rights?

A. Hurt. Whites are starting to wise up what a danger these people can be. They are going to be tough from now on. People are fed up with giving in and giving them everything their little black hearts want.

Q. What do you think the city government could do to keep a disturbance from breaking out here?

A. Ship them all back to Africa. Lock up all the agitators and show them we mean business.

Q. Would you go along with a program of spending more money for jobs, schooling, and housing for Negroes ... or would you oppose it?

A. I'd oppose it. They're getting too much already. If they want something they can damn well work for it. The government would just waste the money anyway. . . .

Q. That finished the interview. Is there anything you would like to add to any of the subjects we've discussed?

A. I just want to say that I don't have anything against Negroes as long as they don't get pushy and stay in their place. One of my best buddies is a nigger so I don't have anything against them.

By contrast, here are some answers from a second respondent:

Q. What do you think was the main cause of these disturbances?

A. Dissatisfaction. They are dissatisfied with the way they live, the way they are treated and their place in the social structure of America.

Q. Have the disturbances helped or hurt the cause of Negro rights?

A. They have helped because they have forced white people to pay attention and have brought the subject out into the open and you can't ignore it anymore. They haven't helped yet but overall it will help . . . .

Q. What do you think the city government could do to keep a disturbance from breaking out here?

A. Not only promise but actually improve conditions, education, housing, jobs, and social treatment . . .

Source: Campbell, A. (1971). *White attitudes toward black people* (pp. 2–4, 17). Ann Arbor: Institute for Social Research, The University of Michigan, Copyright © August 1971.

Open-ended questions have the advantages of eliciting the full range, depth, and complexity of the respondent's own views, with minimal distortion, in his or her own words. They reduce the likelihood of overlooking important possible viewpoints which the investigator has not thought of or not included in the questionnaire. For these reasons they are often used as introductory questions to open up a topic that will subsequently be probed more deeply and intensively with closed-ended questions. (This is called a **funnel sequence** of questioning.) The primary disadvantages of open-ended questions are the difficulty and frequently the unreliability of scoring or **coding** them. That is, trying to decide how the response should be classified or what quantitative point on a scale it best represents can be difficult and time-consuming, and sometimes it cannot be done with adequate agreement between raters. For instance, how would you score the second respondent's answer in Box 3–1 that the disturbances "have helped. . . . They haven't helped yet but overall it will help. . ."?

For these reasons closed-ended questions are likely to make up a large majority of the items on most interviews and questionnaires. They have the advantages of being easy to score and relatively **objective**. That is, independent observers or scorers can reach a high percentage of agreement on which response was given or on what score should be assigned to the response. Of course, unlike open-ended questions, they have the possible disadvantage that they may force the respondent to use the concepts, terms, and alternative answers preferred by the investigator, rather than expressing his or her own ideas and preferences (Schuman & Presser, 1981b; Sudman & Bradburn, 1982; J. Converse, 1984; Schwarz, Groves, & Schuman, 1998; Robinson, Shaver, & Wrightsman, 1999).

Closed-ended questions must be written very carefully so as not to produce biased answers. Without such care in item construction, the results will be far less reliable, and sometimes they may be so slanted that they are seriously misleading. For instance, here are two biased items that were on questionnaires sent out by two political lobbying groups:

Are you in favor of allowing construction union czars the power to shut down an entire construction site because of a dispute with a single contractor, thus forcing even more workers to knuckle under to union agencies? YES__ NO__ (Sudman & Bradburn, 1982, p. 2)

The Soviets and other Communist countries have a record of breaking one treaty after another. They not only shoot down unarmed passenger planes but also lie about it afterwards. Do you agree with those Congressmen who want a so-called political solution based on signing agreements with Communist forces in Central America? YES__ NO__

Obviously, these questions are worded so as to encourage a "No" answer. Consequently, the response percentages reported by their sponsoring agencies will markedly exaggerate respondents' real attitudes about these issues. The lesson of these examples is that one should always look at the question's wording before making or accepting an interpretation of the meaning of survey response figures. For that reason, good practice requires that the exact question wording be stated whenever the quantitative results of survey questions are reported. For readers interested in constructing questionnaires and surveys, a multi-volume series by Fink (2003) is an excellent resource.

The most common way of measuring attitudes is to combine several items on the same topic to form a **scale** (e.g., a scale of political liberalism versus conservatism), and to compute a single score for each respondent for the group of items. In the following section we describe the major ways of constructing such attitude scales.

ATTITUDE-SCALING METHODS

During the late 1920s and early 1930s a number of attitude-scaling methods were developed that are still in common use today, and more recently a few additional methods have been developed. Each of the major attitude-scaling techniques are discussed here rather briefly, primarily to clarify their major characteristics and points of difference. This will not prepare you to use these methods yourself to build an attitude scale, but it will provide you with enough information to understand references to such methods later in this book or in the research literature.

In 1925 Bogardus was one of the first to use quantitative measurement methods in the field of social psychology. Thus, surprisingly, the quantitative study of attitudes is only about 80 years old, even though quantitative research in psychology goes back over 125 years to the founding of Wundt's laboratory in 1879, though the term attitude has been used in the psychological sense for well over a century, and though cognition, affect, and conation have been discussed by philosophers ever since the time of Plato. Given the relatively short history of quantitative research on attitudes and opinions, it is no wonder that many questions remain to be answered.

Bogardus' Social Distance Scale

Bogardus (1925) proposed a scale of **social distance** that could be used to determine attitudes toward various racial or nationality groups, many of which at that time were relatively recent immigrants to the United States. Respondents gave their judgments, following these instructions (p. 301):

According to my first feeling reactions, I would willingly admit members of each race (as a class, and not the best I have known, nor the worst members) to one or more of the classifications under which I have placed a cross.

1. To close kinship by marriage
2. To my club as personal chums
3. To my street as neighbors
4. To employment in my occupation in my country
5. To citizenship in my country
6. As visitors only to my country
7. Would exclude from my country

By use of this scale, people's attitudes toward the English, Germans, Turks, and many other groups could be compared.

As can be seen in the example, the scale points progress systematically from acceptance of members of the racial or national group into the most intimate family relationships, down to complete exclusion of the group. The respondent's attitude score toward that group is taken as the closest degree of relationship that he or she is willing to accept. Some early findings showed that, to the average American, the English were the most accepted national group and Turks were one of the least accepted groups (Bogardus, 1928). A recent study compared the distance scores of 135 U.S. schoolteachers with those reported by Bogardus (Kleg & Yamamoto, 1998). In it, social distance scores were obtained for 39 ethnic and racial groups, and the scores of the teachers were strikingly similar to those found by Bogardus in 1928—the rankings of the

39 groups were highly correlated ($r = 0.86$). However, the distance ratings in the 1998 study were more homogenous, indicating less extreme positive and negative attitudes. As with the findings reported by Bogardus, the English were rated highest and the Turks lowest.

Other variations of this technique have allowed measurement of attitudes toward any social group, not just ethnic or nationality groups, and have also broadened the range of response options (e.g., Triandis, 1964, 1971).

Thurstone's Method of Equal-Appearing Intervals

A few years after Bogardus' work on social distance, Thurstone (1928) proposed the next attitude-scaling method. In contrast to the Bogardus scale, in which the scale points were not designed to be equidistant, Thurstone attempted to develop a method that would indicate rather precisely the *amount* of difference between two respondents' attitudes. The method that he developed is rather complex.

First, the investigator collects or constructs a large number (100 or so) of opinion statements representing favorable, neutral, and unfavorable views about the topic of interest (for instance, Thurstone studied attitudes toward the church, "Negroes," capital punishment, and birth control). Then the investigator obtains a large group of people to serve as judges and rate each statement's favorability or unfavorability toward the topic. Each judge sorts the statements into 11 equally spaced categories, disregarding his or her own attitude toward the topic, and considering only how *favorable* or *unfavorable* the statement is toward the attitude object. If there are statements on which different judges show substantial disagreement, they are discarded as ambiguous; other items may be discarded as irrelevant to the topic; and judges who make too few differentiations are omitted from later computations. The remaining statements are assigned **scale values** based on the median favorability rating of the judges. From these statements, a final scale of about 20 items (or sometimes more) is selected according to two criteria. The aim is to choose items having (a) scale values at approximately **equal intervals** along a 9-point or an 11-point scale of favorability, and (b) high agreement among the judges' ratings (that is, low spread or variability of their ratings).

After the items for the final scale have been chosen, they are randomly arranged on the questionnaire form without any indication of their scale values. Respondents check only the items they agree with and leave the others blank. A person's attitude toward the topic can then be defined as the mean (or the median—both methods have been used) of the scale values of the items that he or she has checked. An example of a Thurstone scale is shown in Box 3–2.

Thurstone's method makes the important assumption that the opinions of the judges do not affect the scale values of the items obtained from their judgments. This assumption has been shown to be reasonably correct when the judges do not have extreme views on the topic. However, if many of the judges have extreme views or are highly involved in the topic, the obtained scale values of the items will be affected (Hovland & Sherif, 1952). Specifically, judges who are highly favorable to a topic rate only a few of the most extreme statements as favorable, and they displace their ratings of most of the statements toward the unfavorable end of the judgment scale. The opposite is true for judges who are highly unfavorable toward a topic.

The other major drawback of Thurstone's method is that it is time-consuming and tedious to apply (Webb, 1955). For that reason it is used much less extensively than the method described next.

Box 3–2 A Thurstone Scale of Attitudes Toward Using Contraceptives

A selection of about half of the items from a Thurstone scale is shown below. Although the items are arranged here in the order of their scale values, on the actual questionnaire they would be arranged in a mixed-up order as indicated by their item numbers, and the scale values would not be shown. Respondents are to check or circle the numbers of the items with which they agree.

Scale value	Item no.	Item
1.28	5	I detest the very word birth control.
2.23	13	I am afraid to use birth control.
3.00	3	My feelings would be hurt if someone advised me to practice birth control.
4.17	6	I am sorry for those who practice birth control.
5.06	11	It frightens me to think that the overcrowding is going to force birth control on us whether we want it or not.
7.38	10	It saddens me that so many persons are ignorant of the advantages of birth control.
8.37	9	I am happy about the positive effects of birth control.
9.37	12	I am so glad people are beginning to accept birth control.
10.77	1	It is a wonderful feeling to take advantage of birth control.

Source: Kothandapani, V. (1971a). *A psychological approach to the prediction of contraceptive behavior* (pp. 26, 69–70). Chapel Hill: University of North Carolina, Carolina Population Center.

Likert's Method of Summated Ratings

Shortly after Thurstone's work, Likert (1932) proposed a simpler method of attitude-scale construction, which does not require the use of judges to rate the items' favorability. Better still, the reliability of Likert scales has been shown to be at least as high as that of the more difficult-to-construct Thurstone scales (Poppleton & Pilkington, 1964).

Likert's method was the first approach that measured the *extent* or *intensity* of the respondent's agreement with each item, rather than simply obtaining a "yes–no" response. In this method, again, a large number of opinion statements on a given topic are collected, but each one is phrased in such a way that it can be answered on a 5-point rating scale. For instance, here is an example from Likert's original scale of internationalism (Likert, 1932, p. 17)—it is interesting to note how many of these attitude items still have an up-to-date ring:

> We should be willing to fight for our country whether it is in the right or in the wrong.
> _____ Strongly approve
> _____ Approve
> _____ Undecided
> _____ Disapprove
> _____ Strongly disapprove

Respondents check one of the five choices, which are scored 1, 2, 3, 4, and 5 respectively. (Of course, items on the opposite end of the continuum—ones expressing a favorable attitude toward internationalism—would be scored in reverse: 5, 4, 3, 2, and 1, respectively.)

Photograph courtesy of Rensis Likert.
Reprinted by permission.

Box 3–3   RENSIS LIKERT, *Attitude Measurement Pioneer*

Rensis Likert's distinguished career included pace-setting work in four major areas: atti-tude measurement, survey research methodology, research on organizational management, and applications of social science to important social problems. He earned his Ph.D. in psychology at Columbia with dissertation research, published in 1932, which developed the attitude measurement technique that bears his name. After teaching briefly at New York University, he moved to full-time research on organizational management. In 1939 he be-came the founding director of the Division of Program Surveys for the U.S. Department of Agriculture, where he made major contributions to methods of survey interviewing, probability sampling, and wartime public opinion research.

Following World War II, Likert founded the University of Michigan's Survey Research Center and later the Institute for Social Research, which under his leadership became the largest university-based social science research agency in the U.S. After retiring, he headed a consultation and research firm on organizational management until his death in 1981. Author of over 100 articles and six books, including New Patterns of Management *and* The Human Organization, *he was elected president of the American Statistical Association, and a director of the American Psychological Association, and he received the highest research award of the American Association for Public Opinion Research.*

This method uses only items that are clearly positive or negative toward the attitude object, whereas Thurstone's method also requires some relatively neutral items.

As the name "summated ratings" indicates, respondents' attitude scores are determined by adding their ratings for all of the items. This procedure is based on the assumption that all of the items are measuring the same underlying attitude. As a consequence of this assumption, it follows that all the items should be positively correlated, in contrast to the Thurstone method, which does not impose this requirement. Although the correlations among the items are not usually high, because each item is measuring its own unique content as well as the general underlying attitude, the assumption can be, and should be, checked. The usual way to do this is to correlate the score on each item with the total score for the whole pool of items combined (these are called item–total correlations). Any item with a correlation near zero is discarded because it is not measuring the common factor shared by other items.

A great strength of the Likert method is its use of **item analysis** techniques to "purify" the scale by keeping only the best items from the initial item pool. A common way of accomplishing this is to compare the group of respondents scoring highest on the total pool of items (say, the top 25%) with the group scoring lowest (the bottom 25%), thus eliminating the middle group, whose attitudes may be less clear, less consistent, less strongly held, and less well-informed. If a particular item does not **discriminate** significantly between these groups—that is, does not have significantly different mean scores for the top and bottom groups—it is clear that it is measuring some other dimension than the general attitude involved in the scale. For example, in a scale of internationalist attitudes, a nondiscriminating item might be concerned with a hope for world peace, because high scorers (internationalists) and low scorers (isolationists) might both share this hope.

The Likert method of attitude scale construction quickly became and remains the most popular method, and a number of variations of it have also gained wide usage. One variation is to eliminate the "Undecided" or "Neutral" category, thus forcing respondents to choose between favorable and unfavorable stances. For instance, an item from the California F Scale, for measuring authoritarian or "fascist" attitudes, is scored as follows (Adorno et al., 1950, p. 68):

An insult to our honor should always be punished.
+ 1: slight support, agreement   − 1: slight opposition, disagreement
+ 2: moderate support, agreement   − 2: moderate opposition, disagreement
+ 3: strong support, agreement   − 3: strong opposition, disagreement

A more serious, and unfortunate, departure from Likert's procedure is the frequent omission of an item analysis. When this occurs, there is no empirical evidence that the items are all measuring the same underlying attitude, nor that they are useful, discriminating items. This situation is often signaled by use of the term "Likert-type" scale, which is apt to be an indication of hasty, slipshod research, quite out of keeping with Likert's own procedures.

Guttman's Cumulative Scaling Method

One of the limitations of both the Thurstone and the Likert techniques is that the respondent's attitude score does not have a unique meaning. That is, any given score can be obtained in many different ways. On a Likert scale, for instance, a respondent can obtain a midrange score by giving mostly "Undecided" responses, or by giving many "Strongly approve" responses offset by many "Strongly disapprove" responses, or by both "Approve" and "Disapprove" responses. Using the summated ratings (or more commonly, the average response to the items) does not tell us much about the pattern of responses or the responses to individual items.

Guttman (1944) proposed a method in which scores would have unique meanings. This was to be accomplished by ensuring that response patterns were **cumulative**. That is, in the Guttman method, a respondent who is moderately favorable to the attitude object should answer "yes" to all of the items accepted by a mildly favorable respondent *plus* one or more additional items. Similarly, a strongly favorable respondent should endorse all the items accepted by moderately favorable respondents *plus* additional one(s).

This reasoning can be clarified by some examples. Actually, the steps on the Bogardus Social Distance Scale, previously discussed in this chapter, apparently meet these requirements. A respondent who was very unfavorable toward Cubans, for instance, might be willing to accept them to citizenship in the country but not to the higher categories. Another person might agree to citizenship and also to equal employment. A favorable respondent might accept both of these items and also endorse accepting Cubans into his neighborhood and his social club; and so on, up to respondents who agreed with all the items.

Box 3–4 An Example of a Guttman Scale

Attitudes toward religious fundamentalism and its role in current American politics were measured in a study of the 1980 U.S. election conducted by the Center for Political Studies at the University of Michigan. Responses to interview questions were obtained from a representative national sample of over 1,200 white adults.

The six-item Guttman scale, which was constructed from the survey responses, is shown below. Items are listed here in rank order of the percentage of respondents agreeing with them, but in the actual interview they were arranged in a mixed-up order. The index of reproducibility of the scale was .925 (meaning only 7½% inconsistent responses). This is a Guttman scale because of the decreasing percentages of pro-fundamentalist answers on the successive questions (though it is unusual to have two items as close together in percentage of agreement as questions 3 and 4 here), and because most respondents who agreed with any given item also agreed with all of the lower-numbered items (as shown by the index of reproducibility).

Some evidence of the scale's validity is that, of 11 current political issues, its highest correlations were with opposition to abortion and support for school prayers.

Items (in rank order, not in their order in the interview)	*% agreeing*
1 Religion is an important part of one's life.	*73*
2 The Bible is God's word and all it says is true.	*44*
3 I feel favorable toward evangelical groups like the Moral Majority.	*30*
4 Religion provides a <u>great deal</u> of everyday guidance.	*28*
5 I am born again.	*21*
6 I feel close to evangelical groups active in politics such as the Moral Majority.	*6*

Source: Miller, A. H., & Wattenberg, M. P. (1984). Politics from the pulpit: Religiosity and the 1980 elections. *Public Opinion Quarterly, 48*, 301–317. Copyright 1984 by The Trustees of Columbia University. Reprinted by permission of the University of Chicago Press.

Guttman suggested that, if a scale displays the cumulative pattern just described, we can be sure that it is **unidimensional**—that is, it is measuring just one underlying attitude. By contrast, Thurstone and Likert scales may be measuring two or more underlying dimensions. Guttman has proposed a quantitative index for determining the unidimensionality of a scale, and scales that meet Guttman's criteria are apt to be quite short (perhaps 4–10 items) and restricted to a narrow topic.

Box 3–4 presents an example of a Guttman scale constructed to measure attitudes toward politicized religious fundamentalism or the "religious right" (the attitude object). Notice that all six items are on a rather narrow topic, concerning various signs of religious fundamentalism, whereas many other aspects of religiosity are not represented. Of course, if desired, these could be measured by other Guttman scales on such topics as specific religious beliefs, frequency of religious activities, or degree of ethical behavior.

To develop a unidimensional scale by Guttman's procedure, an initial pool of items is given to a large group of respondents, each item being stated in a "yes–no" or "agree–disagree" format. Next, the items are arranged according to the number of respondents agreeing with them. In this procedure, by definition, the item agreed to by the *fewest* respondents is the item most favorable toward the attitude object (e.g., the "Moral Majority" in the scale shown in Box 3–4); that is, it is the most-difficult-to-accept item. Each respondent's score is then determined very simply: It is merely the rank number of the most favorable item that he or she endorsed (answered in the scored direction). The answers of each respondent are examined separately (usually by computer). This is done to discover all instances of inconsistent response patterns: that is, cases in which a respondent endorses an item and fails to endorse one of the less-favorable items.

According to the theory of measurement underlying this scaling method, each such instance is considered a response error, and no more than 10% of inconsistent responses are allowed if a scale is to be considered unidimensional. (Guttman refers to this as an **index of reproducibility** of 0.90 or higher.) Items that have many inconsistent responses are probably measuring a different underlying dimension, and accordingly they are deleted from the pool of items. After a number of rounds of computation and discarding of items, a short scale may be developed that meets Guttman's criteria for unidimensionality. However, critical analyses have demonstrated that even more procedural safeguards than those recommended by Guttman are necessary to be sure that a truly unidimensional scale has been developed (Dawes & Smith, 1985).

Osgood's Semantic Differential

In contrast to the preceding methods of constructing attitude scales, Osgood's Semantic Differential is actually a scale in itself. However it is a scale of such a general sort that it can be applied to any attitude object. This has the great advantage that researchers do not have to construct and try out a new scale every time they want to study a new topic. No doubt this convenience is a major reason for the sustained popularity of the Semantic Differential since it was introduced (Osgood et al., 1957).

The reason for the name "Semantic Differential" is that the technique attempts to measure the **connotative meaning** of the concept or object being rated: that is, its implied meaning, or differential connotations to the respondent. In contrast to the other major attitude-scaling methods, the Semantic Differential does not consist of opinion statements about the attitude object. Instead it uses a series of 7-point scales with two opposing adjectives at the ends of each scale (e.g., "good" and "bad"). Respondents check the point on each scale that corresponds to their impressions of, or feelings about, the object or concept being rated. An abbreviated example of the instructions and the rating form is shown in Box 3–5.

Osgood and his colleagues (1957) reported a great deal of research on the application of this Semantic Differential approach to the measurement of a wide variety of concepts, including attitudes toward elderly people, gender groups, substance use, psychopathology, menopause, and work. Notably, the method has been successfully applied in many different cultures and subcultures.

Using the method of factor analysis, Osgood and his colleagues studied the underlying dimensions in connotative meaning, and time after time they came up with generally similar results. They concluded that there are three basic dimensions on which people make semantic judgments, and these are applicable quite universally to varied concepts, varied adjectival rating scales, and various cultures. The three dimensions are as follows: (a) the **evaluative** dimension, involving adjectives such as good–bad, beautiful–ugly, kind–cruel, pleasant–unpleasant, and fair–unfair; (b) the **potency** dimension, marked by adjectives such as strong–weak, large–small, and heavy–light; and (c) the **activity** dimension, identified by adjectives such as active–passive, hot–cold, and fast–slow.

Of these dimensions, the one most heavily weighted in people's judgments is evaluation. Osgood (1965) recommended using it as the prime indicator of attitude toward the object.

Box 3–5 An Example of a Semantic Differential Rating Task

Both the instructions and the rating form are substantially shortened in this demonstration example. Ordinarily many concepts to be rated would be presented to each respondent in a stapled booklet, one concept on each page; and more adjective scales might also be used for each concept. Note that the end of the scale representing the positive pole on the dimension is systematically varied between left and right.

INSTRUCTIONS: The purpose of this study is to measure meanings *of certain things to various people by having them judge them against a series of descriptive scales. In taking this test, please make your judgments on the basis of what these things mean* to you*.*

Here is how you are to use these scale: If you feel that the concept at the top of the page is very closely related *to one end of the scale (for instance, very fair), you should place your check mark as follows:*

fair X : __ : __ : __ : __ : __ *unfair*

If you feel that the concept is only slightly related *to one or the other end of the scale (for instance, slightly strong), you should place your check mark as follows:*

weak __ : __ : __ : __ : X : __ *strong*

The direction toward which you check, of course, depends on which of the two ends of the scale seems most characteristic of the thing you're judging.

If you consider the concept to be neutral *on the scale, both sides of the scale* equally associated *with the concept, or if the scale is* completely irrelevant*, unrelated to the concept, then you should place your check mark in the middle space.*

Rate the concept on each of these scales in order, and do not omit any. Please do not look back and forth *through the items. Do not try to remember how you checked similar items earlier in the test.* Make each item a separate and independent judgment. *Work at fairly high speed throughout this test. Do not worry or puzzle over individual items. It is your first impression, the immediate "feelings" about the items, that we want. On the other hand, please do not be careless, because we want your true impressions.*

SEPARATION OF CHURCH AND STATE	(Dimension)*
good __:__:__:__:__:__ bad	(evaluative)
weak __:__:__:__:__:__ strong	(potency)
active __:__:__:__:__:__ passive	(activity)
large __:__:__:__:__:__ small	(potency)
slow __:__:__:__:__:__ fast	(activity)
unfair __:__:__:__:__:__ fair	(evaluative)

*Of course, the dimensions are not shown on the respondents' forms.

Source: Adapted from Osgood, C. E., Suci, G. J., & Tannenbaum, P. H. (1957). *The measurement of meaning* (pp. 36–38, 82–84). Urbana: University of Illinois Press.

Clearly it is an affective dimension whereas the other two seem more cognitive in nature. Normally each dimension can be measured reliably by the use of only three or four adjective scales, so use of the Semantic Differential is simple and convenient for the investigator and relatively easy for respondents as well.

Final Comments on Attitude Scales

The work by Osgood illustrates the possibility of multidimensional scaling of attitudes. Although most attitude scales have concentrated on measuring the **magnitude** of attitudes—that is, their degree of favorability or unfavorability (also sometimes called their **valence**)—several other dimensions of attitudes have been suggested as worthy of study. In particular, these dimensions include the **complexity** or elaboration of attitudes, their **centrality** or importance to the person who holds them, and their **accessibility** (closeness to awareness, or readiness for expression). The structure of attitudes is considered in more detail in Chapter 5.

It should also be emphasized here, as was mentioned in Chapter 1, that carefully constructed attitude scales have quite rarely been used by researchers and only occasionally utilized by attitude pollers for practical assessment. Instead, the major contribution of these elaborate measurement methods has been to provide theoretical understanding of specific domains of attitudes.

Over the years, a number of other attitude-scaling methods have been proposed (cf. Edwards & Kilpatrick, 1948; Coombs, 1950; Hambleton, 1989; Mitchell, 1990; Kenny & Judd, 1996). In Chapter 4, we examine *implicit measures* of attitudes, which have been developed in the past 10 years and provide a very different approach to measuring attitudes. In addition to implicit measures, there is one other approach that deserves comment. Item response theory (IRT) has become increasingly used by researchers as computer programs became available to perform its required complex computations.

The five measurement approaches previously summarized (Bogardus, Thurstone, Likert, Guttman, and Osgood) all produce scores that are useful in describing a specific sample. However, when scores are based on parameters established with a prior sample (as they are with the Guttman and the Thurstone scales), then the scores are *group-dependent*. That is, they are difficult to compare across dissimilar groups. In addition, all of the scales described above are *test-dependent*, in that the meaning of the scores depends on the specific items used in the scale. It would not be appropriate to replace some of the items in the scale for one sample and then to make comparisons of scores across samples.

Item Response Theory (IRT) has been used primarily in the development of achievement and aptitude tests, but it is also beginning to make its way into attitude measurement. The goal of IRT is to obtain a measure that is applicable to groups and individuals with widely varying ability levels. In attitude terms, this would mean groups with extremely positive or negative attitudes. Items are included in the scale based on extensive testing, and they are selected to range from very easy (i.e., almost everyone agrees with the item) to very difficult (almost no one agrees with it). Different items are given to different samples, but because each item's favorability to the attitude object has been premeasured, comparable scores can be derived for the various samples. In many ways, IRT is an extension of the scale-value aspect of Thurstone scaling, but with a different mathematical approach to obtaining the scale values for each item. Typically, in IRT models, researchers obtain scores for each item in the scale as well as for each respondent. For an overview of IRT, see Hambleton (1989) or Embretson & Reise (2000).

Item response theory has received considerable attention by researchers over the past 20 years, but its merits are still widely debated (Anastasi & Urbina, 1997). Although it has been used sporadically in attitude studies, the most common method used in attitude research continues to be Likert measures. Fortunately, studies comparing the different methods of attitude measurement that we have described have found them to be positively correlated—Fishbein and Ajzen (1974) reported typical intercorrelations of around +.7, though Tittle and Hill (1967) found lower figures averaging around +.5. Both studies showed the Likert scale to be most highly correlated with the various other attitude measures.

In addition to the limitations noted by IRT researchers, another limitation shared by all explicit measures of attitudes is that the scales they produce are **ordinal** scales rather than equal-interval or ratio scales. This means that respondents can successfully be placed in their *rank order* on the attitude dimension, but we cannot be sure that the actual attitudinal distance between two values on the scale is equal to the distance between two other values. For instance, on a Likert scale, is the distance between "Undecided" and "Approve" (3 and 4) the same as the distance between "Approve" and "Strongly approve" (4 and 5)? The two distances are numerically equal, but they may not be psychologically equal. Even though Thurstone's method strives to achieve "equal-appearing intervals," it is nevertheless an ordinal scale rather than an interval scale.

Technically, ordinal scales should be treated with nonparametric, distribution-free statistical techniques involving measures such as the median. For this reason it is statistically improper to add or multiply scores together, compute mean scores, use *t* tests, analysis of variance, or any of the other widely used parametric statistics. However, these restrictions are almost universally disregarded, largely because statistical research has shown that in most instances violations of the assumptions underlying the use of parametric techniques do not lead to serious distortions of their results. Thus scores are customarily derived through summation or averaging, and *t* tests and *F* tests are used on attitude scale results. It is well to keep in mind, however, that occasionally, when distributions are markedly skewed or variances are grossly different, use of parametric techniques may produce misleading conclusions (Dawes & Smith, 1985).

RELIABILITY AND VALIDITY OF MEASUREMENT

There are two essential characteristics for attitude scales, as for all other types of measurement: reliability and validity. **Reliability** means consistency of measurement. A measurement that is unreliable is like an elastic tape measure, which stretches a different amount every time it is used. Two kinds of reliability are commonly reported: **internal consistency** measures, showing the amount of agreement between different items intended to assess the same concept; and **stability** measures, indicating the consistency of scores on the same scale at two different points in time. Both kinds are generally reported in terms of correlation coefficients. Internal consistency measures include *split-half* coefficients, *alternate-form* agreement, and the *alpha coefficient* of internal homogeneity of items (Cronbach, 1984). Stability is usually reported as *test–retest* correlations for the same group of subjects taking the same test or other measurement at two points in time. For verbal attitude or information measures, these two occasions need to be far enough apart that subjects are unlikely to remember their previous answers and simply repeat them on the second measurement occasion—usually a week or two at a minimum.

Unreliability of measurement in verbal scales can often be combated by several means. Sometimes it results from very coarse measurement (e.g., simply "Agree" or "Disagree"), in which case it can usually be reduced by increasing the number of response alternatives (e.g., several degrees of agreement or disagreement). Thus, even if a person gives a slightly different response on another occasion, he or she will not have shifted from one end of the dimension to the other. Another common source of unreliability in multi-item attitude scales is that items are not "pure" measures of the characteristic that one is attempting to measure, and thus they are often only weakly or moderately correlated with each other. The customary way to solve this problem is to add more items of the same sort to the scale, because statistical principles of measurement guarantee that, for any given level of item intercorrelation, a longer scale will be more reliable than a shorter one. However, limits to this approach are the availability of appropriate items and the feasible length of the scale. Other ways of reaching sounder statistical conclusions by improving measurement reliability are discussed by Cook and Campbell (1979), Cronbach (1984), and Thompson (2002).

Validity means accuracy or correctness of measurement. Measuring instruments can be reliable without being valid—for example, a bathroom scale that consistently gives too heavy readings. However, they cannot be valid if they are not reliable—for instance, the many different readings given by an elastic tape measure would almost all (or all) be wrong, and thus the tape measure would not be a valid instrument.

The validity of a measuring instrument is often determined by comparing its results with a **criterion**—an accepted, standardized measure of the same characteristic. For example, butchers' scales are calibrated and tested against a very accurate master instrument. In psychological measurement, a criterion may be a well-established instrument, as in using the Stanford-Binet intelligence test as a standard of comparison for the results of a newly devised IQ test. However, in many cases there may be no well-established criterion instrument for the characteristic being measured, as when research begins on a new topic that has not been measured before. This is frequently true in the area of attitudes, and it necessitates an approach similar to pulling oneself up by one's bootstraps. The typical approach here is termed **construct validation**, which involves computing a network of relationships between the new measure and other relevant characteristics and comparing the obtained correlations with those expected on a theoretical basis. If there is generally good correspondence, that constitutes support for the instrument's validity.

Other aspects of validity are discussed in Chapter 5, and extensive elaborations of threats to validity in reaching conclusions from psychological data and ways of counteracting these threats may be found in Cook and Campbell (1979), Cronbach (1984), and Bickman (2000).

PROBLEMS AFFECTING THE VALIDITY OF ATTITUDE SCALES

Pause for a moment, and think in detail about what respondents have to do in the process of answering an attitude question:

> Respondents first interpret the attitude question, determining what attitude the question is about. They then retrieve relevant beliefs and feelings [from their memory]. Next they apply these beliefs and feelings in rendering the appropriate judgment. Finally, they use this judgment to select a response. (Tourangeau & Rasinski, 1988, p. 299)

Problems can occur at each of these stages, which may reduce the validity of respondents' answers. Also, as mentioned in Chapter 1, the fact that people sometimes *construct* attitude responses on the spot without any prior consideration of the issue, rather than retrieving a previously formed attitude from their memory, would sharply decrease both the reliability and validity of such attitude statements.

The *wording* of attitude questions is one of the main factors affecting the validity of attitude scales. However, because principles regarding the wording of attitude questions are also applicable to the wording of public opinion interviews, they are discussed in detail in Chapter 6.

The major problem to be discussed here is the ways in which response sets can invalidate attitude questionnaire answers. **Response sets** are systematic ways of answering that are not directly related to the question content, but which represent typical behavioral characteristics of the respondents. Several types of response sets are mentioned in the next four subsections, and some possible solutions to them are discussed.

Carelessness

When respondents are unmotivated or careless, their answers will be variable and inconsistent from moment to moment or from one testing session to another. Such a situation will reduce the questionnaire's reliability, and unreliable questionnaires are necessarily low in validity.

Some carelessness and low motivation can be minimized by the researcher building good rapport with the respondent, stressing the importance of the task, and engaging the respondent's interest in it. However, despite such precautions, some respondents may still answer carelessly or fail to follow directions through misunderstanding or poor comprehension. Therefore the response sheets are usually scanned visually, and the data are either discarded or analyzed separately for respondents who (a) omit answers to many items, (b) answer almost all items in the same way, or (c) show systematic patterns of responding (for example, a, b, c, d, a, b, c, d).

Social Desirability

The social desirability response set is the tendency to give the most socially acceptable answer to a question, or to "fake good." It operates both in attitude scales and in public opinion interviews. For example, people will rarely describe themselves as dishonest, even though almost everyone occasionally fudges on the truth or cheats a little bit (by glancing at an opponent's cards, etc.). In extensive studies on this topic, Edwards (1964) showed that personality characteristics that are considered as desirable in our culture are also ones that are claimed by most respondents as applying to themselves, and vice versa. In one study of 140 characteristics, the correlation was +0.87, an almost perfect relationship. Edwards (1964) developed a personality scale that indicates the degree of an individual's tendency to give socially desirable answers, and other authors have constructed similar scales (Crowne & Marlowe, 1964; Schuessler, Hittle, & Cardascia, 1978).

These scales are useful for identifying respondents with a high tendency to provide socially desirable answers, but removing social desirability from the results of a study is more difficult. To control for social desirability responding, Edwards advocated the use of **forced-choice** items. In this technique of scale construction two items of approximately equal social desirability, but indicating, for instance, two different social needs, are paired together. The respondent is asked to choose the one that is most true of himself or herself. This was a creative proposal, but unfortunately the evidence of its success in solving the problem of social desirability responding is disappointing (Barron, 1959; Scott, 1968). Consequently, only a few scales have been built in this way, the best known of which is Rotter's (1966) scale of internal versus external locus of control.

Unfortunately, none of the available methods for combating social desirability responding is entirely satisfactory. The techniques that are most often used are as follows:

(a) selecting innocuous items, for which social desirability does not appear to be an issue; (b) providing anonymity for the respondents; (c) stating that there are no right or wrong answers, because the items cover matters of opinion rather than fact; (d) urging respondents to answer honestly and stressing that it is their own opinions that are desired; (e) use of the forced-choice technique of item construction, previously discussed; and (f) auxiliary use of personality scales to identify respondents who are particularly high or low in social desirability responding, and either excluding these participants from the analyses or statistically removing the variance stemming from their individual differences in social desirability. In his review of techniques for controlling social desirability response bias, Krosnick (1999a) suggested that researchers test for the presence of social desirability responding by having some respondents answer questions in an ordinary self-report fashion, and having others answer in a way that attempts to reduce social desirability through one or more of the approaches discussed above.

Extremity of Response

An extremity response set can occur only on items that have more than two alternative answers. For example, on a Likert-type scale having responses scored from $+3$ to -3, an extremity response set would be demonstrated by a respondent who picked mostly $+3$ and/or -3 answers. Its opposite, a midrange response set, would be shown by a large number of $+1$ and/or -1 answers. In one nationwide study of high school students, black students were found to give many more extreme responses than whites (Bachman & O'Malley, 1984). Other studies have found that Hispanic Americans give more extreme responses than European Americans (Marin, Gamba, & Marin, 1992), and older, less educated, and lower-income respondents give more extreme responses (Greenleaf, 1992).

There has been little study of the effects of extremity response sets or midrange response sets on questionnaire validity. Their effects can be reduced if equal numbers of items on a scale are keyed in the positive and negative directions, for then the $+3$ answers of an extreme responder will tend to counterbalance his or her -3 answers (and similarly for the $+1$ and -1 answers of a midrange responder). Another possible remedy is to eliminate the extremity response set altogether by use of items with only two alternatives (Yes–No or Agree–Disagree).

Acquiescence (Yea-Saying)

The most thoroughly studied aspect of acquiescence is the **agreement** response set, or yea-saying, defined as a tendency to agree with any questionnaire item regardless of its content. It has been studied extensively in the California F Scale measure of authoritarianism (Adorno et al., 1950), but it also is an issue in many other attitude and personality scales, particularly in the Minnesota Multiphasic Personality Inventory (Bradburn & Sudman, 1979). An example of agreement responding is answering "Yes" to both of the following items: "Jews are more willing than others to use shady practices to get ahead" and "Jews are just as honest as other businessmen" (Jackman, 1973). Such patterns of response have been found to be more common among people with lower education and income (Ware, 1978), women, children (Poole & Lindsay, 2001), individuals diagnosed as mentally retarded (Finlay & Lyons, 2002), and in more collectivistic cultures (Cheung & Rensvold, 2000; see also Narayan & Krosnick, 1996). Acquiescence bias occurs most often with difficult questions, or when respondents are fatigued from answering a large number of questions, and during phone interviews more than during face-to-face interviews (Krosnick, Narayan, & Smith, 1996). In a major research review on the topic,

Krosnick (1999a) concluded that "acquiescence occurs when people lack the skills and motivation to answer thoughtfully and when a question demands difficult cognitive tasks be executed in order for a person to answer precisely" (p. 41).

An example of a scale on which acquiescence is a problem is the California F Scale. As the result of an unfortunate decision during the construction of the scale, all 28 items were worded in such a way that agreement indicated authoritarianism and disagreement indicated lack of authoritarianism—that is, all items were keyed in the positive direction. Before 1950, when the authoritarianism studies were being formulated, this was not recognized as a major issue in scale construction, but it has since become so.

One approach for reducing agreement response bias effects during the construction of a scale is to *reverse the wording and the keying* of half of the items from that of the other half. For example, in addition to the item "I like to eat sushi," we might also present the item "I do not enjoy eating sushi." Responses to the latter item would then be *reverse-coded*, so that scores on the two items would be positively correlated. The result is called a **balanced scale**—that is, one having half of the items on the scale scored if the answer is "true," and half scored if the answer is "false." If the two groups of items are equally good, are positively intercorrelated, and have an equal spread of responses, this procedure will cause any agreement response effect to cancel out across the two groups of items.

However, this was not done on the California F Scale, and debates raged for years about the resulting problems. One group of authors (e.g., Bass, 1955; Campbell et al., 1960) claimed that the scale was more a measure of acquiescence than of authoritarianism. Another group, using different statistical methods, concluded that there was little relationship between authoritarianism and acquiescence (Couch & Keniston, 1960). A third group (e.g., Christie, Havel, & Seidenberg, 1958) found that there was some mixture of acquiescence in F Scale scores, but argued that there *should* be, because agreeing with an authoritatively worded statement is really one aspect of being an authoritarian.

The use of reverse-coded items and balanced scales has become common practice in attitude measurement, and as a result it might appear that the problem of acquiescence bias has been solved. However, it is not a simple matter to construct attitude measurement items that are reverse-coded. It is often difficult to devise questions that avoid using the word "not" or another similar negation; and questions containing "not" are apt to be cumbersome and can increase a respondent's fatigue (and thereby inadvertently *increase* acquiescence). In addition, the increased cognitive resources needed to interpret and respond to these reverse-coded items may lead to differential rates of acquiescence across respondents. For example, when confronted with a longer or more confusing item, respondents who are less motivated to think about the item might simply say "yes"—an acquiescent response. In the final analysis, reverse-coded questions are only a partial solution to acquiescence bias, and it is more important to ask a few direct, carefully worded items, encourage respondents to answer honestly, and implement steps to ensure confidentiality or anonymity (Krosnick, 1999a).

A nay-saying or disagreement response set—that is, a tendency to disagree with any item regardless of its content—is the other end of the agreement dimension (cf. Knowles & Condon, 1999). It is relatively rare and has been little investigated. One study found the disagreement response set more common among Republicans than among Democrats (Milbrath, 1962).

THE BOGUS PIPELINE

Because of the response sets discussed in the previous section, the validity of self-report measures is always open to question. However, using them in conjunction with a related objective measure can sometimes increase their validity. For instance, in a study of adolescents' self-reports of smoking, the amount of smoking reported was significantly higher when reports were taken after a demonstration that recent smoking could be detected from the presence of carbon monoxide in their breath (Bauman & Dent, 1982).

This carbon monoxide measure was a true indicator of smoking, but the same effect of increased validity should occur if respondents merely *believe* that there is a true measure of their behavior or feelings available. This principle is the basis of the so-called **bogus pipeline**, in which participants are falsely convinced that some elaborate electronic apparatus can detect their true feelings. This technique typically results in their reporting higher levels of various socially undesirable attitudes or behaviors such as racial prejudice, eating disorders such as bulimia, smoking marijuana, and drunk driving (Jones & Sigall, 1971; Quigley-Fernandez & Tedeschi, 1978; Roese & Jamieson, 1993; Tourangeau, Smith, & Rasinski, 1997).

We should emphasize that using techniques such as the bogus pipeline raises several ethical questions (Aguinis & Henle, 2001). Issues of privacy, informed consent, deception, and debriefing must all be carefully considered. However, these are not clear-cut issues, and researchers differ on how they should be resolved. On the one hand, minor deception is often socially acceptable (as in conventional politeness and "little white lies"), and on the other hand, full debriefing of participants about the research they took part in may sometimes do more harm than good. Dawes and Smith's (1985) often-cited review recommended following social norms about what is considered ethical outside of the laboratory, and using deception only in cases where it seems so innocuous that no debriefing should be needed. A fuller discussion of ethical issues in research is presented in Chapter 12.

Given the ethical issues associated with the bogus pipeline, an important question is whether there are other ways to increase the validity of self-report measures that do not require deception. Several studies have found that using techniques that ensure anonymity can yield equally valid responses (Hill, Dill, & Davenport, 1988).

OTHER WAYS OF MEASURING EXPLICIT ATTITUDES

In the preceding sections, all of the methods that we have described for measuring explicit attitudes have relied on language, either written or oral. But there are other ways of assessing explicit attitudes that do not require linguistic skills.

Graphical Scales

Feeling Thermometer.   One technique for measuring attitudes is through graphical or pictorial rating scales. One example of such a scale is the feeling thermometer. It asks respondents to indicate their attitude on a scale of degrees, typically ranging from 0° (Very cold) to 100° (Very warm), with 50° representing "No feeling at all." The feeling thermometer has been used quite often in public opinion research (Berman & Stookey, 1980), and particularly to measure attitudes toward political candidates (e.g., Granberg & Brent, 1980; Beasley & Joslyn, 2001).

For example, Fox and Smith (1998) used a feeling thermometer to examine how attitudes toward political candidates were affected by the candidate's gender. Students enrolled in American government classes at two universities, in California and Wyoming, rated four hypothetical candidates for the U.S. House of Representatives. The name of each candidate (indicating gender) was followed by his or her positions on a number of issues. On half of the forms the candidate was female (e.g., Lisa Jennings), and on the other half the candidate was male (e.g., Bill Jennings). Results for the California sample (which was selected to be a liberal sample) showed no evidence of gender bias—ratings of the candidates did not differ by their gender. For example, the average rating for Lisa Jennings was 68.3, and for the similarly described Bill Jennings it was 69.4—a nonsignificant difference. However, the more conservative Wyoming sample did show evidence of gender bias—Lisa Jennings' mean was 59.4, whereas Bill Jennings' mean was 65.1.

Body-Shape Preference.   Another example of a graphical scale used to measure attitudes comes from research on female body size and shape. Singh (1993) developed a pictorial measure that assesses preference for female body size (thin, normal, overweight) and shape (waist-to-hip ratio). The waist-to-hip ratio is determined by the smallest width of the waist divided by the largest width of the hips. As shown in Figure 3–1, a waist-to-hip ratio of 1.0 means equal waist and hip sizes, whereas a ratio of 0.7 indicates a waist considerably smaller than the hips. Research with this scale has generally found a preference for "normal" weight combined with a smaller waist-to-hip ratio of around 0.7

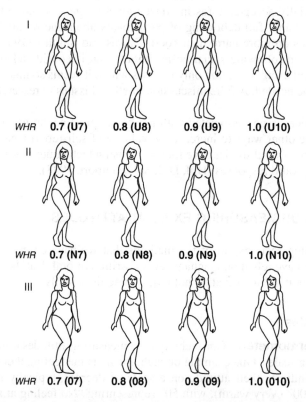

FIGURE 3–1 Stimulus figures representing three body-weight categories: underweight (I), normal weight (II), and overweight (III). Waist-to-hip ratios (WHR) are shown under each figure in each weight category, along with a letter and a number in parentheses that identify the body-weight category and WHR.

Source: Singh, D. (1993). Adaptive significance of female physical attractiveness: Role of waist-to-hip ratio (p. 298). *Journal of Personality and Social Psychology, 65,* 293–307. Copyright © 1993 by the American Psychological Association. Reprinted with permission.

(Markey et al., 2002), although several studies have indicated a tendency for European American respondents to prefer thinner weight (Gordon, 2000). The preference for smaller waist-to-hip ratios has been found among both men and women, across a wide range of ages (sample ages ranged from 25 to 85), and across various ethnic groups (African American, Asian American, Mexican American, and Caucasian).

Observations of Behavior

Compared with verbal self-report measures, behavioral measures of attitudes have been seldom used and consequently are poorly developed and crude in their methodology. In large part this is because they are difficult, time-consuming, and expensive to utilize.

The most straightforward type of behavioral observation is one made in a natural setting, such as watching for aggressive episodes in a schoolyard. However, the time-consuming, tedious nature of such observation has led to use of more standardized situations, which are structured so as to elicit the behavior of interest more easily. Cook and Selltiz (1964) described three different types of such standardized approaches: (a) apparently unstaged standardized situations in which a person's behavior can be observed, (b) staged role-playing situations in which the person is asked either to respond as he or she would in real life, or to take the part of a particular other person, and (c) use of sociometric choices which the participant believes will have real-life consequences (e.g., choice of which members of a group to work with on a joint task). In all three of these approaches, of course, the situation chosen is one in which the attitude objects (e.g., children of a different racial group) are presented in some way.

A key advantage of this approach is that *participants can be convinced that there will be real-life consequences* flowing from their responses (e.g., they will actually get to work with the classmates they choose). Alternatively, it is also possible to represent the attitude objects only *symbolically* (i.e., in words or pictures) rather than having them physically present. An example is Harter and Pikes' (1984) pictorial scale that measures perceived competence and social acceptance in young children (cf. Rainey & Rust, 1999). However, this procedure tends to measure the respondents' behavioral intentions (what they *say* they would do) rather than their actual behavior toward the attitude object—thus it is a return to a self-report form of measurement.

Because Fishbein and Ajzen (1972) have reported very high correlations between behavioral intentions and behavior, the use of behavioral-intention measures may be justifiable here. Cook and Selltiz (1964) defended it on the grounds that it is less sensitive than real-life behavior to a variety of extraneous influences (e.g., previous acquaintance or lack of it with individuals being responded to). However, we should emphasize that it is sometimes possible to observe actual behavior in situations where extraneous influences are relatively inoperative. For instance, slight vertical or horizontal head movements are good indicators of a person's attitude toward a persuasive message (Wells & Petty, 1980). Similarly, in a small-group discussion situation, choice of a seat next to someone in a wheelchair, rather than one farther away, could indicate a person's attitude toward people with disabilities. Because Wicker (1969) and others have shown that there is often only a low relationship between verbal self-report attitude measures and behavior, the use of actual behavior measures may be preferable to behavioral-intention measures.

One famous example illustrates the types of behavioral-intention measures that have been used. DeFleur and Westie (1958) developed a method in which white subjects, after seeing some relevant interracial slides, were asked whether they would be willing to be photographed with a black person of the opposite sex. The subjects were also requested to sign a "standard photograph release agreement" indicating which of a variety of purposes they would be willing to have such a photograph used for—ranging from showings solely to professional sociologists for research purposes to a nationwide publicity campaign in favor of racial integration. The number of uses that they checked was taken as an indicator of favorableness toward blacks.

Unobtrusive Measures

One of the most promising ways of supplementing attitude scale scores is the use of **unobtrusive measures** of behavior (observations made without attracting the attention of the people being studied), as suggested in a fascinating paperback book by Webb et al. (1981). Such measures may be direct observations of behavior, such as standing in a high lookout and counting the number of students taking different paths across campus, or watching children's aggressive behavior in a schoolyard. However, several types of unobtrusive measurement can also substitute for tedious long-term observation as indicators of attitudes: (1) Direct measures of **preference** can be counted, such as candidate bumper stickers in a parking lot (Wrightsman, 1969). (2) **By-products** or waste products can show people's attitudes; for instance, counts of beer cans and liquor bottles in trash can gauge the amount of drinking and the preferred beverages in an area (Rathje & Ritenbaugh, 1984). (3) Measures of **erosion**; for instance, paths worn in the grass across campus, or the rate of emptying of ice cream tubs, can indicate preferred routes or flavors. (4) Measures of **accretion**; people's interests can be estimated from the amount of dirt on pages of library books or the number of fingerprints and nose smudges on glass cases in museums (Webb et al., 1981).

Another good example of unobtrusive measures used in research studies is the percentage size of tips left for a restaurant server (Lynn & Simons, 2000). Similarly, the forwarding of letters in the **lost letter technique**, in which stamped and addressed letters are dropped in shopping areas, can gauge community sentiment toward local organizations or election issues (Simmons & Zumpf, 1983) or attitudes toward specific social groups such as gay men or lesbians (Bridges & Rodriguez, 2000). Recently a newer version of the lost letter technique has been developed for electronic mail—the "lost e-mail" (Stern & Faber, 1997). Further use of such imaginative approaches could help to solve the problems inherent in interpreting the results of attitude-scale and opinion-interview research.

Performance on Objective Tasks

This measurement approach has been used somewhat more widely than the previous ones. Cook and Selltiz (1964) described it as follows:

> Approaches in this category present the respondent with specific tasks to be performed; they are presented as tests of information or ability, or simply as jobs that need to be done. The assumption common to all of them is that performance may be influenced by attitude, and that a systematic bias in performance reflects the influence of attitude. (p. 50)

Thus, in a sense, this approach is similar to observations of behavior. It differs in that the task is structured for the subjects, and that the relevance of their performance to measurement of their attitudes is usually quite thoroughly disguised.

Some examples may clarify how this can be done. Hammond (1948) devised an "information" test with alternative answers that were equally far on either side of the correct response (which was not provided as an alternative). He showed that the respondents' choices of erroneous responses were generally consistent with their own attitudes. For instance, a pro-union person would generally choose an answer that overestimated labor

Photograph courtesy of Lehigh University.
Reprinted by permission.

Box 3–6 DONALD CAMPBELL, *Methodologist and Attitude Researcher*

Donald Campbell received nearly every major honor that psychology had to offer—notably, election to the National Academy of Sciences and the American Academy of Arts and Sciences, the presidency of the American Psychological Association, and its Distinguished Scientific Contribution Award. He was honored as a methodologist and a philosopher, a field researcher and a laboratory experimenter, and for work in anthropology, political science, and sociology as well as psychology.

Born in 1916, Campbell worked on a turkey ranch before taking his B.A. at the University of California at Berkeley. Following wartime service in the Navy he returned to Berkeley and completed a noteworthy dissertation on the consistency of racial attitudes. After teaching briefly at Ohio State and the University of Chicago, he settled in 1953 at Northwestern, remaining there until 1979, when he moved to Syracuse for three years and then to Lehigh University, where he continued to write until his death in 1996.

Campbell was widely known as a coauthor of books on unobtrusive measures and on experimental and quasi-experimental research methods. Among his 200-plus articles, one on indirect methods of measurement is particularly relevant to the topic of this chapter. Chapter 5 cites his research on attitude consistency; and in Chapter 12 his critique of attitude–behavior pseudo-inconsistency is described, and his call for planned experimentation on social and governmental programs is applauded.

unions' membership size, rather than an answer that underestimated it, whereas the opposite would usually be true for an anti-union individual. Similarly, Brigham and Cook (1970) had respondents judge the plausibility of pro-integration and anti-integration arguments, and the judgments were treated as indicators of the person's own attitudes toward racial integration.

Two problems are present in interpreting measures of this sort. If a person shows a consistent bias in performance, it seems safe to infer that the individual's attitudes are responsible. However, if a consistent bias is not shown, it may not be safe to infer that the person's attitude is a weak one, for we do not know how sensitive such measures are. Second, a particular bias in response might reflect either wishes or fears—"a member of the Communist party may overestimate the number of Communists in the United States, but so may a member of [an anti-Communist group]" (Cook & Selltiz, 1964, p. 51). Thus, additional information may be needed to determine the direction of the person's attitude from a biased performance.

In using any of the kinds of measures described in this chapter, it should be emphasized that the researcher's conclusions about people's attitudes is an inference from the particular measures taken. This is true even when the measures used are individuals' self-reports of their own attitudes, for the researcher still has to decide whether the respondents truly are aware of their own attitudes and are reporting them accurately.

SUMMARY

Attitudes and opinions may be expressed in many colorful ways, but for purposes of scientific study, they must be classified into categories or measured on a quantitative scale. The development of attitude-scaling methods in the 1920s and 1930s was the first major application of quantitative measurement in the field of social psychology. In terms of the frequency of their use, the five most widely used scaling methods are Bogardus' scale of social distance toward various ethnic groups, Thurstone's method of equal-appearing intervals, Likert's method of summated ratings (the most popular of all), Guttman's cumulative scaling method of constructing a unidimensional scale, and Osgood's scale of connotative meaning, the Semantic Differential. All of these methods produce scales that are ordinal in nature, and therefore some caution must be exercised if parametric statistics are used in analyzing their results.

It is essential for attitude scales, like all measurement methods, to be both reliable (consistent) and valid (accurate) in their results. Problems that affect the validity of attitude scales include the response sets of carelessness, social desirability, extremity, and acquiescence (yea-saying). With due care in constructing and interpreting attitude scales, all of these problems can be at least partially overcome.

In conjunction with attitude scales, it is recommended that other less-common methods of studying attitudes also be more widely used in research, in order to provide a broader multidimensional measurement approach. These supplementary techniques include methods of increasing the validity of self-report measures, graphical scales, observations of behavior (particularly unobtrusive observations), and measures of performance on objective tasks in attitude-relevant situations. In addition, the following chapter discusses ways of measuring implicit attitudes.

4

Implicit and Indirect Measures of Attitudes

The human mind must think with the aid of categories.... Once formed, categories are the basis for normal prejudgment. We cannot possibly avoid this process.—Gordon Allport, 1954.

There comes to mind the uncertainty of using an opinion [statement] as an index of attitude. The man may be a liar.... Neither his opinions nor his overt acts constitute in any sense an infallible guide to the subjective inclinations and preferences that constitute his attitude.—Louis Thurstone, 1928.

To what extent are we aware of our attitudes and opinions? Is it possible that some of our preferences exist outside of our conscious awareness? Can such unconscious attitudes be "activated" and influence us automatically, without thinking? Or can we control our attitudes so that they don't show? Suppose that you have a negative opinion of your friend's parents; can you control this opinion so that it isn't obvious when you are talking with them?

In the previous chapter, we examined the major approaches that utilize explicit measures of attitudes. These approaches, particularly the use of Likert scales, have dominated attitude measurement since it began around 1930. They have been used to measure attitudes about a multitude of social issues (abortion, school vouchers, gun control, welfare), people (George W. Bush, Bill Gates, Michael Jordan), groups (women, gay men, ethnic minorities), objects (Coke, spotted owls, mass transit), and activities (bungee jumping, surfing, recycling), to name only a few.

Explicit attitudes are deliberate evaluations that are open to introspection and are under conscious control (Ottaway, Hayden, & Oakes, 2001). The traditional model guiding the construction of explicit measures has been referred to as the **file drawer model** (Wilson & Hodges, 1992; Tourangeau, Rips, & Rasinski, 2000). According to this model:

> When people are asked how they feel about something, such as legalized abortion, their Uncle Harry, or anchovies on a pizza, presumably they consult a mental file containing their evaluations. They look for the file marked *abortion, Uncle Harry*, or *anchovies*, and report the evaluation it contains. (Wilson & Hodges, 1992, p. 38)

This basic model characterizes much of the research utilizing explicit measures. It assumes that the attitude exists within the person, that the person can retrieve it accurately from memory, and that he or she is able and willing to express it truthfully in response to the question.

Since the early 1990s, a sizable amount of research has begun to examine **implicit attitudes**—automatic evaluations that occur without conscious reflection and are not necessarily available for introspection or control (Fazio, 1990; Banaji & Bhaskar, 2000;

Photograph courtesy of Mahzarin Banaji.
Reprinted by permission.

Box 4–1 MAHZARIN BANAJI, *Investigator of Implicit Attitudes*

Mahzarin Banaji is a professor of psychology at Harvard University, where she holds the prestigious chair as professor of social ethics that was first held by Gordon Allport. She earned her Ph.D. from Ohio State University in 1986 and taught at Yale until 2001, when she moved to Harvard. She has been associate editor of Psychological Review *and the* Journal of Experimental Social Psychology *and serves on the editorial boards of several other journals in social psychology.*

Banaji's research has focused on the unconscious or implicit processes involved in attitudes, social perception, memory, and self-knowledge. In particular, she has studied self-assessments and feelings and beliefs about other people that are based on their social group membership, such as age, race/ethnicity, gender, and class. She was cofounder of an educational Web site that has accumulated over 2.5 million completed tasks measuring automatic attitudes and beliefs involving self, other individuals, and social groups. Her research uses both cognitive/affective and behavioral measures and neuroimaging (magnetic resonance) techniques, and she explores the implications of her work for theories of individual responsibility and social justice.

Ottaway et al., 2001). In this chapter, we begin with a brief discussion of unconscious cognitive processes, then review types of indirect measures of attitudes, and finally describe several of the methodologies used to measure implicit attitudes: reaction time, priming, and the Implicit Association Test.

Because the research utilizing implicit measures is so new, it is unclear whether they are simply an alternative methodology for measuring a person's attitude, or whether they are measuring something qualitatively different (Fazio & Olson, 2003). Our approach is to view implicit and explicit measures as alternative ways to measure the same underlying attitude. We will return to this issue at the end of the chapter. Let's begin with an examination of indirect measures of attitudes.

INDIRECT MEASURES OF ATTITUDES

As previously discussed, explicit measures of attitudes rely on self-report. Whether obtained through a written questionnaire, an interview, or a telephone call, explicit measures are based on a respondent's self-reports of his or her attitudes or opinions. But can we measure attitudes more indirectly, in ways that do not require awareness or honest responses? Indeed, the search for an attitude "pipeline" has been a recurrent theme in attitude research (Karpinski & Hilton, 2001):

[T]he desire to find a measure that taps attitudes in ways that are impervious to self-presentation represents a kind of "Holy Grail" for attitude researchers. With such a measure, we could explore confidently all the domains of private life. With such a measure, we could explore attitudes that exist outside of conscious awareness. Also, with such a measure, we might gain an important tool for educating the public about our less socially desirable attitudes. Racial prejudice, for example, often fails to emerge on traditional attitude measures. Yet discrimination clearly permeates American culture, and a valid attitude pipeline might provide one way of revealing the unpleasant truth of prejudice. (p. 786)

Lack of Awareness—Studying Unconscious Processes

There is a long history in the science of psychology for the study of thoughts, feelings, and behaviors that occur without conscious awareness. Indeed, systematic studies of unconscious processes date back at least 150 years. The notion of unconscious processes was popularized by Sigmund Freud and the teachers and practitioners who followed his **psychodynamic** approach. Freud (1949) argued that the bulk of mental activity occurs outside of conscious awareness. Unacceptable thoughts about sexuality (*eros*) or aggression (*thanatos*) are pushed into the unconscious mind because thinking about sex and aggression would cause too much anxiety. Although we are not aware of these repressed thoughts and feelings, Freud held that they manifest themselves in our attitudes and actions. Not only do these unconscious feelings have influence, but their influence occurs outside of volition, and we are often unable to control them. Although Freud's theories were provocative and highly influential among the general American public, the evidence supporting them was mixed at best (Kihlstrom, 1987; Kihlstrom, Barnhardt, & Tartaryn, 1992; Cramer, 2000). Yet, more recent empirical research has substantiated claims that our attitudes can exist outside of awareness and can exert an unconscious influence on our thoughts and actions.

But what do we mean by "unconscious"? Indeed, researchers on this topic use a range of terms to describe seemingly related concepts. Some examples include "implicit," "automatic," "unconscious," and "nonconscious." Intuitively, *unconscious* refers to thoughts or behaviors that occur outside of awareness, or those that are automatic. Posner and Snyder (1975) suggested that a mental event (and we would consider an attitude to be a mental event) can be either conscious or automatic. *Conscious* mental processes have four central qualities, according to Bargh (1994):

1. They are intentional,
2. occur within our awareness,
3. use cognitive resources,
4. are controllable.

If a mental process has these qualities, then it is conscious. If not, then it is *automatic*. Although this description is overly simplistic, the opposites of these four qualities are useful for understanding the central features of an unconscious mental process. See Wyer (1997) for a broad set of discussions about automaticity.

We begin our exploration of implicit attitudes by examining two types of indirect measures of attitudes: projective techniques and physiological reactions.

Reactions to Partially Structured Stimuli

One of the first approaches to assessing unconscious thoughts and feelings involved **projective techniques**. In a projective test, stimuli are presented that are not clearly structured, and consequently they do not provide sufficient information from which to draw a conclusion. Therefore respondents must draw on their own needs and dispositions in interpreting or describing the characteristics of the attitude object. For instance, a picture of the head of a Middle Eastern girl may be presented, and the respondent may be asked to describe her characteristics or to make up a story about her. The task is usually presented as a test of imagination or social sensitivity or some similar concept, rather than as a measure of the respondent's attitudes.

Obviously this approach uses the respondent's verbal self-report, and so it has similarities to that measurement approach. The primary differences are the use of a somewhat ambiguous stimulus instead of an explicitly named attitude object, and the disguised goal of the measurement (e.g., as a test of ability to judge people's characteristics rather than an attitude measure). It is assumed that these aspects of the technique decrease the likelihood of respondents distorting their true feelings in an attempt to present themselves in a favorable light to the investigator. However, the literature on projective techniques is full of critiques questioning the validity of their results (e.g., Holt, 1999; Hansemark, 2000; Wood et al., 2003). It is clear that projective responses may reflect an individual's attitude; but they may also merely indicate a person's awareness of the common cultural patterns of response, such as unequal treatment of various minority groups.

As a result of these limitations, systematic use of projective techniques in the study of attitudes and opinions has been rare. One area where they have been utilized is with children, who in many instances may not have the cognitive skills to understand or express attitudes about abstract concepts. For example, Tamm and Prellwitz (2001) measured the attitudes of preschool children toward children with physical disabilities. The task involved drawing a picture of a child in a wheelchair (or selecting a ready-drawn picture). A series of probing questions were then asked about the picture: for example, "Why is the child sitting in the wheelchair?" and "Which games would you play if the person in the wheelchair was your friend?" The responses to these questions were then coded and the attitudes inferred. For example, from these data, Tamm and Prellwitz (2001) concluded:

> Our general impression from this study was that most children had a favourable attitude towards the child in a wheelchair. They were willing to include the child with disability in their games and recreational activities, and they considered that the disabled children would have many friends and high self-esteem. (p. 234)

One of the major limitations with projective techniques, like the one just described, is that they typically do not generate numerical attitude scores. This makes the measures difficult to compare between groups or across time periods, and it limits the extent to which they can be validated with other measures.

This limitation has been addressed in measurement techniques that combine partially structured stimuli with numeric ratings. For instance, Vargas, van Hippel, and Petty (2004) reported a series of studies in which participants provided numeric responses to partially structured stimuli, which were several written vignettes describing social situations. Here is one example:

> Mary didn't go to church once the whole time she was in college but she claimed that she was still a very religious person. She said that she prayed occasionally and that she believed in Christian ideals. Sometimes she watched religious programs on TV like the 700 club or the Billy Graham Crusade. (Vargas et al., 2004, p. 197).

Following each vignette, participants provided numeric responses, using 11-point scales, to a series of questions such as, "How religious was the behavior Mary performed?" and "How religious do you think Mary is, in general?" In addition to these partially structured items, the study also included an established explicit measure of religious attitudes and a 45-item self-report index of religious behaviors. The results showed that the mean score on the partially structured items correlated with both the explicit religious attitudes scale ($r = 0.33$) and self-reported religious behavior ($r = 0.60$). Interestingly, additional analyses showed that the measure of partially structured attitudes explained unique variance in behavior, beyond that explained by explicit measures. Similar results were found for attitudes about cheating and political conservatism. These findings suggest that partially structured stimuli offer a useful alternative to traditional explicit measures, and that they measure something conceptually different.

Physiological Reactions

Another approach to measuring attitudes indirectly is through the use of physiological responses. This approach is based on the principle that people have different physiological responses to stimuli that they like (or agree with) than to stimuli that they don't like (or don't agree with). A fairly wide variety of physiological reactions have been used in the study of attitudes: galvanic skin response (GSR), blood vessel constriction, heart rate, dilation of the pupil of the eye, and even the conditioned response of salivation in humans. One classic study involving physiological measures of attitudes was done by Westie and DeFleur (1959). These researchers showed participants pictures of whites and blacks in social situations and found relationships among GSR, blood vessel constriction, and a self-report measure of attitudes.

In these techniques it is assumed that the amount of the physiological reaction indicates the extent of participants' arousal—the intensity of their feelings—and hence the extremity of their attitudes. Often researchers will utilize multiple measures of physiological arousal, such as skin conductance, heart rate, blood pressure, and muscle tension. However, most physiological measures are **nondirectional** in nature; that is, they do not indicate whether the person is favorable or unfavorable toward the attitude object. Thus additional information is usually necessary to interpret them adequately.

There are two physiological approaches used to study attitudes which offer the possibility of assessing both directionality and strength of the attitude. The first method involves measures of tiny movements in facial muscles by use of **electromyography (EMG)**. A sizable amount of research has demonstrated that exposure to liked and disliked stimuli often induces small expressive facial actions, many of which are not socially perceptible (Ekman, 1971, 1999; Ekman, Friesen, & Ancoli, 1980). Cacioppo and his colleagues reported several studies in which facial EMG measures were used to assess positive and negative affective evaluations of pictorial images (Cacioppo, Petty, & Marshall-Goodal 1984; Cacioppo, Petty, & Losch, 1986). In one study, they assessed evaluations of images that were consistently rated as positive (e.g., a mountain cliff, an ocean beach) or negative (a polluted highway, a bruised torso). They presented these images in randomized order and measured facial EMG for each. The results showed that the facial measures were able to distinguish positive and negative evaluations (see also Cacioppo, Bush, & Tassinary, 1992). The authors reached this conclusion (Cacioppo et al., 1986):

The present results challenge the conventional wisdom in social psychology that physiological measures are sensitive only to changes in general arousal and therefore cannot be used to distinguish positive and negative affect. (pp. 264–265)

Photograph courtesy of John Cacioppo.
Reprinted by permission.

Box 4–2 JOHN CACIOPPO, *Attitude Researcher and Social Neuroscientist*

John Cacioppo is best known for his pioneering work in physiological measurement of attitudes, reflected in his volumes on Social Psychophysiology *and* Foundations in Social Neuroscience. *He is also the coauthor with Richard Petty of the Elaboration Likelihood Model of attitude change, discussed in Chapter 11. Cacioppo earned his Ph.D. at Ohio State University in 1977 and held faculty positions at Notre Dame, the University of Iowa, and Ohio State University before moving in 1999 to the University of Chicago as a Distinguished Service Professor. There he directs the Social Psychology Program and codirects the Institute for Mind and Biology.*

Cacioppo has contributed to the field as editor of Psychophysiology, *served on the editorial boards of 16 other journals, and been elected president of two divisions of the American Psychological Association. As of 2004, his vita listed more than 300 research publications, including 10 books. His numerous research awards include ones from the National Academy of Sciences, the Society for Personality and Social Psychology, and the American Psychological Association's Award for Distinguished Scientific Contributions to Psychology.*

Similar results have been reported by other researchers. For example, Jänke (1994) found that presenting participants with slides having a positive valence spontaneously produced muscle activity in the cheek area, whereas pictures with a negative valence produced an increase in muscle activity in the brow region of the face.

However, Cacioppo et al. (1986) cautioned that EMG facial measures may not be useful for measuring many types of attitudes. First, they are subject to control: "at the simplest level, people are capable of suppressing, falsifying, and distorting their true feelings toward a stimulus using measures of facial actions" (p. 266). Second, facial measures are subject to minor temporary fluctuations in emotions, whereas attitudes are considered to be relatively enduring. For example, individuals may hold a genuinely favorable attitude toward their children, despite experiencing moments of anger or displeasure with them. Given the limitations with EMG measures, Cacioppo and his colleagues have more recently pursued an alternative, brain-based approach to measuring attitudes.

This second physiological approach makes use of **event-related potentials (ERPs)**, which show electrical activity in the brain. ERP measures use electrodes placed on the scalp to measure neural (brain-wave) activity involved in processing information. The ERP reflects brain-activity levels at a specified period of time (in milliseconds) following the presentation of a stimulus, and different time periods have been found to be related to different cognitive activities. That is, the ERP measures the brain activity at different areas of the scalp at specific times (say, 100 or 300 ms) after a stimulus is presented. Cacioppo and colleagues (1993; Cacioppo, Crites, & Gardner, 1996) have developed a technique for measuring attitudes that makes use of a specific ERP (the P300).

> A larger-amplitude P300 along the midline centroparietal region of the scalp is evoked by categorically inconsistent stimuli, such as a high tone preceded by a sequence of low tones, than by categorically consistent stimuli, such as a high tone preceded by a sequence of high tones. (1996, p. 1206)

Utilizing this finding from the P300 ERP measure, Cacioppo and his colleagues developed a paradigm for measuring "evaluative categorizations" (i.e., attitudes). In this **oddball paradigm**, participants are presented with a short series of liked or disliked stimuli (words or pictures) and are asked to indicate which are pleasant and which are unpleasant. The extent to which the stimulus of interest is evaluated favorably or unfavorably can be determined by examining the P300 measures in different contexts: a positive context (in which the attitude object is preceded by positive stimuli) or a negative context (in which it is preceded by negative stimuli).

For example, if we were interested in measuring your attitude about people with disabilities, we could assess it in the context of a series of positive images. We might present eight positive images (e.g., a person smiling, two people holding hands, etc.) and, as the ninth image, show a person in a wheelchair. The extent to which you evaluated this attitude object as negative would be reflected in a higher P300 measure. Results have shown that ERPs generated in this "oddball paradigm" can distinguish between favorable and unfavorable attitudes (Cacioppo et al., 1993, 1994, 1996). Moreover, it appears that these ERPs distinguish favorable and unfavorable attitudes even when participants are instructed to lie (Crites et al., 1995). Thus, although people can control their words by expressing an opinion that is untrue, they cannot control the brain activity that results from exposure to a stimulus. This feature of physiological measures makes them especially useful for the detection of deception.

Lie Detectors. Sensitive electronic recordings of various physiological reactions are also used in the most familiar physiological indicator of emotional reactions, the **polygraph** machine or "lie detector." The use of lie detector tests has been increasing rapidly in industry, government, and law enforcement—for instance, to screen job applicants for honesty, or to identify guilty criminals (Kleiner, 2002). The polygraph makes use of several physiological measures that typically accompany stress, like heart rate, blood pressure, and galvanic skin response (GSR). In the most common form of testing for guilt, physiological reactions to control questions that are arousing but not related to the issue at hand are compared with reactions to test questions that are of interest (Saxe, 1994; Fiedler, Schmid, & Stahl, 2002). For example, reactions to the question "Between the ages of 18 and 34, did you ever deceive someone?" (which is arousing, but not of interest to the tester) would be compared with "Did you take the money from the safe?" If the person had stolen the money, they would be likely to show more elevated arousal levels to that question in comparison with the arousing-but-irrelevant question.

Research on the validity of polygraph tests has yielded mixed results (Fiedler et al., 2002). The accuracy of a polygraph test has been found to be related to several variables, including the type of questions asked, the person being questioned, the experience of the questioner, and the context in which the interview takes place, to name a few. A review of the research on polygraph tests found that, when they were conducted in carefully controlled settings by experienced interviewers, 89% of guilty individuals were correctly detected, and 83% of innocent individuals were detected (Elaad, 1990). Other reviews, based only on "conclusive" determinations of guilt or innocence (that is, disregarding cases that were determined to be inconclusive) reported even higher accuracy scores (98% for guilty determinations, and 82% for innocent determinations—Raskin, Honts, & Kircher, 1997; Fiedler et al., 2002). As a general rule, Ekman (2001) has suggested that for any given case a polygraph is about 85% accurate. This means, of course, that in about 15% of cases they would call an innocent person "guilty," or vice versa.

As a result of this considerably less-than-perfect accuracy rate, polygraphs have typically been ruled as "inadmissible" evidence in criminal courts. However, recent rulings have established clear criteria for the level of accuracy needed in order to be considered legally admissible, and some researchers are optimistic that revised versions of the procedure can increase its validity to a level acceptable in the courts (Ben-Shakhar, Bar-Hillel, & Kremnitzer, 2002). A more recent extension of polygraph measurement principles is aimed at detecting terrorists or other evil-intentioned people at airports. For instance, one recent study reported the results from a thermal-imaging technique for detecting anxiety (and possibly deception) at security screening locations in public places (Pavlidis, Eberhardt, & Levine, 2002). However, the limitations of physiological responses and of projective techniques have led researchers to search for other indirect techniques for assessing attitudes.

IMPLICIT MEASURES OF ATTITUDES

Research on implicit attitudes is based largely on cognitive psychology, especially on studies examining the ways in which the human mind structures and stores information. The concepts of associative networks or "neural networks" (Rumelhart, Hinton, & McClelland, 1986; Martindale, 1991) view human memory as a network of interconnected nodes of information. *Nodes* are basic processing units, and can include a person or object, feature, concept, idea, or evaluation. Nodes can vary in their state of activation, and they are connected to each other through *links*. The *activation* of one node can spread through the associative network to other related nodes. The principles of *nodes*, *associations*, and *activation* are central parts of the theory, and have been applied quite broadly to understanding human cognition, including social cognition. As we stated in Chapter 2, the term **social cognition** refers to the ways in which people think about themselves, other people, and social situations.

Attitudes as Object–Evaluation Associations

Recall from Chapter 1 that a key aspect of an attitude is its evaluative nature. Attitude objects are judged along a continuum of favorability—for example, a person is in favor of gun control, but is opposed to drug legalization. One way to conceptualize an attitude is that it consists of an association between the attitude object and an evaluation. That is, if evaluations (good or bad, positive or negative, like or dislike) are organized as nodes within an associative network, then an attitude can be viewed as an association between two nodes: the attitude object and an evaluation.

Figure 4–1 shows a simplistic example of an associative network concerning dogs, which in turn would be a portion of an associative network regarding pets. The model is hierarchical, such that, linked with the concept PETS, are BIRDS, DOGS, and CATS. At the next level, linked with each type of pet, can be specific types—POODLE, LAB, PUG, and so on. Associated with each of these concepts are some attributes. For example, birds fly, have wings, are colorful, and sing. This is the basic idea of an associative network.

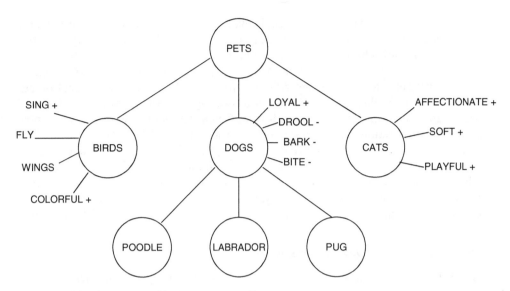

FIGURE 4–1 Sample of an associative network.

However, when the model is applied to attitudes, an additional piece is added: the valence of the attribute. For example, dogs are loyal (a positive attribute), but they also bark (negative), drool (negative), and bite (negative). A person with a favorable attitude toward dogs will have many positive attributes strongly associated with the concept (for example, loyal, lovable, companion, playful, protective), whereas a person with a negative attitude toward dogs will have many negative attributes (e.g., bark, drool, bite, annoying, beg, disobedient).

Early advocates of this approach were Fazio and his colleagues (1982), who proposed that the associative-network model and its principles of nodes, associations, and activation could be applied to attitudes. In the 20 years since this original proposal that attitudes can be viewed as object-evaluation associations, Fazio and his colleagues have conducted many relevant experiments (for a review, see Fazio, 2001). In their view, attitudes can be activated when related nodes are *primed*. For example, seeing a homeless family on a street corner may activate your attitude toward homelessness, or toward social welfare policies. Attitudes that are activated "effortlessly and inescapably" are referred to as **automatic** (Fazio, 1995). Such an attitude association exists within a person's associative network, but is made active without the need for conscious reflection. Indeed, it is even possible for individuals not to know that they have a negative attitude toward homeless people; and, on reflection, they may not want to have such an attitude.

Not all associations are equally strong, and therefore some attitudes are easier to activate than others. **Accessibility** refers to the strength of the attitude-evaluation association. An accessible attitude is one that can be activated from memory automatically when relevant stimuli are encountered, whereas less accessible attitudes are not as easily activated. As Fazio and Williams (1986) stated:

> [A]ttitudes are characterized as object-evaluation associations, and the strength of the association acts as a determinant of the accessibility of the attitude. The stronger the association, the greater the likelihood that the evaluation will be activated spontaneously upon the individual's encountering the attitude object. (p. 505)

Studies of attitude accessibility (and implicit attitudes in general) have relied primarily on the measure of response latency. **Response latency** is the speed, typically measured in milliseconds (ms), with which a judgment is made. Accessible attitudes are those with a small response latency—that is, accessible attitudes can be called to mind very quickly.

A number of studies have been conducted to demonstrate that accessible attitudes are easier and faster to recall. In the basic paradigm, participants are asked to engage in an activity that activates the relevant attitude—for example, copying attitudinal ratings from one sheet to another (i.e., rehearsal) or answering a series of semantic differential questions about the attitude object (recall from Chapter 3 that the semantic differential asks for a variety of ratings such as good–bad, or strong–weak). The goal of these activities is to activate the association between the attitude object and the evaluation. Following this manipulation, participants are asked to indicate their attitude about various attitude objects, and the response latencies are recorded. The findings from these studies consistently show that attitudes that are made accessible are expressed more quickly than attitudes that are not made accessible by the manipulation (Fazio et al., 1982; Roskos-Ewoldsen & Fazio, 1992).

Determinants of Attitude Accessibility

Given that the strength of an attitude can be measured using response latency, what determines how accessible an attitude is? Fazio (1995) listed two determinants:

1. Attitude rehearsal. As we saw in the preceding example, **rehearsing** an attitude by expressing it repeatedly can strengthen the object-evaluation association. In general, the more often a person states his or her attitude, the stronger it becomes. More generally, Fazio suggested that any activity that brings the attitude to mind can strengthen the association, even if the attitude is not stated explicitly.

2. Diagnosticity. The principle of **diagnosticity** refers to the source of information on which an attitude is based, which influences the strength of our belief in the accuracy of our attitude. Fazio (1995) suggested that attitudes tend to be more accessible if they are based on direct experience, are emotionally based, and are freely chosen.

Consequences of Accessible Attitudes

By far the most frequent question about attitude accessibility is: What are its consequences? Research conducted on this issue has used both correlational and experimental methodologies. In the experimental paradigm, attitudes are made accessible through a manipulation (like rehearsal), and then the consequences of increased accessibility are assessed. In the correlational studies, the accessibility of existing attitudes is measured without experimental manipulation, and the relationship between accessibility and an outcome is assessed. The consistency of the findings across both experimental and correlational findings lends support to the following three conclusions:

1. Behavior. Accessible attitudes are more predictive of behavior (Fazio, 1990, 1995). This result has been found in both experimental and correlational studies, and it will be discussed more in Chapter 12.

2. Information processing. Accessible attitudes also influence the ways in which people process information. For example, a sizable amount of research indicates that people tend to search for information that is consistent with their existing views or attitudes (this is the **confirmation bias**, discussed in Chapter 2). Fazio and Williams (1986) found that, when watching a presidential debate, most viewers believed that their candidate performed better. However, people with more accessible attitudes were more prone to this confirmation bias than were people with less accessible attitudes.

Photograph courtesy of Russell Fazio.
Reprinted by permission.

Box 4–3   RUSSELL FAZIO, *Associationistic Attitude Researcher*

Russell Fazio was an early advocate for the study of attitudes as object-evaluation associations. His research over the past 25 years has focused on social cognition, including the topics of attitude formation, change, and accessibility, the functional value of attitudes, and especially the relationship between attitudes and behavior.

Fazio received his Ph.D. from Princeton University in 1978, and he currently holds an endowed professorial chair at Ohio State University. Before moving there in 2001, he spent 23 years on the psychology faculty at Indiana University. From 1980 to 2005, he had 26 continuous years of research support from the National Institute of Mental Health (NIMH) and the National Science Foundation, and he has won awards for distinguished research from NIMH and the American Psychological Association. In addition to his prolific research publications, Fazio was the editor of the Journal of Experimental Social Psychology *and has served on the editorial board of six other journals in social psychology.*

3.   Attitude stability over time. Point 2 regarding confirmation bias in information processing also suggests that accessible attitudes should be more stable across time. If accessible attitudes are associated with a greater tendency to search for confirming information, then they should be less subject to change. As expected, the research findings do show that accessible attitudes are more stable across time (Fazio & Williams, 1986), and also they are more resistant to counterargument (Bassili & Fletcher, 1991).

CONTROL AND AUTOMATICITY: PRIMING

Much research described in the previous section experimentally manipulated the accessibility of an attitude—for example, through rehearsal. However, it is also possible to assess existing attitudes by presenting participants with a stimulus (for example, a picture of a snake or of an attractive woman) and assessing the degree to which the stimulus activates positive or negative reactions. This procedure is known as **affective priming**. As Dovidio et al. (2002, p. 62) point out, implicit attitudes are "automatically activated by the mere presence of the attitude object and commonly function without a person's full awareness or control."

In priming studies, stimuli (most often words, but pictures have also been used) are flashed briefly on a computer screen. The duration of the prime can be as short as a few milliseconds or as long as a few seconds. Primes that are presented below 50 ms often are undetected by participants—that is, they are *subliminal*. Primes that are longer than

50 ms are usually detected, but there are individual differences in how easily the primes are perceived. Following exposure to the prime, participants complete a simple task, such as indicating whether a string of letters comprises a word or not, or indicating whether a word is positive or negative. These tasks are usually quite easy and involve a dichotomous response (e.g., "yes" or "no"), which is indicated by pressing a key on a computer keyboard.

The basic idea in priming is that the primes activate a part of a person's cognitive network, making concepts associated with the prime easier to recall. For example, Meyer and Schvaneveldt (1971) found that response times to words like NURSE were significantly faster when they were preceded by a related word like DOCTOR (the prime). The explanation is that the words DOCTOR and NURSE are connected in a person's associative network, and the activation produced by processing one of the words facilitates a person's reading and deciding about the related word (Neely, 1991; Rosch, 1978). The type of procedure wherein participants make decisions about whether or not string of letters comprises a word is called a **lexical decision-making task**.

The notion of priming can be extended to the measurement of attitudes. For example, if the attitude object *snake* is evaluated negatively, then priming the person with the word SNAKE or a picture of snake should automatically activate negative associations (for example, *disgusting*). However, if the person does not have a negative attitude toward snakes, then the priming effect should not occur. Alternatively, if the attitude is favorable, then we would expect to see facilitation for positive words (for example, *fun* or *interesting*). Indeed, research has found just such automatic activation effects (Bargh et al., 1992; Fazio, 1993; Hermans, De Houwer, & Eelen, 1994; Fazio et al., 1995).

Let's consider a research example of the **automatic activation** of attitudes. Fazio et al. (1995) reported the results from four studies in which priming was used to study the automatic activation of attitudes—in this case, racial attitudes (see Chapter 16 for more extensive discussion of racial attitudes). In their study 1, the researchers primed participants by using color photographs of black, white, or other (Hispanic or Asian) faces. The participant's task was to press a key labeled *good* or a key labeled *bad* as quickly as possible for 24 words: 12 were positive (e.g., *attractive*, *likable*, and *wonderful*) and 12 were negative (e.g., *annoying*, *disgusting*, *offensive*). After a series of baseline trials, the priming trials were presented. In them, a face was flashed on the computer screen for 315 ms, followed by a short delay of 135 ms, and then the target adjective. The average response latencies for the primed words were subtracted from the average baseline response latencies (obtained without the prime) to produce a facilitation score. Thus this score indicates the extent to which the prime sped up a person's responses to positive or negative words.

The results from study 1 by Fazio et al. (1995) showed that white participants had less-favorable attitudes toward blacks than did black participants. That is, when primed with black faces, white participants showed greater facilitation for negative adjectives than did black participants. Study 2 replicated this basic effect and also found a positive correlation ($r = 0.26$) between the facilitation scores for negative adjectives and an explicit measure of racial attitudes (the Modern Racism Scale—McConahay, 1986). Further results from studies 3 and 4 suggested that, unlike explicit measures of attitudes, the facilitation measure was automatic. For example, when tested individually with an explicit measure, participants expressed considerably more-favorable attitudes toward black Americans when the researcher was black than they did when the researcher was white or when the test was mass-administered. The results for the facilitation scores on the implicit measure indicated considerably less reactivity to these conditions (especially for those participants who were motivated to control their attitudes and thus showed high reactivity on the explicit measure). These findings led Fazio et al. (1995) to refer to the priming procedure as a "bona fide pipeline" (in contrast to the "bogus pipeline" procedure that was discussed in the previous chapter).

The research on affective priming has found its effects to be quite robust. Facilitation effects have been found for a range of target stimuli, many different priming stimuli (words, pictures, line drawings), and several decision tasks. Importantly, studies have found that even subliminal primes (those presented so quickly that they go undetected) facilitate response times (Greenwald, Klinger, & Liu, 1989; Wittenbrink, Judd, & Park, 1997). Finally, the effect appears to be limited to a very short predecision period. Studies that allow a long duration between the prime and the decision task, such as 1000 ms (1 second), fail to find priming effects, whereas studies that utilize a shorter duration (e.g., 300 ms) between the prime and the decision task usually find priming effects (e.g., De Houwer, Hermans, & Eelen, 1998). This suggests that the spread of activation produced by the prime either dissipates very quickly, or alternatively, it may be actively inhibited by the individual. We return to the issue of inhibition in a later section of this chapter.

AUTOMATIC STEREOTYPING

The findings obtained with the priming paradigm discussed in the previous section suggest that facilitation scores generated through a priming procedure can provide a measure of a person's attitude. This approach has been extended more broadly to the study of stereotypes. In Chapter 2, we defined a **stereotype** as a generalized set of beliefs that a person holds about most members of a particular group. By their very nature, these beliefs are highly simplified.

Measuring stereotypes adequately can be difficult, because respondents are often unwilling to acknowledge (perhaps even to themselves) that they hold such simplistic beliefs. Stereotypes exist about almost all social groups, including ones based on gender, race, social class, age, political affiliation, athletic roles, and so on. In later chapters of this book, we will examine stereotypes about gender and race in relation to the attitudes that are often associated with them. Here we discuss research on the automatic activation of stereotypes.

In the priming paradigm, when the priming word is the label of a stereotyped group, it follows that adjectives associated with the stereotype may also be activated. This basic effect has been termed **automatic stereotyping**. The argument is that if, for instance, the racial category of *black* and the stereotypic adjective *athletic* are linked in a person's semantic network, then activating the category—for example, by presenting a black face or the word BLACK—should facilitate a person's response to the related adjective. Evidence for the activation of stereotypes has been found for several social categories:

- gender groups (Deaux et al., 1985; Banaji & Greenwald, 1995),
- elderly people (Hense, Penner, & Nelson, 1995; Kawakami, Young, & Dovidio, 2002),
- black Americans (Dovidio et al., 1997; Lepore & Brown, 1997, 1999; Wittenbrink, Judd, & Park, 2001).

Several studies on stereotypes about black Americans demonstrate that the activation of stereotypes occurs automatically, without awareness. For example, Gaertner and McLaughlin (1983) found that priming white participants with the word WHITE produced facilitated response times to positive words, compared with conditions in which the same positive words were primed by the word BLACK or NEGRO. In this study no difference was found between WHITE and BLACK primes for negative words. Even stronger evidence was provided by Wittenbrink et al. (1997), in a study where the primes (BLACK or WHITE) were presented without the participants being consciously aware of them (primes presented for 15 ms). Results showed that the WHITE prime produced faster response times for positive than for negative words, whereas the BLACK prime produced faster response times for negative than for positive words. In addition, the size of this implicit prejudice effect was positively correlated ($r = 0.41$) with an explicit measure of prejudice (the Modern Racism Scale—McConahay, 1986).

The fact that researchers have been successful in demonstrating priming effects for a wide range of stereotypes suggests that stereotypes are quite ubiquitous, and that most individuals within a given culture share these stereotypic beliefs. Indeed, there is evidence that knowledge of a cultural stereotype about groups like African Americans, women, Chicanos, or elderly people *is similar in members of the stereotyped group and in non-members*. In addition, knowledge of the stereotype about different minority racial groups has been found to be similar among high- and low-prejudice white participants (Devine, 1989; Lepore & Brown, 1997).

These findings raise an important question: Given that the content of a stereotype can be activated, can it then be inhibited? Indeed, this question gets to the heart of the issue about automaticity and control. Neely (1977) has demonstrated that priming of related words is automatic if the target immediately follows the prime, but that priming can be inhibited if there is a longer delay such as several seconds. The issue of automatic versus controlled processes in social cognition has sparked considerable debate (Montieth, Sherman, & Devine, 1998; Bargh, 1999; Lepore & Brown, 1999). Devine (1989) suggested that it might be possible for some individuals to suppress stereotype activation. That is, if they had sufficient motivation, time, and cognitive resources, some people should be able to control their cognitions. Specifically, Devine argued that, although most people in the U.S. might share the stereotype content regarding black Americans, people low in prejudice would show a greater tendency to inhibit the activation—if they were given enough time to do so.

Dual-Process Models of Attitudes and Stereotypes

The dual-process notion is that both automatic and controlled processing of stereotype information occurs. Although this viewpoint has received considerable attention, the empirical data are inconsistent. The original supporting data reported by Devine (1989) have been criticized on several levels. One of the criticisms concerns the primes used to activate stereotypes. Lepore and Brown (1997) distinguished between *category primes* and *stereotype primes*. Their results showed that high- and low-prejudice whites did not differ in their reaction times to stereotype-related words when primed by words that were directly related to the stereotype (e.g., LAZY). But, when primed by category labels (e.g., WHITE or BLACK), high-prejudice participants responded faster than low-prejudice participants to stereotype-related words. Because Devine's (1989) study made use of stereotype primes, the procedure may have been measuring the association between traits, and not the association between traits and the social group.

More recently, Kawakami, Dion, and Dovidio (1998) used a word-naming task with white participants to examine the relationships among personal endorsement of the stereotype of blacks, prejudiced attitudes, and stereotype activation. In addition, they manipulated the time interval between the onset of the prime and the onset of the target stimulus word. Following Devine (1989), they hypothesized that, when tested with short intervals, low-prejudice individuals would not have time to inhibit the stereotype and would show the same facilitated responses to negative words primed by BLACK and positive words primed by WHITE that are observed in high-prejudice individuals. In contrast, with long intervals, low-prejudice participants (but not high-prejudice participants) would not show this effect because they would have time to inhibit their responses. However, the actual results showed that high-prejudice participants had facilitated reaction times to stereotype-related words with both long and short intervals, whereas low-prejudice participants showed no facilitation with either long or short intervals.

This pattern of results contradicted Devine's (1989) hypothesis that all individuals share the same stereotype. Instead, it suggested that low-prejudice whites differ from high-prejudice whites in having a lower level of personal endorsement of the common negative stereotype about black Americans. Another, different argument against the controllability of stereotype activation has been presented by Bargh (1999). Thus, although evidence shows that negative attitudes associated with stereotypes can be automatically activated, there is little evidence that these negative attitudes, once activated, can be suppressed or controlled.

IMPLICIT ASSOCIATIONS

Following up the research that we have described on attitude accessibility and automatic versus controlled processes, Greenwald and his colleagues (1995, 1998) wrote influential papers and conducted a series of studies on "implicit social cognition." A product of their work was the development of the **Implicit Association Test (IAT)**, which is a procedure for assessing the degree of association of concepts (e.g., dogs versus cats) with an evaluative dimension (like versus dislike). In many ways, the work was a continuation of the basic associative-network model discussed earlier in this chapter. Within this framework, an attitude can be defined as "the association of a social object or social group concept with a valence attribute concept" (Greenwald et al., 2002, p. 5).

The IAT makes use of reaction times to measure the strength of association between category concepts and valence concepts. Greenwald, McGhee, and Schwartz (1998) presented the first set of data utilizing this approach. To illustrate their approach, consider your attitudes toward insects and toward flowers. If you're like most people, you have a generally unfavorable attitude toward insects but a more favorable attitude toward flowers. The IAT assesses the speed with which a person pairs words from the categories (in this case, insects or flowers) with a valence attribute (i.e., an evaluation like "pleasant" or "unpleasant").

The procedure asks participants to classify words into categories. The words are selected from the categories, typically with 10 or so words from each category. For example, flower words might include DAISY or ROSE, insect words might include FLY or MOSQUITO, pleasant words might include JOY or RAINBOW, and unpleasant words might include DISASTER or GRIEF. The test is presented on a computer screen, and the time (in milliseconds) taken to classify the word into a category is measured. Categories are presented in the corner of the screen and the target words are presented in the center. Participants are instructed to press the "D" key with their left forefinger if the word matches the category on the left of the screen, or the "K" key with their right forefinger if the word belongs to the category on the right. Examples of the procedure are shown in Figure 4–2.

In the typical procedure, participants begin with some easy choices, in which they classify a word into one of two categories—for example, INSECT or FLOWER. Later they are presented with a word and two pairs of categories. In some cases the categories have the same valence (e.g., INSECT and BAD, versus FLOWER and GOOD); these

IAT Instructions

This task involves matching words with categories. Examine the words on the screen. This will tell you what words go with each category. When you are finished, click "Continue." Category names will appear on the left- and right-hand sides of the screen. A word will then appear in the center of the screen that falls into one of the categories. If the word falls into one of the categories on the left-hand side of the screen, press the "D" key. If the word falls into one of the categories on the right-hand side of the screen, press the "K" key.

- Keep your index fingers on the "D" and "K" keys to enable rapid response.
- Two labels at the top will tell you which words or faces go with each key.
- Each word or face has a correct classification. Most of these are easy.
- The test gives no results if you go slow—please try to go fast.
- Expect to make a few mistakes because of going fast. That's OK.

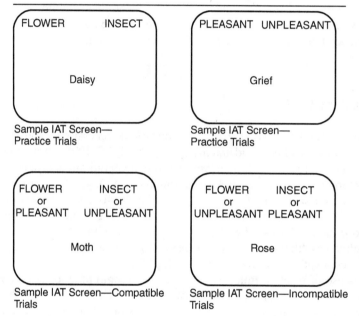

FLOWER   INSECT

Daisy

Sample IAT Screen—
Practice Trials

PLEASANT UNPLEASANT

Grief

Sample IAT Screen—
Practice Trials

FLOWER   INSECT
or   or
PLEASANT   UNPLEASANT

Moth

Sample IAT Screen—Compatible
Trials

FLOWER   INSECT
or   or
UNPLEASANT PLEASANT

Rose

Sample IAT Screen—Incompatible
Trials

FIGURE 4–2 Example of instructions for the Implicit Association Test.

are called **compatible pairings**, and they are easy classifications to make. In other cases the categories have opposite valences (e.g., INSECT and GOOD, versus FLOWER and BAD); these are called **incompatible pairings**, and they are difficult classifications to make, which slows down the participants' responses. The reaction-time data are averaged across many trials, and the average reaction time for compatible categories is subtracted from the average for incompatible categories. This difference shows the ease with which the participant was able to associate words with the categories and valence attributes. In the INSECT–FLOWER example, Greenwald et al. (1998) reported an IAT effect of 176 ms. That is, participants were on average 176 ms (about 1/6 of a second) faster in their decisions for the compatible than for the incompatible associations.

Using this basic procedure, a researcher can assess relative attitudes toward any pair of objects. One of the first uses of this procedure was to assess racial attitudes. As you might guess, the categories were WHITE or BLACK, and the valence categories used were PLEASANT or UNPLEASANT. Categories were represented by African American names (e.g., Jerome, Tyrone, Darnell) or Caucasian names (e.g., Alfred, Barry, Chip). Ottaway et al. (2001) reported an IAT effect of 108 ms, indicating that participants were faster for WHITE–PLEASANT and BLACK–UNPLEASANT trials than for the opposite pairings, and similar results have been reported by other authors.

Methodological Issues

The IAT has become widely used as an alternative measure of attitudes. In the years since the initial publication, it has weathered a number of criticisms, and there is now considerable evidence for its validity and reliability (Greenwald, 2004). Here we briefly review some of the criticisms that have been leveled at the IAT and some of the evidence for its validity.

One of the first criticisms was that the order of trials could influence the ease of associations. For example, a participant who completes the compatible trials (FLOWER–PLEASANT) first may have a more difficult time when the concepts are reversed than would a participant who began with the incompatible trials. Such a finding would be consistent with prior research on mental sets (cf. Schultz & Searleman, 2002). However, subsequent research has shown that, although order is important, it does not explain the IAT effect. Most studies **counterbalance** the order of presentation, so that half of the participants receive compatible pairings first, and the other half receive incompatible pairings first. The findings have tended to show a larger IAT effect when compatible trials were first, but even when compatible trials were second, a smaller but nevertheless significant IAT effect still occurred.

A second criticism of the IAT procedure is that it may confound the familiarity of the words used with the category concept. Consider the IAT procedure for measuring racial attitudes. It is possible that the IAT effect (showing a greater tendency to associate "good" with "white" and "bad" with "black") could have resulted from a greater familiarity with the name words used. That is, white participants would be more familiar with white names and consequently have a bias favoring them, and black participants would be more familiar with black names. However, the study by Ottaway et al. (2001) demonstrated that, although familiarity did play a role in the IAT procedure, it did not explain the overall effect. Their results showed that people were faster in responding to more familiar names than to less familiar names. However, when the IAT effect was tested separately for high- and low-familiar names, white participants still showed an implicit preference for white names on both the high- and low-familiar words, with the effect being stronger for more familiar words. These results showed that familiarity with the concepts can influence a person's responses on the IAT procedure, but that this does not entirely explain the IAT effect.

Some IAT Results

In addition to the basic verbal IAT procedure described in the previous subsection, versions that use pictures have also been created. For example, Banse et al. (2001) created an IAT measure for attitudes toward homosexuality. The homosexual and the heterosexual categories were represented with color pictures of either same-gender or mixed-gender couples. The evaluative concepts were "good" and "bad." Results showed that heterosexual participants had more negative attitudes toward homosexuals (with male heterosexual participants being more negative than females), whereas homosexual respondents showed more positive attitudes toward homosexuals (with the positivity being stronger for lesbians than for gay men). Similar results were reported by Jellison, McConnell, and Gabriel (2004).

Following the 1998 publication of the IAT procedure, an on-line version was posted on the Internet. At the time of this writing, the site was still functioning and available at http://implicit.harvard.edu/. Between 1998 and 2000, 600,000 people completed the on-line IAT (Nosek, Banaji, & Greenwald, 2002b). Although this sample is huge, there are important limitations to consider in using these data. First, the results from this on-line test are based on a convenience sample, and, as discussed in more detail in Chapter 5, there are many problems with self-selected samples. In addition, it is likely that many of the participants completed the items more than once (this author did so). Nevertheless, with these caveats in mind, the findings from such a large sample are interesting to examine. The on-line IAT versions available included a race task (black–white) with names (Tyrone, Jamal–Brad, Walter) and faces (visual images of black and white faces), age (young–old) with words and faces, self-esteem (self–other), gender, and political candidates (Gore–Bush). The findings based on these data are similar to those reported in more controlled lab settings (Nosek et al., 2002b). They include a more favorable attitude toward white than black individuals (which was weaker but also present for black respondents), clear gender stereotypes, and a preference for youth (equally strong for both young and old respondents). We will return to the topics of racial and gender attitudes in Chapters 16 and 17, respectively.

The Relationship Between IAT Measures and Explicit Measures

Although the IAT procedure is relatively new, it has attracted a large amount of research attention. Implicit measures have been developed to assess attitudes about racial groups, gender classifications, sexual preferences, high-fat foods, environmental issues, and political candidates, to name only a few. A very important question is the degree of overlap between implicit and explicit attitude measures, and the results from across these studies have typically found only a small correlation between IAT scores and explicit measures of attitudes (cf. Boniecki & Jacks, 2002). For example, Ottaway et al. (2001) reported a correlation coefficient of $r = 0.21$ between an IAT measure of racial attitudes (using male names) and a feeling-thermometer measure of racial attitudes. They reported a similar correlation between IAT racial attitudes (using male names) and a semantic differential measure. In the Internet study previously mentioned (the one with 600,000 participants), the average correlation between implicit and explicit measures was $r = 0.24$.

The low correlation between IAT measures and explicit attitude measures is an important theoretical issue. Throughout this chapter (and indeed, even in the chapter title), we have been suggesting that implicit measures simply offer another way to assess an attitude. That is, if a particular sort of attitude exists within the person, implicit and explicit measures are thought to provide converging approaches to measuring the attitude. But how then can we explain their low correlation? A possible explanation for the low correlation, and one consistent with the argument that implicit and explicit measures tap the same underlying construct, is that the low relationship is due to the measurement error inherent in reaction-time data (Cunningham, Preacher, & Banaji, 2001). The IAT relies on the average of a series of responses to paired concepts. These reaction times are measured in milliseconds (and they often average less than one second). This means that any distraction in the respondent's concentration will disrupt the reaction time. Any cough, blink, sneeze, twitch, and so on will be included as measurement error in the IAT scores.

Cunningham et al. (2001) tested this measurement-error possibility by presenting participants with a series of IAT procedures measuring attitudes toward blacks and whites on four separate occasions, each separated by two weeks. As found in previous research, the IAT scores were only modestly correlated with each other (correlations for the IAT across occasions ranged from 0.16 to 0.50, with a median $r = 0.32$). However, when they were statistically controlled for measurement error, the results showed a high degree of stability ($r = 0.68$), and the combined IAT scores correlated 0.30 with an explicit measure of racial attitudes (the Modern Racism Scale—McConahay, 1986). These data suggest that the implicit and explicit measures are tapping similar constructs, which raises the possibility that they may be two ways of getting at the same underlying construct, prejudice toward blacks.

However, a different possible explanation for the low correlations is that implicit and explicit attitude measures are really separate constructs (cf. Rudman, 2004). From this perspective, even when IAT scores were corrected for measurement error, the relationship between the IAT and explicit attitudes was only 0.30—not an impressively high relationship. This was the viewpoint espoused by Karpinski and Hilton (2001). Across three studies, their results consistently showed small and nonsignificant relationships between IAT scores and explicit measures of attitudes (a feeling thermometer, semantic differential measures, and Likert scales). These authors concluded that the IAT and explicit measures of attitudes are independent constructs. They further suggested that the IAT measurements can be explained by an **environmental association model**. According to this model, the IAT measures "the association a person has been exposed to in his or her environment, not that individual's level of endorsement regarding the attitude object" (p. 786). That is, most people in the United States show a preference for flowers, youth, white Americans, and so on because those are the stereotypic norms that they are exposed to on a daily basis. Their greater frequency of exposure to particular people or evaluations facilitates the associations (Karpinski & Hilton, 2001):

> IAT scores may reveal little about a person's beliefs and much about his or her environment or culture. By this interpretation, showing a White bias on a Black/White IAT does not necessarily indicate that a person holds deep-rooted prejudices against Blacks or that the person discriminates against Blacks. A more appropriate interpretation would be that the IAT reflects the fact that an individual lives in an environment or culture in which Blacks are devalued relative to Whites. (p. 786)

More recent research has moved beyond the question of *if* implicit and explicit measures are correlated, and instead examined *when* they are correlated. The search for moderators of the relationship has uncovered several possibilities. Drawing on data obtained through the IAT website, Nosek (2004) examined the relationship between implicit and explicit attitudes for 57 attitude objects across a wide range of topics (e.g., vegetables vs. meat, nerds vs. jocks, Democrats vs. Republicans, books vs. television, creationism vs. evolution, and many others). Across the 57 attitude objects, the average correlation was $r = 0.36$, consistent with previous findings. However, there was considerable variability in the strength of the relationships across attitude objects, from a low of -0.05 (females–males) to a high of $r = 0.70$ (prochoice–prolife). Additional analyses revealed that about 50% of the variability in the strength of the relationship could be explained by four possible moderators:

- **Self-presentation**—the relationship tends to be stronger when the person is not motivated to present him(her)self in a favorable manner.
- **Attitude strength**—attitudes that are more important, stable, and elaborated tend to yield stronger implicit–explicit correlations.
- **Self versus culture discrepancies**—implicit and explicit measures tend to be more strongly correlated for attitudes that are believed to differ from those of the average person.

- **Attitude polarity**—the relationship tends to be stronger for attitudes that are conceptually one-dimensional (that is, liking one object implies disliking the other object).

Before concluding this chapter, we need to examine one final issue pertaining to implicit measures. Although there has been considerable research and clarification of *if* and *when* implicit attitude measures correlate with explicit measures, there has been less research on the relationship between *different implicit* measures. For instance, do scores on an affective priming task correlate with IAT scores? This issue gets at the heart of the validity of implicit measures. Initial research findings on this topic revealed little correspondence between the two implicit measurement approaches. Olson and Fazio (2003) reported correlations ranging from +0.05 to −0.13 from four samples with more than 300 participants. More recent research has shown that the low correlations were due in large part to the nature of the measures: The IAT measures attitudes about general categories (e.g., white or black), whereas the affective priming technique measures attitudes toward specific exemplars but not the category itself. If the affective priming task is modified to focus participants' attention on the category rather than on the specific exemplar, it yields correlations with the IAT that are much stronger and more consistent across attitude objects (Olson & Fazio, 2003, Fazio, 2004). These findings indicate that the IAT measures category–valence associations (for example, insect–bad), whereas the traditional affective priming task measures associations between specific items and valence (e.g., mosquito–bad). This is an important contribution, which lends additional evidence to the growing body of research on the validity and usefulness of implicit measures.

SUMMARY

A fast-growing topic in the 1990s was research on implicit measures of attitudes. Unlike explicit measures, implicit measures assess evaluations of an object that occur without conscious reflection and are not necessarily available for introspection or control.

One such alternative to measuring explicit attitudes utilizes indirect measures. For instance, in projective tasks, respondents are presented with an ambiguous image and asked to elaborate on what they see, and the task is presented as a measure of imagination or social sensitivity rather than of their attitude. Because the scoring of the resulting responses is often subjective, there are serious issues with their validity and reliability.

A second type of indirect measure that is useful for measuring attitudes utilizes physiological reactions. In these tasks, respondents are exposed to a stimulus about which they may have an attitude, and measures are obtained of arousal (heart rate, blood pressure), tiny muscle movements in the face (EMG), or electrical activity in the brain (ERP). Much of the early research utilizing physiological measures found that stronger attitudes were positively correlated with physiological measures of arousal, but that these physiological measures were unable to determine the positive or negative direction of a person's attitude. However, more recent studies using EMG measures of facial movements and ERPs in a series of exposures to different objects have been able to discern both direction and strength of an attitude.

One set of approaches to measuring implicit attitudes is based on reaction times to stimuli. These implicit measures are largely an extension of associative-network models developed by cognitive psychologists. Fazio's object-evaluation model suggests that attitudes can be understood as associations between an evaluation (e.g., good-bad) and an attitude object (e.g., a particular person). The extent to which this association is accessible determines its strength. Priming studies attempt to activate the association by presenting stimuli on a computer and measuring the effects of a preceding prime on the respondent's reaction time to related concepts. A widely used measure, which is based on associative network principles, is the IAT. It requires respondents to make many quick associations between evaluative dimensions (e.g., good–bad) and attitude categories (e.g., George W. Bush–Al Gore). The difference in average reaction time for incompatible versus compatible pairings is used to indicate the direction and strength of the attitude.

Research has shown that implicit and explicit attitude measures correlate only moderately. A still-unresolved question is whether implicit and explicit measures are alternative and potentially converging ways of assessing an attitude or whether they tap different underlying concepts.

5

Structure and Functions of Attitudes and Beliefs

My attitude is my greatest asset. As long as a person has a positive attitude, he can always make it.—Glenn Turner, millionaire supersalesman.

If a man would register all his opinions upon love, politics, religion, and learning, what a bundle of inconsistencies and contradictions would appear at last.—Jonathan Swift.

Belief in the general credibility of our senses is the most central belief of all; nearly all of our other beliefs rest upon it, and to lose our faith in it is to lose our sanity.—Daryl J. Bem.

What do attitudes and opinions do for the person who holds them? Some people feel that their favorite football team is the best in the country; others are so negative toward racial minorities that much of their identity is based on their prejudiced attitudes. Do the attitudes that you hold help you to live your daily life, to fulfill your psychological needs, and to get along effectively in your world? Social scientists have traditionally answered these questions with a resounding "Yes." Your attitudes and opinions may not make you wealthy, as the above quotation from a supersalesman suggests, but they probably do help to make you healthy and wise. Let us take a closer look at the functions of attitudes.

FUNCTIONS OF ATTITUDES

One of the first theorists to propose a functional view of attitudes was Daniel Katz (1960), and more recent theorists have largely agreed with his classification of types of attitude functions (cf. Eagly & Chaiken, 1998). Katz suggested that there are four major functions that attitudes perform:

1. Understanding. Many attitudes help us to understand our world and to make sense of occurrences around us. They provide consistency and clarity in our explanation and interpretation of events. This has also been called the **object appraisal** or the knowledge function of attitudes, but the latter term does not imply that attitudes provide a factually truthful picture of the world—merely one that is meaningful and understandable to the particular individual who holds them. That is, attitudes provide a frame of reference for understanding incoming information or new events. For one person, scandals publicized during the last U.S. presidential administration might be understood in reference to an attitude that "politicians are no damn good." Another person might relate the same facts to the belief that "Power tends to corrupt." In each case the person's beliefs or attitudes provide a context for the new information, aiding in its interpretation and assimilation into the person's belief system.

2. Need Satisfaction. Many attitudes are formed as a result of our past rewards and punishments for saying or doing particular things. Once formed, these attitudes usually continue to be useful in helping us to satisfy our needs or to reach our goals. These attitudes have also been termed **adjustive** in the sense of helping us to adjust to life situations, or **utilitarian** in the sense that they are useful in reaching our goals. Examples would include the attitudes of a worker who favors a political party because he believes it will "do more for the working man," or the pupil who comes to like foreign-language classes because she has done well in them in the past and has been rewarded by the teacher's praise and her own feeling of competence.

3. Ego Defense. Attitudes can also help to enhance our self-esteem and to defend us against the thousand "slings and arrows" of life. All people use defense mechanisms to some extent, but they are used much more by individuals who are insecure or feel inferior or who have deep internal conflicts. Prejudiced attitudes against another ethnic group are often used as a crutch to bolster the self-esteem of the holder, a phenomenon that has been called the "scapegoat view of prejudice." Similarly, the employee who shrugs off criticism from the boss by saying "The boss is always bad-tempered" may be using an unrealistic ego-defensive attitude to avoid thinking about his or her own failings.

4. Value Expression. A value-expressive attitude is one that helps to establish a person's self-identity—that is, it portrays the sort of person he or she is, and says, in effect, "This is the way I am." This has also been termed the **social identity** function of attitudes (e.g., Shavitt & Nelson, 2000). Examples include the motorcyclist's liking for his black leather jacket and the teenage girl's preference for her favorite color in all of her wardrobe. More important attitudes often express an individual's basic values, as with the conscientious objector's aversion to all aspects of warfare and violence.

These four types of needs that attitudes can serve for a person are useful in classifying and understanding attitudes. But they also have other uses. As Katz (1960) pointed out, they can also help to explain the types of situation in which different attitudes will be aroused and the types of influences that will be effective in changing different attitudes.

Attitude Activation

Each of us has hundreds of attitudes toward hundreds of different attitude objects, but they are not all active at the same time. Most of the time most of our attitudes are lying dormant while only a few are in the focus of our conscious attention or are directly influencing our behavior. It requires the onset of a particular psychological need or a relevant environmental cue to arouse into an active state a particular attitude that we hold (Fazio, 2000). And, importantly, the question of what type of internal need or external cue will **activate** a particular attitude is largely determined by the function which that attitude serves for the individual concerned.

To illustrate this relationship, consider a common attitude, that of racial prejudice, which involves negative feelings toward people of color. This attitude could serve any of the functions previously mentioned, but Katz has emphasized that the conditions necessary to activate the attitude would be different for the different functions. Attitudes serving the understanding function are apt to be aroused by a cognitive problem whereas attitudes serving the adjustment function may be prompted by a social need. Ego-defensive attitudes can be aroused by threats to the holder's security or by appeals to hate feelings, whereas value-expressive attitudes may be aroused by appeals to a person's ideals or self-image.

Photograph courtesy of Daniel Katz.
Reprinted by permission.

Box 5–1   DANIEL KATZ, *Attitude Theorist and Researcher*

Widely respected and honored as a social psychologist, Daniel Katz retired as Professor Emeritus at the University of Michigan in the 1960s but continued to be active in the field almost until his death at age 94 in 1998. He earned his B.A. at the University of Buffalo and his M.A. and Ph.D. at Syracuse. Before moving to Michigan in 1947, he taught at Princeton, was chairman of the psychology department at Brooklyn College, and did wartime government research on home-front morale and on the effects of strategic bombing in Germany. He wrote many books, including pace-setting texts in social psychology, organizational psychology, and research methods.

In this chapter, Katz's theory of the functions of attitudes is prominently mentioned. He was also influential as a researcher in many different attitude areas and as editor of the premier journal in social psychology from 1962 to 1967. He was elected president of three different divisions of the American Psychological Association, served on its Board of Directors, and was named to membership in the American Academy of Arts and Sciences. His influential early research on racial stereotypes is mentioned in Chapter 15, and he also did seminal research on nationalism, including cross-national studies in Norway, Denmark, Greece, and Yugoslavia.

Many attitudes serve more than one of the types of functions previously discussed, and consequently they can be aroused in several different ways. For instance, one attitude may serve both an understanding and a need-satisfaction function for a person, and so it could be aroused by either a cognitive problem or a need for approval. Despite this potential overlap, it is valuable to know which functions the attitude is serving for the individual in order to know what external cues or internal needs will arouse the attitude into an active state. Ultimately, it would be desirable to be able to measure the degree of importance of the various functions in influencing any given attitude (Eagly & Chaiken, 1998).

Attitude Change

As with attitude activation, it takes different forces and pressures to change attitudes that are serving different functions (Petty, Wheeler, & Bizer, 2000). For example, the conditions that might lead to changing a person's understanding-oriented attitude may be quite different than the conditions necessary for changing an ego-defensive attitude.

Understanding-oriented attitudes are most likely to change in situations that have become ambiguous for the attitude-holder because of new information or a changed environment. For example, prejudiced individuals may learn about the achievements of black doctors, scientists, statesmen, or authors. If the prejudiced attitudes had been serving the understanding function, they would probably then be changed in order to establish a more consistent, complete, and logical cognitive structure.

Need-oriented attitudes, on the other hand, are likely to change only if the holder's goals or needs have changed, or if the person's needs are no longer being satisfied by the attitude in question. An example would be the prejudiced merchant who realizes that the hiring of black employees and the serving of black customers can increase profits. If the merchant's attitudes toward blacks were utilitarian in nature, they would be very likely to change.

Ego-defensive attitudes are unlikely to be changed by the procedures that work with other types of attitudes, such as providing new information or offering positive incentives for change. Because ego defenses are erected to protect the person from threats and conflicts, it is necessary first to remove the threat or conflict before attitude change can occur. This can sometimes be done by establishing a supportive atmosphere, as in a long-term therapy situation. Or individuals may gradually outgrow the emotional conflicts that underlie their prejudices, or they may acquire insight into their defense mechanisms.

Value-expressive attitudes are also usually difficult to change because people's values are apt to be very important and central parts of their cognitive structure. White supremacists whose prejudiced attitudes express some of their most strongly held values are unlikely to change those attitudes. However, change could occur if they were to become seriously dissatisfied with their self-concept or former values, as for instance if they underwent a religious conversion. A more common way in which value-expressive attitudes may change is by the holders becoming aware that the attitudes do not really fit with their values. For example, Rokeach (1971) found that experimental participants' prejudiced attitudes and behaviors were changed following a dramatic demonstration that they were really inconsistent with one of their basic values, the idea of equality for all.

Evaluation of Functional Viewpoints

Functional theories have contributed much to our understanding of why people hold certain attitudes, but they also have limitations. On one hand, the theoretical stance seems very plausible and consistent with the ideas of many authors. On the other hand, for about 25 years after the early statements about attitude functions, very little research was done specifically to test their theoretical hypotheses. As psychological theories, the four functions of attitudes that we have described have a number of serious problems (Kiesler, Collins, & Miller, 1969). To begin with, they are an eclectic compendium of ideas from many past thinkers and researchers (for instance, the ego-defensive function comes directly from psychoanalytic theory), but as a result many of their concepts are ill-defined and therefore their hypotheses are not clearly testable. Even more important is the question of how the underlying functions of attitudes are to be measured. In Chapter 3, we discussed the many approaches that have been developed to measure attitudes, but it is possible for two people to hold the same attitude (e.g., racial prejudice) *for different reasons*. Fortunately, more recent research has developed reliable and valid measurement approaches for measuring the functions of attitudes, and studies using them have demonstrated that attitude functions do relate in predictable ways to relevant cognitive and behavioral variables (cf. Maio & Olson, 2000b).

Since the 1980s there has been a resurgence of interest in the functions of attitudes, and a number of researchers have taken different approaches to studying variables related to the various attitude functions. Fazio (1989, 2000) has emphasized the understanding or "object appraisal" function as primary because it is applicable to all attitudes, whereas the other functions apply to some attitudes but not to all. Other well-known researchers have agreed with that point (Eagly & Chaiken, 1998). In the field of persuasion, theorists have proposed that, under various circumstances, people's responses to persuasive messages may be influenced by motivations toward accuracy (the understanding function), or making a good social impression (the adjustive or utilitarian function), or by ego defensiveness (Chaiken, Giner-Sorolla, & Chen, 1996). The ego-defensive function of attitudes has been particularly emphasized in "terror management theory," which focuses on people's methods for reducing anxiety that stems from awareness of their own mortality (Solomon, Greenberg, & Pyszczynski, 1991; Greenberg et al., 2001). The utilitarian function of attitudes is consistent with many analyses that build on learning theory's emphasis on reinforcement as the major factor in strengthening responses. The value-expressive function of attitudes has been analyzed by Maio and Olson (2000a), and it is highlighted in the research on political ideologies that is discussed in Chapter 7.

Notable advances in operationalizing aspects of functional theories have been made by Herek (1986, 1987, 2000), Snyder and DeBono (1987), Shavitt (1989), and Clary et al. (1994). Herek developed a new instrument, the Attitude Function Inventory, to measure a somewhat revised set of attitude functions. He postulated three types of expressive functions, two of which are similar to Katz's concepts: *defensive, value-expressive*, and *social-expressive* attitudes. The latter term refers to attitude expression that is motivated by a need for acceptance by other people in one's social environment. Three other functions, which are all based on the utility of the attitude object (or person) to the attitude holder, Herek refers to as *evaluative* attitudes; as a group, they are similar to Katz's need-satisfaction function.

New measures such as those just mentioned have been used in studies that demonstrate the results of holding attitudes that serve different functions. For instance, attitude-change studies have shown stronger persuasion effects in conditions where the basis of persuasive appeals **matched** the function served by recipients' attitudes, such as value expression or utilitarian social adjustment (e.g., Lavine & Snyder, 1996; Petty et al., 2000). Similarly, in research that manipulated the momentary strength of attitude functions, Maio and Olson (1995) showed research participants posters that emphasized either value-expressive or utilitarian reasons for donating money to cancer research. This **priming** procedure led participants in the value-expressive condition to align both their attitudes and their intentions to donate money more closely with their values.

THE STRUCTURE OF BELIEFS

We turn now from the topic of function to that of structure—from the question of how attitudes work to how they are built. In doing this, we consider first the structure of beliefs and belief systems, drawing on the thinking of Rokeach (1968) and of Jones and Gerard (1967). To begin, recall that a belief states a relationship between an object and some characteristic (e.g., "my roommate is fun to be with").

Centrality and Intensity of Beliefs

What factors determine how important a belief is to the person who holds it? The concept of a **belief system** may help to answer this question. A system is a set of interconnected parts that function in relationship to each other. Just so, beliefs and attitudes do not exist in isolated separateness, but they are connected with many other beliefs in an organized system.

The **centrality** of a belief, that is, its importance in the person's belief system, may be defined in terms of its degree of connectedness with other beliefs—the number of "implications and consequences it has for other beliefs" (Rokeach, 1968, p. 5). Rokeach has suggested four principles that spell out the concept of centrality in more detail:

1. Beliefs about one's **self**, one's existence and identity, are much more central than other beliefs.
2. **Shared** beliefs about one's existence and self-identity are more central than unshared beliefs (ones held only by oneself).
3. Beliefs that are **derived** from other beliefs (rather than from contact with the object of belief) are *less* central than underived beliefs.
4. Beliefs concerning **matters of taste** are *less* central than other beliefs. They are usually seen by the holder to be arbitrary in nature, and thus they are relatively inconsequential in their impact on other beliefs.

The **intensity** of a belief refers to how strongly the belief is held, or how sure the person is about it. Central beliefs are usually intensely held, but the opposite does not follow: Beliefs concerning matters of taste may be intensely held even though they are not central. I may like pistachio ice cream with a passion (intensely), but that fact probably does not affect my attitude toward people who prefer vanilla or my beliefs about the nutritive value of pistachio nuts. My belief in the tastiness of pistachio ice cream is not central to my belief system because it does not influence other beliefs, and if it were to change, there would be few consequences for my other beliefs.

Primitive Beliefs

Rokeach (1968, p. 6) suggested the term **primitive beliefs** for ones that are very central and that "have an axiomatic, taken-for-granted character." They are generally formed through direct contact with the object of belief (that is, they are not derived beliefs), and they are "psychologically incontrovertible because they are rarely, if ever, experienced as subjects of controversy." Such beliefs are the person's "basic truths" about the world, about other people, and about himself or herself. Examples would be "My name is _____" and "Water is wet." However, they do not have to be shared beliefs. They can be based solely on one's own experience, and thus they can include pathological beliefs such as phobias, delusions, and hallucinations. Examples of unshared primitive beliefs would be "No matter what others may believe, I know that my mother doesn't really love me" and "I believe I am Jesus Christ returned to earth."

The importance of primitive beliefs to the individual holding them can be demonstrated by challenging them and observing the person's response. An effective challenge may produce astonishment, disbelief in the challenge, anger, intense anxiety, or even pathological symptoms of withdrawal and confusion if continued long enough. The humor in the television show *Candid Camera* often came from seeing the astonishment of persons whose primitive beliefs were being challenged—for instance by seeing water apparently running uphill or an inanimate object apparently talking or moving under its own power. Rokeach (1968) observed that when a parent unexpectedly calls a young child by a name that isn't its own, the child will first enjoy it as a new game; but if the parent continues, the child will soon ask for reassurance that it really is a game, and before long intense anxiety will result, with tears, panic, and desperate attempts to get the parent to stop.

Daryl Bem (1970) has described primitive beliefs in an entertaining selection, which is reprinted in Box 5–2.

Box 5–2 Types of Primitive Beliefs

Many beliefs are the product of direct experience. If you ask your friends why they believe oranges are round, they will most likely reply that they have seen oranges, felt oranges, and that oranges are, indeed, round. And that would seem to end the matter. You could of course, ask them why they trust their senses, but that would be impolite.

Consider a more complicated belief. If you ask your friends why they believe the as-teroids are round (that is, spherical), the more sophisticated among them might be able to show how such a conclusion is derived from physical principles and astronomical ob-servations. You could press them further by asking them to justify their belief in physical principles and astronomical observations: Whence comes their knowledge of such things? When they answer that question—perhaps by citing the New York Times*—you can con-tinue to probe: Why do they believe everything they read in the* Times? *If they then refer to previous experience with the accuracy of the* Times *or recall that their teachers always had kind words for its journalistic integrity, challenge the validity of their previous experience or the credibility of their teachers.*

What you will discover by such questioning—besides a noticeable decline in the number of your friends—is that every belief can be pushed back until it is seen to rest ultimately upon a basic belief in the credibility of one's own sensory experience or upon a basic belief in the credibility of some external authority. Other beliefs may derive from these basic beliefs, but the basic beliefs themselves are accepted as givens. Accordingly, we shall call them "primitive beliefs."

Source: From *Beliefs, Attitudes, and Human Affairs*, by Daryl J. Bem, page 5. Copyright © 1970 by Wadsworth Publishing Co., Inc. Reprinted by permission of the publisher, Brooks/Cole Publishing Co., Monterey, CA.

Bem divided primitive beliefs into two categories. **Zero-order beliefs** are so taken for granted that they are normally out of our awareness—"the nonconscious axioms upon which our other beliefs are built" (p. 6). They are mostly beliefs about the trustworthiness of our senses, the size and shape constancy of objects, and the validity of particular authoritative sources of knowledge such as the Bible or the dictionary. **First-order beliefs** are ones based directly on our sensory experience or on an unquestioned authority. They are normally in our awareness, and we can imagine alternatives to them, but they require no justification other than a citation of our experience or of the relevant authority (e.g., oranges are round, not square). Bem (1970) concluded:

We all hold primitive beliefs. It is an epistemological and psychological necessity, not a flaw of intellect or a surplus of naivete. We all share the fundamental zero-order beliefs about our senses, and most of us hold similar sorts of first-order beliefs. For example, we rarely question beliefs such as "This woman is my mother" and "I am a human being." Most of us even treat arbitrary social-linguistic conventions like "This is my left hand" and "Today is Tuesday" as if they were physical bits of knowledge handed down by some authority who "really knows." Finally, most religious and quasi-religious beliefs are first-order beliefs based upon an unquestioned zero-order faith in some internal or external source of knowledge. The child who sings "Jesus loves me—this I know, / For the Bible tells me so" is actually being less evasive about the metaphysical—and hence nonconfirmable—nature of his belief than our founding fathers were when they presumed to interpret reality for King George III: "We hold these truths to be self-evident." (p. 7)

Empirical evidence that there really is a difference between the various types of beliefs discussed above has been presented by Rokeach (1968). He showed that primitive beliefs that are shared with other individuals were most resistant to change, followed by primitive beliefs that are not widely shared. Next in resistance to change came beliefs about authority, such as "The Pope is infallible in matters of faith and morals" or "The philosophy of Karl Marx is basically a sound one, and I am all for it." Next came derived beliefs, such as "Birth control is morally wrong" or "The Russians were justified in putting down the Hungarian revolt in 1956." Finally, easiest to change were inconsequential beliefs concerning matters of taste, like "I think summertime is a much more enjoyable time of the year than winter" or "There is no doubt in my mind that Elizabeth Taylor is more beautiful than Dinah Shore."

Syllogistic Structure of Beliefs

We have seen that nonprimitive beliefs such as the ones just quoted can be derived from other beliefs that we hold. Beliefs exist in interconnected networks, and a useful way of thinking about their connections is to use the syllogistic model proposed by McGuire (1960) and Jones and Gerard (1967)—also termed the **probabilogical model** by McGuire (1985). As you may remember from studying logic, a syllogism is a set of three statements, two of which (the first and second premises) lead logically to the third (the conclusion). Take this example:

1st Premise:	Using birth control protects a woman from getting pregnant.
2nd Premise:	I want to be protected from getting pregnant.
Conclusion:	Therefore, I should use birth control.

The conclusion is a derived belief, and in this case both premises are also derived from other beliefs. Let us trace a possible chain of derivations for this conclusion back to a primitive belief. The next step back toward the source might be this:

- My doctor says that using birth control protects a woman from getting pregnant.
- My doctor is an authority on medical matters.
- Therefore, using birth control protects a woman from getting pregnant.

Here the second premise is a belief about authority, and for many people this step in reasoning might end the matter. They trust their doctor as a reliable source of facts about medical matters, though of course they wouldn't necessarily accept the doctor as an authority in other fields such as car repair or politics. If this is the end of a person's chain of reasoning, then we have arrived at one of her primitive beliefs, an idea so self-evident to her that she takes it for granted: "My doctor knows about medical matters."

The Vertical Structure of Beliefs. Another person, however, might have a longer, more elaborate chain of reasoning, one with more links between the ultimate conclusion and the underlying primitive belief. This characteristic of the belief system has been called its **vertical structure**. The conclusion of each syllogism can be used as a premise in the next syllogism. Thus, starting from a different primitive belief, another person's chain of syllogisms might include beliefs about the doctor's source of information and about his candor as bases for what he says:

- The journal *Science* has reported scientific studies showing that using birth control protects a woman from getting pregnant.
- *Science* is an authoritative source of accurate scientific information.
- Therefore it is true that scientific studies show that using birth control protects a woman from getting pregnant.

- Scientific studies show that using birth control protects a woman from getting pregnant.
- My doctor believes scientific studies.
- Therefore my doctor believes that using birth control protects a woman from getting pregnant.

- My doctor believes that using birth control protects a woman from getting pregnant.
- My doctor says what he really believes.
- Therefore my doctor says that using birth control protects a woman from getting pregnant.

Again, this chain of reasoning is based on a primitive belief about authority as the initial underlying premise. No matter how wise or well-informed we are, many of our beliefs ultimately rest on our faith in some authority: the Bible, the *New York Times*, *Time* magazine, the encyclopedia, the Surgeon General, or some other source of information that we trust.

The Horizontal Structure of Beliefs.   Fortunately, most of our beliefs do not rest on just one line of reasoning or stem from just one authority. There are usually several different routes to the same conclusion. The breadth of support for a given belief has been called its **horizontal structure**. For instance, there may be several other chains of reasoning leading to the same conclusion about personal use of birth control. One such chain, starting from its most central end, might be this:

- My ecology textbook tells me that world overpopulation leads to famine.
- My ecology textbook is an authoritative source of information.
- Therefore world overpopulation leads to famine.

- World overpopulation leads to famine.
- Famine is bad.
- Therefore world overpopulation is bad.

- World overpopulation is bad.
- Birth control programs can reduce world overpopulation.
- Therefore birth control programs are good for the world.

- Birth control programs are good for the world.
- I should take part in programs that are good for the world.
- Therefore I should use birth control.

Another part of the horizontal structure might be this:

- Using birth control produces a more enjoyable sex life.
- I want an enjoyable sex life.
- Therefore I should use birth control.

Of course, these supporting chains of beliefs are not necessarily in the person's awareness at any given time, and the person may not even be able to verbalize them without extensive self-searching and introspection. Also, a person's beliefs are rarely all consistent in leading to the same conclusions. There are usually some contradictory beliefs also present, such as these:

- Using birth control has some medical hazards.
- I don't like to run the risk of medical hazards.
- Therefore I shouldn't use birth control.

The question of the amount and importance of consistency in a person's belief systems is one that has been widely debated by attitude theorists, as we will see in Chapter 11 and, briefly, in the following subsection.

"Psycho-Logic" in Belief Systems.   It is important to realize that, though we have used logical syllogisms to indicate the structure of belief systems, a person's beliefs are not completely logical or rational. In fact, some of the syllogisms stated above would not meet the rigorous specifications of a logician. The following reasoning is no more illogical than the first syllogism supporting birth control presented in this section of the chapter, but it would probably be much less acceptable to most women:

- Never associating with men can prevent a woman from getting pregnant.
- I don't want to get pregnant.
- Therefore I should never associate with men..

Not only might the basic reasoning process be faulty, but even if the reasoning is correct, false premises may lead to incorrect conclusions. Also, even if the premises and the reasoning within each chain are correct, different lines of thought can lead to contradictory conclusions, so a person's higher-order beliefs are often inconsistent with each other. Furthermore, one's evaluative beliefs about an object or a person, based on cognitive reactions, may often be different from evaluations that are based on one's emotional feelings or behavioral reactions (Eagly & Chaiken, 1998).

Thus the typical state of people's belief systems is a kind of rough, partial consistency rather than complete logical rationality. If we look closely, there are usually many gaps, overlaps, and conflicts among the beliefs that we hold. Abelson and Rosenberg (1958) coined the term **psycho-logic** to describe the way in which people's beliefs are based on ideas and concepts that seem to "go together" comfortably from their subjective viewpoints rather than being derived by strict deductive logic. If there are inconsistencies or contradictions, a person can often avoid them by denial, or by redefining concepts, or by other cognitive mechanisms, or simply by refusing to think about the conflict.

Finally, there is evidence that people often choose their beliefs in order to support their feelings about a topic. McGuire (1960) called this process "wishful thinking" in his extensive experimental study, which clearly demonstrated the prevalence of such nonlogical thinking side by side with more logical reasoning processes. Other studies have suggested that people may selectively search for information supporting their feelings or selectively avoid contrary information, rather than rationally considering all the evidence. This common phenomenon of beliefs supporting feelings leads us to our next topic, the question of the relationships among the cognitive (thinking), emotional (feeling), and behavioral aspects of attitudes.

THE STRUCTURE OF ATTITUDES

We move now from discussion of the structure of beliefs to the structure of attitudes, a topic which has had a resurgence of attention in recent years (cf. Eagly & Chaiken, 1998). To begin, we need to distinguish between two important dimensions: the valence and the complexity of attitudes.

Valence and Complexity of Attitudes

Attitudes are, by most definitions, intrinsically evaluative; that is, they involve positive and/or negative feelings toward the attitude object. The **valence** of an attitude is the degree of favorability or unfavorability of the person's feelings toward the object. (As in chemistry, the valence is a combination of the attitude's **direction**—pro or con—and its **extremity**—*how much* pro or con.) An example of valence would be how favorable or unfavorable one feels toward the Democratic Party. It is this evaluative dimension of attitudes that is usually measured by the type of scales that we discussed in Chapter 3.

Another, less-commonly-measured characteristic of attitudes is their **complexity**—that is, the number of elements that they contain. Each of the three aspects or components of an attitude can range from being very simple to very complex. For instance, in the area of political attitudes, the cognitive component for active members of a political party is likely to be highly differentiated (complex)—that is, composed of many different beliefs. In the United States a party member is apt to have information and beliefs about several potential candidates for president, about many issues important to the party's platform, about a number of senators, representatives, and other party leaders, about important events in the party's history, and so on. By contrast, many Americans probably have very simple belief systems regarding Britain's Labour Party, perhaps even just a single dim impression that its leader is Tony Blair.

Similarly, the affective component of attitudes can range from simple liking or disliking for a distant acquaintance to a very complex set of feelings toward someone we know well. Close associates of a political leader such as a U.S. presidential candidate might hold a complex mixture of feelings toward him, possibly including admiration, supportiveness, envy, resentment, amusement, and occasional anger. Likewise, the third component of attitudes, behavioral tendencies toward such a public figure, might range from simply intending to vote for him, to the complex end of the scale, where one might be ready to carry out a varied set of actions such as advising him, helping to write his speeches, soliciting public support from his colleagues, running errands, and even taking the blame for his political mistakes.

A number of researchers have devised various measures of cognitive or attitudinal complexity. One psychologist who has studied complexity extensively is Philip Tetlock (1985, 1986, Tetlock, Peterson, & Lerner, 1996), who has developed a system for coding what he calls "integrative complexity" from written materials such as diplomatic communications, speeches by U.S. presidents, or Supreme Court decisions. A particularly interesting application of this system studied official American and Soviet foreign-policy statements from 1945 to 1983 (Tetlock, 1985). The study predicted and found that higher integrative complexity accompanied periods of coordinative policy initiatives by the two governments, whereas lower integrative complexity was associated with competitive national actions such as military or political interventions in other countries.

Another use of this system studied the complexity of people's ideas about political issues involving conflicting values (e.g., opening public park lands to mining). Findings showed that people display more complex reasoning and attitudes in situations where they see two approximately equally important values in conflict with each other (Tetlock, 1986). Consequently Tetlock (1989) found that politicians in both the U.S. and Great Britain who were relatively middle-of-the-road in their viewpoints were more integratively complex in their political reasoning than were political extremists on either the left or the right wing. Another way of stating this relationship is that complex beliefs are generally accompanied by relatively moderate, rather than extreme, evaluative attitudes (Linville, 1982).

Strength and Ambivalence of Attitudes

Another important dimension of attitudes is their **strength**. It has been measured in various different ways, the most common of which are the *intensity* of the attitude holder's feelings about the attitude object, the *certainty* or confidence with which he or she reports holding the attitude, and the *importance* he or she assigns to it (Schwarz et al., 1998). Comparative studies have found that these three ways of measuring attitude strength (as well as others) are positively correlated with each other, but some of the correlations are low enough that it appears that attitude strength is actually a multidimensional concept (Krosnick & Abelson, 1992; Krosnick et al., 1993). Nevertheless, reviews of published research have established that strongly held attitudes, however measured, are more stable over time, less influenced by persuasion attempts, and better predictors of behavior than are weak attitudes (Krosnick & Abelson, 1992; Petty & Krosnick, 1995).

A theoretical view of attitude strength conceptualizes it in terms of the extensiveness and evaluative coherence of associations (cognitive, affective, or behavioral) with the attitude object in the holder's mind (Eagly & Chaiken, 1998). That is, an attitude is strong if it has many associated beliefs, feelings, and behavioral tendencies, and if most of these associations have a similar evaluative valence. This view of attitude strength is closely related to Rokeach's (1968) concept of the *centrality* or connectedness of a belief in a person's belief system. Attitude strength has also been linked to having vested interests related to the attitude object (Crano, 1995) and to the attitude's relevance to a value that is important to the holder (Johnson & Eagly, 1989).

In keeping with these associative-network concepts, Fazio (1995) has defined attitude strength as the strength of the association between an attitude object and an evaluation. As we saw in Chapter 4, several approaches have been developed within this tradition to measure the strength of these associations. One example is Fazio's (1995) measurement of **accessibility** as the time (in milliseconds) needed to retrieve an evaluation from memory. More accessible attitudes can be recalled quicker. Another approach is Greenwald's measure of the ease with which an attitude object can be paired with a positive or negative valence (cf. Greenwald et al., 2002). Congruent associations are paired more easily and quickly than are incongruent associations.

Ambivalence of attitudes is another key concept that has attracted much recent research attention. It is inversely related to attitude strength, for it is usually defined as a person's having both positive and negative evaluations of the same attitude object, in roughly equal amounts. These evaluations can be measured by use of two unipolar scales, assessing positive characteristics of the attitude object and negative characteristics, respectively (Kaplan, 1972). Another way of measuring ambivalence is by slower response times to attitude questions—that is, weaker accessibility of the attitude (e.g., Bargh et al., 1992; Cacioppo, Gardner, & Berntson, 1997). People with this ambivalent pattern of evaluations of an object or concept (e.g., abortion) usually respond near the midpoint of the typical bipolar attitude scales concerning the object. However, other midscale responders may be individuals who are nonambivalently neutral or indifferent, or ones who have never given the object much thought (the latter group are often referred to as expressing *nonattitudes*—a topic that is discussed further in Chapters 7 and 13).

Research has found that ambivalent attitudes are less stable over time and less closely related to relevant behaviors than are nonambivalent attitudes (e.g., Erber, Hodges, & Wilson, 1995). People with ambivalent attitudes are also more likely than nonambivalent persons to process persuasive messages in a systematic manner (that is, with more careful attention to the messages' arguments—see Chapter 11 for a discussion of systematic versus heuristic processing) (Maio, Bell, & Esses, 1996).

Relationship of Various Attitude Components

The foregoing discussion of attitude complexity has illustrated some issues in a key topic concerning attitude structure: the relationship of the various components of attitudes. Of these, by far the most heavily studied has been the cognitive–affective relationship.

Research Methods.   Three major types of research methods are often used in the attitude area. The first is **correlational** studies, defined as ones that measure the *naturally occurring* covariation in two or more variables. (The term correlational is not limited solely to studies that use correlation coefficients as their statistical procedure.) The second type is **experimental** studies—ones that *manipulate* one or more independent variables and observe their effects on one or more dependent variables. For instance, they may influence one attitude component by an experimental procedure and observe the resulting effects on a different attitude component. The third research method is **quasi-experimental** research, defined as studies in which the investigator does *not* have full control over the independent variable and therefore cannot assign subjects randomly to conditions, but *does* have control over how and when the dependent variable is measured, and usually also over what groups of subjects are measured (Campbell & Stanley, 1966; Cook, Campbell, & Peracchio, 1990). The most common forms of quasi-experiments are nonequivalent control group studies (in which the research groups are not equated by randomized assignment to conditions) and time-series studies (in which a group is measured at several successive points in time, and thus it can serve as its own control). Donald Campbell, who pioneered the concept of quasi-experiments, has stressed that, by a careful choice of measurement procedures and additional comparison groups, one can construct research designs that are almost as powerful and rigorous as true experimental designs.

Early Research.   Empirical study of the relationship of attitude components has been going on since the beginnings of attitude measurement in the 1930s, and there have been several successive waves of such research. The first wave was part of the great burst of empirical research in social psychology that followed World War II, and it was typified by correlational studies. A good example is a study by Campbell (1947), who investigated attitudes toward five different ethnic minority groups (Negroes, Jews, Japanese, etc.) among non-minority-group college students and high school students. He measured the behavioral component of attitudes with a social distance scale, which indicated tendencies to avoid contact with members of each minority group. The affective component was measured by feelings of liking or disliking for each group, and the cognitive component was measured by three scales indicating beliefs in each group's competence, morality, and degree of blame for social problems. In general, the several dimensions for each group were found to correlate around +0.5, showing a substantial positive relationship, but not a complete identity.

Experimental and Quasi-Experimental Research. The second wave of research on attitude components, which peaked in the 1960s, was more experimental in character and typically studied attitude change as a dependent variable. One of its hallmark volumes was produced by the Yale University research group headed by Carl Hovland (Rosenberg et al., 1960) and contained several studies showing the influence of one attitude component on other components. In it, Rosenberg (1960) demonstrated that hypnotically induced changes in the *affective* component (i.e., feelings about a social issue) could create continuing parallel changes in the *cognitive* components of value importance and perceived instrumentality.

Another study in this same volume (McGuire, 1960) began by assessing subjects' beliefs in many different propositions, which included dispersed subgroups of statements having a clear-cut, syllogistic logical relationship to each other. McGuire found a high degree of consistency in beliefs about these cognitive elements, but the consistency was far from perfect because of tendencies toward "wishful thinking" and toward cognitive isolation of inconsistent opinions in "logic-tight compartments." One part of the study demonstrated a so-called **Socratic effect**, showing that the Socratic method of inquiry (merely asking subjects to think about and state their beliefs) was sufficient to produce greater cognitive consistency on a retest one week later. Another portion of the study provided evidence for both *wishful thinking* (a conclusion's desirability influencing belief in its probability) and, on the other hand, for *rationalization* (a conclusion's probability influencing belief in its desirability).

Later Analytical Research. A third wave of research on attitude components accompanied the upsurge of interest in social cognition in the 1980s and 1990s. These studies have gone into great analytical detail concerning the conditions that influence various components and their interrelationships. Some examples of such research were mentioned in the earlier section on attitude complexity.

Another example of analytical research is studies investigating conditions under which the inconsistency-reducing Socratic effect occurs. In general, it is a robust phenomenon, found under most conditions and methods of study (Tesser, 1978; McGuire, 1985), but it is strongest when related belief statements are initially presented in nonsyllogistic order (conclusions mixed with premises) and interspersed with unrelated statements, and when the interval between the original presentation and the retest is short (O'Malley & Thistlethwaite, 1980). Studies using improved measurement methods have indicated that early research may have overestimated the extent of people's "wishful thinking" about such belief statements (C. Miller, 1980). Other research on attitude components has concluded that cognitive-affective consistency is a good indicator of well-defined attitudes, which tend to be resistant to outside attempts to change them (Chaiken & Baldwin, 1981). In Chapters 10 and 11 we will go into more detail on theories and findings concerning attitude change.

From findings such as those stated in the preceding sections, McGuire (1985, p. 245) derived several postulates of nonlogical thinking that amplify the "psycho-logic" viewpoint discussed earlier in this chapter:

1. A person's attitude on one issue is affected by his or her attitudes on other related issues *only* insofar as they are momentarily salient (e.g., the Socratic effect).
2. *Loose linkages* in belief chains cause persuasive impacts to be progressively smaller on more remote related issues (McGuire calls this "spatial inertia").
3. Persuasive impacts on unmentioned related issues filter down gradually over time ("temporal inertia").

4. Because of the loose linkages in belief chains, persuasive effects on a target attitude must exceed some *threshold* amount before change will be induced in remote related attitudes.

5. There is a tendency for one's beliefs and one's desires on any given issue to converge ("hedonic consistency").

Prediction of Behavioral Intentions

Another key question about attitude structure is how closely the behavioral component, often called "behavioral intentions," is tied to the other components. Here we discuss some of the many systems that have been proposed to try to predict behavioral intentions from beliefs, attitudes, and other factors. In turn, behavioral intentions have been used as predictors of actual behavior, but we will save that important topic for extended discussion in Chapter 12.

Fishbein and Ajzen's Theory of Reasoned Action. The most widely cited approach in this area is a theory that has been developed and tested over the past 30 years by Fishbein and Ajzen (1975; Ajzen & Fishbein, 1980, 2000). Their name for it, the "theory of reasoned action," emphasizes the principle that people act on the basis of their beliefs

Photograph courtesy of Martin Fishbein.
Reprinted by permission.

Box 5–3 MARTIN FISHBEIN, *Founder of Reasoned Action Theory*

Martin Fishbein has been doing research on the relationship of attitudes to beliefs, intentions, and behavior for over 40 years, and his theory of reasoned action is the best-known one in this area. After earning his bachelor's degree at Reed College, he took his Ph.D. at UCLA in 1961 and served on the psychology faculty of the University of Illinois for more than 30 years. In the 1990s, he directed a multi-city research program of AIDS-risk-related behavior change interventions for the Centers for Disease Control, and in 1997 he accepted an endowed chair in the area of health communication at the University of Pennsylvania's Annenberg School for Communication, where he remains.

Fishbein is the author or editor of six books and over 200 journal articles and book chapters. He has been president of both the Society for Consumer Psychology and the Interamerican Psychological Society. Among many other consulting positions, he has given advice on attitude and behavior change to the Congressional Office of Technology Assessment, the Center for Disease Control's Office on Smoking and Health, and the NIMH AIDS Policy Subcommittee. As mentioned in this chapter, he has had a long and fruitful collaboration with Icek Ajzen, which has resulted in their joint authorship of two books and over two dozen articles and book chapters.

and available information, though it does not imply the use of strictly logical reasoning. The theory holds that a person's *behavioral intention* is normally the best predictor of how he or she actually will behave, and that behavioral intentions in turn can be predicted by knowing the person's relevant attitudes and beliefs. Specifically, the behavioral intention to perform a certain behavior (for instance, to take a particular college course) is a weighted additive function of two factors: the person's own *attitude toward the behavior (A_B)* and his or her *subjective norm (SN)* about what relevant other people think he or she should do.

$$I = (A_B)w_1 + (SN)w_2$$

Each of these two factors is computed with an **expectancy × value** model—that is, each is a compound involving a series of salient beliefs, with the individual's perceived probability (or expectancy) of each belief statement being multiplied by an evaluative term (the perceived value of that outcome to the individual). Thus, a person's attitude toward the behavior (A_B) is composed of behavioral beliefs (b), which are beliefs about the consequences of performing the behavior, each of which is multiplied by the person's evaluation of that consequence (e). The attitude toward the behavior is the sum of these products:

$$A_B = \Sigma b_i e_i$$

Similarly, the subjective norm is made up of normative beliefs (n), which are beliefs about what each "significant other" thinks the person should do, each of which is multiplied by the person's motivation to comply with that other (m). Again the products are summed to yield the subjective norm:

$$SN = \Sigma n_i m_i$$

Finally, the theory of reasoned action holds that all of these components of the model have their effects on behavior *solely* by acting through behavioral intentions—that is, none of them have independent, direct effects on behavior over and above the effect of intentions.

Triandis' Model of Interpersonal Behavior. Triandis (1977) proposed a model closely related to that of Fishbein and Ajzen, but with some added variables. Triandis agreed that intentions are important in predicting behavior, but he introduced two additional major independent factors: habits and facilitating conditions. Various studies have shown the value of **habit** as a variable in predicting behavior, in situations ranging from donating blood, to attending college classes, to wearing automobile seatbelts (Bagozzi, 1981; Fredricks & Dossett, 1983; Wittenbraker, Gibbs, & Kahle, 1983; Ouellette & Wood, 1998). One reason that Fishbein and Ajzen do not include these two factors as predictors may be that their system is designed to predict behavior that is under "volitional control," rather than being automatic (e.g., taking the same route to work each morning) or being required or prevented by outside forces (e.g., driving to work being necessitated by lack of a public transit system). Within these extremes, however, there are various degrees of voluntary behavior, some of which could well be influenced by learned habits or by facilitating conditions.

Furthermore, in predicting intentions, Triandis (1977) included a separate term directly measuring affect toward the behavior, whereas Fishbein and Ajzen subsumed affect under the attitude term. Triandis also proposed using as predictors several additional social factors, which may add to the predictive power of his model. On the other hand, Fishbein and Ajzen have emphasized the superior parsimony of their system, claiming that it can predict just as well with fewer variables. Of course, the predictive power of these models is an empirical question, and we summarize some of the quantitative findings in a later section.

Ajzen's Theory of Planned Behavior.   In this theory, Ajzen (1988) modified the theory of reasoned action by adding another variable to cover situations in which the actor feels varying degrees of volitional control. He called that variable **perceived behavioral control**, defining it as the person's perception of whether he or she can perform the behavior if he or she wishes to do so. Adding this variable has been shown to give better prediction of less controllable behaviors, such as attempted weight loss (Schifter & Ajzen, 1985), getting an A in a college course (Ajzen & Madden, 1986), and avoiding problem drinking (Schlegel et al., 1992). Madden, Ellen, and Ajzen (1992) investigated students' reports of 10 different behaviors and showed that the added variable of perceived control in Ajzen's system substantially improved prediction of intentions to perform most of the 10 behaviors and also improved prediction of actually performing several of the behaviors, particularly ones that were low in perceived control. Ajzen (1988) specified that, in some situations, perceived behavioral control can have independent effects on behavior as well as acting through its effect on intentions.

Other Approaches in Predicting Intentions.   One feature that the theories of Fishbein and Ajzen, Triandis, and Ajzen all have in common is that they *add* relevant beliefs in an expectancy–value format to obtain an attitude measure. An alternative approach— *averaging* weighted scores of the relevant beliefs—has been advocated by Anderson (1981). Although the two approaches produce similar results in many situations, the averaging method has wider applicability in research because of its flexibility (Eagly & Chaiken, 1998).

Other researchers have suggested using several other variables in predicting intentions. Some studies have shown that a variable of *personal moral obligation* adds to predictability of intentions in morally relevant situations (e.g., returning an undeserved tax refund, or using contraception; Gorsuch & Ortberg, 1983; Pagel & Davidson, 1984). In the same vein, personal values and ideologies have been suggested as an important basis of attitudes and intentions (Lavine, Thomsen, & Gonzales, 1997). As a related finding, Budd and Spencer (1984) demonstrated that the centrality and the certainty of people's attitudes contributed to the predictability of their intentions.

Sheth (1974), like Triandis, proposed a related prediction system, primarily for use in predicting consumer buying intentions and actual purchasing behavior. His system is complex; it includes measures of habits, evaluative beliefs, the general social environment, the anticipated situation, and unexpected events, in addition to affect, behavioral intentions, and behavior. Using this model to predict purchases of a newly introduced instant breakfast product by a sample of 954 housewives, Sheth (1974) found quite high relationships— multiple correlations of almost +0.70 with behavioral intentions and almost +0.50 with purchase behavior.

Quantitative Prediction of Intentions.   Sheth's level of success in predicting behavioral intentions is quite impressive, and the other systems have reported comparable levels of predictive power. Fishbein and Ajzen (1975, p. 310) summarized the findings of 13 studies, involving a wide variety of intentions, ranging from engaging in premarital intercourse to buying eight consumer products. In these studies the average multiple correlation for predicting intentions was a very high figure of +0.75, and in 10 later studies the average multiple correlation was +0.80 (Ajzen, 1988, p. 119). A meta-analysis of research with the theory of reasoned action confirmed that its level of prediction was generally very high (Sheppard, Hartwick, & Warshaw, 1988), and similar results have been reported for the theory of planned behavior (Madden et al., 1992; Armitage & Conner, 2001). Triandis (1977, p. 208) has also reported average multiple correlations, using his system, in the 0.70s.

Thus, it is clear that high levels of prediction of intentions can be attained, and the several systems mentioned here seem to be roughly equivalent in their predictive ability. In more precise comparative studies, no system has been demonstrated to be consistently better, but there is clear evidence that additional predictor variables can add significantly to predictability *in some situations*. Whether this potential improvement outweighs the decrease in parsimony is a matter of personal judgment.

A final interesting point concerns the relative weights (w) of the attitude component versus the subjective norm component in predicting intentions. Fishbein and Ajzen's theory specifies that these weights should vary with the behavior involved, with the surrounding social situation, and for different people. A few findings will illustrate how these weights can provide meaningful interpretive information. In a study concerning intentions to engage in premarital sexual intercourse during a college semester, the subjective norm component (what other people expect) carried all of the predictive power for men, whereas the attitudinal component (summarizing likely consequences) was the major predictor of intentions for women (Fishbein & Ajzen, 1975, p. 311). In cooperative types of interpersonal situations, the normative component is typically the main predictor of behavioral intentions, whereas in competitive situations the attitudinal component is much more important (Ajzen & Fishbein, 1970).

Overview

From this review of research on the components of attitudes, it should be clear that, though there is some general consistency of the three components, nevertheless many situations have been found in which there are meaningful distinctions and differences among them (e.g., Bentler & Speckart, 1981).

Finally, consistent with the preceding discussion, several recent theorists have emphasized that some attitudes may have mostly or entirely cognitive elements, others primarily affective elements, and others primarily behavioral elements (Eagly & Chaiken, 1998). This viewpoint can be linked to the question of attitude functions with which this chapter began, for understanding-oriented attitudes might be more likely to be largely cognitive, whereas value-expressive attitudes might be largely behavioral. Furthermore, ego-defensive attitudes seem most likely to have components that are not consistent, whereas other types of attitudes are more likely to have consistent components.

A DIFFERENT APPROACH—ATTITUDE LATITUDES

A rather different approach to the structure of attitudes has been taken by Muzafer Sherif and his colleagues (Sherif & Hovland, 1961; Sherif, Sherif, & Nebergall, 1965). Sherif has called his viewpoint a social judgment approach, emphasizing that the process by which a person makes judgments about social objects (other people, objects, events, issues, etc.) is both affective and cognitive at the same time. That is, it involves both evaluation of the objects and categorization of them as similar to or different from other objects. Thus he stressed that the "cognitive" and "affective" aspects of attitudes are inextricably intertwined.

Photograph courtesy of Muzafer Sherif.
Reprinted by permission.

Box 5–4 MUZAFER SHERIF, *Proponent of Attitude Latitudes*

Born in Turkey in 1906, Muzafer Sherif did graduate work at the University of Istanbul, Harvard, the University of Berlin, and received his Ph.D. from Columbia in 1935. His dissertation research, published as The Psychology of Social Norms, *achieved fame as a pioneering experimental study in social psychology. Returning to Turkey, he taught at Ankara University, conducted research on social judgment and on adolescence, and translated many American psychological works into Turkish.*

Following World War II, Sherif held research fellowships with Hadley Cantril at Princeton and Carl Hovland at Yale. Each of these collaborations resulted in a well-known book. From 1949 to 1966 he was Professor of Psychology at the University of Oklahoma, and subsequently Professor of Sociology at Pennsylvania State University. His 100 publications include over 24 books that he wrote, coauthored, or edited; and in 1968 he received the American Psychological Association's highest honor, the Distinguished Scientific Contribution Award. Retired in 1972, he continued to contribute to social psychology until his death in 1988, focusing on intergroup conflict and cooperation, and on processes of social perception and judgment. His social judgment theory of attitude change is discussed in Chapter 11, and his contributions to attitude measurement are described in this chapter.

Sherif's major contribution to attitude theory and measurement is the concept of **latitude**—that is, a range of attitudinal positions that a person may accept or reject concerning a given issue. Sherif stressed that *a single score cannot give us sufficient information* about a person's attitude. Because most attitude-measurement techniques yield a single score for each respondent, Sherif felt that they are inadequate to the job of fully understanding attitudes. Although they may be

> ... useful for locating individuals who take a stand on one or the other side of a controversial issue, [they] tell us very little about the person who adopts a moderate or neutral position. They tell us little about the subject's possible susceptibility to change, the direction in which change is most likely, how tolerant the individual is of other positions, or how committed he is to his own stand. (Sherif et al., 1965, p. 21)

How did Sherif propose to determine all this? First, by measuring the individual's latitudes of acceptance, rejection, and noncommitment, and second, by developing an indicator of **ego-involvement**—that is, one's personal commitment to one's own stand on the issue. The **latitude of acceptance** is the set of positions on an issue (or toward a person or object) that a person finds acceptable. The **latitude of rejection** is the set

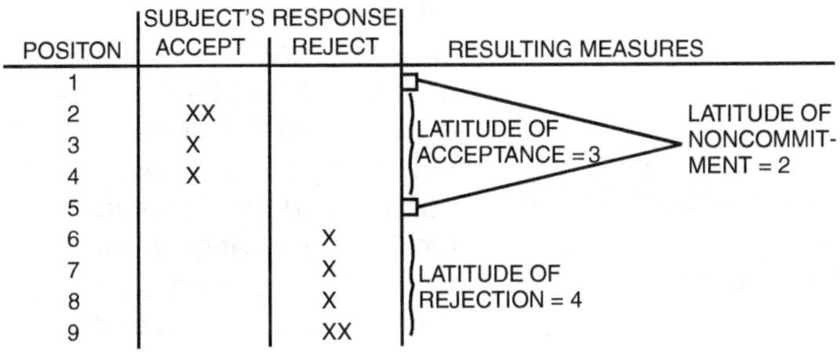

FIGURE 5–1 Responses of a hypothetical respondent, showing computation of attitude latitudes.

of positions that the person finds objectionable. The **latitude of noncommitment** is any other positions on the issue, which the person neither accepts nor rejects. Research findings led Sherif to the conclusion that the best measure of ego-involvement is the breadth of the person's latitude of rejection. (Highly ego-involved people reject more positions as personally unacceptable than do uninvolved individuals.) In short, Sherif held that these three latitudes comprise a *set of categories* that an individual uses in evaluating attitude objects.

The procedure for measuring the three latitudes requires participants to make judgments about the acceptability and then the unacceptability of a fairly large number of attitude positions. In a typical study concerning a presidential election, Sherif et al. (1965) used nine positions ranging from strongly pro-Republican positions, through milder ones, to neutrality, and on to strongly pro-Democratic positions. As examples, here are positions numbered 1, 3, and 5 in the sequence of 9:

1. The election of the Republican presidential and vice-presidential candidates in November is absolutely essential from all angles in the country's interests.
3. It seems that the country's interests would be better served if the presidential and vice-presidential candidates of the Republican Party were elected this November.
5. From the point of view of the country's interests, it is hard to decide whether it is preferable to vote for presidential and vice-presidential candidates of the Republican party or the Democratic party in November.

A typical participant might check position number 2 as most acceptable and numbers 3 and 4 as also acceptable, check positions 6, 7, 8, and 9 as unacceptable, and leave positions 1 and 5 unchecked. Thus, according to Sherif's definitions, this person would have a latitude of acceptance of three positions, a latitude of rejection of four positions, and a latitude of noncommitment of two positions (see Figure 5–1). This measurement technique has also been used with many other attitude issues, such as family size preferences, drinking alcoholic beverages, abortion, and mandatory AIDS testing (Granberg, 1982; Budd & Spencer, 1984; Sarup, Suchner, & Gaylord, 1991; Johnson et al., 1995).

Research Findings on Attitude Latitudes

What would you guess about the relative size of the three latitudes? Would you expect people to accept more positions than they reject, or vice versa? And what kind of people reject the most positions? Results from extensive studies using the latitude concept, summarized by Sherif et al. (1965), are intriguing. They found, first of all, that no matter what

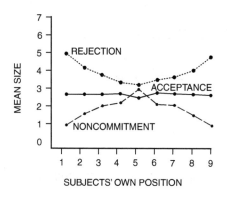

FIGURE 5–2

Average size (number of positions) of latitudes of acceptance, rejection, and noncommitment for persons endorsing different positions as most acceptable in the 1960 presidential election. Positions along the baseline range from 1 (most extreme Republican) through 5 (nonpartisan) to 9 (most extreme Democrat).

Source: Adapted from Sherif, C. W., Sherif, M., & Nebergall, R. E. (1965). *Attitude and Attitude Change: The Social Judgment-Involvement Approach.* Philadelphia: Saunders, p. 52.

the person's own position on the issue was, the average size of the latitude of *acceptance* was about the same (approximately three positions). Second, the latitude of *rejection* was the largest of the three latitudes and, as predicted, its size was greater for participants holding extreme positions than for more moderate or neutral participants. Third, as predicted, the latitude of *noncommitment* was largest for individuals holding a neutral viewpoint and considerably smaller for ones with extreme positions. Thus extreme Republicans and extreme Democrats were found to be nearly identical in their attitude structure (the number of positions which they accepted, rejected, and were noncommittal about) despite their opposition in attitude content. Also, the extreme party supporters on both sides were markedly different in attitude structure from the more moderate supporters of the same party.

These interesting results are graphically displayed in Figure 5–2. Very similar results have been found for some other issues such as right-to-work legislation and federal farm policy questions.

These findings suggest that moderates on any issue typically accept about the same number of positions that they reject. However, people with extreme viewpoints ("far out" on either fringe) typically reject substantially more positions than the number that they accept. There are also usually a few individuals with roughly neutral positions who nevertheless hold to their positions very strongly; for instance, in the political arena such individuals would be dedicated independents. Unlike other neutral or "undecided" respondents, they typically reject nearly as many positions as do the extreme partisans. Sherif et al. (1965, p. 59) concluded that "attitude research has concentrated too exclusively on the subject's agreements or acceptances and far too little on what he rejects."

Assimilation and Contrast

Two additional concepts that are vital to Sherif's theory of social judgment are the principles of *assimilation* and *contrast* (Sherif & Hovland, 1961). These principles derive from research findings in the area of psychophysics, which studies human perception and judgment of physical stimuli like weights, colors, sounds, and so forth. Just as these physical stimuli can be judged on scales of heaviness, brightness, or loudness, so can social stimuli like people or political viewpoints be judged and ranked on attitude scales. For instance, political candidates can be ranked (with some disagreement between judges, of course) on a scale of liberalism–conservatism, or they could be ranked on other more specific scales concerning their stands on civil rights, military spending, welfare programs, and so on. Research findings show that the rater's own attitude on the particular issue serves as an important **anchor**, or reference point for judgment, in making such scale rankings.

The principle of **assimilation** states that social stimuli, such as political candidates or persuasive messages, which are within a person's latitude of acceptance will be assimilated. This means that they (a) will be seen as closer to the person's own attitude than they actually are, (b) will be favorably evaluated, and (c) will produce some change in the person's attitude in the direction advocated by the message. The principle of **contrast** states that when social stimuli are within a person's latitude of rejection, contrast will result. That means (a) they will be seen as farther from the person's own attitude than they actually are, (b) they will be unfavorably evaluated, and (c) they will produce either no attitude change or, in some cases, attitude change opposite to the direction advocated (a "boomerang effect"). Stated in other words, when an attitude object is close to our own attitude, we tend to see it as more similar to our attitude than it really is (assimilation), and when it is quite far from our own attitude, we tend to see it as even farther away than it really is (contrast).

A clear example of assimilation and contrast effects is shown in Figure 5–3, based on a representative national sample of voting-age Americans in the 1972 election between Nixon and McGovern (King, 1977–1978). The figure shows findings for just one of the many issues investigated—attitudes toward busing to achieve school integration—and for only the respondents who actually voted for McGovern. Thus, for these voters, McGovern was clearly in their latitude of acceptance, and Nixon was probably in their latitude of rejection. The seven pairs of data points on the graph represent seven subgroups of McGovern voters whose own attitude toward busing ranged from highly favorable (on the left) to highly unfavorable (on the right). If all voters, regardless of their own attitude toward busing, had perceived a candidate's position on the issue similarly, the plot of data points on the graph would have been horizontal, like the two hypothetical light lines. On the other hand, if there was complete assimilation of the candidate's position to the respondent's own attitude, the plot for McGovern would have been a 45° ascending line; and if there was complete contrast, the plot for Nixon would have been a 45° descending line. What the results actually showed was that these McGovern voters substantially assimilated McGovern's perceived position on busing toward their own attitude (indicated by the areas with dotted shading), and they also contrasted Nixon's position away from their own attitude (the areas with diagonal striping).

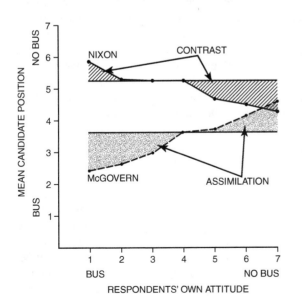

FIGURE 5–3

Mean perceived position of two presidential candidates on the busing issue for McGovern voters who varied in their own attitude toward busing.

Source: Adapted from King, M. (1977–1978, p. 519). Assimilation and contrast of presidential candidates' issue positions, 1972. *Public Opinion Quarterly, 41,* 515–522. Copyright 1978 by Columbia University Press. Reprinted by permission of the University of Chicago Press.

Although both assimilation and contrast effects were clearly displayed on this issue for these McGovern voters, assimilation was a much stronger and more pervasive finding across all the issues studied and for both Nixon and McGovern voters in this research (King, 1977–1978). The greater prevalence and strength of assimilation has been a typical finding in most other studies as well, some of which have even failed to find any evidence for contrast effects (Brent & Granberg, 1982; Granberg, 1984). However, other studies have found substantial contrast effects (e.g., Granberg & Robertson, 1982); and Judd, Kenny, and Krosnick (1983) have argued that common methodological inadequacies have led to underestimation of the strength of contrast effects. Thus both assimilation and contrast seem to be customary ways in which we deal with our social world, leading to greater consistency and comfort in our perceptions of people and of issues with which we have contact (Manis, Nelson, & Shedler, 1988). Extending these questions to research on social comparison processes, Mussweiler (2001) has shown that the assumptions we make about the similarity or dissimilarity of another person determine whether assimilation or contrast occurs: Comparisons with others we consider similar to us result in assimilation, whereas comparisons with others we consider dissimilar yield contrast effects.

We will return to Sherif's social judgment theory in Chapter 10 and examine its performance in the area of attitude change research.

SUMMARY

In this chapter we have seen that attitudes and beliefs can perform several different functions for the person who holds them. They aid in the *understanding* of situations and events; they provide *satisfaction of needs* by helping their holder to adjust to his or her environment; they form a bulwark of *ego defense* against threats to the person's self-esteem; and they provide a channel for *expression of values* that are important to him or her. A particular attitude may serve one or several of these functions, and different forces and pressures are necessary in order to change attitudes that serve different functions.

The *centrality* of a belief is its importance in the person's belief system, whereas a belief's *intensity* is how strongly it is held. *Primitive beliefs* are, by definition, very central in the person's belief system, and they are so much taken for granted that the holder hardly ever has reason to question them. Primitive beliefs are formed either through direct contact with the object of belief or through accepting the statement of an unquestioned external authority such as Mommy or the Bible. Derived beliefs, on the other hand, can be built up from basic underlying beliefs in a syllogistic type of structure. Despite their syllogistic structure, beliefs are not usually completely logical or rational. They are built up of elements that "go together" comfortably in the person's belief system, in accordance with a principle of "psycho-logic" or rough consistency, rather than following the rules of strict deductive logic.

The *valence* of an attitude is its degree of favorability or unfavorability toward the attitude object, and its *complexity* is the number of elements it contains. The *strength* of an attitude has been measured in several different ways but, however measured, strong attitudes generally are more stable, more resistant to persuasion, and more predictive of behavior than are weak attitudes. *Ambivalent* attitudes are ones that contain roughly equal proportions of positive and negative evaluations toward the same object. Ambivalence is inversely related to attitude strength, and it generally results in midrange responses on typical bipolar attitude scales. Research on the relationship between the cognitive, affective, and behavioral components of attitudes has shown that there is very often a general consistency between them, but there are also many situations in which they differ in meaningful ways. Various theories have been developed to predict the behavioral intention component, of which Fishbein and Ajzen's theory of reasoned action is the best-known.

A different viewpoint on the structure of attitudes rejects the notion that a person's attitude can be adequately represented by a single point on a scale. Sherif and his colleagues have emphasized the concept of *latitude*: the range of positions that a person accepts or rejects on a given issue. Research has shown that the width of the latitude of rejection on an issue is a good measure of a person's *ego-involvement* in the issue. Extremists typically reject more positions than they accept. In judging social stimuli within their latitude of acceptance, people commonly *assimilate* them toward their own attitudinal position, whereas stimuli within their latitude of rejection are often *contrasted* (perceived as farther from the person's own attitude than they really are).

6

Public Opinion Polling

I never paid attention to the polls myself.—Harry S Truman.

Carter, Reagan, Bush, and Clinton all designated survey experts to be paid by their respective parties to conduct private research for the White House . . . . these survey researchers have had direct access to the president and served as close political advisors.—Shoon K. Murray & Peter Howard.

Public opinion polls have come to have a pervasive and often dangerous impact in America, an impact which has gone largely unrecognized and uncorrected.—Michael Wheeler.

Polls can help make government more efficient and responsive; . . . they can make this a truer democracy.—George H. Gallup.

In this chapter and the following one we turn to a consideration of public opinion polling—first its procedures and problems, and then its findings about the structure of public opinion.

Public opinion polling is certainly the aspect of psychological measurement with which the general public is most familiar. The major commercial polls, such as Gallup's, appear every week or so in hundreds of newspapers throughout the country. Particularly at national election times, there are almost daily reports about the voting intentions of some part of the public, and aspiring politicians generally hire private polling firms to help determine their "name recognition" and support by voters.

Other groups of pollers are located in academic research institutions, of which the pioneers were the Survey Research Center (SRC) at the University of Michigan and the National Opinion Research Center (NORC) at the University of Chicago. They usually do large-scale and carefully designed research studies that have less-pressing deadlines than those under which the commercial polling firms must operate. For a history of U.S. public opinion research, see J. Converse (1987) or Bradburn and Sudman (1988).

How valid are the results of public opinion polls? The answer to this question depends on several factors, which are discussed in the following sections. Certainly some politicians have concluded that they are not valid. For instance, in 1960, vice-presidential candidate Henry Cabot Lodge said in a campaign speech, "people are going to look back on these polls as one of the hallucinations which the American people have been subjected to . . . . I don't think the polls are here to stay" (Hennessy, 1975, p. 56). On the other hand, President Lyndon Johnson often pulled the latest poll out of his pocket to show visitors his popularity rating, when it was favorable (Altschuler, 1986). It appears that most politicians, whether they complain about the polls or praise them, nevertheless still pay close attention to poll results (Barone, 1997; Murray & Howard, 2002).

Despite the wide circulation of opinion-poll information, there are still many widespread misconceptions about the methods, results, and uses of polls. There have even been attempts by legislators to ban opinion polls as being undemocratic! (*Los Angeles Times*, 1973).

HISTORICAL HIGHLIGHTS OF POLLING

The history of polling in the U.S. began in the hotly contested election of 1824, when a few newspapers started reporting the presidential preferences of groups of interested local citizens or political convention delegates (T. Smith, 1990a). These were **straw polls**, named for the common rural practice of tossing up a straw to see which way the wind was blowing. Their samples were haphazard, and the main reason for reporting them was to sell more newspapers. Many papers adopted this practice and, by 1904, an ambitious poll by a New York newspaper sampled as many as 30,000 registered voters. Two other forms of polling—market research and questionnaire surveys of magazine readers—were first tried out in 1911, and house-to-house interviewing began soon thereafter (Crespi, 1980; Beniger, 1983).

In 1886 a magazine called *Public Opinion* was founded, which addressed major public issues of the day by abstracting and reprinting newspaper editorials from around the nation, influential political speeches, and quotes from public figures, all arranged under broad subject-matter headings. In 1906 it was taken over by the *Literary Digest*, which later became the largest mass-circulation magazine of its era (Sheatsley, 1977).

In 1916 the *Literary Digest* conducted the first of its citizen polls, sending postcards to its subscribers in five key states, asking their preferences for president, and publicizing the results. In each succeeding election, the magazine sent out presidential preference ballots to lists of citizens obtained from telephone books and automobile registration records, increasing the number sent to 20 million by 1932. This was largely a circulation boosting tactic, for each postcard included a subscription blank. Although the ballots that were returned always correctly picked the election winner—until 1936—they usually overestimated the Republican vote by a large margin (Cahalan, 1989). The polling events of 1936 are discussed in the subsequent section on sampling procedures.

In the 1930s the development of large-scale statistical sampling theory set the stage for more scientific polling, first with the quota method that was used in the 1936 election polls of Gallup, Crossley, and Roper, and later with probability sampling (Rossi, Wright, & Anderson, 1983). In 1937 the influential scientific journal *Public Opinion Quarterly* began publication. In 1939 the first private polling was done for potential presidential candidates, and President Roosevelt asked the help of academic pollers in gauging the public's acceptance of his preparations for possible U.S. involvement in World War II (Gallup, 1976). Later in this chapter we discuss several famous polling failures that have occurred since World War II.

CHARACTERISTICS OF OPINION POLLS

In today's society, opinion polls and market research interviews are everywhere. A national study in the U.S. found that 36% of people said they had been interviewed by a poller in the last year, and 73% said that they had been interviewed at some time in their life (Walker Research, 1988). Such polls may be taken on street corners or in shopping malls, but most often they occur over the telephone or sometimes in face-to-face interviews held in the respondent's home. The interview usually contains many questions and may take as long as an hour or more to complete, depending on the topic and type of interview.

Commercial pollers usually use shorter interviews than do academic researchers, but both groups find that most respondents are glad to spend time talking about their opinions, once any initial resistance or suspicion that they may have is dispelled. However, in recent years, the number of potential respondents who refuse to be interviewed has been increasing (Brehm, 1993), and this poses a problem in knowing how much confidence to put in the obtained poll results.

The content of interviews may be highly varied. There are usually questions about attitudes and opinions on important public issues, of course, and questions about demographic characteristics such as the respondent's age, occupation, and voter registration status. Other kinds of information that may be sought include respondents' extent of knowledge on a given topic, typical behavior patterns, personal experiences, and life circumstances. Thus, many factors may be examined together as possible causes or effects of the respondents' attitudes and opinions. Rather than being merely descriptive, in-depth surveys usually study a variety of possibly causal factors by means of correlation techniques or by cross-tabulation of one factor against another. Examples of typical opinion interview questions have already been given in Box 3–1.

The **population** (or **public**) is the whole group of people in which the poller is interested—usually a very large one. It might be the registered voters of a given state, or all citizens over age 18, or a particular subgroup of citizens, such as medical doctors. When such a large population is concerned, it is usually neither necessary nor desirable to contact every member (the national census is the only major exception). Instead, a **sample** of respondents is chosen, whose interview responses will be used as an estimate of the views of the whole population. Therefore, the essential characteristic of any sample is **representativeness**, that is, the degree to which it is similar to the whole population.

A sample does *not* have to be extremely large in order to be representative, but it does have to be very carefully chosen. Of course, there is always some degree of error in any estimate, and the use of a sample necessarily entails some **sampling error** in estimating the population's views. However, in a careful probability sample, the degree of error of the estimate can be computed beforehand by means of a statistical formula, and the size and procedure of the sample can be chosen in such a way as to yield any desired degree of precision.

Contrary to some people's impressions, the factor determining the degree of precision is the size of the *sample—not* the size of the population. This means that just as large a sample is needed to represent a small population as a large population. Thus, a sample of 1,000 respondents will estimate the views of the whole nation just about as accurately as it will estimate the views of a single city's residents. How successfully? Well, a randomly chosen probability sample of 1,100 cases should not miss the true population value by more than 3% in either direction (based on a 95% confidence level). For example, if 55% of such a sample say they favor abolishing the death penalty in the U.S., the true percentage in the overall population is almost surely between 52% and 58%.

A sample size of about 1,000 cases is typical for most of the U.S. national polls. The decision about sample size is necessarily a compromise between the cost (in time, effort, and money) and the degree of precision desired in the final data. More important usually than the size of the sample is the care with which it is chosen, and this is a place where many surveys go astray. Some of the major considerations in choosing the sample are discussed next.

Sampling Procedures

There are many different types of sampling procedures. We distinguish four main categories here: haphazard sampling, systematically biased sampling, quota sampling, and probability sampling.

1. Haphazard sampling is an unsystematic, capricious choice of respondents, selected according to the interviewer's whim, or according to who happens to be available. It is the approach customarily used by "inquiring reporters," who often post themselves on a street corner and ask questions of convenient passersby. It is, most emphatically, *not* identical with random sampling, though "haphazard" and "random" are sometimes used as synonyms in everyday speech. Because of its unsystematic nature, haphazard sampling is not representative of any population, and it therefore has no scientific value.

2. Systematically biased sampling is also an approach to be avoided. As the name implies, it involves systematic errors in a sample that was probably intended to be representative. Some examples of biased samples are ones that include too many old people, too many college graduates, too few minority group members, and so forth. The classic example of this kind of error was made in the 1936 presidential election poll conducted by the *Literary Digest*. The magazine sent 10 million postcard ballots to citizens all over the country, and it received nearly 2,400,000 replies. Because 59% of the replies favored the Republican candidate, Alfred Landon, the magazine predicted his election. Instead, however, Franklin D. Roosevelt won reelection in a landslide, carrying all but two states, and Landon got only 37.5% of the votes.

So what went wrong? Why didn't a sample of over 2 million provide a close estimate of the population? The source of bias in the sample was that the respondents' names were taken from automobile registration lists and telephone books; and in the Depression year of 1936, people who could afford to own cars or even have telephones were systematically different in their presidential voting preferences from their poorer neighbors. Interestingly, this bias had been much weaker in 1932 and previous elections, when similar sampling methods had correctly predicted the winners (Cahalan, 1989). However, ironically, the magazine could have corrected for the sampling bias because it had been pointed out in scientific articles, and George Gallup even predicted the extent and direction of the magazine's error four months before the election (Roshco & Crespi, 1996). After the 1936 fiasco, confidence in the *Literary Digest* was so badly shaken that the magazine died two years later. One clear lesson from this affair is that *a large sample is not necessarily a valid sample!*

3. Quota sampling is the basic method used by many commercial polls. It achieved sudden prominence in the 1936 election, when several young pollers (George Gallup, Archibald Crossley, and Elmo Roper) all used it to predict Roosevelt's re-election, in dramatic contrast to the *Literary Digest* poll's failure. Many refinements have been added since 1936, but the basic principle is unchanged. This approach tries to achieve a representative sample by choosing respondents whose characteristics correspond to those of the national population on several important dimensions. For instance, the dimensions chosen might be geographic region of the country, urban versus rural residence, sex, age, and race. Then an interviewer in Chicago (Midwestern region, urban location) might be assigned a *quota* of respondents with the following characteristics: 10 respondents, all local residents, 5 women and 5 men, 2 of the women and 3 of the men to be black and the other 5 respondents white, 1 woman and 1 man to be in each age decade between 20 and 70.

In quota sampling, the interviewer may be given a free hand as to how and where she finds these respondents, or in some cases there may be further restrictions on where she goes and whom she chooses to interview. (The word "she" is used here because a very large proportion of poll interviewers are women, employed only part-time. This imbalance in the sex of interviewers may, however, sometimes be a source of bias in their results.)

The quota method of sampling avoids the most obvious sources of systematic bias in the sample, and therefore it is much more likely to yield accurate results than either haphazard sampling or systematically biased sampling. However, its major limitation is

*Photograph courtesy of George Gallup.
Reprinted by permission.*

Box 6–1   GEORGE GALLUP, *Public Opinion Poller*

*The best-known figure in public opinion polling during the 1900s, George Gallup was born
in Iowa in 1901 and took his B.A. and Ph.D. at the University of Iowa. Before entering the
polling field, he taught journalism and psychology at Iowa, Northwestern, and Columbia.
He then began doing commercial research on reader interest in newspapers and magazines
and audience interest in radio and motion pictures.*

*In 1935, Gallup founded the American Institute of Public Opinion to measure public
attitudes on social, political, and economic issues. Using the quota system of sampling,
he and several other early pollers became famous by predicting President Roosevelt's
surprising landslide in the 1936 election, and he also correctly predicted how far wrong the
prestigious* Literary Digest *poll would be. Subsequently he pioneered many new trends and
improvements in survey research, including use of some aspects of probability sampling;
and regular research by the Gallup Poll has spread to dozens of foreign countries.*

*Gallup published many articles and 10 books on public opinion. Among his many
honorary degrees and awards were election as president of the American Association
for Public Opinion Research and receipt of its award for distinguished achievement. He
remained actively involved in polling until his death in 1984.*

that it cannot avoid more subtle forms of systematic bias, which may be inherent in
the interviewer's choice of respondents within the limitations of her assigned quota. For
instance, it is common and understandable that interviewers avoid the "seedy" areas of
town, choose to interview only at certain times of the day, and bypass individuals whose
looks or behavior they find offensive. Unfortunately, however, by doing so they also
may be systematically excluding as respondents poor people, night-shift workers, young
"skinheads," or other classes of citizens. As a result, the accuracy of the poll's results is
diminished.

4. Probability sampling avoids all of these problems. By definition, it requires that
every individual in the population must have a known probability (which may or may not
be an equal probability) of being chosen as a respondent. This in turn requires that there
be a complete list of the population or a breakdown of the total population by cities and
counties such as is provided in the national census. With this breakdown as the starting
point, the investigator can choose a sample in such a way that all segments of the population
are included proportionally to their size (e.g., different sections of the country, different
sizes of cities, various racial groups, etc.).

There are several ways of obtaining a probability sample. The simplest is **systematic
sampling**, choosing every *n*th name from a list, such as a college student directory. Next

easiest is **random sampling**, drawing from a container whose contents have been thoroughly mixed (as in a properly run Bingo game), or from a table of random numbers. Both of these methods require a complete list of the members of the population, which is not feasible for any population larger than a small city.

For polls of a larger city, a state, or the whole nation, the probability method usually used is **area sampling** (which is one type of **stratified random sampling**). In this method the total population is broken down into small homogeneous units, such as counties, and a relatively few counties are chosen randomly to be in the sample. In this way the sample includes a group of counties that are typical of the whole country in characteristics such as income and educational level, racial makeup, degree of urbanization, and so forth. The chosen counties are then broken down into smaller units such as precincts or census tracts (the second level of sampling), and again a few tracts from each chosen county are randomly selected to be in the sample. A similar random procedure may be used to select a few blocks or other geographic areas from each chosen tract.

For each of these final areas chosen to be in the sample, a field worker called an enumerator is sent out to list every dwelling unit in the area (including apartments over stores, cottages behind main houses, and all divided-up residences). With this list in hand, the sampling staff randomly chooses a few dwelling units from each sample area, and interviewers are sent to those *specific* dwellings (and they are not allowed to substitute another dwelling if the chosen one is vacant or no one is home). This method is also referred to as **cluster sampling** because a geographically-close "cluster" of a few dwelling units is chosen at this level of sampling.

As the final stage of this process, in each selected dwelling unit the interviewer is instructed to interview a specific person, who is determined by a final random procedure. If the designated person is not at home, interviewers are instructed to come back, several times if necessary, in order to complete the interview. Thus, a stratified random sample uses random selection procedures within each level of the sampling process.

This description suggests how difficult, time-consuming, and expensive a probability sample is. As a result, this method in its entirety is not used by commercial polls, and it is only sometimes used by academic survey researchers. The great advantage of probability sampling methods is that the expected amount of sampling error in the results can be stated exactly; it is an inverse function of the size of the sample (more precisely, of the square root of the sample size). As mentioned in the previous section, the expected error for a sample of 1,100 cases would be no more than plus or minus 3%. By comparison, for a sample of 600 cases, the expected error would be plus or minus 4%; for a sample of 400 cases it would be plus or minus 5%; and obtaining an expected error of plus or minus 2% would require a sample size of 2,500 cases.

Probability sampling has the smallest amount of sampling error of any sampling method. Moreover, it is the only method for which the expected amount of sampling error can be specified. With the sampling methods used by commercial pollsters such as Gallup, Roper, and Harris, one can only guess at the likely amount of error in their results. Thus, though complete probability sampling is expensive and slow, it is the only way to ensure that a sample is really representative of a large population.

Following the 1948 presidential election, when all of the major commercial polling firms made incorrect predictions about the outcome, several of them adopted some aspects of probability sampling in their procedures for selecting areas within which to interview (Perry, 1960, 1979). These changes have undoubtedly improved the representativeness of their samples and the accuracy of their results, but they still allow the interviewer some discretion in choosing respondents, as in the quota method of sampling. Interestingly, however, in England, where most election polls still continue to use quota sampling methods, studies have found their election predictions were usually just as accurate as those using probability sampling (Worcester, 1980).

Telephone Polling

A method of polling that has had rapid growth since the 1970s is interviewing by telephone. It has great advantages in terms of interviewer convenience, reduced costs, increased speed, and closer supervision. In the 1960s, pollers thought that telephone interviews could not be as long as face-to-face ones nor address sensitive subjects with equal validity. However, most of the doubts about the quality of the data they obtain have been allayed by careful research (Groves & Kahn, 1979; Cannell et al., 1987), though they often yield underreporting of illicit behavior such as drug use (e.g., Aquilino, 1994). They typically have somewhat lower response rates and may obtain less complete answers than do in-person interviews, but on the other hand, they sometimes yield higher response rates in large urban areas (Schwarz et al., 1998).

In the U.S., 94% of people now have phones in their home, and some of the rest have access to a telephone nearby. Thus less than 5% of people are unreachable by phone, though these individuals are systematically poorer and more transient than the rest of the population (Thornberry & Massey, 1988; Keeter, 1995). People without phones are also disproportionately nonwhite, young, less educated, rural, and southern (Roll & Cantril, 1980). A potentially more serious threat to representativeness of surveys is the number of unlisted phones, which has reached 30% nationwide and exceeds 50% in many large cities (Dillman, 2000, p. 8). However, this problem can be completely overcome by a technique called **random digit dialing (RDD)**, which uses random methods to determine the numbers to be called. This technique has many variations, but they all have the effect of making all telephone numbers accessible, including those that are unlisted. Thus telephone surveys can use excellent probability sampling procedures.

A problem that cannot be completely overcome is the recent increase in use of telephone answering machines and caller-ID services that can screen incoming phone calls and potentially reduce response rates further. However, a 1999 study by Link and Oldendick found this to be a very minor problem; less than 1% of the numbers they called were consistently screening calls and failing to answer.

An innovation that has become widespread in conjunction with telephone surveys is **computer-assisted telephone interviewing (CATI)**. In this system, telephone interviewers read the questions from a computer-controlled video display terminal and punch the responses directly into a computer data file. This makes interviewing easier and more accurate, and it also completely eliminates the steps of coding and cleaning the data, thus greatly speeding up data analysis (Groves & Mathiowetz, 1984). This computerization also decreases the amount of missing data, but research shows that other improvements in data quality are usually quite small (Nicholls, Baker, & Martin, 1997).

A further step toward automation that is now becoming common in commercial market research is a form of self-administered data collection, sometimes called **touchtone data entry (TDE)**, which eliminates the need for a live interviewer. In this telephone procedure, a computer plays a recording of questions to the respondent, who answers by pressing keys on the handset (or, in some systems, by speaking answers, which are interpreted by voice recognition software). In 1999, the Gallup Organization alone conducted more than one million interviews using this procedure. The major advantages of this system are reduced costs and more honest responding (because of reduced social desirability effects in this impersonal situation), but research has shown that it also produces a lower response rate and many more incomplete interviews than does a CATI procedure, especially if the questionnaire is a lengthy one (Tourangeau, Steiger, & Wilson, 2002).

On-Line Polling

The widespread availability of computers in the U.S. has recently made possible another technological innovation, called **on-line polling** or **Web surveys**, in which the respondents answer questions by using an interactive computer system in their homes or offices (Dillman, 2000). Because of the absence of an interviewer to motivate respondents, the clarity and facilitative design of the survey instrument are crucial in obtaining valid answers and avoiding respondent dropouts (Couper, Traugott, & Lamias, 2001). Most Web surveys have been used in marketing research; they typically are restricted to the subset of the population that already has access to a computer, use haphazard, nonprobability samples of that subset, and suffer from low response rates (Couper, 2000).

However, a few companies have developed true probability panels based on specified population groups, such as college students or Internet users—a procedure that allows computation of the representativeness of each sample of respondents. Scientifically, the best of these systems achieve coverage of the whole national population by contacting a representative and huge group (e.g., 100,000 people) and offering them a free computer and Internet access in return for members of the household completing regular (up to weekly) surveys on the web. Then, for any given study, a representative sample of a few thousand respondents is drawn from this total panel; and panel members are replaced after a year or so, so that their continuing experience as respondents does not make them atypical of the population (Couper, 2000). In the U.S., the pioneering company using this careful approach is Knowledge Networks.

PROBLEMS IN PUBLIC OPINION POLLING

Despite its widespread use, public opinion polling is subject to many potential sources of error. In the following sections we describe some famous polling failures and review the kind of problems that can arise in sampling respondents. Following that, we summarize issues of question wording and context and discuss the other main factors that can influence respondents' answers.

Famous Polling Failures

In 1948 President Truman was running for re-election against Governor Dewey of New York, and all the major polls reported Dewey as the probable winner. Partly for that reason, most people in the country seemed to expect Truman to lose, and the *Chicago Tribune* even hit the streets with a postelection headline proclaiming "Dewey Defeats Truman." Yet when the votes were all counted, Truman won. Whereas the Gallup poll, for instance, had predicted that Truman would receive only 44.5% of the vote, he actually won 49.5% of the vote in a four-party race.

Similarly, in the 1970 British elections the Labour Party led by Prime Minister Harold Wilson was widely expected to win. All except one of the major British polling organizations predicted a Labour win with a vote margin of anywhere from 2% to 9%. Yet on election day the Conservative Party, led by Edward Heath, scored a smashing upset, winning by a margin of nearly 5%. A similar British polling failure occurred in 1992, when almost all of the national polling firms incorrectly predicted a Labour victory, but the Conservative Party again won with a vote margin of over 7% (Jowell et al., 1993).

These three instances represent the most-dramatic failures of scientific polling methods in English-speaking countries since the prescientific era of 1936 when the *Literary Digest* poll failed so ignominiously. Although you may have heard the 1980 U.S. presidential election described as a polling error, it actually was not. Many of the major national polls were reporting the 1980 race as "too close to call" through the end of October, but all of them picked Reagan as the expected winner in their final pre-election report, though they underestimated the margin of his victory over Carter. Careful research has shown that there was a large closing surge in Reagan's voter support, due to three factors: an especially large number of undecided voters in that multiparty election; concurrent developments concerning the American hostages who were being held in Iran; and public reaction to the final candidate debate, held just one week before the election (Ladd & Ferree, 1981). Thus, all the major national polls were on the right track in 1980. Similarly, in the cliff-hanging election of 2000 between George W. Bush and Al Gore, most of the final national polls declared the outcome "too close to call" (Traugott, 2001).

How can the actual failures of 1948, 1970, and 1992 be explained? These three elections have resulted in much scrutiny of the polls, and some of the lessons that have been learned are reported later in this chapter. Before trying to explain these failures, we will discuss some of the basic factors that produce problems in constructing polls and in obtaining valid results. The most important of these factors are: sampling, question wording, respondents' lapses of memory and motivated inaccuracy in reporting, failure to obtain data from some of the designated sample, nonanonymity of responses, interviewer effects on responses, and other practical problems.

Sampling Problems

Many of the problems in quota sampling procedures have been mentioned in the previous section. The most important result of these problems is that the commercial polls, because of their sampling methods, cannot specify the expected amount of sampling error in their data.

In really close elections, such as the 1968 race between Nixon and Humphrey and the 2000 contest between Bush and Gore, the margin between the two candidates' popular vote totals is clearly less than the expected sampling error of the polls, and consequently the pollsters have to admit that their data are not precise enough to be sure of picking the winner. That is a lesson that they learned from their fiasco in 1948 when, to their sorrow, they failed to exercise an equal degree of caution.

Also, it should be kept in mind that the commercial polls indicate the expected percentage of people voting for a presidential candidate nationwide (the **popular vote**). By contrast, the **electoral college vote**, which determines the winner, is based on the popular vote winner in each state separately. (In 2000, for instance, the final vote margin of about 500 votes in Florida determined the nationwide winner in the electoral college). Thus it is conceivable in a close election that the polls could correctly predict the popular vote totals but fail to pick the winning candidate, who was elected by carrying states with a majority of electoral votes.

Despite the few famous polling failures described in the preceding section, the overall record of the national commercial polls in predicting election results has been very good. For instance, in the 1950–1996 periods, the Gallup Poll's average error in predicting 23 congressional and presidential elections was only 1.6% (*Gallup Poll Monthly*, 1996, No. 374). In analyzing the accuracy of poll results, however, it is important to keep in mind the differences in careful sampling procedures and in objectivity between the major national and statewide polls, the often less-sophisticated newspaper polls, and the privately sponsored partisan polls, which sometimes "leak" or distort their results to achieve a political advantage. In other words, *not all polls are equally believable*. Findings in the 1970s showed that careful statewide polls had a good prediction record, even in volatile, multiple-candidate presidential primary contests, and that polls taken just before the elections spotted last-minute trends quite well (Felson & Sudman, 1975). However, in some 1980s statewide elections, there were major prediction errors even by some of the most respected commercial and newspaper polls (Roper, 1983; Goldhaber, 1984). These were probably due in part to a trend toward greater volatility in American voting patterns.

Exit Polls. Also in the 1980s, a new polling technique was widely used on election day because of the TV networks' insatiable desires to be first with their reports of the election victor. So-called **exit polls** are ones that select a representative group of polling places and interview a relatively crude sample of voters as they leave after voting. Respondents are asked to fill out a brief anonymous ballot indicating whom they actually voted for and their views on the main campaign issues. The sample is crude because voters may leave by different exits or in bunches, making systematic selection very difficult, and because different demographic groups tend to vote at different times of day (Busch & Lieske, 1985). Also, some voters refuse to be polled because they are in a rush or do not want to divulge their vote, even anonymously; some who do respond apparently falsify their answers; and absentee voters, who cannot be included in exit polls, are becoming a much larger part of the electorate in many states. Every few hours each interviewer phones the obtained ballot totals in to the central computer room, where they are collated. Thus, by early afternoon the networks may begin to report these results, and they may predict expected winners in statewide or congressional races that seem to be lopsided (Levy, 1983; Mitofsky & Edelman, 1995).

Two major issues have been raised about exit polls. One, the effect of the broadcast reports on citizens who have not yet voted, is discussed later in this chapter. The other issue is the accuracy of exit polls, especially in view of their questionable sampling methods. Some of them have displayed acceptable accuracy (Levy, 1983). However, it is clear that early instances of exit polls contributed substantially to the networks' errors in election-night projections in a number of races, in both England and the U.S., though other more-careful polls were also wrong in some of these races (Worcester, 1980; Roper, 1983). Partly in response to these earlier errors, the U.S. TV networks in 1990 set up a joint exit-poll procedure, which demonstrated outstanding accuracy. In the following four national elections during the whole decade of the 1990s, the joint poll covered about 500 races and made only one incorrect projection (in a 1996 Senate race in New Hampshire—Mitofsky, 1998).

However, by 1996 all the TV networks were again competing to be the first to "call" the results of election races on the basis of exit polls and early returns. In the presidential election of 2000, all of the networks made a highly embarrassing double error, using exit-poll data to project Gore as the winner in the crucial state of Florida but later in the evening changing to project a Bush victory, whereas the actual vote outcome in Florida was still being recounted and disputed a month after the election (Mitofsky, 2001). In the subsequent 2002 congressional election, another kind of failure occurred when the joint exit-poll organization was unable to project the winners of any races during the whole evening of election day because of computer malfunctions (Calvo, Jensen, & Simon, 2002; Plissner, 2003).

Call-In Polls. Another apparently modern polling technique is really a throwback to the old, unscientific straw polls. **Call-in polls** are ones in which respondents phone

Photograph courtesy of Howard Schuman.
Reprinted by permission.

Box 6–2 HOWARD SCHUMAN, *Survey Research Authority*

Howard Schuman taught since 1964 at the University of Michigan, where he is Professor Emeritus of Sociology and continues to conduct research since his retirement in 1996. He earned an A.B. at Antioch College, an M.A. at Trinity University, and a Ph.D. at Harvard, and then briefly directed field research in Pakistan and India. At Michigan he became widely known for his research on survey research methods and on racial attitudes, which is cited in this chapter and in Chapter 16.

Schuman has coauthored eight books, including Questions and Answers in Attitude Surveys, Black Racial Attitudes: Trends and Complexities, *and* Racial Attitudes in America: Trends and Interpretations. *In addition to these topics, his 100-plus articles include notable contributions concerning the attitude–behavior relationship; religious attitudes; authoritarianism; attitudes toward the Vietnam War, gun control, and abortion; and technical issues of question wording and context effects in surveys. He has served as editor of the journals* Sociometry *and* Public Opinion Quarterly *and has been elected president of the American Association of Public Opinion Research and a member of the American Academy of Arts and Sciences.*

their opinions to a special telephone number after a newsworthy event like a presidential candidate debate or a social-issue television documentary. The problem with such audience-response techniques is that there are absolutely no scientific controls on the sample that is obtained. Respondents are self-selected, and a vociferous minority can easily stack the results, as frequently happens in the similar voting for All-Star major-league baseball players. Despite the large response totals and the flashy gimmicks of immediate computer feedback of results, such polls are just as unscientific and invalid as the old *Literary Digest* reports (Cantril & Cantril, 1991).

With the recent proliferation of many different kinds of "polls," it is particularly important for the poll consumer to attend to the sampling methods used and to distinguish the relatively trustworthy, scientific polls from crude, pseudo, or "phony" polls (Orton, 1982; Brady & Orren, 1992). Readers and listeners beware!

Question Wording and Context

Planning and constructing a public opinion interview is a very large and complex task, about which whole books have been written. As early as 1932, Wang presented a comprehensive list of recommendations on the construction and wording of attitude and opinion questionnaires. Because of space limitations, our presentation here can only briefly list the most prominent considerations in wording interview questions. Fuller treatments of a practical sort can be found in excellent volumes by Payne (1951), Sudman and Bradburn (1982), Babbie (1990), and Dillman (2000). In addition, the results of extensive research on question wording and question order are summarized by Schuman and Presser (1996) and Sudman, Bradburn, and Schwarz (1996).

1. Rapport. The interview usually should begin with an explanation of its purpose and sponsorship and then some comments intended to put the respondent at ease as much as possible. The first questions are usually rather simple and factual ones that will be easy for respondents to answer and that will not threaten them in any way.

2. Format of Questions. They may be either multiple-choice, or open-ended ones, which respondents answer in their own words. Both kinds have important and legitimate uses, and many surveys use some of each. Providing a set of response categories, such as a list of possible illnesses, can lead respondents to give answers that they wouldn't have thought of or remembered otherwise. For reviews of research on the format of questions, see Schwarz and Hippler (1991), Schuman and Presser (1996), or Schwarz (1999).

3. Order of Questions. Considerable thought must be given to having the questions in a logical order and to avoiding any influence of earlier questions (i.e., context) on later answers, which can sometimes produce differences in response as great as 20% (Turner & Martin, 1981; Tourangeau & Rasinski, 1988; Moore, 2002c). A common method, which aims toward these goals, is the **funnel sequence** of questions: asking broad, open-ended questions first, followed by somewhat more limited ones, and finally focusing very specifically on narrow aspects of the topic. However, even when the funnel sequence is used, responses to prior questions sometimes may affect later responses.

The effects of different question orders (or different question wording) are often studied by conducting a **split-sample experiment**, in which one sample is given one question order and another comparable sample is given a different question order (cf. Bishop & Smith, 1991). An example of the kind of question-order effects that sometimes occur can be seen in a 1996 survey experiment that asked a national sample whether they were worried or not worried that, in the next few years, (a) "you or your (husband/wife) will lose a job," and (b) "that you will not be able to maintain your standard of living." When the standard-of-living question was asked first, 58% of respondents said they were worried about it, whereas when it was asked after the job-loss question, only 48% said they were worried. In contrast, answers to the job-loss question did not change depending on its position: 36% or 37% expressed that worry in the two orders. The order effect on the standard-of-living question seems to have been due to a carryover of the relatively lower level of worry about job-loss when people were asked about their job-loss worries first (*Gallup Poll Monthly*, 1996, No. 365, pp. 23–24). Note that asking the broader standard-of-living question first is an example of the funnel sequence of questioning.

4. Vocabulary Used. When interviewing a representative sample of citizens, it must be remembered that many respondents will have little education, limited vocabularies, and rather poor understanding of technical terms. In addition to wording the questions carefully, it is essential to **pretest** them with a preliminary sample in order to determine how they are interpreted by typical respondents (Fowler, 1992). An amusing example of this is provided by an item from a widely used standard scale which asked whether "the lot of the average man" was getting worse or better. Pretesting of this item conducted before a major study showed that this usage of "lot" was not familiar to many respondents. "The question was variously interpreted to refer to a lot of average men, to the size of housing lots, and even in one case to cemetery lots!" (Schuman & Kalton, 1985, p. 643), so it had to be reworded.

5. Clarity. Ambiguity can be avoided in the following ways:

a. Keep the questions simple, clear, and direct.

b. Normally keep the questions short, but add repetition or paraphrasing if it will increase understanding.

c. Make the questions as specific as possible (e.g., asking about behavior in a particular time period, such as the last month).

d. Avoid the use of negatives and especially of double negatives.

e. Avoid use of the passive voice.

f. Avoid questions that may be interpreted in more than one way.

g. Avoid "double-barreled" questions, which express two ideas (e.g., Do you favor stronger efforts to eliminate smog and water pollution?—The respondent may have different views on the two topics.)

h. Avoid having so many alternative answers that the question is confusing.

i. Avoid having so few alternative answers that the list is incomplete.

6. Biased Questions. The questions should be as neutral as possible. To avoid **acquiescence effects** (respondents agreeing with the position stated or implied in the question), survey questions should normally present both sides of an issue rather than just one side (Bishop, Oldendick, & Tuchfarber, 1982)—for instance: "Do you favor or oppose increases in the defense budget?" To see why this is important, note the discrepancy in responses to the following two questions (Schuman & Presser, 1996, p. 221):

a. Do you agree or disagree with this statement: Most men are better suited emotionally for politics than are most women.—47% agreed.

b. Would you say that most men are better suited emotionally for politics than are most women, that men and women are equally suited, or that women are better suited than men in this area?—33% said men are better.

Another example of how small changes in question wording can produce major differences in responses is seen in the following two items (Schuman & Presser, 1996, p. 277):

a. Do you think the United States should forbid public speeches against democracy? —21% said yes (forbid).

b. Do you think the United States should allow public speeches against democracy? —48% said no (not allow).

This difference is due to the tone of the verbs, for the verb "forbid" seems to have greater specificity than "not allow" (Holleman, 2000). This effect is actually the opposite of an acquiescence effect, for fewer people said yes to either item than would be expected from responses to the other version (Hippler & Schwarz, 1986). Fortunately, this is one of the largest effects ever found as a result of apparently nonsubstantive wording differences, and most experiments with the "forbid–allow" terms have yielded much smaller response discrepancies. For instance, questions about the government forbidding or allowing the showing of X-rated movies produced only a 5% discrepancy (Schuman & Presser, 1996, p. 282).

Most response effects that are due to wording differences stem from more substantive differences in question wording or context. An understandable example is seen in responses to a question that asked half of a U.S. national sample "What do you think is the ideal number of children for a family to have?" In 1997, 36% of respondents gave answers of three or higher. However, when the other half of the same sample was asked a similar question, beginning with the added phrase, "If money were no object," then 53% said three or more (*Gallup Poll Monthly*, 1997, No. 377, p. 24). Apparently, thinking about the question in terms of realistic financial constraints lessened the percentage of respondents favoring larger families by 17%.

Question-biasing techniques that should be carefully avoided include the use of emotionally laden words or phrases (e.g., "foreign terrorists," "police brutality") and the use of prestige names or symbols in the question. For instance, if an idea is attributed to a well-known and respected person (e.g., "President Bush's policy"), more people will generally agree with the idea than if the prestige name is omitted from the question.

7. Incomplete Specification. It has been said that people will answer what they think you mean rather than what you actually say. In large part, this is a problem of interviewer and respondent having different frames of reference, and it can often be counteracted by asking supplementary questions. (The question "Why?" is often particularly valuable in determining the frames of reference or reasons behind a respondent's attitudes.)

A classic example of the frame of reference problem was provided by Bancroft and Welch (1946) from results of Bureau of the Census interviews designed to determine the number of employed persons in the U.S. The original question used was, "Did you do any work for pay or profit last week?", and it consistently underestimated the employed population. Apparently this occurred because many people such as housewives or students answered it in terms of their main occupation, overlooking the explicit term "any work." The solution adopted was to ask two questions: the first about the respondent's major activity, and a second one (for persons giving "nonworker" responses) as to whether they did any work for pay in addition to their major activity. As a result of this simple change, the official estimate of employment was raised by more than a million persons.

In summary, problems related to question wording and/or context are apt to be the largest source of error in survey results—often much larger than sampling errors, as indicated in this quotation:

> It is far more important in assessing the accuracy of a survey to know the wording of the questions asked than the magnitude of the statistical sampling error. (Roper, 1984, p. 24)

Ignoring the possibility of question-wording and context effects may be viewed as an instance of Ross' (1977) "fundamental attribution error," which was discussed in Chapter 2. That is, it is an overestimation of personal, dispositional factors in the respondent's behavior and an underestimation of situational influences (Schuman & Kalton, 1985).

Memory Errors

We know that human memory is fallible, and many studies have been done to investigate the degree of interviewing errors due to faulty memory. In general they show that less-important facts are forgotten more quickly than more-important facts, and that memory becomes less accurate as the time interval from the event becomes longer. As one example, a survey of known crime victims found that 69% of the crime incidents occurring 1 to 3 months previously were reported to interviewers, whereas only 30% of incidents occurring 10 to 12 months previously were reported (Turner, 1972). Even important past information is apt to be distorted by later events; for instance, reports of past years' income are often distorted in the direction of the respondent's current income. There is also a common phenomenon known as *forward telescoping*, in which past events are recalled as happening more recently than they actually did (Neter & Waksberg, 1964).

A number of means can be used to increase respondents' motivation to remember events accurately and to assist them in their efforts. One common method is to use questions that tap recognition memory rather than unaided recall—for instance, by giving respondents a list to respond to (e.g., illnesses they might have suffered). Other methods include alerting them to the problem of bias in memory so that they can intentionally combat it in their answers, providing contextual information in the question that will help respondents locate an event in time or space, and asking them to consult or keep relevant records (income tax forms, diaries of TV viewing, etc.). Cannell, Miller, and Oksenberg (1981) also recommended giving special instructions about the need for complete and accurate answers, using longer questions which help to symbolize the importance of the topic, asking respondents to sign a pledge of thoroughness, and rewarding their complete answers with verbal approval.

Social Desirability Needs of Respondents

Interview questions are often worded with the implied assumption that the respondent knows something about the topic: "How do you feel about the government's farm policy?" Wanting to be obliging, and not wanting to show their ignorance, many respondents are inclined to fake a knowledge and interest that is not real: "I think it's pretty good." Such uninformed responses have been termed "nonattitudes" by Converse (1974). Often as many as one-third of the respondents will state such uninformed opinions, and this may seriously distort the survey findings (Bishop, Tuchfarber, & Oldendick, 1986). One desirable safeguard is to use **filter questions** to learn the degree of respondents' interest in or knowledge about a topic before asking them detailed questions about it (e.g., Sterngold, Warland, & Herrmann, 1994).

However, social desirability bias is more pervasive than just the nuisance of over-obliging respondents. On any topic where society's norms point to one answer as more socially desirable than another, we can expect an overreporting of the "good" behaviors and an underreporting of the "bad" ones. This tendency is stronger for respondents who are young and/or of lower socioeconomic status (Cahalan, 1968), and it seems to show up most strongly and consistently in questions about voting and voter registration, especially among highly educated respondents who firmly believe in voting (Silver, Anderson, & Abramson, 1986). Some examples of social desirability bias in interview responses are shown in Box 6–3.

Biased responses are particularly likely on sensitive topics—ones that may be embarrassing, threatening, or incriminating to respondents—as illustrated by the large underreporting of drunk driving charges and bankruptcies in Box 6–3. However, a recent review of research on reporting accuracy found surprisingly little intentional denial of undesirable behaviors and attributed much overreporting of voting to the fading of memory (Krosnick, 1999b). Sometimes, on the other hand, motives to shock or impress interviewers, or conform to subcultural norms, can lead to *over*reporting of apparently undesirable behavior. For instance, in research interviews with ex-heroin addicts, many of whom had substantial criminal records, roughly equal percentages overstated and understated their number of past arrests (Wyner, 1980).

Many standard survey techniques help to combat social desirability response bias. First, in wording questions, one can use neutral (unbiased) wording, present two or more opposing alternatives for the respondent to choose between, state that the question is a matter of opinion with no right or wrong answer, and so on (cf. Sudman & Bradburn, 1982). Also, the interviewer should establish good rapport, reassuring the respondent by a supportive manner that any type of response will be perfectly acceptable in the interviewing situation. Detailed **probes** (additional questions following up on a more general one) may often turn up inconsistencies and avoid some overreporting.

Nonresponse Rate

Surveys always fail to obtain data from some of the designated sample members, and the size of this **nonresponse rate** affects the validity of the findings. Nonresponse would

---

Box 6–3 Examples of Social Desirability Bias in Interview Responses

1. *Voter registration—12% overreported (falsely said they were registered), 3% under-reported (falsely said they were not registered). Based on 1976 National Election Study of 2,865 respondents (Katosh & Traugott, 1981).*
2. *Voting in presidential election (1 month previous)—12% overreported, 1% under-reported. Same study as number 1.*
3. *Voting for the winner—14% net overreporting after 4 years. Based on 1964 national survey; 64% of respondents said they had voted for Kennedy 4 years before in 1960, but he only received 50% of the vote (Mueller, 1973).*
4. *Voting in last primary election (8 months previous)—35% overreported, 0% under-reported. Based on probability sample of 157 Chicago adults, half interviewed by phone and half face-to-face (Bradburn & Sudman, 1979).*
5. *Possession of library card—20% overreported, 0% underreported. Same study and interview methods as number 4, different probability sample of 190 adults.*
6. *Donations to community chest—34% overreported, 0% underreported. Based on survey of 920 Denver adults (Parry & Crossley, 1950).*
7. *Possession of driver's license—10% overreported, 2% underreported. Same study as number 6.*
8. *Recent declaration of bankruptcy—30% underreported. Same study and interview methods as number 4, different sample of 79 known recent bankruptcies.*
9. *Recent drunk driving charge—46% underreported. Same study and interview methods as number 4, different sample of 98 respondents all charged with drunk driving 6–12 months previously.*

Of course, in all such checks of official records, it must be realized that sometimes the records may be incorrect, or unavailable because of misfiling, etc. (Marquis, 1978).

---

not matter if the omitted respondents were just like those who answered, but that is never a safe assumption because they usually are systematically different—e.g., poorer, more transient, busier, less cooperative, or less often at home. Thus their loss reduces the representativeness of the obtained sample.

The group of nonrespondents is usually composed of about two-thirds refusals, about one-third not-at-homes who cannot be contacted, even after several attempts, and a variable number of cases lost because of health problems or language difficulties, depending on the geographic area being surveyed (Schuman & Kalton, 1985). Refusals have been rising in recent years, especially in central city areas, and nonresponse rates for national face-to-face surveys with callbacks are apt to be 30% or more (Brehm, 1993). Telephone surveys using random digit dialing (RDD) are likely to have nonresponse rates of 40% or higher, partly because of their unique problem that an unknown percentage of the persistent unanswered calls may be nonworking numbers not currently assigned to anyone (Groves & Kahn, 1979). Fortunately, a careful study of telephone interviews that used RDD found that even one with a relatively low response rate (36%) obtained mean scores on most variables that were almost identical to those from a rigorous study with a much higher response rate (61%) (Keeter et al., 2000).

To reduce the nonresponse rate, it is important not only to call back persistently, but also to explain the survey as clearly and nonthreateningly as possible. Helpful techniques include sending letters in advance explaining the research, and having well-known and prestigious sponsoring organizations for the survey (Fox, Crask, & Kim, 1988). A wide variety of incentives and special questioning techniques have also been tried in efforts to obtain high response rates (e.g., Willimack et al., 1995).Wherever possible, the demographic characteristics of nonresponders (e.g., their census tract or quality of housing) should be obtained for comparison with those of respondents, as an estimate of the amount of bias that is due to nonresponse. Very often, differential statistical weights are applied in the data analysis phase as a way of compensating for nonresponses.

Lack of Anonymity of Responses

Another problem that can distort survey findings, especially on sensitive or threatening topics, is lack of anonymity of responses. Although most respondents apparently do answer honestly under normal conditions, some studies have indicated that anonymity of responses will somewhat increase the accuracy of survey findings (e.g., Bishop & Fisher, 1995). Consequently, a number of the major polling organizations have adopted a "secret ballot" format for obtaining respondents' voting intentions (Perry, 1979).

However, several studies suggest that anonymity may seldom be necessary in order to obtain honest responses, even on sensitive topics. For instance, without anonymity, adolescents and young adults will usually give full reports of socially undesirable behavior such as delinquent acts or drug use (Malvin & Moskowitz, 1983).

When anonymity seems crucial, a relatively new method for ensuring it is the **randomized response technique (RRT)**. In it, the respondent is given two yes–no questions, one threatening (e.g., Have you ever had a venereal disease?) and one innocuous (e.g., Is your birthday in May?). The respondent determines which question to answer by means of a private, random technique such as a coin flip or a choice of different colored beads from a box. Thus, the respondent's anonymity is ensured because neither the interviewer nor the researcher can know which question is being answered. However, the innocuous question has a known probability of "yes" answers (about 1/12 in the case of birth month), so a simple mathematical calculation will reveal what percentage of a group of respondents have said "yes" to the threatening question. However, as this description indicates, RRT can provide meaningful data *only for a group of respondents* and not for any given individual, so its use sacrifices any individual-level analysis of the threatening items. More information about RRT is given by Fox and Tracy (1986) and Antonak and Livneh (1995).

Validation studies have shown that RRT does indeed increase the reporting of socially undesirable behavior such as academic cheating, cigarette smoking, and alcohol use among high school students, and college students' rape-supportive attitudes and actions (Scheers & Dayton, 1987; Fisher, Kupferman, & Lesser, 1992; Jarman, 1997), though it does not eliminate all underreporting (e.g., Bradburn & Sudman, 1979). However, its complexity makes it hard for interviewers to explain, and quite a few respondents remain unconvinced that the randomizing technique will really keep them anonymous (Edgell, Himmelfarb, & Duchan, 1982). In view of these limitations of the RRT method, it is encouraging to remember that many studies have shown relatively little denial of undesirable behaviors or attitudes (Marquis et al., 1981). One reason for this may be the false consensus effect, discussed in Chapter 2—many respondents assume that their own attitudes and behavior are shared by most other people, and so they are not hesitant to express them.

Interviewer Effects on Responses

A vast body of scientific studies shows that the interviewer's behavior and personal characteristics can affect a respondent's answers, though these effects are quite small in most situations (Schwarz et al., 1998). Some of the most interesting and most pervasive factors producing interviewer effects are listed briefly here.

1. Lack of Personal Sensitivity and lack of ability to build rapport with respondents. There is unanimous agreement that such interviewer characteristics can lead to invalid responses (in fact, often to no responses at all).

2. Inadequate Training. Great improvement in interviewing performance can be produced by careful training in field research methods (e.g., Billiet & Loosveldt, 1988).

3. Variations in Putting Questions. Even carefully trained interviewers have been found to vary in minor ways in their reading of questions (Bradburn & Sudman, 1979). Unfortunately, such variation in questions often produces variation in answers. Furthermore, the rules for using additional follow-up questions (**probes**) can never be completely structured, so additional variability in interviewers' behavior occurs here.

4. Variations in Reacting to Respondents' Answers. For instance, an interviewer's reinforcement of answers by frequently saying "good" can systematically influence a respondent's later answers (Cannell et al., 1981).

5. Interviewers' Expectations. One common expectation is that a respondent's answers to related questions will be consistent, and so interviewers often fail to notice inconsistencies that are present. Other expectations about respondents (e.g., that all businessmen are conservative) can also distort survey results, but research suggests that this effect is not strong enough to have much effect on validity (Bradburn & Sudman, 1979).

6. Interviewers' Attitudes. Numerous studies show that interviewers may tend to get (or hear) an excess of responses that are similar to their own attitudes and opinions. Thus the results obtained by interviewers with opposing opinions often vary noticeably (Phillips & Clancy, 1972).

7. Interviewers' Age. This factor may influence the information obtained, particularly across the "generation gap." For instance, when interviewing adolescent girls, older interviewers obtained fewer reports of behavior considered undesirable by middle-class adult standards (Ehrlich & Riesman, 1961).

8. Interviewers' Race. Many studies agree that black respondents tend to give different answers to white interviewers than to black interviewers when the topic is race-related, or sometimes when it pertains to expected social norms such as voting or citizen duties. Such differences in interracial responding generally seem to reflect deference or politeness toward the interviewer. Thus, white interviewers talking to black respondents typically receive fewer indications of distrust of whites or resentment over racial discrimination than do black interviewers (Anderson, Silver, & Abramson, 1988). Parallel findings show that white respondents also avoid offending black interviewers (Hatchett & Schuman, 1975; Schuman et al., 1997), and similar results have been found for other ethnic minority groups (Weeks & Moore, 1981; Reese et al., 1986). These race-of-interviewer effects can distort the findings of research on race-related topics, particularly when the responses of different ethnic groups are compared (Davis, 1997).

9. Interviewers' Gender. Similar to the effects with interviewers' race, when gender effects are found, they usually involve both male and female respondents giving more egalitarian answers to female interviewers than to male interviewers on questions related to gender issues (Kane & Macaulay, 1993).

Finding solutions to these problems of interviewer effects is not easy. Sensitive and well-trained interviewers are a first requirement, but one that many smaller polling organizations fail to meet. Training can at least reduce variability in reading questions, in the use of probes, and in the amount of verbal reinforcement used by interviewers. To some extent training can also help interviewers avoid expectational "halo effects." The effects of interviewers' attitudes, social class, gender, and age can be handled by the principle of "balanced bias"—that is, by attempting to get approximately equal numbers of interviewers from each class, age group, and so forth. Unfortunately, however, this is rarely done, and the majority of opinion-poll interviewers are middle-aged, middle-class women. The problem of respondents' race, and often of their age and social class, can best be met by employing interviewers who have the same race, age, and/or social class as the respondents, and this procedure is often followed when interviews are conducted in ethnic minority areas.

In telephone interviews, interviewers' demographic characteristics present less of a problem, though racial effects may still occur because of recognizable accents (Cotter, Cohen, & Coulter, 1982). Other bases for interviewer effects, such as expectations or variable interviewing behavior, can operate in telephone surveys (Singer, Frankel, & Glassman, 1983). However, one great advantage of telephone interviewing is the possibility of close monitoring and supervision, which should substantially increase the standardization of interviewer behavior (Schuman & Kalton, 1985).

Other Practical Problems

Public opinion polling is a very complex business, whether done by commercial firms or academic research institutions. Between the time of choosing the initial topic for study and the distribution of the final report of findings, there are many phases of the polling operation, each of which can pose its own problems and difficulties. One way of considering these difficulties is in terms of the skilled workers who are needed for the different phases. In addition to the field interviewers, whose characteristics, training, and behavior were discussed in the preceding section, many other talents are needed. First there is the planning staff who develop the interview schedule and specify how and where the sample of respondents will be obtained. Then there are field supervisors who oversee the work of the interviewers. Next, coders in the main office transform the interview responses into quantitative scores on dozens or hundreds of items, and keypunchers transfer these scores into computer data files (though these steps are automated in CATI systems). Then computer experts are needed to process the data, and finally analysts and writers make a coherent picture out of the computer output and prepare a written report of their conclusions.

Another major problem is the cost of polling research. For face-to-face household surveys, the fieldwork costs for interviewers, supervisors, call-backs, and travel typically run $200 or more per interview, and these costs increase each year (Glynn et al., 1999). Interviewing costs depend partly on the length of the interview as well as on the location to which the interviewer must travel, and they are markedly increased when the survey design requires call-backs to find previously not-at-home individuals. Consequently, methods have been developed to weight more heavily the viewpoints of less-frequently-at-home individuals who were successfully interviewed, as a substitute for the more expensive call-back procedure. High-quality telephone surveys with call-backs typically cost less than half as much as face-to-face interviews, and they can be completed much more quickly if a large enough squad of interviewers is employed. However, about 5% of the U.S. population do not have access to a phone and so are overlooked in telephone surveys.

Mailed surveys have the lowest data-collection costs, but their nonresponse rate is usually correspondingly higher, even after follow-up reminders are sent. Other factors that influence the quality of data obtained in mail surveys have been summarized by Schwarz et al. (1998) and Dillman (2000).

Because of the high costs of survey research and the skilled personnel that it requires, very careful advance planning and specification of detailed research goals is essential. A very helpful book that presents a detailed how-to-do-it approach is *Survey Research Methods* by Babbie (1990). Hyman (1972) has written a volume on principles and procedures for **secondary analysis** of survey data that were originally collected by someone else for a different purpose—a very economical procedure compared with fresh data collection. Also, Sudman (1967) has described numerous methods used by the National Opinion Research Center to hold down survey costs.

A final problem of polls comes from their recent extensive use as lead-ins to sales appeals in the marketing of products and services, such as newspaper subscriptions or investment advice. Although these supposed "polls" are not legitimate data-collection surveys, people's overexposure to them may unfortunately lead to more respondent refusals in legitimate and important scientific surveys (Schwarz et al., 1998).

REASONS FOR FAMOUS POLLING FAILURES

Now that we have reviewed many of the issues involved in creating and conducting good opinion polls, let's return to the cases of famous polling failures that we described earlier. The major reasons why opinion polls have sometimes failed to predict election results correctly include end-of-campaign changes in voting intentions, the undecided vote, people who are not at home when the interviewer calls, differential voter turnout, and the effects of the polls themselves on voter behavior.

Late changes in voting intentions were apparently the main factor causing the incorrect predictions in the 1948 election when Truman defeated Dewey (Mosteller et al., 1949). In that year, as in previous elections, some polls stopped interviewing several weeks before the election date. Since that fiasco, the major commercial polls have extended their interviewing to the weekend before the election, and some even take "last-minute" polls on Monday, the day before the election (Bogart, 1998). Thus, by superfast tallying and computations, they can make the morning papers with their final predictions on election day. Even then, a late surge in one candidate's strength could catch them flat-footed, as very nearly happened in Humphrey's uphill fight against Nixon in 1968, and did happen with Reagan's widening lead in 1980.

The undecided vote was also an important factor in the 1948 election, for an unusually high 19% of the voters were still undecided one month before the election (Campbell, Gurin, & Miller, 1954). The usual assumption made is that undecided respondents will divide their votes in the same proportion as those who have already decided, but in 1948 most of those votes apparently went for Truman.

Potential respondents who are not at home are always a headache for the polls, for people who cannot be interviewed until the second, third, or fourth visit are apt to be systematically different from respondents who are home on the interviewer's first visit or phone call. The not-at-homes are more likely to be young adults who are employed outside the home, males, and Republicans (Traugott, 1987). The lesson is clear: To get an adequate sample, it is essential to use **call-backs** to reach those who are less often at home, or some other procedure (e.g., weighting of responses) which gives them fair representation.

Differential turnout seems to have been a major reason for the polls' incorrect predictions in the 1970 British election (Abrams, 1970), and another factor was the lack of last-minute polls to spot late shifts in voting intentions (Worcester, 1980). Whether a particular respondent will actually vote when the election occurs is always difficult to predict. Useful methods for predicting voter turnout have been developed (Perry, 1979) but were little utilized in the 1970 British election. The only polling firm that correctly predicted the Conservative Party to win did so by making a large correction for Labourite voters' traditionally lower turnout. Again in the British election of 1992, late-deciders and differential turnout contributed to the polls' errors, but the most serious factor apparently was the unwillingness of some individuals to respond to the poll questions, which led to a systematic undersampling of Conservative Party voters in the quota sample results (Jowell et al., 1993).

The effects of the polls themselves on voters have not been thoroughly studied, but they are widely believed to have an effect on voter turnout and on the undecided vote. This was illustrated in the 1970 British election when many Labour voters stayed home, trusting in the polls' prediction that their party would win. An even more striking example occurs regularly in the United States because of the differential in time zones between the East and the West Coasts. In several recent elections, the national television networks have predicted the winning party on the basis of East Coast votes well before the close of voting on the West Coast. In 1980, President Carter even broadcast his concession speech over an hour before the voting deadline in the West, and this early concession was apparently a factor in the narrow defeat of several Democratic congressmen, many of whose supporters gave up at that point and failed to vote (Kinder & Sears, 1985). After 1980, early election reports became even more pervasive as the TV networks competed to be first to announce the winners on the basis of their election-day exit polls, though recently the networks have agreed not to declare a statewide winner until the polls close in that state.

Early broadcasts of election results can have a serious effect on the turnout and voting choices of late voters, and legislation has been proposed to prevent their future occurrence (Milavsky et al., 1985). Indeed, many other democratic nations, including France, Germany, Great Britain, Australia, Canada, Brazil, and South Korea, have banned publication of *any poll results* for various periods, even as long as *2 weeks* before an election (Lavrakas & Traugott, 1995; Hodson, Maio, & Esses, 2001). The evidence on the size of the early-broadcast effect, however, is equivocal. Several studies of the influence of early election-day projections on West Coast voting have not shown any clear-cut effects (Tannenbaum & Kostrich, 1983; Lang & Lang, 1984; Epstein & Strom, 1984). However, there are major problems of research design in finding a sample of late voters large enough to yield significance and in choosing a comparison group of other voters that will provide an objective test of the question. Other studies (Wolfinger & Linquiti, 1981; Jackson, 1983; Sudman, 1986) have found evidence that early broadcasting of election returns or projections can reduce turnout by several percentage points, at least under the following special conditions (Sudman, 1986):

> Exit polls appear to cause small declines in total voting in areas where the polls close [later than 8 p.m. EST] for those elections where the exit polls predict a clear winner when previously the race had been considered close. (p. 331)

IMPACT OF POLLS IN POLITICS AND GOVERNMENT

There are many types of polls and innumerable uses for poll information. One type we haven't discussed previously is government polls to establish necessary facts about the population's economic and social circumstances, working conditions, health, and so on. The granddaddy of such surveys is the U.S. census, taken every 10 years since 1790. In addition to the census, the government conducts well over 200 other regular surveys;

the largest of them, the Current Population Survey, contacts over 50,000 households each month. In the 1980s, these government surveys totaled well over 5 million interviews per year, and it was estimated that a total of 30 million survey interviews were conducted with the American public each year (Turner & Martin, 1981; Bradburn & Sudman, 1988). A major purpose of the government surveys is to provide a statistical basis for allocation of government funds to different geographic areas and programs in order to meet demonstrated public needs. In 1979, over $120 *billion* of the federal budget were allocated on the basis of such statistical data (Beal & Hinckley, 1984). Since the 1980s, both the number of surveys conducted in the U.S. and their costs have continued to escalate sharply.

Most of the nongovernmental surveys are conducted for business rather than political purposes. In 1980, one company alone (AT&T) conducted about 5 million survey interviews—about the same number as the entire federal government (Turner & Martin, 1981). Most business surveys are **proprietary**—that is, for the sole use of the sponsor—so their results are seldom made public. In 1997 (the latest available date) there were over 4,000 market research and polling firms doing these kinds of surveys in the U.S.—mostly consumer research on advertising and marketing issues—and their total earnings were nearly $8 billion (U.S. Census Bureau, 1997). Of that total, political polling represented only a few percent, but this tiny fraction was by far the most visible part. Starting in the 1988 U.S. presidential election, political polling became even more ubiquitous because a single media compendium called *Hotline* distributed daily compilations of political polls from all over the country (Cantril & Cantril, 1991). Many of these poll results were unreliable because of small or atypical samples or inferior methods, but that problem was seldom noted in the media reports on them.

Every U.S. President since F. D. Roosevelt has had his own private poller (Worcester, 1987). Since about 1960, most politicians have come to consider poll information as essential in their election campaigns. Privately commissioned polls have become commonplace in races for major state and national offices. By the mid-1960s, 90% of U.S. senators and governors were using private polls, as were up to 80% of newly elected congresspeople (King & Schnitzer, 1968). An analysis of disclosed spending by presidents on survey research suggests large differences among them, but given the amount of money spent, it is clear that survey data play an important role in presidential decisions (Murray & Howard, 2002). For example, reported yearly expenditures on survey research (in 2000 dollars) during election years were: Carter ($3.5 million), Reagan ($3.3 million), Bush ($2.0 million), and Clinton ($1.9 million).

Obviously political polling has become big business. But the question remains: Is it good for the country? Oftentimes excessive public relations zeal can lead to marketing political candidates in the same way that toothpaste is advertised. However, such excesses cannot all be blamed on public opinion polling. And when criticisms of polls are made, it is important to distinguish among several types of polling organizations. The major commercial polls, such as Gallup, Harris, Roper, and a number of statewide polls, use large samples and established scientific methods, and they do not sell their services to individual candidates. By contrast, the thousands of firms that do private political and market polling vary widely in the carefulness and scientific adequacy of their procedures, and some unfortunately have been known to succumb to pressures for biased samples, slanted reports, or other unethical procedures (e.g., Shamir, 1986; Krosnick, 1989). A third group of polls are those conducted by newspapers or radio or TV stations, which again vary greatly in the scientific adequacy of their sampling, interviewing, and reporting.

There is an unfortunate tendency for the news media to concentrate very largely on who is ahead in the political polls—"horse-race journalism"—rather than on public opinion about the current issues and reasons for voter opinions (Graber, 1997). This tendency has been exacerbated in recent elections by use of **tracking polls**, which are series of polls conducted with successive (and often small) samples day after day, to try to monitor fast-changing public opinion on key issues or candidate strength. The various types of polls taken by different methods and different organizations have differing levels of predictive success, which have been summarized in many reports (Felson & Sudman, 1975; Sudman, 1983; Crespi, 1988; Cantril & Cantril, 1991). In general, prediction of election results is much better when the polls are taken only a few days before the election, and when the level of voter interest and turnout is high.

In the following sections we consider, first, the major criticisms and, second, some of the arguments in favor of modern public opinion polling in politics. We concentrate our discussion mainly on evaluation of the major commercial polls, but with some attention to the merits and abuses of private political polling.

Criticisms of Political Polling

As mentioned earlier in this chapter, opinion polls have been accused of influencing the preferences and the turnout of voters. They have also been criticized as "undemocratic" and elitist, because they report the views of only a small and not-wholly-representative sample of citizens. On the opposite flank, polls have been accused of destroying the courage and independence of political leaders and enshrining the conventional and unconsidered opinions of the poorly informed "average man." This reduction of political opinion to the lowest common denominator, it is alleged, may keep good men and women from running for office or prevent incumbent politicians from telling the public unpleasant truths or from adopting unpopular positions. On still another front, polls have been criticized for making little contribution to the essential democratic processes of discussion and reconciliation of opposing viewpoints, because they often emphasize divergence in opinions and thus may discourage compromise or consensus. Obviously, these are all controversial viewpoints, with persuasive arguments on both sides.

Summaries of these arguments against polling have been presented by Bogart (1972a), Wheeler (1976), and Cantril and Cantril (1991), and pointed extracts of the criticisms are highlighted in Box 6–4. Many national politicians have shared these concerns, including congressmen who in 1970 proposed a "truth-in-polling" bill, calling for public disclosure of the detailed methodology and sponsorship of every published poll. These proposed requirements were much like the voluntary standards that have been adopted by the polling industry (see the next section). Another strong critic of political polling was former Senator Albert Gore, Sr., (1960), who raised a commonly heard criticism of the polls about which there is much misunderstanding—the question of how large their samples need to be:

> As a layman, I would question that a straw poll of less than 1 percent of the people could under any reasonable circumstances be regarded as a fair and meaningful cross section test. This would be something more than 500 times as large a sample as Dr. Gallup takes. (p. 16962)

For a country like the United States with a population over 280 million, such a procedure would require a sample of about 2 million adult respondents, which would be impossibly costly in time, effort, and money. By contrast, we have pointed out in an earlier section that a carefully chosen probability sample of 1,100 cases will produce results with an expected error of only ±3%. Thus a sample of 1,000 or more cases can be used to predict the total national vote. However, if it is desired to predict the vote *in each state separately*, 50 separate samples each containing 1,000 or more cases would be needed. Because the Electoral College vote, which determines the winner in presidential elections, is based

Box 6–4 A Critique of the Polls

The polls have a tremendous impact on our political system and other aspects of our life. That the polls can so often be wrong makes that impact all the more disturbing. . . .

Public opinion polls determine who runs for political office and, often, who wins. They also influence the tone and content of debate on great national issues. . . .

The influence of polls extends far beyond elections and government policy-making. The little boxes in twelve hundred homes selected by the Nielsen Company register an electronic thumbs up or down on the television programs which will be watched by the entire country. A shift of a rating point or two can determine whether a program lives or dies, yet each rating point represents only a dozen Nielsen households. . . .

All of these polls are subject to error and manipulation. Even polls which are published in good faith can be dangerously misleading, and of course not all polls are legitimate. . . .

So much now depends on the opinion polls—political candidacies, policies, profits— that there is great pressure on the pollsters to manipulate their surveys. It is not hard to rig a poll. . . . Simply by subtly altering the wording of a question, "you can come up with any result you want." . . .

The high rate of refusals and not-at-homes is just one of the many technical problems which pollsters face, but it strikes at the very heart of public opinion polling, for if a great number of people are not answering the pollster's knock on the door, then opinion surveys cannot be truly representative of the entire population. . . .

The percentages which are printed in banner headlines appear precise and scientific but in fact are based on a great deal of personal judgment. The pollster must decide who is likely to vote and who is not; he must determine which way people are leaning; and he must allocate the undecideds to one candidate or the other. In all of these matters there is more guesswork than science. . . .

Sampling error could throw a poll off by several points either way, but that really is insignificant compared to other sources of error. "Question error—the bias or loading in question wording, or the error that results from the context in which the unbiased question may occur—can cause errors of ten, thirty, or even more percentage points." . . .

In primaries, where a vote is not considered as important, or in early trial heats, when the candidates have not become fully known, people are far less certain of their preferences for the simple reason that they have given them little thought. . . .

The primary results tell us little of national preferences and attitudes, yet the press plays them up. Reporters handicap the candidates like racehorses, picking favorites according to the polls. . . .

Politicians and the press should disregard these early surveys, but because they do not, such polls can easily become self-fulfilling prophecies. . . .

"Polls obviously have an effect. They have a clearer, more dramatic effect on the financial people who give support to the candidates and on the campaign workers, either boosting morale or undercutting it, making the money flow or drying it up, than they do on the electorate directly." . . .

Poor polls kill contributions. Without cash it is hard to get the kind of exposure that will keep the candidate from dropping even further back. It is the Catch-22 of politics. . . .

The polls have come to have a far-reaching and often dangerous impact, largely because the pollsters have intimidated most of their potential critics. The pollsters would have us believe that to criticize their calling is to oppose democracy. . . .

Source: From LIES, DAMN LIES, AND STATISTICS: THE MANIPULATION OF PUBLIC OPINION IN AMERICA, by Michael Wheeler, Copyright © 1976 by Michael Wheeler. Used by permission of Liveright Publishing Corporation. (Extracts from pp. xv–xvii, 23–27, 245–255.)

on the plurality of votes in each state separately, predicting Electoral College returns would require a separate large sample for each of the 50 states. Instead of attempting this overwhelming task, Gallup and the other political pollers have limited themselves to predicting the candidates' percentages of the total national vote.

Another accusation that has very often been made against the commercial opinion polls is that early poll results start "bandwagon" movements toward the leading candidate. It is surprising that this criticism still persists, for very few studies have found support for it (cf. Brady & Johnston, 1987; Skalaban, 1988). Truman's underdog win in 1948 and Humphrey's comeback near-win in 1968 are dramatic illustrations disputing the bandwagon myth, and there is an abundance of other research evidence against it as well.

Improper uses and ethical abuses of private political polls, unfortunately, are widespread (cf. Roll & Cantril, 1980; Cantril & Cantril, 1991). For instance, some firms slant their questions or their "findings" in a direction favorable to their client, and it is common for findings to be "leaked" in attempts to gain political advantage. Early poll results on popularity or "name-recognition" (which are likely to change greatly with time and active campaigning) have nevertheless often discouraged well-qualified candidates from running. Early poll results often set unrealistic goals for a candidate to reach a certain percentage of the vote in the "numbers game" of presidential primary elections; and they are also apt to turn on or off the sluice gates of supporters' financial backing and of media attention (Cantril & Cantril, 1991). Thus there may well be a bandwagon effect among financial contributors and political reporters, if not among voters themselves. As pollster Samuel Lubell has written "Events, not polls, affect people. Polls influence politicians most of all, and, secondly, they influence political writers, and last of all—if at all—they affect the people" (quoted in Roll & Cantril, 1980, p. 28).

Defenses of Political Polling

In response to these criticisms of polling, many defenses have been offered. Roll and Cantril (1980) have cited many ways in which private polls can be genuinely useful to political candidates. They can inform candidates about the public's concerns and indicate which arguments on an issue will probably be best received. They can demonstrate trends in public support or recognition and help to show where campaign efforts will be most effective. Further, they can pinpoint aspects of the candidate's own public image, the opponent's weaknesses, and the likely effects of other candidates and issues. In addition, Altschuler (1982) notes that polls can help target specific demographic subgroups for campaign advertising that is particularly relevant to their concerns, and also can help candidates play the "expectations game" of publicizing a conservative estimate of their expected vote in the coming primaries.

One way that polls should *not* be used by candidates is in deciding whether to run at the beginning of the campaign, because at that time most candidates are still unknown and key campaign issues have not yet crystallized (Altschuler, 1982). Levy (1984) has given an overview of how pollsters have helped the campaigns of U.S. presidential candidates, and Sudman (1982) and Cantril and Cantril (1991) have described a number of effective ways that polls have been used by presidents after they were elected to office.

Early defenders of commercial political polls, though readily admitting that polling methods and results were not perfect, were quick to take issue with many criticisms. Some of their major arguments are stated in George Gallup's (1948) vigorous defense of the polls, summarized in Box 6–5. As he indicated, a major contribution of public opinion polls is an educational one: They encourage both respondents and readers of the results to think about the issues raised. Polls have opened up formerly hush-hush topics, such as

Box 6–5 George Gallup Defends the Polls

Students of government have noted many contributions to our democratic process made by polls....

1. Public opinion polls have provided political leaders with a more accurate gauge of public opinion than they had prior to 1935.
No responsible person in the field of public opinion research would assert that polling methods are perfect. On the other hand,...the indices which were relied on most in the past—letters, newspaper editorials, self-appointed experts, and the like—have been found to be highly inaccurate as guides to public opinion.
2. Public opinion polls have speeded up the processes of democracy by providing not only accurate, but swift, reports of public opinion....
In fact, in many situations—particularly those in which a substantial portion of the population fails to take the trouble to vote—the poll results might be even more accurate as a measure of public sentiment than the official returns.
3. Public opinion polls have shown that the common people do make good decisions....
4. Public opinion polls have helped to focus attention on major issues of the day....
5. Public opinion polls have uncovered many "areas of ignorance."...
6. Public opinion polls have helped administrators of government departments make wiser decisions.... based upon accurate knowledge of public attitudes....
7. Public opinion polls have made it more difficult for political bosses to pick presidential candidates "in smoke-filled rooms."...
8. Public opinion polls have shown that the people are not motivated, in their voting, solely by the factor of self-interest, as many politicians have presumed....
9. Public opinion polls constitute almost the only present check on the growing power of pressure groups....
Poll results show that pressure-group spokesmen often represent only a minority of those within their own groups, and prove baseless their threats of political reprisal if legislators do not bow to their wishes.... more important, [polls] can reveal the will of the inarticulate and unorganized majority of the citizens....
10. Public opinion polls help define the "mandate" of the people in national elections....
At the same time that the views of voters are obtained on candidates, the views of these same voters can be recorded on issues. In this way, election results can be interpreted much more accurately than in the past....

A true statesman will never change his ideals or his principles to make them conform to the opinions of any group, be it large or small. Rather, such a leader will try to persuade the public to accept his views and his goals. In fact, his success as a leader will in large part be measured by his success in making converts to his way of thinking....
Leaders who do not know what the public thinks, or the state of the public's knowledge on any issue, are likely to be ineffective and unsuccessful leaders, and eventually to lose their opportunity to lead....
Great leaders will seek information from every reliable source about the people whom they wish to lead.... The public opinion poll will be a useful tool in enabling them to reach the highest level of their effectiveness as leaders.

Source: *A Guide to Public Opinion Polls* (rev. ed.), pp. ix–xii, 5, 8. Selections from George Gallup. Copyright 1948 by Princeton University Press. © 1972 renewed by Princeton University Press. Reprinted by permission of Princeton University Press.

birth control and mental illness, for public discussion. The main limitation of polling is due to the nature of people's opinions, which are often inconsistent and/or shifting, based on their varied roles and conflicting loyalties—a mixture of desires and fears, prejudices and ideals. If this limitation is kept in mind, the polls can perform a very useful public service.

To improve the quality of polling procedures and reporting, the American Association for Public Opinion Research (AAPOR) and the National Council on Public Polls (NCPP) have adopted codes of professional ethics and practices. These standards specify that any reports of poll results prepared for publication should include information on the poll's sponsor, wording of questions, method and time of interviewing, the population sampled, sample size, likely sampling error, and other details. However, it is unfortunately true that most poll reports in newspapers, much less in radio or TV broadcasts, still do not include all of this necessary interpretive information (Cantril & Cantril, 1991). Usually this is because editors have trimmed the longer reports prepared by the polling organizations, but sometimes it is because incomplete or "leaked" reports have purposely omitted such facts. Adherence to these standards by all pollsters and journalists would be one of the most important possible steps toward making survey findings meaningful and useful to the public.

It is interesting to note that public opinion polling has spread even to Russia and the formerly communist countries of Eastern Europe, where Americans often think of citizens' personal viewpoints as being ignored by the government (McIntosh & Hinckley, 1992; Crespi, 1997). As a final argument in favor of polls in democratic countries, Gallup (1965) has claimed

> that legislators do not follow poll results, and that we would have appreciably better govern-
> ment if they did. As Bryce pointed out, the people are better fitted to determine ends than
> to select means. The task of the leader is to decide how best to achieve the goals set by the
> people. . . . In the last thirty years [polls] have tried out hundreds of proposals, many of which
> are widely approved but may have to wait for years until Congress catches up with the people.
> (p. 463)

SUMMARY

The accuracy of public opinion poll results depends on many factors, but most impor-tantly on the representativeness of the sample of respondents chosen. The commercial polling organizations generally use various modifications of the quota sampling proce-dure, which is faster and less expensive but also less accurate than probability sampling. However, despite occasional failures, the major polls have a very good overall record in predicting election results, even despite the sampling difficulties inherent in exit polls.

In addition to sampling procedures, another problem in public opinion polling in-volves the wording of questions, which is extremely important to the validity of both interview and questionnaire results. Memory errors and social desirability needs of re-spondents can also distort poll results, as can high rates of refusals or nonresponse, lack of anonymity of responses, and variations in interviewers' behavior or characteristics. With proper procedures, there are ways of reducing all of the potential sources of error in poll results. However, many polling organizations do not fully observe these safeguards. Therefore, in reading poll results, it is important to analyze the care and objectivity with which the poll was conducted and to remember that not all polls are equally accurate and believable.

Since about 1980, polling by telephone has replaced face-to-face interviews as the predominant method because it is cheaper, faster, and generally able to produce equally high-quality data. On-line polling is an even more recent method of taking surveys for various specialized purposes.

The main reasons why political polls have sometimes failed to predict election results correctly are last-minute changes in voting intentions, the undecided vote, failure to interview "not-at-homes," the possible effects of the polls themselves on the final vote, and differential voter turnout on election day. Although political polling has become a pervasive part of the American scene, it has critics of its undesirable consequences as well as defenders of its valuable contributions.

7

The Structure of Public Opinion

Q. What do you believe is the most important problem facing the country right now? [early 1960s]

A. Cuba.

Q. Why do you think Cuba is the most important problem . . . ?

A. We should blast Cuba off the map. I don't care why. Just do it. It should be obvious why.

Q. What do you think the government should do about this situation?

A. It's hard to say really. I am really not one to say like my husband was. We should stop sending all our money to the Commies. And we should make all the draft dodgers and those Commies at (state university) fight on the front lines some day. My ex-husband was a retired Army man, you know.—John H. Kessel (1965, pp. 378, 381).

Q. What do the terms liberal and conservative mean to you?

A. Not too much really. For some reason conservative gets identified with the South—identified with drabby looking clothes vs. more something I would wear, drabby clothes, too, but it is just a different type.—W. Russell Neuman (1986, p. 19).

These responses (which were actually given by two survey respondents) are not conspicuous for their informational content nor their logical consistency. Yet they were fairly typical of a substantial portion of respondents in these two studies, which were conducted in largely middle-class, metropolitan areas.

According to the theory of democratic government, an informed populace is the bulwark of freedom. It is the citizen's duty to form an opinion about public affairs and to express it at the ballot box. And democratic governments are expected to be responsive to public opinion on important issues.

But are the average citizen's attitudes on major public issues well-informed? Are they internally consistent? Are they responsive to new information and new situations? And do they have an effect on public policy? The answers to these questions bear on some of the most central assumptions underlying the democratic form of government.

Many authorities have concluded that the populace is ignorant rather than informed. As far back as 1947, Hyman and Sheatsley (p. 412) concluded that "There exists a hard core of chronic 'know-nothing's'" in the American population. Later, Converse (1964, p. 245) declared, "large portions of an electorate do not have meaningful beliefs . . . ." Yet there are arguments and evidence supporting the opposite viewpoint as well, so this issue is by no means a simple one to settle. In this chapter we examine first the extent of public information on current affairs, next the evidence for the elitist view of public opinion, and finally the evidence for the mass-politics view of public opinion.

THE EXTENT OF PUBLIC INFORMATION

As an educated person, learning is a part of your life. You are used to taking in information every day, discussing it, and (we may hope) using it in your regular activities. Most of your friends are probably also educated individuals with an interest in current affairs. From such a position in life, it is often very hard to remember that you are not a typical member of society. Even in this age of mass education, only about half of U.S. adults (51%) have ever attended college, and only 26% of adults have graduated from college (U.S. Census Bureau, 2001).

These facts are important because one's level of education is a strong determinant of how much one knows. Of course there are "self-educated" men and women but, in general, college-educated individuals have a much larger store of factual knowledge than persons with less education. To take only one example, a national poll gave respondents the names of 10 famous men and asked for a simple identification of them. The men ranged from Columbus (the best known with 92% correct identification) through Shakespeare, Napoleon, Freud, Karl Marx, Leo Tolstoy, to Rubens (known by only 24%). The average score for the 10 famous men was 54% correct (Gallup, 1978, p. 596). Moreover, the effect of different levels of education on a task like this is dramatic. In an identical previous survey, these figures were obtained: college-educated respondents, 77% correct; high school-educated ones, 51% correct; and grade school-educated ones, only 26% correct (Erskine, 1963a).

So you are not a typical member of society in your level of information. How much does the "average citizen" know, and on what topics is he or she likely to be well informed or poorly informed? Findings from many different national polls give a rather pessimistic overall picture.

First, let us look at the area of general information. Some items of knowledge are very widespread in our country, but most are not (Sudman & Bradburn, 1982). For instance, in a national survey, only 40% of the American population knew who wrote *Huckleberry Finn* (Mark Twain), and only 22% knew who wrote *A Tale of Two Cities* (Charles Dickens). In the late 1950s, the best-known of many famous statements was "Hi Yo, Silver!", but only 71% of the population knew who said it (the Lone Ranger). Bugs Bunny's greeting, "What's up, Doc?," was identified by only 40%.

In contrast, there are some items of information that are known to most Americans. We may call these **salient** items, meaning that they are in the focus of people's attention:

- During the 1970s, when the proposed Equal Rights Amendment to the U.S. Constitution was being debated throughout the 50 states, 90% of a national sample were aware of it (Gallup, 1978).
- After the 1979 nuclear accident at Three Mile Island, 96% of a national sample had heard of it (*Gallup Opinion Index*, 1979, No. 165);
- In 1986, 98% of the population had heard or read about AIDS (*Gallup Report*, 1986, No. 247), and 92% knew about the recent return of Halley's Comet, though only 7% claimed to have seen it themselves (*Gallup Report*, 1986, No. 246).

- In a 1996 study, 93% of the population could identify Bill Cosby as a comedian; and 96% knew that the U.S. was a member of the United Nations (Delli Carpini & Keeter, 1996).
- On the evening of the September 11, 2001 destruction of the World Trade Center in New York City, an amazing figure of 99% of a national sample had heard about it (Public Agenda, 2001).

What do these items of widely known information have in common? First, they are topics that have been very prominently in the news—in many news broadcasts, on the first page of newspapers, and therefore in the conversation of many people. Second, each of these topics is quite unique, a one-of-a-kind item that stands out in the news because there is nothing else like it with which it can be confused. Third, most of these topics have continued to be in the news day after day and month after month so that it would be almost impossible for anyone except a mental hospital patient or a hermit to escape contact with them.

Knowledge About Public Affairs

Let us compare these data on general information with evidence on citizens' knowledge about public affairs—the facts on which public opinion and political attitudes should be based.

Here again we find there are a few facts that are known to almost everyone. One kind of information that is widely held is **exposure** to terms and issues, as contrasted with knowledge about them. In answering questions of this type respondents merely have to say, "Yes, I've heard of that," rather than giving correct information about the topic. Consequently, percentages of people "knowing" about the topic are usually much higher than for questions which require correct information in the answer. For instance, in the 1990s, 94% of Americans said they had heard about the U.S. dropping an atomic bomb in World War II, but only 75% could correctly report that it was dropped on Japan (T. Smith, 1995b). In 1990, a year when publicity about the imminent U.S. census was perpetual, 66% of the U.S. public knew it was upcoming soon (34% didn't), but knowledge that participation in it was required by law was at a chance level (47% said "yes" and 43% said "no"—*Gallup Poll Monthly*, 1990, No. 294). In 1985, 67% of Americans said they were aware of the Reagan administration's so-called "Star Wars" proposal for a space-based nuclear defense system (*Gallup Report*, 1985, No. 234), and about 70% of the population were familiar with the Peace Corps shortly after it was founded (Erskine, 1963b), but only 49% of respondents in 1990 knew that the United Nations headquarters was in New York (*Gallup Poll Monthly*, 1990, No. 301). These highly familiar events and organizations share the same characteristics mentioned in the preceding section as causes of perceptual salience—they are unique, and they have been in the news prominently and repeatedly.

Turning to items of substantive knowledge, rather than merely exposure to terms or issues, one category of information which is widely known is the names of the very top level of national leaders. Typically, the only Americans correctly identified by more than 90% of our population are the current and past presidents. The best-known senators and cabinet members usually receive between 40% and 60% correct identification (Gallup, 1978). In the early 1990s, when they were repeatedly in the news, Mikhail Gorbachev's name was recognized by 71% of Americans, and Margaret Thatcher was familiar to 53%, but only 17% could identify Nelson Mandela of South Africa (Delli Carpini & Keeter,

1992). In 2000, about 60% of respondents could correctly name the host of TV's "Tonight Show," Jay Leno, and the world's top golfer, Tiger Woods (Carlson, 2000), but most less-illustrious mortals are recognized by only a tiny fraction of the public. For instance, though the Chairman of the Federal Reserve System, Alan Greenspan, was correctly identified by 29% of respondents, only 8% knew that William Rehnquist was Chief Justice of the U.S. Supreme Court in 1992 (*American Enterprise*, 1994). (Do you know who the current Chief Justice is?)

Only a very few other items of information are widely shared by the U.S. population. About three-fourths of Americans can say what the initials "FBI" mean, whereas just over half can correctly describe the term "filibuster" or give the name of the first 10 amendments to the Constitution (*American Enterprise*, 1994). Nearly 90% of young adults can correctly point out California or Texas on a U.S. map, but only two other states (New York and Pennsylvania) were correctly identified by even half of these respondents (National Geographic Education Foundation, 2002). In the same study, only 37% of American young adults could correctly spot England on a map of Europe, 24% could find Saudi Arabia on a map of the Middle East and Asia, and only about 15% could point out Afghanistan, Israel, Iraq, or Iran, despite their almost daily presence in news reports.

Specific factual details are even less well comprehended by most people. Even after several Mideast wars, 40% of respondents mistakenly thought that Israel was an Arab country (Hechinger, 1979); and when the Panama Canal treaty was being debated, well over half of Americans incorrectly believed that the biggest U.S. aircraft carriers and supertankers used the canal, not realizing that they were too large to do so (*Gallup Opinion Index*, 1978, No. 153). Although the long-running conflict over Kashmir has received great publicity because it periodically threatens to escalate into nuclear warfare, only 36% of young American adults are aware that India and Pakistan are the two clashing nations there (National Geographic Education Foundation, 2002). Even during the height of an election campaign, less than one-fourth of U.S. adults can correctly identify either the Democratic or Republican congressional candidates in their own district (Delli Carpini & Keeter, 1992).

When we turn to public issues about which one might expect citizens to be well-informed, that expectation is rudely shattered. There is rarely ever an issue about which even half of the populace is correctly informed, even at the most elementary level. For example, only about 30% of respondents can state the general meaning of the term "affirmative action" (Delli Carpini & Keeter, 1996). In the midst of the "cold war" between the U.S. and the Soviet Union, barely over half of Americans could define that term in a reasonably correct fashion. Civics teachers would shudder still more to learn that less than one-fourth of our population can correctly describe any of the contents of the Bill of Rights (Erskine, 1962). Moreover, despite marked increases in U.S. citizens' education levels, their information about public affairs is, if anything, slightly lower than it was a generation or two ago (Kinder, 1998). Other fascinating examples of Americans' level of knowledge or ignorance on public issues are given in Box 7–1.

These examples of the low level of public information provide the factual background for our next topic, the **elitist** viewpoint concerning public opinion. This view maintains that coherent systems of political beliefs and attitudes are held by only a small minority of citizens, an "elite" group. In considering this viewpoint, it is important to realize that it is descriptive rather than *pre*scriptive. That is, it does not advocate nor defend elite control of public opinion; it merely seeks to describe the way that these processes actually operate, but does not hold that they *should* operate that way.

Box 7–1   The Informed (?) Populace

The following questions from national public opinion polls indicate typical degrees of people's knowledge about U.S. national government and important public issues. All of these questions were open-ended, and the number after each item is the percentage of respondents who were reasonably correct.

How many years are there in one term of office for the U.S. President?	*96%*
What does it mean when a president vetoes a bill sent to him by Congress?	*89*
How many times can an individual be elected President?	*73*
When you read about an economic recession, what does that mean to you?	*57*
What are the first ten amendments to the U.S. Constitution called?	*43*
What majority is required for the Senate and House to override a presidential veto?	*37*
Where are most immigrants to the U.S. coming from?	*35*
Do you know the names of the two U.S. Senators from your state?	*25*
How long is the term of office for a United States Senator?	*25*
Who is the Prime Minister of Canada?	*11*
What percent of the U.S. population is black?	*8*
What country is the U.S.'s largest trading partner?	*8*

Source: Data from Delli Carpini & Keeter (1991, 1992, 1996).

THE ELITIST VIEW OF PUBLIC OPINION

The definitive statement of this viewpoint was given by Philip Converse (1964) in an influential chapter that effectively established the terms of debate for most subsequent work in this area, and provides much of the source material for this section. Converse's major conclusions have also been largely reinforced and extended by several later studies (Converse & Markus, 1979; Converse & Pierce, 1985; Neuman, 1986; Zaller, 1992).

After describing the typical low level of citizens' information about public affairs, Converse (1964) pointed out the resulting consequences for individuals' political belief systems. His major thesis was that, as one moves down the information scale from the best-informed "elites," individuals' *understanding* of public affairs fades out very rapidly. Also, the *objects of belief* that are central in the individuals' belief system

> shift from the remote, generic, and abstract to the increasingly simple, concrete, or "close to home." Where potential political objects [of belief] are concerned, this progression tends to be from abstract, "ideological" principles to the more obviously recognizable social groupings or charismatic leaders and finally to such objects of immediate experience as family, job, and immediate associates. (p. 213)

Furthermore, these differences in belief systems seem crucial in understanding different individuals' political behavior.

What evidence did Converse have for these conclusions? Most of it came from a series of major research studies concerning U.S. national elections conducted every two years by the Survey Research Center (SRC) at the University of Michigan. These studies polled national samples of 1,000 to 1,800 citizens and were reported in a very influential volume called *The American Voter* (Campbell et al., 1960). Converse stressed several different types of findings from these studies, which we summarize in the following sections.

Use of Ideological Concepts

The first finding concerned the amount of use of ideological dimensions in understanding public affairs. By **ideological dimension** Converse meant a basic principle (such as conservatism or internationalism or socialism) that underlies and helps to determine an individual's beliefs on many different political issues. The respondents in the SRC studies were asked open-ended interview questions which allowed them to evaluate current political issues and candidates in their own words, showing what evaluative dimensions they used spontaneously. Almost the only ideological dimension used was the *liberal–conservative* one, and only 2.5% of the population used any such dimension in a clear and consistent way. A second group of respondents (about 9%) mentioned such an ideological dimension but used it very little or were unclear in their use and understanding of the term. A third group of respondents (the largest one—42%) evaluated political candidates and parties in terms of their expected favorability toward particular subgroups within the nation (e.g., "A Republican victory will be better for farmers").

A fourth group of respondents, with even less concern for broad considerations of political policy, were those (about 24%) who emphasized only a single narrow issue, such as social security, war versus peace, taxes, or the nature of the times when one of the political parties had previously governed during a period of national prosperity or depression. Finally, a fifth group of respondents (22.5%) entirely ignored policy issues in making political evaluations. They might mention personal qualities of the candidates (e.g., "honest," or "handsome"), or favor a party without showing any knowledge of its program, or be completely uninterested in politics. The distribution of these groups in the national population is depicted in Table 7–1, which also shows that the more ideological groups were more likely to have voted in the previous presidential election. The dramatic conclusion from this table is that no more than 10%–15% of the population, at most, thinks about political questions in terms of the broad public policy principles or ideological dimensions which underlie many different specific issues.

Converse went on to present evidence that the level of education declined quite regularly from the first to the fifth category. More important for our purposes, the level of political activity also declined dramatically in the same direction. On average, the first category of respondents had over three acts of political participation (e.g., party membership, campaign

TABLE 7–1   Use of Ideological Concepts Among Total National Sample and Among Voters in the 1956 Presidential Election

Ideological category	Total sample	Voters
1. Used ideological dimension clearly	2.5%	3.5%
2. Mentioned ideological dimension (unclear)	9	12
3. Stressed interests of a particular group	42	45
4. Emphasized a single narrow issue	24	22
5. Ignored policy issues completely	22.5	17.5
	100%	100%

Source: Adapted and reprinted with permission of Macmillan Publishing Co., Inc., from Converse, P. E., "The nature of belief systems in mass publics," in D. Apter (Ed.), *Ideology and Discontent*, p. 218. Copyright © 1964 by The Free Press of Glencoe, a Division of The Macmillan Co.

contributions, attendance at political rallies, etc.) in addition to voting, whereas the fifth category of respondents had less than one such act.

A number of later studies have used a variety of methods to compare more recent levels of ideological thinking with Converse's findings. For instance, Neuman (1986) found a somewhat similar distribution of people in the five ideological categories, but a substantial increase in the top category (13% used ideological concepts clearly) and a decrease in the bottom category (only 8% ignored issues completely).

Relationships Between Beliefs About Specific Issues

A second major finding in Converse's chapter concerned what he called **constraints** among respondents' beliefs on various political issues. That is, are beliefs interconnected ("constrained") in logically or psycho-logically meaningful patterns? Or, on the contrary, are an individual's beliefs on different political issues isolated into separate clusters— even "logic-tight compartments"—such that beliefs about one issue do not affect beliefs on another issue, even where they may be logically contradictory? This latter viewpoint is the one that Converse emphasized, and it is very similar to Abelson's (1968) theory of isolated "opinion molecules" about a given topic—viewpoints that are not logically interconnected to opinion molecules on other topics.

To support this viewpoint, Converse cited correlational data relating beliefs about seven different political issues in (a) a national cross-section sample, and (b) an elite sample made up of congressional candidates in the 1958 election. There were four domestic issues and three foreign-affairs issues, as follows:

1. Federal programs for full employment
2. Federal aid to education
3. Federal funds for public housing and electric power
4. Federal Fair Employment Practices Commission (FEPC) to prevent discrimination in employment
5. Foreign economic aid
6. Foreign military aid
7. Isolationism versus commitments abroad

In addition, the respondents' party preferences were obtained. Scores on these eight variables were interrelated by use of a statistic called tau–gamma, which yields results similar to but somewhat smaller than conventional correlation coefficients. A summary of the results is shown in Table 7–2.

In interpreting these results, it is important to remember that the cross-section sample contained its fair share (about 10%) of "ideologues" and "near-ideologues," the first two categories of people in Table 7–1, and the structure of their political belief systems might be much more like that of the elite sample than like that of the remainder of the cross-section sample. Thus the difference between the two samples was undoubtedly diminished by the inclusion of some "elites" in the cross-section sample. In spite of that, the difference between the samples was marked. The elite sample showed a much greater degree of structure, that is, higher relationships between beliefs about different issues. The elite sample also showed a markedly higher relationship between party preference and beliefs on the seven issues than did the cross-section sample.

In sum, this finding and many similar ones led Converse to conclude that elites do have a meaningful structure for their political belief systems, but that the "average man" generally does not. Other experts on political behavior have agreed with this point of

TABLE 7–2 Average Relationships ("Constraints") Between Beliefs on Various
Political Issues and Party Preference in Two Samples

Sample	Among domestic issues	Between domestic and foreign issues	Among foreign issues	Between 7 issues and party preference
Elite	0.53	0.25	0.37	0.39
Cross section	0.23	0.11	0.23	0.11

Note: Coefficients are tau–gammas.

Source: Adapted and reprinted with permission of Macmillan Publishing Co., Inc., from Converse, P. E.,
"The nature of belief systems in mass publics," in D. Apter (Ed.), *Ideology and Discontent*, p. 229.
Copyright © 1964 by The Free Press of Glencoe, a division of The Macmillan Co.

view. For instance, a similar comparison of 1978 congressional candidates with voters in
that election found a much higher level of relationship among attitudes toward various
issues in the candidate group than in the general electorate (Bishop & Frankovic, 1981).
In the 1996 National Election Study, a comparison of high-information respondents with
low-information ones showed much higher relationships between policy issues for the
high-information group (as one example, a tau–gamma of 0.66 versus one of 0.07 for the
low-information group—Erikson & Tedin, 2001, p. 73). Citing findings such as these,
Hennessy (1970) even went so far as to state that

> political attitudes are an elite phenomenon. Most people do not have political attitudes. Even
> in modern high-energy societies most people do not have political attitudes. (p. 463)

Importance of Groups in Political Belief Systems

If it is true that most people don't have clearly structured political attitudes, do they
have any substitute for them? Or are they completely without political belief systems?
Converse would not be willing to carry his argument that far, primarily because of the
importance of **reference groups** (either positive or negative), which provide a basis for
the belief systems of many people.

Take the case of a male lathe operator who works in a large factory, has several children
to educate, has a large mortgage on the family home, and has occasionally been laid off from
work for several months when the company was having financial troubles. This person is apt
to organize many beliefs around "what is good for workers" (just as the boss may organize
many beliefs around "what is good for industry"). Thus, if asked, the lathe operator might
favor reducing taxes, but might also favor increasing unemployment benefits, as both of
these measures would be good for workers, his reference group. That would be logical from
this person's standpoint, and it would demonstrate at least a rudimentary type of political
belief system. But note a discrepancy here: The worker's two answers fall on opposite sides
of the major ideological dimension underlying American political positions, liberalism–
conservatism (reducing taxes is a "conservative" position, whereas welfare measures like
unemployment benefits are "liberal" programs). Thus, on Converse's scale, this worker
would not be classified in the top two ideological categories, but in category 3, the group-
benefit category (along with about 40% of the total population—see Table 7–1).

As the third major point in his argument, Converse proposed that, below the well-
informed and ideologically oriented top 10% or so of the population, the main organizing
principle underlying individuals' political beliefs is their attitudes toward major societal

groups. That is, whatever political beliefs such individuals have are apt to be organized around their concept of the interests of their own most important reference group, be it a social class, an ethnic or nationality group, a religious group, a regional group (e.g., Easterners), or an occupation (e.g., farmers).

However, below the top 50% or so of the population, the importance of groups in determining individuals' political beliefs drops off quite rapidly. Converse suggested that this finding is due to the very low level of political information held by individuals in the lower half of the distribution. They literally know so little about most political issues that they can't determine how the issue would affect their own group, even when they are aware of being a member of a group that has common interests. As an example, many Americans who know that they are members of the working class have so little information about the political party platforms and policies that they cannot tell whether a Democratic or a Republican victory would benefit them. As a result, they form their political opinions on the basis of isolated issues, such as which party will lower taxes (these individuals fall in category 4 of Table 7–1), or on the basis of such factors as the candidate's attractiveness (these people fall in category 5).

Stability of Beliefs Over Time

A fourth major finding that supports the elitist theory of public opinion concerns the stability of particular political beliefs over time. Saying that a person has a "belief system" implies that most of his or her beliefs will be relatively stable and unchanging over a few-year period, rather than fluctuating markedly from time to time. This question was studied by a longitudinal design in which the same panel of respondents was reinterviewed several times about 2 years apart. They were questioned about political issues such as the seven listed on page 146. The results were dramatic (Converse, 1964):

> Faced with the typical item of this kind, only about 13 people out of 20 manage to locate themselves even on the same *side* of the controversy in successive interrogations, when 10 out of 20 could have done so by chance alone. (p. 239)

By contrast, Converse has deduced from repeated congressional roll-call votes on comparable bills that about 18 out of 20 members of an elite office-holder sample would show stable opinions over time. Thus you can see that there is a marked difference in the temporal stability of political beliefs, with elites being highly stable in beliefs and mass samples being quite changeable over time. This conclusion was corroborated more recently in a comparison of political elites (delegates to the Democratic and Republican national conventions) and members of the mass public (Jennings, 1992).

A further question may be raised as to which beliefs are most stable and which most changeable. Of all the items reported, one was by far the most stable—party preference, with a tau–beta reliability coefficient of more than +0.7. This stability of people's party identification was one of the major findings of *The American Voter*. By contrast, all of the seven issues listed on page 146 had tau–beta reliability coefficients close to +0.3 or +0.4, indicating some continuing temporal stability but also a great deal of change over the 2-year period. The issue that had the highest stability (close to +0.5) was an item about federal action to promote school desegregation, and the next highest in stability were the items concerning a federal FEPC and federal programs for full employment. Converse (1964) concluded that

> stability declines as the referents of the attitude items become increasingly remote, from jobs, which are significant objects to all, and Negroes, who are attitude objects for most, to items involving ways and means of handling foreign policy. (p. 241)

When a third interview was held with the respondents, 4 years after the first interview, another fascinating finding emerged. The data showed that the "turnover correlations" between the same beliefs at three different points in time remained very nearly the same from one time to the next. This meant that a person's opinions at time 3 could be predicted just as well from his or her opinions at time 1 as from those at time 2. This was a surprising finding because test–retest correlations usually tend to decrease with longer time intervals between the original test and the retest, as one would expect if opinion change is a relatively steady or continuous process.

Analyzing the obtained pattern of turnover correlations further with complex statistical techniques, Converse found that they could be explained quite well by an "all-or-none" model of stability. That model postulated that some respondents had clear-cut opinions that were perfectly stable over time, whereas others (a much larger group) had no opinion in any meaningful sense and were just as likely to change their response randomly when reinterviewed as to give the same response a second time. This "all-or-none" model fit the obtained pattern of turnover correlations on one issue perfectly, and it came close to a perfect fit on the other issues as well. Converse suggested that it needed only a slight modification, adding the postulate of a *small* third group of genuine converts, to make it fit the data for all the issues measured.

This is a very important finding, for it indicates once again in a new way that on any given issue the public can be meaningfully divided into a small elite group of the well-informed and a large mass of politically naive individuals. Moreover, this finding goes further and says that most of the latter group have *no meaningful opinions at all*, for the changes in their responses over time were completely random in nature. As Converse (1964) summarized the conclusion:

> large portions of an electorate do not have meaningful beliefs, even on issues that have formed the basis for intense political controversy among elites for substantial periods of time. (p. 245)

Later analyses of political opinion stability over the 1972–1974–1976 elections have produced similarly low stability estimates for the overall population, though some moral attitudes (e.g., toward marijuana or abortion) were found to have higher stability, and party identification remained very stable (Converse & Markus, 1979). Other studies also agree that there has been little change in the stability of Americans' political opinions since Converse's early research (Abramson, 1983), and similar low levels of stability have been found in survey research of the British and French populaces (Butler & Stokes, 1974; Converse & Pierce, 1986).

In further research on the stability of attitudes, a new method of measuring stability was introduced in the 1990s. It records precise measures of the time that a respondent takes to answer attitude questions in a computer-assisted telephone interview. Thus it uses the same response-time procedure to study explicit attitudes that was pioneered in the measurement of implicit attitudes discussed in Chapter 4. Data obtained by use of this technique "lend support to [Converse's] notion that stable preferences are due principally to crystallized attitudes . . . while unstable preferences result when those without such attitudes improvise their answers" (Bassili & Fletcher, 1991, p. 344).

This reference to "improvising answers" alludes to another reason for the apparent instability of many people's attitudes. A number of authors have suggested that most people's survey answers are the result of an on-line **construction process**, basing responses on whichever of their relevant beliefs and feelings are most salient or accessible at the moment they are asked for their opinion (e.g., Zaller, 1992; Nayakankuppan & Priester, 2003). This viewpoint harks back to our discussion in Chapter 2 of *schemas* as a shorthand

Photograph courtesy of Philip Converse.
Reprinted by permission.

Box 7–2 PHILIP CONVERSE, *Analyst of Political Attitudes*

Widely known for his research on political behavior, Philip Converse spent many years as Professor of Sociology and of Political Science at the University of Michigan, and served terms as director of the Center for Political Studies there and of its parent body, the Institute for Social Research. Born in 1928 in New Hampshire, he earned a B.A. at Denison University, studied in France, served in the Army, and took his Ph.D. in social psychology at the University of Michigan in 1958. He remained there on its faculty for over 30 years, authoring numerous, widely cited books and articles. In 1989 he moved to Stanford University to become director of the Center for Advanced Study in the Behavioral Sciences for 5 years and then a trustee there until 2000.

Converse is most famous for his books on voting written with Campbell, Miller, and Stokes: The American Voter, *and* Elections and the Political Order, *which are cited in Chapters 13 and 14 and elsewhere in this book. He also coauthored a social psychology text, wrote pivotal papers on the structure of public opinion which are described in this chapter, and collaborated on* The Quality of American Life, *discussed in Chapter 13. Converse's research was honored by his election to the American Academy of Arts and Sciences as well as the National Academy of Sciences. He also served as president of the American Political Science Association and the International Society of Political Psychology, and received the distinguished achievement award of the American Association for Public Opinion Research.*

basis for thinking about social groups and issues. For instance, Tesser (1978) has written that

> An attitude at a particular point in time is the result of a constructive process.... And, there is not a single attitude toward an object but, rather, any number of attitudes depending on the number of schemas available for thinking about the objects. (pp. 297–298)

Every Issue Has Its Own Public

The final major conclusion of Converse's chapter was that there is not just one political elite group, but there are different **issue publics** for different topics. This means that each important political issue has its own group of interested citizens, partially unique and partially overlapping other issue publics. On major topics, these issue publics vary in size from about 20% to about 40% of the total population. A tiny group of people were found to be members of all eight issue publics that Converse studied, and many individuals were not concerned nor informed about any of the issues. Most people were members of only a few of the issue publics; for instance, they might be concerned about racial issues but not about economic ones nor about foreign affairs.

THE MASS-POLITICS VIEW OF PUBLIC OPINION

Having discussed the major research findings supporting the elitist view of public opinion, we turn now to its antithesis, which we term the **mass-politics** viewpoint. Here some of the best-known contributions have been Robert Lane's (1962) book, *Political Ideology*, and his later writings (1973). Lane argued that common men and women do have political ideologies, though they may not be expressed as easily and articulately as the elites'. However, as he himself recognized, his method of in-depth interviews with a few individuals can only provide suggestive evidence but not prove his case (1962, p. 4). Other researchers have found support for the same theoretical viewpoint with empirical work in several areas.

In general, adherents of the mass-politics view do not dispute most of the evidence concerning political belief systems that we have already summarized. Rather, they interpret its meaning differently and present additional evidence that tends to throw a different light on the question. They comprise a diverse collection of critics of the elitist view, each stressing certain kinds of arguments. The several types of research evidence that are discussed in the following sections can be classified as having one or another of three main bases: (a) the pluralism or variety of ideologies, (b) methodological problems and refinements, or (c) changes in the political characteristics of the American public (Neuman, 1986).

Core Values Instead of Ideologies

One criticism of the elitist viewpoint stresses that many people make sense out of political issues and events by relating them to their own key values instead of classifying them ideologically. "While individuals may not have an overarching ideology, they do hold enduring and strong core values and beliefs" (Alvarez & Brehm, 2002, p. 7). **Core values** are deeply held, enduring, and oftentimes widely shared standards in life. Such central values might include equality and freedom, as proposed by Rokeach (1973), or individualism or humanitarianism (cf. Feldman & Zaller, 1992), or capitalism, piety, industriousness, or many others.

Any one of these core values may be invoked in determining a person's stand on a political issue, such as tax cuts or welfare programs. However, a person can have many such values, which are likely to be at least partially conflicting, and holding conflicting values frequently leads people to be ambivalent in their views about public policy issues (Feldman & Zaller, 1992). Also, conflicting values are hard to sum up systematically in a generally consistent viewpoint such as an ideology. Thus, in this respect the core values approach does not dispute the key tenet of the elitist position, which is that many people do not think in ideological terms.

A Search for Other Ideological Dimensions

Another approach that departs only modestly from the elitist viewpoint is to search for alternative ideological dimensions, other than the liberal–conservative one, around which individuals' political beliefs might be organized. Because only 10% or 15% of the population are verbally articulate about their ideological viewpoints, as Converse has shown, this search has usually taken the form of examining empirical correlations between different political beliefs in a large population, rather than asking people directly about their ideologies.

An increasingly widespread methodological approach used in many such studies is **secondary analysis** of data already collected and analyzed in other ways by another investigator—for instance, the huge repository of successive national sample survey data collected by the SRC at the University of Michigan.

A good example of a secondary-analysis study that focused on ideological dimensions was conducted by Axelrod (1967), using SRC data from the 1956 election. In that survey a national sample of nearly 1,800 persons had been asked, among many other questions, about their beliefs on 16 political issues, including the 7 listed previously in this chapter. Campbell et al. (1960) had reported the results in terms of two clusters of issues, a welfare scale and a foreign-policy scale, both of which had rather weak interrelationships among their several items (the average r between items within each cluster was less than $+0.3$). Moreover, there was no relationship at all between these two scales (average r very close to 0.0). This finding had demonstrated once again that there was no clear liberal–conservative dimension underlying most people's political views, because a liberal on welfare issues was no more likely to be liberal on foreign-policy issues than he or she was to be conservative on them.

In his reanalysis of these same 16 political issues, Axelrod found a single cluster of interrelated items that he termed a **populism** cluster because of its similarity to the principles of the American Populist political movement of the 1890s. This cluster included more issues (six), and the issues had slightly stronger intercorrelations than either of the clusters analyzed by Campbell et al. The American Populist movement had advocated domestic social reforms but was opposed to foreigners and to U.S. foreign involvement. Similarly, Axelrod's populist cluster of items favored federal programs for full employment, aid to education, and medical care, but also favored tax cuts and the firing of suspected Communists, and opposed U.S. foreign involvement. Perhaps most surprisingly, this cluster of issues had its strongest intercorrelations for the subsample of *nonvoters* in the total sample. The cluster was less coherent for more politically active and informed individuals, and it had the lowest intercorrelations for the college graduate subsample.

Axelrod emphasized that, for a large segment of the American public, "domestic liberalism is not correlated with internationalism," and his evidence for the populism dimension of political attitudes showed that "much of the public views policy questions as they were seen in the 1890s and not the 1930s" (1967, p. 59).

A later study of people's attitudes toward 12 political issues, using the statistical technique of cluster analysis, found, rather than a single liberal–conservative dimension, a variety of ideological patterns (Fleishman, 1986). In addition to liberals and conservatives, it identified distinct groups of people who were primarily prolabor, or who advocated limited government, or who were middle-of-the-road on government economic policies.

Another possible ideological dimension, as an alternative to liberalism–conservatism, is **libertarianism**, a viewpoint that opposes government intervention in both economic and social realms. Libertarians tend to be "conservative on economic issues and liberal on life-style issues" (Zaller, 1992, p. 27). However, their numbers in the U.S. are small enough that they rarely show up in research on political ideology.

Measurement Problems

A different critique of the elitist viewpoint has emphasized that vague and/or ambiguous questions, and the resulting low reliability in measurement of attitudes on various political issues, contribute markedly to the apparent lack of stability in people's attitudes on these issues over time. One proposed solution that has shown promise is posing questions in ways that reduce their apparent ambiguity (Krosnick & Berent, 1993). Another approach is correcting for the unreliability of measurement of respondents' issue attitudes, in order to determine what the "true" stability of attitudes would be if they were measured without any error. There are several complex statistical ways of estimating such corrections, and all of them that have been tried yield substantially higher estimates of attitude stability—in other words, lower estimates of the number of respondents whose attitude reports are haphazard or meaningless (Achen, 1975; Erikson, 1979; Inglehart, 1985). Judd and Milburn (1980) stated such a conclusion:

> Both the highly educated and the uneducated public show evidence of an underlying ideological predisposition, show remarkable stability in their attitudes, and show equal consistency or constraint between different attitude areas. (p. 627)

However, these various statistical techniques produce somewhat differing results, and their application has provoked sharp controversies in the research literature (e.g., Converse, 1980; Judd, Krosnick, & Milburn, 1981). Converse and Markus (1979) analyzed the longitudinal data from the Center for Political Studies 1972–1974–1976 election panel study, and concluded that there had been little change in the political-attitude stability of the American public since the 1950s. Unfortunately, this historical comparison is tenuous because of intervening changes in item response format and wording (Abramson, 1983); these changes are described later in this chapter in the section on attitude consistency. In a review of this issue, Kinder and Sears (1985) concluded that findings of attitude instability partly indicate a real phenomenon, but are also partly due to difficulties in accurate attitude measurement.

Consistency Within Single Individuals. A different methodological objection to the evidence for the elitist viewpoint was offered by Bennett (1975), following the conceptual approach of Lane (1973). Both authors stressed that various individuals may organize their political attitudes in different ways—that is, using a variety of dimensions, not just liberalism–conservatism or populism. Also, for each person, some topics may represent "nonissues"—questions that the individual hasn't thought about and has no opinion about. Other, more recent authors have also stressed the heterogeneous ways in which people decide about political issues (e.g., Sniderman, Brody, & Tetlock, 1991).

This individualistic conception of belief organization suggests the need for a different research methodology to investigate it. Whereas Converse studied the consistency of attitudes *on each separate issue* across a large number of people, Bennett (1975) advocated studying the consistency of attitudes *within each person* on a large number of political issues. The difference in results for these two methods is dramatic. Using 20 specific political issues, including Converse's familiar 7, Bennett found test–retest stability figures *across people* that were very similar to Converse's (1964) findings—correlations ranging from about +0.1 to +0.4, even though the respondents were college students and the retest was only three weeks after initial testing. However, when the stability of attitudes *within individuals* was examined (that is, stability in which ideas they evaluated most favorably and most unfavorably), the average test–retest correlation was an impressively high +0.74. Bennett (1975) concluded that "not all people make sense of politics in the same way, but most people make sense of politics in some way" (p. 25).

Use of Heuristics

A fourth line of attack on the elitist viewpoint is to propose that a large part of the populace thinks heuristically about political topics rather than ideologically. **Heuristics**, as we described in Chapter 2, are shortcut routes that people can use in making decisions. As described by Sniderman et al. (1991):

> Citizens frequently can compensate for their limited information about politics by taking advantage of judgmental heuristics. . . . [In so doing] people can be knowledgeable in their reasoning about political choices without necessarily possessing a large body of knowledge about politics. (p. 19)

A common way to use heuristics here is to rely on some source that one trusts—presumably a better-informed one—for guidance on how to think about a topic or vote on a candidate (Kinder, 1998). This process relies more on one's affect or emotions than on any detailed cognitive reasoning. That is, one merely has to know what sources one likes and/or trusts, and adopt their views.

Sniderman et al. (1991) suggested that both politically sophisticated elites and common citizens use affect and heuristics in their political decision making. They proposed two main heuristics that people use in this process: The *likability heuristic* focuses on how one feels toward a particular social group that is involved in a political issue (e.g., flood victims), and the *desert heuristic* focuses on whether that group deserves help, a feeling that is based on one's attributions about the causes for the group's predicament (e.g., are particular flood victims innocent sufferers, or should they have known better than to build houses in a flood plain?).

Emphasis on Parties Instead of Issues

A heuristic guide that many people use in considering public issues is the views of a political party or some other group that they identify closely with. This approach downgrades the importance of *policy issues* as major aspects of political attitudes. It posits that, instead of being oriented around the details of policies or issues, the mass public's belief systems are more rudimentary, less detailed, and less differentiated (Wilker & Milbrath, 1970). They are apt to be organized around individuals' *party identification* (Democratic or Republican) or their loyalty to one or another group (unions, farmers, Catholics, blacks, etc.), whose perceived interests influence their vote and their political attitudes.

The importance of a person's party identification for his or her political belief systems was stressed by Kirkpatrick (1970a, 1970b). Reanalyzing data from SRC election surveys, he developed a measure of an individual's "total partisan affect" (the number of things that the individual liked better about one party and its presidential candidate than about the other party and candidate). Then, following a balance theory model, he showed that there was a high degree of consistency among individuals' party identification, their total partisan affect, and the candidate for whom they intended to vote. In a sample of more than 1,500, 86% of individuals were consistent and only 14% were inconsistent (for instance, one inconsistent pattern would have been Republican party identification, but partisan affect favoring the Democratic side and an intention to vote for the Democratic presidential candidate). Thus Kirkpatrick showed that when party identification is considered instead of specific policy issues, an overwhelming majority of the population have consistent political attitudes.

Kirkpatrick (1970a) carried the emphasis on parties as a source of attitude consistency a step farther by relating (a) individuals' *issue* positions to (b) their party identification, and

(c) their beliefs about the parties' stands on the same issues. He reanalyzed SRC election survey data for four of the domestic issues discussed earlier in this chapter, examining the responses of relatively small subsets of the total population who had an interest in one or another of these issues ("issue publics"). Within these select groups, he found that consistency among the three belief elements ranged from 83% to 90% for different issues.

From such studies the conclusion seems clear that party preference forms the foundation for consistent political attitudes in a large majority of the population, regardless of whether these individuals have information or beliefs about specific issues. Similarly, people's liking or disliking for other groups in society (e.g., racial or religious groups) has been shown to help determine their political attitudes on particular issues (Brady & Sniderman, 1985). Of course, Converse would classify such group- or party-linked political attitudes at the third level of Table 7–1, as group-related rather than ideological. In Chapters 13 and 14 we will consider further data from recent studies comparing party identification, policy issues, and candidate images as influences on individual voting decisions.

Attitude Structure on Local Issues

A fourth objection to the elitist viewpoint stresses that average citizens may be a good deal more interested in local issues than they are in national or international ones. For instance, Luttbeg (1968) studied attitudes toward 10 issues such as urban renewal, bringing in new industry, annexation of suburbs, creation of a metropolitan park along the major river in the area, and so forth. He sampled over 1,200 representative citizens in two Oregon cities and 117 community leaders from the same two cities, who were selected by a reputational technique. Using the technique of factor analysis, he found that five different conceptual dimensions were needed to explain the structure of attitudes on these 10 issues. These five factors did explain a large amount of the variance (74%) in the attitudes of community leaders, but they also explained nearly as much (65%) of the variance in the citizens' attitudes. Luttbeg concluded, contrary to the elitist viewpoint, that community leaders' attitudes on these local issues were complex (based on several different dimensions) rather than unidimensional (e.g., based on a single liberal–conservative continuum), and second, that average citizens' attitudes on local issues were very nearly as highly structured as the leaders' attitudes.

Salient Issues—A Better Methodology

Another objection to the elitist viewpoint is that most studies have not allowed respondents to specify issues that were important (salient) to them (Litwak, Hooyman, & Warren, 1973). In 1960 the SRC election surveys rectified this situation by adding to their previous closed-ended (multiple-choice) questions a new set of open-ended questions. These questions asked respondents to describe in their own words any "problems you think the government in Washington should do something about," how worried they were about these problems, and which party they thought would be most likely to do what they wanted done about the problems. The interviewees' free responses were coded into about 25 different categories, and the results were studied by RePass (1971).

RePass analyzed primarily the high-salience issues, that is, ones that respondents were very worried about. He did this because he found that below this level of salience there was a lower level of information about the issue and a poorer perception of party differences concerning it. Thus he was essentially dealing solely with a concerned "issue public" on each issue, and one that had volunteered its concern without any prior cues from

TABLE 7–3   Relationship of Party Identification to Perception of Party's "Issue Advantage" in 1964 Election

Party having perceived "issue advantage"	Party Identification				
	Strong Democrat (N = 332)	Weak Democrat (N = 308)	Independent (N = 272)	Weak Republican (N = 175)	Strong Republican (N = 150)
Democratic	78%	53%	39%	26%	7%
No perceived difference	14	26	26	27	11
Republican	8	21	35	47	82
	100%	100%	100%	100%	100%

Source: Adapted from RePass (1971, p. 399).

the interviewer. It is interesting to note the content of these high-salience problems. In 1960, 62% of them were in the area of foreign affairs and defense (largely problems in relation to Communism), whereas in 1964, 60% concerned domestic issues (most prominently, racial problems).

In general these issue publics perceived differences in the party positions concerning the issues which they mentioned, and they showed a fairly accurate perception of these party differences despite some tendency toward distorted perception favoring their own preferred party. As shown in Table 7–3, there was a very strong relationship between their party identification and their perception of which party could handle their salient issues better; however, a minority of individuals from each party perceived the other party as better on the issues than their own party. Going beyond the table, it is interesting to note that, among respondents for whom this "issue advantage" strongly favored the other party, over 90% ended up voting against their own party. In other words, when issues are important to individuals, and when they can see a clear difference between party positions on these issues, they do tend very strongly to vote in accordance with their issue belief.

The overall relationship between these individuals' perception of a party's "issue advantage" and their presidential vote was +0.57 (tau–beta). By way of comparison, the relationship between their vote and their overall attitude toward the candidates was almost identical (tau–beta = +0.60); and this was in 1964, when attitudes toward the candidates were unusually salient (Kessel, 1968). RePass (1971) concluded that:

> When we allow voters to define their own issue space, they are able to sort out the differences between parties with a fair degree of accuracy.... [W]e have shown that the public is in large measure concerned about specific issues, and that these cognitions have a considerable impact on electoral choice. (p. 400)

Findings similar to these have led several later investigators and reviewers to conclude that, despite the acknowledged limitations in individual citizens' political knowledge and reasoning, *aggregate* public opinion on important issues generally changes in ways that are coherent and rational (e.g., Page & Shapiro, 1992; Kinder, 1998; Glynn et al., 1999). Converse (1996) has agreed that the lack of ideological thinking among most citizens does not prevent these rational aggregate patterns of public attitude change from occurring in response to changing conditions of the times.

Temporal Increases in Ideology

Another basis for criticism of the elitist viewpoint is the claim that the American public has become much more ideological since the 1950s, when Converse's original research was done. Those were the years of Eisenhower's presidency, when partisan politics and ideological disputes were quite muted in comparison with those of later elections. Several research teams have provided evidence that the number of Americans who used ideological concepts increased markedly in the elections of 1964 through 1972 (e.g., A. Miller et al., 1976; Nie, Verba, & Petrocik, 1979, 1981). This change paralleled the sharply increased issue-based voting produced by the ideological disparities between the candidates and platforms in those elections (i.e., in the 1964 contest between Johnson and Goldwater, in George Wallace's third-party candidacy in 1968, and in the 1972 election between Nixon and McGovern).

The strongest proponents of this increased-ideology viewpoint were Nie, Verba, and Petrocik (1979), in their book *The Changing American Voter*. They computed the percentage of ideologues and near-ideologues (the top two levels in Converse's classification) as totaling over 45% in each of these three elections (Nie et al., 1981). However, their coding scheme was substantially different from the one used by Converse, and most analyses by other researchers have reached less-extreme conclusions, putting the total figure for ideologues and near-ideologues for those years close to 25%. This is about twice the 1956 level reported by Converse (1964), and he agrees that there was a substantial increase in Americans' ideological thinking in the 1960s and 1970s (Converse, 1975). This increase was probably due in part to the rising educational levels of the populace and in part to the political battles of the 1960s over civil rights and the Vietnam War.

Since 1972, the level of ideological thinking in the American public seems to have decreased somewhat and then stabilized, with ideologues and near-ideologues totaling around 20% of respondents. In these elections into the 1990s, about 30% of the public stressed group interests, about 30% emphasized a single issue or the nature of the times, and about 20% ignored policy issues altogether (Erikson & Tedin, 2001, p. 70). In summarizing the disputes about levels of ideological thinking, Kinder (1998) concluded that:

> Converse's original claim of ideological naiveté stands up well, both to detailed reanalysis and to political change. . . . most citizens continue to be mystified by or at least indifferent to ideological terminology. (p. 794)

Increases in Attitude Consistency?

A final criticism of the elitist viewpoint took aim at Converse's (1964) emphasis on most people's low levels of political attitude consistency ("constraint"). Nie and Andersen (1974) and Nie et al. (1979) demonstrated that the average relationship between attitudes on different issues (i.e., "constraint") rose markedly between 1960 and 1964, stayed high through 1972, and declined somewhat in 1976. However, the importance of this finding has been challenged because there was a concurrent change in 1964 in the response format and wording of the questions used by the SRC to measure respondents' issue attitudes (from a 5-choice Likert format to a dichotomous pro–con choice). Although these changes seemed innocuous at the time, careful later experiments with question wording demonstrated that they were sufficient to account for *all* of the apparent increase in issue consistency (Bishop et al., 1978; Sullivan, Piereson, & Marcus, 1978).

Following that demonstration, Nie and his colleagues came to agree that their earlier finding was a methodological artifact, and that there has not been any long-term increase in citizens' issue consistency (Nie & Rabjohn, 1979). Because neither question format is clearly better, it is hard to say whether the "true" level of consistency of the population is as low as Converse's research with the original items indicated, or as high as the more-reliable new items suggest. However, a review by Kinder and Sears (1985) favored the newer items and the conclusion that, all along, the American public has *not* been so distressingly low in issue consistency. Likewise, appreciable levels of political attitude consistency have been reported in the British populace (Himmelweit et al., 1981).

RESOLUTION OF THE CONTROVERSY

It is possible to resolve the controversy between the elitist and the mass-politics view-points, at least in part. Converse (1964) himself emphasized that he was *not* claiming that:

> poorly educated people have no systems of beliefs about politics . . . . We do not disclaim the existence of entities that might best be called "folk ideologies," nor do we deny for a moment that strong differentiations in a variety of narrower values may be found within subcultures of less educated people. (pp. 255–256)

Rather, he asserted that, below the top elite fraction of the population (10% to 25%, depending on one's calculations and the year in question):

> Instead of a few wide-ranging belief systems that organize large amounts of specific information, one would expect to find a proliferation of clusters of ideas among which little constraint is felt, even, quite often, in instances of sheer logical constraint. (p. 213)

What can supporters of the mass-politics view add to this conclusion? First, they would agree strongly that the average person does have beliefs, values, and ideas about some aspects of public affairs. Second, they would probably agree that on national and international issues of government policy, the average person's attitudes are less clear and consistent than the elite's, and less likely to be organized along a liberal–conservative dimension. Third, they would point to a variety of core values and to heuristic decision methods as important factors in most people's political attitudes. Fourth, they would suggest the presence of a populist ideology or other ideological dimensions among many members of the mass public, and they would stress the importance of political parties and other reference groups as central elements around which many average citizens organize a consistent set of political attitudes.

Fifth, critics of the elitist view would point to local issues, and also issues that are highly salient to the individual, as areas where the mass public's political attitudes are apt to be very nearly as well-organized and coherent as the elite's. Sixth, they would cite the increasing education levels of the American public (Bishop, 1976) and the issue-oriented character of the elections after 1960 as two factors that have raised the overall level of ideological thinking of the populace. Seventh, they would claim that consistency of political attitudes among the mass public has always been higher than Converse concluded, but that this fact was obscured by the unfortunate choice of attitude measures used in the early studies. Also, they would stress the measurement problems resulting from use of vague or ambiguous questions, and point out that, when computations are corrected to compensate for unreliability of measurement, the stability of political attitudes over time is substantially higher than earlier reported. All of these points tend to support the view that many common citizens do have a meaningful political ideology.

Finally, a resolution between the elitist view and the mass-politics view of public opinion might point out that in our complex modern world no one can be well-informed in all the areas that touch on one's daily life, so a large degree of ignorance is inevitable for everyone. In this situation, it makes sense to concentrate on the knowledge and opinions that are important in one's own job and to turn over most responsibility for other areas of life to people who are seen as experts in those areas (doctors in health questions, legislators in politics, community leaders in local issues, etc.). It is simply not functional for most people to develop an integrated system of political information and attitudes concerning issues that do not closely affect their everyday lives. This viewpoint has been stressed by Lane (1973) and by Litwak et al. (1973), who gave the following example of the unmanageable complexity of modern life:

> To deal with the problems of water supply in a city like New York, knowledge of at least five major bureaucracies is necessary. If someone had no water, he would contact the health department; if not enough water—the department of water supply; if no hot water or water leaks—the buildings department; if these were major water leaks—the department of water supply; if water was overflowing from the apartment above—the police department; if there was water sewage in the cellar—the sanitation department. (p. 330)

Tying the preceding points back to our discussion of attitude structure and functions in Chapter 5, we can conclude that attitudes serve the same general functions for members of the mass public as for political elites. However, it is much less likely (and less necessary) for political beliefs and attitudes to be central and salient in the belief systems of the average citizen than in those of the highly educated, of community leaders, and of people who are employed in politics or active in political affairs.

SUMMARY

Although the "informed citizen" is often claimed to be a necessary ingredient of democratic government, most citizens in our society are not very well-informed. A few items of knowledge are very widespread, but most are not. The *salient* bits of information that known to almost everyone are ones that have been very prominently in the news, that are unique and different from other events, and that have continued to receive public attention over long periods of time.

In the field of public affairs, *exposure* to terms and events (such as the Enron scandal or genocide in Rwanda or the former Yugoslavia) is much more widespread than factual knowledge about them, and knowledge about specific public issues and policies is almost always confined to a minority of the population—often a very small minority. Each important political issue has its own group of informed and involved citizens, called an *issue public*.

The *elitist* view of public opinion holds that only the "elite," the top 10% to 25% of the public, have political attitudes and belief systems that provide a broad and coherent basis for understanding public affairs. Only these elites use ideological concepts (such as liberalism–conservatism) in discussing public affairs, and their attitudes on political issues are much more stable over time and more closely connected to relevant beliefs and attitudes on other issues than are those of the rest of the populace. Below this elite level, attitudes toward major societal groups (e.g., union members, blacks, the middle class, a political party) provide a major focus for organizing whatever political attitudes are present. Many people's answers to survey questions really represent *nonattitudes*, which are constructed on the spot, based on whatever relevant beliefs and feelings are momentarily accessible, rather than being firmly held views.

The *mass-politics* view of public opinion generally does not dispute the facts cited by the elitist proponents, but does interpret them differently and add many other sorts of evidence. For instance, measurement problems have resulted from potentially ambiguous questions, and correcting computations to compensate for unreliability of measurement yields substantially higher estimates of the stability of political attitudes over time. Other methodological studies have shown high consistency in political attitudes within individuals, though different individuals may differ widely in the dimensions they use to judge political issues. Some of those dimensions are various core values and others are heuristic shortcuts, such as following the lead of trusted groups or sources. For example, political party preference is a key factor which forms the foundation for consistent political attitudes in a large portion of the population, many of whom are not concerned about specific policy issues. Other evidence shows that, for local community issues and for issues that are highly salient to the individuals concerned, the mass public's attitudes are apt to be very nearly as well-organized as are the elite's. Also, there is general agreement that the U.S. public's level of ideological thinking increased substantially in the 1960s and 1970s and has remained higher than in the early studies of political ideology. These types of findings have helped to diminish the controversy over the political attitudes of the elite versus those of the average citizen.

8

Formation of Attitudes and Opinions

The greatest part of mankind have no other reason for their opinions than that they are in fashion.—Samuel Johnson.

Opinions should be formed with great caution and changed with greater. —Josh Billings.

Attitudes and opinions are usually learned—that much is agreed on by all authorities. But how are they learned? The processes of attitude formation, and the factors that can be important in the development of attitudes, are numerous. Some researchers stress the role of family influences in a child's early years, others underline the importance of the educational system or of peer-group pressures, and still others emphasize the mass media of communication, particularly television. Undoubtedly all of these factors play a part in attitude formation, which may occur through several different learning processes. The research summarized in this chapter has begun the task of classifying and understanding the processes and the determining factors involved.

The term **attitude formation** refers to the initial change from having *no* attitude toward a given object to having *some* attitude toward it, either positive or negative. But what is it like to have no attitude toward an object? For an infant, the situation was described by William James as a world of "blooming, buzzing confusion" in which all stimuli are new and strange. For adults to have no attitude might mean that they have never had any experience, either direct or vicarious, with the object (for instance, your attitude toward "Cromelians," a group of people you have never heard of), or simply that they have never thought evaluatively about it (an example might be your attitude toward the planet Jupiter).

Starting from this zero point, what determining factors can cause a person to acquire an attitude toward Cromelians or toward Jupiter? In answering that question we consider several different factors, starting with internal and personal determinants and moving toward external influences. Then in the latter part of the chapter we briefly examine the various *processes of learning* by which a new attitude or opinion may be acquired.

First, one distinction is needed. Attitude formation and attitude change are often hard to distinguish from each other and are therefore often spoken of together, as if they were synonymous. Indeed, many of the same processes and influences are at work when attitudes and opinions are being changed as when they were originally formed. However, the research literature on attitude change, which is voluminous, involves a variety of issues and methods that differ from much of the work on attitude formation. Because the topic of attitude change is taken up in two subsequent chapters, this chapter focuses primarily on attitude formation. However, in some cases where the amount of available research evidence is small, we occasionally cite studies of attitude change in this chapter as well.

WHAT LEADS TO ATTITUDE FORMATION?

Because an attitude is a predisposition to respond favorably or unfavorably toward a given object (person, idea, etc.), you can't have an attitude until you have some feeling about the object in question, and feelings are usually based on at least some fragmentary information. Thus an attitude *may* be formed if your early experience with an object elicits a favorable or unfavorable feeling about it. However, oftentimes early experience and information concerning an object may not be accompanied by evaluative feelings, and if so, no attitude would yet exist toward the object. What then would lead to formation of an attitude?

In a theoretical analysis of attitude and opinion formation, Gerard and Orive (1987) stressed that a key circumstance for attitude formation is that the person expects to interact with the object and needs to be prepared for that interaction. They posited that when a person expects to interact soon with an object, the person feels an "opinion-forming imperative," which motivates him or her to form a relatively clear evaluative stance toward the object. For instance, you may have met several other students once or twice and noticed a few facts about them without having formed any particular favorable or unfavorable impression. But now if you learn that one of them will be paired with you as a lab partner, you will be motivated to decide which ones you like or dislike. In doing so, you will try to reduce ambivalence toward them. Gerard and Orive concluded that, as your attitude becomes clearer, it will tend to get more strongly favorable or unfavorable.

Similarly, Jamieson and Zanna (1988) have described the "need for cognitive structure" as an important factor in attitude formation. An interesting example of this principle can be seen in people's reactions to the campaign debates between U.S. presidential candidates. Kennamer (1985) found that anticipation of an ensuing discussion was enough to motivate the formation of an attitude in participants who watched a televised presidential debate. In addition, several studies have found that attitudes about candidates are less closely linked to having watched the debates than to participating in discussions about them—with or without having watched them (Lenart, 1994). These findings are consistent with Gerard and Orive's point that we form attitudes because they are functional and necessary in preparing us for our daily interactions.

As a related point, Tybout and Scott (1983) have made a useful theoretical distinction. When individuals have direct sensory information about an object, their attitude toward it will normally be determined by their adding up that information, for instance in ways specified by the theories of Fishbein and Ajzen (1975) or Triandis (1977). However, if their internal knowledge is weak or ambiguous, they may infer their attitude from observation of their own behavior and the surrounding circumstances, as specified in Bem's (1972) self-perception theory. This raises an important issue about attitude formation, and attitudes in general. Traditionally, attitudes have been viewed as existing cognitive structures that are relatively stable across time. However, there are many instances in which a person may not have an existing attitude but, when asked a question, can easily construct one. It is also possible for an individual to have several, partially inconsistent attitudes about the same object.

It is useful here to distinguish between *attitude construction* and attitude formation. Attitude formation is the process by which an individual develops a favorable or unfavorable evaluation of an object. That is, attitude formation is based on experiences that lead a person to hold a specific attitude. In contrast, **attitude construction** is the process by which a person comes to *express* an attitude. As Tesser (1978) and others (Zanna, 1990;

Wilson & Hodges, 1992; Tourangeau et al., 2000) have argued, people may hold many (and in some instances conflicting) attitudes toward an object: "An attitude at a particular point in time is the result of a constructive process.... *there is not a single attitude toward an object* but, rather, any number of attitudes depending on the number of schemas available for thinking about the object" (Tesser, 1978, pp. 297–298). That is, expressing an attitude often involves selecting which of several evaluations that one holds is most relevant and should be stated.

Alternatively, attitude construction can sometimes be the first step toward the formation of an attitude. Consider the situation in which a man is asked about his attitude toward the death penalty. If he has a strong existing attitude, such as one based on direct experience (for example, an acquaintance who was sentenced to the death penalty), it seems likely that he will express this attitude and that it will remain fairly stable across time. However, if this question were asked of a man who had no direct experience with or past evaluative thought about the death penalty, he would need to construct an attitude (Nayakankuppam & Priester, 2003). Wilson and Hodges (1992) suggested that when people construct an attitude they draw from a large database of information, including their past behaviors, their mood, their surroundings, the context in which the question was asked, and a range of beliefs about the attitude object. These points tie our discussion of attitude formation back to the attitude definitions and theories that were discussed in Chapters 1, 2, and 3.

Given these principles and circumstances regarding attitude formation, let us consider the various factors that determine what particular attitudes an individual will form.

GENETIC AND PHYSIOLOGICAL FACTORS

The first type of factor that we consider is a surprising one, for it is rarely mentioned in discussions of attitude formation. Because attitudes are generally agreed to be learned, citing genetic or physiological factors in their formation may sound like support for the fallacious viewpoint that acquired characteristics can be inherited (the discredited theory of the Russian geneticist Lysenko and French biologist Lamarck). However, McGuire (1985) has pointed out that it is often wise to question any universally accepted principle—at the very least, it may have some exceptions that have been overlooked.

In the case of genetic factors in attitude formation, the most plausible way they might operate would be in establishing a *predisposition* for the development of particular attitudes (Tesser, 1993). For instance, there is good evidence for genetic factors determining an organism's general level of aggressiveness, as in Scott and Fuller's (1965) studies of different breeds of dogs. In humans, a person's level of aggressiveness might help to determine his or her attitudes of hostility toward outgroup members, which could be seen in prejudice against other groups (for instance, Arabs or foreigners or teenagers). Such intergroup hostility may once have had survival value, though it appears counterproductive in our nuclear age. Another example of possible genetic influences is the widespread human characteristic of feeling nurturant toward individuals with large head-to-body-length ratios—that is, infants (Alley, 1981). It is important to realize that the notion of genetic determinants of some attitudes does not imply that those attitudes could not be changed under the right environmental conditions, though it might make the change process more difficult (Tesser & Crelia, 1994).

Physiological factors in attitude formation can be seen particularly in such conditions as aging, illnesses, and the effects of various drugs. For instance, there is evidence that as people age they become less open to new ideas and more rigid in their thinking (Schaie & Willis, 1991; Schultz & Searleman, 2002). This gradual decrease in cognitive flexibility is

*Photograph courtesy of Yale University,
Office of Public Information.
Reprinted by permission.*

Box 8–1 WILLIAM McGUIRE, *Psychological Systematizer and Gadfly*

William McGuire has made a multiple reputation in social psychology as an experimental-ist, theorist, systematizer, editor, and administrator. Born in New York in 1925, he served in the Army in World War II, and then received his B.A. and M.A. from Fordham. Moving to Yale for his Ph.D., he was one of the fruitful group of scholars who worked with Carl Hovland in experimental research on communication and attitude change. Following brief periods of teaching at Yale and Illinois, he spent longer periods on the faculty of Columbia and the University of California at San Diego before returning to Yale as chairman of the psychology department in 1971. More than 30 years later, he remains an active faculty member there, writing and doing research on cognitive systems, persuasion processes, and research methods.

McGuire was influential as editor of the Journal of Personality and Social Psychology *from 1968 through 1970. In 1988 he received the Distinguished Scientific Contribution Award of the American Psychological Association, and since 1990 he has published five more research volumes. He was cited in Chapters 1 and 5 for his landmark handbook chapter on attitudes and attitude change, and Chapters 10 and 11 describe his theoretical contributions to consistency approaches, personality research, and resistance to attitude change, as well as his role as a gadfly and prophet for the field.*

likely to affect new attitudes, such as the person's feelings toward a new political candidate or social groups like "yuppies," and ultimately to more conservative political attitudes. Certain illnesses are frequently associated with predispositions to particular attitude states: Encephalitis often increases general aggressiveness, whereas tuberculosis paradoxically seems to increase optimistic attitudes. Such effects are more understandable in light of the attitudinal effects of certain drugs, which are clearly physiological in nature. The euphoria produced by marijuana and the opiate drugs is well-known, as are the calming and anxiety-reducing effects of tranquilizers; so both of these are conducive to forming more favorable attitudes. In sum, it is clear that physiological states can influence people's general levels of aggressiveness and persuasibility and their readiness to adopt certain attitudes.

Evidence that attitudes can have a partially genetic basis can also be found in studies of twins. One approach is to examine the strength of the relationship between the attitudes of twins—comparing identical twins (who share 100% of their genetic material) with fraternal twins (who share 50% of their genes). Such studies have consistently demon-strated a sizable heritability coefficient for many attitudes (Perry, 1973; Eaves, Eysenck, & Martin, 1989; Olson et al., 2001). For example, Olson et al. (2001) compared the attitudes of identical and fraternal twins toward 30 attitude objects. The attitude objects included controversial issues (e.g., euthanasia, death penalty, organized religion), personal activities (e.g., playing chess, exercising, roller coaster rides), and social settings (big parties, athletic activities, being the leader of groups). The participants evaluated each item on a Likert scale from –3 (extremely unfavorable) to +3 (extremely favorable). Analyses showed that 26 of the 30 attitude topics displayed significant genetic effects, with a median heritability coefficient of 0.35. Similar results have been obtained in studies comparing twins (both identical and fraternal) who were raised together with twins who were raised apart (Arvey et al., 1989; Waller et al., 1990; Keller et al. 1992).

In summary, there is considerable evidence for the operation of genetic and physiological factors in the formation of attitudes. However, that does *not* mean that genes or physiology cause specific attitudes—indeed, it seems very unlikely that a specific gene sequence or physiological process could cause favorability or unfavorability toward something such as the death penalty. Rather, genes and physiological factors influence personal characteristics that can serve as mediators or moderators of the relationship between experience and attitude formation. Olson et al. (2001) provided evidence for three such mediating characteristics: sociability, physical attractiveness, and aggressiveness. As an example, consider sociability and attitudes toward leadership, both of which were found to be heritable. Olson et al. (2001) suggested that:

> It is possible that attitudes toward leadership were heritable, in part, because other inherited characteristics led to particular experiences relevant to leadership. For example, perhaps physiologically more attractive persons were treated deferentially and developed more confidence in their leadership abilities. Similarly, perhaps individuals who were naturally outgoing (sociable) gravitated to positions of leadership and developed positive attitudes. (p. 857)

DIRECT PERSONAL EXPERIENCE

No matter what factors may predispose people to adopt particular attitudes, the formation of an attitude still requires experience. The earliest and most fundamental way in which people form attitudes is through direct personal experience with the attitude object. For example, an infant who is given orange juice to drink for the first time is apt to like it because it is sweet, flavorful, pleasantly cool, and filling. Following that encounter, the infant has an attitude toward orange juice that is likely to be confirmed and strengthened with further experience. The child's physiology (e.g., sweetness taste buds, preference for sugar, and desire to satiate hunger) provided the foundation, but it was the experience that led to attitude formation.

Attitudes formed through one's own personal experience with the attitude object are generally stronger than those formed through indirect or vicarious experience (Fazio, 1988). For instance, research shows that they are more likely to influence one's behavior, and more resistant to counterinfluence. As indicated in Chapter 5, a major reason for this is that attitudes based on one's own sensory experience are apt to involve primitive, first-order beliefs. Here we discuss two aspects of personal experience in the formation of attitudes: salient incidents and repeated exposure.

Salient Incidents

Many authors have stressed the importance of salient incidents, particularly traumatic or frightening ones, in the development of attitudes. Psychoanalysts and clinical psychologists have described many phobias that originated in a single traumatic experience, for instance with a runaway horse or a fierce dog. Other examples of single incidents markedly affecting attitudes can be seen in religious conversion experiences (Paloutzian, 1981), which were written about by William James as long ago as 1902, and in the clinical descriptions of war neuroses (e.g., Sargant, 1957). A typical case is that of a naval pilot who crashed in flames on an aircraft carrier's deck, was rescued with relatively minor injuries, but was never able to approach a plane again because of extreme, uncontrollable fear and trembling.

It is easy to understand the importance of traumatic incidents as influences on attitudes (Read, 1983). Fishbein and Ajzen's (1975) attitude theory posits that a person's attitude toward an object at any given time is based on a few (perhaps 5–10) salient beliefs that he or she holds about the object. Obviously, a belief like "It almost killed me" is likely to remain very salient and very powerful in determining the person's attitude for a long time. In the attitude-change literature, a number of studies have shown marked changes in public opinion stemming from a single dramatic event such as President Nixon's precedent-setting trip to mainland China or the assassination of Martin Luther King, Jr. (e.g., Riley & Pettigrew, 1976). However, even the effects of dramatic or traumatic incidents are often counterbalanced by the cumulative effect of other events, leading attitudes to return to their earlier levels.

Repeated Exposure

Another way in which attitudes are often formed is through repeated exposure to an object (or person or idea) over time. The research literature on this topic was recently summarized by Zajonc (2001), who has conducted many experimental studies with his coworkers to clarify how this effect occurs (e.g., Zajonc, 1968a). The essence of the **mere exposure effect** is that repeated exposure to a stimulus object without any associated reinforcement is sufficient to enhance a person's attitude toward the object. This effect operates most strongly during the first few exposures, but attitudes continue to increase in favorability at a gradually slower rate over any number of exposures (see Figure 8–1). In fact, the effect can even occur in situations where people are not aware of being exposed to the stimulus object (Wilson, 1979; Zajonc, 1980; Monahan, Murphy, & Zajonc, 2000).

A number of different theoretical explanations of the mere exposure effect have been suggested (Grush, 1979; Bargh, 2001; Murphy, 2001). Zajonc (2000, 2001) has highlighted three key findings in this research area. First, the changes in preference that result from repeated exposure do not depend on subjective *impressions of familiarity*—that is, a person's preference for the object doesn't require any thought about it. Second, the effect appears, and is even stronger, when the stimuli are presented subliminally (i.e., below a person's detection threshold). These two findings indicate that preferences can exist independently of any beliefs or cognitions about the object. Third, repeated exposure generally leads to an increase in positive mood. For instance, Monahan et al. (2000) found that participants who were repeatedly shown 5 Chinese ideographs (5 times each) reported being in a better mood than participants who were shown 25 different ideographs. In interpreting these findings, Zajonc has proposed that the repeated exposure of a stimulus first leads to an increase in participants' positive mood, and then they associate their positive mood (or possibly their lack of negative mood) with the stimulus.

The attitude-enhancing effect of repeated exposure is not confined to the research laboratory. It has also been found in field studies, such as in elections—there the relative amount of candidates' name exposure often closely predicts the election results (Grush, 1980; Schaffner, Wandersman, & Stang, 1981). Indeed, this principle seems to underlie

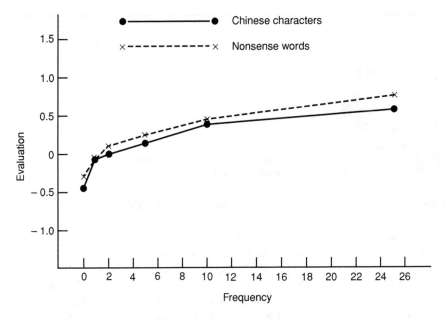

FIGURE 8–1 Relationship between frequency of mere exposure of an object and attitude to it.

Source: Data from Zajonc (1968a); figure reprinted from Fishbein & Ajzen (1975, p. 282). Reprinted by permission of Addison-Wesley Publishing Co.

much commercial advertising and political campaigning. A rather frightening corollary of this principle is that a harmful product or a political demagogue can become more popular just by getting more public exposure, despite their injurious nature. For example, this would suggest that the heightened media coverage of Saddam Hussein in 2003 would lead people to have a more favorable attitude toward him.

Fortunately, this alarming prospect has been shown to be unlikely, for several studies have demonstrated that the attitude-enhancement effect holds only for positive and neutral stimuli, and it may even be reversed for repeated exposure to stimuli that were originally negative in their impact on the individual (Perlman & Oskamp, 1971; Grush, 1976). In addition, it should be remembered that the mere exposure effect is only one of many influences on attitude formation, and it would not be expected to be as strong as many others, for instance the effect of *reward or punishment* associated with exposure to the stimulus. Thus, if the voice of a particular politician always grates on your ears, or you dislike his insincere manner, you are very likely to become less fond of him with repeated exposure, rather than more fond of him.

Another area where repeated exposure has been studied is the effect of interracial or international contact on attitude change (Stephan, 1985). In this area, also, repeated contact can lead to more-favorable or less-favorable attitudes, depending on the presence or absence of several crucial factors. These factors, therefore, are very important to the success of programs designed to reduce prejudice or racial tensions in schools, or to promote international tolerance and understanding (cf. Bochner, 1982; Marcus-Newhall & Heindl, 1998; Stephan & Banks, 1999). A number of authors have emphasized that interracial contact is more likely to lead to increased friendliness if it has most or all of the following characteristics: if it is (a) continued over a long period, (b) felt to be voluntary, (c) in relatively close relationships, (d) in cooperative activities, between individuals having

Photograph courtesy of Robert Zajonc.
Reprinted by permission.

Box 8–2 ROBERT ZAJONC, *Outstanding Experimentalist*

Born in Poland in 1925, Robert Zajonc completed his elementary and secondary education there. After World War II, he escaped to the U.S., quickly learned English, and later became a graduate student at the University of Michigan. Following his Ph.D. in 1955, he became a researcher there at the Research Center for Group Dynamics, where he rose through the academic ranks and eventually became its director, Professor of Psychology, and finally director of the Institute for Social Research. In 1994 he moved to Stanford University, where he continues to write and conduct research.

Known for his elegant experimental work, Zajonc has investigated many topics in addition to his research on the mere exposure effect, mentioned in this chapter. Among them are psychological balance, small-group processes, social facilitation of behavior, effects of birth order, the confluence of emotional and cognitive processes, and animal social behavior. He has served on the editorial boards of 14 journals and written nine books, the most recent of which is Massacres: The Psychology of Mega-Violence. *In 1978 he received the American Psychological Association's Distinguished Scientific Contribution Award.*

(e) equal status, (f) common or supportive goals, and (g) similar belief systems, and in situations that are (h) supported by authorities or by social custom. (Chapters 15 and 16 present more information about the details of international and racial attitudes.)

PARENTAL INFLUENCE

The amount of parental influence over a young child's behavior and attitudes is so great that some authors have referred to childhood as a "total institution," comparable in its degree of control to confinement in a penal institution or a concentration camp. Parents have almost total control over the young child's informational input, the behaviors demanded of the child, and the rewards and punishments meted out. Thus they have great power to shape the child's attitudes, particularly because the infant has no preexisting attitudes that would be contrary to the parental influence.

A child's attitudes are largely shaped by his or her own experience with the world, but much of this experience consists of explicit teaching and implicit modeling of parental attitudes (e.g., "Nice kitty. Kitty won't hurt you. Pet the kitty gently."). Thus many childhood attitudes are probably a combination of the child's own experience and what he or she has heard parents say or seen them do. However, there are many other areas with which the average child has no direct experience at all, and in these areas parental influence on the child's attitudes may be very great. Examples include attitudes toward war, toward foreigners, toward other countries, toward nature and environmental issues, toward political parties and candidates, and toward abstract concepts like freedom and justice.

Gender-role attitudes are greatly influenced by parents' teaching and examples (Ruble & Martin, 1998). Children's gender-role attitudes are positively correlated with the gender-role attitudes of their parents, and with the division of housework they witnessed in their parents (Blee & Tickamyer, 1995; Cunningham, 2001). For instance, children of mothers who were employed outside the home generally have less-traditional attitudes about gender roles than those whose mothers were housewives (Thornton, Alwin, & Camburn, 1983; Blair, 1992). Similarly, daughters whose fathers encouraged their independence and achievement are more likely to undertake and succeed in demanding careers (Hoffman, 1977). The attitudinal influence of parents tends to be stronger for their same-sex children (fathers are a stronger influence on their sons, and mothers on their daughters). (For a fuller discussion of gender-role attitudes, see Chapter 17.)

Prejudice and racial attitudes are prominent areas in which parental influence has been studied. Many studies have shown that, by age 4, children usually know about and endorse cultural stereotypes (Augoustinos & Rosewarne, 2001). Also, research shows that, in general, children's level of prejudice is related to their parents' prejudice and that, at least in part, they take over that prejudice directly (Ashmore & Del Boca, 1976). In addition, it is quite possible for children to learn from parental behavior indirectly and without any intentional teaching. Once learned, prejudiced attitudes tend to be generalized to many outgroups, so there are high positive correlations among the levels of prejudice toward various different minority groups such as blacks, Chicanos, Jews, Japanese, and so forth (Frenkel-Brunswik & Havel, 1953). However, as children grow older, there are many other influences on their attitudes in addition to their parents, and by adolescence the degree of parent–child similarity is only a low positive one.

Many studies have attempted to trace children's development of prejudice to the child-rearing methods used by their parents. There is general agreement that emotionally cold, status-oriented parents who stress obedience, discipline, and physical punishment are likely to have highly prejudiced and authoritarian children (Adorno et al., 1950). However, research has not clarified whether this effect occurs indirectly, through the psychodynamic mechanisms posited in *The Authoritarian Personality* (i.e., that harsh childrearing produces children with low tolerance for frustration and high repressed hostility, which later generate prejudiced ethnic attitudes). A plausible alternative view is that these children learn their prejudice directly by identifying with and copying their parents' attitudes and behavior (Peterson, Smirles, & Wentworth, 1997; Peterson & Duncan, 1999). In any case, there is clear evidence that authoritarian attitudes are generally established during childhood and persist across a substantial period of a person's life (Vollebergh, 1996). The research also shows that boys and men are more authoritarian than girls and women, and that greater education is strongly associated with lower levels of authoritarian attitudes (Peterson & Lane, 2001).

Development of Political Attitudes

The area where children's attitudes and parental influence have been most extensively studied is the development of political attitudes—a topic known as **political socialization**. Because of the large amount of research in this area, we can summarize only a few of the most interesting findings. For more extensive reviews of political socialization, see Kinder and Sears (1985) or Buckingham (2000).

The first major finding is the early age at which political attitudes begin to develop. As early as age 6 or 7, many children have developed strong emotional and cognitive associations about their nation, its leaders, and national symbols such as the flag (Lambert & Klineberg, 1967; Helwig, 1998).

Youthful Chauvinism and Idealization.   A second finding is the very high degree of chauvinism that has typically been displayed by young children. For instance, in Hess and Torney's (1967) large nationwide sample of white children from grades 2 through 8, over 95% of the children at every grade level agreed that "the American flag is the best flag in the world" and that "America is the best country in the world."

Third, this positive view of the nation has been found to extend to attitudes of idealization toward the government and toward specific "benevolent leaders." For instance, 77% of fourth-graders in another study agreed that "the government usually knows what is best for people" (Easton & Dennis, 1965). Idealization of the president occurs not only in the United States, but also in Puerto Rico, Australia, Chile, and Japan (Hess, 1963). Although the president is rated highest, other political leaders are also favorably evaluated by children, being seen as less selfish than most people, more honest, and almost always keeping their promises. Not surprisingly, these positive views in the early grade school years are accompanied by relatively little factual information about the government and how it works. This first stage of attachment to the system involves an undifferentiated view of one's own nation and its leaders as "good," and associating them with conventional national symbols (e.g., for U.S. children, the flag, the Statue of Liberty, and George Washington).

By junior high school ages, children's chauvinistic attitudes become much more differentiated, and they typically state reasons for their national pride such as "freedom," "democracy," and "the right to vote." They also idealize the president less and become more cynical and doubting of politicians (Hess & Torney, 1967). By about this same time, many of them begin to develop partisan political preferences, which are discussed in the following paragraphs.

Amount of Parent–Child Correspondence.   Although parents are quite influential in children's earliest political attitudes, during their primary and secondary school years other sources of attitudes are added, and parents' degree of influence wanes. By college age, the correspondence in political attitudes between parent–child pairs from the same family is typically fairly low (Niemi, Ross, & Alexander, 1978). A particularly thorough study was done by Jennings and Niemi (1968), who independently interviewed a representative national sample of over 1,600 high school seniors and their parents. Their findings demonstrated rather low positive correlations (between 0.0 and +0.4) for parent–child pairs on about 15 measures of political attitudes (political cynicism, attitudes on specific issues and toward various groups, etc.). However, there was one measure with a notably higher relationship, which is discussed next.

Party Identification.   The single high relationship in the political area found by Jennings and Niemi (1968) was between U.S. parents' party identification and their child's party identification—a product–moment correlation coefficient of about +0.6. This finding is quite consistent with Converse's (1964) report, described in the previous chapter, of singularly high stability over time for the party-identification measure. In addition to being stable, party identification is a highly salient attitude in the American political system. As a result, it turns out to be the only political attitude transmitted very effectively from parents to their children, though even here there are many cases of noncorrespondence

(Niemi & Jennings, 1991). In addition, its level of transmission has been somewhat lower in recent decades than it was in the 1950s and 1960s (Luskin, McIver, & Carmines, 1989).

The prominence of party identification as an attitude transmitted by parents is paralleled by findings from the area of religious attitudes. There parent–child correspondence in denominational preference was found to be quite high (about 74%, yielding a contingency coefficient of +0.88, the highest relationship reported by Jennings & Niemi, 1968). However, just as in the political arena, parent–child agreement on other religious questions displayed a very modest positive relationship. Thus we may conclude that transmission of parental values is apt to be strongly successful only when they deal with simple and highly visible questions of group membership.

Disaffection Toward Government.   An exception to the common findings of idealization mentioned earlier in this section is the fact that some groups of children have been found to be far less favorable toward the government and political leaders than the typical picture among American middle-class youth. For instance, several studies have shown greater feelings of political powerlessness among black and Mexican American children and a marked decrease in their political trust following the urban ghetto riots and assassinations of political and civil rights leaders in the late 1960s (e.g., Greenberg, 1970; Garcia, 1973). These beachheads of disaffection toward government increased and spread among adolescents in all demographic groups as a result of the controversy over the Vietnam War and the Watergate scandal that led to President Nixon's resignation from office (Sigel & Hoskin, 1981). Similarly, during the 1999 presidential impeachment hearings, a national sample of adolescents was quite critical of President Clinton, but nevertheless they remained more trusting and supportive of the U.S. government in general than adults were at that time (Owen & Dennis, 1999).

In a longitudinal follow-up of their former high school seniors, Jennings and Niemi (1974) found that both they and their parents had increased considerably in political cynicism. Although studies of early grade school children still found considerable idealization of the government, political disaffection had become more common among various demographic subgroups of older children (Tolley, 1973). During the 1980s, approval of President Reagan was relatively high among middle- and upper-class youth, but substantially lower among racial minority groups and poor children (Kinder & Sears, 1985). It now appears that, to a greater extent than formerly thought, children's attitudes toward political institutions are shaped by the events of the times rather than being invariably positive and idealistic.

GROUP DETERMINANTS OF ATTITUDES

Another important influence on the formation of attitudes is the pressure of various groups. Here we touch briefly on four kinds of group pressure: school indoctrination, peer groups, conformity pressures in general, and reference groups.

Schools

Second only to parental influences in determining children's attitudes are school teaching and indoctrination. This has become especially clear in the area of political attitudes, where many studies have emphasized the importance of school influence (e.g., Torney, Oppenheim, & Farnen, 1975; Rutter et al., 1979; Schonbach, 1981). The highly favorable attitudes previously mentioned, which young children develop toward government, and

FIGURE 8-2
The schools instill prosystem attitudes.

their idealization of the president and other leaders (even down to the local policeman) are undoubtedly largely due to schoolroom teaching. Schools in all nations are given the task of instilling respect for and obedience to local and national authorities (Torney et al., 1975).

We have all experienced this kind of indoctrination, but it is easy to forget or overlook how hard the schools work to instill patriotism. For example, Hess and Torney (1967) found that teachers, especially in the lower grades, consciously tried to "emphasize the positive" and to avoid discussion of conflict within the country. They reported that 99% of their sample of teachers displayed the American flag prominently, over 85% at each grade level required the Pledge of Allegiance to be said daily, and in the lower grades most classrooms spent some time every day singing patriotic songs. Although children may not always understand the words ("one nation, invisible"), it is no wonder that they get the message clearly—"my country, right or wrong" (see Figure 8-2).

Despite the schools' dedicated efforts to teach civic values and knowledge, they seem to be far less successful than might be desired. For instance, in the late 1990s, barely 50% of U.S. high school seniors knew that the right to religious freedom was a principle in the Bill of Rights, and 35% of them failed the national civics test in the National Assessment of Educational Progress (Niemi & Junn, 1998; Hedges, 1999). The average effect of *college* attendance, for the half of American youth that go on to that level, is for them to become more politically tolerant and supportive of democratic values, as well as more liberal on most political issues, but not on economic ones (Nie, Junn, & Stehlik-Barry, 1998). However, societal changes over the decades have made current U.S. college students less liberal than those in the 1960s and 1970s (Sax et al., 1998).

Peer Groups

Following family and school, the next major determinant of attitudes, both chronologically and in relative importance, is the child's peer group. From the end of grade school onward, peer-group contacts become increasingly important and time-consuming (Renshon, 1977). Where peer-group norms agree with parental or school standards, previously existing attitudes and values may be strengthened (Youniss, 1980). However, peers also frequently introduce and reinforce new viewpoints, attitudes, and behavioral patterns, ranging from fads like hairstyles through preferences for particular music, films, or political parties, to lifestyle choices involving career planning, drug use, and sexual behavior (Conger, 1981; Yankelovich, 1981).

The many "generation gap" differences in attitudes between youth and the older generation are undoubtedly due in part to youthful peer-group influences. Some typical examples of research findings concerning generation differences are young people's greater political liberality, toleration of nonconformity, advocacy of civil liberties, and racial tolerance (e.g., Jennings & Niemi, 1968). That such generational differences are related to peer-group influences was shown in an interesting study of moral attitudes in Israeli *kibbutzim*. There the age-group system of childrearing produced greater differences in attitudes between parents and children than were found with more traditional family living arrangements (Rettig, 1966). However, it is also true that many attitude differences between generations are due to having grown up under the impact of differing overwhelming societal forces, like the Great Depression, World War II, the civil rights movement, or the Vietnam War (Abramson, 1983).

Conformity Pressures

Not only peer groups, but a variety of other conformity pressures, can lead to attitude formation and change. One key example is the impact of major societal events of the era, such as wars or depressions, as just mentioned. As another example, the overall cultural context within which we live can provide a set of assumptions and salient "facts" that determine the attitudes we will develop, without our even being aware of any influence. For example, Pettigrew (1971) estimated that about three-fourths of Americans who are racially prejudiced are simply reflecting the assumptions and norms of their culture. Moreover, almost everyone believes that others are more prejudiced than themselves—a phenomenon termed **pluralistic ignorance**—and this creates added resistance to change in attitudes or behavior (Taylor, 1982).

However, intergroup contact under the right conditions can ameliorate such prejudice, especially when cooperative efforts toward common goals are required by the circumstances (Pettigrew & Tropp, 2000). For instance, such beneficial effects of intergroup contact have been demonstrated in preschool children (Crooks, 1970) and in boys' summer camp groups when conditions conducive to cooperation rather than competition were established (Sherif et al., 1961).

Changes in social roles can often exert powerful influences on attitudes, such as when a prounion worker is promoted to the management job of foreman (Lieberman, 1956). Even more far-reaching changes in attitudes and behavior can be induced when there is relatively complete control over the social environment, rewards, and punishments, as in military basic training, in some religious cults, or in brainwashing of political prisoners (Lifton, 1963; McEwen, 1980; Pavlos, 1982). See Cialdini and Trost (1998) for a summary of research on conformity.

Reference Groups

A milder form of influence on attitudes, and one that is often unintentional, is seen in **reference groups**. These are groups whose standards and beliefs one accepts and measures oneself against, regardless of whether one is a member of the group or not. For many teenagers, movie stars or rock musicians serve this function, whereas for others, the "in crowd" at school serves as a reference group.

The central point here is that reference groups often influence people's attitudes, even without any overt attempts to do so. In various studies this effect has been found for racial and religious issues, for economic and political attitudes, and for authoritarian attitudes (Pettigrew, 1967). One of the most important studies of reference groups was the famous Bennington College study by Newcomb (1943). Bennington began as a very liberal college during the Depression years, but its incoming students were mostly from upper-class, highly conservative families. Thus there was a conflict between the college community's standards and those of the new students. Although some students retained their family as their reference group, most of the students resolved this conflict by adopting the faculty and advanced students as their reference group and gradually changing their own attitudes in a more liberal direction throughout their stay in college. A typical student comment described this process (Newcomb, 1943):

> It's very simple, I was so anxious to be accepted that I accepted the political complexion of the community here. I just couldn't stand out against the crowd unless I had made many friends and had strong support. (p. 132)

Follow-up studies 25 years later (Newcomb et al., 1967) and again after nearly 50 years (Cohen & Alwin, 1993) showed that a surprisingly large amount of the Bennington graduates' college-induced liberalism had persisted throughout their lives. Apparently this occurred largely through the women's choices of postcollege social environments (e.g., friends, jobs, and husbands) that were supportive of their attitudes.

MASS MEDIA

The final factor in attitude formation that we discuss here is effects of the **mass media** of communication—the channels through which information, images, and ideas are communicated to large groups of people. These media include newspapers, magazines, books, movies, radio, television, and the Internet. There is no doubt that these communication channels have had enormous impacts on our society and on other nations around the world. Just try to imagine what your life would be like if there were no TV or radio, for instance!

Yet there is much less hard evidence on their precise effects than we would like. We know much more about media *exposure* than about media effects. For instance, we know that American children typically spend 2–3 hours per day watching television, and that by the time they finish high school they will have spent more hours in front of the TV set than in school classrooms, churches, and all other educational and cultural activities combined (Andreasen, 1994; Robinson & Godbey, 1997). Thus the *informational* impact of TV, and to a lesser extent of the other media, is potentially very great. By the time children are 10, TV and school have replaced the family as the most frequently mentioned sources of their information; and attention to news media then becomes the most important influence on children's political socialization (Conway et al., 1981; Garramone & Atkin, 1986). Adults, too, generally say that they rely on television for most of their daily information (Comstock et al., 1978), although the percentage of young adults who report watching news shows has decreased steadily over the past 40 years (Buckingham, 2000). A major British study of the impact of TV reported that the carefully planned BBC programs broadened children's views of other nations and peoples, making them more objective and less evaluative. Importantly, the programs also had their greatest effect on children who were not already familiar with their subject matter (Himmelweit, Oppenheim, & Vince, 1958).

These findings are relevant to attitude formation, because people's information and beliefs are important factors in their attitudes. However, the media do not simply transmit information. They also aim to produce favorable attitudes toward products, behaviors, and political candidates; and a relevant finding here is the fact that attitude formation can often occur in the absence of conscious awareness and recognition (Olson & Fazio, 2001, 2002). Perhaps even more important, the media select, emphasize, and interpret particular events, and publicize people's reactions to those events. By so doing, they help to structure the nature of "reality" and to define the crucial issues of the day, which in turn impels the public to form attitudes on these new issues (Kinder & Sears, 1985; Roberts & Maccoby, 1985).

In brief, what can we say about the attitudinal effects of exposure to specific mass media messages? For example, will watching a commercial that pairs a product with positive images or words produce a positive attitude toward the product? The early years of media research accepted this **direct effects model** of mass media influence on audiences, but the picture has been found to be more complex than this. More recent research has favored an **indirect effects model**, wherein audience members are seen as active processors of media information, not simply passive recipients of persuasive messages (Petty, Priester, & Briñol, 2002; Rubin, 2002). Overall, the research findings indicate that exposure to mass media messages is more likely to reinforce existing attitudes, rather than to change them. Thus the mass media are often an effective means of creating new attitudes, but less effective at modifying existing attitudes.

For example, consider research on mass media persuasion campaigns. Such campaigns are often aimed at specific attitudes or behaviors such as participating in recycling, quitting smoking, or preventing drug use. Research has shown that these mass communication persuasion campaigns often have only minor effects (Derzon & Lipsey, 2002; Donaldson, 2002), but they are most likely to be effective in creating opinions and attitudes on *new issues*, for which there are no predispositions to be changed, or on topics or political candidates about which current attitudes are weak or absent (e.g., Patterson, 1980). For instance, research on the national publicity campaign to "take a bite out of crime," which featured the cartoon dog character "McGruff," showed that it had considerable effects on viewers' beliefs, attitudes, and behaviors about the novel topic of crime prevention (O'Keefe, 1985). Similarly, children's viewing of prosocial TV entertainment programs has been shown to affect their racial and gender-role attitudes (Zuckerman, Singer, & Singer, 1980; Morgan, 1982).

The topic of media effectiveness will recur again at greater length in the following chapter on attitude communication. In the meantime, we turn to an examination of the various learning processes by which attitudes can be formed.

LEARNING PROCESSES IN ATTITUDE FORMATION

As we have seen throughout this book, most attitudes are learned. As Walther (2002, p. 919) has stated, "there is substantial agreement in the literature that attitudes can be formed through simple learning mechanisms." This section briefly describes different learning processes that can be involved in attitude formation. It summarizes three main types of learning—classical conditioning, operant conditioning, and observational learning—plus two other processes of attitude formation that utilize learned information.

Classical Conditioning

Classical conditioning is the process investigated by Pavlov, who presented meat powder and the sound of a bell to dogs and observed that later the bell alone would cause the dogs to salivate. The paradigm uses a stimulus, called the unconditioned stimulus (UCS), which automatically elicits an unconditioned response (UCR) from the organism; in this case the meat powder caused the dogs to salivate. Another stimulus that does not automatically elicit that response is presented simultaneously with or just before the UCS on several trials. To test the presence of learning, the UCS is then omitted. If the response is given to the other stimulus alone, we say that it is a conditioned response (CR), which has been conditioned to that stimulus, termed the conditioned stimulus (CS).

Applying this paradigm to attitude formation, we might consider being knocked down roughly as the UCS, which would automatically produce negative, unhappy feelings in a child. If this occurs every time the child is with a particular dog, the dog will soon become a CS, and seeing it even without being knocked down will produce negative feelings (an attitude). Of course, positive attitudes (for instance, toward a particular medicine) can be produced in the same way if the object is frequently paired with unconditioned stimuli, like tasty food or a hug, which make the child feel good (see Figure 8–3). This paradigm is most relevant to formation of the evaluative or feeling aspect of attitudes, and it has

FIGURE 8–3 Classical conditioning (top) pairs a new stimulus object (the pill) with one that already produces a response from the person, and eventually the new object will produce the same response. Instrumental conditioning (bottom) applies a reinforcer (such as a reward) after the person has made a particular response, and as a result the person's tendency to make that response is strengthened.

been referred to as *evaluative conditioning*, "the learning of likes and dislikes" (Walther, 2002, p. 920).

The classical conditioning paradigm has been used in attitude research by many investigators, involving topics such as attitudes toward different nations, opinions about future scientific discoveries, and children's racial attitudes (e.g., Weiss, 1968; Zanna, Kiesler, & Pilkonis, 1970; Cacioppo et al., 1992; De Houwer, Thomas, & Baeyens, 2001; Olson & Fazio, 2002). In a recent example, Olson and Fazio (2001) presented participants with novel stimuli (Pokemon characters) paired with either positive words ("excellent," "awesome") and images (puppies, a hot fudge sundae) or negative words ("terrible," "awful") or images (a cockroach). After viewing these pairings repeatedly on a computer screen, participants rated the Pokemon characters that had been paired with positively valenced stimuli more positively than the Pokemon characters that had been paired with the negative stimuli. That is, by pairing the CS (Pokemon characters) with a UCS (positive or negative words or images) over many trials, eventually the CS (Pokemon characters) were able to elicit the CR (positive or negative evaluation). In a parallel study involving the classical conditioning of *implicit attitudes*, the researchers found the same effect, but somewhat stronger, when using the Implicit Association Test as the attitude measure (Olson & Fazio, 2001).

Importantly, in both of these studies, there was no evidence that the participants were aware of the newly developed associations. This fact is critical, because a major question in performing classical conditioning is whether participants are *aware* of the S–R connection that the investigator is trying to establish. If they are aware, the participants' learning may be of an instrumental sort (trying to do what will gain the researcher's approval), or alternatively it may be of a cognitive, information-processing sort, rather than being classical conditioning (Page, 1974).

Stimulus generalization is a principle that is associated with classical conditioning, and which is highly relevant to attitude formation. Generalization is a process that occurs after an S–R connection has been established by conditioning. Then, researchers usually find that the conditioned response can be elicited, not just by the CS, but by other similar stimuli (for instance, a bell of a different pitch in Pavlov's experiments with dogs). An example in attitude formation might be the establishment of a negative reaction to one dog, an attitude that would then generalize to other dogs of different sizes and degrees of roughness. Moreover, through the use of language, humans can display **semantic generalization** to other stimuli having similar *meanings*. So, for instance, a negative attitude to a big black dog can further generalize to the words "hound" and "black" and to other words or objects that have a similar meaning (e.g., Edwards & Williams, 1970).

Extinction is another key principle in conditioning, defined as the process of eliminating an association. In the Pavlovian example of the dog and the bell, extinction would occur after a series of trials in which the bell was rung, but no meat was presented. Eventually, the bell would not produce the salivation response. Several attitudinal studies have suggested that, once formed, an evaluative association is particularly resistant to extinction, and can last for a long period of time, even in the absence of confirming evidence. Furthermore, once the association is formed, there is a tendency for people to attend selectively and notice instances that are consistent with the association. For example, consider a negative attitude toward dogs, which was formed as a result of bad childhood experiences with a particular dog. Once that attitude is formed, its holder has a tendency to attend to the negative aspects of any new encounters with dogs and to ignore the positive aspects. Through this process, a negative attitude toward dogs can continue, even in the absence of additional negative experiences. Thus attitudes are particularly difficult to extinguish through simple lack of reinforcement.

Operant Conditioning

This process, sometimes called **instrumental conditioning**, is the kind of learning stressed by Skinner and his followers. It is called *operant* because the organism is allowed to operate freely on its environment instead of being constrained to make one particular response to one particular stimulus. It is *instrumental* in the sense that the organism's behavior is instrumental; that is, the behavior is the means by which reward or punishment is achieved. The researcher does not usually know or care what the original stimulus was for the organism's behavior. Instead, he or she waits until the organism makes a desired response (say, scratching its ear) and then immediately *reinforces* the response by presenting a food pellet or a piece of candy (see Figure 8–3).

In human attitude formation, the reinforcer is apt to be verbal—either praise or criticism—or nonverbal signs of approval or disapproval. For instance, a child might say "nasty Arabs" and be rewarded by an approving smile from the parent. As a result, the child would not only be likely to say "nasty Arabs" more often in the future, but also to form a negative attitude toward Arabs. Examples of attitude research using this paradigm have been conducted on opinion statements (Insko, 1965; Weiss, 1968), liking for stimulus persons (Byrne, 1971), and children's racial attitudes (Williams & Morland, 1976).

Selective learning is an extension of instrumental conditioning, which has also been studied experimentally by Weiss (1968). In this situation the organism has several alternative responses, and they are differentially reinforced by someone presenting different degrees of reward or punishment. As a result, the more reinforced responses increase in their likelihood of being emitted. An example in the attitude area might be a youthful baseball fan who has expressed liking for several different teams on different occasions. If one attitude ("I like the Dodgers") was reinforced more quickly, more strongly, or more frequently than his statements favorable to other teams, his positive attitude toward the Dodgers would gradually be selected as his dominant attitude on the topic of baseball teams. Like instrumental conditioning, this paradigm is most directly relevant to formation of the behavioral aspect of attitudes.

Observational Learning—Imitation or Modeling

A common type of learning, which can occur without any external reinforcement, is **imitation** of the behavior of another person who serves as a model. Parents are often disconcerted to find that their children imitate not only their admirable behavior (e.g., helping to feed the baby) but also their antisocial acts (e.g., swearing at the disliked neighbors). In many such modeled actions, the behavioral aspect of attitudes begins to be formed without any explicit instruction or reinforcement by the parent. In fact, children will often imitate what they see their parents practice instead of what they preach (Rushton, 1975). Much research has shown the effectiveness of models in shaping attitudes and behavior—for instance, in the areas of aggression (Bandura, 1977; Sparks & Sparks, 2002), helping behavior (London, 1970; Berkowitz, 1972), and attitudes toward learning and science (Fisch, 2002).

Information Integration

Another process of attitude formation, **information integration**, is emphasized by many cognitive theorists and researchers. They stress that a person's attitude toward an object is based on the beliefs that he or she holds about it, some of which may be favorable and others unfavorable. In forming their attitudes, people must integrate their beliefs about the object, combining the beliefs that are salient to them into an overall impression. For instance, your friend may tell you that a political candidate of whom you knew nothing before is honest, unwilling to make any deals to get elected, but not a good speaker. To form an attitude toward the candidate, you then have to combine those beliefs (and perhaps also your opinion of your friend's political judgment) in some way. This process often occurs when attitudes are constructed "on the spot."

Of course, the evidence on political attitudes cited in Chapter 7 indicates that many people are relatively inattentive and/or inconsistent in their reaction to political information. However, theorists have constructed many different models suggesting ways in which their sets of beliefs are typically combined. These include additive models, in which the valences of the beliefs are added together, and averaging models, in which they are averaged. In expectancy-value models, the person's degree of belief in each of the attitude object's characteristics is combined with his or her evaluation of those characteristics, as described in Chapter 5. Major contributors to research on information integration have been Anderson (1971), who favors weighted-averaging approaches, and Fishbein and Ajzen (1975), whose theory of reasoned action is an expectancy-value model using additive formulas.

Persuasion

Persuasive communication is probably the most common way of trying to change a person's attitude, and it is discussed at length in Chapters 10 and 11. It can also be used to form attitudes for the first time, as when a friend tells you the good or bad points about a local political candidate with whom you were unfamiliar. The typical contents of such a persuasive message include one or more suggested conclusions or recommendations for action, usually together with some supporting facts or arguments (e.g., "She's a good candidate because she's honest and won't make any political deals to get elected. You should vote for her."). The format of persuasive messages can be infinitely varied: long or short, logical or emotional, organized or disorganized, and so on. They are apt to influence the cognitive aspect of attitudes most directly, and sometimes also the behavioral aspect. Some of the most influential early research in this area was done by the group of researchers working with Carl Hovland at Yale (e.g., Hovland et al., 1953; Rosenberg et al., 1960).

It is important to point out that the various learning processes that we have just described are not antagonistic, mutually exclusive theories of attitude formation. Several or all of these processes may take place in the acquisition of various attitudes, depending on the stimulus situations a person is exposed to.

SUMMARY

Attitude formation, the step from no attitude to some attitude toward a given object, is similar but not identical to attitude change. It is generally agreed that most attitudes are learned, but many different factors can operate in the acquisition process. The most fundamental factor in attitude formation is direct personal experience—either salient incidents or repeated exposure over time. Attitudes formed through personal experience can be very potent and long-lasting. Although genetic and physiological factors are often overlooked, they may establish a predisposition for the development of particular attitudes.

Among other important factors, parental influence is a key variable in forming children's early attitudes, as shown in extensive studies of prejudice and of political attitudes. However, by the time a child is of high school age in the United States, the parent–child similarity is only a low positive one, except on measures of party identification and religious denomination preference, where it remains high. Studies of political socialization have found that most young children display strong positive attitudes toward the government and national leaders, but older children in some population subgroups display greater disaffection, indicating that idealization of government is largely a middle-class phenomenon.

The schools are very important in instilling attitudes favorable to the political system. Other group determinants—peer groups, conformity pressures in general, and reference groups—become more important as children grow older. Finally, the mass media not only provide much of our information, but also help to form our attitudes, particularly on new issues where no attitudes existed before.

There are several different learning processes by which attitude formation occurs. Classical conditioning, which involves the repeated pairing of two stimuli, can lead to attitude formation. Stimulus generalization can spread the resulting attitude to other similar stimuli, and in both of these procedures the person is often unaware of the associative process. Operant (or instrumental) conditioning and its extension, selective learning, both involve the explicit reward or punishment of a behavior. Observational learning, involving imitation or modeling of attitudes, on the other hand, often occurs without any reinforcement or any explicit instruction. Information integration is a cognitive process of combining one's salient beliefs into an overall attitude toward an object. Explicit persuasion attempts are one of the most common methods of attitude change, but they are equally applicable to attitude formation.

9

Communication of Attitudes and Opinions

Every new opinion, at its starting, is precisely in a minority of one.—Thomas Carlyle.

In the United States, the majority undertakes to supply a multitude of ready-made opinions for the use of individuals, who are thus relieved from the necessity of forming opinions of their own.—Alexis de Tocqueville.

All effective propaganda must be limited to a very few points and must harp on these in slogans until the last member of the public understands what you want him to understand.—Adolf Hitler.

The amount of money devoted to communication and advertising in the United States, and worldwide, is staggering. In the United States, advertising campaigns through the mass media cost over $200 *billion* per year (U.S. Census Bureau, 2002). That's over $700 for every person in the country, spent to persuade them to change their attitudes and actions—far more than the total per capita income of many developing countries! The four primary media for advertising in the United States are television ($57 billion), newspapers ($49 billion), direct mail ($44 billion), and magazines ($42 billion). In 2001, General Motors and Proctor & Gamble, the two companies with the largest advertising budgets, spent more than $3 billion dollars each to advertise their products (*Adage.com*, 2003).

What do the advertisers get for all their expenditures? Do mass media campaigns successfully sell products or attract voters? Do people rely on the media for information and advice, or do they turn to their families, friends, and neighbors? What are the communication processes by which mass information, propaganda, and advertising efforts are spread and transformed into individual beliefs, attitudes, and actions? This chapter considers these questions regarding the communication of attitudes, beginning with a very brief sketch of the history of communication research.

EARLY STUDIES OF COMMUNICATION AND PROPAGANDA

Much of the early research on communication was motivated by deep concern over the effects on society of political propaganda. By the 1930s numerous demagogues had attained political power, in part through the clever use of propaganda techniques: Hitler and Goebbels in Germany, Mussolini in Italy, Huey Long as Louisiana governor and senator in the United States. Radio broadcasting had begun in 1920, and by the 1930s the widespread ownership of radios made possible a mass audience of millions for propagandists like the American priest, Father Coughlin. There was deep fear that democracy could not withstand this onslaught, for the propaganda analysts of that era assumed that the millions listening to demagogic broadcasts were an easily swayed, captive, and gullible audience. It was also assumed "that propaganda could be made almost irresistible with sufficiently clever use of propagandistic gimmicks in the content of the communication" (Sears & Whitney, 1973, p. 2). An analysis of Father Coughlin's radio speeches made by the Institute for Propaganda Analysis (Lee & Lee, 1939) ascribed his persuasiveness to tricks like name-calling, use of "glittering generalities," a "plain folks" approach, and "card-stacking" techniques of argument. Other fascinating analyses were made of the principles involved in Goebbels' propaganda campaigns (Doob, 1950) and of the successes and failures with the use of Allied propaganda leaflets in World War II (Herz, 1949).

Gradually it became apparent that these propaganda efforts were not nearly so successful as had first been thought. For instance, careful experimental studies of U.S. Army orientation films showed that they failed to achieve many of the attitude and motivational changes that were intended (Hovland, Lumsdaine, & Sheffield, 1949). Similarly, the first major field study of American voting behavior showed amazingly small effects traceable to the large amount of media exposure during the political campaign (Lazarsfeld, Berelson, & Gaudet, 1948). Also, in commercial advertising it has become clear that, instead of a captive, easily persuaded, and gullible audience, the communicator is faced by an inattentive, difficult-to-persuade, "obstinate audience" (Bauer, 1964).

Two major changes in the orientation of research occurred as a result of these findings. First, attention largely shifted from mass communication to face-to-face interpersonal communication, which was felt to be considerably more influential in affecting people's attitudes and behavior. Second, attention shifted from the content of the communication to other factors in the communication process, such as the source and the audience. To understand these trends in research, we need to describe briefly the various factors in the persuasive communication process.

FACTORS IN PERSUASIVE COMMUNICATION

There are two sets of factors to be considered here: independent variables and dependent variables. Independent variables are the elements of the persuasion situation that can be varied or manipulated in some way. The dependent variables are the various aspects of the persuasion process that may occur in response to the communication—that is, the effects of communication.

Independent Variables.   The process of communication can be analyzed in terms of who says what to whom, how, with what intent, and with what effect. The final item, "with what effect," summarizes all of the dependent variables, whereas the other five items constitute the major independent variables in communication. More frequently used terms for the major independent variables are source, message, audience, medium, and target behavior variables.

Source variables are characteristics of the source of the message, such as its expertness, credibility, or likeability. **Message variables** include both the content and structure of the message, how it is organized, its use of emotional appeals, and so on. **Audience variables** are characteristics of the people who are receiving the message, their personalities, interests, and involvement in the communication process. **Media variables** include the printed word, radio, television, and face-to-face interpersonal transmission. **Target behavior variables** are the goals of the communicator, which parallel the possible dependent variables. That is, sometimes the goal may be merely to convey knowledge (comprehension); more often it is to change attitudes, or to instigate action; or it may be to create

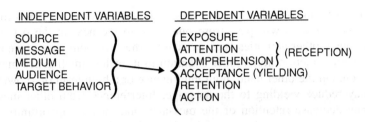

FIGURE 9–1 The major independent variables and dependent variables that are involved in the study of persuasive communication.

resistance to later persuasion. Useful overviews of research on all of these variables have been provided by McGuire (1985) and Roberts and Maccoby (1985).

In this chapter, we confine our attention primarily to media factors, particularly stressing mass communication media versus personal face-to-face persuasion. Chapters 10 and 11, on attitude change, will present considerable detail on source, message, audience, and target variables.

Dependent Variables. In the process of persuasion there are at least six distinguishable steps that must occur in sequence, each one involving a separate stage of persuasive effect. These steps are generally termed **exposure, attention, comprehension, acceptance, retention,** and **action.** Other authors have used other terms, for instance **reception** to include both attention and comprehension, and **yielding** instead of acceptance (see Figure 9–1).

Whatever terms are used, it is important to be clear about which stage is being studied in any given research. For instance, the television Nielsen ratings and newspaper circulation figures pertain to the first stage, exposure to the communication. Research on readership of magazines or recall of TV commercials is using the second stage, attention, as the dependent variable—a common procedure because it can be much more easily and precisely measured than other variables at later stages. Studies of the amount of information obtained from messages are relevant to the third stage, comprehension. Most experiments on persuasive communication or attitude change measure the fourth stage: yielding, or acceptance of the message. Experiments with delayed posttests can study the fifth stage: retention of the information or the attitude change. Finally, voting research or studies using advertising sales data are dealing with the sixth stage: action.

Importance of Specifying Variables. These distinctions are quite clear conceptually but are often forgotten when authors make generalizations about the effectiveness of persuasive communication. A message may be quite effective at one of the early stages but ineffective at some of the later stages. Success at each stage is generally necessary but not sufficient for effectiveness at each following stage. Hence it is essential to specify, for any given study, what the dependent variables were and which ones showed significant effects.

To illustrate these points, think of a persuasive message in a television commercial. Many homes will not be tuned in, or no one will be in front of the set, so the residents will not be exposed to the message. Among the thousands of viewers of that TV program, many will not pay attention to the commercial. Of those who do, some will not understand it for one reason or another. Many of those who understand the message will not agree with it nor yield to its suggestions. Further, those who are persuaded may not remember the suggestions for more than a short time. And finally, even those who are persuaded and remember the message may not act on it.

An important point to notice in this example is that different variables may help to determine which viewers will pass from one stage to the next in the persuasion process. For instance, other activities such as visiting the bathroom may prevent exposure to the message, distraction may hinder attention to it, or low intelligence may decrease comprehension. On the other hand, high intelligence or a high level of knowledge about the topic may reduce yielding to the message. Interference from other messages and activities may decrease retention of the message, and lack of opportunity or lack of money may prevent acting on the suggestion. Thus the effects of persuasive communication are the complex result of many different variables working in interaction with each other.

A Different Approach—Uses and Gratifications of Mass Media.   The mass media serve many functions for people—not just providing new information or attitudinal persuasion. This fact has been recognized and studied by the approach called "uses and gratifications" research (e.g., McLeod & Becker, 1981; Rubin, 2002). Among the other basic needs which the mass media serve, three main clusters stand out: The media help to provide self-identity (e.g., comparing oneself with media characters), social contact (e.g., discussing recent episodes with friends), and diversion and entertainment (Murray & Kippax, 1979). Of these, *entertainment* is the reason most often given by people for their media attention, though social scientists have studied it much less than the persuasive (attitude-change) function (cf. Tannenbaum, 1980; Bryant & Miron, 2002).

The uses and gratifications approach differs markedly from the early communication studies, which worried about the effects of propaganda on a passive and gullible audience. In contrast, it stresses the active role of viewers or readers in choosing what media to "consume" and in interpreting the content of messages in accordance with their own interests, needs, and fantasies. For instance, a message which was intended to be objective and informative may be interpreted by a viewer as supporting her own pet prejudice, or the theme of a persuasive message may be missed entirely by a viewer who is ogling the speaker's beautiful figure or costume (Rubin, 2002):

> Uses and gratifications [research] sees a medium or message as a source of influence within the context of other possible influences. It sees media audiences as variably active communicators, rather than passive recipients of messages. (pp. 525–526)

With these distinctions and cautions in mind, let us examine some of the research on mass communication, and on personal communication, and see what effects they have on the various stages of persuasion.

PERSUASIVE EFFECTS OF THE MASS MEDIA

What is the effect of the mass media on public opinion? In the early days of opinion research, this was viewed as a simple question with a simple answer, but now we know that it is a very complex question with many different answers, depending on the circumstances.

In the first place, mass communication rarely serves as a necessary and sufficient cause of persuasive effects. Instead it operates in conjunction with other variables in the audience and the situation to produce combined or interaction effects (McGuire, 1985). Second, the six different types of dependent variables in communication studies can produce six different answers to the question of media influence. Third, one medium of communication can have markedly different effects from other media.

There is widespread agreement that the various media have differing advantages and disadvantages. **Print** media (books, magazines, and newspapers) and computerized on-line media allow readers to determine the time and pace of their exposure and also permit easy reexposure if desired. Research suggests that these media produce better comprehension and retention of complex material than other media, but that this advantage does not hold for simple material. The **broadcasting** media (radio and television) now reach nearly everyone in the industrialized world, including groups such as the aged, young children, and people with low education, who are not easily reached by other media (in the U.S., 98% of all households have at least one television set). Moreover, they are harder to escape than the print media, as exposure can occur whenever they are within view or earshot, without any conscious action of the recipient.

The **visual** media (television and films) are unique in the "you are there" immediacy conferred by their combined audio and visual nature. As a result, they typically receive more complete attention and are better liked than other media, particularly by children (Lichty, 1982). Also, they produce more yielding and retention than print media when their message is relatively simple, but less when the message is complex (Chaiken & Eagly, 1976). However, despite these advantages of the visual media, people's knowledge of current affairs is more closely related to their use of print media—see the subsequent discussion of research on comprehension (Roberts & Maccoby, 1985).

In the next sections we discuss each of the communication dependent variables in turn and report a few of the studies that have found results relevant to that variable.

Studies of Exposure

There is a great deal of exposure to the mass media in the United States and other industrialized nations. The Nielsen ratings of television programs measure this variable by recording the times and channels when TV sets are tuned in. The average U.S. television set is turned on about 7 hours per day—but up to 40% of the time no one is watching it (Allen, 1965; Gerbner et al., 2002). Children typically watch TV from 2 to 4 hours per day, depending on their ages, and by the end of high school they will have accumulated about 20,000 hours of TV viewing—far more time than they have spent in school classrooms (Adler et al., 1980; Kunkel, 2001). The average U.S. adult also watches TV about 3 hours per day, though there are wide individual differences related to age, sex, education, social class, and employment (Robinson & Godbey, 1997; Comstock & Scharrer, 1999). In many of the world's developing nations, movies (very often American movies) provide much of the information about life and conditions in other countries (Gerbner, 1977; Morgan & Shanahan, 1997).

Despite the time dominance of television, reading in the United States has not yet become a lost art. True, daily newspaper readership has dropped off substantially in the past 30 years, and younger adults who grew up in the television era are much less likely to read newspapers regularly than are older adults. However, there has been a moderate increase in the reading of magazines and books over the same time period, and younger adults report more increases in such reading than do older adults (Robinson, 1980; Robinson & Godbey, 1997). Although many general-interest newspapers and magazines have declined or ceased publication since the advent of TV, the circulation of special-interest magazines and books has climbed sharply (Roberts & Maccoby, 1985). In general, there is little evidence that time devoted to television has displaced time spent reading, though it has reduced comic book reading, radio listening, and movie attendance (Anderson & Collins, 1988).

In the advertising area, it is well known that people often try to avoid commercial messages, for instance, by taking bathroom breaks or making refrigerator raids. However, advertisements are so ubiquitous in our society, not only on TV and radio, but also on billboards, bus and train placards, and in newspapers and magazines, that most people are exposed to over 1,000 every day. This high level of exposure, though, emphatically does not mean that attention and comprehension are also high.

Is There Selective Exposure to Communications?

The concept of **selective exposure** refers to the notion that people actively avoid information that is inconsistent with or threatening to their beliefs and attitudes, and that they seek supportive information. As a current example, most people who choose to listen to Rush Limbaugh's talk show (70%) are politically conservative (Cappella, Turow, & Jamieson, 1996). Many of the early public opinion researchers invoked the hypothesis of selective exposure in interpreting their findings. For instance, Hyman and Sheatsley (1947) used it in explaining reasons why information campaigns often fail. Selective exposure was a key explanatory concept in the first major voting study (Lazarsfeld et al., 1948) and in Klapper's (1960) widely cited review of the effects of mass communication, and it assumed an important place in Festinger's (1957) influential theory of cognitive dissonance, as we will see in Chapter 11.

Photograph courtesy of Columbia University. Reprinted by permission.

Box 9–1 PAUL LAZARSFELD, *Pioneer Communication Researcher*

Probably the most famous early figure in the field of communication research, Paul Lazarsfeld was founder and director of the Bureau of Applied Social Research at Columbia University, becoming a professor of sociology there in 1940. Born in Austria in 1901, he took his Ph.D. at the University of Vienna, and taught and published sociological research there before coming to the U.S. in the 1930s. Before moving to Columbia, he taught briefly at the University of Newark and Princeton University.

Lazarsfeld was known for many research volumes on the mass media, such as Radio and the Printed Page, Radio Research, *and* Communication Research. *He pioneered many new approaches to interviewing, attitude measurement, and survey research, including the panel technique of repeated surveys. His research on personal influence and opinion leadership is cited later in this chapter. Chapter 14 describes his famous work as the originator of large-scale voting studies, reported in the* The People's Choice *and* Voting. *Among his many honors were the first distinguished achievement award of the American Association for Public Opinion Research (AAPOR), presidency of AAPOR and the American Sociological Association, and election to the National Academy of Sciences. Following retirement, he continued a vigorous research career until his death in 1976.*

Despite the intuitive appeal of the selective-exposure concept, the early research found inconsistent results. Sears and Freedman (1967) made a careful summary of the research evidence and reached some surprising conclusions. First, Sears and Freedman distinguished two different aspects of the concept: **de facto** selectivity, and **motivated** selective exposure. De facto selectivity means a greater than chance agreement between the opinion of an audience and the viewpoint of a communication directed to that audience. For instance, it is mostly Republicans who take the trouble to go to a speech by a Republican political candidate, and similarly, most readers of *Mother Jones* are apt to be liberal in their political and social attitudes. However, for actions as easy to perform as reading a newspaper editorial favoring one candidate or listening to the president speak on TV, there is probably much less of a tendency for the audience to be biased in favor of the communicator's position. In fact, political campaigning on television has been transformed since it began in the 1950s—changing from long televised speeches to 5-minute commercials in the 1970s, and most recently to 30-second and 1-minute spots that are sandwiched in with other commercials, and thus are almost impossible to avoid intentionally.

Sears and Freedman concluded that, in many situations and for many people, *de facto* selectivity of communication exposure is an established fact, though not nearly as general a phenomenon as had earlier been thought. In contrast, they found very little firm evidence of a *motivated* search for supportive information or avoidance of opposing information. This is the kind of selectivity that most previous writers had postulated, perhaps partly because it fit so well into a Freudian defense mechanism perspective. Despite that fit, it seemed to occur only rarely. For example, in a study on smoking and lung cancer, Feather (1962) found that neither smokers nor nonsmokers showed a significant preference for reading either of two articles, one that argued smoking causes lung cancer and the other that claimed it does not. Further, when smokers were divided according to whether they believed that the evidence linking cancer and smoking was convincing or not convincing, both groups preferred the article *opposed* their own viewpoint—a surprising preference for nonsupportive information by these ego-involved subjects.

In explaining findings such as these, several other determinants of exposure to information have been stressed: (a) As already mentioned, supportive information is much more extensively available than nonsupportive information in most people's normal environments. (b) *Refutability* of information may be a factor, weak opposing information being desired but strong opposing arguments being avoided. (c) Even more important, the *usefulness* of information will make it desired, whether it is supportive or not (as in obtaining knowledge about a potentially dangerous defect in one's new car). (d) A person's recent exposure history is important because people who are aware of having received one-sided information generally will seek exposure to the other side. (e) Educational level is a very powerful predictor of increased exposure to all kinds of information, both supportive and nonsupportive (Janis & Mann, 1977).

Recent research has demonstrated other specific conditions that may encourage motivated selective exposure: commitment, perception of free choice, and a sequential presentation of choices (Frey, 1986; Frey, Schulz-Hardt, & Stahlberg, 1996; Lundgren & Prislin, 1998; Jonas et al., 2001). People are more likely to seek out information that is consistent with a past behavioral choice if they believe that their behavior was freely chosen, and they are committed to the chosen behavior. Also, if two or more choices (usually one pro and one con) are presented simultaneously, selective exposure is unlikely to occur. But when choices or a selection of information are presented sequentially, people are more likely to selectively expose themselves first to information that is congenial. Television viewing and Internet use are good examples of sequential information seeking because the user makes a choice (click or flip) whether to view each channel or web page. However, the current data are unclear concerning the degree of selective exposure to these media (Mastro, Eastin, & Tamborini, 2002).

Thus the topic of audience selectivity is a complicated one. However, it is encouraging that research does not show much evidence for a general head-in-the-sand avoidance of all information that challenges one's presuppositions or attitudes. At the same time, it is clear that most people most of the time are surrounded by a higher proportion of supportive information than of opposing information.

Studies of Attention

In the United States, most news events are first learned about through the mass media. A summary study of several major events showed that about 35% of people first heard of them on TV compared with about 25% each for radio and the print media (Ostlund, 1973). However, sensational events, such as the shooting of President Kennedy or the terrorist attacks on the World Trade Center showed a different pattern—as much as half of the population first learned of them through word-of-mouth contact with another person, and then most people turned to the media for further information (e.g., Sheatsley & Feldman, 1965). In such calamities news travels very fast—99% of the U.S. adult population knew of the destruction of the World Trade Center on September 11, 2001, within hours of its occurrence (Public Agenda, 2001).

Even children attend to a substantial amount of media news information (Egan, 1978; Chaffee & Yang, 1990). Most Americans report that they learn more about news and politics from television than from newspapers, and they perceive television as the fairest and most objective news source (Comstock, 1988). Yet roughly three times as many adults read the newspaper each day as watch the evening TV news, and people's knowledge about government and current affairs (i.e., comprehension) is more strongly related to newspaper reading than to TV news viewing (Robinson & Levy, 1986b). In particular, people tend to use the print media more for information on complex topics such as science and health.

In contrast to the breadth of public attention to the mass media, the *quality* of attention generally leaves much to be desired. Although most people "read" a newspaper, the average reader looks at no more than one-fourth of the stories, and less than half of the readers even examine the front-page stories (Cutlip, 1954). Among the most popular sections of the paper are the comics, entertainment, and sports sections (Frank & Greenberg, 1980). Similarly, in television, entertainment generally takes precedence over information, and regular viewing of TV network news has dropped steadily over the past 40 years (Buckingham, 2000). Viewing is often a secondary activity, being combined with such other daily events as cooking, eating, conversation, sorting wash, playing games, disciplining children, and reading. Such interrupted or sporadic viewing contributes to very low levels of recall of news stories that have been viewed (Neuman, 1976).

In the area of advertising, it has been found that frequency of presentation of ads per se does not lead to higher levels of attention, but the quality of the ads does. Ads are better attended to if they are entertaining, usefully informative, humorous, professional in appearance, or feature novel or "catchy" elements (Atkin, Bowen, et al., 1973). The average television viewer is exposed to about 60,000 commercials each year. Of these, less than 1% are noticed, and of those that are noticed, only one-sixth are important enough to be classified as enjoyable, informative, annoying, or offensive (Bauer & Greyser, 1968). In addition, advertising that offends or annoys some people entertains or informs others, so the effects of ads are rarely if ever consistent across all members of the mass audience.

These findings of audience indifference to most persuasive messages and varied reactions to any given message help to explain the fact that public mass information and persuasion campaigns so often fail, as pointed out long ago by Hyman and Sheatsley (1947). However, research shows that, despite general public disinterest, information campaigns can be relatively successful if they carefully consider specific target audiences and their lifestyles, value systems, and media habits (Roberts & Maccoby, 1985; Donaldson, 2002; Hornik, 2002). Although only a small proportion of the total population may be reached by such campaigns, that audience may still comprise a great many people in a major metropolitan area such as Los Angeles or New York.

There is also evidence that viewers display **selective perception** in attending to various aspects of a message (Oliver, 2002). In essence, people typically attend to those aspects of a message that reinforce their existing views. In a classic study, Vidmar and Rokeach (1974) found that prejudice levels of viewers influenced their interpretation of an episode in the TV comedy series *All in the Family*. Although both high- and low-prejudiced groups reported enjoying the show, high-prejudiced viewers saw the program as primarily affirming the views of the bigoted main character (Archie), whereas low-prejudiced viewers saw the primary message as supporting Archie's liberal son-in-law. A more recent study of *In Living Color* reported similar findings (Cooks & Orbe, 1993).

Studies of Comprehension

Comprehension of mass communication has been less studied than attention. Most studies have focused on news or educational programs, measured comprehension with objective tests of knowledge, and investigated the amount of self-determined exposure to a particular area of information, a design that allows the findings to be confounded by many other viewer characteristics such as education, interests, or personality. Some studies (e.g., Mendelsohn, 1973) have shown successful communication of knowledge, for instance through television special programs such as "The National Drivers Test." Public comprehension is usually increased when the conclusion or moral of a communication is explicitly stated rather than left implicit or subtly suggested (Weiss, 1969). However, numerous studies have found either no effects or limited effects, with relatively little comprehension and even less attitude change (e.g., Peterson et al., 1984). Some other investigations have documented examples of widespread misunderstanding of messages.

As mentioned earlier, individuals' amount of current affairs knowledge and information is usually more closely related to their use of print media than to their amount of television news viewing (Chaffee & Yang, 1990). Two reasons for this are that network TV news uses a short-snippet "headline" format featuring 20-second "sound bites" (Sawyer, 1988), and that it searches for exciting visual images, a process which leads to an emphasis on action, events, and peripheral "human interest" aspects of the news rather than on substantive issues and policy positions. As Buckingham (2000) summarized:

> Viewers themselves appear to look to television news as a significant source of information about the world and frequently claim that they trust it above any other source. Yet research consistently suggests that it [television] is comparatively ineffective in actually communicating. (p. 17)

In the area of political information, many studies have found that amount of media exposure to relevant messages is either unrelated to knowledge gained or has only a low positive relation to it (Roberts & Maccoby, 1985; Erikson & Tedin, 2001). However, *attention* to messages is more closely related to knowledge gain (Atkin, Galloway, & Nayman, 1973). Patterson and McClure (1976) found that televised political ads had marked effects on voters' beliefs (that is, they were well comprehended), but they had practically no effects on voters' attitudes (they did not produce yielding).

Other variables such as demographic background, political interests, or particular motivations can interact with media variables to affect the amount of comprehension of messages. For instance, highly educated individuals grasp new information presented by the media more quickly than do less-educated ones (Price & Zaller, 1993). This finding has given rise to the **knowledge gap hypothesis**—that higher-status individuals, who typically have more knowledge to start with, will gather information from the media faster than low-status individuals, thus increasing the disparity between the two groups (Donohue, Tichenor, & Olien, 1975; Viswanath & Finnegan, 1996). As one example, Cook et al. (1975) demonstrated this effect in the differential amount of learning from *Sesame Street* by relatively advantaged and disadvantaged children.

Studies of Acceptance or Yielding

What effect do you think the mass media have on your attitudes or actions? Do they influence you—convince you to buy a new product or to vote for a specific candidate? Interestingly, most people answer "no" to such questions. But when individuals are asked about the effect of persuasive messages on *other people*, they generally *do* believe that other people are influenced.

The **third-person effect** refers to an individual's belief that a persuasive message will exert a stronger influence on others than on oneself (Davison, 1983; Perloff, 2002). This effect has been demonstrated for messages like cigarette advertisements and public service announcements, and for some highly publicized events such as the O. J. Simpson trial. In a meta-analysis of 32 studies on the third-person effect, Paul, Salwen, and Dupagne (2000) found a large and consistent discrepancy between estimates of the media's influence on oneself (low) and on others (higher). In the subsections that follow, we summarize some of the research findings with respect to yielding. As you read, keep in mind that if such effects are true for other people, they are also likely to be true for you.

Yielding, or acceptance of the persuasive message, is the dependent variable studied most extensively in the voluminous research on attitude change and conformity. Although yielding cannot occur without reception of the message (that is, attention and comprehension, the two variables previously discussed), the amount of yielding is not necessarily positively related to the amount of reception. Indeed, the most common finding is a lack of any clear relationship between reception and attitude change (Fishbein & Ajzen, 1972). A major factor in this lack of relationship is that "any personality characteristic [such as self-esteem] that has a positive relationship to reception, tends to be negatively related to yielding, and vice versa" (McGuire, 1968a, p. 172). Similarly, in the area of political attitudes, Zaller (1987) has shown that political involvement increases exposure to political messages but decreases acceptance of them.

Types of Yielding. An important distinction was made by Kelman (1958), who described three types of attitude change that have different underlying bases: compliance, identification, and internalization. **Compliance** is public yielding to an influence attempt without private acceptance; its basis is the expectation of gaining rewards or avoiding punishment. **Identification** is yielding to influence in an attempt to emulate an individual or group; its basis is satisfaction in being like the admired other(s). **Internalization** is yielding to influence in situations where the new attitude is intrinsically rewarding, useful, or consistent with one's value system; its basis is the intrinsic value of the new attitude to oneself. Different characteristics of the source of the influence attempt will help to determine which of these types of yielding will occur. A source who is powerful (and who has continuing surveillance over one's activities) will be likely to produce compliance. An attractive source will be more likely to produce identification, whereas a credible source tends to produce internalization. Experimental results that generally support this theory have been summarized by Moscovici (1985).

Importance of the Social Setting.   Research on attitude change has most often been done in an experimental laboratory situation, with audiences of selected individuals, compulsory exposure situations, and single communications. These conditions are desirable for their control of experimental variables, but they are far different from the typical situation in which an individual is exposed to mass communication in everyday life. There the audience is mostly self-selected, the message can easily be turned off or avoided, and communications are frequently repeated. In this chapter we are focusing mostly on factors affecting the typical mass communication situation, whereas the following two chapters deal more with experimental attitude-change research findings.

Even in the real-world mass communication situation, there can be considerable control of the communication conditions if the media content is highly standardized, as is frequently the case in totalitarian nations. In that case the influence of the mass media on individual attitudes can be great, though even in oppressive dictatorships there are usually underground and foreign sources of competing information and attitudes. However, in nations with relatively free mass communication systems, there will be many conflicting viewpoints expressed in the media on almost any topic. Consequently the influence of the media on yielding is apt to be much smaller there than in totalitarian societies.

Three Models of Media Influence.   Since the early part of the twentieth century, when research on the mass media began, three successive views concerning media effects have held sway. The first, a **powerful effects** model, was dominant from the 1920s through the 1940s, as illustrated in the deep fear of the possibly irresistible effects of propaganda on a defenseless public described at the beginning of this chapter. It was followed by the **minimal effects** model, articulated by Klapper (1960), based on the many empirical studies which found no effects or very limited effects of the media in changing people's beliefs, attitudes, and behavior. More recently, a model of **powerful effects under limiting conditions** has gained more adherents (Roberts & Maccoby, 1985). It denies the early all-powerful view of the media, but stresses that they have important effects in particular circumstances and with particular individuals. Thus current research is apt to focus on the interacting variables and contingent conditions under which media effects will emerge most clearly (McLeod & Reeves, 1980)—for instance, under conditions of heavy viewing and weak prior predispositions. Furthermore, current conceptions include a wide range of media effects—not just changing attitudes, but also forming new attitudes, beliefs, or behaviors, reinforcing already existing ones, and crystallizing previously vague or unstated beliefs or attitudes.

A number of general principles about the mass media's effects on attitudes have been well stated by Klapper (1960, 1963) and are summarized in Box 9–2. The fifth principle, concerning creation of attitudes and opinions on new issues, has been dealt with in the preceding chapter. The other four principles are illustrated here with the results of a few key studies.

1. Other Factors Mediate Mass Communication Effects.   In a classic study, Peterson and Thurstone (1933) found that the famous film *Birth of a Nation*, which extolled the Ku Klux Klan, had its strongest effects on children who had had little or no contact

---

Box 9–2   Five General Principles Concerning the Influence of Mass Media

1. The influence of mass communication is mediated by factors such as personal pre-dispositions, personal selective processes, group memberships, etc.

2. Because of these factors, mass communication usually serves to reinforce existing attitudes and opinions, though occasionally it may serve as an agent of change.

3. When mass communication does produce attitude change, minor change in the extremity or intensity of the attitude is much more common than is "conversion" from one side of an issue to the other side.

4. Mass communication can be quite effective in changing attitudes in areas where people's existing opinions are weak, as in much of commercial advertising.

5. Mass communication can be quite effective in creating opinions on new issues where there are no existing predispositions to reinforce.

Source: Adapted from Klapper (1960, p. 15; 1963, pp. 70, 76).

---

with blacks. A similar effect occurred in the 1984 election debates between Reagan and Mondale. The first debate, in which Reagan appeared old and confused, led to a definitely improved public image for Mondale, but the effect was mostly limited to previously undecided voters.

2. Mass Communication Usually Reinforces Existing Attitudes.   That is, the net effect of many mass media campaigns is often no overall change (McGuire, 1986). This point is also illustrated by the presidential campaign debates. In each of the elections where they have been studied, their main effect was to reinforce viewers' prior candidate preferences and to increase the consistency of their attitudes about the various issues and aspects of the campaign (Sigelman & Sigelman, 1984; Kinder, 1998).

3. Mass Communication Can Produce Minor Changes in Attitudes, but It Rarely Produces Conversion to an Opposite Viewpoint.   Examples of minor change have been shown both with adolescents' traditional sex-role attitudes and with their racial attitudes, which can be shifted in either direction by appropriate television portrayals (e.g., Johnston, Ettema, & Davidson, 1980; Christenson & Roberts, 1983). Analogous findings of minor shifts in the area of political attitudes started with the pioneering study of Lazarsfeld et al. (1948). Similarly, a large-scale panel study of television's influence in British elections showed again that attitude changes of most voters were either small or absent altogether. Only about 10% of voters changed their intended vote from one party to another during the campaign (Blumler & McQuail, 1969). Even such a major political upheaval as the Watergate scandal, with its massive media coverage, caused relatively small changes in political attitudes among the American public (Robinson, 1974).

4. Mass Communication Is Most Effective Where Attitudes Are Weak. This principle applies particularly to advertising, for most people's product preferences are weakly held, but it also holds true in politics and many other opinion areas. In politics, many studies have shown that the least-involved voters are most apt to change opinions and most likely to be influenced by TV campaigning (e.g., Patterson, 1980). In advertising, research as well as common parental experience indicates that children can be more strongly influenced by TV commercials than adults usually are (Goldberg & Gorn, 1974).

Studies of Retention

When persuasion changes a person's attitude, how long does that change usually last? This issue of retention has been and still is the least-studied dependent variable in attitude-change research. Much of the research that does exist was done in classroom experimental settings, so its generalizability to more typical media exposure settings is unclear. There is a particular need for research on the continuing, cumulative impact of the media over a prolonged period of time (cf. Comstock, 1985).

Two types of retention are of interest: retention of message content (i.e., memory for the message) and retention of attitude change. In general, these two variables usually show a low-to-moderate positive correlation ($r = +0.2$ to $+0.5$), though some studies have shown that recall of specific message content is not essential to attitude change (e.g., Cacioppo & Petty, 1979).

Often the content of media presentations is not well learned, in part because the messages may have received only sporadic attention. For instance, one study showed that only a couple of hours after a network news broadcast, the average viewer could recall only 1.2 of the 20 stories in the broadcast, though about half of the stories were correctly recognized when respondents were given a list of potential story headlines (Neuman, 1976). Moreover, as is true of any learned information, retention of message content tends to drop off rather sharply in the first hours and days after exposure, and then gradually to level off. After a period of 4 to 6 weeks, retention of newly learned material may range from a low of about 10% (Watts & McGuire, 1964) to a high of about 75% (Fitzsimmons & Osburn, 1968)—the wide range being due partly to differences in messages (printed selections vs. TV) and partly to differences in methodological procedures for measuring recall versus recognition. However, some experimental studies have shown substantial amounts of information retention for periods as long as 6 months; and oft-repeated exposure to a message, as in media advertising campaigns, may make it almost impossible to forget a product slogan.

Retention of any attitude change that may have occurred tends to follow a rather similar declining pattern. After 4 to 6 weeks, the amount of attitude change retained may be from one-third to two-thirds of the initial change, which of course may have been small to begin with (Watts & McGuire, 1964). In a study of five different TV documentaries shown to college students, Fitzsimmons and Osburn (1968) found that only one retained a significant attitudinal effect after 4 weeks. However, many experiments have found attitude changes lasting as long as 6 months (McGuire, 1969), and a very impressive classroom study by Rokeach (1971) showed significant attitude changes lasting well over one year. Keep in mind that all of these findings stem from studies in which the persuasive message was delivered only once, and that fact makes it hard to achieve long-lasting attitude change (Cook & Flay, 1978).

Research has shown that repeated re-exposures to a persuasive message will strengthen and prolong any prior opinion change (Cook & Insko, 1968). A dramatic example of this principle may be seen in the 25-year follow-up of Newcomb's Bennington College students, whose attitudes had been changed in a liberal direction by their college experiences (Newcomb et al., 1967). The authors found that many of these women had chosen a supportive postcollege environment of husbands and associates, and as a result they retained much of the attitude change that had been created 25 years before. Similar results were reported in a later follow-up after nearly 50 years (Cohen & Alwin, 1993).

Whether or not message retention is *essential* for attitude change has been a bone of contention. On one hand, there is strong evidence that message retention is positively correlated with attitude change (Chaiken, Wood, & Eagly, 1996), but other researchers have argued that there is not a necessary connection (Petty & Wegener, 1998). In the previous chapter, we saw two examples of attitude acquisition that occurred in the absence of awareness. The research on *mere exposure* showed that attitudes toward a neutral stimulus became more favorable with repeated presentation, and that this effect occurred even when the stimuli were presented subliminally. Similarly, research on *classical conditioning* has shown that attitude formation can occur by repeated pairings of an attitude object with a positive or negative stimulus, and that participants are generally not aware that any association has been made. Thus it appears that message retention can lead to greater attitude change, but that retention (or even awareness) is not required.

In summarizing research findings on retention, Petty and Wegener (1998) suggested that message retention may lead to *greater* attitude change if the message recipient does not already hold a strong, well-thought-out attitude, and if there are no major peripheral cues, such as an expert source, that would influence the attitude. In such situations, the extent to which the individual recalls the content of the persuasive message will lead to attitudes that are more consistent with it.

Selective Memory. The preceding discussion raises the issue of selective memory for messages. As we have seen, there is a tendency for people to surround themselves with, and attend to, information that is consistent with their existing attitudes or beliefs (de facto selective exposure and selective perception). This tendency can be further enhanced by our tendency to selectively remember information that is consistent with our attitudes and beliefs. For example, Oliver (1999) found that prejudice levels among viewers moderated their memory for a criminal suspect. In this study, white participants were shown a newscast depicting either an African American or a white criminal suspect. Three months later, high-prejudice white participants were more likely to misidentify the African American suspect as the criminal, and they were less likely to identify the white suspect as the criminal.

Studies of Action

The final dependent variable to be considered in studies of mass communication is behavioral—taking overt action as a result of the persuasive message. The relationship between attitudes and behavior may range from zero to very strongly positive, and we will consider the nature of this relationship between attitudes and behavior at length in Chapter 12. This section describes some of the typical behavioral effects of the mass media.

We know that occasionally the mass media can have very dramatic effects on people's behavior. Perhaps the most famous example is Orson Welles' 1938 radio broadcast dramatizing an invasion of Earth by Martians, a broadcast so realistic and compelling that over a million people were driven to panic and many fled their homes (Cantril, 1940). Of course, in realistic situations involving imminent danger, such as hurricane warnings along the Gulf Coast, we take it for granted that millions of people will be influenced by media warning messages. However, what are the more typical behavioral effects of the media?

Allocation of Time. Comstock and Scharrer (1999) have summarized studies of the amount of time that people spend with the mass media, particularly television. American children, from the age of three onward, spend one-sixth or more of their waking hours watching television. However, despite fears and claims that children's television attention would sharply reduce their reading, outdoor play, hobbies, or social activities, careful research has shown very little evidence of such effects—except perhaps some decrease in organized outdoor activities (Timmer, Eccles, & O'Brien, 1985; Anderson & Collins, 1988). Both children and adults often find time for media attention by coordinating viewing or listening with other household activities such as cooking, cleaning, and meals, and even with more demanding cognitive activities such as reading or homework.

Alleged Passivity.   A number of authors have claimed that the availability of TV, and earlier of radio, has increased the passivity of their audiences, perhaps even causing them to behave like "zombies." However, Anderson and Collins' (1988) careful research review concluded that there is no evidence of any such effect. An elaborate study in England found no evidence that children's TV viewing produced any of the five different sorts of passivity that concerned school teachers (Himmelweit et al., 1958). In fact, viewing in their early years may give children a faster start in school because it promotes a larger vocabulary and a larger store of knowledge.

Scholastic Performance.   The research evidence with respect to scholastic achievement is clear—despite the possible advantage in preschool years just mentioned, school-age children who watch more television score lower on a wide range of academic outcomes. The effect is consistent across different academic domains (reading, writing, math) and across different socioeconomic levels. This negative relationship has been found in several extremely large-scale studies (see Comstock & Scharrer, 1999).

Although watching more television is related to lower school performance, the issue of *causality* is unclear. Gaddy (1986) argued that the effect was spurious and disappeared when demographic and other background characteristics were controlled. However, in their extensive review, Comstock and Scharrer (1999) found that other background variables cannot fully explain the negative relationship. They concluded that the relationship is complex and potentially mediated by a number of psychological variables:

> Television viewing is inversely related to achievement when it displaces intellectually and experientially richer stimuli. Viewing is positively related to achievement when the stimuli it supplies are intellectually and experientially richer than the available alternatives. (p. 259)

In sum, the link between television viewing and performance depends on what the viewer watches, and on what activities are replaced by watching television.

Social Behavior.   Research on the media and social behavior has focused most heavily on aggressive behavior, and the overall findings on this topic as well as on prosocial behavior have been summarized in a number of reviews (Hearold, 1986; Comstock & Scharrer, 1999; Fisch, 2002; Sparks & Sparks, 2002).

The amount of violence shown on U.S. TV entertainment programs is horrendously high, and by far the most violent time of the week is on Saturday morning programming for children, which averages 18 or more violent episodes per hour (Signorielli, Gross, & Morgan, 1982). Many large-scale reviews of the research have concluded that watching these very high levels of violence causes an increase in aggressive behavior (National Commission on the Causes and Prevention of Violence, 1969; Scientific Advisory Committee on Television and Social Behavior, 1972; American Psychological Association, 1993; National Academy of Science, 1993), though a few reviews have concluded that the effect is so small as to have no practical importance (Milavsky et al., 1982; Freedman, 1984). Careful experimental studies have demonstrated that watching violent media

Photograph courtesy of George Gerbner.
Reprinted by permission.

Box 9–3　GEORGE GERBNER, *Watchdog on TV Content and Effects*

George Gerbner was born in Budapest, Hungary, in 1919 and won first prize in a national literary competition as a teenager. In 1939 he emigrated to the United States, quickly learned English, and earned a B.A. in journalism from the University of California at Berkeley in 1942. After briefly working as a reporter and columnist for the San Francisco Chronicle, *he became a U.S. citizen in 1943 and enlisted in the army. He served overseas with the secret services and received a field commission and Bronze Star for operations behind enemy lines.*

After the war, Gerbner worked as an editor for the U.S. Information Service and taught at junior colleges before earning his Ph.D. in communication at the University of Southern California in 1955. After teaching 9 years at the University of Illinois, he moved to the University of Pennsylvania as the Dean of the Annenberg School of Communication. Since 1989 he has been Dean Emeritus and has held visiting professorships at universities in five countries, most recently at Temple University.

Gerbner has directed many research projects on mass communications, studying topics as diverse as the portrayal of film heroes, media treatments of aging, press coverage of foreign news, and violence on television. He served for 17 years as editor of the Journal of Communication, *and he is especially noted for his theories about the "cultivation effect" of television in influencing viewers' norms of expected social behavior, and for developing "cultural indicators" through analysis of trends in television content and effects.*

presentations has larger effects on initially aggressive youngsters, and that viewers are more likely to respond aggressively when the violence is portrayed as rewarded, useful, or justified (Roberts & Maccoby, 1985).

The other side of the coin—much less studied—is that television can also stimulate prosocial behavior and behavioral intentions (Rushton, 1982), and that the effects of intentional prosocial programming can be quite strong (Hearold, 1986). Viewing programs such as *Sesame Street* and *Mister Rogers' Neighborhood* has been shown to encourage children's sharing, cooperation, and self-control (Friedrich & Stein, 1975; Huston et al., 2001). Similarly, preschool children who watched selected prosocial episodes of programs like *Barney* later displayed increased levels of helping behavior (Fisch, 2002). Finally, several science-oriented shows (*Bill Nye, the Science Guy, 3-2-1 Contact*, and *Cro*) have been found to produce more positive attitudes toward science among children (Fisch, 2002). However, there is very little prosocial programming available on U.S. television, and Fairchild (1988) has given an interesting account of the difficulties involved in pioneering and producing a TV program that was aimed primarily at prosocial themes.

Political Behavior.   The cost of U.S. election campaigns for president and congress exceeded the staggering total of $3 billion in 2000 (Ackerman & Ayres, 2002). Much of this money goes for paid political ads, but in addition a huge amount of unpurchased television and radio time is devoted to election news, predictions, interviews, and debates.

Nevertheless, the mass media have shown very little ability to change voting intentions from one party to another, probably in large part because publicity on one side is usually quickly counteracted by publicity on the other side. Paid political advertisements have quite small effects on voting decisions, affecting mostly the small group of still-undecided voters (Kaid, 1981), and they fairly often influence decisions *against* rather than for the advertised candidate (Raj, 1982). However, it is clear that candidates' expenditures for media ads are related to their overall vote totals, particularly where the candidates are not already well known, so advertising definitely is not useless (Grush, 1980). Also, in cases where television coverage of a public issue is unbalanced in a pro or con direction, public opinion is likely to shift in that direction subsequently (Page, Shapiro, & Dempsey, 1987).

Research has demonstrated that the major effects of the mass media during election campaigns are *reinforcement* of voters' current attitudes, and *activation* of any latent motivational predispositions (such as party loyalty or strong issue commitments) that would lead people to vote in the desired direction. There is also some suggestive evidence that media exposure can help to increase voter turnout (Weiss, 1969). Kinder (1998) summarized the situation as follows:

> Activation and reinforcement may not be as glamorous (or as sinister) as persuasion, but they are important processes nonetheless. Campaigns activate voters by arousing their inter-est...[and] campaigns reinforce voters by providing good reasons and reminding them why they are Democrats or Republicans. (p. 818)

Until 1987, the broadcast media in the U.S. were required to follow the FCC's "fairness doctrine," which mandated equal coverage of both sides of controversial issues, and they still generally avoid partisan candidate endorsements. In contrast, the print media have historically been free to editorialize and even to slant the news on behalf of their preferred candidates. In almost every election, the great majority of newspapers support the Republican presidential candidate. In keeping with the "minimal effects" conclusion discussed in an earlier section, such editorials may influence only a few percent of voters. However, when other factors are held constant, careful research has shown that these lopsided newspaper endorsements have led several million readers to follow their paper's editorial advice—far more than needed for the winning margin in a close election (Robinson, 1972; Coombs, 1981). Thus newspapers can sometimes have a crucial influence on elections—similarly, television coverage which is largely favorable or unfavorable to an issue, often has an effect in swaying public opinion in that direction (Page et al., 1987).

In Chapter 14 we will return to a more extensive discussion of factors affecting political behavior and voting.

Advertising.   In developing countries, where mass media availability is new and information about products and fashions is not widespread, advertising in the media may be very effective (Schramm, 1964). Likewise, with child audiences, who have not yet learned to discount the persuasive impact of commercials, the 60,000 TV ads that they are exposed to each year may both influence specific product preferences and also carry the broader message that "to consume is to be happy" (Adler et al., 1980; Comstock & Scharrer, 1999).

In the United States and other media-saturated countries, much advertising is directed at maintaining the share of the market already held by a particular toothpaste, automobile, or detergent (that is, it is aimed at *reinforcing* existing preferences). Frequently, research has shown no relationship between advertising budgets and sales, but other studies have shown small increases in sales resulting from advertising campaigns (Gorn & Goldberg, 1982; Assmus, Farley, & Lehmann, 1984). Paradoxically, though a major ad campaign may cost millions of dollars, it does not have to influence large percentages of people in order to be successful. A highly successful sales campaign may increase a brand's share of the market by only 1%, and it may even alienate more people (not current buyers) than it wins over as new buyers (Bauer, 1964; Raj, 1982). Thus small percentage effects may have a great dollar value, and yet the advertiser may not care at all what you or I think of his "pitch" or his product, as long as somebody likes them. Comstock and Scharrer (1999) concluded:

> Television commercials do not sell products. They sell a position in the cognitive space of the viewer that will make it more likely that the product in question will fall within the universe of considered options when a purchase is under way, whether it is of a $33,947 sport utility vehicle or a $1.09 bar of soap. (p. 44)

PERSUASIVE EFFECTS OF PERSONAL COMMUNICATION

There is general agreement that personal communication usually has a stronger influence on people's attitudes and behavior than does mass communication. Initial evidence for this conclusion came from studies of face-to-face speeches versus radio versus printed messages (Cantril & Allport, 1935), and similar conclusions were reached in the early election surveys, which failed to find the expected strong mass media effects (Lazarsfeld et al., 1948; Berelson, Lazarsfeld, & McPhee, 1954). As a result of their findings of greater exposure to personal political conversation than to the mass media, the authors proposed the hypothesis that communication follows a **two-step flow**: from media to "opinion leaders" to other citizens. We discuss this two-step flow concept in more detail later in this section.

Critics have pointed out that the early data only suggested but did not prove that personal communication had a stronger influence on voting than did the media (O'Keefe & Atwood, 1981). However, Katz and Lazarsfeld (1955) showed that personal contacts were more effective than the media in influencing women's decisions about marketing, fashion, and movie-going. Similarly, there is very convincing evidence that personal contact increases voter turnout, though it does not seem generally successful in changing people's voting choice (e.g., Kraut & McConahay, 1973; Traugott & Katosh, 1981). Huckfeldt and Sprague (1995) have highlighted the importance of political discussion and interpersonal communication as an aspect of democratic citizenship.

Many reasons can be given to explain the apparent superiority of personal communication. Because it is a face-to-face situation, attention is likely to be higher than with the media, and the message can be given at an appropriate moment and planned to be relevant to the recipient's motives and attitudes. Because such communication is two-way, feedback from the recipient can be used to increase comprehension, counter any objections, and stress particularly effective arguments. The communicator will probably have many traits and interests in common with the recipient, and he or she can repeat part or all of the message, if necessary. The personal relationship may cause the recipient to relax any defenses against being influenced, and it may encourage yielding (compliance) in the interests of maintaining smooth social relations. Finally, if the recipient is also participating actively in the conversation, he or she may occasionally express agreement with the communicator—a form of public commitment—and such commitments have been found to increase attitude change and retention (e.g., Pallak, Cook, & Sullivan, 1980).

Studies of Personal Communication

Although all of these advantages do seem to be available, personal communication rather seldom makes use of them. Any political or buying influence which does take place is apt to be just part of an ordinary everyday conversation rather than a planned influence attempt. Altough research studies usually focus on *changes* in opinion or behavior, personal conversations are much more apt to *reinforce* currently held views. As Huckfeldt and Sprague (1995) noted, "few people intentionally expose themselves to repugnant political views" (p. 158). Berelson et al. (1954) found about 30% of political conversations did not involve voting preferences (they concerned predictions of who would win, exchange of information, etc.), and over 60% involved reinforcing comments about mutual views on the candidates or the issues. That left only 6% of political conversations that involved any argument or attempt to change opinions!

There have been three major methods used to determine which citizens are **opinion leaders** in personal communication with others. The original method used was *self-designation* as an advice-giver in response to questions like "Have you recently tried to convince anyone of your political ideas?" Many later studies used one or the other of two nomination approaches. In the *sociometric* method, all members of a group (for instance, all local doctors) are asked to list the group members who are most influential in giving information and advice (for instance, about the merits of new drugs). In the *key informant* approach, a limited number of knowledgeable individuals are asked to list the group members who are most influential concerning a given topic, such as choice of fashions. In some studies these "influentials" have also been interviewed to determine who or what had influenced them. Using any one of these methods, about 20% to 25% of a group are typically found to be opinion leaders on any given topic. Although there are some differences in the individuals identified as leaders by the several methods, there does appear to be substantial consistency in the methods' results (Jacoby, 1974).

What are the characteristics of opinion leaders that have been found in research? In general, they are very like those people whom they influence, usually from the same social class, though perhaps with a bit more status and a bit more contact with the media (Katz, 1957). The finding that opinion leaders are more likely than others to split their vote suggests that they may be unusually independent and self-reliant in making up their own mind on political questions (Kingdon, 1970). The breadth of their leadership across different areas of decision-making is somewhat at issue. Early studies found no generalization of opinion leadership across different areas such as public affairs and fashion (Katz & Lazarsfeld, 1955), but later studies showed considerable overlap of leadership, particularly across somewhat similar product categories such as clothing and cosmetics (Jacoby, 1974).

There are a number of sequential steps in the process by which a person adopts an innovation such as a new farming method or cosmetic product. First, awareness of the innovation must occur, and next, interest must be developed and information obtained. Third, this information must be evaluated for its usefulness, and fourth, the person may try out the innovation in his or her own situation. If this proves successful, full-scale and continuing adoption may follow. In general it has been found that mass media sources are most important in the early stages of the adoption process (awareness and perhaps also information gathering), whereas personal sources are more important in the later stages, particularly in evaluation and final decision (Rogers, 1982).

This finding returns us to our earlier question about the direction of flow of communication in the influence process.

The Flow of Communication

Two-Step? The original two-step-flow hypothesis postulated that communication about public affairs flowed first from the media to attentive "opinion leaders," who in turn passed it on to other citizens, but that most average citizens did not attend to the media sources directly. There is considerable evidence supporting this sequence (e.g., Katz, 1957; Huckfeldt & Sprague, 1995), but additional findings cited by Katz and later authors make the picture much more complicated. One recent study found that opinion leaders did not use mass media more than other citizens, but they used "higher-quality," more specialized media sources (Weimann, 1994).

Multi-Step? A multi-step theory posits that information flows from the media to opinion leaders and then down through several levels of individuals having decreasing amounts of interest and knowledge concerning the topic. For instance, Katz and Lazarsfeld (1955) proposed that opinion leaders were most interested in the topic, but the people they talked with were moderately interested rather than completely uninterested. Other studies have shown quite definitively that most opinion-givers are also opinion-receivers. For instance, Troldahl and Van Dam (1965) found that 30% of their respondents had asked someone about their opinion on a major news topic in the previous 2 weeks, and two-thirds of those individuals had also been asked for such an opinion. From these data it appears clear that opinion leaders are also listeners, but that a great many citizens neither talk nor listen to anyone about newsworthy events (63% in this study had not discussed any major news topic with anyone, and the comparable figure in a later study was 40%—Robinson & Levy, 1986a). These noninteractive individuals do get a certain amount of information directly from the media, however (Robinson, 1976).

Circular Flow. Probably the most accurate view of persuasive communication is that its flow is usually circular, involving much alternation between media sources and personal sources (Page & Shapiro, 1992; Huckfeldt & Sprague, 1995). For instance, we have already described the important finding that different sources are dominant at different stages of the innovation adoption process. In addition, even though one source may be predominant at a given stage, other sources are usually involved (Rogers, 1982).

Several studies illustrate the close alternating or circular relation between obtaining information from the media and from interpersonal discussion (Lenart, 1994; Mondak, 1995a). People's comprehension of news events depends as much or more on discussion of the news with other people as on the amount of media news exposure (Robinson & Levy, 1986a). The same pattern is found in election campaigns—watching the presidential debates on television is normally associated with personal discussions of them, but the interpersonal communication is apt to contribute more heavily to people's understanding of campaign issues and to their later voting decisions (McLeod et al., 1979; Kennamer, 1985). In calamities, such as the assassination of President Kennedy, diffusion of the news is largely achieved by word-of-mouth (over two-thirds of the population learned of it within half an hour), but then people turn to the media for confirmation and further details (Greenberg, 1964).

The circular flow of communication has been summarized by Klapper (1960) as follows:

Personal influence may be more effective than persuasive mass communication, but at present mass communication seems the most effective means of stimulating personal influence. (p. 72)

Combining Media and Personal Influence. As a result of research findings about the mutual importance of both methods of communication, a number of attempts have been made to combine them in order to achieve greater persuasive effect. An approach that proved effective for developing community action programs in rural areas was to bring groups of citizens together for a media presentation, immediately followed by a group discussion and consideration of possible action (UNESCO, 1960). With children, following up a TV episode from *Mister Rogers' Neighborhood* with a discussion by the teacher that focused on the same message about helpfulness proved successful in increasing cooperative behavior (Friedrich & Stein, 1975—see Figure 9–2). Similar cumulative effects of media presentations plus discussion have been found in encouraging preschoolers' helping behavior, reducing sex-role stereotyping among grade school students, and deterring smoking by adolescents (Ahammer & Murray, 1979; Johnston et al., 1980; Evans et al., 1981). These studies illustrate the potential practical importance of some of the research on persuasive communication.

OTHER EFFECTS OF MASS MEDIA

Although the mass media are generally not very effective in changing public attitudes, they have other effects which are important to consider. Shrum (2002) has proposed that, beyond any direct effect on people's attitudes, media exposure does lead to an increase in the accessibility of information. Recall from Chapters 4 and 5 that accessibility is a central concept in Fazio's (1988) model of attitudes, and a topic of considerable social psychological research. **Accessibility** refers to the ease with which a cognitive element

FIGURE 9–2 Combining media presentation and personal communication on the same topic can have a stronger effect than either alone.

can be activated. Three potential consequences of differential accessibility are cultivation of reality, agenda-setting, and conferral of prestige, which we discuss in the following sections.

The Media Define Reality

The first of these important effects of mass media has been termed the creation of "secondhand reality"—that is, the definition of what is really happening in the world beyond one's own firsthand experience. Each one of us has a very limited range of experiences that we have actually participated in firsthand. Beyond that range, all our knowledge, beliefs, and attitudes come from others, and the great majority probably come from some mass communication medium (ranging from books to billboards to radio and television).

If you have ever participated in an event which was written up in the press or described in broadcasts, you have probably discovered how different the media's "secondhand reality" is from what you have experienced firsthand. Inevitably the media select certain details to mention and omit many others. In this process they highlight and emphasize some aspects of the event and obscure others. Often this results in distortion and misleading reports, even when there is no intention to mislead the public at all. When the personal beliefs, values, and motives of the reporters or of the editorial staff enter into the reporting process, as they often do, the resulting picture can be even farther from an objective, complete, and unbiased account. In fact, careful research in recent U.S. presidential elections has shown that some TV network news anchors displayed systematically different amounts of positive facial expressions when they were mentioning different candidates (Friedman, DiMatteo, & Mertz, 1980). Furthermore, the smiles they bestowed on candidates had a favorable impact on viewers' voting on election day (Mullen et al., 1986). These smiles are very subtle stimuli—probably outside the usual awareness of both newscasters and viewers— but this research dramatically indicates how potent television's effects can sometimes be.

The ways in which media selectivity occurs in the reporting process have been described in many empirical studies. Cutlip (1954) demonstrated that only about 10% of the news copy stemming from national news agencies ends up in small-town daily newspapers, so obviously the editors' interests and biases play a very strong part in determining what is available to the public to read. Even large-city dailies rely heavily on the news items selected by the national agencies' staffs. The three major weekly news magazines, *Time*, *Newsweek*, and *U.S. News & World Report*, have been strongly criticized for the amount of bias and slanted editorial opinion that creeps into their news reporting (Bagdikian, 1962). The titles of several in-depth scholarly volumes clearly highlight the reality-defining nature of the news media: *Deciding What's News* (Gans, 1979), *Making News: A Study in the Construction of Reality* (Tuchman, 1978), and *Creating Reality: How TV News Distorts News Events* (Altheide, 1976).

Television news broadcasts are particularly prone to creation of their own "reality" because of limitations on what is possible and easy to put on the air and what will attract audience attention (Epstein, 1973; McCombs & Reynolds, 2002). The TV network camera crews are normally located in only a handful of major U.S. cities and a few foreign capitals, so their geographic coverage is sharply limited. Buying film footage from other sources is expensive, so most of what we see as supposedly up-to-the-minute network "news" is confined to events which happen in those major cities. The inputs from other locations are usually confined to human interest stories or continuing events such as strikes and warfare, for which footage from several recent days can be spliced together to make a coherent story. Furthermore, news organizations, both in Europe and the U.S., exercise much selectivity in deciding what events are "newsworthy" and in trying to highlight a theme or pattern in the events that are broadcast (Gurevitch & Blumler, 1982).

In the past, because of the FCC's "fairness doctrine," political news on American television has been limited to stories that could be presented as having two sides. The networks generally still maintain this quest for "balance," even when almost all experts are on one side of an issue, as they are in proclaiming the occurrence of global warming. Thus U.S. television emphasizes controversy more than consensus, and it also stresses the horse-race aspect of "who's ahead" in political campaigns much more than the substantive issues and policy questions of the campaign (Patterson, 1980; Lichter & Noyes, 1995). The nightly newscasts constantly strive to present flashy pictures—"hecklers, crowds, motorcades, balloons, rallies and gossip" (Patterson & McClure, 1976, p. 22). The result, as Lang and Lang (1984) have pointed out in numerous research examples, is that the picture on the TV tube is often much different from the reality on the streets of the city or the battlefield overseas. Particularly clear examples of this TV creation of reality occurred in selective coverage of natural disasters around the world (Adams, 1986), and in reporting the contentious aftermath of the 2000 presidential election between Al Gore and George W. Bush.

However, this creation of secondhand reality by TV should not be confused with polemical slanting of the news. Despite the claims of antiadministration bias in TV reporting of the Vietnam War, Russo's (1971) careful content analysis study concluded that, on the average, network newscasts of the war did not present any noticeable bias against administration policies. Such claims of partisan bias are an inescapable aspect of media coverage of any highly controversial issue, for research shows that people with extreme views on such an issue will always tend to see the media as biased *against them* (Vallone, Ross, & Lepper, 1985).

The broadest aspect of the media's creation of reality is the very widespread effect known as **enculturation**. This is "the process of instilling and reinforcing the values, beliefs, traditions, behavioral standards, and views of reality that are held by most members of a given culture" (Oskamp & Schultz, 1998, p. 265). As far back in human history as Homer and other oral storytellers, this has always been one of the main functions of the media. Because this effect is so pervasive in any given culture and so consistent with the existing cultural patterns, it can easily be overlooked, and it is very hard to study objectively. Nevertheless, it is extremely important, and it has received considerable research attention in recent years.

One example of enculturation is what George Gerbner and his colleagues have called the **cultivation effect** of television—that is, that it "cultivates" or inculcates in its viewers a set of shared assumptions about the nature of social reality (e.g., Gerbner et al., 1980; Gerbner et al., 2002). These assumptions are shown, for instance, in commonly held beliefs about which individuals and groups are important and powerful, about what we should believe in ("the free enterprise system") and what we should fear ("crime in the streets"), and so forth. An example of TV's cultivation effects is its pervasive negative stereotyping and underrepresentation of low-power groups in society, such as women, ethnic minorities, and older persons. Another example is its overemphasis on crime, in comparison with the actual amount in our society—a TV picture of a "mean" or "scary" world. Although there has been criticism of the cultivation hypothesis (Hirsch, 1980), there is considerable empirical support for it when it is carefully operationalized—for instance, viewers who watch mostly situation comedies would not be expected to perceive a scary world (Hawkins & Pingree, 1982; Kinder, 1998).

A social psychological concept closely related to defining reality, or the cultivation effect, is the **framing** of a public issue—that is, which of its many possible features are emphasized or de-emphasized in discussing it (Kinder, 1998). For instance, the issue of abortion policy can be framed as the woman's right to control her body or the fetus's right to life. Similarly, affirmative action policy can be framed as a desirable remedy for past discriminatory actions or as unwarranted preferential treatment in hiring (Stoker, 2001). Many recent studies demonstrate that public opinion can be markedly affected by the way in which the media and spokespersons frame such current issues (e.g., Iyengar, 1991; Nelson & Kinder, 1996).

The Media Determine the Public Agenda

Probably the most important effect of the mass media is their **agenda-setting** function. There is clear evidence that people attend to, are interested in, and talk about the information and ideas that they receive through the media. Because the media do not reflect reality completely and faithfully, it follows that their selectivity has a marked effect on what most people learn about and respond to.

The selectivity shown by the media in determining the public agenda has been demonstrated across many studies (Dearing & Rogers, 1996; Wanta & Ghanem, 2003). Funkhouser (1973) found that coverage of major public issues in the three major U.S. news magazines from 1960 to 1970 did not show a close correspondence to the occurrence of important actual events. For instance, coverage of the Vietnam War reached its peak and began to decline before the war itself reached a peak. However, media coverage showed a close relationship to, and probably largely determined, people's responses to poll questions about the most important national problem. In a similar study, MacKuen (1981) found strong agenda-setting effects of media coverage on four different issues: the Vietnam War, race relations, campus unrest, and energy problems. On the local scene, also, media investigative reporting on an issue such as police brutality has been found to influence citizens' judgments about the importance of the issue (Leff, Protess, & Brooks, 1986). The individuals who are most influenced by the media's agenda-setting effect are ones having low education, low interest in politics, and low party identification (Iyengar & Kinder, 1987).

The causal direction of agenda-setting effects is an important question. If both media content and the public's concerns were measured at only one point in time, it could be the case that public concerns or interests determine media coverage, rather than vice versa. Or both might be reacting to the external reality of events in the world, which certainly do provide a starting point for both media coverage and public concerns (Behr & Iyengar, 1985). However, a number of careful longitudinal studies have shown that the direction of influence about which events are important is primarily from media coverage to the public agenda (McCombs, 1977; MacKuen, 1981; Behr & Iyengar, 1985); and, interestingly, the print media seem to have stronger agenda-setting effects than does television (Patterson & McClure, 1976; McCombs, 1977).

Definitive experimental studies have recently been done that subtly manipulated the amount of coverage of various topics in TV newscasts by unobtrusively combining stories from previous news programs. When these specially structured programs were shown, the viewers' judgments of the importance of various issues mirrored the amount of coverage in the programs, thus clearly establishing that the programs were the causal factor. In fact, the program content even helped to determine what specific issues the president would be judged on when viewers rated his overall performance in office (Iyengar et al., 1984; Iyengar & Kinder, 1986). Thus television works to "prime" viewers' notions about what topics are important, and in so doing it can even influence the outcomes of national elections (see McCombs & Reynolds, 2002, for a review).

Photograph courtesy of Shanto Iyengar.
Reprinted by permission.

Box 9–4 SHANTO IYENGAR, *Media Effects Researcher*

Shanto Iyengar is Chair of the Department of Communication and also a professor in Political Science at Stanford University, where he conducts research on political communication and the effects of mass media. His six books include Going Negative: How Political Advertisements Shrink and Polarize the Electorate, Do the Media Govern?, *and* Is Anyone Responsible?: How Television Frames Political Issues. *This chapter discusses his research on the agenda-setting or "priming" effect of the mass media.*

Iyengar earned his Ph.D. in political science from the University of Iowa in 1973, taught at Kansas State University and UCLA, and later received a postdoctoral fellowship to study social psychology at Yale. He has done extensive research on media agenda-setting, political campaign advertising on TV, and racial stereotyping. His honors include a Lifetime Career Award from the American Political Science Association, and in his free time he is an avid cricket player.

In sum, it appears clear that the various mass media all fulfill the agenda-setting function described by Cohen (1963):

> The mass media may not be successful much of the time in telling people what to think, but the media are stunningly successful in telling their audience what to think about. (p. 16)

The Media Confer Prestige

A final major effect of the media is that, by their very mention of people, events, and issues, they confer importance on them in the public eye (Lazarsfeld & Merton, 1948). In politics, the previously unknown candidates who win early presidential primary elections in small and atypical states (and often even nonwinners who did better than expected) get massive media attention, which gives their campaigns a major, though often short-lived, boost (Adams, 1984). Some media celebrities, such as Bill Cosby and Jay Leno, have become so famous that they have been widely credited with personal persuasive power in selling products or ideas. But even formerly obscure nonentities whose actions or thoughts are picked out for coverage by TV or in print are suddenly invested with a seeming importance out of all proportion to their status in life—an outcome that has been called "15 minutes of fame." As a result, the media audience will pay attention to them and their ideas. Dramatic examples of this process have occurred even with individuals who attempted to assassinate presidents and then were featured on the covers of news magazines. As Lazarsfeld and Merton (1948) put it,

The audiences of mass media apparently subscribe to the circular belief: "If you really matter, you will be at the focus of mass attention and, if you are at the focus of mass attention, then surely you must really matter." (p. 102)

SUMMARY

Early studies of communication and propaganda were motivated by the fear that demagogues could easily sway the gullible audience. Since then, research has shown that persuasive communication is much less successful and much more complicated in its effects than had first been thought.

The main *independent* variables in persuasive communication are factors related to the source, the message, the medium (the topic of this chapter), the audience, and the target behavior. The main *dependent* variables involve the sequential steps of audience exposure, attention, comprehension, acceptance (yielding), retention, and action. Each of these stages may display different findings about communication effects because different independent variables and mediating variables may be important at each stage. Although the mass media often have minimal effects, they can have powerful effects under certain conditions, and personal and situational characteristics are important mediators of any media effects.

Personal communication is generally agreed to have stronger effects than mass communication. However, most personal communication is reinforcing or informative rather than persuasive in nature. The *two-step flow* of communication (from mass media to opinion leaders to other citizens) was proposed by early studies to help account for the low direct effectiveness of the media. However, it appears that communication flow tends to be circular, alternating between media sources and personal sources.

Although the mass media are generally not very effective in changing public attitudes, they define "reality" for us in areas beyond the limited range of our firsthand personal experience, and in so doing, they *enculturate* or instill in their audience the shared beliefs and values of their society. Also, by their selection of events to cover, the mass media determine the public agenda, and they confer prestige and apparent importance on the people, events, and issues that they decide to cover.

10

Attitude-Change Theories and Research: Methodology; Learning and Judgment Approaches

We are incredibly heedless in the formation of our beliefs, but find ourselves filled with an illicit passion for them when anyone proposes to rob us of their companionship.—James Harvey Robinson.

Some praise at morning what they blame at night
But always think the last opinion right.—Alexander Pope.

If you give me any normal human being and a couple of weeks...I can change his behavior from what it is now to whatever you want it to be, if it's physically possible.—James McConnell.

These three statements about attitudinal and behavioral change illustrate the widely discrepant viewpoints that different authors have held on this subject. The topic of attitude *change* has probably occupied the attention of psychologists more than all the other aspects of attitudes put together. One reason for this is the great importance of attitude changes in human affairs—for example, in events such as religious conversions, political persuasion, commercial advertising campaigns, and changes in personal prejudices. Another major reason for interest in attitude change was expressed by Kurt Lewin: To really understand something, such as the concept *attitude*, one must study it as it changes—not while it remains stable. For instance, in studying prejudiced attitudes, it is not enough to know that prejudice exists; to learn more, we must study situations in which the amount of prejudice differs, or create programs and educational activities aimed at reducing prejudice.

This chapter and the following one summarize the major theories about attitude change and some selected portions of the huge body of research evidence in this field. We organize our discussion primarily around six broad theoretical orientations toward attitude change—learning, judgment, consistency, dissonance, attribution, and cognitive-response approaches. However, before beginning those topics, we must briefly summarize various kinds of attitude-change research and the major methodological problems involved in doing research in this area.

*Photograph courtesy of
M.I.T. Historical Collections.
Reprinted by permission.*

Box 10–1   KURT LEWIN, *Theorist, Researcher, and Founding Father*

*The most influential single figure in shaping modern social psychology, Kurt Lewin was
born in Prussia in 1890. After studying in Freiburg and Munich and receiving his Ph.D. at
Berlin in 1914, he served in the German Army in World War I. Subsequently, as Professor of
Philosophy and Psychology at the University of Berlin, he was a member of its influential
group of Gestalt psychologists until he left Germany in 1932 to escape Nazism. After
teaching briefly at Stanford and Cornell, he settled on the faculty at the University of
Iowa. In 1944 he founded the Research Center for Group Dynamics at M.I.T., where he
died suddenly in 1947. As a professor, he produced many graduates who became famous
researchers and leaders in social psychology.*

*As a theorist, Lewin was known for his development of psychological field theory. As
a researcher, he introduced methods which allowed scientific study of groups in real-life
situations. He was famous for studies of democratic and autocratic group leadership styles,
and of group discussion and decision-making processes. Advocating "action research,"
he pioneered practical projects to lessen prejudice, reduce wartime attitude problems, and
introduce group-participation methods into industrial management. He helped found the
National Training Laboratories, where his group dynamic principles were put to work in
"T-groups" designed to improve social adjustment and group effectiveness.*

TYPES OF ATTITUDE-CHANGE RESEARCH

There are two common approaches to attitude-change research: group settings, such as
testing a class of students, and experiments with individuals. Both types of research have
their advantages and their liabilities. In group research, many variables can be manipulated
or measured at the same time, and complex statistical designs are necessary to analyze
the data, which often show complicated interactions between variables. Because of the
limited ability to control conditions and weak manipulations of independent variables,
there is apt to be considerable error variance, which in turn necessitates large groups of
participants to obtain significance. In contrast, experiments with individual participants
usually concentrate on manipulation of one or two independent variables and control
of other variables, and they focus much less on measurement techniques for the dependent variable. The manipulation procedures are apt to be complicated and precise, with
careful checks on their success, so that a relatively large effect may be found. Because
other contaminating variables have been controlled experimentally, a simple statistical
design is often sufficient, and significance may be obtained even with small numbers of
participants.

TABLE 10–1   Most-Studied Variables Involved in Persuasion

Source Variables
- Credibility (expertise and trustworthiness)
- Attractiveness and likability
- Power
- Other (speed of speech, demographic variables, majority or minority status, similarity to recipient)

Message Variables
- Message topic, position, and style (issue relevance or importance, position, discrepancy, conclusion drawing, use of rhetorical questions)
- Message content (argument quality, argument quantity, positive versus negative framing, fear appeals, emotion versus reason, one-sided versus two-sided arguments)
- Message organization

Recipient Variables
- Attitudinal (accessibility, issue-relevant knowledge)
- Demographic (age, gender)
- Personality and skills (intelligence, self-esteem, self-monitoring, need for cognition)

Context Variables
- Distraction
- Audience reactions
- Forewarning (of positions, or of persuasive intent)
- Anticipated discussion or interaction
- Channel of communication or message modality
- Mood
- Repetition of message

Source: Topic headings from Petty & Wegener (1998).

Another way of categorizing attitude-change research is by the types of variables studied. In these two chapters we focus primarily on three major classes of variables involved in the process of communication—namely, the *source, message*, and *recipient*. (A fourth type of variable, the *medium* of communication, was discussed in Chapter 9). Table 10–1 also lists some variables of the *social context* surrounding the communication, many of which are discussed in the next chapter. A further account of research findings concerning attitude change in an area of great social importance can be found in Chapter 16, on racial attitudes and prejudice.

A multitude of topics have been studied in research on attitude change. A useful view of research on the process of attitude change is displayed in Figure 10–1. The figure shows the main independent variables and the mediating processes through which they produce attitude change. The study of attitude change has been an extremely active and continuous area of research for nearly a century, and Table 10–1 presents a brief list of the variables that have been most thoroughly studied, based on the summary of attitude-change research in Petty and Wegener's (1998) chapter in *The Handbook of Social Psychology*. Other reviews of recent research on attitudes and attitude change are published regularly in the *Annual Review of Psychology* (e.g., Petty et al., 1997; Wood, 2000; Fazio, 2003).

In these two chapters we discuss many of the variables that are involved in the process of attitude change, particularly those which have had the greatest amount of research attention. Interested readers may also wish to consult the review chapters just mentioned for further detailed information.

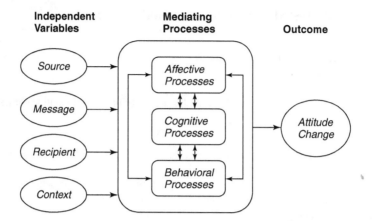

FIGURE 10–1 Types of independent variables and the moderating processes through which they affect attitude change.

Source: Petty, R. E., & Wegener, D. T. (1998). Attitude change: Multiple roles for persuasion variables. In D. T. Gilbert, S. T. Fiske, & G. Lindzey (Eds.), *The handbook of social psychology* (4th ed., Vol. 1, pp. 323–390). Boston: McGraw-Hill. Reprinted with permission of The McGraw-Hill Companies.

METHODOLOGICAL ISSUES

As an introduction, we briefly describe some of the most important methodological problems in attitude-change research. It should be noted that these problems are not unique to the area of attitude change, being frequently found in most experimental and quasi-experimental research in social psychology.

Research Design

The psychological knowledge that has been developed over decades of study is grounded in empirical research. Although there are a variety of research methodologies, most attitude research can be classified as either correlational, quasi-experimental, or experimental.

Correlational Studies.   In correlational studies, researchers make no effort to manipulate or change any aspect of the situation, but instead study aspects which are already there. They measure two or more variables and assess the relationships between them. This is the type of research often conducted by polling organizations, or in studies of attitude change resulting from mass media exposure.

Experimental Studies.   When they are possible, experiments are the most preferred method of attitude-change research. They are studies in which researchers achieve a high degree of *planned manipulation* of variables, and participants are *randomly assigned* to experimental conditions. Because of the level of control required (random assignment and great control over the manipulated variables), these studies are most often conducted with college students in university laboratories.

Quasi-Experiments.   In some instances, researchers have partial control over the independent variable, but may not be able to assign participants randomly to conditions.

There are a large number of possible quasi-experimental designs, ranging from simple ones with many threats to internal validity to more complicated and rigorous ones (cf. Cook et al., 1990). One example is research situations in which random assignment of participants to specific conditions is not possible, but where there is reason to believe (or evidence to show) that the groups being compared were not systematically different before the intervention that constitutes the key variable (e.g., a specific stimulus or experience).

The choice of a research design is always an important step in research. The requirement for an internally valid design becomes more difficult to meet when attitude-change studies move from the laboratory to more natural settings, as is often the case in research on marketing, political attitudes, media influence, racism, and many important social issues. There it is often difficult or impossible to assign people randomly to conditions. In such quasi-experimental situations, investigators usually cannot manipulate all of the crucial variables, but they can control the conditions under which the dependent variables are measured.

Although pretest–posttest experimental designs offer a great deal of control of variables, they also have potential dangers to be aware of. The use of a pretest may either sensitize participants to the issue and promote attitude change, or alternatively it may commit them to their initial viewpoints and deter attitude change (Rosnow & Suls, 1970). Fortunately this kind of experimental artifact does not seem to occur frequently (McGuire, 1966). Another procedure requiring great caution is the use of change scores in pretest–posttest designs (Cronbach & Furby, 1970). Both of these problems can be circumvented by use of posttest-only designs, in which participants are randomly assigned to treatment and control groups and are not given pretests before the experimental manipulation, as well as by other more complex research designs.

Measurement Methods

The most common way of measuring attitudes, verbal self-report, has many limitations, particularly if participants have any reason not to report accurately (e.g., laziness, defensiveness, saving face, etc.). As we discussed in Chapter 4, there are a number of alternative measurement techniques that do not require self-report. Some of these methods are indirect or disguised verbal techniques, physiological indicators, or implicit measures like the Implicit Association Test or affective priming techniques. Others are unobtrusive, nonreactive methods of observation, which are particularly useful in field studies. In these methods, subjects are not aware of being studied; examples include observation of political bumper stickers, or of racial seating patterns in a classroom.

Physiological and biochemical measures of attitudes have also been proposed (Cacioppo & Petty, 1983; Ito et al., 2002), as have methods which use bogus electronic instruments as a means of reducing participants' tendencies to give socially desirable responses (Jones & Sigall, 1971). At present, little is known about the comparability of these many differing methods of measurement, and the confusion of noncomparable dependent variable measures may account for many of the conflicting findings in the attitude research literature.

Demand Characteristics

This term, coined by Orne, refers to perceptual cues that indicate what is expected of people in a given situation (Orne, 1969). Such cues may be explicit or implicit, and they are present in all situations, though it is in laboratory experiments that they are most apt to present a problem in the interpretation of results. Orne and others have shown that participants in experimental situations may try to cooperate with the experimenter and thus respond in ways that will support the experimental hypothesis (Orne, 2002):

> For example, one task was to perform serial additions of each adjacent two numbers on sheets filled with rows of random digits. In order to complete just one sheet, the subject would be required to perform 224 additions! A stack of some 2,000 sheets was presented to each subject—clearly an impossible task to complete. After the instructions were given, the subject was deprived of his watch and told, "Continue to work; I will return eventually." Five and one-half hours later, the *experimenter* gave up! In general, subjects tended to continue with this type of task for several hours, usually with little decrement in performance. (p. 779)

The tendency for participants to be "good subjects" has serious implications for research on attitude change. For example, participants who learn or are told the experimental hypothesis more often perform in ways that will support it than do other subjects (Weber & Cook, 1972).

The effects of demand characteristics on research data can be minimized in several ways. Probably the most important way is through replication of studies in different laboratories and by experimenters with differing theoretical viewpoints. Also important are greater use of nonartificial settings, and detailed postexperimental inquiries about participants' suspicions. Other helpful procedures include careful development of experimental procedures and "cover stories" to conceal the point of the research, separating the experimental manipulation from collection of the dependent variable measures so that participants will not see a connection between them, and avoiding designs using pretests which may alert participants to the focus of study (Rosenthal & Rosnow, 1991). Fortunately, there is some evidence that participants are quite conscientious in following experimental instructions even if they are suspicious about the procedures (Cook et al., 1970).

Subject Effects

In addition to the set to be a cooperative participant, there are several other sets that participants in experiments can adopt. Weber and Cook (1972) have discussed the uncooperative, "negativistic subject"; the "faithful subject" who scrupulously follows task instructions and avoids acting on any suspicions which he or she may have; and the "apprehensive subject" who is worried about how his or her behavior may be evaluated. Weber and Cook's extensive review of the research literature concluded that there is much evidence for the operation of **evaluation apprehension**—that is, attempts by individuals to act in socially desirable ways because of their concern about evaluation by other people (e.g., Rosenberg, 1969).

Fortunately, there is little or no clear-cut evidence for operation of the other three subject roles except in certain very restricted situations (Spinner, Adair, & Barnes, 1977; Carlston & Cohen, 1980). Nonetheless, careful researchers will try to minimize the possibility that subject roles are influencing their findings. Appropriate precautions include carefully disguising the experimental hypothesis, doing research in natural settings where individuals are unaware that their behavior is being studied, and/or reducing evaluation apprehension by avoiding anxiety-arousing instructions and maintaining subject anonymity.

Another possible subject effect that has been studied stems from the frequent use of *volunteers* as participants in experiments. Many studies have found that volunteer participants differ in various ways from nonvolunteers, and these differences may affect their experimental performance (Rosenthal & Rosnow, 1975). For instance, volunteers are apt to be more educated, intelligent, and sociable, but also higher in need for approval. Because of the possibility of such effects, it is wise to avoid using volunteer participants whenever that is feasible.

As you are undoubtedly aware, college students are the participants most commonly used in social psychological research. Despite long-standing recommendations for use of a wider and more representative pool of subjects, the use of college students tested in laboratory situations has remained a large majority of all published social psychological studies (Sears, 1986; Vitelli, 1988). College students are not only younger, better educated, more intelligent, and more affluent than the average citizen, but they are also more likely than older adults to have less-crystallized attitudes, self-concepts, and peer relationships. The consequences of overreliance on such an unrepresentative database may be to distort some of our scientific findings about human nature in the direction of overemphasizing compliance, inconsistency, easy attitude change, and cognitive responses, and underemphasizing emotions, personality characteristics, and group norms (Sears, 1986). This potential danger needs to be considered in interpreting research findings and particularly in planning future studies.

Experimenter Effects

Distortions of research results produced by biases of the experimenter have been extensively studied by Rosenthal (1976, 2002). These biases can lead to errors in observation, recording of data, or computation of results, but the most-studied type of experimenter bias is **expectancies** that affect the participants' behavior. The experimenter's expectancies can be unintentionally transmitted to participants by subtle cues of voice tone, gestures, and facial expressions that display warmth and provide feedback (Rosenthal, 1976; Snodgrass & Rosenthal, 1982). Although there have been vigorous criticisms of some of Rosenthal's research conclusions (e.g., Barber & Silver, 1968), there is widespread agreement that experimenter effects can occur under some conditions. Thus attempts to eliminate or minimize them are desirable. Some of the best ways to do so include cutting down on experimenter–participant contact by mechanizing as much of the procedure as possible, using several different experimenters and testing for differences in their results, ensuring that the experimenter cannot reinforce participants' behavior differentially, keeping experimenters "blind" to the research hypothesis and/or to the experimental condition assigned to specific participants, and using extra control groups which differ only in the expectancies given to their members about the research hypothesis.

Deception and Suspicion

Because of the many extraneous variables, such as those discussed in the preceding sections, which can affect the results of attitude-change studies, investigators in this area have often felt it necessary or desirable to increase their control of conditions by deceiving participants during the course of experiments (Pittenger, 2002). Indeed, in the 1960s and 1970s, the percentage of studies published in the major social psychological journals that used deception rose significantly to about 60% (Gross & Fleming, 1982), though it has since dropped somewhat to around 47% (Sieber, Iannuzzo, & Rodriguez, 1995; Nicks, Korn, & Mainieri, 1997). Deception itself, and the participants' suspicion that may result, can become additional confounding variables that sometimes bias research results (Stricker, Messick, & Jackson, 1969). On the other hand, an equal number of studies have shown that prior deception and/or current suspiciousness do not necessarily bias subjects' responses (Fillenbaum & Frey, 1970; Holmes & Bennett, 1974). Thus, situational differences and the carefulness of the researcher are apt to determine whether use of deception poses a threat to valid conclusions.

Another reason which has been stressed for avoiding experimental deception wherever possible involves questions of ethical propriety (Kelman, 1967, 1972; Baumrind, 1985). When deception is used in psychological studies, it is generally of a mild and innocuous sort. Indeed, studies show that most psychologists would impose more stringent ethical safeguards in research than are advocated by typical citizens or by college undergraduates (Sullivan & Deiker, 1973; Wilson & Donnerstein, 1976; Christensen, 1988). The American Psychological Association (APA) (1973, 1982, 2002) has established ethical guidelines for all aspects of research, including the following points about deception in research (APA, 2002):

(a) Psychologists do not conduct a study involving deception unless they have determined that the use of deceptive techniques is justified by the study's significant prospective scientific, educational, or applied value and that effective nondeceptive alternative procedures are not feasible.

(b) Psychologists do not deceive prospective participants about research that is reasonably expected to cause physical pain or severe emotional distress.

(c) Psychologists explain any deception that is an integral feature of the design and conduct of an experiment to participants as early as is feasible, preferably at the conclusion of their participation, but no later than at the conclusion of the data collection, and permit participants to withdraw their data. (pp. 11–12)

Having discussed research methods and methodological problems, we turn now to theories of attitude change, beginning in this chapter with learning theories and judgment theories.

WHY HAVE THEORIES?

In considering theories of attitude change, we should first ask, What good are theories? Why do we have them? A number of answers have been given to these questions. First, theories provide a path to guide our steps in research; they suggest factors that are important to study, ones that we might not think of otherwise. Second, theories help us to understand research findings by putting them into a context; they explain the meaning of the facts that have been discovered—how and why they fit together. Third, theories allow us to predict what will happen under various conditions in the future. In turn, correct prediction of events provides a stringent test of the adequacy of any theory. As Deutsch and Krauss (1965) put it, "Theory is the net man weaves to catch the world of observation—to explain, predict, and influence it" (p. vii).

Another point that should be stressed is that *theories are never proven*. They can be disproven at crucial points by negative evidence, but an accumulation of positive evidence merely adds support to a theory rather than proving it in any final sense. These supportive data may also be compatible with another, different theory. When a theoretical relationship between two variables has been confirmed so many times that all authorities agree on its correctness, it is usually called a **law** (such as the *law of effect*, which states that any behavior that is rewarded is more likely to occur in the future). Even with scientific laws, there are often exceptions and limits to the breadth of their applicability (for instance, there are situations in which rewards will actually lead to a reduction in behavior—the so-called *overjustification effect*). In the social sciences there are very few relationships that have been so thoroughly established that we would call them laws. Consequently our theories are held tentatively rather than with certainty. They are more like road maps, which display some of the connections between major points, than like detailed topographic maps, which show every feature of the landscape.

There are also different types or levels of theories that vary in their scope or range of applicability within the field of attitude change. At the narrowest end are *principles*, which describe a pattern of results in a limited subarea of attitude change. At the other extreme are broad, general orientations toward ways of thinking about and explaining attitude change (for example, learning-theory approaches, and consistency-theory approaches). In between are numerous midrange theories with varying degrees of scope.

There is no classification of attitude theories generally agreed on. Shaw and Costanzo (1982) described 38 different social psychological theories, whereas Eagly and Chaiken (1993) summarized 17 models of attitude formation and change. It is important to realize that these theoretical approaches, though stressing different processes, can only rarely be pitted against each other in opposing predictions. Different theories sometimes make similar predictions, and often they stress different independent variables and different areas of applicability. In many cases, these theories are like ships that pass in the night without making contact with each other (Suedfeld, 1971).

One system for classifying attitude changes that has gained favorability in recent years is **dual-process models** (Chaiken & Trope, 1999). This approach involves the classification of attitude changes into those that involve high-effort processes and those that do not.

Photograph courtesy of Alice Eagly.
Reprinted by permission.

Box 10–2 ALICE EAGLY, *Noted Authority on Attitudes*

Alice Eagly has published widely on the psychology of attitudes, especially attitude change and attitude structure. She is especially famous for her research on the psychology of gender, which is discussed in Chapter 17, and for her many meta-analysis studies of social psychological topics such as leadership and social influence. Among her six books are influential volumes on Sex Differences in Social Behavior *and* The Psychology of Attitudes, *and she has served on the editorial boards of 14 psychological journals.*

Eagly graduated from Radcliffe College and earned her Ph.D. from the University of Michigan in 1965. She held faculty positions at Michigan State University, the University of Massachusetts at Amherst, and Purdue University before moving to Northwestern University in 1995. She has been elected president of the Midwestern Psychological Association and the Society of Personality and Social Psychology, and has served as chair of the Society of Experimental Social Psychology and the Board of Scientific Affairs of the American Psychological Association. Her many honors include the Donald Campbell Award for Distinguished Contribution to Social Psychology, the Distinguished Scientist Award of the Society of Experimental Social Psychology, and a citation as a Distinguished Leader for Women in Psychology.

High-effort processes include cognitive responses, information integration, and cognitive dissonance, among others. These high-effort processes require mental resources, thought, and evaluation. In contrast are attitude-change processes that do not require effort—for example, forming a favorable attitude toward the beverage Gatorade because of seeing a commercial featuring Michael Jordan. We discuss these dual-process models at some length in the next chapter.

LEARNING APPROACHES TO ATTITUDE CHANGE

Learning approaches to attitudes have been the subject of much research. We have presented a summary of some of this research in Chapter 8, which dealt with the formation of attitudes. There we described several different learning processes (e.g., classical and instrumental conditioning) that can be involved in initial attitude formation. Here we should note that any of these processes can also be involved in attitude change.

The key feature of **learning approaches** to attitude change is their emphasis that learning processes are responsible for attitude change. Although this may seem obvious, it has several less-obvious corollaries. First, because all learning theories are based on the principles of **reinforcement** and/or temporal **contiguity** as being responsible for learning, there is a strong emphasis on reinforcement and, to a lesser extent, on association through contiguity in explaining attitude change. Second, because learning theories emphasize **stimulus–response** (S–R) connections, their application in the field of attitude change has focused much attention on the characteristics of the persuasive stimulus—particularly on the source of the message and on its content.

Third, researchers with a learning orientation have tended to emphasize the learning part of the communication process (that is, attention and comprehension) more than other researchers and to be less concerned with the acceptance or yielding stage of the process (Eagly & Chaiken, 1984). Fourth, because much of learning theory has been established through research with animals, a good deal of extension and translation of concepts and procedures is often needed to make them applicable to humans and to the kind of intangible intervening variable that we call an attitude. The gap between animal learning and human attitudes has led to many questions about what extensions and translations were reasonable and proper and what conclusions should be drawn if previously supported findings with animals failed to be duplicated with humans. In a word, was it the original theories or their translations and applications that were at fault?

A final consequence of applying learning theory to human attitudes has been the profusion of approaches. There are several major competing theories of learning, and there are even more ways of translating and applying them to new situations. As a result, many different attitude researchers claim a "learning-theory" orientation, but the details of their approaches often have little in common other than the underlying concern with learning, reinforcement, and S–R associations.

Out of this profusion of approaches we can describe and illustrate only a few of the most influential ones. In the sections that follow, we review three theoretical perspectives (conditioning theories, Bem's behavioral theory, and Hovland's communication research program), along with a number of basic principles of attitude change.

Conditioning Theories of Attitude Change

One of the first authors to propose the application of conditioning and learning principles to the attitude area was Doob (1947). His approach was derived from Hullian learning theory and suggested that attitudes are a type of implicit (nonobservable) response and are learned and modified through reinforcement just like all other responses. Other researchers who have investigated attitudes within a framework of classical conditioning and/or instrumental conditioning have described their approaches in a volume by Greenwald, Brock, and Ostrom (1968). The following sections give three examples of the relationship of conditioning to attitude change.

Reward for Advocating a Position. Scott (1959) studied this subject in a debate context, where some college students were assigned to take the side opposite to their own attitudes ("counterattitudinal advocacy"), whereas others argued for a position less distant from their own, and still others supported their own real viewpoint in the debate. "Winners" and "losers" were randomly determined by the experimenter, though the debaters thought the decision reflected their classmates' votes. In all conditions, the reward of winning produced attitude change toward the position which the student had advocated, but the losers showed no change in attitude as a result of participating in the debate.

Verbal Reinforcement of Opinions. Students' existing opinions were directly reinforced in an experiment by Insko (1965). Undergraduates in a psychology course were telephoned at home by student interviewers and reinforced with comments like "good"— half being rewarded for stating opinions favorable to a possible new campus festival, and half for unfavorable opinions. A week later in class the students participated in an apparently unconnected activity, filling out a long questionnaire, one item of which asked for opinions on the creation of the same proposed festival, thus providing a delayed test of attitude change in a completely different setting from the experimental manipulation. Results showed that the telephone verbal reinforcement had a significant effect on the students' attitudes. Many other studies have provided ample evidence that reinforcement can have a strong effect in modifying attitudes and opinions.

Attitude Accessibility. A modern attitude conception that relies on conditioning principles is Fazio's (1986, 2001) viewpoint that an attitude is an association in memory between an object (e.g., horses) and an evaluation (e.g., "good"). Based on past conditioning, the strength of this association determines the degree to which the attitude will be activated if one is exposed to or thinks about the object. Two factors that have been found to increase the attitude strength are direct (rather than vicarious) experience with the attitude object, and the number of times that the attitude has been expressed (Fazio et al., 1982). As in some other conditioning approaches, attitude strength in this system is measured in terms of the reaction time when a person is asked evaluative questions about the object—that is, a quick evaluative reaction indicates a strong attitude.

Bem's Behavioral Theory

Daryl Bem (1965) suggested another learning approach to attitude change, stemming from Skinnerian behavioristic principles. Although he used cognitive concepts such as beliefs, attitudes, and self-awareness, he attempted to give them rigorously objective definitions, following the behavioristic tradition. Furthermore, as previously discussed in Chapter 2, he proposed that the way that people know about their own internal processes, such as attitudes, is the same way they learn about other people's attitudes and feelings— through observation. That is, a person's cues for *self-perception* are primarily the same publicly observable responses by which he or she perceives and evaluates the feelings and attitudes of other people.

Because we have described Bem's theory at some length in Chapter 2, we will not expand further on it here. One rather uncommon feature that it shares with dissonance theory is its emphasis that attitude change often follows from behavior change, rather than the opposite sequence which many theories suggest. However, another important aspect of Bem's theory is its critique of dissonance theory concerning the underlying reasons for attitude change (Bem, 1967). This dispute will be described when we discuss dissonance theory in Chapter 11.

Hovland's Communication Research Program

At Yale University after World War II, Carl Hovland gathered a gifted and productive group of researchers, whose work dominated the attitude area in the 1950s and continues to be highly influential to this day. This group published many volumes of research findings, the most important of which in outlining their conceptual approach was *Communication and Persuasion* (Hovland et al., 1953).

Hovland and his coworkers were very explicit in stating that they were not presenting a systematic theory, but rather an initial framework of working assumptions about factors affecting attitude change. However, it is clear that their working assumptions derived primarily from a learning and reinforcement point of view. They likened the process of attitude change to the learning of a habit or skill. Just as with learning, they postulated, attitude change will occur only if there is (a) practice ("mental rehearsal" or thinking about

Photograph copyright 1958 by the
American Psychological Association.
Reprinted by permission.

Box 10–3   CARL HOVLAND, *Early Persuasion Researcher*

One of the most outstanding researchers on attitude change, Carl Hovland was born in Chicago in 1912 and died an untimely death in 1961. Following a B.A. and M.A. at Northwestern, he took his Ph.D. at Yale in 1936 and joined the Yale faculty, where he remained for the rest of his life. For many years he was chair of the psychology department and director of the Yale Communication Research Program.

During World War II, Hovland directed the Research Branch of the U.S. War Department's Information and Education Division. There he studied the effectiveness of Army training films and morale problems. His many years of communication research led to volumes on Experiments on Mass Communication, Communication and Persuasion, The Order of Presentation in Persuasion, Personality and Persuasibility, Attitude Organization and Change, *and* Social Judgment. *He was honored by election to the National Academy of Sciences, and in 1957 he was one of the first recipients of the American Psychological Association's highest honor, the Distinguished Scientific Contribution Award.*

the new attitude), and (b) an incentive (a reward or reinforcement) for accepting it. Also they stressed the sequential process described in Chapter 9: Attention to the persuasive stimulus is necessary before there can be comprehension, and comprehension is necessary before there can be acceptance of the new attitude.

Because of their stimulus–response viewpoint, the research of Hovland et al. (1953) concentrated heavily on variables in the stimulus situation that might help to determine the amount of attitude change (the response). In particular, they studied aspects of the source of the message, many elements of the content of the message, some characteristics of the audience, and a few target behavior variables. Here we briefly describe a few of the specific variables they investigated and their key findings.

Source Variables. The **credibility** of the communicator was the major source variable studied, and it was found to be positively related to the degree of acceptance of the message, though not very closely related to attention, comprehension, or later retention of the message. Other studies divided credibility into two separate aspects: the source's *expertness* (degree of knowledge), and its *trustworthiness* (lack of intention to deceive or manipulate the audience). Later research studied the **power** of the source over the audience, and its **attractiveness**, which was operationalized in several ways, including the audience's *liking* for the source, the source's *similarity* to the audience, and its *familiarity*. The three main variables of source power, attractiveness, and credibility parallel Plato's classic behavioral–affective–cognitive distinction, and they are closely related to Kelman's (1958) three processes of attitude change. That is, compliance stems primarily from the power of the source, identification from its attractiveness, and internalization from its credibility. Research on source credibility is discussed more fully in a subsequent section.

Message Variables. Effects that were due to the content of the message were quite extensively studied by Hovland et al. One variable that has stirred continuing interest, the presence of fear-inducing arguments in the message, is also discussed in a later section. Other message content factors studied by the Hovland group included where to place the strongest argument in a persuasive communication, and whether to use only arguments on one side of the issue or to include and refute a few of the opposing arguments. In general, this "two-sided" presentation was found to be more effective, especially with intelligent audiences or when followed by contrary messages. Related studies showed that drawing conclusions explicitly was more effective than leaving them implicit.

A great deal of work has been done on the question of whether the first side of a controversy to be presented, or the most recent side, has a persuasive advantage. This **primacy** versus **recency** question involves two opposing messages. Early research results appeared to support a universal "law of primacy," both in debate-type situations (Lund, 1925) and in forming first impressions of other people on the basis of a few bits of information (Asch, 1946). However, Hovland's work and other related research effectively challenged this conclusion and showed that recency effects were regularly obtained under some conditions (Hovland, Mandell, et al., 1957).

Subsequent research showed that recency effects are more likely as the time interval between the two opposing messages is increased (Miller & Campbell, 1959; Wilson & Miller, 1968). Although these results were predicted from a learning framework, they do not seem to depend heavily on forgetting of the first message during the following time interval. In general, research on order effects has found many variables which interact with each other to determine whether primacy effects or recency effects or neither will occur (e.g., Anderson & Farkas, 1973; Johnson & Eagly, 1990; Haugtvedt & Wegener, 1994; Petty et al., 2001).

One consistent finding in the research on order of presentation is that motivation can largely determine whether a primacy or recency effect will occur. Several studies have demonstrated that when the topic is personally relevant, or when the person is otherwise motivated to think about the issue, recipients tend to weigh information presented in early messages more heavily than information presented later (Kassin, Reddy, & Tulloch, 1990; Haugtvedt & Petty, 1992). In contrast, when the recipient is not motivated or is otherwise unable to fully process the information contained in messages, there is a greater likelihood of a recency effect. Kassin et al. (1990) argued that when people are motivated to process the contents of a message, they are likely to form an opinion early. Once it is formed, they tend to search for information that is consistent with their initial opinion—the **confirmation bias** we discussed in Chapter 2.

Audience Variables.   Personality factors that are related to persuasibility were extensively studied by Hovland et al. (1953) and by Janis, Hovland et al. (1959). Another important audience variable which they studied is active participation in stating or making up arguments for a persuasive message. The topic of personality and persuasibility is discussed later in this chapter, and research on active participation is summarized in Chapter 11 in the section on dissonance theory.

Target Behavior Variables.   Several types of target behavior were also studied by the Hovland group. *Persistence* of attitude change was investigated in a number of studies by the inclusion of repeated posttests or several groups having posttests after different periods of time. A related issue, the surprising occurrence of delayed rather than immediate attitude change—dubbed the **sleeper effect**—attracted considerable interest, and studies on this topic are described in a later section. In addition, generalization of changes beyond the specific target issue to other related topics was studied by McGuire (1960) and Rosenberg (1960). Finally, though most research concerned the direct impact of persuasion, a few early studies were directed at creating *resistance* to future persuasion (e.g., McGuire, 1964).

In summary, though Hovland and his colleagues did not present a systematic theory, their approach was very influential in expanding the interest in attitude research among U.S. psychologists. Their research was prolific and well-done, and they opened up many productive areas of inquiry. Their concepts of attention, comprehension, and acceptance have provided a fertile way of analyzing attitude-change effects, even though the interrelationships of these concepts are still not fully understood.

In the next four sections of this chapter we summarize some of the research evidence concerning four topics that have been studied mainly within a learning framework: source credibility, fear appeals in messages, recipient personality and persuasibility, and persistence of attitude change.

Research on Source Credibility

Variables concerning the communication source have most often been studied by presenting a given message to several groups of subjects and telling each group that the message comes from a different source (for instance, Thomas Jefferson or Karl Marx; a Nobel Prize-winning physiologist or the director of a local YMCA). The **credibility** of a source such as these has been subdivided into two aspects: *expertness* and *trustworthiness*. Although both aspects of credibility are usually positively related to the amount of attitude change, the findings for expertness are typically stronger and more consistent (Hass, 1981; Wilson & Sherrell, 1993), so we confine this discussion mostly to the expertness aspect of credibility. In experiments, expertness is usually manipulated by ascribing to the source a high degree of knowledge, intelligence, age, prestige or social status, or a relevant professional or occupational background.

A large body of research indicates that a message from a highly credible source will produce more attitude change than one from a low-credibility source (McGuire, 1985; Petty & Wegener, 1998). However, this greater acceptance of the message is not due to greater reception, for the arguments of low-credibility sources are remembered as well as those of highly credible sources. Even minimal cues about the source's credibility, such as the communicator's height or erect posture, can have some persuasive effect (Weisfeld & Beresford, 1982; Hastie, Penrod, & Pennington, 1984).

Although in general an expert source produces more opinion change, there are a number of interesting exceptions and special conditions limiting this conclusion. A source who is only somewhat more knowledgeable, older, and so forth, such as a somewhat older child, may have more influence than a greatly superior expert. The expertise usually must be relevant to the topic being addressed (not, for instance, an eminent physiologist giving advice on dressmaking). However, sometimes high status can increase a source's persuasiveness even in irrelevant areas (Aronson & Golden, 1962). For the source's expertise to be most effective, it must be known to the audience before the message is delivered—a good reason for the practice of introductions, which describe the speaker's qualifications (Mills & Harvey, 1972).

A number of important moderator variables have been found that influence the size of the source-credibility effect. The source's credibility is most likely to influence people's attitudes when they are not highly involved in the issue, whereas when people are highly involved in the issue, the credibility of the source is less likely to increase persuasion (Johnson & Scileppi, 1969; Petty, Cacioppo, & Goldman, 1981). Also, expert credibility alone, if not supported by cues indicating trustworthiness, is apt to have relatively little effect on many attitudes (McGinnies & Ward, 1980). A strong cue for trustworthiness, leading to a greater persuasive effect, is a communicator who advocates a position contrary to his or her own personal interests (such as a salesclerk recommending the cheaper of two products—Eagly, Wood, & Chaiken, 1978; Harmon & Coney, 1982). In addition, there is some evidence for interaction among multiple source characteristics. In most of the research just summarized, the researchers manipulated one aspect of the source (e.g., credibility or likability), but little is known about the combination of these source variables—for example, a source who is credible but not liked, or an expert who is not trustworthy (Ziegler, Diehl, & Ruther, 2002).

Research on Fear Appeals

One of the most provocative early studies on message content was Janis and Feshbach's (1953) experiment, in which they varied the extent of fear-arousing information about tooth decay in persuasive messages about proper dental care. With three levels of fear arousal, they found that a very weak fear appeal produced the most reported change in toothbrushing practices a week later, whereas the least change was produced by the strongest fear appeal (containing gruesome pictures of diseased jaws and personalized threatening information). Their interpretation of this finding stressed that arousal of negative emotions can produce avoidance and defensive reactions to a communication. Despite this early evidence, Madison Avenue advertising copywriters have continued to use fear appeals in abundance (in HIV-prevention campaigns, messages on drug prevention, seat belt use, and so on). One clear example can be seen in smoking-prevention messages, like the Canadian one shown in Figure 10–2.

FIGURE 10–2   Images like this one make use of fear appeals to induce behavior change. This image is from recent programs in Australia and Canada, where it was printed on packages of cigarettes!

Source: Australian National Tobacco Campaign. Reprinted by permission of the Commonwealth of Australia.

Importantly, later research on fear appeals found that they can be effective, and there is a great deal of research showing that strong fear appeals produce more attitude change than weak ones (e.g., Leventhal, 1970; Boster & Mongeau, 1984; Witte & Allen, 2000). Many of these studies have dealt with important real-life issues such as stopping smoking, using seat belts, getting breast examinations, or taking tetanus inoculations.

To explain the conflicting findings of an occasional negative relationship between fear appeals and attitude change and the more commonly found positive relationship, **curvilinear** theories have been proposed (e.g., McGuire, 1968b). According to this viewpoint, there is an inverted-U-shaped relationship between amount of fear arousal and attitude change, with the greatest attitude change at moderate fear levels. Accordingly, a positive relationship to attitude change might be found for conditions low on the fear continuum, but a negative relationship for higher fear conditions. McGuire's theory relates this curvilinear pattern to the intermediate processes of reception of and yielding to the persuasive message. Thus, at very low fear levels, audience interest and reception will be low. At higher fear levels, interest and reception will be good, and credible fear appeals will also increase yielding. However, at very high fear levels, the aversive affect created by the message motivates audience members to defensively avoid the situation and/or to discount the message—mechanisms that reduce both reception and yielding, so that attitude change is sharply lower (Axelrod & Apsche, 1982; Leventhal & Nerenz, 1983).

A curvilinear theory of fear-arousal effects also implies a number of interactions with other variables. One example of an interaction that has received some empirical support is that a higher level of fear arousal is optimal when highly specific and detailed recommendations are made concerning actions to be taken to reduce the fear—for instance, directions about where to go and what to do to get a tetanus inoculation. (Leventhal, 1970; Rogers, 1983; Rogers & Prentice-Dunn, 1997). A combination of immediately relevant fear appeals with specific behavioral instructions had the strongest positive effects on both attitudes and actual behavior in a study by McArdle (1972).

An important model in this area has been labeled **protection motivation theory**, and a sizable amount of research has demonstrated its usefulness in understanding when fear appeals will lead to attitude change (Milne, Sheeran, & Orbell, 2000; Ruitter, Abraham, & Kok, 2001). Overall, the research indicates that the relationship between fear appeals and protective behavior is a complex one, involving perceptions of risk (including such variables as personal relevance, arousal, risk, and benefits of the behavior), and the ability to avoid the dangers posed by the fear-inducing stimulus (including such variables as self-efficacy, coping, effectiveness of specific actions, and costs associated with the protective behavior). For reviews of this research, see Wood (2000) or Ruitter et al. (2001).

Research on Personality and Persuasibility

Another research topic of interest concerns audience personality characteristics which are related to susceptibility to persuasion. Early work by Hovland and his colleagues sought to determine to what extent persuasibility is a general personality trait that holds across various topics and situations (Hovland et al., 1953; Janis, Hovland, et al., 1959). Their hypothesis, and the general tenor of their findings, was that there is a significant but small degree of general persuasibility that is topic-free. In the years since the original Yale studies, persuasibility has been studied in relation to a number of personal characteristics such as age, gender, anxiety, self-esteem, dogmatism, self-monitoring, need for cognition, and intelligence. We focus here on three of the most frequently studied variables: gender, need for cognition, and self-esteem.

Gender.   Are women easier to persuade than men? Over the years, this question has attracted considerable research interest. Early findings showed women generally to be more persuasible than men, but later research indicated that this finding might be largely an artifact of the types of topics or issues usually used in influenceability studies. Many of the early studies focused on topics that were traditionally "masculine" issues, about which women might be less interested or knowledgeable. But when the studies concerned "feminine" issues (ones in which women have more interest and knowledge), men have been found to be more persuasible (Sistrunk & McDavid, 1971; Cacioppo & Petty, 1980; Eagly & Carli, 1981; Karabenick, 1983). Although reasonable, this methodological explanation for gender differences has not been universally accepted, and several authors still interpret the evidence to indicate an overall tendency for women to be more persuasible than men (Burgoon & Klinkle, 1998).

Need for Cognition.   Individual differences in the motivation to think about issues have been found to affect persuasibility in complex ways (Petty & Wegener, 1998). Some people enjoy and are more prone to think about issues than are others (Cacioppo, Petty, et al., 1996). These people, who are high in need for cognition, are more likely to scrutinize and attend to the content of a message than are people low in need for cognition. As a result, they are more persuaded by the substantive content of the message than they are by the source or other cues peripheral to the message itself (Haugtvedt & Petty, 1992). For example, a study conducted during a national election campaign showed that people high in need for cognition thought more about the election issues and candidates than did those who were low on the scale (Cacioppo, Petty, Kao, & Rodriguez, 1986).

Self-Esteem.   Early studies of persuasibility searched for linear relationships between amount of attitude change and personality traits such as self-esteem (Janis & Field, 1959). When that line of inquiry proved unproductive, more complex theories were proposed, which involved multiple processes mediating between personality characteristics and attitude change—particularly reception (including both attention and comprehension),

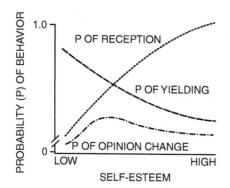

FIGURE 10–3

Predicted relationship of the personality variable of self-esteem to the mediating processes of reception and yielding and to the resulting amount of opinion change.

Source: Adapted from McGuire (1968b, p. 1151).

and yielding (acceptance) (McGuire, 1968b). We have previously referred to this **Yale–McGuire Model** in relation to fear appeals, and also in Chapter 9 in discussing these mediating processes as some of the dependent variables of communication studies. The complexity of the theory stems from the fact that any personality characteristic (such as intelligence or self-esteem), which is positively related to reception, is expected to be negatively related to yielding, and vice versa. For instance, a more-intelligent person may comprehend a message better than a less-intelligent one, but be less inclined to yield to it.

An example of this predicted relationship and the expected combined result of reception and yielding on opinion change is shown in Figure 10–3. Although McGuire suggested that very simple or very complex messages might produce linear relationships to the amount of opinion change, the curvilinear, inverted-U relationship between self-esteem and opinion change is the one that would be expected to occur in the majority of situations, rather than the linear relationship sought by earlier investigators.

There is a rather large body of research reporting interaction effects that are supportive of McGuire's viewpoint (e.g., Lehmann, 1970). For example, Nisbett and Gordon (1967) showed that simple but poorly substantiated messages produced most attitude change in lower self-esteem recipients, whereas complex but well-substantiated messages were most effective with high self-esteem recipients. A meta-analysis of the research literature provided strong evidence for the curvilinear relationship proposed by McGuire (Rhodes & Wood, 1992), although not all reviews have reached the same conclusion (cf. Petty & Wegener, 1998).

Research on Persistence of Attitude Change

In Chapter 9 we discussed research on retention of both message content and attitude change, so we will not repeat that information here. A learning-theory approach postulates that attitude change should be based on the new information learned or on rewards or incentives presented to the audience member. Thus it implies that there should normally be a positive relationship between the amount of message content remembered and the amount of attitude change that persists over time. However, the time course and the shape of the decay curves for content memory and attitude change are often so different that it is clear that there is no simple relationship between message learning and attitude change (McGuire, 1985).

This pattern of findings has cast doubt on the adequacy of a learning-theory approach to attitude change and has encouraged work on several of the cognitive approaches that we discuss in the next chapter. Also, research on the persistence of attitude change has shown that it interacts in complex ways with many other variables such as source, message, medium, or audience characteristics. For instance, attitudes that people consider person-ally unimportant change more over time than ones that are important to their holders (Krosnick, 1988). One of the most interesting of these interaction effects involves a sur-prising interaction of time passage and source credibility, which has been quite extensively studied and named the "sleeper effect."

The **sleeper effect** refers to delayed attitude change in the direction advocated by a *non*credible communicator (such as a person identified as a convict arguing for lighter court sentences). Such a noncredible source or, alternatively, inclusion of a warning that the persuasive message is not necessarily factual, is considered a **discounting cue**—one that signals the receiver not to be influenced by the message. Early studies (e.g., Kelman & Hovland, 1953) found that the amount of attitude change produced by a credible source decreased from its initial level over a period of several weeks, but that attitude change produced by the same message from a noncredible source *increased* from its initial low level and eventually reached the same level as that for the credible source. This effect was found to be due, not to the participants' forgetting the source per se, but apparently to their ceasing to connect the source with the message content (i.e., "dissociating" the message content from the source).

These "sleeper effect" findings were fascinating because they were originally unex-pected and yet seemed plausible on further consideration. However, the sleeper effect was almost "laid to rest" by several studies in the 1970s that failed to replicate the finding (e.g., Gillig & Greenwald, 1974). These studies showed that, though a gradual decrease in attitude change produced by a credible source is customary, a delayed *increase* in atti-tude change produced by a noncredible source is a rare and fragile phenomenon (Pratkanis et al., 1988). More recently, though, careful research has revived the sleeper effect, demon-strating that such delayed increases in attitude change can be found under the following conditions: (a) the persuasive message is strong and plausible, (b) the discounting cue is a strong warning that the message content is inaccurate, and (c) the discounting cue is deliv-ered *after* the message itself, thus allowing the message a better chance of reception and acceptance (Gruder et al., 1978; Cook et al., 1979; Greenwald et al., 1986; Pratkanis et al., 1988). Under those conditions any initial persuasive effect of the message is suppressed, but later on it is apt to be displayed in delayed attitude change in the direction advocated by the message. Pratkanis et al. (1988) interpreted this effect, not in terms of dissociation of the message and the discounting cue, but as being due to faster forgetting of the discounting cue—thus keeping the sleeper effect firmly within a learning-theory framework.

An alternative interpretation of these findings has been offered, suggesting that they are consistent with an *elaboration likelihood* model of attitude change—a cognitive-response approach that we will discuss further in the following chapter. Thus Priester et al. (1999) proposed that the sleeper effect will occur only when the message is thoughtfully elaborated by the recipient. They argued that conditions (a) and (c) listed in the preceding paragraph are consistent with the recipient's doing effortful processing of the information in the message. In contrast, if people are told that the communicator is not trustworthy *before* hearing the message, they won't be likely to think about or elaborate on the contents of the message. Thus, from this viewpoint, what appears to be essential is that the message is elaborated by recipients upon hearing it, following which they learn that the information presented by the message communicator is not trustworthy.

Evaluation of Learning Approaches

As mentioned earlier, there is no single unified learning theory of attitude change, and each of the approaches we have discussed is at best a partial, incomplete theory. Some, like the Hovland group's approach, are not theories at all in the technical sense of the word. Despite their common characteristics, these approaches do not really build together toward a unified theory. They differ among themselves in many details, such as their procedures and operational definitions of their concepts; they apply most clearly to different types of situations; and they all fail to cover some other types of attitude-change situations.

McGuire, who was a member of the Hovland group of researchers, concluded that learning-theory approaches to attitude change may have been "a fertile error" (McGuire, 1969, p. 266). These approaches were fertile in suggesting areas and procedures for research, but they have often been wrong in the details of their experimental predictions. Clearly, theories of conditioning and learning can explain many attitude-change phenomena, and particularly also findings in the area of attitude formation. Yet even in this area of their greatest applicability, they are vulnerable to the criticism that participants' *awareness* of the conditioning procedures may be responsible for much of the effect obtained. If so, then cognitive or judgment theories would be more appropriate ways of understanding and explaining attitude changes. However, in his review of the research literature, Jones (1985, p. 75) has stressed the value of learning and reinforcement concepts as providing "an ever-present alternative to more subtle, cognitive explanations."

We turn now to a discussion of judgment theories, and in the following chapter we will examine cognitive theories of attitude change in some detail.

JUDGMENT APPROACHES TO ATTITUDE CHANGE

Judgment theories are ones that give central attention to how we make judgments about other people and objects in our environment. They postulate that all stimuli can be arranged in a meaningful order on various dimensions (hot–cold, good–bad, etc.), and they aim to describe the principles according to which people make such comparative judgments.

Probably the best-known judgment theory is Helson's (1964) **adaptation-level theory**. Its central concept, the **adaptation level**, is a person's psychological neutral point on any given dimension—that is, the level that the person has gotten used to, or "adapted" to. Other stimuli are judged in terms of how far they depart from this adaptation level. A concrete example can clearly illustrate that such judgments are relative. If you simultaneously put your left hand in a bucket of cold water and your right hand in a bucket of hot water, each hand will gradually adapt to the temperature of the water that it is in, with the result that the temperature will soon feel less extreme than at first. Then, if you take both hands out and put them in a pail of water having an intermediate temperature, your left hand will feel the water as being warm while your right hand will feel it as cool. This example is dramatic because we usually are adapted to only one level at a time, so experiencing two apparently different temperatures in the same pail of water vividly demonstrates that such judgments are relative.

The adaptation level constitutes an **anchor** or reference point with which stimuli are compared. When a stimulus is judged as more different from the adaptation level than it actually is, as in the preceding example of water temperature judgments, we have a **contrast effect**. On the other hand, sometimes a stimulus may be judged as closer to the adaptation level than it actually is, and that is termed an **assimilation effect**. Most of the research on adaptation-level theory has dealt with judgments of physical stimuli on dimensions such as temperature, weight, brightness, or noise of objects. However, the same principles apply to judging the friendliness, intelligence, attractiveness, or any other characteristic of people, or to judging aspects of abstract concepts, such as the humor of a story. For instance, Kenrick and Gutierres (1980) demonstrated contrast effects in ratings of the attractiveness of women after the male raters had been exposed to pictures of extremely beautiful women—for example, after watching *Charlie's Angels*, men rated pictures of average-looking potential dates as less attractive than if they had not watched the TV program.

Adaptation-level theory clearly illustrates the approach of judgment theory. However, because it has rarely been applied in attitude-change research, we now move on to another judgment theory that has been used more extensively in attitude studies.

Sherif and Hovland's Social Judgment Theory

We have described the structural aspects of this theory at some length in Chapter 5. To recapitulate briefly, Sherif and his coworkers have presented the concept of three **attitude latitudes**—the latitudes of *acceptance, rejection*, and *noncommitment*. They have also concluded that the size of a person's latitude of rejection on an attitude issue is the best indicator of his or her ego-involvement in that issue: The more involved a person is in the issue, the larger the latitude of rejection.

The attitude-change aspects of the theory, as presented in Sherif and Hovland's (1961) major theoretical statement, emphasize the principles of assimilation and of contrast. The theory postulates, first, that a person's *own attitude* on any given issue *serves as an anchor*, or reference point, for judging other people's attitudes or persuasive messages on that issue; and second, that the boundaries of the individual's latitudes of acceptance and rejection will determine what kind and amount of attitude change will result from exposure to persuasive messages. Regarding attitude change, the principle of *assimilation* states that social stimuli such as persuasive messages which are *within a person's latitude of acceptance* will be assimilated: that is, they will produce some attitude change in the direction advocated. On the other hand, the principle of *contrast* states that social stimuli which are *within a person's latitude of rejection* will be contrasted: that is, they will produce no attitude change, or else attitude change opposite to the direction advocated (a "boomerang effect"). The relationship of amount of attitude change to the discrepancy between the person's attitude and the position advocated by the message will be positive in the latitude of acceptance and negative in the latitude of rejection—a curvilinear relationship (Freedman, 1964). Both assimilation and contrast effects on *judgment* will be greater for highly ego-involved individuals than for uninvolved ones, but their effects on *attitude change* will be smaller for involved individuals.

Research Related to Social Judgment Theory

Chapter 5 presented an example of assimilation and contrast effects involving *judgment* of the positions of U.S. presidential candidates on the issue of school busing in relation to the respondent's position on that issue. In this section, we briefly describe some of the social judgment theory research that involves *attitude change*. The theoretical topics that have received most research attention are the discrepancy of the message from the recipient's position and the ego-involvement of the recipient.

Message Discrepancy.   When a persuasive message is quite discrepant from the recipient's own attitude, he or she may change the attitude, or may resolve the incongruity in one or more of several other ways: perceptual distortion of the message, derogation of the source, increased counterarguing, disparagement of the message, or underrecall of its contents. Several studies have shown the functional equivalence of these mechanisms, indicating that they may be used interchangeably as alternatives to attitude change, or they may be used in combination, depending on the situation (McGuire, 1969; Sears & Abeles, 1969).

Two different relationships have been postulated to hold between message discrepancy and attitude change. Some researchers have predicted and found an approximately linear rising relationship: More discrepant messages produce more attitude change (e.g., Zimbardo, 1960; Eagly, 1967). However, the more frequent finding is the inverted-U curve predicted by social judgment theory, with the curve's downturn occurring in the latitude of rejection (e.g., Hovland, Harvey, & Sherif, 1957; Peterson & Koulack, 1969). Because the peak of the curve usually occurs at a high discrepancy level, the studies that obtained roughly linear findings may not have used messages which were extreme enough to produce a downturn in influence. With either linear or curvilinear findings, the amount of attitude change obtained is apt to be markedly less than the amount advocated by the message, though in the same direction.

An interaction between message discrepancy and source credibility has often been found, as predicted by both social judgment theory and consistency theories. The rationale behind this interaction is that source derogation and message disparagement are less likely with a highly credible source, and therefore attitude change continues to increase up to higher levels of message discrepancy than it does with a less-credible source who can be more easily disparaged.

Figure 10–4 illustrates this pattern of findings in a study where the same basic message was attributed to a Nobel Prize-winning physiologist (the highly credible source) for half of the subjects, or to the director of the Fort Worth YMCA (the less-credible source)

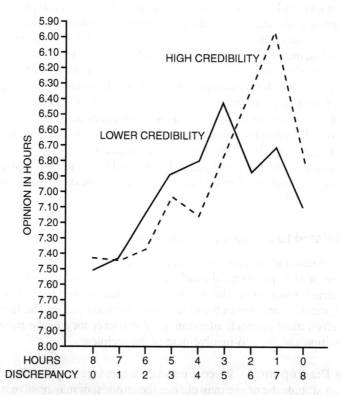

FIGURE 10–4 The inverted-U relationship between message discrepancy and attitude change, for high- and lower-credibility communicators.

Source: Bochner & Insko (1966, p. 618). Copyright 1966 by the American Psychological Association. Reprinted by permission.

for the other half (Bochner & Insko, 1966). The message gave reasons to support the view that the average young adult needed only a given number of hours of sleep a night, and nine different groups of subjects received messages saying that the number of hours needed was either 8, 7, 6, or on down to 2, 1, or 0 hours per night (whereas the average subject had indicated that 7.9 hours per night were needed). Consistent with the theory, both communicators had inverted-U-shaped curves of attitude change, and the peak of the curve for the high-credibility communicator was at a greater discrepancy than for the lower-credibility communicator. Note, however, that for both message sources the amount of attitude change was positive, and that for all but the small discrepancies it was much less than the amount advocated (peaking at roughly 2 hours of *change* in the recipient's belief about how much sleep was needed). In this experiment, even with the most-extreme messages, there was no boomerang effect leading to inverse attitude change. However, boomerang effects are sometimes found with very extreme messages, or when the source and the recipient are on opposite sides of a psychological neutral point, as with a Democratic communicator soliciting votes from a Republican audience (Lange & Fishbein, 1983).

Congeniality Hypothesis. The research on message discrepancy described previously suggests that people may actively avoid information that is discrepant from their existing attitudes or, if exposed to it, be less likely to remember it. Eagly and Chaiken (1998) have referred to this as the **congeniality hypothesis**—that people are more likely to remember information that is consistent with their attitudes. However, in a review of 70 relevant experiments, Eagly et al. (1999) found that there was only a small tendency for research participants to remember messages that were congenial with their attitudes. Consequently,

> it may be more likely that under many circumstances people expose themselves to [information that challenges their attitudes], attend to it, scrutinize it carefully, encode it accurately, and thus remember it fairly well, even though they dislike the information and are not persuaded by it. (Eagly et al., 2001, p. 7)

Other studies have shown that congenial and uncongenial messages are processed differently (Eagly, Kulesa, et al., 2000). Participants presented with congenial information were passive and simply agreed with the message. In contrast, when the message was uncongenial, participants actively processed the message; they were skeptical, generated counterarguments, and scrutinized the message in greater detail. These findings suggest that memory for the content of the message is not a key component in its persuasiveness, but rather persuasiveness is due to differences in the types of cognitive processing that the message evokes (see the Chapter 11 section on cognitive-response theories).

Ego-Involvement. Research on ego-involvement has had rather mixed results. The construct of **ego-involvement** refers to the extent to which an individual cares about a particular topic. This can involve personal relevance, self-identity, or pertinence to one's core values. Although some relationships between ego-involvement and attitude change have been found, the specific details of Sherif's theory have not been well-supported, and many of the research results seem contradictory.

Zimbardo (1960) attempted to clarify this situation by distinguishing between **issue** involvement (interest and concern about the issue) and **response** involvement (concern about making a desirable response—appearing well-adjusted, acceptable to the experimenter, etc.). Zimbardo's results showed that high-response involvement produced more attitude change. This finding is opposite to Sherif's theory, but it appears that the theory really concerns issue involvement rather than response involvement. Chaiken and Stangor (1987) have suggested a still-finer breakdown of types of involvement, citing findings that people for whom the topic of a message is important ("personal relevance") may often be more open-minded and ready to be persuaded by good arguments than Sherif's issue-involvement hypothesis suggests (Petty & Cacioppo, 1984; Leippe & Elkin, 1987). However, such individuals are still somewhat biased by their initial attitudes (Howard-Pitney, Borgida, & Omoto, 1986), and people who have a strong vested interest in their initial opinion ("position involvement") generally confirm Sherif's hypothesis of low attitude change (Sivacek & Crano, 1982; Abelson, 1986).

There is active debate in the research literature about many different proposed ways of conceptualizing involvement and about their effects on the amount of attitude change (Johnson & Eagly, 1990; Petty & Cacioppo, 1990; Sears, 1997). Recent studies of involvement and attitude change have taken an *attitude-strength* approach (Chaiken, Pomerantz, & Giner-Sorolla, 1995; Pomerantz, Chaiken, & Tordesillas, 1995), in which strong attitudes are associated with narrow latitudes of acceptance, and ego-involvement is one determinant of the strength of the attitude. Other determinants include centrality to the self, knowledge of the topic, and personal commitment. Recently, a number of constructs have been introduced that on the surface appear similar to ego-involvement (e.g., importance, certainty, accessibility, lack of ambivalence). Unfortunately, there is no evidence that these constructs reflect a single underlying construct (Krosnick et al., 1993). As a result, the safest conclusion is that, although these constructs are related, they should be treated as distinct.

The topic of ego-involvement is rather closely related to the concept of commitment, which we discuss in the section on dissonance theory in the next chapter. People who are high in issue involvement (especially if it is position involvement) are also high in commitment to their opinion on the issue. Ego-involvement is also an important variable in the cognitive-response approaches to attitude change that are discussed in the next chapter.

Evaluation of Social Judgment Theory

Appraising this theoretical perspective fairly is not easy. On one hand, it has stimulated quite a bit of research, though many studies have been aimed at resolving controversies between it and dissonance theory. Its concepts of latitudes of acceptance and rejection have proved useful in resolving disputes between dissonance theory and self-perception theory (Fazio, Zanna, & Cooper, 1977). Also, much of the social judgment research has dealt with important real-world issues in a field setting (e.g., a referendum on prohibition in Oklahoma, voter attitudes in a presidential election). On the other hand, its assimilation and contrast principles can also be derived from consistency theories and from dissonance theory, as can some of its attitude-change predictions. Social judgment theory as it concerns *attitude change* is quite narrow in scope, dealing mainly with the variables of the person's ego-involvement and the message's discrepancy from the person's attitude, whereas dissonance theory has the advantage of much broader applicability and inclusion of additional variables, such as the amount of incentive and degree of perceived choice. Also, much of the theory has been empirically derived from the results of experiments, so it has some undesirable gaps, inconsistencies, and ad hoc aspects.

The theory has been more successful in dealing with human judgment than with attitude change. In general, studies are consistent with the theory in showing that people's own attitudes influence their judgments about the extremity of social stimuli, but they have not supported many of the theory's more specific predictions about attitude change (Zavalloni & Cook, 1965; Eiser & Stroebe, 1972). In fact, it is possible that *judgmental* assimilation or contrast effects may sometimes substitute for the attitude-change effects predicted by the theory—for instance, a large assimilation effect could make a message appear identical to one's own opinion and thus prevent the need for any attitude change (Lammers & Becker, 1980).

The relationship found between attitude change and message discrepancy has most often been the curvilinear one predicted by social judgment theory, but there are many exceptions in the literature, and the theory's postulates about the latitudes of acceptance and rejection as determining the effects of discrepancy on attitude change do not seem to be well supported (Eagly, 1981). In the area of ego-involvement the theory is somewhat confusing in predicting opposite effects of involvement on judgment and on attitude change, and predictions about involvement have suffered many setbacks in experimental studies, leading to a rash of ad hoc concepts and modifications of the theory. In applied research, however, Varela (1971) has claimed good success in using Sherif's notion of the latitude of acceptance in producing planned attitude change—for instance, in creating a script by which salesmen could persuade resistant customers to buy more lavishly.

All in all, despite social judgment theory's intriguing aspects and the research that it generated, interest in it declined after 1980 as other new theories of attitude change emerged and gained prominence. Portions of the theory (most notably message–attitude discrepancy) were incorporated into other models of attitude change like the cognitive-response theories and elaboration likelihood model, which we discuss in the next chapter.

SUMMARY

The topic of attitude change has generated much more research than other aspects of attitudes, inspiring a profusion of competing theories. This chapter has discussed many of the methodological problems that are met in attitude research, such as demand characteristics, experimenter effects, subject effects, and problems related to use of deception. However, alternative research designs and attitude-measurement methods can often be used to overcome those problems and obtain more valid data.

Although all current theories of attitude change have serious limitations and none has achieved a predominant position, they still have an important role to play. Theories guide our research efforts, provide a context for understanding observed facts, and help us to predict future events. Theories are always held tentatively and never considered proven in any final sense, though they may be disproved by contrary evidence. The many theories discussed in this and the following chapter are largely complementary—that is, they often have different areas of applicability, and they rarely make directly opposing predictions.

The many different *learning* approaches to attitude change have generated a great deal of research. They all stress stimulus–response connections, the importance of reinforcement or contiguity in learning, and extension or translation of concepts from animal learning experiments. Among the important topics studied within this research tradition are the credibility of the communication *source*, order effects and the use of fear appeals in the *message*, the persuasibility of *audience* members, and the *target behavior* of persistent, long-lasting attitude change. The various learning approaches to attitude change conflict with each other in many details and do not approach the status of a unified theory. Although they have been fertile in stimulating research on attitude change as well as attitude formation, many of their specific predictions have not been supported.

Judgment approaches to attitude change focus on the principles by which people make judgments by placing objects along any given dimension. The major example is Sherif and Hovland's social judgment theory, which has been used to study some important real-world issues, though it is quite narrow in scope. It has generated a good deal of research on message discrepancy and ego-involvement, but enough of this research has been nonsupportive that the theory's prominence in the field of attitude change has declined.

11

Attitude Change: Cognitive Theories and Research

Americans have, more than any other people I know, a willingness to change their opinions.—Gunnar Myrdal.

Most of our so-called reasoning consists in finding arguments for going on believing as we already have.—James Harvey Robinson.

It requires ages to destroy a popular opinion.—Voltaire.

Attitudes can sometimes change very rapidly, whereas in other situations they may prove very resistant to change. It is the goal of theories of attitude change to define the conditions under which attitudes will change and the ways in which this will occur. It is unlikely that any single theory will ever provide all of these answers, but recent studies have uncovered a number of fundamental principles of attitude change, and several broad theoretical models have emerged that offer integrated perspectives on attitude change.

Before we become overly impressed with the state of our current theoretical knowledge, it may be well to recall a statement by Thomas Edison: "I have constructed *three thousand* different theories in connection with the electric light. ... Yet in only two cases did my experiments prove the truth of my theory."

In that spirit of continually searching for closer approximations of the truth, this chapter discusses several kinds of cognitive theories of attitude change—ones stressing consistency or dissonance or reactance as explanatory variables, ones emphasizing people's cognitive responses to persuasive messages, and attitude-change research stemming from attribution theories.

CONSISTENCY THEORIES

Over the years, **consistency theories** of attitude change have drawn a great deal of attention and inspired much research. These theories are, first of all, cognitive theories; that is, they emphasize the importance of people's beliefs and ideas. As their name implies, their key feature is the principle that people try to maintain consistency among their beliefs, attitudes, and behaviors. Awareness of one's own inconsistency is viewed as an uncomfortable situation that every person is motivated to escape. Thus, attitude change should result if individuals receive new information that is inconsistent with their previous viewpoints, or if existing inconsistencies in their beliefs and attitudes are pointed out to them.

Consistency theories view people as essentially thoughtful and rational, adjusting their attitudes and behavior in accordance with incoming information. However, they do not assume a strict logical consistency, but rather a value- and emotion-tinged "**psycho-logic**," to use Abelson and Rosenberg's (1958) clever term. For instance, strict logic does not lead to the conclusion that "My enemy's enemy is my friend," but psycho-logic does (McGuire, 1969). Also, consistency theories have room for such "illogical" ways of maintaining consistency as denial of the truth of new information that conflicts with a person's present viewpoints, or searching for supportive data to bolster present attitudes when they have been challenged by new information (Abelson, 1959).

The original idea leading to consistency theory is usually credited to Fritz Heider's (1946) short paper, which he followed with a major book 12 years later (Heider, 1958). In the meantime, Festinger (1957) had launched his dissonance theory, which is a form of consistency theory, but which is sufficiently different that we discuss it separately in the following section. Soon many other variants of consistency notions arose so that, just as with learning theory, there sometimes seem to be as many different consistency theories as there are consistency theorists. The major ones we discuss in this section are Heider's balance theory and Osgood and Tannenbaum's (1955) congruity theory.

Heider's Balance Theory

Heider's theory concerns the way in which we perceive other people, objects, and ideas. For simplicity, he limited his discussion to three elements: the perceiver (P), another person (O), and some object or idea (X). Between each pair of elements there can be two types of relationships: a liking relationship, L (either positive or negative); or a unit relationship, U (also either positive or negative). The liking relationship is self-explanatory; the unit relationship refers to elements that are perceived as belonging together—for instance, due to ownership of one by the other, or similarity, or membership in the same group.

With three elements in a system and either a positive or a negative relationship between each pair of elements, there are eight possible patterns. These eight patterns are shown in Figure 11–1. The characteristics of the relationships determine whether the pattern is balanced or unbalanced. A **balanced** state is one in which the relationships are in harmony so that there is no cognitive stress in the perceiver's view of the system, and consequently the system is stable and resists change. Conversely, an **unbalanced** system is unstable because it produces psychological tension in the perceiver, which pushes toward change

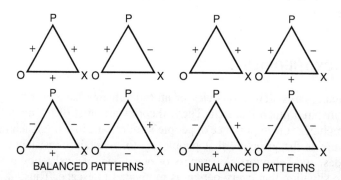

FIGURE 11–1 Balanced and unbalanced patterns according to Heider's theory. The lines between elements represent either liking or unit relationships. Positive relationships are shown by +, negative relationships by −.

in the perceived relationships. Specifically, *triadic* systems are balanced when they have an odd number of positive relationships (either 3 or 1); otherwise they are unbalanced. As shown in Figure 11–1, the system is balanced if all three relationships are positive (P likes O, P likes X, O likes X) or if only one is positive (e.g., P likes O, P dislikes X, O dislikes X). However, when two relationships are positive and one negative (e.g., P likes O, P likes X, O dislikes X), the situation is cognitively uncomfortable and presses toward change. The definition of balance is less clear when all three relationships are negative (P dislikes O, P dislikes X, O dislikes X), but Heider stated that this situation is unstable, so it is usually also considered unbalanced.

Heider also discussed *dyadic* situations involving either two people or one person and one object. He stated that balance exists if both the liking and the unit relationship have the same sign (e.g., P owns X, and P likes X). Also, with two people, balance requires that liking or disliking be reciprocated (that is, P likes O and O likes P is balanced; P likes O and O dislikes P is unbalanced). Again, unbalanced states "induce" or press for a change toward balance.

Heider's theory has been very influential in stimulating other cognitive consistency approaches. Its greatest limitation is its rather extreme degree of simplicity. It has no provision for degrees of liking or for degrees of balance. Systems with more than three elements are not considered. In the *triadic* system, only unidirectional relationships are discussed (e.g., from P to O, but not from O to P), and the possibility of having both liking and unit relationships between a single pair of elements is not allowed. The opposites of liking and unit relationships have different implications that the theory does not consider—disliking is negative, whereas lack of a unit relationship is neutral in character. Also there is no specification of *which* changes will be made in order to restore balance in any given situation.

Some other theorists have modified Heider's basic formulation. Most notably, Cartwright and Harary (1956) applied mathematical graph theory to problems of cognitive balance and made many valuable revisions to Heider's theory. In particular, they extended it to any number of elements, allowed nonreciprocated relationships and different types of relationships simultaneously, took neutral relationships into consideration, and presented a way to determine degrees of balance. Feather (1967) used some of the same improvements suggested by Cartwright and Harary, and applied his more precise theory specifically to persuasive communication and resulting attitude change. Wiest (1965) quantified each of the three relationships among P, O, and X on a 7-point scale and used Heider's principles to derive a complex "tetrahedron" model of balance, which has received good support in empirical research by Tashakkori and Insko (1981).

Despite the influential impact of Heider's thinking, his theory has not generated a great deal of research. In part this has been due to its simplicity and lack of precision, the same factors that stimulated revisions and extensions of the theory. The most common form of research in this area has been to obtain ratings or other indications of the pleasantness or unpleasantness of hypothetical situations to test the theory's underlying postulate that balanced situations are more pleasant than unbalanced ones. This research has not been consistently supportive, and it has suggested a number of needed revisions in the theory (e.g., Morrissette, 1958; Price, Harburg, & Newcomb, 1966).

The most important findings from this research have demonstrated that people have other cognitive preferences (or biases—cf. Chapter 2) that are often just as strong or stronger than their preference for consistency. Specifically, people tend to prefer (a) **positivity** in personal relationships (i.e., a positive P–O relation), and (b) **agreement** rather than disagreement of opinions (i.e., the same sign for the P–X and O–X relations); and either of these two tendencies can often override the tendency to prefer balanced cognitive structures (Zajonc, 1968b; Sears & Whitney, 1973). For instance, contrary to balance theory, people may often disagree with their friends, find their opponents likable, or be pleased that an opponent agrees with them. Additional research has shown that the positivity or attraction preference is common because it is the simplest of these three cognitive tendencies (involving just one sign, a positive P–O relation), whereas agreement is somewhat more complex (involving two signs), and balance is the most complex of the three (being a combination of positivity and agreement—Cottrell, 1975; Mower-White, 1979; Cacioppo & Petty, 1981a).

Another kind of revision to Heider's theory was proposed by Rosenberg and Abelson (1960; Rosenberg, 1960). They gave a clear-cut classification of different ways of resolving imbalance and predicted the order in which these methods would be used. Their general principle is that the easiest ways of restoring balance will be tried first and used most frequently, and they presented experimental evidence supporting this principle (Rosenberg & Abelson, 1960). In addition, Rosenberg (1960) emphasized the importance of consistency between the cognitive and the affective components of an attitude. Whenever these two components are not consistent, Rosenberg postulated, a homeostatic process will operate to bring them back into equilibrium. Several experiments have shown that a change in either the cognitive or the affective component can produce a change in the other component (e.g., Carlson, 1956). In related research, Chaiken and Baldwin (1981) used degree of affective–cognitive consistency as an index of well-defined attitudes.

Osgood and Tannenbaum's Congruity Theory

Among consistency theorists, Osgood and Tannenbaum (1955) were unique in the degree of quantification of their approach. They measured attitudes by means of the evaluative dimension of the semantic differential (see Chapter 3), and they made precise predictions about the direction and amount of attitude change. However, in compensation for its increased precision, their theory has a narrower scope than most other approaches. It deals solely with the results of communications in which a source (S) makes an evaluative assertion about some attitude object (O), and its predictions are based on the **congruity**— that is, the degree of similarity—of an individual's evaluation of the source, the object, and the message (M).

An example will help to clarify the details of this approach. Let us suppose that the U.S. president (S) said something favorable about Fidel Castro (O). The attitude toward each of these men held by a particular individual must have been previously measured, normally on a scale from +3 to −3. If the person's prior attitude toward the source is different from his or her attitude toward the object, the theory makes several predictions:

1. The person's attitudes toward both the source and the object will change (rather than only the attitude toward the object, as many theories would expect).
2. The amount of change in each attitude will be inversely related to the polarization (extremity) of the attitude. In other words, the more extreme attitude will change less than the milder attitude.
3. If S said something good about O, the person's final attitudes toward both S and O will be the same.
4. If S said something bad about O, the person's final attitudes toward S and O will be equidistant from zero (one positive and one negative).

In our example, if the person's prior attitude toward the president was +1 and toward Castro was −2, and the message was favorable, the final equilibrium point would be −1, with the rating of the president decreasing two points and the rating of Castro increasing one point. The same result would occur if Castro had said something good about the president. However, if one said something bad about the other, then their ratings would end up on opposite sides of zero, the president at +1 2/3 and Castro at −1 2/3. (The fact that, in the latter case, both ratings would increase following an unfavorable assertion is one of the most paradoxical consequences of the theory.)

Congruity theory indicates that this amount of attitude change will occur as the result of a single communication, though it would not be expected to happen instantaneously. However, the theory also has some escape hatches. One is the *correction for incredulity*, which becomes necessary when a communication tries to bridge too large a discrepancy in attitudes (e.g., "U.S. president praises terrorist leader," or "the Pope condemns official Catholic doctrine"). In such instances, an incredulous recipient of the message will just reject it as false. Another correction is the *assertion constant*, which is necessary because attitudes toward the object of a message have been found to change somewhat more than attitudes toward the source (about 1/6 of a point more, according to the findings of Tannenbaum, 1953). Further details about the theory and formulas for computing the attitude change may be found in Kiesler et al. (1969).

How adequate is the theory? On one hand, with the corrections just mentioned, Tannenbaum (1953) found a correlation of +0.91 between the predicted and the observed attitude change in response to specially made-up newspaper stories—nearly perfect prediction. On the other hand, later research showed that the theory did better at predicting the *relative amount* of change of attitudes toward S and O than the absolute amount of change (Tannenbaum, 1967). Also the extensive research literature on "prestige suggestion" has demonstrated many other factors, in addition to the prestige of the source, which can affect the amount of attitude change. For example, Rokeach and Rothman (1965) showed that considering the importance of S and O to the message recipient could markedly improve the predictions of attitude change. Similarly, Kerrick (1958) showed that the theory predicted better when a prestigious source was *relevant* to the topic of the message than when the source was not relevant (e.g., a professional football star commenting on American foreign policy). The artificial simplicity of the theory in not allowing for degrees of positiveness or negativeness in the message is another major limitation.

In spite of these limitations, congruity theory seems to have performed quite well in its narrow goal of predicting attitude change in response to a persuasive communication from a relevant source (Tannenbaum, 1967).

Research on Consistency Principles

If we focus on the general ideas underlying consistency theories, rather than on the specific details of a particular version, we can find many areas where consistency theory has proved fruitful in research and applied work. For instance, consistency principles have been used to explain attitudes toward political candidates (Kinder, 1978), jurors' confidence in their verdicts (Fischoff, 1979), and international attitudes of people from different nations (Moore, 1979). Cialdini (2000) has cited consistency as one of the six central principles that direct human behavior—a principle that salespeople, advertisers, and fundraisers use extensively in trying to influence you and me.

The Foot-in-the-Door Effect. One well-established application of consistency principles, which salespeople and charitable organizations frequently use, is the foot-in-the-door phenomenon (named for the old door-to-door salesperson's trick of putting a foot in the door to prevent it from being closed and thus allow time for completion of the sales pitch and promotion of a sale). The principle involved is that if you can persuade an individual to perform a small requested action, consistency pressures and a feeling of commitment will make it more likely that the person will later perform a larger request of the same general sort.

The initial research in this area by Freedman and Fraser (1966) had volunteers go door to door, asking people to display a tiny sign saying "Be a safe driver" in their window (the small action). Because it was such a trivial request, almost all of them did so. Two weeks later, a different volunteer came by and asked them to allow a very large and unattractive billboard saying "DRIVE CAREFULLY" to be installed on their front lawn. Over three-quarters of them complied with this large request, compared with only 17% of a control group who had not received the first small request. In another condition, where the initial request was to sign a petition supporting "keeping California beautiful" (an entirely different topic), about half of the people agreed to place the DRIVE CAREFULLY sign in their yard. Because the small-request groups complied with both of the large requests so much more than the control group did, the authors concluded that performing the small request had changed their self-image, and that they complied with the large request because of a pressure to be consistent with their new self-image as someone who supported public-spirited campaigns.

Reviews of many later foot-in-the-door studies have shown that the effect, though not always easy to create, does often increase compliance with large requests; and research has supported the consistency-based explanation of the effect in terms of changes in the individual's self-image (DeJong, 1979; Beaman et al., 1983; Cialdini & Trost, 1998; Burger & Caldwell, 2003). For instance, people whose initial compliance is explicitly labeled as helpful or generous become even more likely to accede to the later large request. However, it is also possible that performing the initial small request serves as a commitment, which in turn induces later consistent behavior without any necessary change in self-image (Gorassini & Olson, 1995; Burger & Guadagno, 2003).

Despite the potential power of the foot-in-the-door technique, it is not equally effective across individuals. Cialdini, Trost, and Newsom (1995) showed that there are individual differences in a person's **preference for consistency**. Individuals who are high in preference for consistency desire to be and to appear consistent. Individuals who score low prefer unpredictability, change, and spontaneity. Cialdini's research has provided clear evidence that the foot-in-the-door effect is particularly strong among people who are high in preference for consistency. Interestingly, there is also evidence for a reverse foot-in-the-door effect (that is, *less* compliance following an initial request) among people *low* in preference for consistency (Guadagno et al., 2001).

Liking for the Source of a Message.   According to consistency principles, one's degree of liking for a person who is the source of a persuasive message should be positively related to the amount of one's resulting attitude change. In general, many studies have provided support for this principle (e.g., Janis, 1983). However, a number of exceptions have also been found, which fit better into other theoretical frameworks (McGuire, 1983).

One exception that follows an adaptation-level type of pattern is the "praise from a stranger" phenomenon. Praise from a stranger has more effect than praise from a family member or friend, probably because it is more novel and unexpected. Following the same principle, criticism has more impact when it comes from a friend than from a stranger (e.g., A. Miller et al., 1980). Aronson and Linder (1965) have suggested a gain–loss principle of interpersonal attraction, specifying that an *increase* in praise from another person will produce greater liking for that person than will continuing high levels of praise, whereas a *decrease* in praise will lead to much lower liking.

Another exception to the normal relationship between liking and persuasiveness is the case of a disagreeable communicator delivering an unpopular message—a situation that follows dissonance-theory predictions (see next section). More acceptance of unpopular messages may be produced by a disliked source than by an attractive one (presumably because liking for the source cannot be used as a reason for listening, and therefore dissonance is reduced by increasing the acceptance of the message). For example, Army reservists were persuaded to eat fried grasshoppers—definitely a counterattitudinal behavior—by an officer who behaved in either an unpleasant, officious manner or a pleasant, friendly manner. Although equal numbers of men ate the disliked food in the two conditions, the men who did so for the unpleasant communicator showed more increase in liking for the grasshoppers than did those who ate them for the pleasant communicator (Zimbardo et al., 1965).

As to what characteristics of people make them *likable*, research has identified a number of variables associated with greater liking. They include physical attractiveness, similarity, giving complements, and exhibiting cooperation (Cialdini & Trost, 1998).

Similarity of the Source. One of the central elements of liking is similarity—we like (and are more influenced by) individuals who are more similar to ourselves (Silvia, 2002). The research is clear in showing that source–audience similarity normally tends to produce more attitude change, and that is one reason that so many TV commercials use testimonials from average-appearing people, who are presumably like the viewers, rather than from celebrities (Simons, Berkowitz, & Moyer, 1970; Stoneman & Brody, 1981). However, various exceptions to this principle have also been demonstrated. In the area of race relations, many studies have been directed to the issue of whether ethnic similarity or attitudinal similarity ("race or belief") is more important in determining liking for and persuasion by another person (e.g., Robinson & Insko, 1969). The results show that attitudinal similarity is more important for abstract evaluation of another person, but ethnic similarity carries more weight in determining behavioral acceptance; however, attitudinal similarity has gained increasing weight in the U.S. in recent years (Insko, Nacoste, & Moe, 1983).

It is also important to distinguish between similarities that are relevant or irrelevant to the topic of the message. Relevant *attitudinal* similarities generally produce positive effects on attitude change, relevant dissimilarities produce negative effects, and irrelevant similarities have little or no effect. However, the effect of relevant *group-membership* similarities is determined by the relative status of the source and the audience. For instance, if the source is expert on the topic and the audience is not (e.g., T. S. Eliot giving his opinion on the merits of a poem), this dissimilarity will produce more attitude change than a similar but nonexpert source (Simons et al., 1970).

Balanced Identity Designs. Recent research on implicit attitudes has extended Heider's original notion of balance. Recall from Chapter 4 that studies of *implicit attitudes* have treated attitudes as object-evaluation associations. Greenwald et al. (2002) have expanded on this basic model by incorporating the "self" as another key element and examining *balanced sets* of relationships among the self, a group, and an attribute. A balanced identity and attitude design is shown in Figure 11–2. The theory defines four sets of associations: self-evaluation associations (self-esteem), self-group associations (identity), group-attribute associations (stereotypes), and attribute-evaluation associations (attitudes).

Following balance theory notions, Greenwald et al. (2002) analyzed the relationships among the self, a group, and an attribute. They proposed that the presence of two positive

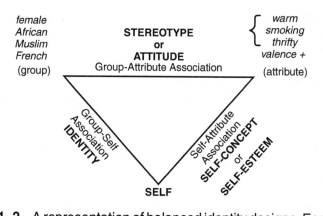

FIGURE 11–2   A representation of balanced identity designs. Each vertex of the triangle represents a concept. A balanced identity design always includes *self* as one of the concepts (bottom vertex), and it also includes both a social category (group) concept and an attribute concept. In italics, above the group and attribute vertices, are examples of concepts that could play those roles in the design.

Source: Greenwald, A. G., Banaji, M. R., Rudman, L. A., Farnham, S. D., Nosek, B. A., & Mellott, D. S. (2002). A unified theory of implicit attitudes, stereotypes, self-esteem, and self-concept (p. 9). *Psychological Review, 109,* 3–25. Copyright © 2002 by the American Psychological Association. Reprinted with permission.

links among these concepts should lead to the development of a third positive link. For example, in the case of a woman with a favorable self-concept: "If self ('me') has the expected (for women) associations with both positive and female, the conditions exist for the development of a balanced association of positive with female" (p. 9). In a series of studies, Greenwald et al. (2002) provided evidence for balanced identity designs, but *only when the associations were measured implicitly.* Surprisingly, when the associations were measured explicitly through self-report measures, the data were inconsistent with the balanced identity design model.

Resolutions of this provocative discrepancy between results with implicit and explicit measures will require future research. One possibility is that implicit and explicit measures should correspond more closely "when subjects have little motivation to disguise their attitudes on explicit measures" (Greenwald et al., 2002, p. 18). Thus, for associations involving gender (which is a sensitive topic), explicit measures did not fit with the balanced identity design, whereas we might expect that the balanced design would hold for explicit measures of attitudes about political candidates, or attitudes about commercial products.

Evaluation of Consistency Theories

The popularity of consistency theories has waned since the 1960s, but they still continue to stimulate research and practical applications (balanced identity designs being a current example). The profusion of consistency approaches and their individual incompleteness have already been mentioned. Osgood and Tannenbaum's congruity theory is the most detailed and explicit in its predictions (and also one of the narrowest in its applications). Although it has had relatively good success in some experimental research, the ad hoc corrections that it requires and the many factors that it does not consider demonstrate its limitations and cast some doubt on the value of its quantifications. The many other consistency approaches, though less precise in their predictions, have generally had less empirical support when put to experimental tests, though they have been fruitful in suggesting many new and interesting areas of research. Despite the disagreements among consistency theorists and researchers, there remains considerable agreement on the underlying importance of *consistency* as a construct, and on the general tendency for individuals to prefer consistency. As Greenwald et al. (2002) concluded, "In part, reduced attention to consistency theories may be due to their having been so thoroughly woven into the fabric of social psychology as to have acquired the character of unquestioned wisdom, no longer requiring research investigation" (p. 3).

However, as we have seen in the preceding sections, not everyone prefers consistency, and there are wide individual differences in the degree to which attitude change can be motivated by a desire for consistency. Despite the value of consistency theory, it is clear that people do not live by consistency alone. Further, it seems likely that psychologists and other highly educated people are much more concerned with maintaining consistency in their thoughts, feelings, and actions than are the great majority of humankind. Bem (1970) has stated this viewpoint vividly:

> Inconsistency is probably our most enduring cognitive commonplace. . . . I suspect that for most of the people most of the time and for all the people some of the time inconsistency just sits there. (p. 34)

In corroboration of this viewpoint, we have seen in Chapter 7 that most citizens display a great deal of inconsistency in their political attitudes and opinions. Similarly, in the next chapter we will see that people's attitudes and behaviors are only moderately correlated.

A theoretical viewpoint that helps to explain this widespread inconsistency has been suggested by Abelson (1968). He proposes that much of our knowledge and attitudes exists, in isolated "opinion molecules," each of which contains one or a few facts, feelings, and sources of support. These opinion molecules serve us well in social conversation by giving us something to say on many topics (for instance, the national budget deficit, or the dangers of nuclear energy). However, when not brought out for such use, they are generally kept in "logic-tight compartments," where we do not need to think about them in relation to other topics that might contain contradictory facts or feelings. Thus, most of us probably tolerate a great deal of inconsistency among our attitudes and beliefs all the time, and yet we are hardly ever even aware of it.

DISSONANCE THEORY

Our next major topic, cognitive dissonance theory, is a type of consistency theory. However, it has some unique aspects, and it has received so much attention and stimulated so much research that it deserves separate treatment. Conceived by Leon Festinger (1957), it has been modified by a number of researchers, including Brehm and Cohen (1962), Festinger himself (1964), Aronson (1968, 1992, 1999), Wicklund and Brehm (1976), Steele (1988), and Cooper and Fazio (1984), and it has been studied experimentally by a whole generation of social psychologists. Without a doubt, dissonance theory has aroused more controversy and received more praise and criticism than any other current theory in social psychology.

Nature of Dissonance Theory

The theory deals with the relations between "cognitive elements." These elements are items of knowledge, information, attitude, or belief that a person holds about himself or herself, or about the surrounding world. Two elements can be **consonant** with each other (that is, compatible or consistent), or dissonant, or irrelevant. The definition of a **dissonant** relationship is that *the opposite of one element would follow from the other element*—that is, X and Y are dissonant if non-Y follows from X. What "follows from" a cognitive element is determined by the person's expectations; thus dissonance can be the result of logical inconsistency, of the person's past experience concerning what things go together, or of cultural norms and values. The basic principles of the theory are as follows (Festinger, 1957):

1. Dissonance, being psychologically uncomfortable, will motivate the person to try to reduce the dissonance and achieve consonance . . . [and to] avoid situations and information which would likely increase the dissonance.
2. The magnitude of the dissonance (or consonance) increases as the importance or value of the elements increases.
3. The strength of the pressure to reduce dissonance is a function of the magnitude of the dissonance. (pp. 3, 18)

To use one of Festinger's examples, the cognition "I know I smoke" is consonant with the cognition "I know I enjoy smoking" but dissonant with "I believe smoking is bad for my health." (It would also be irrelevant to many other cognitions, such as "I know that I live in the United States.") Faced with a dissonant situation, if the elements are personally important to a woman, she will try to reduce the dissonance in one or more of the following four ways: (1) She may change a cognition about the behavior, for instance by giving up smoking, or by deciding "I only smoke a little." (2) She may change a cognition about the environment, for instance by deciding that smoking is not harmful, or that only heavy smoking is harmful. (3) She may add new cognitions to bolster one or the other of the dissonant elements, which reduces the dissonance by lowering the proportion of elements that are dissonant—for instance, "I know most of my friends smoke," or "I believe the evidence linking smoking and cancer isn't conclusive," or "I know the dangers from smoking are no greater than the dangers from driving a car." (4) Because the amount of dissonance depends on the importance of the cognitions, she may reduce dissonance by deciding that one or more cognitions are less important, e.g., "It really isn't very important that smoking is bad for my health. I'm going to live fast and die young."

Although it is not always possible to reduce dissonance successfully, if the amount of dissonance is great enough, one or more cognitive elements will be changed. Moreover, cognitions are generally responsive to reality, so it is hard to change a cognition about one's behavior without also changing the behavior.

Areas of Application of the Theory

That is the basic skeleton of the theory, but it does not do justice to the richness of its applications. As Markus and Zajonc (1985) pointed out, the theory is basically an open one which can be applied to many different situations (in contrast, for instance, to congruity theory, which only concerns communications in which a source makes an evaluative assertion about an object). Dissonance theory is stated in broad conceptual terms and does not make specific predictions about particular situations until additional

Photograph courtesy of Leon Festinger.
Reprinted by permission.

Box 11–1   LEON FESTINGER, *Eminent Theorist and Experimentalist*

Leon Festinger was probably the most famous of Kurt Lewin's many renowned students. Born in New York in 1919, he studied at CCNY and took his M.A. and Ph.D. with Lewin at Iowa. He taught briefly at the University of Rochester before rejoining Lewin at M.I.T. Following Lewin's death, he moved with the Research Center for Group Dynamics to the University of Michigan. At the age of 32, he became a full professor at Minnesota, subsequently moving to Stanford in 1955, and back to New York at the New School for Social Research in 1968.

Festinger's famous theoretical contributions included articles on social communication and on social comparison processes, and his 1957 book, A Theory of Cognitive Dissonance, *wich stimulated a prolific outpouring of research on attitude change. His fame as a clever experimentalist and a role model for productive students was also widespread. In addition to theoretical and experimental writings, his work included field and observational research and statistical contributions. He was elected to the National Academy of Sciences, and he received the American Psychological Association's Distinguished Scientific Contribution Award in 1959. In the early 1960s he left social psychology and concentrated his research on the area of perception until his death in 1989.*

facts or assumptions are stated. For instance, in any situation it is necessary to specify the dissonant cognitions that are present and the feasible and infeasible ways of reducing the dissonance. When such additional assumptions are specified, the theory can be applied to countless situations, including many beyond the realm of attitude-change research. It has even been applied to an understanding of partial reinforcement effects in rats as well as in human beings, and to participant observation studies of religious cults!

In spite of the fact that it is a cognitive theory, dissonance theory has led to many hypotheses and experiments about people's overt behavior. It has been innovative in emphasizing that attitude change often *results from* a person's behavior rather than causing the behavior. In his original statement of the theory, Festinger suggested four major areas of its application. Here we briefly summarize the relevant recent evidence on each of these areas.

The Consequences of Decisions.   The theory posits that dissonance is aroused by making a decision between two or more alternative objects or courses of action. The dissonant elements are the negative features of the chosen alternative and the positive features of the unchosen alternative(s). The resulting dissonance is greater when (a) the decision is an important one, (b) the unchosen alternative(s) is(are) nearly as attractive as the chosen one, and (c) there is low similarity between the various alternatives (e.g., choosing between going to an enjoyable sports event or reading an enjoyable book would create more dissonance than would choosing which of two enjoyable books to read, because the two similar alternatives have many of the same positive aspects and the same negative aspects). Ways of reducing postdecision dissonance include decreasing the subjective attractiveness of the unchosen alternative, increasing the subjective attractiveness of the chosen alternative, or, occasionally, increasing the perceived similarity of the alternatives in other ways (e.g., deciding that both sports events and reading are forms of recreation).

In this area of postdecision dissonance, the experimental findings have generally supported the theory (e.g., Festinger, 1964), though there have been some contrary reports (e.g., Harris, 1969). An intriguing real-world study done at a racetrack showed that bettors' confidence in their chosen horse increased markedly immediately after they placed their bet—clear-cut support for the theory (Knox & Inkster, 1968).

Revisions of the Theory.   In the course of these studies, the theory has been revised to stress the importance of **commitment** and **volition (choice)** as necessary conditions for dissonance to be aroused (Brehm & Cohen, 1962). If people do not feel committed to (bound by) their decisions, there is no reason for them to experience dissonance, and the research findings show no evidence of dissonance reduction (Kiesler, 1968). Similarly, if they feel that they had little or no choice in their actions, then their dissonance is apt to be minimal (Harmon-Jones et al., 1996; Harmon-Jones, 2000a), though some evidence suggests that choice is not always necessary for the arousal of dissonance (Insko, 1967).

Other revisions of dissonance theory were suggested by Aronson (1968, 1992, 1999), who proposed that inconsistency of cognitions with a person's self-concept was the crucial factor leading to dissonance. Thus, for anyone with a positive self-concept, doing or saying something embarrassing or nonsensical or immoral would be dissonance-arousing. Similarly, Steele and Liu (1983) posited that dissonance is aroused by threats to the self-image, and that it can be reduced by any action that affirms one's important values (not just by attitude change). More recently, Steele and his colleagues have argued that people with high self-esteem are *less* likely to experience dissonance because they have more resources with which to protect themselves and to affirm their positive self-esteem, despite the inconsistency (Steele, Spencer, & Lynch, 1993). This viewpoint is opposed to Aronson's prediction that embarrassing or disapproved behavior would be more dissonant for a person with high self-esteem. To date, the available data are consistent with Steele's *self-affirmation* model, showing more dissonance and attitude change for people with low self-esteem (Holland, Meertens, & Van Vugt, 2002; Stone, 2003).

A possible resolution to the conflicting predictions and research findings regarding the role of self-esteem in dissonance-induced attitude change was proposed by Stone and Cooper (2001, 2003). Their **self-standards model** suggests that the role of self-esteem in cognitive dissonance depends on the standards that an individual uses to evaluate the discrepant act. In an experiment, they had university students write a counterattitudinal essay under high-choice conditions that would create dissonance. After this task, some students engaged in a task designed to prime thoughts about the self that were relevant to the essay topic, while other students engaged in a task designed to prime self-thoughts irrelevant to the essay topic. The results showed that, in the self-irrelevant condition, students *low* in self-esteem displayed significantly more attitude change in the direction of the essay than did students high in self-esteem. This finding is consistent with the research cited at the end of preceding paragraph. However, participants in the self-relevant condition showed the opposite pattern: students with *high* self-esteem showed significantly more attitude change than did students with low self-esteem (Stone & Cooper, 2003). These findings suggest a possible resolution to the controversy over the role of self-esteem in dissonance-induced attitude change.

Another revision to the theory involves the basic assumption that inconsistency is aversive and that everyone is motivated to resolve it (Aronson, 1968). Indeed, research is clear in showing that there are individual differences among people in their ability to tolerate dissonance and in their preferred ways of reducing dissonance when it occurs (e.g., Wicklund & Brehm, 1976). A good example is the research by Cialdini et al. (1995) on preference for consistency, described previously in the section on the foot-in-the-door effect. Following this line of reasoning, it seems likely that there are cultural differences in the importance of dissonance or the discomfort that results from inconsistency (Fiske et al., 1998). Several researchers have found that North Americans and others in western cultures place greater importance on consistency among attitudes, beliefs, and behaviors than do people from eastern cultures (Kashima et al., 1992; Heine & Lehman, 1997; Choi & Nisbett, 2000).

Finally, other dissonance theorists have proposed that a key factor in arousing dissonance is a person's feeling of *responsibility* for some negative consequences to someone (Wicklund & Brehm, 1976). This aspect of the theory is particularly applicable to research on induced compliance or counterattitudinal behavior (see that topic on the next page).

Voluntary and Involuntary Exposure to Information.   Dissonance theory holds, in general, that dissonance-reducing information will be sought out and dissonance-increasing information will be avoided. However, it is often difficult or impossible to avoid contact with information which is being spread by the mass media or by one's acquaintances. If such new information were opposite to cognitions which one already held, then dissonance would result and, according to the theory, efforts would be made to reduce that dissonance. That might be accomplished in many different ways: by defensive misperception or misunderstanding, discrediting the information or its source, seeking other consonant information, or changing one's attitude. There are studies that provide evidence for each of these processes occurring under some conditions.

However, there are also many reasons that one might want to receive supposedly dissonant information: It may be valuable to know what the opposition is saying, especially on personally important issues; one may be highly confident of one's own position and expect the opposition arguments to be weak; one may want to appear open-minded; or one may not care much about the issue and be interested in hearing divergent viewpoints. There are research findings supporting all of these processes as well (McGuire, 1985).

For a time, reviews of these conflicting findings generally stressed lack of support for the dissonance-theory predictions regarding selective exposure (e.g., Greenwald & Ronis, 1978). As we discussed in Chapter 9, there is much less evidence for *motivated* selective exposure to information than for de facto selective exposure (Sears & Freedman, 1967). However, in recent years, a number of studies have found more support for general selectivity and also have pinpointed conditions under which it is less likely (Frey, 1986; Jonas et al., 2001). For instance, dissonant information is valuable if the decision might be reversible or if its consequences are very great (e.g., Frey, 1982), but people who avoid threatening information ("repressors") are most likely to display selective exposure (Olson & Zanna, 1979).

Dissonance and Social Support.   Disagreement with other people is another source of dissonance, and agreement with people can reduce dissonance. This part of the theory was foreshadowed by Festinger's (1954) theory of social comparison processes, which emphasized that people often compare their opinions with those of others around them. Dissonance theory posits that dissonance will be high if a disagreement is (a) extensive; on a topic which is (b) important and (c) difficult to verify through observation; and if the disagreeing persons are (d) many, (e) attractive, and/or (f) credible. In such situations, one can reduce dissonance either by changing one's own opinion, or by persuading the disagreeing person(s) to change their opinions, or by discrediting or derogating the other person(s). Alternatively, one may seek out others who agree with one's views, or try to obtain social support by communicating with and persuading others who are currently uninvolved in the issue.

Festinger (1957) gave several examples of such group social-support phenomena, including mild denial of reality ("It isn't really going to rain on our picnic"), spread of rumors, and mass proselytizing for causes. The book *When Prophecy Fails* (Festinger, Riecken, & Schachter, 1956) illustrates how dissonance theory can explain the initiation of proselytizing by a formerly secretive religious cult. However, Hardyck and Braden (1962) studied a somewhat similar religious group and pointed out additional conditions that were necessary in order for proselytizing to occur.

Because of the difficulties of such field studies (Thompson & Oskamp, 1974), and also because of the many ways in which dissonance can be resolved in social situations, there is relatively little clear-cut evidence concerning this part of dissonance theory. However, a number of laboratory experiments on induced counterattitudinal behavior have shown that the presence of social support (i.e., other people performing the same counterattitudinal acts) reduces the resulting attitude change, as dissonance theory predicts (White, 1980; Stroebe & Diehl, 1981, 1988; Zanna & Sande, 1987).

Effects of Forced Compliance.   This area of research is the most controversial one and, in recent years, by far the most active one spawned by dissonance theory. It is also misleadingly named for, as indicated by the comments concerning volition in a previous section, it is important for the creation of dissonance that participants not feel "forced" to comply. A better name for this research area would be **induced compliance** or **counterattitudinal behavior**. The typical research procedure is to induce participants to do or say something contrary to their opinions, with two or more levels of inducement being used for different participants. The experimental prediction is that maximum dissonance (and dissonance reduction) will be created by the *minimum successful* inducement, whereas larger inducements will create less dissonance because their very size offers a reason for having performed the behavior.

In the famous Festinger and Carlsmith (1959) study, participants were paid either $1 or $20 to act briefly as assistants to the experimenter (and to be available for similar future assistance) by falsely telling another participant that a very dull experiment had been enjoyable and interesting. As predicted, the $1 group of participants subsequently resolved their dissonance by changing their actual attitude toward the experiment to a more favorable level than did the $20 group. This is an effect of perceived amount of choice ("If I said that for only $1, I must really believe it" vs. "I said it because I was paid so much").

The controversy over this area of research is not primarily concerning the effects of perceived choice, but rather it stems from the role-playing task that the participant typically has to perform. One group of researchers, following learning-theory principles, has proposed and done experiments to show that the size of *incentive* for role-playing is positively related to the amount of attitude change—directly opposite to the dissonance prediction (e.g., Elms, 1967). However, it was soon pointed out that the occasional findings that supported incentive theory did not thereby disprove dissonance theory, and attention shifted to a search for *conditions* under which one or the other theory was upheld. Carlsmith, Collins, and Helmreich (1966) offered one resolution by showing a dissonance effect in interpersonal role-playing but an incentive effect in counterattitudinal essay writing. However, Linder, Cooper, and Jones (1967) showed that even essay writing could produce a dissonance effect under high-choice conditions. Freedman (1963) supported dissonance theory in showing greater enjoyment of boring tasks when there was relatively little justification given for complying. However, Collins (1969) failed to find dissonance effects in most of a long series of forced-compliance experiments.

Later research findings in the induced-compliance area have converged on the following conclusions. Dissonance effects are very likely to occur when counterattitudinal behavior is performed under conditions of (a) low incentive, (b) high perceived choice, with (c) unpleasant consequences of the behavior (for someone), and (d) awareness by the actor of personal responsibility for the consequences (Collins & Hoyt, 1972; Wicklund & Brehm, 1976; McGuire, 1985). The question of whether the unpleasant consequences must be foreseen in order for the dissonance effect to occur has been answered by research showing that dissonance is aroused even if the person realizes retrospectively that he or she could have foreseen them (Goethals, Cooper, & Naficy, 1979). A major reappraisal of the forced-compliance literature from a nondissonance perspective also seems to be quite consistent with these conclusions (Nuttin, 1975).

Despite the generalizations about counterattitudinal behavior in the preceding paragraph, other research has demonstrated that effects of commitment to *pro*attitudinal behavior can be predicted by dissonance theory, even in situations with no aversive consequences (Aronson, 1992). In reviewing the literature, Harmon-Jones (1999) concluded that "feeling personally responsible for producing aversive consequences is not necessary to generate dissonance . . . but it may enhance the magnitude of dissonance effects" (p. 92).

An offshoot of the research on induced compliance is the topic of **overjustification**, which involves using rewards, threats, or surveillance to induce a person to perform an *attitude-congruent* action rather than a counterattitudinal one. The usual effects of this procedure are to "undermine" or weaken the person's former attitude toward the action (Lepper & Greene, 1975; Deci & Ryan, 1985; Tang & Hall, 1995; Deci, Koestner, & Ryan, 1999, 2001). Because there is no reason for dissonance in doing something that one likes, this effect has been interpreted in attribution terms (cf. Kelley, 1972a) as being due to discounting of the attitudinal cause for the action because of the presence of another possible cause (the reward or threat)—"If I'm getting paid to do this, it must not be such an enjoyable thing to do after all." This analysis stresses that the undermining effect is due to the controlling aspect rather than to the informational aspect of the external pressures (Deci & Ryan, 1985), and it has important implications for teachers and parents who want to maintain children's interest in various intrinsically enjoyable activities, such as school learning or musical or athletic participation—don't force, bribe, or threaten!

Bem's Critique of Dissonance Theory

Bem (1967) suggested a different approach to the forced-compliance area and to the postdecision attitude-change area, based on his theory of **self-perception**. As we described in Chapter 2, his theory postulates that one learns about one's own attitudes through observation of one's behavior. Thus, in the experimental situation with large versus small rewards for counterattitudinal performance, Bem did not question the basic experimental predictions from dissonance theory, but instead gave a different theoretical explanation for them. He posited that people will observe the fact that they have said something unusual for them, and the size of the inducement, and will interpret their true attitude in light of the size of reward (e.g., "I only said it because I was paid a lot; I don't really believe it").

Bem's method for studying his theory was to perform an "interpersonal replication," in which "observers" were simply told about the procedures experienced by a participant in one of the classic dissonance studies (e.g., Festinger & Carlsmith, 1959), and were asked to estimate the original participant's true attitude. In general, these simulated replications quite closely paralleled the results of the earlier experiments.

However, R. A. Jones et al. (1968) pointed out that some crucial information about participants' initial attitudes was not provided to Bem's observers; and when they did "interpersonal replications" incorporating that information, the results no longer paralleled the original experimental findings. Thus they concluded that mere observers and involved participants were not always comparable and that "To explore the processes by which the attitudinal responses of involved subjects are determined it appears necessary to study involved subjects" (p. 267).

In his original theoretical statement, Bem (1967) had stated that involved individuals participating in a behavioral episode and observers of the same episode are "isomorphic" (that is, identical) in their inference processes and conclusions about behavior. By 1970, Bem had retreated from this viewpoint and only claimed, "In identifying his own internal states, an individual *partially* relies on the same external cues that others use when they infer his internal states" (1970, p. 50; italics added). This is a much harder hypothesis to disprove—almost impossible, in fact—so the controversy has mostly been waged over Bem's earlier, more extreme formulation. Despite an occasional finding of actor–observer

Photograph courtesy of Daryl Bem.
Reprinted by permission.

Box 11–2   DARYL BEM, *Advocate of Self-Perception Theory*

When Daryl Bem earned his B.A. degree in physics from Reed College in 1960, the civil rights movement had just begun, and he became so intrigued with the changing attitudes towards desegregation in the American South that he switched fields from physics to social psychology, specializing in attitudes and public opinion. He earned his Ph.D. degree from the University of Michigan in 1964 and subsequently taught at Carnegie-Mellon University, Stanford, and Cornell University, where he has been since 1978.

Bem has published on many topics in psychology, including group decision making, self-perception, personality theory and assessment, ESP, and sexual orientation. He is coauthor of two introductory textbooks in psychology and the author of Beliefs, Attitudes, and Human Affairs *and* Exotic Becomes Erotic: Explaining the Enigma of Sexual Orientation *(forthcoming).*

similarity, the research evidence is quite conclusively opposed to the hypothesis that their perception is similar (Jones & Nisbett, 1972; Nisbett et al., 1973; Storms, 1973).

Although Bem's theory of a passive process of self-perception was not disproven by these results, it was also not clearly supported. Moreover, if passive observers can replicate experimental findings, it is quite possible that they are doing so because of their intuitive understanding of common ways of dissonance reduction. As Zajonc (1968b, p. 375) commented, "Most subjects are also able to guess the trajectory of an apple falling from a tree, without doing serious damage to the laws of classical mechanics." Thus it has proven difficult to find situations that clearly pit the two theories against each other.

However, one clear difference between the theories is that dissonance theory posits motivational arousal in the form of an unpleasant emotional state arising from counterattitudinal actions, whereas self-perception theory does not make such motivational assumptions. Research over the past 30 years has demonstrated considerable support for dissonance theory by showing that counterattitudinal advocacy does produce emotional arousal (Zanna & Cooper, 1974; Losch & Cacioppo, 1990; Elliot & Devine, 1994; Harmon-Jones, 2001). This research has largely resolved the conflict between the two theories by concluding that dissonance theory applies to behavior and ideas in the person's latitude of rejection (i.e., ones that are counterattitudinal), whereas self-perception theory applies to behavior and ideas within the latitude of acceptance (i.e., attitude-congruent ones—Fazio et al., 1977). Thus Bem's theory is applicable to the overjustification effect described in the preceding section. We may conclude that Bem's theory has been provocative and heuristically useful, but that he has understated people's use of internal cues about their attitudes and overstated their use of external cues (Fazio, 1987).

Impression Management Theory

Another theoretical viewpoint that has arisen to challenge dissonance theory is **impression management theory** (Tedeschi, Schlenker, & Bonoma, 1971; Schlenker, 1980; Tedeschi, 1981). Its major principle is that people try to manage their self-presentations so as to maintain a favorable public image—the same basic motive posited in the concept of social desirability response set (see Chapter 3). A closely related motive in self-presentation is to maintain a public image consistent with *one's own* ideal (Baumeister, 1982). When people have done something inconsistent or socially undesirable, they make excuses or deny responsibility or look for justifications that minimize the negative consequences. Attitude statements are one form of social communication that people try to manage for purposes of self-presentation. Accordingly, the theory views attitude change following counterattitudinal behavior as being just an attempt to maintain a favorable impression in the eyes of the experimenter or other witnesses by not appearing inconsistent—not a true change of views. That is, people are more concerned about *looking* consistent than about being consistent.

Because the theory views purported attitude change as false and self-presentational in nature, it has generally been tested by comparing the usual paper-and-pencil attitude-change measures with techniques intended to tap people's "true" attitudes, such as the "bogus pipeline" (refer to Chapter 3 for details). A number of studies of induced compliance have found much less dissonance-based attitude change when the bogus pipeline was used than when standard attitude question methods were used (e.g., Gaes, Kalle, & Tedeschi, 1978). In addition, there is much evidence of other sorts that people are concerned about the impressions they make in self-presentation (Jones & Pittman, 1982; Schlenker & Britt, 1999). However, that does not mean that impression management is people's only concern or even their main focus when they have acted counterattitudinally.

A number of studies have continued to support the dissonance findings and explanation (e.g., Rosenfeld, Giacalone, & Tedeschi, 1983; Stults, Messe, & Kerr, 1984); and it is quite likely that both dissonance reduction and impression management are jointly involved in much of the induced-compliance research.

Further developments in impression management theory have made it more compatible with dissonance theory and reduced much of the conflict between the two approaches. Schlenker (1980, 1982) proposed an *identity-analytic* approach, which grants that induced-compliance attitude change can be real, but explains it in terms of people's attempts to avoid being held responsible for the negative consequences of their actions. This is very similar to the view of current dissonance theory, which stresses that awareness of personal responsibility for someone's negative consequences can enhance the magnitude of attitude change. Also, Tedeschi has conceded that self-presentation can be accompanied by arousal in the form of discomfort, anxiety, and embarrassment, which brings his views much closer to the concepts of cognitive dissonance theory (Tedeschi & Rosenfeld, 1981).

Other Research Related to Dissonance Theory

Before concluding our discussion of dissonance theory, let's examine two additional procedures that dissonance theory holds should be related to attitude change: making a public commitment to a particular viewpoint, and active participation in stating persuasive arguments.

Commitment.   Interest in the topic of commitment goes back to the early theory and research of Kurt Lewin (1947), who proposed that making a decision would "freeze" a person's beliefs and make them resistant to future counterpressures. Bennett (1955) confirmed that both private and public decisions had that effect, though most studies have found public commitment more effective (e.g., Wicklund & Brehm, 1976; Pallak et al., 1980).

More complex effects of commitment were studied by Kiesler (1971) and his colleagues, usually in situations involving commitment to consonant positions, but allowing participants no choice about the commitment. Their results often parallel dissonance research findings for commitment to counterattitudinal positions. For instance, defense of one's beliefs for a small reward produces more resistance to later attacks than does defense of one's beliefs for a large reward. When individuals have made a public commitment, they tend to become more extreme in their position and to avoid thinking about the implications of their behavior. Commitment also makes people more responsive to extreme but reputable messages that agree with them, and more inclined to act on their beliefs if they are disputed (Kiesler & Munson, 1975). Being reminded of attitudes to which they are committed makes people act in ways more consistent with their attitudes (Aronson, 1992).

Active Participation.   Early studies by the Hovland group showed that active participation in improvising persuasive arguments produced more attitude change than did passive listening to the same arguments (King & Janis, 1956). Active participation also produces longer-lasting attitude change (Watts, 1967).

An extension of this method is the technique of **role-playing**—that is, acting out the feelings and behavior that another person might display in a particular situation. This technique was shown to be effective in reducing the prejudice of whites who played the role of an advocate of peaceful racial integration (Culbertson, 1957). Another study had smokers play the part of a lung-cancer victim who had to undergo surgery. This dramatic emotional experience was found to reduce smoking significantly, an effect that lasted for at least 18 months (Mann & Janis, 1968). Undoubtedly the emotional impact of imagining, and in a sense experiencing, consequences that could happen to oneself is a powerful factor in producing attitude change through role-playing.

But why should active participation be effective in the less-emotional situation where a person merely improvises or states arguments for a position with which he or she disagrees? A variety of research studies have suggested several different explanations, any or all of which may apply in a particular situation. Preparing to argue against one's own position stimulates open-minded and unbiased evaluation of controversial information. Actually stating the arguments has been found to produce more attitude change than does just preparing them, perhaps because greater effort is involved. People also remember their own improvisations better and judge them more favorably than others' improvisations. We return to these points in more detail in the final section of this chapter, on cognitive-response approaches to attitude change.

Despite all the evidence for greater attitude change stemming from active participation, there are also situations in which the opposite effect is found. Primarily this is true in the area of "cultural truisms" or beliefs that are so common that people have rarely ever heard them challenged (e.g., "you should brush your teeth after every meal"). In such situations, a person may be unmotivated or unable to improvise supportive arguments, and thus passive reception of someone else's arguments may have more effect than active participation (McGuire, 1964, 1969). Notice that these situations are generally ones where individuals are arguing *for* their own beliefs, which may later be attacked, whereas in situations where they are arguing *against* their own beliefs, active participation generally produces more attitude change.

Evaluation of Dissonance Theory

Dissonance theory must be given credit, first of all, for being exciting and influential enough to stimulate research by hundreds of followers and critics. This in itself is perhaps the most important function of a theory. The theory is also much broader in its applications than other consistency theories. Because of its unique way of defining inconsistency, it is particularly applicable to choice behavior in conflict situations, an arena that other consistency theories do not enter. Moreover, dissonance theory is particularly intriguing for its numerous "nonobvious" hypotheses—for instance, the inverse relationship of dissonance to incentive size in the $1 versus $20 forced-compliance situation. Dissonance experimenters also became known for their ingenious experimental procedures, some of which require a high degree of theatrical talent and stage-setting, though they also raise the problems of believability and the ethics of deception.

Dissonance theory has also been severely criticized, most notably by Chapanis and Chapanis (1964), and defended just as stoutly by others (Silverman, 1964; Aronson, 1969). Many of the criticisms revolve around dubious methodological practices such as the discarding of some subjects or the citation of marginally significant findings—what Suedfeld (1971) termed "inviting weaknesses" in the research. These criticisms are well-taken, but there are many supportive findings to which they do not apply. Another set of criticisms proposes alternative theoretical interpretations of the experimental findings (for instance, based on participants' suspiciousness, or anxiety, or degree of reinforcement, or expectation of future unpleasant consequences, etc.). One or another of these explanations may seem plausible in any given experiment, but they are almost always after-the-fact interpretations. Moreover, they rarely have the parsimony, and never the broad range of applicability, of the dissonance predictions. Because of these kinds of criticisms, the

Chapanises concluded their critique by stating that, after 5 years of dissonance research, they must return "a verdict of NOT PROVEN" (1964, p. 21, capitals in original). However, critics should be aware that no theory is ever proven! Theories can be disproved by contrary data, but at most they can only be supported by confirming data, never proven in any final or ultimate sense. As Aronson (1969) replied, "Happily, after more than 10 years, it is still not proven; all the theory ever does is generate research" (p. 31).

Some more crucial criticisms of the theory can be made, however. Most important is the difficulty in making clear-cut predictions from the theory for a specific situation. This difficulty arises from two facts: that the same situation may create different amounts of dissonance in two individuals who have different prior cognitions, and especially that dissonance can be reduced in many different ways and even in several ways at once. These difficulties are usually overcome in experiments by contriving a situation in which the crucial cognitions are relatively clear-cut and in which most of the ways of reducing dissonance are blocked or are unlikely, so that clear-cut predictions can be made and tested. But in everyday-life situations, it is usually very difficult to tell what important cognitions a person has or what ways of reducing dissonance may be most likely. Thus specific predictions are on shaky ground except in relatively rare or artificially controlled situations. This problem could be greatly reduced if an independent, quantitative measure of the amount of a person's dissonance could be developed, or if objective manipulation checks could be devised in experiments to verify the approximate amount of dissonance aroused. However, we would still have to deal with the problem of individual differences in the tolerance for dissonance or the preference for consistency. Other criticisms and strengths of dissonance theory can be found in the 13 chapters of a volume edited by Harmon-Jones and Mills (1999).

Following the great initial impact of dissonance theory and its domination of social psychological research in the 1960s, interest then shifted to other approaches, particularly attribution theory. However, in the 1990s and early 2000s, dissonance theory had a substantial resurgence, and recent reviews have emphasized its central and important contributions to understanding attitude change as well as its numerous practical applications (e.g., Harmon-Jones & Mills, 1999).

REACTANCE THEORY

An indirect offshoot of dissonance theory was J. W. Brehm's (1966) reactance theory. The key principle of the theory is that people are motivationally aroused whenever they feel some aspect of their freedom is being threatened or restricted. This arousal, called psychological reactance, motivates the person to try to restore the threatened freedom, with the result that the potentially restricted behavior becomes more attractive to the person. For example, if one is told, "Sorry, that item is already sold, and no more are available," it suddenly becomes even more attractive to the would-be buyer. A large-scale example of reactance was seen in 1985 when the Coca-Cola Company decided to stop selling original flavored Coke, resulting in widespread public rejection of "New Coke" (Ringold, 1988).

Threats to an individual's freedom can occur through the actions of a powerful other person or group, such as the government or the police, or through the mere implication that someone else is attempting to influence one's behavior or attitudes ("eat this lovely eggplant; you'll like it"). Also, the restrictions can be social in origin or nonsocial, as

Photograph courtesy of Jack Brehm.
Reprinted by permission.

Box 11–3 JACK BREHM, *Originator of Reactance Theory*

Widely known for his contributions to cognitive theory, Jack Brehm is Professor Emeritus of Psychology at the University of Kansas. Following high school, he served in the U.S. Navy after World War II and then took his B.A. at Harvard and his Ph.D. at the University of Minnesota. During 3 years as a faculty member at Yale, he was a member of the highly creative communication research program under Carl Hovland. Then he taught for 17 years at Duke University, before moving to Kansas in 1975, where he has remained active since his retirement in 1996.

Brehm was one of the earliest researchers on Festinger's cognitive dissonance theory, to which he made major contributions in books titled Explorations in Cognitive Dissonance *and* Perspectives on Cognitive Dissonance. *He has also published two books about psychological reactance, the original theory for which he is best known. He has been honored by election as chair of the Society of Experimental Social Psychology and receipt of its Distinguished Scientist Award. His current research interests are centered on emotions, such as sadness, and how the intensity of emotion relates to motivation and goal-setting.*

when the physical environment prevents an action. When a freedom is threatened, the magnitude of the psychological reactance is determined by the importance of the freedom, the proportion of freedoms that are threatened, the person's subjective confidence that he or she really had that freedom to begin with, the degree of restriction experienced, the illegitimacy or lack of justification of the restriction, and the absence of any available similar alternative actions. The consequences of reactance can be observed in verbal reports of attitudes or perceptions, or sometimes in behavior directed at exercising the threatened freedom or attacking the source of the restriction (Brehm, 1966).

Reactance theory is relatively simple and logically consistent, but it is not precisely quantified, so statements about the degree of reactance, the importance of a freedom, the amount of confidence concerning its possession, and the consequences of reactance have to be phrased in relative (more than or less than) terms (Shaw & Costanzo, 1982). However, considerable research has supported the principles of the theory (e.g., Wicklund, 1974; S. Brehm & J. Brehm, 1981), sometimes even finding a "boomerang effect" of reverse attitude change (Heller, Pallak, & Picek, 1973; Fishbein et al., 2002). As one example, housewives whose freedom to use detergents containing phosphates was eliminated by a local law expressed more favorable attitudes toward those detergents than did a non-deprived control group in a nearby city (Mazis, 1975). The theory further suggests that *forewarning* of a communicator's persuasive intent will arouse reactance motivation, thus producing less attitude change; and some studies have supported this general hypothesis (e.g., Petty & Cacioppo, 1979a).

As with dissonance-theory research, impression management theory has challenged reactance findings as being due, not to concern about the actual loss of freedom, but to attempts to maintain the outward appearance of being free (e.g., a politician claiming, "No, I haven't changed my viewpoint; I've always believed that. . . .") (Baer et al., 1980; Schlenker, 1980). However, Wright and S. Brehm (1982) have disputed the impression-management view by showing that reactance effects are found even when the resulting behavior could not be interpreted by others as a sign of autonomy.

ATTRIBUTION THEORIES AND ATTITUDE CHANGE

We have discussed attribution theories at some length in Chapter 2, noting that they replaced dissonance theory as the most frequently studied topic in the social psychological research literature of the 1970s and 1980s. However, most of the research discussed in Chapter 2 did not deal with attitude *change* and, in general, attribution theories have not been widely applied to the traditional topics of attitude-change research. However, it is clear that attributions can play an important role in attitude change, and in this section we summarize several areas where attribution theories have made useful contributions.

One such area, which we have discussed in previous sections, is the research on Bem's self-perception theory, which pitted it against dissonance theory in explaining attitude change following counterattitudinal advocacy. Another topic utilizing attributional explanations, also discussed in previous sections, is the overjustification or undermining effect, which is found when rewards or threats are offered for performing attitude-congruent behavior. Either Bem's theory or Kelley's (1972a) discounting principle is applicable to that situation. A third topic where attribution principles were invoked was in research on the foot-in-the-door effect, which was discussed earlier as an example of consistency motivation. One of the popular explanations of that effect adds an attributional element to the consistency interpretation, specifying that a person who complies with the first small request is influenced to make a self-attribution of helpfulness, and consequently is more likely to comply with a later large request: "I put the small sticker in my window, so I'm a supporter of public-spirited campaigns."

Attribution of Physiological Responses. A number of attributional studies of physiological responses have involved the variable of attitude change. One was the classic experiment of Schachter and Singer (1962), in which they injected individuals with physiologically arousing epinephrine and then put them in a waiting room with an accomplice of the experimenter who began to act either euphoric or angry. The participants who had not been given an explanation of the drug's arousing effects apparently used the cue provided by the accomplice's behavior as the basis for self-attribution, for they later reported themselves as being either happy or angry, depending on which condition they had experienced.

An experiment by Valins (1966) extended this principle to false physiological feedback—specifically, sounds that the male subjects believed were their own heartbeats. The results showed that *Playboy* pictures which were accompanied by either increased or decreased "heart rates" were later judged as more attractive than the other pictures. However, this *misattribution* of attitudes that is based on physiological information has limits. Taylor (1975) showed that bogus physiological feedback did not significantly influence women's ratings of men's pictures in the condition where they expected there would be future consequences of their ratings (i.e., that they would be able to meet one of the men).

Other research has utilized misattribution of physiological arousal for therapeutic ends in treating anxiety, insomnia, and phobias (Reisenzein, 1983). For instance, in a laboratory setting, Brodt and Zimbardo (1981) increased social responsiveness and emotional comfort among very shy college women by misattributing their shyness symptoms to the environmental impact of bombardment by high-frequency noise in the experiment. More clinically feasible examples of attribution-based treatments have been used to reduce anxiety and improve performance in mixed-sex social interactions and in college examinations (Wilson & Linville, 1982; Haemmerlie & Montgomery, 1984; Noel, Forsyth, & Kelley, 1987).

Communicator Credibility.   An attributional analysis of persuasion has been offered by Eagly, Chaiken, and Wood (1981), based on inferences that people make about the credibility of communicators. Credibility is seen as being determined by recipients' inferences about the *causes* of a communicator's advocacy of a particular position. The cause of the communicator's message may be a strong commitment to that position (referred to as a **knowledge bias**), or situational pressures such as trying to please a particular audience (implying a **reporting bias** on the part of the communicator), or simply a veridical view of the issue. Recipients are less likely to be persuaded if premessage cues give them an expectancy that the communicator has a knowledge bias or a reporting bias. However, in cases where that expectancy is disconfirmed by the communicator advocating an unexpected position, persuasion is likely, because then the recipient attributes the message as being based on the true weight of evidence on the issue (Eagly et al., 1978). This analysis helps to explain why statements that appear contrary to the speaker's self-interest are apt to be quite persuasive to the hearer. Cialdini (2000) has used this principle to point out the social-influence effects of self-deprecating humor, and of waiters who suggest one of the cheaper dishes to diners (and then use the credibility conferred by that action to recommend expensive wines or fancy desserts).

A related topic is the way in which people decide about a communicator's true viewpoint. People generally attribute a statement as being due to the speaker's true attitude, even when they are told that the person had no choice about making the statement (Jones & Harris, 1967). This is an example of the **fundamental attribution error**—the tendency to overestimate the extent to which a person's behavior is due to dispositional factors and to underestimate the influence of situational factors. For example, Ross et al. (1977) showed that, in a simulated game show, viewers consistently attributed greater knowledge and ability to the questioner than to the contestant (see also Block & Funder, 1986). This effect persisted even when the viewer was told that the determination of contestant and questioner roles was arbitrary.

Minority Influence in a Group.   A topic that has been pioneered by Moscovici (cf. 1985) is the influence that can be exerted by numerical minorities in group decision or discussion situations. This European perspective represents a contrast with American social psychology's preoccupation with conformity of minorities in a group to the majority opinion (e.g., Asch, 1956). According to Moscovici and Nemeth's (1974) attributional account, single individuals or small subgroups in a group can have considerable influence on the group's decisions if they state positions that are *consistent* and *distinctive* from the majority viewpoint. Such a stance leads other group members to attribute certainty and confidence to the minority, and this in turn may influence the majority decision. A meta-analysis of 97 minority-influence experiments found that numerical minorities who were perceived to be consistent in their advocacy were particularly influential (Wood et al., 1994).

However, the research also indicates that directly changing the attitudes of majority-group members can be extremely difficult. Even in instances where numerical minorities are consistent and distinctive, they often fail to produce attitude change among the majority (De Vries et al., 1996; Martin, 1998). A number of studies have demonstrated that majority-group members are often resistant to arguments by the minority and may even show boomerang effects (Wood et al., 1996). Thus, group members who advocate a minority viewpoint are usually unlikely to change the attitudes of group members successfully. However, there is some evidence that minorities can produce change on topics *indirectly related* to the persuasive appeal (Wood et al., 1994), provided that they are *ingroup* members (not from an outgroup) and that their arguments do not threaten the group's existence (Crano & Chen, 1998; Crano, 2000). Majority members don't want to be identified with the minority viewpoint, but at the same time they want to avoid intragroup conflict. Thus, although they are unlikely to be persuaded on the focal topic (e.g., abortion), their attitudes toward related topics (e.g., birth control, euthanasia) might change (Crano & Chen, 1998; Gordijn, De Vries, & De Dreu, 2002).

Evaluation of Attribution Approaches. It is clear that attribution theories have been applied productively to many different aspects of attitude change. There are some areas in which they provide the best or only explanation, other areas where they have been less successful than other theories such as dissonance, and quite a few areas where they offer a useful alternative viewpoint or a needed complement to other theories in explaining a phenomenon more completely. Attribution theorists have modestly granted that some social situations may engage other social motives more than (or rather than) attribution, and also that attribution processes, which are relatively thoughtful, may be more typical among college students, the most commonly used research participants, than among the general public (Jones et al., 1972). Despite their limitations, attribution theories have stimulated a great deal of research and will undoubtedly continue to be extended to new research topics and additional practical applications.

COGNITIVE RESPONSE THEORIES

A more recent, important, theoretical viewpoint about persuasion emphasizes the cognitive responses that people make when they are exposed to persuasive messages (Petty & Cacioppo, 1981; Petty & Wegener, 1998; Petty, Wheeler, & Tormala, 2003). These **cognitive responses** are thoughts that recipients themselves generate, and they can be favorable to the message, or opposing counterarguments, or neutral or irrelevant thoughts. Usually there will be some mix of these different types of thoughts, and the relative balance of favorable and unfavorable thoughts is a key variable.

These self-generated thoughts are subjective. They are not linked directly to the objective characteristics of the message, and they can vary widely across recipients. Consequently, measuring a person's cognitive responses to a message requires an individual-level measure. The most frequently used method is called the **thought-listing technique**. In it, research participants are given a specified period of time, such as 3 minutes, in which to write down brief statements of the thoughts they had as they listened to or read a persuasive message. These statements are then coded by independent raters for their degree of favorability to the message or for other aspects of the responses (Cacioppo & Petty, 1981b; Rosselli, Skelly, & Mackie, 1995; Hafer, Reynolds, & Obertynski, 1996).

Theoretical Principles

The cognitive-response viewpoint assumes that when people receive (or even anticipate) a persuasive message, they are likely to try to relate its arguments to knowledge, beliefs, and attitudes they already hold on that topic, and in doing so they generate a number of thoughts that are not part of the message itself. As one researcher (Baumwoll, quoted in Gordon, 1987) put it, "What people do to messages is more important than what messages do to people" (p. 25).

The theory holds that the balance of favorable or unfavorable self-generated thoughts will determine the success of the persuasive message. That is, the cognitive responses *mediate* between characteristics of the message or the recipient and the effect of the message, and they are considered to be crucial in determining what effect the message will have. They represent a step between comprehension of the message and yielding to or acceptance of it, as described in McGuire's (1985) fine-grain analysis of the communication process.

The first ideas contributing to the cognitive-response viewpoint developed from the early research on *active participation* in persuasion (see the section on dissonance research earlier in this chapter). There, studies found that people who improvised their own

Photograph courtesy of Richard Petty.
Reprinted by permission.

Box 11–4 RICHARD PETTY, *Originator of the Elaboration Likelihood Model*

Richard Petty graduated from the University of Virginia and earned his Ph.D. in social psychology from Ohio State University in 1977. He taught for 8 years at the University of Missouri, where he was honored by appointment to an endowed professorship. In 1987 he returned to teach at Ohio State, where he has served as chair of the psychology department and remains today as a Distinguished Professor. He has been elected president of the Midwestern Psychological Association.

In the past 30 years, Petty has published almost 200 articles, written 7 books, served as the editor of the Personality and Social Psychology Bulletin, *and worked on the editorial boards of 6 other journals. He is perhaps best known for his collaboration with John Cacioppo as originators of the Elaboration Likelihood Model of attitude change, which is summarized in this chapter. The two began their collaboration as fellow graduate students, and they have shared authorship on more than 60 papers and 5 books, notably including* Communication and Persuasion: Central and Peripheral Routes to Attitude Change *(1986). Petty has also been active in applying his research findings to issues of health and substance abuse, racial and ethnic prejudice, to marketing and consumer psychology, and to combating global environmental degradation.*

persuasive talk based on a written counterattitudinal communication displayed more attitude change than did people who read the written message silently or read it aloud into a tape recorder (King & Janis, 1956). The difference was not due to satisfaction with their own performance, which was higher in the read-aloud group, but rather to the element of improvising their own statement of the arguments. Later studies showed two factors that contribute to this improvisation effect. First, when people know what position they are going to have to defend, they engage in a *biased information search*, which selectively concentrates on arguments that favor that position, and this process encourages more attitude change in that direction (O'Neill & Levings, 1979). Second, people *value* the arguments that they generate themselves more than other people value them and more than they value other people's arguments (Greenwald & Albert, 1968).

Another key conclusion is that active participation in generating a talk on an assigned topic produces longer-lasting attitude change than does passive exposure to the same or equivalent arguments (Watts, 1967). An underlying reason for this difference is that people are *able to recall* their own arguments on a topic better than they can recall arguments presented by someone else (Greenwald & Albert, 1968).

Research Findings

Effects of Mere Thought.   One of the areas of research that supports the cognitive-response viewpoint is studies of people merely thinking about an issue without being exposed to any persuasive communication. In a series of studies, Tesser (1978) came to the conclusion that mere thought about an issue generally results in a person's attitude becoming more extreme than it was before (termed a **polarization effect**). This effect occurs because on many topics people have viewpoints or schemas that make some aspects of the issue salient and provide guides for inferences about other aspects. Thought under the direction of such a schema leads to changes in beliefs, which are generally in the direction of greater belief consistency. Mere thought leads to more extreme attitudes only when people have such a schema or bias to guide their thinking (Tesser & Leone, 1977; Tesser, Martin, & Mendolia, 1995).

In a typical study of mere thought, participants were introduced to either a likable partner or a dislikable partner through a tape recording. The likable partner was pleasant, describing himself confidently but without bragging, whereas the dislikable partner was arrogant and insulting. Then half the participants were instructed to think about their partner, while the other half were given a distracting task to perform, which would limit their thinking about the partner. Next, they rated their partner on a series of scales and listed their thoughts about him. The results showed that participants who thought about their partner were more favorable to the likable partner than were distracted participants, and those who thought about the dislikable partner were more negative toward him than were the distracted participants (Sadler & Tesser, 1973). Further research demonstrated that giving people a few more minutes for thinking resulted in more polarization of attitudes, but that after a relatively brief time all the thinking possible on the topic had been done and no further polarization occurred (Tesser, 1978). Studies of a longer duration (up to 2 weeks) have shown that repeated trials do not lead to further polarization, but that the initial polarization of attitudes is long-lasting and does not dissipate (Liu & Latane, 1998).

Forewarning of Persuasion.   The topic of forewarning is somewhat like mere thought in that attitude change often occurs even before the persuasive message is delivered (an **anticipatory attitude change**). The direction of the change depends on whether the recipient is highly involved in the issue or not (Cialdini & Petty, 1981; Wood & Quinn,

2003). People who expect to receive a message on an issue that is not very personally relevant to them generally become more moderate (less extreme) in their attitudes (Chen et al., 1992). On the contrary, people who expect to receive a message on a highly relevant topic usually become more polarized in their attitudes (i.e., more extreme in the direction of their original views).

Several explanations have been offered in the research literature for these findings concerning anticipatory attitude change. One possibility is that uninvolved individuals may moderate their views in the service of impression management—trying to present an acceptable appearance to the communicator and other recipients—and if they do not receive the message, their attitudes will "snap back" to their original position. However, individuals who are involved in the topic will be motivated to defend their true opinion, and they will rehearse arguments supporting their own viewpoint, resulting in more extreme attitudes. If the message they expect is proattitudinal, their rehearsal of favorable arguments can be explained by self-perception theory, whereas if it is counterattitudinal, their counterarguing may be seen as motivated by psychological reactance (Cialdini et al., 1976; see also Romero, Agnew, & Insko, 1996).

Resistance to Persuasion. The research just discussed shows that forewarning can produce resistance to persuasion by encouraging counterarguing. This effect is particularly strong if the forewarning comes long enough before the message (e.g., 2–10 minutes) to allow time for counterarguing and if the person is not distracted (Hass & Grady, 1975; Chen et al., 1992; Wood & Quinn, 2003). For a thorough discussion of resistance processes, see Knowles and Linn (2004).

A famous early study on resistance to persuasion was McGuire's (1964) research on "inoculation" against persuasion. He used the medical analogy of creating resistance to a disease by inoculating a person with a weak form of the disease-producing germ and thus producing antibodies against the disease. The beliefs that he aimed to protect from attack were "cultural truisms"—beliefs so common in our culture that people have rarely ever heard them attacked (for instance, "mental illness is not contagious"). With such beliefs, people do not have supportive arguments readily at hand, so they need some help in defending them from attack. McGuire accomplished the inoculation by presenting individuals with some weak arguments against the truisms followed by refutations of those arguments, and he showed that this approach produced more resistance against a later attacking message than did a "supportive defense" which merely presented some arguments for the truisms before receipt of the attacking message. Consistent with a cognitive-response viewpoint, participants listed more thoughts supportive of the truisms in the inoculation condition than in the supportive defense condition. For more recent research on inoculation, see Pfau, Kyle, and Koerner (1997).

Head Nodding. While listening to a persuasive message, recipients often nod or shake their head in response to specific elements of the message. What effect does this have on the persuasiveness of the message? Wells and Petty (1980) had college students listen to a tape-recorded editorial advocating either an increase or a decrease in college tuition. They were randomly assigned either to nod their head up and down, or to shake their head from side to side while listening (ostensibly to test the durability of the earphones). Results showed that nodding produced more agreement with the message than did shaking—a result consistent with several different theoretical viewpoints.

However, recent research showed that this occurred only when strong arguments were presented. When the arguments were weak (which was likely to stimulate unfavorable thoughts), head nodding produced *less* attitude change than did shaking (Briñol & Petty,

2003). The authors concluded that the findings were "consistent with the self-validation hypothesis that postulates that head movements either enhance (nodding) or undermine (shaking) confidence in one's thoughts about the message" (p. 1123).

Issue Involvement. We have seen in previous chapters that involvement is an important variable in various theories of attitude change, and it is also a key concept in cognitive response theory. People who are highly involved in an issue will be more motivated to generate thoughts on the topic, and so their attitudes will normally become more extreme, as previously noted in regard to forewarning. That means they will usually shift *toward* a strong proattitudinal message but become more extreme in the direction *opposite* to a counterattitudinal message. However, an exception to this common pattern is based on the quality of the arguments in the message. If a counterattitudinal message presents many strong arguments on an issue in which they are highly involved, people will tend to generate thoughts favorable to these strong arguments, but if the message arguments are weaker, they will generate mostly counterarguments (Petty & Cacioppo, 1979b, 1984; Leippe & Elkin, 1987). Thus research shows that high issue-involvement produces more careful processing of the message content—but not always biased processing, though that often occurs (Abelson, 1986; Howard-Pitney et al., 1986).

Central Versus Peripheral Routes to Persuasion

The complex pattern of interactions that we have discussed in preceding sections can be much better understood by using a concept of two different routes to attitude change (Petty & Cacioppo, 1986; Petty & Wegener, 1999; Petty et al., 2004). The fundamental distinction between the two routes is whether the person engages in effortful processing of the persuasive message. Some messages are processed more fully—elaborated and thought about—whereas others are dismissed or processed in a more cursory manner. In recent years, a large number of studies have been devoted to identifying the personal and situational variables that lead to high versus low effortful processing, the attitude changes that can occur through these two routes, and the consequences of attitudes formed or changed through each route. In this section, we review the basic theory and some of the variables that are associated with elaboration.

The **central route** to persuasion is based on the *information* that a person has about the attitude topic or issue. It stresses the individual's prior knowledge and interest in the topic, the degree of comprehension and learning of arguments in a message, and the self-generated thoughts of the individual in reaction to a message. Thus it involves a relatively rational process of considering facts, arguments, and thoughts, though it is not completely logical, for it often considers a biased group of thoughts or arguments and combines them in psychological rather than logical ways. Its hallmark is a *thoughtful* consideration of information.

The **peripheral route** to persuasion is far less thoughtful, and it ensues when a person's motivation or ability to process message content or other information is low. It relies on cues *peripheral to the content* of the message instead of on the arguments in the message and the thoughts which it arouses. The peripheral cues provide a *shortcut procedure* by which a person can decide how to react to a message without taking the trouble to think about all the pros and cons. For instance, one type of peripheral cue is the source's credibility or likability or power, and a recipient may rely on any one of these to determine his or her response, without thinking about the message in detail.

Another type of peripheral cue is message characteristics that have been associated with rewarding or punishing experiences in the past, as in product commercials or political ads that develop a mood of sexual arousal or happy relaxation or patriotism. Also, recipient characteristics, such as low issue involvement, often lead to response by the peripheral route, as illustrated by findings in the preceding sections of this chapter. Although the peripheral route is cognitively "lazy," it is not necessarily illogical. You cannot possibly think in detail about every persuasive message, advertisement, or commercial that you are exposed to, and it may often make sense to rely on the recommendation of an expert or on the feelings of pleasure or threat which a message arouses, particularly if the topic is not important to you.

Figure 11–3 presents a schematic diagram of the main factors involved in determining whether the central route or the peripheral route will be followed and the consequences of the two routes. Petty and Cacioppo (1986) have emphasized that persuasion via the peripheral route is apt to be weak, temporary, and susceptible to counterpressures, whereas persuasion via the central route is apt to be stronger, relatively persistent, and resistant to counterattack. They call their theory of attitude change the **elaboration likelihood model**

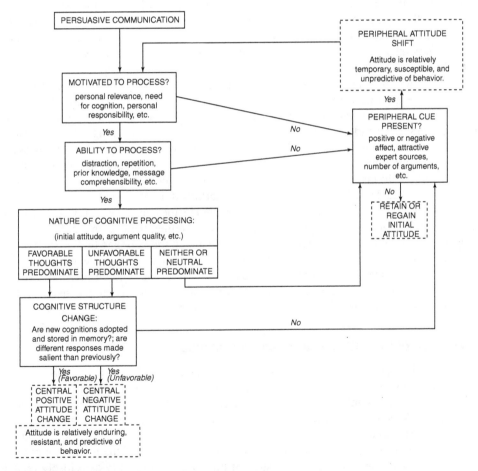

FIGURE 11–3 Schematic diagram of major factors involved in the central route and the peripheral route to persuasion, according to the elaboration likelihood model.

Source: Reprinted from Petty & Cacioppo (1986, p. 4).

because it stresses that an individual's cognitive elaboration of issue-relevant arguments plays a crucial role in attitude change and persistence.

Rather similar concepts have been proposed by other researchers working in the fields of attitude change and social cognition. For instance, Petty and Cacioppo's distinction between central and peripheral routes to persuasion has considerable similarity to distinctions between **systematic** versus **heuristic** processing (Chaiken, 1980; Chen & Chaiken, 1999), thoughtful versus "scripted" or "mindless" processing (Abelson, 1976; Langer, Blank, & Chanowitz, 1978), and cognitive versus affective evaluation of information (Zajonc, 1980). The use of simple heuristic decision cues (e.g., "more is better," "experts can be trusted") and unthoughtful, mindless reactions are special cases of the peripheral route, which is typified by the energy-saving "cognitive miser" approach (Fiske & Taylor, 1984).

In addition to the research topics cited in the preceding section, several other areas of research support the value of the central–peripheral distinction. For example, the effect of *distraction* during receipt of a message is to reduce cognitive elaborations and thus to weaken what would otherwise be the person's reaction to the message. Ironically, this means that distraction can lead to some favorable attitude change toward the viewpoint of a counterattitudinal message, which would otherwise be rejected if the recipient were not being distracted (Petty, Wells, & Brock, 1976; Lammers & Becker, 1980). On the other hand, *message repetition* allows an opportunity for more cognitive elaboration, and if the arguments in the message are strong ones, this can lead to more favorable attitudes toward either a proattitudinal or a counterattitudinal message (Cacioppo & Petty, 1979). However, if the message is repeated several times in a relatively short period, boredom and reactance are likely, resulting in more counterarguing and reduced attitude change. If the message arguments are weak ones, repetition can quickly lead to counterarguing and unfavorable attitude change (Petty & Cacioppo, 1981). Presenting a larger *number of arguments* in a message also allows for more cognitive elaboration. As with message repetition, if the arguments are strong ones, more favorable thoughts and more attitude change will result; but if the arguments are weak, more counterarguing and less attitude change occur (Calder, Insko, & Yandell, 1974; Harkins & Petty, 1981).

Finally, *persistence of attitude change* is explained by the cognitive-response viewpoint as being due to favorable thoughts being rehearsed and remembered over a period of time. However, importantly, it is not recall of the arguments in the message that is crucial, but rather recall of the self-generated thoughts about the message that is significantly predictive of persisting attitude change (Love & Greenwald, 1978). This finding presents a major quandary for a message-learning theory of attitude change, but it is quite consistent with cognitive response theory (Cook & Flay, 1978; Chaiken, 1980).

Evaluation of Cognitive Response Approaches

Cognitive response viewpoints see attitude change largely as a process of **self-persuasion**, holding that "a person's own thoughts are a more powerful determinant of persuasion than is information that originates externally" (Petty & Cacioppo, 1981, p. 251). As demonstrated in the preceding discussion, this principle has received support in research on a wide variety of topics. However, questions can be raised about the thought-listing technique, which is the most common measure of the mediating process of self-generated thinking. Because results of this measure typically are closely related to measures of attitude change, it is possible that the thought-listing measure is just an alternative measure of attitude change, rather than an index of an intervening process (Sears, 1988a). If so, the obtained relationships would be far less important, and other methods of measurement would be needed. Although there are few data related to this issue, several studies have experimentally manipulated the types of thoughts a person has about the persuasive message (the so-called directed-thought technique). These studies suggest that thoughts about the persuasive argument precede attitude change, as cognitive response theory would expect (Killeya & Johnson, 1998).

The distinction between central and peripheral routes to attitude change has gone far in making sense out of a diverse and often apparently conflicting set of research findings. Thus, this approach is a hopeful step toward a truly general theory of attitude change, and it is closely in tune with the recent growth of a cognitive emphasis in social psychology. In addition, it has been applied to various practical topics such as advertising and counseling (Brock & Shavitt, 1983; Heesacker, 1985).

However, even proponents of cognitive response theory admit that it is not sufficient in itself to explain all attitude change (Petty & Cacioppo, 1981). Cognitive responses tell us *how* a person thinks about a message or an issue, but other (motivational) theories are necessary to tell us *why* a person generates favorable or unfavorable thoughts in response to a message. Examples of such other theories are ones discussed in this chapter, stressing motivational concepts such as a need for consistency, dissonance that is due to feeling responsible for some unpleasant consequences, or reactance against threats to one's freedom of action or thought. The principles of cognitive response theory provide an important explanatory link between the arousal of such motives and the resulting changes in people's attitudes and behavior.

A FINAL COMMENT ON THEORIES

It is obvious from our discussion in this chapter that all theories of attitude change have limitations. Some have greater problems than others, but all have rather crucial failings. Does that mean that we should abandon them, in effect saying "a plague on both your houses"? No, definitely not. Although that course might be emotionally satisfying, it would not be good science. The scientific reasons for developing and using theories have been presented earlier, in Chapter 10. As scientists, when we are faced with the inadequacies of our theories, our job is twofold: first, to try to determine the range of conditions under which each theory holds, and second, to endeavor to construct better theories that will more fully explain the existing research evidence. This is an exciting and an urgent task.

SUMMARY

Cognitive *consistency* theories have generated a great deal of research, but they are fractionated into many partially conflicting minitheories. The basic principle of all consistency theories is that awareness of inconsistency among one's ideas is an uncomfortable situation which will motivate cognitive changes, though not necessarily strictly logical ones. In general, consistency theories have been heuristically provocative but relatively low in the empirical validity of their research predictions. In part, this is probably due to the common and pervasive occurrence of *in*consistency in human psychological functioning.

Festinger's *dissonance* theory is a type of cognitive consistency theory, but it is unique in both its form and its ability to stimulate controversy and research. The theory is stated in an open way which allows it to be applied to many diverse areas. With later revisions that stressed the importance of volition and commitment and the centrality of the self-concept in the dissonance-arousal process, the theory has done quite well in predicting the consequences of making decisions. However, there is less-complete support for its predictions about selective exposure to information, the role of social support in reducing dissonance, and the effects of induced counterattitudinal behavior.

Brehm's *reactance* theory posits that people are motivationally aroused whenever they feel some aspect of their freedom is being threatened, and consequently they try to restore the threatened freedom. The theory has had relatively good success in predicting research findings, including the topic of forewarning of persuasive intent. *Attribution* theories, in recent years, have been increasingly applied to attitude change issues such as research on overjustification effects and the foot-in-the-door phenomenon.

Cognitive response theories are a major new approach, which emphasizes that attitude change is based largely on people's self-generated thoughts in reaction to persuasive messages, rather than on the message content itself. Support for this principle comes from many research topics: effects of active participation in improvising arguments, polarization of attitudes that is due to mere thought, anticipatory attitude change that is due to forewarning of persuasion, resistance to persuasion developed by methods such as the inoculation procedure, and effects of issue-involvement on attitude change. Petty and Cacioppo's *elaboration likelihood model* posits two contrasting routes to persuasion: The central route depends on information and thought about the message content, whereas the peripheral route uses noncontent cues to arrive at attitude changes that are apt to be weaker and less persistent.

Although each of these theoretical approaches has had some success in predicting and explaining research findings, each is a partial theory in that it explains only certain phenomena. Other theories are complementary in explaining other findings, and much of the research cited in this chapter shows that, if used in combination, they can take us closer to the eventual goal of an adequate general theory of attitude change.

12

Attitude–Behavior Consistency and Related Issues

Attitude and action are linked in a continuing reciprocal process, each generating the other in an endless chain.—Herbert C. Kelman.

We have too many high sounding words, and too few actions that correspond with them.—Abigail Adams, 1774.

What I want is to get done what the people desire to have done, and the question for me is how to find that out exactly.—Abraham Lincoln.

The politician who sways with the polls is not worth his pay.—Richard Nixon.

This chapter takes up several key issues in the study of attitudes and opinions. First we consider two long-standing questions that are still being debated—how are attitudes related to behavior, and how are they related to personality? Next we explore some methodological problems and ethical issues—what differences are there between the findings of laboratory research and field research, and what ethical problems are raised in attitude and opinion research? Finally, extending our examination of attitudes and behavior into the public arena, we look at the relationship of public opinion to public policy.

ATTITUDES AND BEHAVIOR

The topic of attitude–behavior consistency has been a subject of debate since the early days of social psychology (e.g., LaPiere, 1934), and in the years since whole books have been written on the subject (e.g., Deutscher, 1973; Zanna, Higgins, & Herman, 1982; Canary & Seibold, 1984). In the space available here we will highlight the most important aspects of this issue.

The question of what relationships exist among the cognitive, affective, and behavioral components of attitudes (or between beliefs, attitudes, and behavioral intentions as separate concepts) was discussed in Chapters 5 and 11. Now our attention shifts from the components or aspects of attitudes to the link between attitudes and behavior (that is, overt responses).

Is what we say always consistent with what we do? Obviously not, as Abigail Adams noted in 1774, before the American Revolution, in the quotation at the beginning of this chapter. We can all think of cases of discrepancy between our own words and deeds, just as between the statements and actions of others. Because attitudes are usually measured through a person's verbal report, there is a likelihood that attitudes and actions often may not correspond. Let's suppose for a moment that we pushed this idea to its extreme and asserted that attitudes were completely unrelated to actions. If that were the case, what would be the value of having the concept of "attitude"? On reflection, it should be clear that there would be very little value to it, for as an intervening variable, "attitude" is a useful concept only if it conveniently summarizes, or predicts, or is related to patterns of actual behavior. (For instance, recall Allport's 1935 definition that an attitude is a state of readiness that influences an individual's responses to objects and situations.)

Thus you can see that the verdict about the usefulness of the concept "attitude" depends largely on the empirical evidence regarding its relationship to behavior. What is the evidence? From the great mass of research in this area, we will mention a few studies which illustrate important points.

A Famous Early Study

In the early 1930s, when racial prejudice toward blacks, Asians, and most other foreigners was at a high level in the U.S., LaPiere (1934) traveled extensively around the country with a young, foreign-born Chinese couple. In a careful empirical manner he kept records on their acceptance and the quality of service they received in hotels, "auto camps," and restaurants. In addition, LaPiere attempted to vary the conditions experimentally by frequently having his Chinese friends enter restaurants first or do the negotiation for rooms. The results were dramatic: In about 10,000 miles of travel, the party was served (often with great hospitality) at 250 establishments and rejected at only one (a "rather inferior auto camp"). That was the behavioral measure.

To determine these establishments' attitudes toward Chinese as guests, LaPiere waited 6 months after the time of their visit and then sent each one a questionnaire asking, "Will you accept members of the Chinese race as guests in your establishment?" With persistence, he was able to get replies from 128, of which one auto camp replied "Yes," nine respondents said it would depend on the circumstances, and 118 said "No." Identical questionnaires sent to 128 similar businesses that they had *not* visited produced exactly the same distribution of responses. As a result of this massive discrepancy between questionnaire responses and actual behavior, LaPiere concluded that in many social situations questionnaire data cannot be trusted, and that attitudes generally must be studied through observation of actual social behavior. Results highly similar to LaPiere's have also been obtained in other studies, such as one involving racially mixed parties of diners in New York restaurants (Kutner, Wilkins, & Yarrow, 1952).

Can we conclude from these findings that the attitudes and behavior of these businesspeople were basically inconsistent? No, we cannot! Although at first glance it would appear so, there are major methodological problems involved, which cause what we may term "pseudo inconsistency."

Pseudo Inconsistency

One important point about the question of consistency was made by Campbell (1963), who emphasized the importance of **situational thresholds**. He stressed that often the verbal attitude statements and the overt behavioral measures that are studied have quite different thresholds, or levels of probability of occurrence. The reason for this discrepancy may be any of a number of factors, which will be discussed a bit later in this section. As an example, take a political party member who doesn't contribute financially to his party. For convenience, let us say that about 50% of the adult registered voters belong to the party; yet we know that the number of financial contributors is never more than about 5%.

Campbell pointed out that it would be grossly unfair to call the 45% who don't contribute "inconsistent." They are merely doing the easy (or common) thing and avoiding the difficult (or uncommon) behavior. The only true case of inconsistency would be a person who did the difficult, uncommon thing but failed to perform the easy, common action—in this example, one who contributed to the party but was not a member (e.g., one who gave money to "Democrats for Bush"). Such individuals are not only rare, but their behavior after the election is over often suggests that their *attitude* (stated party affiliation) was misclassified. For instance, in 1995 U.S. Senator Ben Nighthorse Campbell of Colorado switched from the Democratic to the Republican party after the Senate defeated a constitutional amendment requiring a balanced budget, which he favored. In explaining his move, he said "I have always been considered a moderate, much to the consternation of the Democratic party" (Patterson, 2001).

This analysis of **pseudo inconsistency** clearly applies to the LaPiere study of the Chinese couple's acceptance in restaurants and hotels. Its famous "inconsistency" was probably primarily a matter of differences in situational thresholds, for discrimination against members of another race is much harder in the face-to-face personal situation than in the abstract written-letter situation. Another example of this point is shown in Box 12–1. However, not all attitude–behavior comparisons display such differences in situational thresholds (Raden, 1977).

Other methodological critiques of the famous "inconsistency" studies have also been made. For example, in phoning or sending questionnaires to a restaurant or hotel, there is no certainty that the attitude measure was provided by the *same person* whose behavior was earlier observed (Dillehay, 1973). Also, the base rate or commonness of the behavior can markedly affect the attitude–behavior correlation—if almost everyone chooses one response (as in the LaPiere study), a single inconsistent case can lower the attitude–behavior correlation to nearly zero; whereas if the base rate is closer to 50%, one inconsistent case will have very little effect on the correlation (Fishbein & Ajzen, 1975, p. 373).

We can conclude that much (but by no means all) of the alleged inconsistency in the attitude–behavior research literature is actually pseudo inconsistency.

How Much Consistency?

But what about cases of real inconsistency between attitudes and behavior? How common are they, and what explanations can be found for them? Considerable attention has been directed to these questions. In an early review article, Wicker (1969) examined more than 30 studies bearing on the attitude–behavior relationship and concluded pessimistically that in most cases verbal measures of attitudes were only slightly related or were even unrelated to the overt behaviors. In only a minority of cases was the correlation coefficient between attitude and behavior higher than 0.30, and even this high a relationship indicates that the two measures have only about 10% of their variance in common; that is, they show only a small degree of overlap or similarity. Thus, Wicker concluded that it is risky to conceptualize attitudes as a latent process underlying behavior and/or to try to predict behavioral responses from verbal attitude measures.

However, some of the articles reviewed by Wicker suffered from the pseudo-inconsistency problems we have just described, whereas others did not really have a genuine measure of attitude or an actual behavioral criterion (Fishbein & Ajzen, 1975, pp. 359–361). One reanalysis of the same studies concluded that only seven of them had adequate measures of both attitudes and behavior, and these studies found substantially higher attitude–behavior correlations (M. E. Shaw, cited in Severy, 1974). Also, we should

Box 12–1 *Pseudo Inconsistency of Attitude Measures: Differing Situational Thresholds*

Minard (1952) described a group of white and Negro coal miners who worked together in the same mines, but whose interaction patterns were very different in the mines than in the town where they lived. Campbell (1963) has clarified the misleading analyses that have been made of this supposed inconsistency, as follows:

> Minard's . . . comments on the Pocahontas coal miners involve two items which can be diagrammed as [below]. His report clearly indicates that the setting of mine and town have markedly different situational thresholds for nondiscriminatory reactions of white miners, only 20 percent being friendly in town, 80 percent being friendly in the mines. He reports no instances of true inconsistency, i.e., being friendly in town and hostile in the mines. From this point of view, . . . [it is] clearly wrong to conclude that the middle 60 percent are persons "whose overt behavior provides no clue as to their attitudes." Their behavior clearly indicates that they have consistently middling attitudes. The two items, mine and town, correlate perfectly.

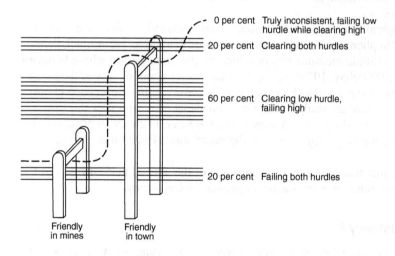

0 per cent Truly inconsistent, failing low hurdle while clearing high

20 per cent Clearing both hurdles

60 per cent Clearing low hurdle, failing high

20 per cent Failing both hurdles

Friendly in mines   Friendly in town

Source: D. T. Campbell, 1963, p. 161.

realize that correlations from 0.30 up to over 0.60, as found in the more successful studies, actually represent a high degree of accuracy in predicting a complex social behavior. Donald Campbell has pointed out that the correlation between two different but conceptually related *behaviors* (for instance, willingness to serve a minority-group member, and sitting beside the same person on a bus) is probably lower still (cited in A. G. Miller, 1972).

Supporting this point, Triandis (1964) has shown that behaviors involved in social distance and prejudice do not all cluster together with high positive correlations, but rather form five relatively distinct factors. Behaviors indicating general respect may be largely uncorrelated with acceptance into friendship relations, which in turn may be unrelated to marital acceptance. Similarly, low correlations might often be found between the same behavior in two different situations; for instance, Dutton (1971) found that enforcement of stated dress regulations in some Canadian restaurants was often different depending on whether a white couple or a black couple were the first ones to arrive informally dressed—interestingly, enforcement was often more lenient for black customers.

Despite low correlations in some studies, there is much evidence of general attitude–behavior similarity (Kraus, 1995). The election campaign opinion polls almost always show a close correspondence between *aggregate* public opinion and voting behavior, and Crespi (1971) has described other examples in which polls have shown good ability to predict aggregate criteria such as movie attendance and food brand preference. Similarly for *individual-level* comparisons, many reviews of the research literature have concluded that attitudes and behavior are generally related (e.g., Schuman & Johnson, 1976; Cialdini et al., 1981; Cooper & Croyle, 1984). In a meta-analysis of 88 studies of the attitude–behavior relationship, Kraus (1995) reported that "attitudes significantly and substantially predict future behavior (mean $r = 0.38$; combined $p < 0.000000000001$)" (p. 58).

Thus there is much evidence that attitudes can usually predict future behavior. More detailed research has gone beyond this fundamental issue to examine methodological and conceptual variables that moderate the strength of the relationship.

Methodological Improvements

There are several methodological refinements that have been shown to yield higher attitude–behavior relationships. Two are broader methods of measurement: using a multi-item attitude scale instead of measurement by a single item (e.g., Snyder & Kendzierski, 1982), and using a behavioral criterion scale made up of several actions instead of just one (Fishbein & Ajzen, 1975, pp. 359-363; Jaccard, 1979). Provided that the several items in a scale are positively correlated, this procedure will necessarily increase the scale's reliability and the size of the attitude–behavior correlation (Dawes & Smith, 1985).

Another methodological improvement is to measure attitudes toward a particular action (with a particular person) rather than using the more traditional measure of attitudes toward a person or a whole category of persons, such as "blacks" in general (e.g., Schwartz & Tessler, 1972). For instance, in predicting how often students will cut a particular course, we should achieve better prediction by measuring the students' attitudes concerning the importance of the course and the act of cutting class than by measuring only the students' attitudes toward the instructor.

The most often-cited methodological improvement affecting attitude–behavior correlations is to ensure **compatibility** in the level of measurement. Many of the early studies in this area correlated *general* attitudes with *specific* behaviors—for example, attitudes toward "blacks" with specific discriminatory behavior, or general attitudes about "environmental problems" with specific behaviors like recycling newspapers. A large amount of research has demonstrated that specific attitudes that are *compatible* with the behaviors being studied are more strongly associated with them (Fishbein & Ajzen, 1975; Ajzen & Fishbein, 1977; Ajzen, 1988; Ajzen & Sexton, 1999). Lack of compatibility regarding the attitude object was obviously a problem in LaPiere's (1934) study, for the attitude questionnaire asked about Chinese guests in general whereas the behavioral decision was made regarding a particular Chinese couple, well-dressed, well-spoken, smiling, and accompanied by a middle-class white companion.

Further research on the principle of compatibility has indicated that it also applies to general measures—that is, a measure of general attitudes on a given topic will usually correlate quite strongly with an aggregate measure of actions within a relevant class of goal-directed behaviors (Kaiser & Gutscher, 2003).

Photograph courtesy of Mark Zanna.
Reprinted by permission.

Box 12–2 MARK P. ZANNA, *Analyst of Attitude–Behavior Consistency*

Mark Zanna is Professor of Psychology and Health Studies at the University of Waterloo. He received both his B.A. and Ph.D. from Yale. After completing his Ph.D., he taught for 5 years at Princeton University, and then moved to Waterloo, Canada, in 1975. He has held visiting professorships at Stanford, Princeton, McGill, and the Universities of Exeter, Minnesota, and California at Santa Cruz.

As an attitude researcher, Zanna has conducted extensive research in the areas of persuasion, overcoming resistance to change, and the relationship between attitudes and behavior. He has also led a number of applied research projects in the areas of drinking, safer sex, and dangers from smoking. His publications include 2 books and more than 100 journal articles. In addition, he has served as editor or coeditor of two influential series of volumes: Advances in Experimental Social Psychology *since 1990, and the* Ontario Symposium on Personality and Social Psychology *since 1981.*

Explaining Variations in Attitude–Behavior Consistency

Zanna and Fazio (1982) characterized the history of research on attitude–behavior consistency as passing through three stages. The first stage, in the 1960s, asked the "Is" question—Is there a relation between the two? Although the answers suggested were often pessimistic, as in Wicker's (1969) review, many studies did report high correlations. Therefore research moved on to the second stage, asking the "When" question—Under what conditions are certain attitudes related to certain behaviors? During the 1970s, studies of this type identified many situational, personality, and attitudinal factors that *moderated* (i.e., helped to determine) the attitude–behavior relationship. (Most of these factors are discussed later in this section.) Finally, beginning in the 1980s and continuing to the present, many studies moved on to the "How" question, examining the processes by which attitudes guide behavior.

This section summarizes the main **moderator variables** that influence the relationship between attitudes and behavior. A moderator is a variable that increases or decreases the strength of a relationship between two other variables. Later in this chapter, we describe some conceptual systems that aim to understand the processes linking attitudes and behavior. First, we discuss the variables that moderate the relationship between attitudes and behavior, dividing them into aspects of the attitude, person, behavior, or situation.

1. The Attitude.   Some of the strongest moderators of the attitude–behavior relationship are features of the attitude itself (Kraus, 1995). The variables of certainty, stability, consistency, and direct experience have all been found to influence when an attitude will predict a behavior. Attitude **certainty** refers to the internal consistency of the attitude; for example, the extent to which the cognitive and affective components of the attitude are in agreement, or the degree to which there are competing attitudes toward the behavior. An uncertain attitude is one that is ambivalent, and typically is not a good predictor of behavior (Schuman, 1972; Canon & Mathews, 1972; Armitage & Conner, 2000). For instance, you might have a favorable attitude toward a political party but not contribute to it financially (the behavior measure) because you have a stronger favorable attitude toward other organizations seeking your donations, or because you have a strong motive to save money.

Attitude **stability** is another important moderator. Instability of attitudes and intentions over time can reduce the strength of the attitude–behavior relationship. Many studies have shown that attitudes and intentions shift over time, sometimes quite sharply. Consequently, the longer the time period between attitude measurement and behavioral observation, the greater the chances for inconsistency (Schwartz, 1978).

Direct personal experience is another aspect of the attitude that moderates its relationship with behavior. Attitudes that are the result of a direct encounter with the attitude object tend to be better predictors of behavior than do attitudes acquired through indirect experience (e.g., hearing about it on the radio or from a friend).

Attitude **accessibility** has received considerable attention in recent years. An accessible attitude is one that is more likely to be activated by the presence of (or thinking about) the attitude object. A number of studies have shown that accessible attitudes tend to be better predictors of behavior (Fazio & Williams, 1986; Kraus, 1995). As an alternative conceptualization, Krosnick and Petty (1995) have suggested an opposite causal direction, but one having similar implications for behavioral prediction. Rather than searching for features of an attitude that lead to a strong attitude–behavior relationship, they have instead proposed that attitude–behavior correspondence is one element of attitude strength (the other elements, they say, are persistence, resistance, and impact on information processing).

2. The Person.   A second set of variables that have been studied as moderators of the attitude–behavior relationship is characteristics of the individual. The most-studied of these variables is self-monitoring. **Self-monitoring** is the extent to which an individual modifies his or her behavior to match the situation. People who are high in self-monitoring pay close attention to their surroundings, and they frequently override their attitudes in order to behave "properly" in accordance with others' expectations. In contrast, people who are low in self-monitoring are less influenced by their surroundings, and more often rely on internal, attitudinal cues in determining how to act (Snyder, 1987). A number of studies have found, as predicted, that low self-monitors show a greater degree of attitude–behavior correspondence (Snyder & Kendzierski, 1982; Kraus, 1995).

Another personal moderator is *inadequate skills*—either intellectual, verbal, or social skills. If a man lacks the intelligence or the information to recognize that his behavior does not match his attitude, inconsistency is not surprising. This might happen, for instance, with a poorly informed voter backing a candidate whose views are actually contrary to his own.

3. The Behavior.   Research has also found that not all behaviors are equally predicted by attitudes. Some behaviors, such as a mother's ability to breast-feed her newborn baby, are not completely under *voluntary control*. In one study, about 25% of mothers with positive attitudes were nevertheless unsuccessful at breast-feeding (Newton & Newton, 1950). Also, habitual behaviors that we perform without thinking about them are generally not under our voluntary, intentional control—this is why Triandis (1977) included *habit* as well as intentions as factors in his system for predicting behavior.

Three other moderating aspects of the behavior are availability of alternative behaviors, normative prescriptions, and consequences of the action. *Unavailability of alternative behaviors* has been found to decrease the strength of the attitude–behavior relationship. A good example is the man who regularly buys a daily newspaper even though he detests it, because it is the only one conveniently available in his city. Also, situations involving *normative prescriptions* of "proper" behavior decrease the strength of the attitude–behavior relationship. A familiar example is that we are taught to be polite to people even though we don't like them. Similarly, the norms held by other people present in the situation are important: A strong racist would be less likely to walk out of a racially mixed gathering if she knew that most of the others present supported social integration of the races.

Finally, the *severity of expected consequences* of the behavior can decrease its relationship to one's attitude. It has been well-established that many restaurant and hotel managers, despite strong antiblack attitudes, nevertheless began serving black customers following the passage of antidiscrimination laws, when they were faced with the prospect of legal punishment for racial discrimination. In a weaker form, this consideration of likely consequences is probably also involved in the preceding category (norms regarding proper behavior).

One possibility for integrating the research on the behavioral moderators is the **effort hypothesis**. Schultz and Oskamp (1996) proposed that behaviors that are very easy are less likely to be determined by one's attitude. This reasoning was extended by Stern (2000) who suggested that the attitude–behavior link will be strongest for behaviors that have few incentives or barriers. That is, attitudes are less likely to correlate with behaviors that are very difficult *or* very easy. Kaiser and Schultz (2004) provided evidence supporting this position, but also noted that the lack of correspondence for very easy and very difficult behaviors may be a methodological artifact resulting from low variability across individuals on such behaviors.

4. The Situation.   Finally, aspects of the situation can reduce the correspondence between attitudes and behaviors. One example would be *unforeseen extraneous events.* For instance, even a family with a strongly favorable attitude toward church attendance might miss Sunday service if they had a seriously ill child, or if their car wouldn't start, or if a heavy thunderstorm intervened.

We may conclude from this list that attitudes are by no means the only factors necessary to predict behavioral responses, and sometimes they are not even among the most important factors. Thus a certain amount of inconsistency between attitudes and behavior is to be expected, the amount depending on the particular attitude, person, behavior, and situation. It is also clear from this list that there are many variables that affect the size of the attitude–behavior relationship. In several places, we have suggested that two or more of these variables may be linked to an underlying process—for example, the ease or difficulty of the behavior could be used to integrate several of the behavioral moderators. Several researchers have gone farther down the conceptual path and developed broad theoretical models of the attitude–behavior relationship. In the following section, we discuss two of these models: the theory of planned behavior, and the mode model of motivation and opportunity as determinants.

Models for Understanding the Attitude–Behavior Linkage

One of the first broad theoretical models for understanding the relationship between attitudes and behaviors was the **theory of reasoned action** (Fishbein & Ajzen, 1974, 1975), which we discussed in Chapter 5. According to the theory, a person's intention to act is the best determinant of his or her actual behavior. The theory presents a mathematical formula in which intentions are determined by both attitudinal and normative factors: (a) the person's beliefs about the consequences of performing a particular behavior, (b) his or her evaluation of those consequences, (c) his or her normative beliefs regarding the expectations of relevant others, and (d) his or her motivation to comply with those expectations. These two pairs of factors are combined mathematically by multiplying each pair together, weighting them appropriately, and then adding the two products (see p. 103). This equation is then used to predict behavioral intentions, rather than behavior. Note that, in this theoretical approach, the attitude measure typically refers to a specific behavior, rather than being a general attitude toward a group of behaviors or a whole class of objects.

Across many studies in which the predictor variables were combined in a multiple correlation to predict intention, the average multiple correlation has been found to be a very high figure. In a review of 13 studies, Fishbein and Ajzen (1975) reported an average multiple correlaton of +0.75, and a similar analysis of 10 later studies found an even higher average multiple correlation of +0.80 (Ajzen, 1988, p. 119). Moreover, many studies have shown that, in turn, behavioral intentions that are carefully measured are usually good predictors of overt behaviors, with correlation coefficients ranging from +0.4 to as high as 0.95 (Kothandapani, 1971b; Fishbein & Ajzen, 1975, pp. 373–374; Davidson & Jaccard, 1979; Ajzen & Fishbein, 1980; Ajzen, 1988, p. 114; Kaiser & Gutscher, 2003). For instance, a person's intention to attend church on Sunday morning is likely to be highly correlated with the behavior of actually attending.

A more recent modification of this model is known as the **theory of planned behavior** (Ajzen & Madden, 1986; Madden et al., 1992). As depicted in Figure 12–1, this theory incorporates perceived behavioral control as a third antecedent of behavioral intention. **Perceived behavioral control** is a person's belief about his or her ability to perform the behavior. The theory of planned behavior has been used extensively in basic research and also applied to a number of social issues—most notably health behaviors like condom use, alcohol consumption, and seat belt use, but also environmental behaviors like recycling and water conservation. A meta-analysis of 185 published studies that used the theory of planned behavior found the model to work very well, with a multiple correlation of 0.63 for predicting behavioral intention (Armitage & Conner, 2001). The added component of perceived behavioral control improved the model's predictions significantly.

An example of recent research using the theory of planned behavior will illustrate its basic elements and how it can be used in applied research settings. Since the early 1980s,

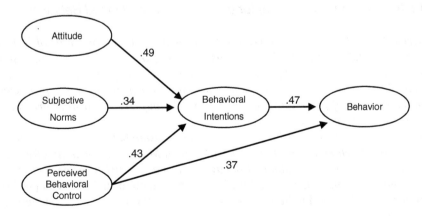

FIGURE 12–1 The theory of planned behavior.

Note: Regression coefficients shown are from Armitage & Conner (2001, p. 481).

researchers have worked to understand the attitudes and behaviors associated with HIV-risky behavior. In a large-scale project, Fishbein and his colleagues (1996) applied the theory of planned behavior to a group of people who were at high risk for contracting HIV: prostitutes. Interviews were conducted with 634 prostitutes who were recruited on the streets of five cities that were sites for the research project. Items in the interview were designed to measure intentions to use a condom for vaginal sex with their main partner and with paying partners, attitudes toward condom use, subjective norms about condom use, and perceived behavioral control for using a condom. The multiple correlation of the several predictor variables with behavioral intentions was 0.69 (Jamner et al., 1998).

Subsequent research created intervention materials aimed at targeting attitudes, subjective norms, and perceived behavioral control with the goal of increasing HIV-preventive behavior among high-risk groups (Fishbein et al., 1996; CDC ACDP Research Group, 1999). Pamphlets and other "small media" provided HIV-prevention messages in the form of role-model stories designed to increase positive attitudes toward condom use, increase pertinent social norms, and promote greater perceived behavioral control. The intervention materials were delivered by members of the community who had been trained to encourage acceptance of the message and to reinforce attempts to reduce HIV-risk behaviors. Results from the sample of prostitutes showed that, compared with those in matched control areas that did not receive the messages, prostitutes in intervention areas showed greater intentions to use condoms with their main partners and with their paying partners. Results also showed a substantial increase in the number of prostitutes who were carrying condoms (from 17% to 30% in the intervention areas—CDC, 1999).

Photograph courtesy of Icek Ajzen.
Reprinted by permission.

Box 12–3 ICEK AJZEN, *Originator of the Theory of Planned Behavior*

Icek Ajzen (also spelled Aizen) received his B.A. from the Hebrew University of Jerusalem, Israel, and his M.A. and Ph.D. in social psychology from the University of Illinois at Urbana-Champaign. He taught for 2 years at the University of Illinois before moving in 1971 to the University of Massachusetts at Amherst, where he remains as a professor and head of the division of personality and social psychology. He has also returned several times to teach at universities in Israel.

Ajzen is most well-known for his work on the relationship between verbal attitudes and overt behavior, which he began in collaboration with Martin Fishbein, and for his later development of the theory of planned behavior. He has published extensively on these topics, including 3 influential books: Belief, Attitude, Intention, and Behavior *(1975),* Understanding Attitudes and Predicting Social Behavior *(1980), and* Attitudes, Personality, and Behavior *(1988).*

The MODE Model of Attitude–Behavior Processes. A second system for understanding the relationship between attitudes and behavior is the Motivation and Opportunities as Determinants (MODE) model (Fazio, 1990; Fazio & Towles-Schwen, 1999). The basic premise of the MODE model is that attitudes are conditioned associations between an object and an evaluation (Fazio, 1986; see Chapter 4). As an example, a person's attitude toward penguins is the strength of his or her cognitive association between the object (penguins) and the valence (good). The MODE model postulates two pathways through which attitudes can lead to behavior: spontaneous and deliberate. The *spontaneous* path begins with an "environmental trigger"—something in the person's experience that activates the object association. Continuing with our example, this might be a newspaper story with a picture of a penguin. Then, if a behavioral opportunity presents itself (e.g., donate money to the Wildlife Penguin Fund), the person acts or fails to act.

When the spontaneous pathway is followed, there is no critical evaluation of the message or "environmental trigger." The attitude exists, presumably from past experience, and it is merely activated by the presence of an external stimulus. But not all stimuli activate an attitude enough to produce a behavior. Indeed, Fazio and his colleagues (1982, 1989, 1995, 1999) have argued that the degree to which an attitude is accessible moderates the attitude–behavior relationship. That is, a person with a weak-and-favorable attitude is less likely to act in ways consistent with the attitude than is a person with a strong-and-favorable attitude. The degree to which an attitude is automatically activated from memory when the individual encounters the attitude object is termed **accessibility**. If the association between the object and the evaluation is strong, the evaluation is very likely to come to mind when one is exposed to, or thinks about, the object—and as a result, the attitude is likely to influence subsequent behavior. An easily accessed attitude will also be likely to influence perception and processing of new information about the object (Fazio & Williams, 1986; Houston & Fazio, 1989.)

Unlike the spontaneous pathway, the *deliberate* pathway requires an effortful processing of the attitude object and behavioral alternatives. "This type of deliberative processing is characterized by considerable cognitive work. It involves the scrutiny of available information and an analysis of positive and negative features, of costs and benefits" (Fazio & Towles-Schwen, 1999, p. 98). The deliberate pathway is data-driven—that is, based on an evaluation of the given situation rather than the activation of an existing attitude.

Figure 12–2 shows the sequence of steps in Fazio's (1986) proposed model of the attitude-to-behavior process. The two lines in the figure show two components involved in determining behavior, quite similar to Fishbein and Ajzen's (1975) model: an attitude component and a normative component. However, if the person's attitude is not activated (because the association is weak or is blocked in some way), the attitude will not enter

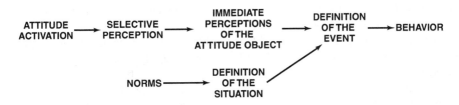

FIGURE 12–2 A diagram of the attitude-to-behavior process.

Source: Fazio, R. H. (1986). How do attitudes guide behavior? In R. M. Sorrentino & E. T. Higgins (Eds.), *The handbook of motivation and cognition: Foundations of social behavior* (p. 212). New York: Guilford. Reprinted with permission.

into the immediate perceptions of the object, and the resulting behavior may be quite inconsistent with the attitude. Thus, for researchers in this tradition, the interesting process-oriented question is this: What factors will strengthen the learned association (i.e., the accessibility of the attitude)?

The MODE model of attitude–behavior processes differs in several ways from predictive models such as the theory of planned behavior. The predictive approach typically uses correlational methods and often studies important real-world behavior (e.g., contraceptive use, voting, or energy conservation behavior). In contrast, the MODE process studies have usually been experiments conducted in laboratory settings, and often with attitudes that were trivial or developed solely during the experiment. In addition, they define attitude strength in terms of response latency—that is, the speed of a person's evaluative response when presented with an attitude object—whereas the predictive studies typically use self-report questionnaire responses to define attitude direction and extremity. Thus, findings from the two streams of research are hard to compare because they use quite different behavioral tasks and different operational definitions of "attitude."

Nevertheless, very useful light has been shed on the attitude–behavior relation by some of the MODE process studies. Several variables have been found to moderate the attitude–behavior relationship because they influence the accessibility and thus the activation of attitudes. They include (a) direct rather than vicarious experience with the attitude object (Fazio & Zanna, 1981; Borgida & Campbell, 1982), (b) the number of times that the attitude has been expressed (Fazio et al., 1982; Houston & Fazio, 1989), (c) attitude objects that are prototypical rather than unusual members of their category (Lord, Lepper, & Mackie, 1984), (d) attitude topics that are central or involving to the respondents (Sivacek & Crano, 1982), (e) respondents who are in a state of introspective self-awareness (Gibbons, 1978), and (f) respondents who are low self-monitors, because they tend to be consistent in their attitude expression, regardless of the situation (Snyder & Kendzierski, 1982). Each of these variables increases an attitude's accessibility, and hence they increase the consistency between the attitude and subsequent behavior.

Planned Behavior and Dual-Process Models. One other feature of the MODE approach is that it applies both to routine, habitual behavior (i.e., what Langer, 1978, called "mindless" actions), and to voluntary, nonhabitual behaviors. In contrast, recall that Fishbein and Ajzen's theory of reasoned action applies only to behavior that is under volitional control—its name as well as its formulas indicate that a person's behavior is determined in a reasoned, thoughtful way by summing his or her salient beliefs about any object to form an attitude and combining the attitude with information about relevant social norms. This rationalistic approach has been noted as a limitation of the theory of reasoned action (Fazio, 1986), and Fazio and Towles-Schwen (1999) have argued that the theory of planned behavior also represents a deliberate processing model. Because the theory of planned behavior focuses on *intention*, they say, it is thought out and incorporates an evaluation of the costs and benefits associated with it.

However, Ajzen (2002; Ajzen & Fishbein, 2000) has argued that the theory of planned behavior can apply to instances in which behavior is largely automatic. "The theory of planned behavior does not propose that individuals review their behavioral, normative, and control beliefs prior to every . . . behavior" (Ajzen, 2002, p. 108). Rather, he proposes that, once formed, the attitudes and intentions can be activated automatically by the context and produce behavior without conscious deliberation. Thus, although the attitudes and intention components of the theory of planned behavior are formed through a deliberate, reasoned process, after they are formed they can influence behavior without the need for additional reflection or cognition.

The Effect of Behavior on Attitudes

The preceding sections have presented considerable evidence for a substantial relationship between attitudes and behavior. However, this evidence does not demonstrate that attitudes *cause* behavior. Because most of the research previously summarized was correlational in nature, it does not allow for a clear causal inference. (One notable exception is predictive studies in which the behavior was measured substantially after the attitude—in some cases, several weeks later.)

Thus, although it may seem that attitudes cause behavior, there is much research demonstrating that people's behavior also has a reciprocal effect on their attitudes. For example, Lieberman (1956) showed that being promoted to (or demoted from) the positions of foreman or union shop steward had clear-cut effects on workers' job-related attitudes. Other prominent examples include the effects of "forced compliance" or counterattitudinal advocacy (discussed in Chapter 11 in relation to dissonance theory and impression-management theory), effects of commitment and of active participation on attitude change (also discussed in Chapter 11), and the prointegration attitudinal changes that followed U.S. school desegregation (described in Chapter 16).

As an example, consider several studies by Stone and his colleagues regarding attitudes toward condom use (Aronson, Fried, & Stone, 1991; Stone et al., 1994, 1997). The studies followed a cognitive dissonance paradigm in which research participants were induced to make a public statement regarding favorable attitudes toward condom use, following which they were reminded that their sexual behaviors were at least partially inconsistent with this statement—that is, they were hypocrites! Consistently across several studies in which this *hypocrisy* manipulation was used, the results showed that engaging in a behavior (making public statements in favor of condom use), and being reminded that one's actions were not entirely consistent with these statements, led to a greater recognition among participants that they did not use condoms as often as they should have in the past (and led later sexual behavior to become more consistent with these attitudes favorable to condom use.).

Thus we may conclude with Kelman (1974) that "attitudes are alive and well and gainfully employed in the sphere of action," for we have good evidence of

> the engagement of attitude and action in a continuing, reciprocal, circular process. Not only is attitude an integral part of action, but action is an integral part of the development, testing, and crystallization of attitudes. (p. 324)

ATTITUDES AND PERSONALITY

To what extent are people's attitudes related to their personality? In previous chapters we have seen evidence that both attitudes and personality have a partially genetic basis. The major issue to be discussed here is whether or not attitudes have a systematic and close relationship to personality traits. Note that this is a different question than whether attitude *change* is related to personality, a topic discussed in Chapter 10 under the heading of Personality and Persuasibility.

Classic Studies of Attitudes and Personality

There are several classic studies that link attitudes and personality. One of the best-known of all attitude studies, *The Authoritarian Personality* (Adorno et al., 1950), began as a study of anti-Semitic attitudes. As the project developed, the focus broadened to include conservatism, ethnocentrism (a generalized attitude of prejudice toward many ethnic groups), and finally authoritarianism, which was conceptualized as a basic personality characteristic. Each of the major topics of the research, in turn, was studied through development of a scale to measure it. The authors reported that the Anti-Semitism (A-S) Scale correlated +0.53 with the first version of the F (Fascism) Scale, which became the dominant measure of authoritarian personality tendencies. This relationship was at least partly due to the fact that each successive measurement scale was constructed by using the correlations of its items with the preceding scales as a basis for item selection. However, despite this methodological problem, the point here is that this highly influential research project both assumed and found a close relationship between the personality characteristic of authoritarianism and certain attitudes (e.g., negative attitudes toward Jews).

Some of the relationships that were reported, obtained by methods of personality testing and intensive depth interviews, were as follows: Highly prejudiced individuals were found to have rigid personality characteristics; they were highly conventional in values and standards; they rejected any negative implications about themselves or their parents; and they projected socially unacceptable impulses or characteristics onto other people. They typically reported having had parents who were concerned about status, who were cold and unloving, who used harsh physical punishment for infractions of family rules, and who gave love only for "proper" behavior.

Similar patterns of relationships between personality characteristics and attitudes have been reported in studies of political conservatism (McClosky, 1958), of international attitudes (Smith, Bruner, & White, 1956), and of prejudice (Martin & Westie, 1959). A cross-national study of prejudice showed that, in both Greece and the United States, insecure individuals were generally high in prejudice, though the typical target groups for prejudice differed in the two nations (Triandis & Triandis, 1962).

Methodological Critiques

Individual Prejudice Versus Social Conformity. Although personality-based theories of prejudice have received some empirical support, they by no means account for all prejudice. Because they deal with *individual* prejudice, they are least applicable in situations where social norms prescribe prejudiced and discriminatory behavior from all members of the dominant group—that is, situations of **institutional racism**—as has been true in the American South. Despite the high degree of racial prejudice that has existed in the South, Southerners in general were no higher than Northerners on measures of authoritarian personality traits. Instead of personality being the source of most prejudiced attitudes, the evidence suggests that *social conformity* may be the more potent source of prejudice in those cultural settings where such clear-cut norms of discrimination exist (Pettigrew, 1959). (See Chapter 16 for a fuller discussion of racial prejudice.)

The Authoritarian Personality. Methodological critiques of the authoritarian personality research have been extensive and varied (Christie & Jahoda, 1954; Kirscht & Dillehay, 1967; Meloen, 1993). Here we can mention only a few of the points most relevant to our discussion of personality and attitudes. For thorough reviews of the topic, see the chapter on authoritarianism by Brown (1965) or more recent volumes (e.g., Stone, Lederer, & Christie, 1993; Altemeyer, 1996).

Four methodological criticisms of the early authoritarian personality research were most damaging. First, the sampling procedures were far from representative because most participants were obtained through organized groups such as labor unions, Kiwanis clubs, and university classes. However, Martin and Westie (1959) and McClosky (1958) studied representative samples of adults living in a major U.S. city, and their results also showed clear connections between attitudes and personality traits. Second, the interviewers, who were allowed wide discretion in their choice of questions, were shown the participants' F Scale scores before the interview, and thus they may have consciously or unconsciously tried to obtain interview responses consistent with the questionnaire data. However, again, this criticism is not applicable to Martin and Westie's and McClosky's similar findings because they used questionnaires for collecting their data.

A third methodological criticism of authoritarianism research is the problem of acquiescence response set (yea-saying), which occurred because all the items of the F Scale were worded in the authoritarian direction (as discussed in Chapter 3). However, Martin and Westie's research methods did not suffer from this problem, and their results were highly similar to those of Adorno et al. The fourth criticism of authoritarianism research is that demographic characteristics such as education and social class are quite strongly correlated with F Scale scores, in a negative direction (Selznick & Steinberg, 1969). There is no escaping this fact, but it does not vitiate the relationship between personality and attitudes. It appears that underprivileged groups in the United States and many other countries are more likely to develop authoritarian personality structures and the typical pattern of accompanying attitudes than are middle- or upper-class groups.

More Recent Findings

Despite these criticisms of the methodology used in early research relating attitudes and personality variables, later, improved studies have continued to report clear-cut relationships (e.g., Peterson, Doty, & Winter, 1993). Research consistently finds that attitudes toward many social issues tend to cluster together (cf. Saucier, 2000). Departing somewhat from the approach of the authoritarian personality, other perspectives have been offered in recent years.

Conservative ideology has been studied in a particularly interesting and influential group—U.S. Senators—by Tetlock (1983a). He classified them as liberal, moderate, or conservative on the basis of their voting record, and he analyzed their published policy statements with his systematic coding measure of "integrative complexity"—a characteristic which is usually low in authoritarian personalities. The findings showed that conservative senators were significantly less complex in their thinking than were their liberal or moderate colleagues. Similarly, Tetlock (1981) found that senators who were consistently isolationistic in their foreign-policy votes made policy statements that showed several features of the authoritarian personality: low complexity of thought, unusually positive ingroup attitudes, and negative affect toward outgroups.

Right-Wing Authoritarianism. A major program of research conducted over 20 years by Altemeyer (1988, 1996, 1998) has focused on right-wing authoritarianism (RWA), which he conceptualized as a personality trait that includes three main aspects: authoritarian submission, authoritarian aggression, and conventionalism. Altemeyer's carefully developed RWA scale has been found to correlate strongly with attitudes of acceptance of governmental injustice and illegality, punitiveness toward common criminals, ethnocentric prejudice, true-believer religiosity, and conservative political views among people interested in politics. Although Altemeyer (1996) has acknowledged the possibility for a genetic basis for this constellation of attitudes (see Corson, 1996, for genetic evidence), he has argued in favor of a learning-based explanation: "(O)ur best present model of how people become authoritarian, or nonauthoritarian, again proceeds from Bandura's (1977) social learning theory" (p. 78). In essence, Altemeyer suggests that authoritarian qualities are taught and modeled by parents, with the critical period for children to learn them occurring during adolescence.

Although most of the research on authoritarianism has used correlational methods, several experimental studies have measured the effect of contextual variables on authoritarianism, and on cognitive processes among people high and low in authoritarianism. One consistent finding in this line of research is that *threat* tends to produce an increase in authoritarianism (Altemeyer, 1988; Doty, Peterson, & Winter, 1991; Duckitt & Fisher, 2003; Feldman, 2003). The idea that threat mediates the relationship between authoritarianism and social attitudes, at least in part, offers a potentially unifying theme. In the years since the first authoritarian personality research, a number of related constructs have been proposed (e.g., dogmatism, intolerance of ambiguity, need for closure, terror management, social dominance orientation). Jost et al. (2003) have argued that this constellation of conservative attitudes emphasizes resistance to change and the justification of inequality. These tendencies in turn are motivated by the need to manage uncertainty and threat, whether they are dispositional in nature (i.e., insecurity, authoritarianism) or situational (e.g., physical or social threats).

Another recent model linking personality to attitudes focuses on **social dominance orientation** (SDO—Sidanius & Pratto, 1993, 1999). According to this perspective, people differ in their preference for hierarchical social relationships versus equal ones, and in their degree of belief that their ingroup is superior to outgroups. Clearly, such a disposition is similar to authoritarianism, which includes submission to authority and hostility to perceived outgroups. However, the SDO scale was developed to measure something different from authoritarianism, and research has shown that measures of SDO and RWA tend to be only weakly correlated. Studies that used the SDO scale have been conducted in many different countries, and consistent relationships have been found with prejudice, nationalism, and patriotism, as well as with a number of social attitudes like support of the Gulf War, capital punishment, and immigration policy. Duckitt et al. (2002) suggested that both SDO and RWA can lead to similar attitudes, but through different processes. Specifically, authoritarianism appears to function primarily through social conformity, and through beliefs in a dangerous world where one's values and way of life are threatened by bad people. In contrast, SDO leads to attitudes through tough-mindedness (being "harsh" and uncaring) and beliefs in a competitive world.

Overview

Research on the relationship between attitudes and personality has continued steadily over many decades. Although early studies of the authoritarian personality were challenged on methodological grounds, later studies using improved methods have continued to find that attitudes toward many social issues tend to cluster together with relevant personality characteristics. Altemeyer's long-running program of research on right-wing authoritarianism has adopted a social-learning perspective and demonstrated a number of relationships to attitudes such as punitiveness toward criminal suspects and ethnocentric prejudice. Recent years have seen advances in research on related constructs such as conservative ideology, political intolerance, and social dominance orientation. Theoretical models incorporating both dispositional and situational variables have offered promising new lines of research for understanding the processes (such as motivated social cognition) associated with the link between personality and attitudes.

LABORATORY RESEARCH VERSUS FIELD RESEARCH

We turn next to a topic that has received increasing attention in recent years—what differences are there, if any, between the results of experimental, laboratory research and

Photograph courtesy of Jim Sidanius.
Reprinted by permission.

Box 12–4 JIM SIDANIUS, *Investigator of Social Dominance Orientation*

Jim Sidanius earned a B.A. in psychology from the City University of New York and a 1977 Ph.D. in political psychology from the University of Stockholm, Sweden, where he taught for 10 years before returning to the U.S. in 1983. He is currently a professor of psychology and head of the social psychology area at UCLA, having also taught at Carnegie-Mellon University, the University of Texas at Austin, New York University, Princeton, Yale, and the University of Wisconsin.

Sidanius is best known for developing the concept of social dominance orientation. His research in political psychology has focused mainly on the interface between political ideology and cognitive functioning, including topics of political socialization, the political psychology of gender, theories of intergroup conflict, and the dynamics of hierarchical social systems. He has more than 100 journal publications, and has written or edited books on Racialized Politics *and* Social Dominance: An Intergroup Theory of Social Hierarchy and Oppression.

those of studies done in real-life field settings? One initial clarification may be needed: Although most research in field settings uses survey methods and correlational (nonmanipulative) designs, these are not necessary characteristics of **field research**. Swingle (1973) and Reich (1982) have presented collections of field research studies, most of which are true experiments, with all of the advantages in manipulation, control, precision, and stronger causal inferences that the term "experiment" implies. (For a discussion of the advantages and disadvantages of different types of research methods, together with examples of each method, see Oskamp & Schultz, 1998.)

Many of the differences between laboratory and field studies of attitudes have been summarized by Hovland (1959) and Shadish (2002). One interesting finding that emerged from a meta-analysis of studies examining the relationship between attitudes and behavior was that those studies conducted outside the laboratory with nonstudents tended to find stronger relationships than did laboratory studies with students (Kraus, 1995). However, in research on persuasion and attitude change, laboratory studies typically show *stronger* effects than field studies. For instance, the greater impact of lab studies has been demonstrated in research on the effects of TV violence on viewers' aggressiveness (Freedman, 1984). This contrast is probably due largely, if not entirely, to a number of methodological differences that are frequently *confounded* with the laboratory–field distinction. To clarify this point, here is a list of some of the typical methodological characteristics of laboratory studies—ways in which they are apt to differ from field studies:

1. An authoritative, prestigious situation. The experimenter or other communicator is in a position of power and authority, and demand characteristics encourage attitude change.
2. No distractions. In contrast, field studies often have to compete with many other distracting stimuli.
3. Less ego-involving or important topics. These are chosen so as to maximize attitude change, whereas field research has often studied more important issues such as political attitudes, which are less likely to change.
4. College students as subjects. Students are better informed, quicker to understand, and more responsive to rational persuasion than are average citizens.
5. Disguised persuasive intent. Often experiments cover up their true purpose, whereas commercial advertisers, politicians, and other real-world communicators usually make a direct persuasive appeal, thus allowing the recipients to evade the message if they are so inclined.
6. No counterpersuasion. In everyday life there are almost always messages from competing products, groups, or individuals, which tend to lessen the original message's effect.
7. Better measures of attitude. The laboratory situation allows more extensive and careful attitude measurement than do most real-world situations.
8. Attitude change is usually measured immediately. By contrast, in field research the measurement of change may be many days or weeks after the message, thus showing a diminished effect due to the passage of time.

The Importance of Field Research

The issue of *generalizability* is one in which field research usually has an advantage, due to the real-world nature of the tasks and settings involved. The degree of similarity of a research situation to circumstances in the outside world has been termed its **mundane realism**. When laboratory research uses highly unusual tasks and settings, and particularly when the participants are very aware of performing as subjects under the experimenter's scrutiny, its results may not be applicable to most situations in the world outside of the laboratory. However, well-known experimentalists have emphasized that the supposed artificiality of experimental situations need not be an obstacle to the generalizability of results as long as the situation is convincingly constructed to have **experimental realism** (believability and impact) for the subjects (Berkowitz & Donnerstein, 1982; Aronson, Brewer, & Carlsmith, 1985). These authors have also pointed out many of the challenges and difficulties inherent in conducting field research.

The lab-versus-field issue is by no means a one-sided one. Even dedicated laboratory researchers usually grant the importance and necessity of field research and recognize its relation to their own investigations. For instance, Leon Festinger (1953), one of the most noted laboratory experimenters in social psychology, wrote:

> Laboratory experimentation, as a technique for the development of an empirical body of knowledge, cannot exist by itself. Experiments in the laboratory must derive their direction from studies of real-life situations, and results must continually be checked by studies of real-life situations. (pp. 169–170)

Since the 1970s many behavioral scientists have issued calls for more field research and broader application of scientific theory and methods to a variety of social problems in the real world (e.g., McGuire, 1973; Rodin, 1985). As a result, increased attention has been directed toward field methods, as illustrated in various recent research reviews (e.g., Reich, 1982; Rodin, 1985; Schultz & Oskamp, 2000; Shadish, 2002). In keeping with this verbal attention to field research, its small share of the research literature published in the major American social psychology journals has increased somewhat—it was around 5% of the articles in the 1960s (Fried, Gumpper, & Allen, 1973), whereas it was a bit over 20% in the mid-1980s (Sears, 1986).

ETHICAL PROBLEMS IN ATTITUDE RESEARCH

Ethical questions arise in any kind of research activity, and attitude and opinion research is no exception. Psychologists and other attitude researchers have been attentive to ethical questions for many years, and ever since 1953 the American Psychological Association has published and updated thorough guidelines to protect the interests of research participants and of society in general (APA, 1953, 1967, 1973, 1981, 1982, 1992, 2002). Empirical studies of ethical issues in social science research have been conducted with regularity (Korn, 1984; Adair, Dushenko, & Lindsay, 1985; Adair, 1988), and Kelman (1982) has offered a scheme for classifying these issues and their specific manifestations in different types of research. Many volumes have analyzed, criticized, and proposed solutions for potential ethical problems in the social and behavioral sciences (e.g., Beauchamp et al., 1982; Sieber, 1982, 1992; Stanley, Sieber, & Melton, 1996).

The recent history of concerns about scientific research ethics is a fascinating one. In the 1960s, media publicity and a resulting public outcry led to congressional investigations of occasional ethical lapses in *biomedical* research, involving failure to protect research participants from possible harm—for example, injecting senile patients with live cancer cells without their understanding what was being done, or observing the long-term progression of syphilis in destitute black males while misleading them into believing they were being treated (Pattullo, 1984). Consequently, the U.S. Surgeon General issued an order in 1966 requiring that procedures for federally funded research projects be reviewed and approved in advance by an impartial committee at the research institution, and more extensive regulations were later promulgated by the U.S. Department of Health, Education, and Welfare (1971). Although biomedical research was the main target of the regulations, all social and behavioral science research was also included until 1981, when the federal rules governing it were greatly simplified and redirected toward the few such studies that do carry potential risks for the participants (Fields, 1981).

Although most attitude and opinion studies do not pose major ethical problems, the federal government requires that the potential threats of all research with human participants must be weighed and approved by an *institutional review board* (IRB). The following important issues must be considered by anyone working in this field.

Harmful Consequences. This is the most serious ethical problem in research, but it arises mostly in medical research, or in behavioral research involving the administration of drugs, threatening or emotional situations, or use of painful stimuli like electric shocks. Only rarely does the risk of harmful consequences occur in attitude and opinion research, though it is possible in studies of the effects of stress (e.g., Berkun et al., 1962) or of threats to participants' self-esteem (e.g., Bramel, 1963; Walster, 1965). However, these few atypical cases have generated a great deal of comment and concern (Warwick, 1982).

Deception. Far more common in attitude and opinion research than the problem of harmful consequences is the issue of deceiving research participants by giving them false information. One survey of the social psychological literature found that deception was used in 66% of the research reports published in 1969. The figure dropped to 47% in 1978 and 32% in 1986, but climbed again to 47% in 1992 (Sieber et al., 1995). Questions have been raised not only about the morality of deceiving participants, but also about the effect this will have over the long run on public attitudes toward psychology and sociology as disciplines, and the possible impact on society of an erosion of public trust in its institutions (Kelman, 1967, 1982).

On the other hand, to obtain valid results in experimental studies, it is often essential that the research participants not be aware of the hypotheses being tested. Thus some secrecy is usually necessary, and often this can be accomplished only if the participants are actively misled, though various alternatives to deception have been proposed (Geller, 1982). In general, the currently accepted ethical principles prescribe that deception should only be used if there are no other legitimate ways to accomplish the same research goal, if the importance of the research warrants the amount of deception used, if participants are allowed to withdraw from the research at any time without penalty, and if they are fully debriefed at the end of their participation (APA, 2002). In actual practice, some surveys have shown that psychologists are more concerned about the use of deception than are research participants (Sullivan & Deiker, 1973; Christensen, 1988). And even when participants have had previous experience with deception in research, it does not necessarily bias their responses in later studies (see the discussion of deception and suspicion in Chapter 10).

Informed Consent.   Since 1966, it has become an essential ethical requirement of experiments that participants have given their informed and knowledgeable consent, after an explanation of any possible risks or unpleasant aspects of participation (APA, 2002). If participants agree to be involved in the study after a full and open explanation of the attendant risks and benefits, it is generally felt that they are doing so as free agents and that the researcher's ethical obligation in this area has been satisfied. However, in survey studies of public opinion, the risks involved in participation are limited to minor inconvenience at most; and consequently the requirement for informed consent has generally been considered to be fulfilled by the researcher's obtaining implicit consent (i.e., the respondent answering the questions instead of refusing), and perhaps also by telling respondents that any bothersome question can be skipped (Schuman & Kalton, 1985). And in observational studies of public behavior, such as marching in a demonstration or buying a particular product, the informed consent of participants is hardly ever obtained—largely because it would be very difficult or impossible to do so, and it might be more of a bother than a service to the participants (Aronson et al., 1985).

Invasion of Privacy.   A related question concerns when and how participants' privacy must be protected. Of course, anonymity and confidentiality of data are essential—participants' names or identification must never be linked with their behavior or opinions in reporting research results. But particularly in observational studies, the line where invasion of privacy begins is apt to be very fuzzy. Is a concealed tape recording of an interview acceptable? What about listening to shoppers' conversations as they examine the merchandise? Or how about checking the number of liquor bottles in people's trash (Webb et al., 1981)? Probably the line which most researchers would draw is that public behavior or behavior in public places may legitimately be observed and/or recorded, whereas private behavior in private places must be protected from observation through invasive techniques such as "bugging," high-powered microphones, and so forth. But even the line between "private" and "public" can be blurred. For example, is a stall or urinal in a public restroom a private place? Or are messages sent by means of an Internet "chat" program private?

Such decisions are typically made in the context of the local community's norms, and the researcher's proposed procedures must be approved by an institutional review board.

Inconvenience to Participants. Although most attitude studies involve only minor inconvenience at most, researchers must be vigilant to avoid any unnecessary inconvenience. For example, in survey interviews, questions must be worded so that embarrassment is minimized, time requirements must be reasonable, and repeated calls or inconvenient hours should be avoided (Crossley, 1971). A deplorable example of respondent inconvenience is the misleading tactics of some salespeople who disguise their initial approach as a consumer survey. One study found that very recent experience with such a deceptive practice lowered response rates to a legitimate survey interview *by 75%* (Sheets et al., 1974).

Debriefing of Participants. In experimental research it has been a traditional requirement that participants are interviewed and informed at the end of the experimental session. This accomplishes several goals: The investigator usually thanks them and gives them information about the research topic in return for their cooperation; any deception is carefully explained, the need for it described in detail, and its effectiveness checked on; participants' questions are answered and any remaining anxiety that they may have is allayed; and appeals for secrecy about the research procedure are often made so that future participants will not learn information that might invalidate the research results. Detailed and helpful suggestions for debriefing procedures have been offered by Aronson et al. (1985). If this debriefing is done thoroughly and sensitively, most investigators feel that participants come to appreciate the value of the research, accept the need for any deception, and leave with a positive feeling about their experience (Aronson et al., 1985; Christensen, 1988).

In field research, by contrast, it is rare and often impossible to debrief individuals after their participation in a study. Usually there is little or no deception that needs to be explained and no reason for participants to have been upset or anxious; so debriefing is less necessary. Particularly in observational research, such as a study of traffic violations, if individuals did not know they had been observed, informing them about it might only raise their concern rather than lowering it (Sieber, 1984, pp. 74–75).

Reporting of Results. In scientific publication, standards for reporting research results are carefully specified and overseen by journal editors. However, studies involving important social issues, particularly survey research findings, are often reported in the public press without the careful details and safeguards that reputable scientists would insist on. In fact, some unscrupulous pollsters have been known to slant their data collection or reporting for devious political ends (Roll & Cantril, 1980). To help eliminate these unfortunate instances, the American Association for Public Opinion Research (AAPOR) in 1968 made an important addition to its code of professional ethics and practices (Field, 1971). The added standards specify that any report of survey or poll results which is made public should contain information on the sponsor of the survey, the wording of questions, the method and dates of interviewing, the population sampled and sample size, and the likely amount of sampling error in the results. Adherence to these standards will not prevent all abuses of polls, but it will make their interpretation much more open to the scrutiny of other investigators and informed citizens.

The Obligation To Do Research. Although researchers must give careful thought to all of the ethical problems discussed here, they cannot just throw up their hands in defeat and give up the research enterprise. The duty of the trained scientist to gather information and knowledge that can be put to public use is also an ethical obligation. To withdraw from that responsibility would be just as unethical as to do research in ways that ignored the rights of participants (APA, 1982):

> The distinctive contribution of scientists to human welfare is the development of knowledge and its intelligent application to appropriate problems. Their underlying ethical imperative, thus, is to conduct research as well as they know how. (p. 15)

PUBLIC OPINION AND PUBLIC POLICY

Related to ethical issues in attitude research are the questions about uses and abuses of opinion polls in practical politics that we considered in Chapter 6. Now, as the final major topic in this chapter, we turn to broader policy questions concerning whether and how public opinion affects or is reflected in public policy. First, *should* public opinion affect public policy? Second, *does* it do so, and if it does, in what ways and under what circumstances? And finally, what uses are there for social science research in the public policy arena?

Should Public Opinion Affect Public Policy?

This is a question that has been asked by political philosophers for centuries. In general, there are three main answers that have been given. One position, which we may call the **"will of the people"** viewpoint, holds that legislators and political administrators should make their decisions entirely in accordance with the opinion of their constituents (see Figure 12–3). This view was stated before the French Revolution by Jean-Jacques Rousseau in his treatise *The Social Contract*, and it was strongly supported by Thomas Jefferson. Later Abraham Lincoln expressed it well in the quotation at the beginning of this chapter: "What I want is to get done what the people desire to have done, and the question for me is how to find that out exactly."

In contrast, another viewpoint holds that the calm, reasoned **"judgment of the representative"** should guide that representative's vote, rather than the popular clamor or the shifting winds of public opinion. This position was prominently espoused by the British parliamentarian Edmund Burke and by Alexander Hamilton in *The Federalist Papers*. A later and less-elegant statement of the same principle is seen in Richard Nixon's admonition against "swaying with the polls."

A third viewpoint might be called the **"party responsibility"** approach. It became popular after the rise of strong national parties, and it holds the representative responsible, not to his or her own local constituents, but to the program developed by his or her party, designed to satisfy the needs of the whole nation. Clearly, in this approach, national public opinion is an important determinant of the party platform.

There is another dimension of the question about the role of public opinion—*Which* public opinion? As we discussed in Chapter 7, mass public opinion may differ greatly from elite public opinion. On any given political issue, a large majority of the whole population is usually unconcerned and/or uninformed. Therefore, is it reasonable to guide policy by overall public opinion, with its weak preferences and shifting viewpoints? Or, on the other hand, should the "involved public," the minority who are concerned over a particular issue, be the ones who guide official policy? But if that approach is followed, how can we avoid giving undue weight to vocal pressure groups and self-interested lobbyists?

FIGURE 12–3
Should political leaders be guided by the "will of the people"?

These are difficult questions, and no final philosophical answers can be given to them. However, it is clear that, if public opinion is to be consulted, modern opinion polls give us a greatly improved method of doing so. Before the 1930s, political leaders had to seek the "will of the people" through newspaper editorials, through letters from the few involved citizens who took the trouble to write them, or through discussion with their highly selective circle of acquaintances. Now, with modern polling techniques, national leaders can learn with great accuracy the views of the total electorate *or* the opinions of the most concerned citizens, and they can balance these against the claims and demands of pressure groups and lobbyists (Gallup, 1965; Bogart, 1972a).

Another question is whether there are certain types of issues about which the public should be consulted more than on other issues. Many authorities have concluded that the public should determine the decisions on broad, general questions having to do with the goals of public policy, rather than the specific means of achieving these goals. As Childs (1965) expressed it, the public is most competent

> to determine the basic ends of public policy, to choose top policy makers, to appraise the results of public policy, and to say what, in the final analysis is fair, just, and moral. On the other hand, the general public is not competent to determine the best means for attaining specific goals, to answer technical questions, to prescribe remedies for political, social, and economic ills, and to deal with specialized issues far removed from the everyday experience and understanding of the people in general. (p. 350)

Clearly, official policy cannot follow opinion-poll results or specific questions in detail because the results are often unclear, shifting, uninformed, or ill-considered. For instance, in 1954 during the Korean War, over 60% of respondents to a Gallup Poll said they favored using atomic artillery shells against the Chinese army, and one-third advocated dropping hydrogen bombs on China (Bogart, 1972a, p. 19). Similarly, during the buildup to the invasion of Iraq in 2003, 6 in 10 Americans said that they would support using nuclear weapons against Iraq if it attacked U.S. forces with biological or chemical weapons (*ABC/Washington Post* Poll, 2002). Fortunately, such simplistic and genocidal "ultimate solutions" were not adopted by the U.S. government. However, polls inherently have great difficulty in focusing on the more complex and varied alternative policies that have to be considered by diplomats and politicians.

Although there are dangers in public opinion influencing national policy too greatly, there are also undesirable consequences when government has so much power that it can readily manipulate public opinion. An extreme instance was the use of propaganda in Hitler's Germany, but a trend in the same direction seems to have occurred in the United States with the increase in presidential power and official secrecy—one example is the Bush administration's use of distorted or fabricated intelligence information about Iraqi "weapons of mass destruction" in 2003 to persuade Congress and the American people to support a preemptive war against Iraq.

Although social scientists have studied public opinion extensively, there have been relatively few studies of what effects it actually has on government actions and the process by which it is or is not translated into public policy. We look next at some of the studies that bear on these questions.

Does Public Opinion Affect Public Policy?

Research in this area has shown, not one typical pattern, but several different ones, depending largely on the issue involved. Some issues have displayed a direct effect of public opinion on government policy, others no effect, and still others a reverse effect (policy influencing public opinion). Other terms that have been used for these three patterns are official responsiveness to public opinion, unresponsiveness, and management or manipulation of public opinion (McGraw, 2002). Bennett (1989) estimated that each of these patterns occurs about one-third of the time.

Direct Effects of Public Opinion.
One of the issues where public opinion had its greatest effect on policy was the civil rights struggle of the 1950s and 1960s. A famous study of this topic by Miller and Stokes (1963) compared the attitudes, perceptions, and roll-call votes of a sample of 116 congressional representatives with the attitudes of their election opponents and of a sample of their constituents, district by district. The correspondence between constituents' attitudes and the legislator's roll-call votes on civil rights questions was shown by a correlation of almost +0.6, much the highest of the three issues studied. Moreover, additional analyses indicated that representatives by and large correctly perceived their constituents' attitudes and chose to vote accordingly, regardless of their own attitudes (Cnudde & McCrone, 1966). This pattern is quite different from the ones found on some other issues. A similar, but improved, study of congressional voting patterns in 1977–1978 showed relatively high correlations with constituents' opinions in the areas of social welfare, women's rights, and racial issues (Page et al., 1984). Another area in which congressional actions closely followed public opinion was the spurt in defense spending in the early 1980s (Wlezien, 1995).

Other research has shown that legislators vote more closely in accord with public opinion in the year before their next election than at other times in the electoral cycle (Kuklinski, 1978; Thomas, 1985), and that they change their voting patterns toward the attitudes of their new constituency when their legislative district boundaries are changed (Glazer & Robbins, 1985). Similarly, in statewide referenda issues, there is a fairly close relation between representatives' original votes on the legislation and their district's later vote on the referendum (Snyder, 1996). In the U.S. Senate, the liberalism of statewide electorates is closely related to liberal voting by their senators (Wood & Anderson, 1998).

Three large-scale studies have investigated all the U.S. public issues for which there were poll data on citizens' policy preferences *and* clear subsequent federal policy actions. Studying 222 issues during the period from 1960 to 1974, Monroe (1978) found that the federal actions were consistent with the public's majority preferences 64% of the time— 70% of the time for *salient* issues, on which there was a high level of public concern. In a later study of 566 federal actions from 1980 to 1993, Monroe (1998) found a lower overall rate of policy corresponding to public opinion—only 55% (where a chance level would be 50%), but over 60% for salient issues that were currently among the top five in their level of public concern. Page and Shapiro (1983) studied quantitative *changes* in public preferences over the whole period from 1935 to 1979 and found 357 issues for which there was a significant amount of change (but not necessarily a preference by a majority of the public). As in Monroe's earlier study, they reported a fairly high correspondence in subsequent changes in federal policy actions—66% of these actions taken within 1 year after the public opinion changes were congruent with it (i.e., in the same direction), and the figure was 90% in cases where public opinion changed by 20% or more. Page and Shapiro found more congruence on salient *social* issues than on economic or welfare policies or foreign-policy issues.

Even where public opinion does not determine government policy, it quite often sets limits on the policy options that leaders feel free to consider (Roll & Cantril, 1980; Glynn et al., 1999; Sobel, 2001). This appears to have been true both in the Vietnam War, when Lyndon Johnson was forced to withdraw from the 1968 presidential race, and in more recent U.S. military actions in the first Persian Gulf War, in Bosnia, and Kosovo. It was also a factor in the gradual U.S. mobilization before World War II. Starting in 1939, President Franklin D. Roosevelt was probably the first national leader to use poll results in a planned, programmatic way. He commissioned the noted psychologist Hadley Cantril to do repeated public opinion polls, and endeavored very successfully to manage the buildup in aid to Britain so that a majority of citizens would continue to respond that the pace was "about right."

Lack of Effect of Public Opinion.   A common case in which public opinion does not get translated into national policy is where one or both houses of Congress throw up roadblocks against a popularly endorsed proposal. For instance, Congress turned down Medicare legislation for many years in the 1960s (Childs, 1965) and refused to pass national health insurance in the 1980s and 1990s, even though both of those programs have had strong public support (Jacobs, 1993). In 1970 there were sharp discrepancies between general public opinion and congressional attitudes on treatment of suspected criminals, family income-maintenance approaches to welfare programs, and wage and price controls (Backstrom, 1972). Even more extreme is Congress's 50-year record of disregarding the very large majority of the population who favor more stringent gun control laws (Erskine, 1972b; Schuman & Presser, 1981a; Blendon, Young, & Hemenway, 1996; Glynn et al., 1999).

Although the House of Representatives was planned as the branch of government that would be directly responsive to public opinion, that has often not been the case. The Miller and Stokes (1963) study showed that House roll-call votes on foreign policy were essentially unrelated to constituents' attitudes. Similarly, Page et al. (1984) found no significant relationship on the issues of abortion and legal rights of accused individuals. Monroe (1978) found the greatest discrepancies between public opinion and federal action in the areas of defense issues and internal governmental reforms. Page and Shapiro (1983) pointed to public–governmental disagreement concerning foreign military and economic aid in the 1950s and on the issue of U.S. adoption of the metric system in the 1970s.

Reverse Effects—Policy Influences on Public Opinion.   It is in the field of foreign affairs that public opinion most often follows rather than leads official policy (Etzioni, 1969). This is probably because public ignorance of and indifference to policy issues tend to be proportional to the issues' geographic distance from home, so most foreign affairs engage little citizen attention and develop public attitudes that are weakly held and rather easily changed. A specific example can be seen in the many twists and turns of public opinion which followed changing administration decisions regarding nuclear testing from 1954 to 1963 (unilateral suspension of tests, an international nuclear moratorium, resumption of testing, preparation for atmospheric tests, and finally the test-ban treaty with the Soviet Union). Through all these events, public opinion rather faithfully followed official policies (Childs, 1965; Rosi, 1965). Other similar cases show continued public approval for the tremendously mounting U.S. military budget since 1945 and for many presidential decisions regarding the deployment and use of U.S. troops around the world (examples include the Gulf War and the invasions of Afghanistan and Iraq in 2001–2003). In both of Monroe's (1978, 1998) studies, the highest level of agreement between public opinion and government actions was in the area of foreign policy, though it declined from 92% in the 1960s and 1970s to only 67% in the 1980s and 1990s.

Despite public willingness to follow the administration's lead in foreign affairs, there are some limits to public acquiescence. The most clear-cut example is the Vietnam War. Early in the war it appeared that President Johnson could lead and influence popular opinion at will (Lipset, 1966); but as U.S. casualties, budgets, and impatience with the military stalemate increased, popular approval of the war gradually changed to disapproval and finally forced a change in administrations and a withdrawal from the war (Mueller, 1973). In 2004, a similar process of public reaction against the Iraq occupation seemed to be starting.

Uses for Social Science Research

In the public policy arena there are many uses for social science research. Although it gets far less attention and funding than the physical sciences, engineering, and economics, social science research is still generally acknowledged to have substantial applied value. For instance, note this passage from an official report of the National Science Foundation (1969):

> Policies for handling the nation's most pressing issues and problems—whether they relate to the cities, pollution, inflation, or supersonic transport—must rest not only on knowledge drawn from the physical and biological sciences, but also on the best available knowledge about human individual and social behavior. Many of our most urgent domestic policy issues, indeed, are more closely related to the social sciences than to the other sciences. (pp. xiii–xiv)

Abt (1980) provided a list of major social science research projects sponsored by the federal government, in areas ranging from child care to housing to criminal justice; and Oskamp and Schultz (1998, Chapter 17) have summarized many of the findings about how social research has been used in the public policy arena. Tornatzky et al. (1982) have given examples suggesting that even larger investments in social science research would pay major dividends in increasing U.S. innovation and productivity. Because a large part of the problem concerns how to ensure that available knowledge is *used* by policymakers, various proposals have been made, such as establishing a presidential Council of Social Science Advisors, parallel to the influential Council of Economic Advisors (Kiesler, 1980).

George Gallup (1965) and other pollers have long insisted that more attention to legitimate scientific opinion polls could improve the processes of government. A sad example was provided by the abortive Bay of Pigs Cuban invasion attempt in 1961, which was apparently based on the assumption that many Cubans were ready to rise up against the Castro regime. However, in 1960, Lloyd Free had conducted a careful opinion poll of 1,000 urban Cubans which showed that they backed Castro overwhelmingly, and attention to those findings could have avoided the Bay of Pigs debacle (Cantril, 1967, pp. 1–5).

Similarly, Ralph White (1970) has suggested that a careful analysis of South Vietnamese public opinion toward the Viet Cong versus the Saigon government could have kept the United States from its disastrous military involvement in Vietnam.

In recent decades, survey research has become "indispensable in the public and private sectors" (Cordes, 1982, p. 40). An area in which poll information is widely used is in political election campaigns for state and federal offices, as discussed in Chapter 6. Specialized governmental agencies also have many uses for social science research. One interesting example was the report of the Committee on Community Reactions to the Concorde (1977). This report was ordered by the U.S. Secretary of Transportation to assess the amount of disturbance to nearby residents caused by that extremely loud supersonic aircraft, and it led to heavy restrictions in the number of U.S. cities to which the Concorde was allowed to fly.

Although many public officials are receptive to the use of social science research (Caplan, Morrison, & Stambaugh, 1975), there are also many cases in which good research is done but then ignored by the government. For instance, the Supreme Court has sometimes disregarded and sometimes badly misunderstood social science research findings in several important cases (Saks, 1974; Grofman, 1980). In the 1980s, the Attorney General's Commission on Pornography drew conclusions in its final report that misrepresented the social science research findings on which they ostensibly were based (Wilcox, 1987). A different, but equally sad, fate befell the social research done for the earlier Surgeon General's Advisory Committee on Television and Social Behavior (Bogart, 1972b), and the President's Commission on Obscenity and Pornography (Zillmann, 1992). The latter commission's findings, gathered at a cost of $2 million, were not just ignored but were actively repudiated by many congressional representatives and by President Nixon, who called them "morally bankrupt" (*Los Angeles Times*, 1970).

Obviously, this is not the sort of research utilization that one would hope for. By contrast, Campbell (1988) has advocated that we become an "experimenting society," in which new social and political programs will be tried out as planned scientific experiments with careful evaluation of their effects. Such an honest, nonpartisan, and accountable approach would be a great improvement over today's typical extremes of complete lack of evaluation of government programs or overadvocacy of programs whose value has not been established. In fact, some very large-scale policy experiments of this sort have been carried out, notably on income-maintenance programs to combat poverty (Rossi & Lyall, 1976; Heclo & Rein, 1980), and on housing-assistance programs to help low-income families upgrade their housing (Field, 1980; Friedman & Weinberg, 1983).

Training for social scientists to participate in policy issues is not usually included in most behavioral science curricula, and there should be more emphasis on such preparation. However, in giving advice to policymakers, we should keep in mind the earlier section of this chapter on attitude–behavior discrepancies. As Deutscher (1965) underlined, social scientists should be very cautious about giving such advice unless they have studied behavioral outcomes as well as people's attitudes and opinions. And, in proposing or carrying out interventions in any kind of social situation, they should give careful thought to the ethical principles regarding such interventions (Bermant, Kelman, & Warwick, 1978).

SUMMARY

This concluding chapter of Part I has discussed five important continuing issues in the field of attitudes and opinions. Research on the relationship between attitudes and behavior has shown that attitudes usually are significantly related to behavior, and it has identified a number of methodological, attitudinal, personal, behavioral, and situational variables that moderate the strength of that relationship. Two broad theoretical models for understanding the attitude–behavior relationship are the theory of planned behavior, which has been well supported by many studies, and the conditioning-based MODE model, which proposes two processes (spontaneous and deliberate) by which attitudes can lead to behavior.

A close link between personality and attitudes has been expected and found in many research studies. More than 50 years of research on authoritarian personality characteristics have established their relationship to a cluster of attitudes, including ethnic prejudice and political conservatism. Recent studies examining the relationship between personality and attitudes have indicated that perceptions of threat (whether dispositional or situational in nature) can lead to increased authoritarianism and more conservative attitudes.

Laboratory experimental studies of attitudes generally show stronger effects than field studies, largely because of a number of methodological differences that are frequently confounded with the laboratory–field distinction. Although field research is still much less common, its popularity has been growing gradually. Ethical issues in attitude research have received much attention over the years, and guidelines have been developed to protect research participants while simultaneously affirming the scientist's societal obligation to provide new knowledge.

The relationship of public opinion to public policy has been a topic of debate. It appears that the public is most competent to determine broad questions of the goals of government policy rather than the means for achieving them. Modern survey methods provide reliable ways of determining both mass and elite public opinion, but there are dangers in political leaders' either following public opinion too slavishly or leading it too manipulatively. On some issues, government policy has followed public opinion, on others it has ignored majority viewpoints for decades, and in the area of foreign affairs official policy tends to lead and shape public opinion. In addition to attitude survey data, there are many other important uses for social science research in the public policy arena.

Public Opinion on Socially Important Topics

13

Political Attitudes I

[The President] is the last person in the world to know what the people really want and think.—James A. Garfield.

Our government rests on public opinion. Whoever can change public opinion can change the government practically as such.—Abraham Lincoln.

Popular opinion is the greatest lie in the world.—Thomas Carlyle.

Political attitudes and behavior have received far more attention than any other area of public opinion. As the quotes above show, they have been the subject of great controversy as well as great interest. Some authorities, like Abraham Lincoln, have claimed that government decisions were based firmly on public opinion. Others, such as George Gallup (1965), have doubted that they were, but felt that they should be. Still others, like Thomas Carlyle, have scoffed at the concept of public opinion and the notion that it could or should affect governmental decisions.

The political attitude area is almost unique among areas of public opinion in having an easily measured behavioral concomitant, the vote. Therefore voting behavior is frequently used as the criterion in political attitude surveys, or as the dependent variable of greatest interest. However, voting occurs only periodically, and only a few specific political issues are presented directly to the public for their vote, as in a referendum or constitutional amendment or bond issue. Therefore we cannot confine our interest to voting behavior alone, but we must also consider public attitudes on various other important political issues.

This chapter and the next one are organized in three major sections, based on the dependent variable being studied. In this chapter we consider political attitudes per se, particularly attitudes on important issues that are not put to public vote. In the following chapter we will first consider factors influencing *individuals'* voting behavior and then shift the focus to **aggregate voting** as a dependent variable, adding together all the individual votes and studying the patterns which occur within an election and the changes from one election to the next. For convenience in considering various presidential elections, Table 13–1 lists U.S. presidents since 1932 and summarizes major events in their presidencies.

PRESIDENTIAL POPULARITY

Probably the most familiar single index in all of political polling is the presidential "popularity" rating or, more accurately, the rating of people's approval of the president's performance in office. For decades, stretching back to the first administration of Franklin D. Roosevelt, the Gallup Poll and other survey organizations have been asking a question such as "Do you approve or disapprove of the way George W. Bush is handling his job as President?" It is widely known that fluctuations in these poll results can send shivers up and down the backs of White House staff members, or raise presidential spirits (and campaign dollars) when the results are favorable.

TABLE 13–1 U.S. Presidents and Major Events in Their Presidencies
Since 1932

Year	President	Major events
1932	Franklin D. Roosevelt	Great Depression 1929–1941
1936	" "	Hitler attacks Poland 1939, World War II begins
1940	" "	U.S. in World War II, 1941–1945
1944	" "	" " ; FDR dies April 12, 1945
1945	Harry S Truman	World War II ends Aug. 14, 1945 Cold War with USSR begins in 1946
1948	" "	Marshall Plan gives aid to Europe NATO is founded Korean War starts June 25, 1950
1952	Dwight D. Eisenhower	Korean War armistice July 27, 1953 Supreme Court rules against segregated schools 1954
1956	" "	USSR launches first satellite 1957 Fidel Castro becomes premier of Cuba 1959
1960	John F. Kennedy	Peace Corps founded Civil rights movement gains in South 1961–1963 U.S. troops in Vietnam 1961 USSR blockade of Berlin fails 1961 Bay of Pigs invasion of Cuba fails 1961 Cuban Missile Crisis Oct. 1962 JFK assassinated Nov. 22, 1963
1963	Lyndon B. Johnson	Major civil rights law passed Many U.S. troops fight as Vietnam War grows
1964	" "	Martin L. King Jr. assassinated 1968 LBJ does not seek reelection in 1968
1968	Richard M. Nixon	Vietnam War grows U.S. lands men on the moon Vice President Agnew resigns Nixon visit to China reverses past U.S. nonrecognition
1972	" "	Israeli–Arab War, 1973, leads to OPEC oil embargo to West Watergate break-in cover-up scandal Nixon resigns Aug. 1974
1974	Gerald Ford	Vietnam War ends with U.S. withdrawal 1975
1976	Jimmy Carter	Another oil shortage 1978–1979 U.S. embassy staff taken hostage in Iran
1980	Ronald Reagan	Major tax cut Reagan condemns USSR as "evil empire"
1984	" "	Mikhail Gorbachev becomes head of USSR, begins *perestroika* restructuring
1988	George Bush	Berlin Wall torn down Nov. 1989 Persian Gulf War to free Kuwait 1991 USSR broken into separate nations 1991
1992	Bill Clinton	First attack on World Trade Center 1993
1996	" "	Major federal budget surplus Monica Lewinsky scandal Impeachment fails

(continued)

TABLE 13–1   (continued)

Year	President	Major events
2000	George W. Bush	Disputed election Major tax cuts World Trade Center terrorist attack, Sept. 11, 2001 Afghanistan invasion 2002 War on Iraq 2003

What do these approval ratings demonstrate about presidential popularity? In most cases they start relatively high when a president comes into office (a "honeymoon period") and decline later as his actions or inactions displease various subgroups of the populace. After this decline to a middling level, approval levels may fall further or rise, mainly in response to major national and international events and the president's handling of them. We can illustrate some of these patterns by summarizing approval trends for the past two presidents.

Bill Clinton entered office in 1993 with a relatively high approval rating of 58%, which remained in the low 50s for three months and then declined to a low of 37% within the next two months as domestic policy controversies developed. For most of that year his approval score hovered in the 40s, but it gradually returned to a high of 58% at the 1-year point after some legislative successes. It declined again and stayed in the 40s for most of Clinton's second year, which ended with a strong Republican victory in the midterm election of 1994. Clinton's approval rating stayed in the high 40s for most of his third year, but rose into the 50s briefly after the bombing of the federal building in Oklahoma City and more permanently after a deadlock with the Republican Congress over the proposed budget led to a shutdown of government services at the end of the year. Thereafter his approval remained in the 50s and hit a high of 60% in the fall before the 1996 election.

Following Clinton's victory in the 1996 election, his approval score stayed in the high 50s and low 60s for the whole of his second term. It reached a high of 69% in January 1998 shortly after Monica Lewinsky's charge of having had sexual contact with Clinton, and it persisted in the mid-60s for the rest of that year despite the House hearings and vote to impeach the president. When the Senate acquitted Clinton in February 1999, his approval rating hit its all-time high of 70%, and it stayed above 60% most of that year, during which U.S. and NATO military forces were engaged against the Serbian army that was occupying Kosovo. For the rest of his second term, Clinton's job approval hovered in the high 50s and low 60s, and it ended at an unprecedentedly high figure of 65%, which contrasted with the low public ratings of his personal character (Moore, 2001a).

George W. Bush began his term in 2001 with a relatively high approval rating of 57% despite the preceding weeks of court suits over who had won the election. In his first month in office, his rating increased to a high of 63%, but it quickly dropped back and stabilized in the mid-50s. Its low point was 51% just before the terrorist attacks on the World Trade Center on September 11, after which it skyrocketed to the highest peak ever recorded, 90%. Subsequently, despite the military victory over the Taliban in Afghanistan, Bush's approval rating steadily declined, reaching a low of 58% in February, 2003, nearly 1$\frac{1}{2}$ years after the WTC attack. Then, with the start of the U.S.-led war on Iraq, it briefly jumped up to 71%, but again decreased quite speedily and reached a new low of 46% in May, 2004 (Jones, 2004; Newport & Saad, 2003).(Because of sharp fluctuations in public attitudes accompanying the WTC attacks and the subsequent U.S. military campaigns in Afghanistan and Iraq, we will usually terminate most attitude measures described in this chapter in mid-2001.)

In addition to the usual tendency for a president's popularity to decline over time, presidential approval ratings are apt to rise markedly for a short while after a decisive action or event in international affairs, such as Carter's peace-making initiative between Israel and Egypt. Sometimes this even occurs after an unsuccessful action or crisis, when many previously apathetic citizens rally around the president because he symbolizes the nation as a whole—a pattern that Mueller (1973) dubbed the "rally-round-the-flag phenomenon." For instance, George W. Bush's approval rating surged upward 35 percentage points immediately after the terrorist attacks on the World Trade Center on September 11, 2001, and his father's presidential approval rating jumped 14 points after Iraq invaded Kuwait in 1990. Similarly, Franklin Roosevelt's approval increased 12 points after the Japanese attack on Pearl Harbor.

Both favorable and unfavorable events can stimulate such rally effects. For instance, Kennedy's popularity rose from 78% to 83% following the fiasco of the attempted invasion of Cuba at the Bay of Pigs, and it increased from 61% to 74% after his successful handling of the Cuban missile crisis. A majority of such rally effects have lasted no more than 10 weeks (Hugick & Gallup, 1991). In an analysis of 193 military disputes between 1933 and 1992, Baker and Oneal (2001) found that the size of the rally effect was heavily dependent on media coverage. Rally effects were more likely in situations where there were bipartisan supporters and clearly articulated statements from the White House.

In contrast to these rally effects, presidential popularity sags markedly during economic recessions but may not rebound as much during economic booms (Kinder, 1981; Adams, 1984). Wars can also depress public approval of the president, as shown by the fact that presidential popularity dropped steadily in close relationship to the increasing cumulative number of U.S. combat deaths in both the Korean and Vietnam Wars (Mueller, 1973; Kernell, 1978). Careful quantitative studies have shown that the following types of events, in addition to economic conditions and wars, all have clear and predictable effects on presidential approval ratings: international crises, diplomatic meetings and agreements, sympathy concerning personal events such as health problems or attempted assassinations, government scandals, domestic unrest, and dramatic policy initiatives (Ostrom & Simon, 1985; Ostrom & Smith, 1992). However, highly publicized presidential speeches and foreign travel have much less effect on public approval than commonly thought (Simon & Ostrom, 1989).

A politically important fact about presidential approval ratings is that they are strongly predictive of success in the subsequent election. Specifically, an approval rating of 50% or above during the summer preceding a presidential election is usually enough to ensure the subsequent electoral victory of the incumbent president or of whatever candidate his party nominates (Brody & Sigelman, 1983), though this indicator failed by a hair in the 2000 election when Al Gore lost by 4 votes in the electoral college.

Consistent with our discussion in Chapter 9, these public perceptions of the president are influenced by the agenda-setting power of the mass media, particularly television. A single news commentary on network television can sometimes stimulate as much as 4 percentage points of opinion change (Page, Shapiro, & Dempsey, 1985). Content analyses of television campaign stories have found that they focus largely on the candidates' personal traits, such as competence or integrity of character, rather than on policy issues; and they present these traits in small, easily understood packages, which are then repeated with slight variations, night after night (Graber, 1987).

Researchers in the field of social cognition consider this media agenda-setting power an example of **priming**. That is, presenting certain topics in campaign news stories makes those topics more accessible in viewers' thinking (*primes* them), and as a result these topics assume more weight in viewers' judgments about the candidates. An extreme example of this occurred in the last few days of the 1980 campaign, when the unresolved problem of the U.S. hostages in Iran was constantly emphasized in the news, and President Carter's standing with the voters took a sharp last-minute tumble.

To show that this kind of effect is really due to the content of the news stories, rather than to other concurrent events, carefully controlled experiments have been done. These experiments presented groups of participants with actual network news stories that had been unobtrusively augmented by added segments that all focused on a particular national problem, such as defense capabilities, pollution dangers, or economic problems. Such studies have shown conclusively that viewers exposed to a TV news diet emphasizing a particular national problem used that problem area heavily in their evaluations of the president's overall performance (Iyengar & Kinder, 1986). Analyses of actual, unmodified TV network news coverage as an influence on presidential approval have also demonstrated this priming effect (Krosnick & Kinder, 1990).

Despite the eye-catching headline appeal of presidential approval ratings, they are at best a very crude indication of the public's political attitudes. They cannot be relied on as a guide for governmental decisions because of their oversimplicity and the fact that they can be quickly changed by the impact of events. A particularly dramatic example of their rapid fluctuation is the fact that less than a year before his unexpected victory over Dewey in the 1948 election, President Truman's rating stood at a dismal figure of only 36%. An opposite change occurred after President Nixon's peace settlement of the Vietnam War, when his 67% approval rating sank to 31% only six months later because of the public revelations about his administration's role in the Watergate scandal, and a year later he was forced to resign the presidency. Somewhat similarly, when George Bush's victory in the 1991 Persian Gulf War was followed by an economic recession, his approval ratings plummeted from a peak of 89% to a low of 29%, and he lost the subsequent election to Bill Clinton (Newport, 1998).

CONCERNS OF CITIZENS

A better indicator of political attitudes would focus on the issues and concerns that are uppermost in people's minds, for instance by asking a question such as "What do you think is the most important problem facing this country today?" Questions similar to this have been repeatedly asked of national samples by many polling organizations. It may surprise you to learn how much the answers have varied from time to time, depending on the course of national and international events. Some examples will illustrate the range of responses.

At the beginning of George W. Bush's presidency, in March 2001, the Gallup Poll asked this question to a representative nationwide sample of 1,060 people, and a summary of their answers is shown in Table 13–2. At that point in time, a rather wide variety of problems was mentioned, with economic issues (including taxes, poverty, and unemployment) leading the list with 37% of respondents mentioning them (*Gallup Poll Monthly*, 2001, No. 426). Also of substantial concern were crime and violence (including school shootings and gun control issues), mentioned by 17% of respondents, and education as a national problem (16%). Next in prominence was a group of concerns about ethics (moral and religious issues, such as family decline, dishonesty, and lack of integrity), listed by 11%, closely followed by concerns about international issues, war, national security, and defense (10%).

Many other problems, though less salient in early 2001, were high on the list of people's concerns in some other years. For instance, worry about international problems shot up to 67% late in 2001, after the terrorist destruction of the World Trade Center. Fears of crime hit a peak level of 52% in August 1994, concerns about health-care costs and availability

TABLE 13–2   Responses of a National Sample to a Question About Our Nation's
Most Important Problem, March 2001

Problem	% Mentioning
Economic problems (summary)	37%
Economy in general	10
Taxes	7
Poverty/hunger/homelessness	5
Unemployment/jobs	4
Recession	3
Other economic	8
Crime/violence/school shootings/guns/gun control	17
Education	16
Ethics/moral/religious/family decline/lack of integrity	11
International issues/problems/fear of war/national security	10
Poor health care/hospitals/cost of health care	7
Children's behavior/way they are raised	6
Drugs	6
Dissatisfaction with government/politicians/leadership/corruption	5
All others	19
No opinion	7
Total (some people gave multiple responses)	141%

Source: Data collated from *Gallup Poll Monthly* (March 2001, No. 426, pp. 22–23).

registered 31% in January 1994, and worries about drugs and drug abuse reached 63% in September 1989 (*Gallup Poll Monthly*, 1995, No. 358). Severe energy crises were the main problem listed by 46% in 1974 and by 33% in 1979, whereas 27% named lack of integrity in government during the Watergate scandal in 1974 (Smith, 1985). Within the overall area of economic problems, the U.S. budget deficit was a specific worry for 21% of respondents in July 1990, whereas unemployment reached a peak level of concern of 62% in October 1982, but less than two years earlier, inflation was the primary worry of 73% in February 1981 (*Gallup Report*, 1983, No. 219).

An overview of trends in these public concerns since the end of World War II shows some clear patterns. From the late 1940s to the early 1960s, the greatest public worry was foreign affairs, particularly threats to world peace. Between 1963 and 1965 the focus shifted to the civil rights struggle, including problems of racial strife and racial discrimination, but that concern faded to a vestige by 1971. Between 1964 and 1972 the Vietnam War claimed the bulk of public concern, after which economic problems took over the spotlight and kept it continuously up through 2001 (Smith, 1985). The only times when international problems again became primary were during the Persian Gulf War of 1991 and after the World Trade Center terrorist attack in 2001 and the subsequent war buildup against Afghanistan and Iraq.

These trends in public concerns over a 55-year period since 1947 are clearly shown in Figure 13–1. The graph lumps together all mentions of war, peace, and foreign affairs as the nation's single most important problem, and it compares their level with that of racial problems and of all economic problems such as unemployment, cost of living, poverty, taxes, and government spending. The data are from the Gallup Poll (e.g., Gallup, 1972; Smith, 1985; *Gallup Poll Monthly*, 1991, No. 308; 1999, No. 400). This graph shows dramatically how briefly racial problems held center stage as the greatest American

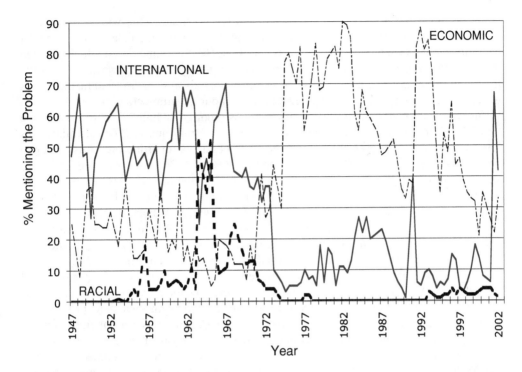

FIGURE 13–1 A 55-year summary of the public's view of our nation's most serious single problem, comparing international, economic, and racial problems from 1947 to 2002.

Source: Data are from the Gallup Poll.

concern and how quickly both racial and international problems were forgotten when economic worries increased in the early 1970s.

In comparing research findings such as those just described, readers should be alert to the fact that they are influenced by the type of response required, the wording of the question, and the basis used in tabulating responses. Different findings may sometimes be obtained with free-response questions (e.g., "What are our biggest problems?") than with ones in which a list of problems is read or handed to the respondent (e.g., "How worried are you about each of the following problems?"). For instance, when the latter format was used in a January 1987 Roper Poll, a much higher level of public concern was reported about the problems of drug abuse and of crime and lawlessness than in the free-response question of the Gallup Poll during the same month (*Public Opinion*, 1987, No. 4; *Gallup Report*, 1987, No. 260). Additionally, in comparing studies, it is important to note not only the question wording, but also the basis of tabulating responses. When several responses per person are requested (e.g., "What are our nation's two or three biggest problems?"), the resulting percentages of mentions are not comparable with studies that ask about only the single most important problem, such as those summarized in Table 13–2 and Figure 13–1.

TRUST IN GOVERNMENT

Another aspect of political attitudes is how much the citizens trust their government—not the current administration, but the government as a whole. The Survey Research Center has been measuring this topic since 1958, and its findings have raised questions about the prospects for political stability in the United States. One widely used index of trust in government is based on four or five questions about the federal government's performance, of which the most central is "How much of the time do you think you can trust the government in Washington to do what is right—just about always, most of the time, or only some of the time?" Answering "just about always" or "most of the time" has generally been interpreted as a high level of trust in our government.

Initially, on this item, many more U.S. citizens reported a "high" level of trust than a "low" level. In 1958, 73% of respondents showed high trust, and in 1964, the figure was 76%. From there, however, the percentage of respondents reporting high trust dropped progressively to 53% in 1972, then plunged to 36% in 1974, and continued its steady slide to a low of 25% in 1980 (Newport, 2001d). At that point, nearly three times as many Americans had low trust in their government as had high trust. Research has shown that the sharp decline in the early 1970s was partly due to the Vietnam War and partly to the impact of the Watergate scandal, which eventually forced President Nixon to resign. During the 1980s, the high-trust figure recovered somewhat (to 44% in 1984), but despite the U.S. victory in the 1991 Persian Gulf War, it suffered another steep drop-off to an all-time low of 21% in 1994. This downturn accompanied a recession in the U.S. economy and preceded the 1994 election, when a Republican resurgence took over control of the House of Representatives. Since then, however, despite the failed impeachment proceedings against President Clinton and the controversies over U.S. military actions in the former Yugoslavia, Americans' trust in government rose steadily and again reached the 44% level before the 2000 election. Interestingly, the trust score shot up to 60% immediately after the World Trade Center (WTC) terrorist attacks in September 2001—a level not seen since 1968, and possibly an indication of wishful thinking by the public (Newport, 2001d).

As these findings show, trust in government is not solely an assessment of the overall government system; it is sensitive to national events such as economic cycles, and it is partially an evaluation of the performance of the incumbent administration (Abramson & Finifter, 1981; A. Miller, 1983; Citrin & Luks, 2001). Major factors that reduce it are scandals in Congress or the administration and public concerns about high crime rates (Chanley, Rudolph, & Rahn, 2000). Further confirmation of its sensitivity to political and economic reality is shown by the fact that black Americans, who were more trusting during the 1960s era of civil rights progress, have displayed lower trust in government than whites in most years since 1968 (Howell & Fagan, 1988; Alford, 2001). Another main element contributing to declining trust in government has been the increasingly negative coverage of politics in the U.S. media that began in the 1960s (Ansolabehere & Iyengar, 1995; Jamieson & Cappella, 1996).

Here are the main reasons that Americans give for distrusting government:

- It is inefficient and wasteful,
- It spends money on the wrong things,
- Special interests are too powerful,
- Politicians lack integrity (Blendon et al., 1997).

These findings about trust have been linked to research on social cognition that investigates which people are most inclined to be cynical. There is evidence that the greatest cynicism or distrust of government occurs in those individuals who think about politics in terms of *schemas* about issues or leaders *and* who feel their own political position is far from that of the policies and leaders on the current political scene (Erber & Lau, 1990).

Trust in government can also be shown by citizens' ratings of how good a job various branches of the government are doing compared with their ratings of other institutions in our society. What would you guess to be the most approved institutions in our country?

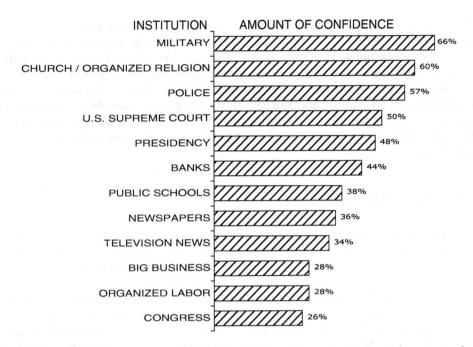

FIGURE 13–2 Public confidence in 12 American institutions (percent of respondents saying they themselves have "a great deal" or "quite a lot" of confidence).

Source: Data are from Newport (2001b, p. 52).

The results of such a comparison are shown in Figure 13–2. In the summer of 2001, the 2 most-approved institutions of the 12 included were the U.S. military and the church/organized religion. For three decades, the church and the military have typically held the top places in public confidence, with the church leading in the 1970s to the mid-1980s, but being surpassed by the military since 1986. Next in the 2001 distribution came the police, the Supreme Court, and the presidency. Among the three branches of government, the Supreme Court has almost always outranked the presidency, and Congress has always trailed far behind in public confidence. In the middle of the 2001 ranking came banks, public schools, newspapers, and television news. Finally, the lowest ranking of the 12 institutions were big business, organized labor, and Congress—three groups that have almost always been near the bottom of the distribution (*Gallup Report*, 1988, No. 279; Newport, 2001b). Later in 2001, the military and the presidency showed sharp jumps in public confidence following the destruction of the World Trade Center—another example of the "rally-round-the-flag effect" (*Gallup Poll Tuesday Briefing*, June 2002).

Comparative data regarding changes in public trust since 1973 show that all the institutions measured *declined* in public confidence during that time, most of them quite markedly, with the sole exceptions of the military and the Supreme Court, which increased (*Gallup Report*, 1988, No. 279; Newport, 2001b). This substantial drop in Americans' trust in almost all institutions, including the executive and legislative branches of our government, plus business, labor, and many other aspects of our society, raises serious questions of whether citizens will continue to believe in the legitimacy of our social and political order (Lipset & Schneider, 1983). A. Miller stated, "A democratic political system cannot survive for long without the support of a majority of its citizens" (1974, p. 951); and

Hetherington concluded, "Low trust helps create a political environment in which it is more difficult for leaders to succeed" (1998, p. 791). However, to keep this picture in perspective, it is helpful to know that, even after this decline in trust, the American public was more confident in every one of its major institutions than were the citizens of West Germany, France, Great Britain, and Spain (Parisot, 1988). Research has shown that this disaffection with government does not generally cause people to withdraw from political participation and voting, though it does often lead to a more confrontational style of political activity, including protests, demonstrations, boycotts, and even violence (Kinder & Sears, 1985).

THE QUALITY OF LIFE

A fascinating trend in measuring political attitudes is to develop standardized **social indicators** as indices of the quality of life in various spheres, analogous to the well-known economic indicators such as the gross national product, unemployment rate, and the cost of living index. This development is part of a general trend toward increased consideration of human values and personal satisfactions in business and industry and in economic and political decision-making. Interest in the development of social indicators began in the early 1960s and was fostered by support from various foundations and government agencies (Bauer, 1966). The goal was to construct meaningful measures of the psychological and sociological aspects of our national life patterns (for instance, such measures might include an index of Gross National Happiness, or Work Satisfaction, or even a "Cost of Loving Index" to measure marriage and family satisfaction). Once they are built, these indices should be measured at regular intervals to show trends and changes in our national quality of life. Highly useful sets of such long-term longitudinal trend indicators have been developed by the National Election Studies, for political variables, and by the General Social Survey, for attitudes on many social issues.

Unfortunately, there are no reliable psychological survey data to tell us whether the "good old days" were really so good for most people as we often think they were in retrospect. Certainly today's assembly-line jobs, high divorce rate, urban crowding, and air pollution are factors which diminish general satisfaction. Yet past centuries had problems of equal or greater impact, such as child labor, high death rates, slum tenements, and unpaved roads covered with horse manure. In fact, objectively;

> The nation's health (as measured by life expectancy, which has increased by 20 years in the last century); standard of living (as measured by real income, which has doubled since [World War II]); cultural development (as measured by mean years of education); and family life (as measured by the proportion of people who are married or who expect to marry) are higher than they have ever been in the past. (Greeley, 1981, p. 16)

Objective factors such as these have been incorporated in many rating systems that have been proposed for measuring and comparing the quality of life in different cities, states, or countries (e.g., Marlin, 1992; Thomas, 1994; Prescott-Allen, 2001).

A major goal of the social indicators movement is to supplement these objective measures with carefully constructed indicators of the subjective side of life, such as happiness and well-being. Since the 1960s, many research reports have been produced based on time-series data examining measures of subjective well-being as they changed over time (e.g., Converse et al., 1980; *Public Perspective*, 1997b; Blanchflower & Oswald, 2000; Lane, 2000). The first large-scale national surveys of this sort were conducted in 1971 and 1972 by several different research organizations. They focused on a variety of areas which affect people's satisfaction with their lives, including marriage and family, health, satisfaction with job and income, leisure activities, race relations, civil liberties, women's rights, political alienation, and general happiness (Wilcox et al., 1972).

An example of survey findings on the quality of life comes from a Survey Research Center (SRC) study (Campbell, Converse, & Rodgers, 1976). Interviews were conducted with a national sample of over 2,100 persons 18 years of age and older. In general, respondents were more likely to say that life was getting worse in this country than that it was getting better, a finding very similar to the ones previously cited about citizens' trust in government. About half of the sample saw no change in the quality of life, about one-third felt it was deteriorating, and only about one-sixth saw it as improving. The most common complaints cited were increasing alienation, public protests and disorders, crime, drug usage, declining morality, behavior of young people, inflation, government policies, taxes, and environmental problems.

Although many of these problems are still worrisome, recent data show that public satisfaction with "the way things are going in the U.S." has increased greatly from its all-time low point in 1979, when only 12% of Americans said they were satisfied. This measure of *satisfaction with national affairs* is quite sensitive to economic and political events, reaching two of its peaks (66% satisfied) during the prosperity of early 1986 and again in 1991 just after the victory in the Persian Gulf War. From that point it dropped precipitously to a low of 14% satisfied during the recession of 1992, and then increased steadily throughout the 1990s. It reached an all-time high of 71% satisfied during the economic boom of early 1999, remained in the 50s and 60s through 2000, but sank to 46% by mid-2001 as the recession deepened (Moore, 2001b; Newport, 2001a). In early 2001, the aspects of national life that provoked the greatest dissatisfaction were the amount of federal taxes, the availability of affordable health care, the problem of poverty and homelessness, and the moral and ethical climate (Moore, 2001b).

In contrast to people's satisfaction with national affairs, their *satisfaction with personal life* is always much higher. Its low point was 73% satisfied in mid-1979 when satisfaction with national affairs hit an all-time low of 12%, and it reached a high of 91% satisfied in mid-2001 (Hugick, 1992; Saad, 2001d). When personal satisfaction is divided into different domains, satisfaction with marriage and family life is typically highest. Only 5% of Americans were dissatisfied in that area in mid-2001, and only 7% were dissatisfied with their housing. Levels of dissatisfaction with one's job, health, education, community, safety from physical harm or violence, and opportunities for success were intermediate, and the highest level of dissatisfaction was 22% for one's financial situation (Saad, 2001c). Earlier research showed that the domains most closely related to overall personal life satisfaction were satisfaction with self, with standard of living, and with family life (Campbell, 1981). Levels of personal satisfaction have been found to change very little in response to economic and political conditions (Caplow, 1982). However, U.S. citizens' enjoyment of work decreased notably between 1955 and 1980, but recovered substantially by 2001 (Glenn & Weaver, 1982; Moore, 2001d).

The individuals most extremely dissatisfied with public aspects of American life were identified by a 3-item "index of political alienation" in the 1971 SRC study. During that Vietnam War era, this 2% of the sample mostly consisted of people who were young, well-educated, metropolitan residents, and/or blacks rather than members of other population subgroups (Campbell et al., 1976). However, by mid-2001, the most dissatisfied population groups were Democrats, lower-middle-income households ($20,000–$30,000 annual income), nonwhites, those with a high school education or less, women over 50, and senior citizens (Newport, 2001a).

Photograph courtesy of Seymour M. Lipset.
Reprinted by permission.

Box 13–1   SEYMOUR M. LIPSET, *Political Attitudes Researcher*

Credited as being the most-cited living political scientist, Seymour M. Lipset is Emeritus Professor of Political Science and Sociology and Senior Fellow of the Hoover Institution at Stanford University, and also Professor Emeritus of Public Policy at George Mason University. He graduated from the City College of New York and Columbia University and taught for many years at Harvard University before moving to Stanford in 1975. He has written extensively on political sociology, social stratification, trade union organization, public opinion, the conditions for democracy, and the sociology of intellectual life.

Lipset has served as president of the American Political Science Association, the American Sociological Association, the International Society of Political Psychology, the Sociological Research Association, and the World Association for Public Opinion Research. He has been honored by election to the National Academy of Sciences, the American Academy of Arts and Sciences, and the National Academy of Education. He has authored, co-authored, or edited nearly 400 articles and nearly 50 books, among which Political Man, The Politics of Unreason, *and* American Exceptionalism *are particularly well-known. In this chapter we mention his research on political attitudes, including the book* The Confidence Gap.

POLITICAL ATTITUDES OF POPULATION SUBGROUPS

These findings about dissatisfaction bring us to another very important topic, the differing political attitudes of various subgroups in the population. In this area there is a great mass of demographic information, so we can only summarize some of the major trends.

The commonly accepted beliefs about the relationship of demographic factors to political attitudes and behavior are partly a myth and partly based on Depression-era political alignments that have changed markedly in more recent elections. For instance, the Republican Party was traditionally considered the party of older people, farmers and rural residents, the well-to-do, and upper educational and occupational groups, whereas the Democratic Party was expected to be favored by the opposite groups, particularly by union members, blacks, and Catholics. Although many of these conclusions were correct during the Great Depression and World War II, their validity declined substantially during the Eisenhower era of the 1950s (W. Miller, 1960). Since then, the process of change has continued, so that much of the "traditional wisdom" is no longer applicable.

TABLE 13–3 Degree of Democratic Preference in Party Identification for Major Social Groups, Showing Changes from 1952 to 2000

Group	1952– 1960	1962– 1968	1970– 1976	1978– 1984	1986– 1992	1994– 2000
Females	+16	+24	+21	+23	+18	+20
Males	+22	+24	+18	+15	+ 5	+ 2
Whites	+18	+19	+13	+10	0	+ 1
Blacks	+37	+67	+75	+75	+70	+73
Lowest income (0–16 percentile)	+21	+29	+31	+37	+29	+35
Middle income (34–67 percentile)	+24	+27	+25	+20	+13	+11
Highest income (96–100 percentile)	−31	− 8	−29	−19	−39	−22
Union members	+40	+46	+39	+36	+30	+31
South	+47	+43	+33	+29	+24	+10

Note: Numbers indicate Democratic percentage minus Republican percentage. For instance, among men in 1952–1960, an average of 56% were Democratic and 34% were Republican, a 22% difference.

Source: Data are from the National Election Studies (2001). http://www.umich.edu/~nes.

Recent Research Findings

Table 13–3 illustrates these changes from the 1950s through 2000 by displaying patterns of expressed party identification for several of the major population groups that had supported FDR's New Deal voting coalition. The figures are based on the National Election Studies (NES) 7-point scale, with positive figures in the table showing the degree of Democratic advantage and negative numbers meaning a Republican advantage in party identification. The findings demonstrate that women maintained an approximately 20% Democratic preference for the whole 50 years, whereas men decreased steadily from about a 20% Democratic preference to a 2% one. The overall pattern for whites across the country was a steady decrease, whereas blacks started at about a 40% Democratic preference and increased to over 70% by the 1970s. Union members decreased their initial strong Democratic preference by about one-fourth, whereas Southerners decreased it by over three-fourths (and white Southerners actually moved to a Republican advantage). Over the 50 years, the lowest-income group increased their Democratic preference somewhat, while the middle-income group decreased their Democratic preference about 10% in the mid-1980s, and the highest-income group, although quite variable in their strength of preference, always maintained a substantial Republican advantage.

Data not reported in the table showed that Catholics and Jews decreased their Democratic preference whereas, overall, regular churchgoers changed from a moderate Democratic preference to a moderate Republican one, and married Americans also adopted a 10% or greater Republican preference (Petrocik & Steeper, 1987; Weisberg, 1987). In general, these changes in party identification were paralleled by changes in actual voting patterns. Other analyses of racial and gender differences are presented in later chapters.

Age. The "traditional wisdom" holds that, as people get older, an increasing percentage of them tend to identify with the Republican Party, and there is some empirical evidence for the correctness of that conclusion during the 1950s (Crittenden, 1962). However, people's political attitudes are influenced not only by their age, but also by the specific political experiences of each successive generation, such as living through depressions, wars, etc. The effects of these differing experiences on different generations can be determined through a **cohort analysis**—an analysis which follows each generation, or cohort, longitudinally as they get older. (In contrast, the more common cross-sectional analysis collects data at a single point in time and compares the responses of 25-year-olds with those aged 50, 75, and so on, thus comparing people who were born in different eras and who consequently may have had very different early political experiences.)

Cohort analyses that have been done on the variable of party identification have demonstrated a relatively small linkage between age and increasing conservatism—much less than commonly thought (Converse, 1976; Davis, 1992). During the 1980s, an increasing proportion of young people (traditionally expected to be liberals) became Republican supporters (Axelrod, 1986). Similarly, on many issues of morality and lifestyle, the "generation gap" in attitudes between older Americans and young adults diminished markedly in the 1980s (*Gallup Report*, 1989, No. 282/283). Although young adults still tend to be somewhat more liberal than their elders, there are many issues on which the age groups do not differ appreciably. One current major area of difference is that the young generation in recent years is less involved in public affairs issues, more "turned off" by politics, and more politically ignorant than previous generations were (Bennett, 1998).

Geographic Region.   Despite the "melting-pot" notion of social homogenization in the United States, very great regional differences persisted through the nineteenth century. Since then, most of these differences have decreased greatly (e.g., per-capita income in the various regions has become much more similar), though some differences still remain prominent (Ladd, 1998). Politically, the southern states as far west as Texas and Oklahoma used to be nearly 75% Democratic in party identification, but by 1980 the Democratic portion dropped below 50%, and by 1996 it was down to 35%. At that point, about 32% of their residents considered themselves Republicans and about 33% were Independents. (Note that these three proportions would be different if the figure for "Independents" excluded respondents who admitted that they "leaned" toward one party or the other, as some measurement scales do.) Furthermore, these southern states now quite regularly elect Republicans to major offices (Erikson & Tedin, 2001).

There are still regional differences on many religious and moral views, and on social issues such as gun control or racial attitudes, but these differences are shrinking. For instance, on a 100-point scale, people in the old South were 11 points more conservative than the rest of the country in 1964 but only 4 points more conservative in 1998 (Erikson & Tedin, 2001). The western states and New England are more favorable than other regions to issues such as legal abortion, gun control, and legalization of marijuana, and the same is true for urban areas as compared with small towns and rural areas (Yang & Alba, 1992; Ladd, 1998). On some issues, such as women working and integrated schooling, the whole nation has become markedly more favorable in the past 50 years, and the attitude gap between regions has greatly diminished.

Social Class.   Economic disparities are greater in the U.S. than in any other western democracy, and they have been increasing in recent decades. In 1999, the richest 1% of Americans received 13% of all income, and they had more wealth than the bottom 50% of Americans; the richest one-fifth of the population took home more than 50% of all income (Johnstone, 1999). Yet class-based cleavages are smaller in the U.S. than in Europe. It is an interesting fact that over 70% of Americans reject the notion that U.S. society is divided into two distinct groups, the "haves" and the "have-nots" (*Gallup Report*, 1988, No. 276).

Although upper-income and upper-occupation groups still tend to be more conservative politically than other subgroups, these differences have blurred over the decades. The general pattern is that higher social class groups tend to be conservative on economic policy but more liberal on social policy issues. On noneconomic domestic issues, having higher levels of education adds to the liberal trend; and on foreign-policy issues, higher education groups are more favorable than other citizens toward U.S. international involvement (Erikson & Tedin, 2001). Class-based differences in *voting* declined continually during the 1950s and 1960s, then held steady through the 1970s and 1980s, and reached their lowest levels in the Clinton elections of the 1990s. However, class-based differences in *party identification* remained prominent and actually grew stronger in the 1970s and 1980s, with upper-class and middle-class individuals identifying more strongly with the Republican Party (Glenn, 1973; Petrocik & Steeper, 1987; Stanley & Niemi, 2000).

Another phenomenon related to social class is the emergence of "yuppies" (young upwardly mobile professionals) as a possible new force in politics. Research has shown that these well-educated and well-paid young people tend to be fairly conservative on economic issues, like other members of the postwar "baby boom" generation, but quite markedly liberal on social issues such as school prayer, school integration, women's rights, and abortion (Hammond, 1986). This mixture, as well as their affluence and political activism, make the yuppies a prized potential target group for both political parties.

Psychographic Groupings.   Instead of looking just at single variables, such as age or social class, many recent analyses of political attitudes have focused on patterns of key values, attitudes, and demographic factors in combination—a procedure that has been called **psychographics** because it involves a psychological profile of voting groups. One example of this approach was based on in-person interviews by the Gallup Poll with over 4,200 respondents. It used the statistical technique of cluster analysis to classify the American electorate into 11 relatively distinct groups, each of which had many characteristics in common and as few similarities as possible to the other 10 groups (*Times Mirror*, 1987). Kohut and Ornstein (1987) have summarized the voting pattern of these groups in President Reagan's election victories. Without going into detail on the method or the findings, here are brief descriptions of the 11 groups:

- Bystanders (11% of adults): Almost no interest in politics and no voting history. Tend to be young, white, and poorly educated.
- Enterprise Republicans (10% of adults): Probusiness and antigovernment. Affluent, educated, and white.
- Moral Republicans (11% of adults): Swayed by moral issues, anticommunist, middle-aged, middle-income, conservative, many Southerners.
- New Deal Democrats (11% of adults): Older blue-collar, union members, moderate income, fairly traditional and anticommunist.
- Sixties Democrats (8% of adults): Upper-middle-class, tolerant, committed to social justice and peace, many women.
- Partisan Poor (9% of adults): Low-income, heavily black, highly politicized, concerned with social justice, vote Democratic.
- Passive Poor (7% of adults): Low-income, less politicized, older, less critical of America, vote Democratic.
- Upbeats (9% of adults): Young, optimistic, strong believers in America, middle-income, lean toward Republicans.
- Disaffecteds (9% of adults): Middle-aged, pessimistic, distrust business and government, middle-income, lean toward Republicans.
- Seculars (8% of adults): Nonreligious, affluent, well-informed, tolerant, peace-oriented, lean toward Democrats.
- Followers (7% of adults): Poor, young, uninformed, little faith in America, little interest in politics, lean toward Democrats.

Sources of Political Attitudes

As indicated in Chapter 8, there are many possible sources of people's political attitudes in addition to general ideological principles, which were discussed at length in Chapter 7. Kinder and Sears (1985) have suggested six different types of sources. First, some attitudes may stem from self-interest (e.g., voting against higher taxes), but much research has shown that political attitudes are often symbolic (e.g., reverence for the flag or the military) rather than directly linked to one's self-interest. Second, many people's attitudes are strongly related to the views or concerns of salient social groups that they belong to or identify with (e.g., political parties, the middle class, or ethnic minorities). Third, people are often influenced by opinion leaders whom they respect, especially the nation's president. Fourth, some attitudes seem based on the expression of individuals' central values (e.g., individualism or equalitarianism); this value-expressive function of attitudes was discussed in Chapter 5. Other attitudes may be rooted in personality needs or motives (this seems to be particularly true of attitudes based on authoritarian tendencies or political intolerance). Finally, political history may help to shape attitudes, as in public reactions to economic recessions, wars, government scandals, hostage dramas, terrorist activities, and other foreign and domestic events.

ATTITUDES TOWARD CIVIL LIBERTIES

A particularly important area of political attitudes is people's views on civil rights—a topic so central to our democratic form of government that it is enshrined in the Bill of Rights. People's tolerance toward the expression of opposing points of view has been called "the pivotal dilemma of democracy in a pluralist society" (Marcus et al., 1995, p. 3). In the early 1950s, during the anticommunism witchhunt period fostered by Senator Joseph McCarthy, this topic was the subject of a classic study by Stouffer (1955). His findings demonstrated in great detail Americans' unwillingness to grant basic constitutional rights to avowed communists and to other dissenters such as atheists. Studying a careful probability sample of nearly 5,000 respondents, Stouffer showed that two-thirds to three-fourths of Americans would not allow communists to speak publicly and would favor tapping their telephone conversations and revoking their citizenship, and 90% would not allow them to teach in public schools. One-third of the respondents even favored jailing communists for their private beliefs—a far cry from the protections for unpopular beliefs supposedly guaranteed by the Bill of Rights!

To what extent has this public intolerance changed since the 1950s? One hopeful sign in Stouffer's study was that the well-educated young adult generation was much more tolerant of dissent than was the less-educated older generation. If people's tolerance does not change as they age, the process of generational replacement should automatically increase the overall level of public tolerance. In fact, some later studies confirmed this expectation. In the 1970s, nearly twice as many Americans were willing to grant constitutional rights to communists and to atheists as in the 1950s (Davis, 1975; Nunn, Crockett, & Williams, 1978), and the increase in tolerance continued at a slow pace in the 1980s and 1990s (Mueller, 1988; Page & Shapiro, 1992). Research shows that community leaders tend to be markedly more tolerant than the average citizen (Kinder, 1998), and young people, people who live in large cities, and those who have moved to a new community are also high in tolerance (Stephan & McMullen, 1982; Wilson, 1991, 1994).

However, some questions still remain. Because internal communism is no longer seen as such a sinister danger to our form of government, the apparent increased tolerance for communists may merely reflect the decreased threat of communism. This view suggests that Americans may merely have redirected their intolerance at other groups rather than becoming genuinely more tolerant. Sullivan, Piereson, and Marcus (1979) tested this notion by asking a probability sample of respondents who their least-liked group was (examples included communists, the Ku Klux Klan, the John Birch Society, the Black Panthers, and proabortionists), and then they determined tolerance toward that group. Findings from this methodological approach demonstrated that respondents were less tolerant toward their least-liked group than they were toward communists or atheists, though both tolerance figures were higher in the 1970s than Stouffer's data from the 1950s. For instance, only half of the respondents were willing to allow members of their least-liked groups to make a public speech, 40% favored tapping of their telephones, and 70% thought the group should be outlawed completely. The authors concluded that "although tolerance of communists and atheists has increased, the overall extent of tolerance may not have changed much" (p. 788). Not a heartening conclusion about the preservation of civil rights in America!

An intensive analysis of political tolerance by McClosky and Brill (1983) has shown that Americans express much higher levels of support for tolerance in the abstract than when they are asked about possible restrictions on specific groups or individuals. And they are even less tolerant of rights on "emerging issues" (e.g., abortion or sexual preference) than on well-established issues. Among the more-tolerant people in our society are most elites—those who are well-educated, well-informed, and politically active; people who are younger, less religious, more liberal religiously and politically; ones who are psychologically more secure and flexible; and those who have a strong commitment to democratic values (Sullivan & Transue, 1999). Among the least tolerant are advocates of "law and order," superpatriots, and foreign-policy hawks.

One hopeful finding is that people's actions are usually less intolerant than their attitudes (Kinder, 1998). Traumatic events, such as the World Trade Center destruction of September 2001, can shift many people's attitudes toward intolerance of group differences and willingness to sacrifice civil liberties in order to prevent more terrorism. However, a year after that attack, Americans' concern for not violating civil liberties had risen again to 62% of the populace—nearly twice the proportion who said they were willing to violate civil liberties (Carlson, 2002).

LIBERAL–CONSERVATIVE IDEOLOGY

One of the most basic aspects of people's political attitudes is their ideological viewpoint. We have discussed political ideology extensively in Chapter 7, but a few additional issues are important to consider here. The first issue is what people mean when they answer the poller's question about whether they consider themselves "liberal" or "conservative." When they are given an in-between option, about 30% to 40% of respondents typically choose it, and when they are asked a filter question such as "or haven't you thought much about this?", roughly one-third tend to agree that they haven't (Robinson & Fleishman, 1988). When asked a series of questions on different issues, many people give conservative answers on some and liberal answers on others. Following up this finding, Kerlinger (1984) did careful measurement work which concluded that liberalism and conservatism are two separate (and only somewhat negatively correlated) factors, rather than opposite ends of a single continuum.

Nevertheless, for respondents willing to classify themselves, you might assume that the liberal–conservative question would give very similar results to the question about

Democratic versus Republican party identification. However, data from the NES (2001) show that is not the case. For the past 60 years, the number of Americans stating a Democratic identification has almost always been at least 1.3 times the number of Republican identifiers, whereas since 1980 the number of self-reported conservatives has always been at least 1.5 times as high as the number calling themselves liberals. Thus, though the two measures are positively correlated, there are many people who respond inconsistently on them (i.e., conservative Democrats and liberal Republicans). Moreover, whereas party identification is the best predictor of actual voting, "self-identified liberals and conservatives differ more meaningfully and significantly on political issues than do self-identified Democrats and Republicans" (Robinson & Fleishman, 1988, p. 137).

Changes over time in the liberal–conservative balance in America have been the subject of much discussion and considerable misinformation. Over a 60-year period, it is clear that most social and political attitudes of Americans have moved in an increasingly liberal direction (*Gallup Report*, 1985, No. 241; Glenn, 1987; Smith, 1990b). Here are a few examples from these and other sources: In 1937 only 33% of the U.S. population said they would be willing to vote for a woman for president, whereas in 1999 92% said they would (*Gallup Poll Monthly*, 2000). In 1938, only 22% of Americans approved of married women holding a paid job, whereas in 1972 the figure was 65%, and by 1986 it had climbed to 78% (*Public Perspective*, 1997a). As recently as 1969, 68% of Americans said premarital sex was wrong, but this figure decreased to 39% by 1985 and remained at approximately that level through 2001 (Saad, 2001b). In 1969, only 4% of American adults reported having tried marijuana, whereas by 1999 the figure increased to 34% (Robison, 2002). In the 1950s, only 37% said they favored allowing an atheist to speak in their community, compared with 65% in 1985. As recently as 1973, only 34% of Americans favored a law that homeowners could not refuse to sell their house to someone because of the purchaser's race or color, but by 1996, 65% favored such a law. In 1977, 56% of the population endorsed homosexuals having equal rights in job opportunities, compared with 84% in 1996 (*Public Perspective*, 1997b). In contrast, a few issues have changed in a conservative direction, such as increases in support for capital punishment and being "tough on crime" (Flanagan & Longmire, 1996).

What about changes in *self-reported* liberalism or conservatism? Surprisingly, during a period when public attitudes toward many specific issues have become more liberal, an increasing percentage of Americans have been reporting themselves to be conservative. The balance of liberals and conservatives in the U.S. population was approximately equal from the 1930s through the 1960s, but by 1970 the balance changed sharply toward more conservatives, and this ratio continued through 2000 (see Figure 13–3). The picture in 1998 was representative, with 30% of a national sample rating themselves as conservative and 18% as liberal (a ratio of 1.7), whereas 28% described themselves as middle of the road (4 on a 1–7 scale), and 23% said they didn't know or hadn't thought about it. It has often been claimed that there was a strong trend toward more conservatism accompanying Ronald Reagan's election as president in 1980, but the major change occurred by 1970, and the conservative edge remained relatively stable after 1976 except for a short-lived spurt in conservative self-identification in 1994 (Robinson & Fleishman, 1988; National Election Studies, 2001).

Another question is this: What differences distinguish conservatives from liberals? People who call themselves conservatives are, in fact, more likely to take conservative stands on various issues, but on many issues the differences are quite small (Ladd, 1981; Robinson, 1984). Examples of issues on which the liberal–conservative difference in

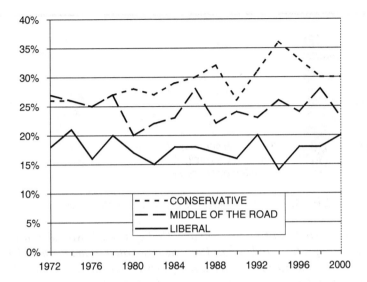

FIGURE 13–3 Trend in percentages of Americans who identified themselves as liberal, conservative, and middle of the road, 1972–2000. (Omitted are the 23% to 36% of respondents in various years who said they didn't know or hadn't thought about the topic.)

Source: Data are from the National Election Studies (2001). http://www.umich.edu/~nes.

agreement has usually been less than 10% include the following: The courts are not hard enough on criminals; divorce should be more difficult to obtain; the federal income tax is too high; and the U.S. should stay out of world affairs. Somewhat larger differences (less than 20%) have been found on these items: approval of the death penalty for murder; there should be laws against pornography; whites have a right to exclude blacks from their neighborhoods; and the country spends too much on solving urban problems. The few items with the largest differences between liberals and conservatives (more than 20%) generally are morality and lifestyle issues, such as approval of abortion, legalization of marijuana, and premarital sex. Even on these issues, the majority of both groups are often on the same side of the neutral point (Robinson, 1984). Moreover, there are usually much greater differences among demographic subgroups *within* the conservative camp or the liberal camp than *between* the two groups; for instance, differences between the most-educated and the least-educated conservatives on an issue like abortion or spending for space exploration may be as large as 40%—roughly twice as large as the difference between the average conservative and the average liberal (Ladd, 1981).

Ideological Conservatism but Operational Liberalism

An important point about ideological positions was made by Free and Cantril (1967). In their study of a national sample of over 3,000 respondents, they found that, ideologically, Americans tended to lean in a conservative direction. Using five questions on abstract, general views regarding federal interference in state and local matters, government regulation of business, local solutions of social problems, belief in economic opportunity in America, and belief in individual initiative, they constructed an index of **ideological**

Photograph courtesy of
Princeton University Archives.
Reprinted by permission.

Box 13–2   HADLEY CANTRIL, *Pioneer Survey Researcher*

Best known for his studies of public opinion, Hadley Cantril was also a researcher in perceptual psychology. Born in Utah in 1906, he graduated from Dartmouth College and received his Ph.D. from Harvard. After a few years of teaching, he joined the faculty of Princeton in 1936, later becoming chairman of the psychology department. He founded Princeton's Office of Public Opinion Research but left in 1955 to form the Institute for International Social Research. He died of a stroke in 1969.

Before World War II, Cantril was asked by President Franklin D. Roosevelt to assess Americans' feelings about potential U.S. involvement in the war, and later he advised both Eisenhower and Kennedy. His text Gauging Public Opinion *is a classic, and he wrote 17 other books and over 100 articles, including* The Invasion of Mars, *a study of panic reactions to Orson Welles' famous radio drama. He directed the Tensions Project of UNESCO, edited* Tensions That Cause Wars, *and conducted survey research in at least 14 nations, from Nigeria to Poland to Brazil.*

---

liberalism or conservatism. The results showed that the American public fell in the following categories:

Completely or predominantly liberal	16%
Middle of the road	34%
Completely or predominantly conservative	50%

However, the results were markedly different for an index of **operational** liberalism or conservatism, which involved attitudes toward five specific government programs—federal aid to education, Medicare, the federal low-rent housing program, urban renewal, and federal efforts to reduce unemployment and poverty. At this specific, or operational, level the public leaned strongly in the liberal direction:

Completely or predominantly liberal	65%
Middle of the road	21%
Completely or predominantly conservative	14%

When scores on these two scales were cross-tabulated, a fascinating picture emerged: 78% of the ideological middle-of-the-roaders and 46% of the ideological conservatives were operational *liberals*! These results demonstrate that New Deal-type government programs aiming at the welfare of all citizens have gained very wide public support, even among professed conservatives. The authors concluded that the operational dimension is "the most significant (one) from any functional point of view" (p. 50), for it indicates the kind of specific government programs that people will support.

In more recent years, the same general pattern holds true: Many ideological conservatives support government policies and programs that are liberal in nature, such as Social Security, Medicare, farm price supports, and pollution control. Even "welfare," which has recently become a pejorative term to Americans, is supported by a substantial majority of Americans if it is called "assistance to the poor" (Smith, 1987). In a national-sample study using open-ended questions about government social welfare programs, Feldman and Zaller (1992) found that people's abstract responses were mostly opposed to such programs, whereas their concrete responses were mostly favorable. Similarly, in a national telephone survey, Cantril and Cantril (1999) found that even those respondents who were "mostly critical of government" on the abstract level were heavily supportive of specific government activities, such as job training for low-income people, clean-air standards, or Head Start programs—69% of these government critics favored maintaining or increasing federal funding levels for at least 8 of 10 such activities. The combination of ideological conservatism and operational liberalism is especially clear in the following quotation from Ladd (1983):

> At the very moment three-fourths of the people are saying tax money spent for human services is poorly used, three-fourths are arguing that the federal government should provide medical care and legal assistance for everyone who can't afford them. While seven Americans in ten think government has gone too far in regulating economic life, the same proportion believes that government should make sure everyone has a good standard of living. Overwhelming majorities say federal spending is too high—but majorities just as big say even more should be spent for basic services like education and social security. (p. 2)

LEADING PUBLIC OPINION VERSUS FOLLOWING IT

We have previously mentioned at several points that public attitudes change from time to time in response to events. The growing acceptance over the years of operationally liberal government programs is one example of such attitude change. Another example is the frequent fluctuations in presidential popularity, and particularly the typical increases in the president's ratings after he takes some decisive action in international affairs.

As these examples show, the public is usually more concerned with reaching a goal (stopping a war, ending a recession, etc.) than with the methods whereby the goal is reached. Thus, as far as the public is concerned, the president has a rather wide latitude in choosing specific programs, as long as they seem to be directed toward the important goal of that period. Because of most people's lack of information, low level of involvement in specific issues, and eagerness to believe that progress is being made, the public will usually give a favorable rating to any newly-proposed presidential solution to national problems, even to programs that it had formerly rated unfavorably, such as greater recognition for Communist China, or war against another country such as the first President Bush's defense of Kuwait against Iraq (Zaller, 1992).

These conclusions are doubly true in the unfamiliar and mysterious (to most Americans) area of foreign affairs. Lipset (1966) illustrated this point with many examples from the Vietnam War era. During that period of national frustration and discontent, President Johnson was able to present clear-cut escalations of the conflict (e.g., extensions of U.S. bombing raids, mining of Haiphong harbor) as attempts to bring peace closer, and a majority of Americans accepted this rationale. In the long run, as American casualties climbed to painfully high levels, public opinion gradually shifted and produced pressures to end the war (Mueller, 1973). But in the short run at least, as Lipset (1966) stressed, the president can lead public opinion very effectively rather than following it:

> The opinion data indicate that national policy-makers, particularly the President, have an almost free hand to pursue any policy they think correct and get public support for it. (p. 20)

The same pattern seems to have occurred in President George W. Bush's proposed "war on terrorism" and invasions of Afghanistan and Iraq. Recent research studies have suggested that the end of the Cold War has given presidents even greater latitude than before to lead or manipulate public opinion (Shapiro & Jacobs, 2000). On the other hand, however, analysis of U.S. involvement in foreign conflicts since the Vietnam War shows that public opinion frequently sets limits or constraints on the policy options that leaders can consider in their decision-making (Sobel, 2001).

In domestic affairs as well, citizens are often ready to accept new and unfamiliar programs (Gallup, 1965). In fact, because of their lower degree of ideological commitment, the public is often way ahead of the politicians in this regard. Charles Farnsley, a U.S. Congressman and former mayor of Louisville, Kentucky, agreed with this view, as he stated in this backstage glimpse of political life (Farnsley, 1965):

> I found surveys particularly helpful, when I was Mayor, in overruling my advisors. Political advisors have a lot of stereotyped "don'ts": don't do thus and so; the public's against it; it'll be fatal to you if you do. But my surveys would frequently show me that such timidity and caution were unwarranted. The public was not only willing to go along with unorthodox and presumably politically dangerous actions, they were ready and eager for them. (p. 464)

However, it is not just the public at large that politicians have to be responsive to. As we have seen in this chapter and in Chapter 7, a large proportion of the mass public are so uninformed and uninvolved in public affairs that their views may be termed "nonattitudes" rather than consistent political beliefs and attitudes (Converse, 1974). Consequently, it is various "elite" segments of the populations, who have more clear-cut views on particular issues, that help to shape overall public opinion and influence public policy. Moreover, the political process involves the interactions of competing and cooperating *groups and organizations*, and the political attitudes of any individual are largely irrelevant unless they are expressed through group pressures (Goldner, 1971). Despite these qualifications, however, many studies of election campaigns have clearly demonstrated the value to candidates of reliable polling information about the current state of public opinion.

SUMMARY

Presidential approval ratings are the most familiar measure of public political attitudes. They tend to decline during a president's term in office, especially in response to economic recessions or international problems, but they often rise for a time after decisive presidential actions. Concerns of citizens about problems facing the country are a better index than presidential popularity because they help to identify the source of people's discontent or satisfaction. In successive eras, the most serious U.S. public concerns have been foreign affairs and war-peace issues from the late 1940s to the early 1960s, racial problems from 1963 to 1965, then the Vietnam War until the early 1970s, and economic worries almost continuously from 1974 until the World Trade Center destruction in 2001, when international anxieties again took center stage.

Another useful measure is the index of public trust in our government, which declined sharply and steadily from the late 1960s to a very low point in 1980, partially due to the Vietnam War and the impact of the Watergate scandal. It recovered less than half of its loss by the late 1980s, then dropped steeply to an all-time low in 1994, and again climbed back to its late-1980s level before the 2000 election. Among important American institutions, the military and organized religion have usually had the highest degree of public confidence in recent years, whereas big business, organized labor, and Congress have generally been near the bottom of the ratings. An important trend in measuring political attitudes is the recent development of standard social indicators of the quality of life, analogous to the familiar economic indicators such as the gross national product. Findings indicate a generally high level of satisfaction for most people in most areas of their personal lives, but their satisfaction with national affairs is highly sensitive to economic and international events. Accordingly, it hit its all-time low points during recessions in 1979 and 1992, and reached its peaks after the 1991 Persian Gulf military victory and during the economic boom of 1999.

Traditional patterns of political attitudes among population subgroups, based on Depression-era alignments, began to change rather markedly during the Eisenhower era of the 1950s. For instance, age differences and regional differences on many issues have decreased greatly. However, social class differences, which had diminished in the 1950s and 1960s, increased again beginning in the 1970s, with middle- and upper-income groups becoming much more strongly Republican than before.

Americans' attitudes about granting civil liberties to dissenters are not nearly as tolerant as the principles specified in the Bill of Rights, though they seem to have become somewhat more tolerant since the anticommunist scares of the 1950s. Over the past 60 years, the long-term trend of most social and political attitudes of Americans has moved in a strongly liberal direction, though since about 1970 attitudes on a few issues have become somewhat more conservative. Although more Americans espouse a conservative position than a liberal one on ideological issues, on operational questions concerning specific government programs they are generally liberal. The president can often lead public opinion very effectively rather than following it in his choice of specific programs and operational procedures, but the viewpoints expressed by pressure groups and organizations can have an influence on public policy.

▬ 14 ▬

Political Attitudes II: Voting

Democracy substitutes selection by the incompetent many for appointment by the corrupt few.—George Bernard Shaw.

Our government is a government of political parties under the guiding influence of public opinion. There does not seem to be any other method by which a representative government can function.—Calvin Coolidge.

I always voted at my party's call, and I never thought of thinking for myself at all.—W. S. Gilbert.

In this chapter we discuss two aspects of voting behavior: *individual* voting decisions and *aggregate* voting patterns. Because many of the demographic factors that influence voting behavior as well as political attitudes per se were examined in the preceding chapter, those factors are mentioned only briefly here. Instead, we focus on several other major determinants of individual voting decisions that have been discovered in a series of major election studies.

SOME DETERMINANTS OF INDIVIDUAL VOTING DECISIONS

Cross-Pressures

Historically, the first such factor to be analyzed came from the earliest large-scale scientific election study, conducted by researchers at Columbia University (Lazarsfeld et al., 1948). This research on the 1940 election, reported in a landmark volume called *The People's Choice*, was a **panel study** in which 600 residents of Erie County, Ohio, were each interviewed seven times between May and November to investigate factors involved in changing voting preferences. (Interestingly, and unexpectedly, nearly 70% of the respondents showed *no changes* in voting intentions from start to finish of the study; and similar results have been found for elections in the 1990s—Erikson & Wlezien, 1999.)

Because Lazarsfeld was a sociologist, he adopted a sociological approach in this research, focusing primarily on demographic groups. Predictions of the respondents' voting patterns were made from a score called the Index of Political Predisposition (IPP), based on a combination of three demographic variables—religion, social class, and urban or rural residence. At the various levels of this index, the proportion of respondents voting Democratic ranged from 26% at one extreme to 83% at the other, indicating a strong relationship of the index to voting decisions. (Although most demographic variables no longer relate as closely to voting behavior as they did in the 1930s and 1940s, it is still possible to make reasonably accurate forecasts of election outcomes based solely on demographic groupings—Axelrod, 1986. For instance, in presidential elections of the 1990s, African Americans, Hispanics, and Jews voted heavily Democratic, as did Catholics and women to a lesser degree; whereas Protestants, especially fundamentalist Protestants, and Southerners tended to vote Republican—Erikson & Tedin, 2001.)

In the study by Lazarsfeld et al. (1948), **cross-pressures** were defined as contradictory voting predispositions on the three variables (e.g., being a middle-class Catholic, or a working-class rural resident). Respondents who were under such conflicting pressures were also found to fluctuate in their voting intentions, to show less interest and attention to the campaign, to be more influenced by other persons' views, and to reach their voting decision later than other citizens. These results of political cross-pressures, however defined, still seem generally to hold true (Kinder, 1998), though cross-pressured voters do not necessarily display lower turnout than other voters (Pool, Abelson, & Popkin, 1964). In every presidential election since 1950, the percentage of cross-pressured voters has been at least 12%, and sometimes as high as 25%–30% (Lawrence, 2001).

Personal Influences

Following the Erie County study, a very similar panel study of the 1948 election was conducted by the same research group in Elmira, New York (Berelson et al., 1954). Here a major variable of interest was the personal influence stemming from the voting intentions of the respondents' closest friends and family members. The investigators found this kind of influence to be strongly associated with the person's own voting intentions (Kitt & Gleicher, 1950). For instance, in this heavily Republican area, the following relationships were found between the voting intentions of the respondent and those of his or her three closest friends:

3 friends Republican	93% intended to vote Republican			
2 Republican, 1 Democratic	68%	"	" "	"
2 Democratic, 1 Republican	50%	"	" "	"
3 friends Democratic	19%	"	" "	"

The same kind of pattern held for differences of voting intentions between the respondent and his or her immediate family and changes in the respondent's voting intentions between June and August. In cases where all of the family agreed with the respondent, 80% to 90% held to their original voting intention in August. On the other extreme, where all family members disagreed with the respondent's voting plans, nearly half changed their intentions by August.

There are similar findings about the importance of personal communication in more recent elections. For instance, Huckfeldt and Sprague (1993) showed that presidential voting intentions were influenced by conversations with spouses, and also by discussion with nonspouses who were strongly interested in the campaign if the respondent was relatively uninterested.

Party Identification

Party identification as a determinant of voting decisions has been emphasized in the highly influential series of studies conducted by the SRC at the University of Michigan (Campbell et al., 1954, 1960)—a much more psychological analysis than that of the Columbia University group. Measurement of party identification does not involve official party membership, registration, or campaign activity, but depends entirely on the

Photograph courtesy of Angus Campbell.
Reprinted by permission.

Box 14–1   ANGUS CAMPBELL, *Trail-Blazing Survey Researcher*

Director of the Survey Research Center at the University of Michigan for over 20 years, Angus Campbell was a pioneer in attitude and opinion research. Born in Indiana in 1910, he attended the University of Oregon and took his Ph.D. at Stanford in 1936. After teaching at Northwestern, he assisted Rensis Likert in the Division of Program Surveys of the U.S. Department of Agriculture during World War II, and moved with him to Michigan when the Survey Research Center was founded in 1946. In 1970 he succeeded Likert as director of the Institute for Social Research, and he continued as an active researcher until his death in 1980.

Best known for his research on political attitudes and voting, Campbell led survey studies of U.S. elections beginning in 1948, resulting in pace-setting volumes such as The Voter Decides, The American Voter, *and* Elections and the Political Order. *Toward the end of his career, he published influential work on racial attitudes and the quality of life. His many achievements were honored by his receipt of Distinguished Contribution Awards from both the American Association for Public Opinion Research, and the American Psychological Association.*

respondent's self-classification as a strong or not-so-strong Republican or Democrat or as an Independent. So measured, party identification is quite a stable personal characteristic (e.g., a correlation of about +0.85 over a 2-year interval), and the changes that do occur are mostly ones in and out of the Independent category rather than from one major party to the other (Converse, 1964; Converse & Markus, 1979). Among major-party identifiers, 82% retained the same party identification in three interviews between 1956 and 1960; however, by contrast, only 40% of Independents kept the same self-classification over the 4-year period.

In recent years, party identification has become somewhat less stable, but it still remains a key factor in voting (Kinder, 1998). Historically, ever since the end of World War II, more Americans have stated a Democratic identification than a Republican one. Important political variables such as party identification have been tracked at every biannual national election since 1952 by the University of Michigan's SRC. Later the SRC established the National Election Studies (NES), which is the premier survey research program on political behavior, administered by a prestigious nationwide group of academic researchers. On the NES 7-point scale, the "party ID" margin in large national samples in presidential election years has varied from a 2-to-1 Democratic advantage in 1964 (52% to 25%) to an 8% edge in 1988 (W. Miller, 2002). (The Gallup Poll uses a simpler measure, which does not consider people who "lean" toward one party or the other as party identifiers; that measure produces data that parallel the NES measure, but generally with a somewhat smaller

Democratic edge—cf. Saad, 1999). Surprisingly, the fluctuations in the party identification measure have not at all paralleled fluctuations in the electorate's self-reported liberalism or conservatism (Erikson & Tedin, 2001). Despite the importance of party identification in voting, other factors are also important, and consequently actual voting does not always closely follow party identification, as discussed later. (If it did, there would have been no Republican presidents since World War II.)

In elections of the 1950s and 1960s, party identification was found to be more highly correlated with voting behavior than any other factor studied, such as attitudes toward campaign issues or toward the candidates (Declercq, Hurley, & Luttbeg, 1975). For instance, in 1952, party identification correlated nearly +0.6 with presidential choice, whereas the other attitude measures correlated only in the range of +0.2 to +0.5 (Campbell & Stokes, 1959). In most later elections, party identification has continued to correlate very highly with voting behavior. Exceptions occurred in two presidential elections, 1964 and 1972, when the correlation was substantially lower (around +0.5), but in the 1980s the relationship climbed above +0.7 (W. Miller, 1991), and it has remained high since then.

Party loyalty is the percentage of party identifiers who actually vote for their party's candidate. The 1950s saw about 83% of major-party identifiers voting for their party's presidential candidate, and those were the Eisenhower years when Democratic defectors were relatively numerous (Campbell et al., 1960). During later decades, party loyalty decreased to a level below 70% in the Reagan elections of the 1980s, and then increased to about 76% by 1996. In elections for Congress and other less-important offices, party loyalty has usually been even higher, although roughly paralleling the presidential-year levels; its peak was about 85% in the 1958 congressional election (Jacobson, 2001). A persistent pattern ever since the 1950s has been that Republican identifiers display greater party loyalty and turnout than do Democratic identifiers (W. Miller, 1991).

One important change in the pattern of party identification has been a substantial increase in the number of citizens who identify themselves as **Independents**. This figure rose from about 26% in the 1950s, to about 36% in the 1970s and 1980s, and exceeded 40% in 2000 (W. Miller, 2002). This group can be divided into those who admit "leaning" toward Republicans or Democrats and the "pure" Independents (currently about 12%—NES, 2001). The "leaners" are apparently covert partisans because they act and vote very much like party identifiers, whereas the "pure" independents are less well-informed and less likely to vote, and they swing widely in their voting from one election to another in accordance with short-term forces (Kinder, 1998). The increase in these politically uninvolved "pure" Independents parallels and reflects the rise of disillusionment and lack of trust in our government and institutions, described in the preceding chapter.

A second major change is in **ticket-splitting** (an individual not voting a straight party ticket for all offices), which also increased sharply to 25%–30% of voters in the 1970s and 1980s (Fiorina, 1992), though it has since dropped below 20% (NES, 2001). As a result, amazing proportions of all congressional districts elected a congressperson of the opposite party from the party that won their presidential vote—45% in 1972 and 44% in 1984 (Wattenberg, 1987). These processes have gone so far as to lead some analysts to refer to the "decomposition" or "disintegration" of the party system (Burnham, 1970, 1985). Although weakened, however, party identification still remains the strongest predictor of voters' presidential choice in most elections (Keith et al., 1992; W. Miller & Shanks, 1996).

Candidate Images

Next to party identification, the candidate's characteristics can also have a major impact, particularly in certain elections. In 1960, Kennedy's Catholic religion became the most crucial issue of the campaign, and studies estimated that about 4 1/2 million anti-Catholic voters switched to Nixon whereas about 3 million normally Republican Catholics voted for Kennedy (Pool et al., 1964). The public's personal images of Barry Goldwater in 1964, George McGovern in 1972, and Jimmy Carter in 1980 all had negative values on various important characteristics, which contributed substantially to their electoral defeats (Field & Anderson, 1969; A. Miller et al., 1976). (A similar event occurred in Britain's 1983 election when the Labour Party under an unpopular leader, Michael Foot, lost to the Conservatives and Margaret Thatcher, even though her party got only 44% of the vote—Worcester, 1984.)

Some election studies have compared the relative contribution of party identification, candidate images, and issue positions in individuals' voting decisions, using techniques such as multiple regression analysis. Whereas research on earlier elections showed party identification to be the strongest factor, in 1964 and again in 1972, when negative images of a candidate were prominent, a measure of candidate images was the best predictor of people's votes (RePass, 1971; Declercq et al., 1975). In rather similar analyses for 1980 and 1984, the candidate characteristic of presidential approval was the strongest predictor of voting decisions (Wattenberg, 1987).

Contrary to Converse's (1964) conclusion that only the less-educated and less politically-involved citizens focus on candidate personal characteristics, later research has shown that well-educated voters give more attention to candidate characteristics (Glass, 1985). Their judgments tend to be centered on performance-relevant traits such as competence, integrity, and reliability; and these judgments often weigh strongly on their voting decisions (A. Miller, Wattenberg, & Malanchuk, 1986; Mondak, 1995b; W. Miller & Shanks, 1996). The greatly increased emphasis on candidate characteristics instead of party positions in campaigns over a 30-year period is dramatically shown in Figure 14–1.

An interesting group of studies has demonstrated how people's images of political candidates can influence their perceptions of the candidates' issue positions (Granberg & Brent, 1980; Judd et al., 1983). Their findings support the principles of Heider's (1958) balance theory and also of social judgment theory (Sherif & Hovland, 1961) concerning the assimilation or contrast of persuasive messages. In all of the presidential elections that were studied, American voters tended to assimilate the issue positions of their preferred candidate and preferred party—that is, they perceived them as being closer to their own views than they actually were. For example, an environmentalist who favored Reagan for president would typically perceive Reagan's stand on issues as being more proenvironmental (i.e., closer to the voter's own position) than it actually was, as objectively measured. Results showed that people also contrasted the positions of their nonpreferred presidential candidates, but less than they assimilated the position of their preferred candidate. As social judgment theory would predict, voters who were very involved in and concerned about an election campaign showed especially strong tendencies to assimilate the positions of their preferred candidate.

Most research that has examined candidate images has considered perceived personality traits such as competence, honesty, and warmth; but some research has also studied the emotions that candidates arouse in voters (e.g., hope, pride, anger, or fear). These studies found that, unlike personality trait ratings, summary scores of good feelings toward a candidate and bad feelings toward the same candidate were nearly independent, indicating that candidates often arouse simultaneous conflicting emotions in voters. Moreover, the summary affect measures strongly predicted voting preferences, and their contribution was greater than and independent of trait ratings (Abelson et al., 1982; Kinder, 1994). This research is consistent with other findings about the relation of cognitive and affective judgments (Zajonc, 1980—see Chapter 8), and it provides a new methodological approach for studying candidate images.

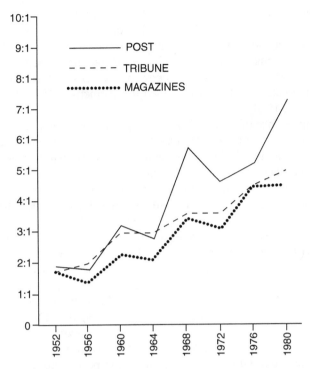

FIGURE 14–1 Ratio of mentions of candidates to mentions of parties in campaign stories in the *Washington Post, Chicago Tribune*, and three news magazines, *Newsweek, Time*, and *U.S. News and World Report*, from 1952 to 1980.

Source: Wattenberg (1984, p. 94). Reprinted by permission of the publishers from THE DECLINE OF AMERICAN POLITICAL PARTIES, by Martin P. Wattenberg, Cambridge, Mass.: Harvard University Press, Copyright © 1984 by the President and Fellows of Harvard College.

Issue Positions

If you ask them, most citizens and most politicians will tell you that "the issues" are the key factor in people's voting decisions, but such self-reports have doubtful validity because respondents may just be giving the socially desirable or expected answer. In fact, the early election studies disputed the importance of issues in determining people's voting behavior (e.g., Campbell et al., 1960). However, since 1964 that picture has changed quite markedly.

In the 1964 election, Goldwater's strongly conservative stand on issues gave a marked ideological tone to the campaign and was clearly a factor in his low vote total (Field & Anderson, 1969). In 1968, George Wallace's third-party candidacy stressed racist and nationalist issues, and he won 13% of the total vote—enough to reverse the winning party in eight states and give the presidency to Richard Nixon instead of Hubert Humphrey (Mitofsky, 1969). In 1972 McGovern stressed the issues of the Vietnam War, urban unrest, and government aid to the poor; and in this election for the first time people's issue orientation had as much impact on their vote as did party identification (Declercq et al., 1975).

The cumulative effect of these three elections introduced a "new era of issue politics" in America (A. Miller et al., 1976; Nie et al., 1979), and this trend has continued, particularly in Reagan's strongly ideological campaign in 1980 (Abramson, Aldrich, & Rohde, 1982; Aldrich, Sullivan, & Borgida, 1989; MacDonald, Rabinowitz, & Listhaug, 1995). In turn, this polarization of the electorate on important current issues seems to have contributed substantially to the soaring public distrust of government—a feeling that politicians are apt to be dishonest and unconcerned about the common citizen's welfare. This is a paradoxical drawback not anticipated by those who called for distinctive ideological stands in party platforms (A. Miller, 1974).

The central importance of economic issues in presidential campaigns has been dramatized by the creation of the **misery index**—the sum of the unemployment rate plus the inflation rate. Carter popularized the concept in his 1976 campaign criticisms of Republican handling of the economy, and Reagan turned it against him very effectively in 1980. In the 1984 and 1988 elections, a major factor in the Republican victories was considered to be the low level of the misery index; and similar relationships have been found in elections in many other industrialized nations (Lipset, 1982; *Gallup Report*, 1988, No. 278).

Emphasis on economic issues, such as the misery index, suggests that voters primarily follow their own self-interest and "vote their pocketbook," thus throwing out the incumbent party whenever times are bad and returning it to office when times are good. At the aggregate level, this generalization about the crucial importance of a prosperous economy has held true in every U.S. presidential election since 1970, except for the disputed election of 2000, when Al Gore lost to George W. Bush by a hairsbreadth (Brewer, 2002). Thus it appears that voters do give strong weight to the *overall performance* of the administration— more so than to the fine-grain details of campaign issues and policies. Fiorina (1981) termed this **retrospective voting**, and concluded that peace, prosperity, and civil rights were the aspects of government performance that voters considered most strongly.

However, rather than voting primarily in terms of their own individual pocketbook situation (e.g., personal unemployment), citizens have been found to vote more closely in accordance with their view of the national economic conditions—an outcome that has been termed **sociotropic voting** (Kinder & Kiewiet, 1981; Markus, 1988). Some of the evidence on this topic has come from studies of **symbolic politics**, which show that individual self-interest (e.g., having a relative in the Vietnam War, or an unemployed family member) is usually less important in people's policy preferences and voting decisions than are long-standing symbolic attitudes such as anticommunism or liberal–conservative ideology (Sears et al., 1980; Sears & Citrin, 1985). This conclusion brings our discussion of determinants of voting full-circle because, for most voters, party identification is one of their long-term symbolic attachments.

EFFECTS OF POLITICAL PERSUASION ON VOTING

Another major element influencing voting decisions is all of the persuasive communication that abounds during an election campaign—political propaganda, candidate oratory, editorials, personal appeals from acquaintances, and local "grassroots" political activity. In Chapter 9 on Communication of Attitudes and Opinions, we have discussed the general findings concerning persuasive communication. Here we consider just a few of the most salient influences which affect political voting decisions.

Most studies of electioneering propaganda have shown relatively little resulting attitude change—often no change at all (Kinder & Sears, 1985). However, this finding does not mean that propaganda is ineffective, and it can have many effects besides directly influencing voting decisions (Iyengar & Simon, 2000). In many cases the most important effect of political persuasion may be **reinforcement**—that is, strengthening people's already existing attitudes (Mendelsohn & O'Keefe, 1976). In occasional elections, like 1980, the number of undecided voters remains unusually large through most of the campaign and even right up to election day, and then persuasive messages may have an unusually great effect (Wattenberg, 1984). In other cases, less than half of the change in partisan preference from one election to the next may actually occur during the campaign period (Blumler & McQuail, 1969). Thus a major function of campaign propaganda may be to support people's already changed attitudes and to extend the amount of change where possible.

Problems in Political Persuasion

For persuasive arguments to have any effect on attitudes and/or behavior, they must first be received and then accepted, at least to some extent; and both of these processes pose problems for the political communicator.

Reception of persuasive arguments is a problem mainly because of low levels of public exposure and attention to political information. As we have pointed out in Chapter 7, many citizens are political "know-nothings," and most of the rest are relatively uninterested in political issues. As a result, most people simply do not "catch" the available political information, even when it is presented in a highly novel or dramatic way.

Another potential problem in the reception of political arguments is people's general tendency to expose themselves selectively to communicators and channels of information with whom they already tend to agree. As we have discussed in Chapter 9, this effect seems to be largely due to people following customary and convenient modes of information exposure, rather than to any strongly motivated search for supportive ideas or avoidance of contradictory ideas (Sears & Freedman, 1967). In recent elections, campaign managers have combated selective-exposure tendencies by purchasing time for short 30-second or even 10- or 15-second campaign "ads" in popular prime-time shows. Thus it is almost impossible to avoid exposure to many campaign messages, but the public's low level of interest and attention still pose problems for reception of their content.

Acceptance of persuasive arguments, once they are received, is also a problem for the political communicator. If individuals are committed to their party identification, or have strong loyalties to racial, religious, or ethnic groups, or see clear bases of economic self-interest for their views, it is unlikely that contrary political arguments will be effective in changing their attitudes or votes. Longitudinal panel studies of both U.S. and British election campaigns have shown that a large majority of the public—as much as 80% in some elections—have made up their minds how to vote before the formal campaign even starts. In most elections no more than 10% of citizens change their voting preferences from one side to the other during the campaign—the other changers move from undecided to some candidate preference, or vice versa (Lazarsfeld et al., 1948; Benham, 1965; Blumler & McQuail, 1969). However, it is also true that most people are not strongly committed to any position on most political issues (Converse, 1964). Thus, if a clear and effective argument can be presented to them on any given issue, it may be easy to sway their attitude—and even their vote, if the issue is an important one.

The result of the preceding factors is that in elections where people's enduring commitments are relevant, political propaganda generally serves merely to reinforce their preexisting attitudes. But in elections where enduring commitments are not called into play, attitudes and votes are more labile, and political persuasion may have major effects. This is especially true in nonpartisan and primary elections, in which party identification does not provide a guide for voting. It is also applicable to partisan elections in which economic, racial, or religious issues are not centrally involved or where the candidates have taken "me-too" positions.

Photograph courtesy of David Sears.
Reprinted by permission.

Box 14–2   DAVID SEARS, *Authority on Political Psychology*

Widely known for his research on political and racial attitudes, David Sears grew up in California, received his B.A. from Stanford, and earned his Ph.D. at Yale in 1962. He then became a faculty member at UCLA, where he still remains, having served as Professor of Psychology and Political Science and as Dean of Social Sciences. He has been honored by election as a member of the American Academy of Arts and Sciences and as president of the International Society of Political Psychology.

Sears' books include Public Opinion, Political Cognition, Racialized Politics, *the* Handbook of Political Psychology, *and a widely used textbook in social psychology. He has also authored or co-authored chapters on political behavior in two successive editions of* The Handbook of Social Psychology. *This chapter discusses his work on political attitudes and voting; previous chapters have referred to his research on political persuasion and on selective exposure to information, and in Chapter 16 we describe his studies of symbolic racism.*

The greatest amount of attitude change in national election campaigns occurs in individuals who have a relatively weak party identification (Abramson, 1983). It also occurs among people with a relatively low level of interest in the campaign and a resulting low level of exposure to political propaganda. Thus, surprisingly, the amount of attitude change is often *negatively* related to amount of exposure to the mass media (Dreyer, 1971).

Some interesting research findings on the effects of *particular kinds* of influences are presented in the following pages.

Campaign Expenditures

"Money is the mother's milk of politics," according to a well-known politician. The importance of money to the political process is evident in the huge amounts that are spent for campaigns. The 2000 presidential and congressional campaign cost about $3 billion. In it, more than $1.2 billion was spent by the two major political parties, about $700 million by the Republicans and about $500 million by the Democrats. Of these totals, George W. Bush raised $194 million alone, and Al Gore took in $132 million (La Raja, 2002). In addition, "outside" political-interest groups, ranging from the National Rifle Association to the trucking industry to the Sierra Club, dedicated huge amounts of money to running purported "issue" ads, beyond their direct support for candidates. To keep these figures in perspective, the nation's leading commercial advertisers, General Motors and Procter &

Gamble, each spent more than $3 billion in 2001 to advertise its products (*Adage.com*, 2003).

Campaign expenditures by candidates for the U.S. Senate and House of Representatives have escalated dramatically in recent years. The average amount spent by a candidate in a House race in 1998 was over $700,000, and candidates in close races each spent an average of about $1.5 million (La Raja, 2002). Senate races are much more expensive. As of 2000, the record for spending in one campaign for the U.S. Senate was held by Jon Corzine, who spent over $60 million to win a Senate seat from New Jersey—more than $37 for every vote that he received (*Time*, 2000; Abramson, Aldrich, & Rohde, 2003). Special-interest political action committees (PACs) gave about $220 million to candidates for the U.S. House and Senate in the 1998 election—$45 million from labor unions, $144 million from corporations and trade associations, and $30 million from other issue-oriented PACs (Stanley & Niemi, 2000). A large portion of these campaign expenditures go for TV commercials, which we discuss in the next section.

As a general rule, the bigger spender in each congressional or U.S. Senate race is highly likely to be elected (Jacobson, 2001). The number of exceptions is few, but even some rich candidates who poured millions of dollars into their own campaigns have lost. Having the highest campaign budget is also usually crucial for the several candidates in presidential primary elections (Grush, 1980; Mutz, 1995). Because most of the candidates who campaign in open-seat races are relatively unfamiliar to most voters, these results support Zajonc's (1968a) theory of the effects of repeated exposure to previously unfamiliar stimuli (discussed in Chapter 8). On the level of individual voter attitudes toward candidates, similar exposure effects have been found for the amount of exposure to political advertising (Atkin & Heald, 1976). However, repetitive political advertising is likely to be more successful in changing voting intentions in low-involvement elections such as local or state legislature races, but not very effective in high-involvement elections such as presidential campaigns (Kinder, 1998).

Television

One of the main effects of TV coverage of elections has been to make the candidates' personality and "image" more crucial factors in the campaign (Wattenberg, 1984; Keeter, 1987). Since its first large-scale use in the 1952 presidential election, television political advertising has leaped to a total of almost one million political ads in 2000, with broadcasting costs of about half a billion dollars—just for presidential, Senate, and House candidates alone (Franz & Goldstein, 2002). This approach is clearly the most efficient way of reaching a large proportion of the electorate, but there are conflicting views about its effects.

In Chapter 9 we briefly summarized the research findings about television's impact on political information as well as on political attitudes and voting behavior. Starting in the 1960s, most researchers supported the *minimal effects* model, but more recent evidence indicates that TV and campaigns in general can have *powerful effects under limiting conditions* (Iyengar & Simon, 2000). On the minimalist side, television viewing typically adds only a marginal amount to citizens' political knowledge during campaigns (e.g., Patterson, 1980). A major reason that it is uninformative about the issues of the campaign is that it focuses very largely on the candidates' personal style and on trivia such as campaign tactics and blunders, rather than on important ideological and policy positions of the parties and the candidates. Also, by constantly presenting the latest poll standings and emphasizing who is ahead in the race, television campaign coverage has justly earned its description as "horse-race journalism" (Arterton, 1984; Stovall & Solomon, 1984). In the words of one research report (Patterson & McClure, 1976), the networks

> devote most of their election coverage to the trivia of political campaigning that make for flashy pictures. Hecklers, crowds, motorcades, balloons, rallies and gossip—these are the regular subjects of network campaign stories. (p. 22)

Yet recent research points out that citizens do gain useful information from television, especially when political campaigns are hard-fought and when the candidates' actions and personality traits seem relevant to the issues that voters care about (Brians & Wattenberg, 1996; Popkin, 1996; Kahn & Kenny, 1997).

Attitude change resulting from televised political ads is mostly limited to undecided voters with a low interest in the campaign and a high level of customary television usage (e.g., Blumler & McQuail, 1969; Patterson, 1980). Atkin et al. (1973) found that a large number of TV ads for a candidate produced greater viewer *exposure*, apparently overcoming any tendencies toward selective exposure. However, the quantitative frequency of advertising did not influence viewer *attention* levels; instead, attention was related to the ads' qualitative characteristics, such as informative or entertainment value. These same qualitative factors influenced voting intentions also, particularly among undecided voters. More than half of them reported that the political ads for their chosen candidate helped them reach their decision, and many also mentioned the other candidates' ads as a factor weighing *against* them (in agreement with the findings of Raj, 1982). As a result of findings like these, media consultants have spent great effort and expense to make their political ads entertaining as well as sharply focused on a single issue or emotion that they want voters to absorb about their candidate.

Another key process by which campaign ads and news influence voter attitudes is by *priming* the topics that audiences will consider important, or *agenda-setting*, as we have discussed in Chapters 9 and 13 (Dearing & Rogers, 1996; McCombs & Reynolds, 2002). For instance, in the last week of the 1980 election between Carter and Reagan, the media focused heavily on the unresolved situation of American hostages being held by Iran, and this was a major factor leading to a massive shift in people's voting intentions, from an election that was "too close to call" to a severe loss for Carter (*Public Opinion*, 1980/1981, No. 6; Iyengar & Kinder, 1987). Similarly, in cases where TV commentaries are one-sided, they have been found to produce several percentage points of opinion change (Page et al., 1987). The greatest overall effects of television exposure might be expected to come from dramatic events with very high viewership, such as the "great debates" between presidential candidates. The first such debates between Kennedy and Nixon in 1960 reached a huge audience (55% or more of the adult population), but this was partly because they were broadcast by all three television networks; in one city where an alternative TV program was also on the air the debate audience was reduced to 35%—still an exceptionally high figure (Katz & Feldman, 1962). The candidate debates in later presidential elections were watched by smaller audiences, and research showed that their main effect was to reinforce the preexisting preferences of viewers (Kinder & Sears, 1985). Nevertheless, key events in each series of debates, involving gaffes or weaknesses by a candidate, were given heavy negative publicity by the media and were often cited as being crucial to the final election outcome. For instance, in September of 2000, Gore was slightly ahead in the preelection polls until his weak performance in his first debate with Bush led to a reversal of the lead (Abramson et al., 2003).

Other instances of TV's political power can also be cited. Recently, televised facial expressions of political leaders have been found to influence the attitudes and emotional responses of viewers, so news departments' choices of which film clips to show can potentially affect audience reactions (Lanzetta et al., 1985). Rather similarly, studies of network news programs noted that the anchor of one network (Peter Jennings of ABC) smiled more when referring to President Reagan than when mentioning his 1984 campaign opponent, Walter Mondale. Surprisingly, this subtle and probably unconscious cue was found to be significantly related to the presidential votes of viewers of that network's news programs (Mullen et al., 1986). Although this particular election outcome was not close, the researchers raised a provocative question: Can a newscaster's smile elect a president?

Further evidence of behavioral effects of TV on voting can be seen in the impact of negative, attack, or "mud-slinging" ads, which have comprised as much as 70% of the TV ads run by political parties in some recent election campaigns (Franz & Goldstein, 2002). Research has shown that attack ads can be quite effective, particularly if they attack the opponent on issues rather than on personal characteristics, and if they come from a source supposedly independent of the attacking candidate (Garramone, 1985; Roddy & Garramone, 1988). These studies also show that it is vital to rebut attack ads, and that the rebuttals decrease support for the attacker. Attack ads are most effective with independents or uninvolved voters, but among strong partisans of the attacked candidate they may boomerang and create reactance (Merritt, 1984). Despite their effectiveness as a propaganda tool, attack ads can also reduce voter *turnout*, particularly among independents and uninvolved citizens—in effect, people seem to say "a plague on both your houses" (Ansolabehere & Iyengar, 1995; Houston, Doan, & Roskos-Ewoldsen, 1999; Kahn & Kenny, 1999). However, some studies have disputed these conclusions (e.g., Freedman & Goldstein, 1999; Lau et al., 1999; Vavreck, 2000; Wattenberg, 2002), so the effects of negative political ads are still an unresolved topic for research.

Newspapers

Americans got most of their campaign information from newspapers until television was introduced following World War II. Since then, newspaper reading in the U.S. has declined, especially among young adults (Robinson, 1980), and the public's increasing trust in television as a news source made it the preferred political news medium by the 1970s. However, as we discussed in Chapter 9, people's knowledge of current affairs and politics is more closely related to newspaper reading than to television news viewing (Robinson & Davis, 1990; Erikson & Tedin, 2001). There is also research evidence that newspapers have a greater agenda-setting effect than television, that they influence audience attitudes more, and that they are particularly influential on local issues (Palmgreen & Clarke, 1977; Patterson, 1980). People tend to rely on newspapers more for information on complex topics, and newspaper readers pay less attention to political candidates' personal traits than do TV viewers (Keeter, 1987).

Concerning influence on voting, newspapers have a historical tradition of backing their preferred candidates with editorial endorsements and even, at times, with slanted news coverage. In contrast, until 1987, the FCC's "fairness doctrine" required U.S. television and radio stations to give roughly equal coverage to both sides of controversial issues, and this tradition still persists in TV's general avoidance of candidate endorsements. Research has found that, although respondents typically rank television as their most important source of campaign news, they are more likely to *vote* in accordance with their newspaper's election preference than with their impressions from TV (Robinson, 1972). This effect may have played an important role in the very close 1968 election, for about 80% of the nation's newspapers were pro-Nixon. In an analysis that held other influential factors constant, Robinson (1972) concluded that the pro-Nixon newspaper endorsements had swayed about 3% of the overall vote to Nixon—enough to give him the election, since his winning margin was only 1% of the total vote.

Studies of newspaper editorials in other elections have reached similar conclusions about their potentially crucial influence, especially in local elections (Erikson, 1976; Scarrow & Borman, 1979; Coombs, 1981). Much of the effect of editorials or other one-sided commentaries is due to the way in which they *frame* a particular issue—i.e., which of its many possible features are emphasized or deemphasized in discussing it (Kinder, 1998).

Personal Contact

In Chapter 9 we discussed general findings about the persuasive effects of personal communication. In the area of voting, some researchers have claimed that personal contact is a more effective influence on political decisions than any of the mass media (e.g., Katz & Lazarsfeld, 1955), whereas others have disputed that conclusion (e.g., Mendelsohn & O'Keefe, 1976). The original study of this topic (Lazarsfeld et al., 1948) found that less than half of the respondents mentioned personal contact as a campaign influence, and only one-fourth mentioned it as the most important factor. Yet some studies that have compared specific media exposure to political topics, such as watching presidential debates, with personal discussion of them have found the personal interaction to be a stronger influence on people's understanding of the campaign and their voting decisions (McLeod et al., 1979). Such discussions are very often held with like-minded individuals, and so they may serve more to reinforce existing voting intentions than to change them (Deutschmann, 1962). Young first-time voters are particularly likely to rely on personal sources of information (O'Keefe, 1973), and people who interact more with their friends and neighbors are more likely to vote (Knack, 1992).

In politics, **mobilization** is the term used for inducing people to participate in the political process, and much of it is accomplished through personal contact. In recent national elections, about one-fourth of potential voters have been contacted by party workers in person or by phone to discuss the election and urge participation (Rosenstone & Hansen, 1993). Several studies have shown clear-cut effects of such personal contact. Rossi and Cutright (1961) found that contacts by political workers had only a slight effect on voting in presidential elections, but they were absolutely crucial to the outcome of primary elections and very important in local partisan elections. Both field experiments and national survey findings have shown that *turnout* on election day was markedly higher for voters contacted by telephone or in person than for voters who received only a mailed appeal to vote or ones who were not contacted at all (e.g., Yalch, 1976; Adams & Smith, 1980; Abramson et al., 2003; but see Gerber & Green, 2001, for a methodological objection).

Dramatic support for the effectiveness of personal contact was found in a careful experimental test by Kraut and McConahay (1973). Exposure to a short political-opinion interview, without any appeals to vote, more than doubled the voting turnout rate at a primary election held 2 weeks later. Even more surprising, the effect persisted strongly to another primary election 4 months after the interview, in which turnout was still 60% above that of the uninterviewed control group. Another study found that people who had taken part in several lengthy research interviews were more likely to vote than those who had been surveyed only once—that is, several interviews had a cumulative effect on turnout (Traugott & Katosh, 1979).

These research findings corroborate political lore about the importance of canvassing to get out the vote, and they suggest a potent method of increasing citizen involvement in politics (see Figure 14–2). As a related point, some authors have explained the major

FIGURE 14–2
A way to increase citizen involvement.

decline in U.S. voter turnout (decreasing from a high of 63% of the voting-age population in 1960 down to 51% in 2000) as being largely due to a drop-off in party mobilization efforts (Rosenstone & Hansen, 1993).

Other Types of Public Exposure

Several other factors affecting individual voting decisions should be briefly mentioned. As several social psychological theories predict, the *familiarity* of the candidate, either in terms of having a regional reputation, or more previous media coverage, or name exposure through advertising, adds to the probability of a favorable vote (Grush, 1980; Schaffner et al., 1981). Top *positions on the ballot* also add a bit to a candidate's vote, and honorary titles confer a voting advantage, especially in Britain (Mueller, 1970; Kelley & McAllister, 1984; J. Miller & Krosnick, 1998). *Endorsements* by activist groups also yield an electoral bonus. All of these factors were clearly demonstrated in a study of an unusual election for positions on a newly created junior college board of trustees, for which there were no incumbents, no party labels, and 133 eager candidates, about most of whom voters knew very little (Mueller, 1970). Other evidence of the advantage conferred by celebrity status can be seen in the election of first-time candidates Clint Eastwood and Sonny Bono as mayors of California cities, and Jesse "The Body" Ventura as governor of Minnesota. These influences on voting results, which can be seen so clearly in these unusual elections, are probably also operative to a lesser degree in many other campaigns.

FACTORS AFFECTING AGGREGATE VOTING

Before the development of public opinion surveys allowed us to study factors influencing individuals' voting decisions, the only way to analyze election outcomes was in terms of aggregate voting results for different geographic areas. This is still a useful analytic approach, and it has produced some interesting findings. Since 1920 the Census Bureau has published data on the demographic and social characteristics of each small census tract in the United States, and these data can be very illuminating when linked with aggregate voting results for the same areas.

Other facts about our society can also be tied to aggregate voting trends; for instance, Campbell (1962) has shown that the advent of radio as a nearly universal household possession was accompanied by a dramatic rise in voter turnout for elections in the 1930s. Undoubtedly this was at least partly due to radio's ability to carry political information and appeals to the less-educated and less-involved portions of the populace who were unlikely to get the same type of information by reading. By contrast, the advent of nationwide television in the 1950s was not accompanied by any clear increase in voter turnout. Although television has replaced radio as a major source of information and has increased the importance of candidates' visual images, Campbell's data showed that it did not produce any noticeable increase in the information level or political involvement of the electorate.

Typical Aggregate Voting Patterns

Some of the facts about aggregate voting patterns are relatively well known. First, voter **turnout** in presidential election years is markedly higher than in the intervening midterm or "off-year" congressional elections. The percentage of the voting-age population that actually voted in presidential elections since World War II has ranged from 63% down to 49%, whereas it has been between 45% and 33% in the midterm elections. The difference in turnout at successive elections has always been at least 10% of the electorate and sometimes as much as 20%, so the drop-off in voting after each presidential election ranges from one-fifth to nearly two-fifths of the previous election's voters. It is also well-known that the party in power typically loses seats in the House of Representatives at the midterm election; this has happened at every midterm election since 1900 except 1934, 1998, and 2002 (the last two points suggest that this long-standing pattern may no longer be a dependable outcome—Reiter, 2003).

Two less-well-known facts about voting patterns are related to the preceding observations. In presidential elections the variation in percentage of voters choosing a given party is about twice as great as in midterm elections (Stokes & Miller, 1962); that is, there are larger swings in party dominance of the vote in presidential years. Also, when there are large increases in voter turnout, the added votes usually go very heavily to one party rather than being split more equally.

Campbell (1964) offered an explanation for these facts of aggregate voting, based on two important characteristics of individual voters, their *party identification* and their degree of *interest in politics*. SRC panel studies have found that these two attributes are both quite stable over time for most individuals. What's more, they are related; in general, people who are highly interested in politics are likely to have a strong party identification. Such people tend to vote regularly in every election, whereas less-interested individuals vote only when strong situational forces push them to do so. Thus voters in the lower-interest off-year elections tend to be the core group of politically interested citizens with strong party identifications. They are rather unlikely to shift parties, so the division of the vote is quite stable from election to election. By contrast, the greater ballyhoo and hullabaloo of presidential elections bring many additional voters to the polls, most of whom are only marginally interested in politics.

Moreover, at any given time there are a variety of **short-term forces** which influence people's voting intentions—such factors as important recent events, the candidates' personal characteristics, the public images of the majority parties, and current issues developed in the campaign (Shively, 1992). When these short-term forces are approximately balanced in the degree to which they favor one party or the other, the division of the total vote will be determined mainly by the pattern of **long-term political characteristics** in the population, that is, by political interest and party identification. However, the short-term forces often build up and favor one candidate and party over the other—"an honest man," "end the war," "repair the economy," "no new taxes," etc. When that occurs, strongly committed voters may not shift their vote, but marginal voters are attracted to the favored party in droves.

Thus it sometimes happens that in high-interest presidential elections, which stimulate a high voter turnout, there is a dramatic surge to the favored candidate. But in the next congressional election, most of those off-and-on voters stay home, the division of the vote returns close to its normal level, and the party that is in the White House loses seats in Congress.

Several other aspects of voter turnout are also of interest here. Overall turnout increased markedly from 1920, when women gained the right to vote, through 1940 and reached new peaks in 1952 and 1960. However, a topic of concern to many analysts has been the quite-steady decrease in turnout at each presidential election since 1960 (Abramson, 1983; Burnham, 1985). This figure was only 53% in 1980 and 1984, 50% in 1988, and in 1996 it fell to a new low of 49%, meaning that over half the adult population—more than 100 million people—failed to vote. It also means that the winner received the votes of less than one-fourth of the American electorate. In the next *congressional* election, in 1998, only 33% of Americans voted. Voter turnout in the U.S. is strikingly lower than in many other industrialized democracies (for instance, turnout in the most recent elections has averaged 81% in Sweden, 73% in the Netherlands, and 62% in Britain), though almost all European countries have also experienced markedly declining turnout since the 1960s (Wattenberg, 2002). In part, the European advantage is because those countries have automatic or less-complicated registration systems or allow registration right up to election day, and because they vote on weekends. The American post-World War I maximum turnout figure, 63% of the electorate in 1960, is misleadingly low because of the multiplicity of state registration laws which prevent many citizens (and, of course, noncitizens) from voting if they are ill or disabled, or felons, are traveling or living abroad, or have recently moved. In 1984, the election turnout of citizens who had met all the state registration requirements was actually 74%, compared with 53% overall (Burnham, 1985). However, the 1993 Motor Voter Act and a prior federal law that set a later registration deadline for presidential elections, though they led to somewhat increased registration, did not succeed in increasing voter turnout (Teixeira, 1987; Wattenberg, 2002).

A final important trend in aggregate voting is the steady increase in **ticket-splitting**, which has been going on throughout this century (Fiorina, 1992). The number of people who voted for different parties for president and House of Representatives averaged 15% in the 1952–1968 period, then spurted to an average of 27% for the 1972–1988 elections, and dropped back to 19% in the 1992–2000 period (NES, 2001). The increase in ticket-splitting is part of the process of party dealignment, which is discussed later in this chapter, and it has two notable corollaries. First, it allowed the Democrats to keep control of the House continuously from 1948 to 1994, and usually of the Senate too, despite Republican landslides for President in 1972 and 1984.

A second aspect of ticket-splitting is its close linkage to the electoral advantage of being an **incumbent**, that is, holding the office for which one is running. A huge majority of people who split their tickets vote for incumbents, and as a consequence incumbent representatives almost always win, often by very heavy margins (Ornstein, Mann, & Malbin, 1998). In the years 1980–1998, on average, only 1% of House incumbents who sought reelection were defeated in primary elections, and only 5% lost in the general election.

A major reason for incumbents' success is their greater ability to raise campaign funds; Jacobson (2001) has shown that to have a competitive chance of winning, a challenger for a House seat must raise at least $600,000, and as much as ten times that amount for a race in the largest states. Senate incumbents are more likely to face strong challengers, but nevertheless their overall success rate in reelection campaigns averaged 80% in the 1980s and 90% in the 1990s. Another reason for the success of incumbents is that, following each census, many congressional district lines are redrawn to make them noncompetitive one-party districts. As a result, 20% or more of House incumbents may run unopposed, and only about 15% of House challengers have competitive districts and adequate resources to run a close race (Herrnson, 2000). This pattern gives stability to congressional membership that would otherwise have been lost in the trend toward party dealignment.

Flaws in the Voting System

The publicity and turmoil regarding the contested results of the 2000 election between Al Gore and George W. Bush cast a spotlight on errors and irregularities that probably occur to a small degree in every election. However, the closeness of the final determining vote margin (only 537 votes in Florida out of nearly 6 million cast there) made these faults of the system crucial in deciding who would be the next president of the U.S.

The first claim was that many voters had been improperly excluded from voting. In particular, many black citizens stated that their names had been omitted from the voting rolls, or that they had been told that they had already voted by absentee ballot, or that police had set up intimidating roadblocks near the polls and checked the IDs of minority voters (White, 2000).

Another problem was caused by carelessness of voters and imperfections in the punched-card system of voting that was widely used in that area. This became famous as the problem of "hanging chads"—the little chips of the cardboard ballots that were punched out with a stylus, but sometimes clung to the back of the ballot or were only depressed rather than fully punched out. These became the focus of heated disputes in the manual recounts of ballots that were required in many voting districts. Tallies in one Florida county found over 10,000 ballots without a machine-recorded vote for president (about 2.5% of the ballots), and hand inspections showed that in many cases the reason was that hanging chads prevented the machines from counting the voter's choice (Duffy et al., 2000).

A third problem was voter confusion about how to record their vote, which was dramatically highlighted by the unique problem of the "butterfly ballot" that was used only in one Florida county (Palm Beach County). This was a ballot with names of 6 of the 10 presidential candidates appearing on the left-hand page and the other 4 candidates appearing on the right-hand page (the butterfly's wings), and slots where the voter was to punch down the middle (the body). It happened that George W. Bush appeared as the top candidate on the left-hand page; Pat Buchanan of the Reform Party was the first candidate name on the right, placed a bit below the first name on the left and a bit above the second one; and Al Gore was the second candidate name on the left. Thus the slot to vote for Buchanan was between the slots to vote for Bush and Gore (see Figure 14–3).

Because people are accustomed to reading down the left-hand page first, they might think that votes for the second candidate on the left should be put in the second, rather than the third, slot, particularly because the dividing lines above and below Gore's listing actually touched the second and fourth slots, as well as the third. In fact, after the election, thousands of voters in Palm Beach County submitted affidavits saying that they had done this, thus voting for a candidate other than their intended one. Also, over 19,000 voters punched two slots (nearly 5% of those who voted in the county), perhaps misled by the instructions "Vote for Group" to think that they should punch a vote for both president and vice president, or perhaps trying to correct their first punch (Brady et al., 2001; Wand et al., 2001).

Going beyond the after-the-fact and possibly biased protests of misled voters, crucial evidence on the impact of the butterfly ballot problem comes from a careful empirical study by Wand et al. (2001). Using multiple methods of analysis, they showed that well

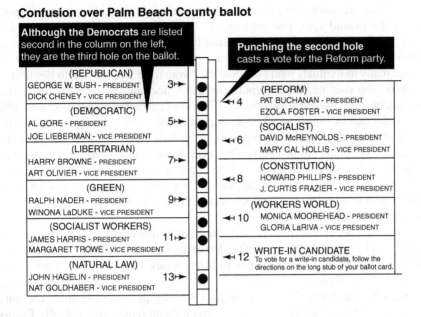

FIGURE 14–3   Illustration of the confusing Florida butterfly ballot.

Source: Photo and graphics from South Florida Sun-Sentinel. Available online at: http://www.sun-sentinel.com/graphics/news/ballot.htm. Reprinted with permission.

over 20,000 votes were miscast because of the confusion the butterfly ballot caused. In particular, because the second slot was assigned to Pat Buchanan, whose name was on the right-hand page, a substantial number of confused Gore voters punched that slot and were recorded as voting for Buchanan. In heavily Democratic Palm Beach County where the butterfly ballot was used, Buchanan was recorded as having received more than 3,400 votes (close to 1% of the 400,000+ ballots cast there), in spite of having no campaign activity in the county. The highest figure he got in any other Florida county was about 1,000 votes, and he himself said publicly that he didn't think all his Palm Beach votes had been meant for him. In fact, careful statistical calculations indicate that over 2,000 of these votes were intended to be cast for Gore, and that about 11,000 of the double punches were also intended for Gore (Brady et al., 2001; Wand et al., 2001, Dillman, 2002). Adding to Gore's total vote just the 2,000+ votes that were mistakenly cast for Buchanan would have far surpassed Bush's small official vote margin in Florida and elected Gore as president. Thus the flaws in the voting system became tremendously consequential in this election, and the butterfly ballot actually elected a president.

Switchers and Standpatters

One way of classifying groups of voters is to lump together all those who switched their party vote from one presidential election to the next, the **switchers**, and compare them with those who voted for the same party at both elections, the **standpatters**. There is also a third group, whom we can call **new voters**, consisting of young adults who have reached voting age since the last election *and* of older individuals who did not vote then, for whatever reason. These three groups were thoroughly analyzed by Key and Cummings (1966). The switchers are the group most responsible for changing patterns of party victory and defeat. They are much more numerous than you might think, based on changes in the division of the overall vote. For instance, in 1992 George Bush got about 47% of the two-party vote, a decrease of about 7% from his winning margin in 1988. However, far more than 7% of voters switched their choice that year. The 7% figure was a net change, made up of many individuals who switched their vote from Democratic to Republican and many others who switched from Republican to Democratic. Historically, the proportion of vote switchers has ranged from about 10% to about 20% in various elections, although in Nixon's election in 1968 it reached an unprecedented 33% (Converse et al., 1969).

The standpatters are a much larger group, about 60% to 75% of total voters, making up the backbone of support of each party. However, standpatters alone would rarely ever be numerous enough to win an election, and the out-of-office party in particular is compelled to direct its appeals at potential switchers and new voters. The "new voters" (who include many older people with low political interest) generally number from 15% to 20% of the voters at each presidential election.

Typically, switchers come more from the ranks of Democratic Party identifiers than from the Republican Party, partly because of the lower average interest in politics of Democrats, and partly because there are more registered Democrats. However, in elections following a heavy Republican victory, such as Reagan's in 1984, there are apt to be more defections from those who voted Republican in the past election than from Democratic ranks. Of course, many of these "defectors" from the Republican ranks were actually Democratic party identifiers returning "home" after previously defecting to vote Republican.

Let's look at a recent election to examine the nature of the switchers, who often determine the overall outcome. From 1996, when Clinton won a three-party race with just over 49% of the votes, to 2000, when Gore received over 48% of the total vote in a three-party race, here are the population groups that changed their party vote the most: Both blacks and Hispanics, though voting heavily Democratic, decreased about 5% from their 1996 level. Among whites, Southerners decreased over 15% in their level of Democratic voting, working-class members decreased about 15%, as did members of union households, and Catholics dropped about 10% between 1996 and 2000 (Abramson et al., 2003).

The "Normal" Vote

These fluctuations in voting figures lead us to another important question: What is the **"normal" vote**—that is, the most likely division of the popular vote? Because the percentage vote for the winning presidential candidate varies widely across elections, a more stable indication of the usual vote is provided by the parties' percentage of the votes for House members (averaging across all 435 races). Because there are two major parties, and they frequently succeed each other as election winners, you might assume that the "normal" state of affairs is a 50–50 division of party strength. However, that has not usually been the case in votes for Congress. From 1936 to about 1990 the "normal" Democratic Party proportion of the vote was 54%, but since then it has been just under 50% (A. Miller, 1979; Stanley & Niemi, 2000). A higher proportion of party identifiers are Democratic; but Republican party identifiers, on the average, are higher in ideological orientation (as conservatives), higher in political interest and in turnout, and lower in voting defection (Abramowitz & Saunders, 2002). Also, the increasingly large group of Independents tends to divide their votes, somewhat unevenly, between the two parties. The net result of these group loyalties and interests is that, since 1990, in national elections where short-term forces do not favor either party, each party can expect to receive about 50% of the votes cast.

In the preceding period of Republican Party ascendancy, from 1896 to 1928, the "normal" expected Republican proportion of the vote was 54%—the same as the expected Democratic proportion from 1936 to 1990. The fact that these two percentages are identical led Sellers (1965) to speculate that this level of partisanship may represent a natural limit within our political system. He concluded that:

> There seems to be at work a constant tendency toward equilibrium that is built into the structure of the American two-party system. The persistent narrowness of the margin between the parties is one of the most striking characteristics of the system.... There is a tendency not only for a minority party to readjust its image so as to detach groups from the majority coalition, but also for a party with an oversized majority to force out groups in the process of deciding which part of its coalition its policies will favor. (pp. 28, 30)

In the current, closely divided state of the U.S. electorate, both major parties have to find issues and candidates that will appeal to the nonideological marginal voters (weakly committed party identifiers and Independents) who can swing the election to them. Clearly, despite their past position as the minority party, the Republicans have been very successful in doing that. After the Eisenhower era, the Republican party won 6 of the next 11 presidential elections, some of them by landslides. Kinder (1998) summarized that:

> Deviations from the electorate's normal vote seem motivated primarily by three forces...: the emergence of new candidates, changes in national circumstances, and the introduction of new issue divisions. (p. 842)

We turn now to consideration of how these forces have played out over time.

PARTY DOMINANCE AND REALIGNMENT

The historian Charles Sellers (1965) has analyzed changes in the electoral fortunes of U.S. political parties all the way back to the nation's first election in 1789. On the basis of his careful quantitative study, he concluded that, over a series of elections, "the parties supplant each other by blocks of elections," and the parties' majorities tend to "rise and fall by regular, graded steps" (p. 19). A period of **ascendancy** of one party is followed by a period of **equilibrium,** in which the difference between the two parties' share of the presidential and congressional vote is small and shifting in direction. Then forces in the nation or the world lead to a period of **realignment** "in which the underlying pattern of party identifications is substantially and durably altered" (Sellers, 1965, p. 22). The realignment phase is usually accompanied by a third-party movement or even multiple parties, which provide a temporary home for many of the voters whose party identifications are shifting. Surprisingly, the end result of the pressures toward realignment may be a renewed ascendancy of the previously dominant party, just as often as a shift to ascendancy of the former minority party. A rather similar analysis has been made by Burnham (1970).

Classification of Elections

The three phases of the party voting cycle described by Sellers are paralleled by three basic types of presidential elections. Campbell (1966) termed these types maintaining, deviating, and realigning elections.

Maintaining Elections. These are elections in which the underlying pattern of party identifications is maintained and is reflected in the distribution of the vote. In other words, the majority party of that era retains power or is returned to power. Carter's victory in 1976 is an example, though that has also been termed a reinstating election because the majority party had previously been out of power. Maintaining elections typically have no overriding policy issues nor particularly attractive candidates impelling marginal voters disproportionately toward one party. They also typically have a relatively low voter turnout because of the lackluster campaign.

Deviating Elections.   These are campaigns in which the pattern of party identification remains unchanged, but short-term forces lead to the defeat of the majority party. These forces may be strong candidate personalities or important events or issues that impel many citizens to shift their vote temporarily away from their basic party allegiance. After these personalities or events have passed from the current political scene, the balance of the vote reverts back to an advantage for the current majority party. Examples of deviating elections occurred in 1980 and 1984, when Carter's poor presidential performance and a bad economy, and then Reagan's personality and a healthy economy, exerted a major effect on the vote. Another example was the 1916 election, where Woodrow Wilson was reelected during a period of Republican dominance as the majority party.

Sellers (1965) has shown that, throughout U.S. history, in every election which displayed a particularly strong surge of voters to one candidate in a two-party race, the winners—

> Washington, Jackson, Harrison, Taylor, Grant, and Eisenhower—were "popular hero" candidates who were widely revered for their military achievements and personal characteristics before entering politics. . . . Apparently, only such candidates have the power to draw to the polls the previously apathetic citizens who mainly create the surge effect. (p. 22)

Because Reagan was not a military hero, his massive victory in 1984 does not seem to fit this description—unless perhaps he could qualify as a hero based on his movie-star roles (?).

Realigning Elections.   In a period of realignment, popular political feelings are so intense and issues and/or events have such an impact that there is a shifting of the basic party loyalties of part of the electorate. Such periods are rare, but very important to our political system. Since the emergence of the Republican Party in 1856–1860 in the conflict over slavery, there have been only two other clear periods of basic political realignment: the reascendance of the Republicans with McKinley's election in 1896, and the shift to Democratic dominance during the Depression with Roosevelt's victories in 1932–1936 (Campbell, 1964; Burnham, 1991). The differences between these three realignment periods and the deviating "surge" elections are fascinating (Campbell, 1964):

> Neither Lincoln, McKinley nor Roosevelt, it may be noted, was a military figure and none of them possessed any extraordinary personal appeal at the time he first took office. The quality which did distinguish these elections was the presence of a great national issue and the association of the two major parties with relatively clearly contrasting programs for its solution. In some degree, national politics during these realigning periods did take on an ideological character. The flow of the vote was not a temporary reaction to a heroic figure or a passing embarrassment of the party in power; it reflected a reorientation of basic party attachments growing out of a conflict regarding governmental policies. (p. 753)

The issues which lead to major political realignment leave their effects, not just on individual citizens, but on the party loyalties of whole groups within society. In 1856 and 1896 the groups that changed their political views were mostly regional ones; in 1936 the Depression-induced issues led to political changes related to voters' social class and economic status. During the Depression, and probably also in earlier realignments, it was largely the young, first-time voters who switched party identification permanently, whereas older voters who switched their votes tended to change back again in subsequent elections (Campbell et al., 1960).

Another Realigning Period?

If realignments are cyclical, a 40-year cycle would lead us to expect another realignment around 1976. That does not seem to have happened, and there are highly divergent accounts of what we should expect in the future (cf. Ladd, 1991; Silbey, 1991; Nardulli, 1995). Let's examine presidential elections since the 1960s. Johnson's win over Goldwater in 1964 was clearly a maintaining election, with an extra surge of votes related to candidate images and policy issues. Nixon's victory in 1968 is a bit harder to classify. It was probably a deviating election, but the presence of a vigorous third-party challenge and the importance of circumstances and issues rather than candidate images raise the possibility that 1968 may have been the beginning of a period of realignment. The 1972 election, with its landslide victory for the former minority party and the great importance of ideological issues in the campaign, was a further indication of strong realigning forces at work in the electorate (A. Miller et al., 1976). However, just as with Goldwater in 1964, the negative candidate image of McGovern in the 1972 election was a factor which suggests classifying it not as a realigning election, but as a deviating one. Then Carter's victory in 1976 would appear to be a maintaining (or reinstating) election, and if so, no realignment was yet established.

Moving on in time, Reagan's two victories in the 1980s raise the same questions as Nixon's in 1968 and 1972. The 1980 campaign was highly ideological, and there was a third party challenge from John Anderson, a Republican congressman—both possible indicators of a realigning trend—but Carter's negative candidate image suggests the likelihood that it was a deviating election. The 1984 landslide for the former minority party and the increasing proportion of young adults identifying and voting Republican are consistent with a realignment hypothesis (Norpoth, 1987; *Public Opinion*, 1985, No. 5); but Reagan's great personal popularity and the lack of ideological emphasis in the campaign are more indicative of another deviating election. More clearly, with Bush's substantial win in 1988, when he received 54% of the vote despite lacking Reagan's popularity and despite the absence of strong ideological issues in the campaign, the series of Republican victories began to look like a developing realignment toward a Republican majority.

In 1992, there was a strong third-party challenge by Ross Perot, who won 19% of the votes, thanks largely to his investing about $73 million of his own fortune in the campaign (Kinder, 1998). The multiparty campaign was again an indication of the presence of realigning forces, as was the dominance of economic and ideological issues in the election. However, Clinton's win with 43% of the vote to Bush's 37% postponed any thoughts that the Republicans might emerge as the new majority party. Again in 1996, Perot's third-party campaign won 9% of the votes, but Clinton's 49% to 41% triumph appeared to be a maintaining election, with the Democrats still the majority party. If so, the 2002 election must be seen as a deviating one, for George W. Bush carried the electoral vote by a hair, though Al Gore led in the popular vote by the small margin of 0.5%. In this election, ideological issues were more muted, though a third-party candidate (Ralph Nader of the Green Party) won nearly 3% of the votes and, in doing so, took enough votes away from Gore to make him lose both Florida and New Hampshire and thus the final electoral vote (Scammon, McGillivray, & Cook, 2001).

Thus, nearly 30 years after the mid-1970s, when a cyclical political realignment might have been expected, no definite national one has appeared. However, regionally, a very clear realignment has occurred in the South in those years. Spurred by the civil rights reforms of the 1960s, black Southerners began to vote, and blacks nationally moved massively into the Democratic Party. Meanwhile, white Southerners shifted steadily to the Republicans, so that now the formerly Democratic "solid South" is solidly Republican (Kinder & Sanders, 1996). However, these developments and other changes in the parties' coalitions have largely offset each other, and have not yet made the Republicans a clear majority party in the popular vote. On the other hand, their gaining control of both Houses of Congress in the 2002 election, as well as the presidency, gave them a powerful position from which to try to consolidate their gains.

If and when a definite political realignment does become clear, Seller's (1965) analysis of electoral cycles reminds us that we still cannot tell what its ultimate shape will be, for despite the Republican victories a realigning period may end with either party in the ascendancy. In the 1970s, the twin blows of Watergate and recession thwarted Republican hopes of building a new dynasty based on the "silent majority." Likewise, Reagan's popularity was dimmed considerably by the Iran–Contra scandal, but it was aided by the nation's continuing economic health and by foreign-policy rapprochement with the USSR. The Democrats' resurgence under Clinton was blunted by the Lewinsky scandal and his impeachment trial, offsetting the economic prosperity during his administration and the achievement of a budget surplus for the first time since 1960. George W. Bush's lofty approval ratings after the Afghanistan and Iraq military victories dropped steeply, as his father's did after the Persian Gulf War of 1991, and may remain low if he doesn't appear to be solving the nation's economic and foreign-policy problems. Thus the future prospects for political realignment are still cloudy.

However, there is another alternative future other than realignment, which has received increasing attention by political researchers. It is **dealignment**, or decomposition of the party system. Burnham (1985), a noted authority on this topic, proposed that dealignment started about 1968 with the decline in party identification and turnout, an increase in vote-switching and ticket-splitting, the precipitous drop in trust in government, heightened attention to candidate images, and the importance of incumbency in congressional races. Other features include greater importance of short-term situational forces, a lessened value of presidential coattails to other candidates of the same party, and a smaller shift to the opposition party in off-year congressional elections (Tuckel & Tejera, 1983).

The net result of all these aspects has been a substantial disintegration of party coalitions—erosion of the role of parties and increased prominence of individual candidates and of the media, through which they wage a "permanent campaign" to woo increasingly fickle supporters (Blumenthal, 1982). Burnham (1985) concluded that dealignment made the nation increasingly difficult to govern because of the impotence of party platforms and party discipline, the proliferation of many special-interest groups trying to obtain or buy influence, the spurt of single-issue campaigning that ignores all other policy concerns, and the sharp polarization of the electorate along class lines of "haves" versus "have-nots." Thus, dealignment is a marked change in our political system, but not the expected one of a political party achieving a newly dominant position. Other authorities have agreed that dealignment is an appropriate description for a party system that is currently in "disarray" (Abramson et al., 2003, p. 295).

However, not everyone is so pessimistic about the occurrence of dealignment and its effects. Warren Miller, one of the original SRC researchers who stressed the primacy of party identification, has disputed the dealignment thesis and pointed to a "limited version" of political realignment with an increase in Republican party identification, which occurred in 1984–1988 (W. Miller, 2002, p. 90). Other authors have challenged the dealignment theory's thesis that the emergence of a large group of independent voters has made American

Photograph courtesy of the
Arizona Board of Regents.
Reprinted by permission.

Box 14–3 WARREN MILLER, *Founder of the National Election Studies*

A central figure in voting research for four decades, Warren Miller grew up in South Dakota and graduated from the University of Oregon after serving in World War II. Before earning his doctorate at Syracuse University, he worked under Angus Campbell at the University of Michigan, conducting the first comprehensive national survey of a U.S. presidential election in 1952. With Campbell and other researchers, he served as coauthor of the resulting volume, The Voter Decides, *and of subsequent pioneering volumes,* The American Voter, *and* Elections and the Political Order.

Remaining at the University of Michigan, Miller founded the Center for Political Studies and the National Election Studies (NES), and was awarded an endowed professorial chair. In 1982 he moved to the political science department at Arizona State University, where he continued research until his death in 1999. He led the NES's nationwide collaborative research on every U.S. national election until 1992, and he was honored as president of the American Political Science Association.

politics less partisan. In rebuttal, they have pointed to a steady increase in partisan polarization of political views among the American electorate, starting in the 1980s, and a parallel increase in voters' ideological (liberal–conservative) orientation and voting (Bartels, 2000; Abramowitz & Saunders, 2002; Fleisher & Bond, 2002; Jones, 2004). A major result, especially as Southern voters moved more to the Republican Party, has been that the two parties have become more ideological and more dissimilar in their congressional legislative programs. This is especially true of the Republican Party, which has become more homogeneously conservative in its policies and candidates (Abramson et al., 2003).

PREDICTING THE VOTE

Is it possible to predict electoral outcomes successfully with polling methods? There are several ways to answer this question. First, we know that in U.S. presidential elections the major commercial polls have not made a major error since their failure to predict the 1948 election. They correctly noted Humphrey's last-minute comeback in 1968, pronouncing the outcome "too close to call"; they all reflected Reagan's final surge in 1980; and again in 2000 the final polls concluded that the Bush versus Gore contest was "too close to call" (Wlezien, 2001). Historically, in 23 congressional and presidential elections from 1950 to 1994, the Gallup Poll's average error in predicting the outcome was only 1.6%, a figure well within the poll's expected margin of sampling error (*Gallup Poll Monthly*, 1994, No. 350).

However, looking at national poll predictions in nine countries over a period of 40 years, 15% of published predictions have gone astray in close elections (Buchanan, 1986).

Studies of many different elections have shown that, quite typically, 80% of voters have their minds made up by August and do not change their voting intentions in the 3 months between then and election day. This was true in the first major scientific election study by Lazarsfeld et al. (1948) in the small area of Erie County, Ohio. It was also true for representative national samples in the photo-finish election of 1960 and the landslide election of 1964 (Benham, 1965). And it was true in the Reagan landslide of 1984 (Cronin, 1985), though not in the unique surge toward Reagan in 1980, when 35% of voters made up their minds in the final week of the campaign after the last debate (*Gallup Opinion Index*, 1980, No. 183). In the 2000 cliff-hanger election, 22% of voters said they decided in the last 2 weeks of the campaign (Abramson et al., 2003). Thus in most elections, except for the closest ones:

> The campaign for the underdog becomes nothing more than running out a pop fly and hoping his opponent will drop the ball. (Benham, 1965, p. 188)

Early Forecasting of the Vote.   We will distinguish between *forecasting* election results, often many months beforehand, on the basis of overall economic, public opinion, and demographic measures, and *predicting* the vote, based on survey respondents' statements about their election preferences and intentions. A variety of techniques have been developed to forecast the results of elections in elaborate detail. A pioneering approach in the 1960 election demonstrated that computer simulations of the electorate could be quite accurate in forecasting the vote of many voter groups (Pool et al., 1964). Since then, various similar but competing systems have been developed, all basing their forecasts on factors such as national economic conditions and overall presidential approval (e.g., Lewis-Beck & Rice, 1992). Most of these methods, months before the election, correctly forecasted Clinton's victories in 1992 and 1996, and even accurately pinpointed his percentage of the vote within about 2%. However, though they all correctly picked Gore as the popular vote winner in 2000, they badly overestimated his percentage of the vote by an average of 6% (Wlezien, 2001). Thus, in the 2000 election, other determining factors were clearly at work beyond national economic conditions and overall presidential approval.

A somewhat different system for forecasting election results has been based on separate computations for the 50 states, because the states' Electoral College votes, not the overall popular vote, are the final determinant of the outcome (Rosenstone, 1983). This system has performed excellently in foretelling the results of presidential elections. Forecasting schemes have also been proposed for House and Senate elections, using input variables such as the state of the economy and of presidential popularity. Though these systems performed well in their early trials, they overpredicted Republican House losses in 1982 and 1986 and underpredicted Republican Senate losses in 1986 (Lewis-Beck, 1987). These errors are consistent with our previous discussion of dealignment, and they suggest that more complex models are needed for forecasting outcomes of congressional races.

Predicting Voters' Decisions.   It is important to realize that opinion surveys that make so-called "predictions" of election outcomes are simply a snapshot at one point in time of the respondents' intentions, which may change before the election is held. In addition to changes in voters' attitudes, one major reason that both national and state or district elections are hard to predict accurately is the crucial importance of *turnout* and of *undecided voters* in determining the outcome (see the discussion in preceding sections and in Chapter 6). As an example of the difficulties in estimating turnout, the percentage of respondents who say they are "absolutely certain" to vote is generally about 20% higher than the actual turnout in a presidential election. Consequently, elaborate systems have been devised for predicting the overall level of turnout and which survey respondents will actually vote (cf. Voss, Gelman, & King, 1995; Erikson & Tedin, 2001). Although not always successful, these methods have definitely improved the accuracy of polls' election predictions (Traugott & Tucker, 1984; Crespi, 1988).

Whereas the major national election polls have had a very good record of correct prediction, statewide election polls have sometimes been less carefully done and somewhat less accurate. In a study of 79 statewide polls in 2000, 15% of them picked the wrong major-party candidate as the winner, though all of these results were within the poll's expected margin of sampling error and several of these "errors" were in very tight races, including the Florida presidential race, which was not decided for over a month (Rademacher & Smith, 2001). Relatively few of the organizations that continued to poll until 2 days before the election made prediction errors.

Two kinds of election situations have proved to be particularly hard to predict correctly—i.e., primary elections and referendum campaigns. This is true partly because the efforts of local political workers are very influential in these campaigns, and partly because the overarching factor of party identification is irrelevant to voters' decisions, so other less-stable voting determinants are called into play. However, development of careful procedures has helped the state polls to predict primary results quite accurately, particularly when the polling is done within a few days of the election (Felson & Sudman, 1975).

Another kind of election prediction is seen in the television election-night projections, which have usually had very high levels of success. In the 1960s and 1970s, before the development of "exit polling," the television projections of election winners were made after the polls closed, based on counts of the first few ballots from "key districts," carefully chosen to be representative of the voting patterns of the state. In 1964 and 1966 the predictions made in this way by both NBC and CBS Television proved to be over 99% correct (Skedgell, 1966; Abelson, 1968).

However, not content with these results, the networks extended their competition with the goal of continually being earlier in broadcasting projections of the election outcome. To this end, by 1980 they changed their prediction method and began to rely on exit polls (described in Chapter 6), which potentially allow them to predict the results of apparently lopsided contests many hours before the close of voting. As we discussed in Chapter 6, the inaccuracy of sampling inherent in this method has caused incorrect network predictions in several high-profile contests, but almost all of their early projections have continued to be accurate (Levy, 1983; Roper, 1983; Mitofsky, 1998). However, a serious question remains as to how much these early afternoon election projections discourage voters from going to the polls, and thus diminish public involvement in the electoral process (e.g., Wolfinger & Linquiti, 1981).

A final issue concerning prediction of voting is how well *individual* voters' decisions, rather than aggregate outcomes, can be predicted. Among the many studies on this topic, ones using Fishbein and Ajzen's theory of reasoned action are most numerous, and a summary of their approach to predicting voting behavior is provided by Fishbein, Ajzen, and Hinkle (1980). Their theory emphasizes voters' cognitive beliefs about and affective evaluations of candidates as predictors of voting intentions, and they reported a high correlation of +0.80 between voting intention and voting behavior, with very little addition to this figure when other more-traditional political variables were added to the prediction equation. A study by Jaccard, Knox, and Brinberg (1980), using this theory, found that voting intentions correctly predicted 97% of the respondents' presidential votes, 85% of their senatorial votes, and 76% of their congressional votes. In turn, the theory's formulas correctly predicted the voting intentions of over 85% of the respondents; and voters' beliefs predicted their attitudes toward the candidates with a multiple correlation of about +0.75. These findings show an excellent ability to predict a group of voters but at least a modest margin of error in predicting individuals' votes (see also Netemeyer & Burton, 1990; Singh, Leong, & Tan, 1995).

SUMMARY

Individual voting decisions are affected by several major determinants, including personal influences from friends or family members and cross-pressures that are due to a person's noncongruent demographic characteristics. An individual's party identification is often the most important determinant in voting, but the increasing number of people who identify themselves as independents has somewhat reduced its impact. In some elections since the 1960s, the public's image of the candidates has become an even more important factor, and many campaigns have been more stridently ideological in nature, with more attention given to issue positions.

Political persuasion is generally much more likely to reinforce existing attitudes than to change contrary attitudes, for both reception and acceptance of political persuasion attempts are limited. Campaign expenditures, largely for television commercials, are typically the strongest factor in determining election winners. The advent of television in politics in the 1950s made the personality and "image" of a candidate more important in the campaign, and television advertising and major events such as the presidential debates can sometimes swing election outcomes in close races. Newspapers' political endorsements frequently have a noticeable effect on readers' voting, and personal contact is particularly effective in local or primary elections. In low-interest elections, even factors such as order on the ballot or a familiar name can markedly affect vote totals.

Aggregate voting patterns in presidential elections reflect the turnout of many marginally interested voters, who are more influenced than regular voters by the short-term forces favoring one party or the other at that time. Citizens who switch their vote at successive elections make up only 10% to 20% of the electorate, but they have often determined the election outcome, particularly during the post-1968 era, which has been called a period of decomposition or dealignment of the former U.S. party system. Flaws in the U.S. voting system were dramatically highlighted by the contested 2000 presidential election.

The "normal" or average division of the vote, since 1990, has changed to about 50% for each major party, whereas historically it had been 54% Democratic since 1936, and 54% Republican between 1896 and 1928. Over time, a period of ascendancy by one party is usually followed by a period of rough equilibrium, and then eventually by a period of realignment when the electorate's pattern of party identifications is markedly altered. Many observers have been expecting a major national political realignment since the 1970s, but no national one had definitively appeared by 2002. However, a very clear regional realignment did occur, with the South becoming quite solidly Republican.

Since 1950 the major U.S. polling organizations have had a remarkably good record in predicting the division of the popular vote, and a variety of more complex methods have been developed to predict the results for specific voter groups and special types of elections.

15

International Attitudes

Wars begin in the minds of men.—UNESCO Charter.

Peace, in the sense of the absence of war, is of little value to someone who is dying of hunger. . . . Peace can only last where human rights are respected, where the people are fed, and where individuals and nations are free.—The Dalai Lama.

O wad some Power the giftie gie us
To see oursel's as ithers see us!—Robert Burns.

This chapter discusses people's attitudes toward other nations and their images of foreign peoples. How are these attitudes developed, and to what extent are they stereotyped or based on limited sources of information? Attitudes concerning war and internationalism are central topics here, and attitudes toward terrorism have become a new focus since the 2001 attacks on the World Trade Center. Other topics covered include the kinds of people who tend to develop warlike attitudes or isolationistic viewpoints. Finally, how do international attitudes change over time?

If you agree that wars begin in people's minds, the importance of international attitudes is clear. Because a nuclear war could devastate the whole planet and possibly wipe out all human life, nations' warlike actions and the beliefs and attitudes that lead up to them are literally life-and-death issues for all of us. In addition, nations' preparations for preventing or fighting a war have an overpowering impact on everything else they do or don't do, as illustrated in this quotation (Hiatt & Atkinson, 1985):

> By 1990, nearly enough will have been spent on defense during the Cold War—$3.7 trillion in constant 1972 dollars—to buy everything in the U.S. except the land: every house, factory, train, plane and refrigerator. (p. A1)

In 1995, the United Nations Children's Fund (UNICEF) estimated that it would cost an additional $34 billion per year to pay for the unmet worldwide needs for basic child health and nutrition, primary education, safe water and sanitation, and family planning. In comparison, the world spent $800 billion per year on military expenses, so about 2 weeks' worth of military expenditures would have covered all of those needs of children around the world.

Much of what we have already learned about political attitudes applies directly to international affairs. However, there are some special ways in which international attitudes are unique. One characteristic feature is that many people's attitudes are formed despite their having little or no direct contact with other nations, foreigners, or issues of foreign affairs. As a result, the attitudes may be quite unrelated to the realities of world affairs. Of course all of our attitudes are based on our perception of the environment rather than on the actual, objective situation. But in the field of foreign affairs, the gap between perception and reality is apt to be especially large.

Images.   A number of authors from different disciplines have emphasized the gap between international attitudes and international reality by using the term *images* to describe our often-distorted views of other nations and peoples (e.g., Jervis, 1970; Holt & Silverstein, 1989; Blanton, 1996). The following quotation clearly conveys that point of view (Stagner, 1967):

> Americans do not know Russia; they know an image of Russia, subject to many errors and misconceptions. In fact, they do not know America, but only an image thereof; and it is sometimes amazing to find how we differ among ourselves as to the attributes of our nation. (p. 12)

THE IGNORANT PUBLIC

Even more than in the area of political attitudes, public information about world affairs is sharply limited. For example, in a 1988 study of basic geographic knowledge, the average American who was given an outline map of Europe could correctly name only slightly more than 3 of 12 European nations, whereas in 1947 Americans could name almost twice as many. In late 2002, after the U.S. war on Afghanistan and shortly before the war on Iraq, a survey of young Americans 18–24 years old found that only 13% could locate Iraq on a map and only 17% could find Afghanistan. The Americans scored much worse than young adults from seven other industrial nations (*CNN.com*, 2002). On other foreign-affairs questions, in 1988, half of Americans were unaware that Nicaragua was the country where Sandinistas and American-backed Contras were fighting; 45% didn't know that apartheid was a government policy in South Africa; and 32% couldn't name *any* of the member nations of NATO (*Gallup Report*, 1988, No. 277).

In 1984, 81% of the American public falsely believed that the U.S. had a no-first-use policy for nuclear weapons in case of war, and only 49% of a 1994 sample were aware that the Soviet Union and the U.S. had fought on the same side in World War II (Public Agenda Foundation, 1984; Smith, 1995b). In 1996, more than 2 years after the North American Free Trade Agreement went into effect, 48% of Americans said they didn't know enough to say whether they favored or opposed it. Also in the mid-1990s, when Americans were asked what amount of our gross national product they thought the U.S. gave as humanitarian and economic aid to developing countries, their median response was 10%, whereas the true figure was less than 0.2%, one-fiftieth as much (*Public Perspective*, 1997b, No. 5).

The implications of this lack of public information are clear: Many people in our society are "know-nothings," and if you ask their opinions, especially about world affairs, you will very likely be measuring what Converse (1974) has called "nonattitudes," based on a complete lack of information and understanding. Thus it is important for attitude surveys to eliminate or isolate such respondents by use of careful screening questions so that their "attitudes" are not lumped together with those of more knowledgeable citizens. The best-informed people, the "issue publics" in Converse's terminology, are the ones whose attitudes are more likely to be meaningful and stable. However, in between the two extremes, there is a large middle group with limited knowledge, who nevertheless display an understandable pattern of foreign-policy preferences and beliefs (Jervis, 1986; Hurwitz & Peffley, 1987). One indication of this is the amount of attention given to foreign affairs, both by candidates and by voters, in many presidential election campaigns (Aldrich et al., 1989).

Another methodological reminder is also pertinent here—it is important to remember that the exact wording of survey questions is often crucial in determining people's answers to them. As an example, Mueller (1993) analyzed answers to several national polls taken at the same time, about 2 months before the start of the Persian Gulf War of 1991. Depending on the question's wording, he noted:

> One might conclude from this array of results that . . . 28% of the population was willing to initiate war, 38% was willing to go to war, 46% was willing to engage in combat, and 65% was willing to use military force. (p. 81)

Clearly, correctly interpreting the implications of these data required careful attention to the wording of the questions being asked.

CHILDREN'S VIEWS OF FOREIGN PEOPLES

How do our international attitudes originate and develop? When do children begin to become aware of foreign nations and peoples, and how do their attitudes change with increasing age?

A classic study of these questions was conducted by Lambert and Klineberg (1967), following a research plan developed by the United Nations Educational, Social, and Cultural Organization (UNESCO). The study used a careful cross-cultural approach in 11 different areas of the world: the United States, Bantu children in South Africa, Brazil, English Canada, French Canada, France, Germany, Israel, Japan, Lebanon, and Turkey. In each area 300 children at three age levels (6, 10, and 14 years) were interviewed at length by native interviewers. The sample was carefully selected from among lower-class and middle-class urban children, but was not representative of the whole nation's child population.

The structured interviews with the children concentrated on their conceptions of their own national groups, on which foreign peoples were similar to or different from them, and on liked and disliked nationalities. Table 15–1 shows a sample of the findings, comparing children's descriptions of their own nationality with the most typical descriptions of their nations by other national groups.

Of course, these national descriptions are stereotypes, frequently based on little information and having doubtful validity at best. Nevertheless, this glimpse of children's national images provides intriguing food for thought. For instance, nearly all nations' children regarded their own people as "good," but (in 1959, when the interviewing was conducted) the Bantu and the Japanese did not—perhaps the result of racial oppression and disastrous defeat in war, respectively. Similarly, positive evaluations were foremost in descriptions of almost all other nations, though Russians were seen as "good" less often than they were seen as "aggressive" (keep in mind that this study was done during the "Cold War" period and almost entirely in nations allied to the United States rather than to Russia). The other descriptive terms showed much greater differences—from wealthy and free, to intelligent, cultured, and happy. Undoubtedly some of these stereotypes have changed substantially since then with the flow of international events (economic recovery, wars, superpower agreements, and the end of the Cold War).

Development of Children's Attitudes

The process of development and change in these attitudes toward foreign peoples is particularly important. At age 6, many of the children could give only very sparse responses about foreign peoples—mostly simple factual information and evaluations of "good" or

TABLE 15–1 Most–Typical Descriptions of Various National Groups as Seen by Children in Their Own and Other Nations

Nationality	Self-description	Description by other nations
American	good, wealthy, free	good, wealthy, intelligent, aggressive
Bantu	factual statements (e.g., dark-skinned) and similarity references (e.g., like us)	(description of "Negroes from Africa") good, uncultured, unintelligent, dominated, poor, bad, aggressive
Brazilian	good, intelligent, cultured, happy, unambitious	good (no other terms)
French	good, intelligent, cultured, happy, bad	(not obtained)
German	good, ambitious, wealthy, intelligent	good, aggressive, intelligent, bad
Israeli	good, religious, peaceful, intelligent	(not obtained)
Japanese	poor, intelligent, bad	(not obtained)
Turkish	good, peaceful, ambitious, religious, patriotic, clean	(not obtained)
Chinese	(not interviewed)	good, poor, aggressive, bad
Indians from India	(not interviewed)	good, poor
Russians	(not interviewed)	aggressive, good, intelligent, bad, dominated

Note: Terms are listed in approximate order of their frequency of usage in each national description.

Source: Adapted from W. E. Lambert & O. Klineberg, *Children's Views of Foreign Peoples*, 1967, pp. 102, 143. Reprinted by permission of Irvington Publishers, Inc.

"bad." At ages 10 and 14, the children displayed a progressive increase in the range of evaluative categories used, such as intelligent, aggressive, poor, wealthy, peaceful, dominated, and ambitious. At the same time their types of descriptive statements shifted—from physical characteristics, clothing, and language, to a greater emphasis on personality traits, habits, political and religious characteristics, and material possessions. Interestingly, children described well-liked nations with many factual, descriptive terms and with relatively few evaluative terms, whereas less-liked nations were characterized with many evaluative terms (often negative) and few factual descriptions.

Lambert and Klineberg (1967) concluded that the stereotyping process gets its start in children's early conceptions of their own group, and that between the ages of 6 and 14 children develop increasingly stereotyped views of foreign peoples. A basic finding of many studies is that children as young as 6 generally express strong positive feelings for their own nation and for traditional national symbols (e.g., Hess & Torney, 1967). By about the age of 10, many children develop fairly strong negative feelings for enemy or rival nations (Middleton, Tajfel, & Johnson, 1970). Like other political attitudes, international attitudes tend to be relatively malleable during the "impressionable" teenage years and even into the early twenties, after which they become more resistant to change (Sears, 1991).

These early national preferences and aversions are based largely on ingroup–outgroup relationships and are fostered by *consistency* motives that produce a **self-serving bias**—preferences for "us" and related groups, and aversions for groups that are seen as different from or opposed to "us." In a long series of experimental studies, Tajfel and his colleagues have shown that ingroup-versus-outgroup, "we-versus-they," feelings can be generated simply by separating people into categories, even on characteristics as unimportant as their estimation of the number of dots in a random pattern (Tajfel, 1981). Once such cognitive distinctions are established, they take on emotional significance as well, and people come to consider them important as a basis for self-esteem as well as personal consistency (e.g., "It's great to be an American"). Furthermore, these stereotypes serve as guides for assessing new information, so actions of an outgroup are usually remembered and interpreted in ways consistent with a person's existing stereotype of the group (e.g., Howard & Rothbart, 1980).

Principles of attribution theory are also relevant here, such as the "fundamental attribution error" of attributing individuals' or groups' behavior to their internal dispositions rather than to the situational pressures they face. Pettigrew (1979) extended this line of thought, describing a common tendency which he called the **ultimate attribution error**— that is, attributing *negative* behavior by outgroup members to their dispositions ("They're just naturally aggressive"), while ignoring or explaining away their *positive* behavior as situationally determined (e.g., "Our threats made them behave properly"). Coles (1986) has offered another discussion of the development of international images, and an important collection of research papers on enemy images is contained in Holt and Silverstein (1989).

International images do not apply only to nations (Tetlock, 1998); the same ingroup–outgroup principles apply to images of supranational groupings (e.g., Europeans) or to subnational ethnic or religious groups (e.g., Muslims, Jews, Kurds, Eritreans, Quebecois, immigrants). Other valuable theoretical contributions about international decision-making come from **prospect theory** (Kahneman & Tversky, 1979), which posits that people's decisions are influenced by how choice problems are framed, and that people are particularly averse to perceived losses. For instance, in bargaining situations, viewing one's own concessions as losses is counterproductive, and it is easier to defend the status quo than to argue for a modification of it (Levy, 1992).

ADULTS' VIEWS OF FOREIGN PEOPLES

In adulthood, attitudes toward foreign nations and peoples tend to remain fairly stable unless influenced by strong pressures or events. However, studies in life-span developmental psychology have shown that important changes can occur at any stage of life if the pressures are strong enough (Kinder & Sears, 1985).

A pioneering study of adult attitudes, rather similar to the one with children described in the previous section, was conducted under UNESCO sponsorship in 1948–1949 (Buchanan & Cantril, 1953). The study was carried out in six European nations plus Australia, Mexico, and the United States, and a quota sample of about 1,000 adults was interviewed in each country. Instead of open-ended questions being used, as in the study with children, a list of 12 adjectives was presented for respondents to choose from in describing two foreign peoples (Americans and Russians) and also natives of their own country. Thus the sampling was broader and more representative than in the children's study, but the interview content was much less extensive.

The results of this study largely reflected alignments in the recently concluded World War II and the subsequent Cold War between the eastern and western blocs of nations. When the survey was conducted in 1948, the United States was clearly the best-liked foreign country in the eight western nations studied (an average of 33% of respondents so listed it), whereas Russia was least-liked (by an average of 36% of respondents). Britain was second best-liked, with an average mention of 12%, and the Scandinavian countries as a whole were third with 8%. In the least-liked category, Germany was second with 16% and Japan third with 7%. Nations that shared a common language and/or culture in most cases had strongly friendly feelings for each other, but sharing a common boundary was slightly more likely to lead to disliking than to liking. Interestingly, the bordering countries that were well-liked were all smaller than the country that liked them, and thus unlikely to be a military or economic threat.

Of course, the adjectives that respondents chose to describe the various countries represent very gross stereotypes of the peoples described, but each nation's stereotype was relatively clear-cut. In that post-World War II era, Russians were seen in mostly unflattering terms: domineering, cruel, hardworking, and backward. Americans (partially because of the Marshall Plan for aid to Europe) were generally viewed as practical, progressive, hardworking, and generous. The respondents' own country, no matter which one it happened to be, was usually seen in highly favorable terms: peace loving, hardworking, intelligent, and brave.

Changes in the degree of favorability of American samples toward various other nations have been tracked from the 1950s up to the present (e.g., *Gallup Opinion Index*, 1980, No. 176; *Gallup Report*, 1989, No. 287; *Public Perspective*, 1997b, No. 5; Saad, 2002b). A recent snapshot of Americans' views of 25 other countries is shown in Table 15–2, which presents, for each country, the percent of Americans who had a very or mostly favorable view of the country and a net favorability score (percent favorable minus percent unfavorable). The survey was taken in February of 2002, and Saudi Arabia's rating had decreased markedly after the 2001 destruction of the WTC (from +1 net favorability in

TABLE 15–2   Americans' Favorability Toward 25 Countries in 2002

Country	Favorability %	Net	Country	Favorability %	Net
Canada	92	+87	China	44	− 5
Great Britain	90	+83	Cuba	31	−30
Germany	83	+72	Pakistan	30	−33
France	79	+63	Colombia	28	−32
Japan	79	+63	Saudi Arabia	27	−37
Mexico	72	+50	Afghanistan	26	−42
Russia	66	+39	North Korea	23	−42
Taiwan	62	+40	Libya	15	−53
Israel	58	+23	Palestinian Authority	14	−62
India	56	+23	Iran	11	−73
Philippines	56	+22	Iraq	6	−82
South Korea	54	+21			
Egypt	54	+20			
Vietnam	46	+ 4			

Note: The net score is the percent of Americans who were very or mostly favorable toward the country minus the percent who were very or mostly unfavorable (e.g., for Canada, 92% favorable minus 5% unfavorable equals +87 net favorability).

Source: Data from the Gallup Poll World Affairs survey of 1,011 American adults, February, 2002 (Saad, 2002b).

2001 to −37 in 2002), whereas no other country had changed more than 14 points in net favorability (Saad, 2002b).

In these data, three of the top four favorability ratings were held by historic allies of the U.S., Canada, Great Britain, and France. Americans' favorability to these countries has been gradually increasing since the 1950s and 1960s, as has their favorability to many of the other countries (*Gallup Report*, 1989, No. 287; *Public Perspective*, 1997b). However, a remarkable finding was the very high favorability ratings of nations that were our enemies in World War II or in the Cold War (Germany and Japan, +72 and +63 respectively, and Russia, +39). Even Vietnam had a slightly positive rating of +4, though China and North Korea remained negative at −5 and −42, respectively. These high favorability ratings of former deadly enemies show that old enmities can have an amazing malleability when confronted with new circumstances and alliances. They are consistent with Buchanan and Cantril's (1953) conclusion that national images are more likely to be determined by the relationship between nations than to be a major determinant of such relationships.

Another interesting aspect of these ratings is that respondents aged 18–29 were less repudiating, giving notably more favorable ratings than older Americans for most of the low-favorability countries and some of those in the +20 range. Specifically, they were substantially more favorable to The Philippines, India, Vietnam, China, Cuba, Colombia, North Korea, Libya, The Palestinian Authority, Iran, and Iraq; however, they were less favorable than older Americans to Afghanistan (Saad, 2002b). This leniency on the part of young citizens is consistent with Mueller's (2002) conclusion that foreign affairs have become much less important in American political campaigns since the end of the Vietnam War in 1975, and this same effect is shown in the graph of public opinion about America's most important problem, shown earlier in Figure 13–1.

FOREIGNERS' VIEWS OF THE U.S.

Other nations' attitudes toward the United States have not been studied nearly as thoroughly as U.S. attitudes toward other nations, largely because doing comparable studies in many countries is difficult and costly. However, it is clear that attitudes toward the U.S. have varied quite markedly over time. Since the post-World War II era of favorability depicted in Buchanan and Cantril's (1953) survey, there have been three main periods when our major allies were much less favorable to us. One was during the Vietnam War. The second was early in the 1980s, when President Reagan was seen as a dangerous warmonger, partly for his bellicose rhetoric and partly for sending U.S. troops to Grenada and Lebanon, bombing Libya, and sending arms to the Contras fighting against the government in Nicaragua. The third was in 2000–2004, when President George W. Bush was seen by other nations as initiating a unilateral, nonconsultative foreign policy, and then as a dangerously aggressive militarist in his campaigns against Afghanistan and Iraq (*Eurobarometer*, 2003).

In 1982, respondents in six western European countries were asked how much confidence they had in the ability of the U.S. to deal wisely with present world problems. In five of the countries (Switzerland, France, Denmark, Belgium, and Britain—all except West Germany) the percentage saying they had "little" or "very little" confidence exceeded the percentage saying "considerable" or "very great" confidence (Wybrow, 1984). The attitudes of the British toward the U.S. provide a key example, as they have been our strongest allies throughout this century. On the question about confidence in the U.S. to deal wisely with world problems, a relatively stable average of only 30%–34% of Britons expressed at least considerable confidence during the presidencies of Nixon, Ford, and Carter, but this figure sank to 25% during the first six years of Reagan's administration. On more specific items, majorities of about 70%–75% of Britons agreed with statements like these:

- The United States is as great a threat to world peace as is the USSR.
- The United States forces its policies too much on Britain and other European countries.
- The military and organizations like the CIA have too much influence on United States policies.

Moreover, these anti-American attitudes were much stronger in the younger generation (aged 18–35) than in older ones (Crewe, 1987, p. 52). By 1986 the U.S. and USSR were seen by Britons as about equally unresponsive in trying to prevent a third world war, whereas only a few years earlier the difference between the two nations had been much more in America's favor.

However, it is important to note that these criticisms were primarily of U.S. government policies—not mainly of the U.S. people, for whom Britons still retained a reservoir of goodwill. For instance, majorities of over 80% and over 60%, respectively, agreed with the following items (Crewe, 1987):

- Americans are, on the whole, pleasant and friendly people.
- The United States does much good for poor countries in the world by food and other aid. (p. 52)

And when asked how trustworthy people from 17 other countries were, Britons placed Americans fourth, only behind citizens of three nearby, small, and peaceable nations, Switzerland, the Netherlands, and Denmark.

Another aspect of America's broad impact on the world—our culture and way of life—was studied in a broad 30-nation survey in 1998 by Roper Starch Worldwide (Crispell, 2001). Respondents were asked "Please tell me if you feel very close, somewhat close, somewhat distant, or very distant from the American culture and way of life." The average figures for the 30 countries were only 3% feeling very close, 22% somewhat close, and 71% feeling somewhat or very distant. Although the question asked here was different than the question about favorability shown in Table 15–2, note that using the same scoring convention would give almost all of these nations *negative* closeness scores to American culture.

As you might guess, Canada was the only country where a majority of people (55%) felt somewhat or very close to the American culture and way of life. The next four countries in order were all in the Far East—Korea, Japan, The Philippines, and Australia—ranging from 48% down to 39% close. European countries were mostly near the global average of 25%, whereas Latin American countries were mostly a bit lower. The lowest scores in the countries studied were in The Netherlands, Thailand, and Argentina (17% close), Malaysia and Russia (13%), Indonesia (11%), and Saudi Arabia (7%). Another interesting finding was that, in most of the countries, young people with some college education felt much closer to American culture (averaging 33% close) than did older adults (only 12% of those without a high school education felt close). In 1998, the younger generation's feeling of greater closeness to American culture contrasted with their earlier greater criticism of U.S. government policies. Worldwide, 6% of the respondents said that they felt Americans caused change *for the worse* in their societies, whereas only 4% said they felt Americans created change *for the better* (Crispell, 2001).

Muslim countries, in particular, tended to be unfavorable to the U.S., at least by the end of 2001, shortly after the Afghanistan War had begun, but well before the U.S.-led war against Iraq in 2003. An in-person Gallup Poll survey of nine Muslim nations in December 2001 and January 2002, asked people if they felt very or somewhat favorable, or very or somewhat unfavorable, to the United States. Only in Turkey, Jordan, and Morocco were more respondents on the favorable side than on the unfavorable side. Turkey had the largest favorable group (38%), with 23% unfavorable and 39% "no opinion," for a net favorability rating of +15. Morocco recorded a +7 net favorability score, and Jordan had +4. In ascending order of unfavorability, Indonesia scored −7, and even Kuwait, which was liberated from Iraq's occupation by the Persian Gulf War of 1991, scored −8. Pakistan scored −17, Lebanon −28, Saudi Arabia −30, and Iran −62 (Moore, 2002a).

Perhaps unsurprisingly, these negative attitudes of Muslim countries were reciprocated by Americans who were asked their favorability toward Muslim countries in general. Only 24% said they were somewhat or very favorable, 41% were unfavorable, and 35% expressed no opinion, producing a net favorability score of −17 (Moore, 2002a). At this time in early 2002, over 80% of Americans realized that the U.S. was viewed unfavorably by people in Muslim countries, but they attributed that fact to misinformation spread by governments and media in the Islamic world. Large majorities of Americans saw the U.S. as caring about poorer nations, eager to have better relationships with Muslim countries, taking fair positions toward Muslim countries, and respecting Islamic values (Saad, 2002a). These perceptions represent a good example of the double standard in evaluating international actions of nations (see p. 355).

The Meaning of "Socialism" and "Capitalism"

Another aspect of disagreement between the U.S. and other nations—particularly our European allies—is the differing meanings attached to the words "socialism" and "capitalism." This was studied by White (1966), who summarized U.S. Information Agency (USIA) surveys of public opinion in Britain, France, West Germany, and Italy. When representative samples in these four countries were asked to rate the United States on a scale from completely capitalistic (0) to completely socialistic (10), an amazing 63% of them said the United States was completely capitalistic (0 on the scale) whereas 25% more put it at 1 or 2 on the scale. By contrast, in groups of Americans whom White asked the same question, no one ever rated the United States at 0, and the typical response was usually about 5—roughly halfway between complete capitalism and complete socialism.

When the USIA surveys asked western Europeans how much capitalism or socialism they wanted for their own countries, by far the most common answer was 5 on the 0–10 scale, given by 35% of the respondents; 65% chose answers in the range from 3 to 7, with 23% higher and 12% lower. White cited this and other evidence to show that in many countries "capitalism is on balance a slightly dirty word" and "that in most of the world the word socialism is more unequivocally positive than the word capitalism is negative" (1966, p. 219).

White pointed out that, when Americans speak of socialism, they often refer to government ownership of industry, whereas in most other countries the term is used much more to refer to government responsibility for social welfare and government regulation of industry and labor. Similarly, to Americans, capitalism primarily means private ownership of industry, whereas in most other countries it means excessive political power for the rich (capitalists) and lack of social welfare for poor people. In addition, most other peoples dislike communism, which they associate with dictatorship and violence, and they make a sharp distinction between it and socialism. (Indeed a dominant party in many countries is named Democratic Socialists or some variation thereof.) In contrast, many Americans use the words "communist" and "socialist" almost interchangeably as pejorative terms.

An important substantive lesson can be drawn from these semantic distinctions. White concluded that American social welfare programs and government regulative laws have given us an intermediate level of socialism (probably not far from the level preferred by many Europeans). However, there is a great ignorance of that fact overseas, and Americans compound that problem by often referring to our system as capitalistic and by "confusing socialism with Communism and condemning both in the same breath" (p. 228). White (1966) recommended, in the interest of clearer communication and understanding with other nations, that we should try

> to avoid needless emphasis on issues in the area of socialism that we and they may disagree on, and to emphasize instead the principles of democracy that we and they have in common. ... We can then define what America stands for unambiguously as a maximum of democracy, a minimum of government ownership, and a medium-to-high amount of social welfare. (p. 228)

Bringing these differences on views of socialism up to date, Lipset (2000) summarized:

> Not only has the United States never had a significant socialist movement, but as of the year 2000, it has the weakest labor movement and remains the least statist western nation in terms of public effort, ownership, taxes, welfare benefits and public employment. (p. 33)

An example of these differences in terms of public opinion is shown in answers to a question asked in the U.S. and in 9 European countries and several former Soviet states (*Public Perspective*, 1991). Samples of about 1,000 people in each country were asked whether they completely agreed, mostly agreed, mostly disagreed, or completely disagreed with this statement: "It is the responsibility of the government to take care of very poor people who can't take care of themselves." The percentage who "completely agreed" in the U.S. was only 23%, whereas the next-lowest country was Germany with 50%. Complete agreement in other representative western countries was 56% in Poland, 62% in the United Kingdom and in France, 66% in Italy, 70% in Russia, and 71% in Spain.

U.S. ATTITUDES ABOUT FOREIGN POLICY

Foreign affairs are often listed together with domestic issues as the two main areas for government policy. Indeed, U.S. foreign policy is crucial in affecting the life-and-death issues of war and peace, as well as determining U.S. relations with other countries and peoples all around the globe. However, since the end of the Vietnam War, foreign affairs have only rarely been viewed as a major national problem by U.S. citizens (see Chapter 13), and since the end of the Cold War with the USSR, foreign policy has become less important in political presidential campaigns (Mueller, 2002). Mueller has summarized several aspects of the American neglect of foreign policy, pointing out that the American public generally pays little attention to international issues, and asserting that it typically uses reasonable cost-benefit principles in evaluating proposed foreign activities. However, he showed that, "it values the lives of Americans very highly and tends to undervalue the lives of foreigners" (p. 156). Consequently, the president can lead the nation into many foreign ventures, including military actions and wars (see Chapter 13), but if any appreciable number of American lives are lost there, the public is likely to reject the activity quite quickly (Mueller, 2002).

Images of the USSR

Since the end of World War II, the Cold War between the U.S. and the Soviet Union was the dominant foreign policy issue until the dissolution of the USSR in 1991. Therefore a key aspect of international attitudes was the views of each other's country held by Americans and Russians. The attitudes of Soviet citizens were rarely studied by systematic surveys until the 1990s, so other methods of estimating Soviet public opinion had to be used. A unique opportunity to study Russian attitudes came to Urie Bronfenbrenner, a social psychologist who was one of the first American scientists to visit Russia during a thaw in U.S.–Russian relations in 1960. He was allowed to travel quite freely without a guide in a number of cities, and because he spoke fluent Russian, he was able to converse in a systematic manner with many common citizens. Bronfenbrenner's (1961) main conclusion was that Soviet citizens viewed the world almost exactly as American citizens did, but with a reversed evaluative direction—a **mirror image** in international perceptions. For instance, each nation saw itself as peace loving and could give many reasons and arguments to support that view. Similarly, both Americans and Russians viewed the other nation as aggressive and threatening to foment a war at any moment, as evidenced by the other's huge expenditures for armed forces and military weapons. Consequently each nation felt that it must arm itself heavily for "defensive" purposes—to prevent the warlike other from carrying out its aggressive plans. In these respects the two countries held exact mirror images of each other (Bronfenbrenner, 1961).

Many other aspects of the mirror image were described by White (1984). He pointed out that most Americans and most Russians viewed the vast bulk of the other country's citizens as good, peace-loving individuals. But each country had a "black-top" image of the other—a belief that their leaders were evil, aggressive, and reckless. Although each country lived in constant fear of reckless aggressive actions by the other, neither was able to see that the other's actions were often motivated by fear rather than by hostile intent. Surprisingly enough, each side used similar standards in judging themselves and the other side—truthfulness, strength, material advancement, courage, unselfishness, and so forth—but because they did not see any given event from the same viewpoint, they applied these standards to an entirely different perception of world affairs. Finally, each side claimed that the other's statements were propaganda, intended to deceive, and therefore it paid little attention to them.

In spite of these many similarities, U.S.–Soviet perceptions were not a perfect reflection of each other. The mirror image had "flaws"—points at which the reciprocal perceptions didn't match exactly. One such wrinkle in the mirror was the Russians' strong feeling of warmth and friendliness for the American people, which was only feebly reciprocated by Americans. Another was the Russians' admiration for America's wealth and material progress, whereas Americans viewed Russia as poor, drab, and inefficient. Although both nations highly valued "democracy," they held quite different meanings of that term: Americans emphasized free elections and individual freedoms, whereas Russians stressed citizens' responsibilities to serve the common good (White, 1984).

If Russians and Americans observed the same world events and emerged with opposite conclusions, then it follows that both sides were probably using a **double standard** for evaluating international affairs. Oskamp (1965) demonstrated that a double standard of evaluation did indeed underlie the mirror image. He developed a list of 50 international actions that had been taken in substantially equivalent forms by both the U.S. and the USSR—both countries had increased their military budgets, blockaded foreign areas, made disarmament proposals, signed joint treaties, sent great musicians to perform in the other country, and so forth. When American college students were asked to indicate how favorable they felt toward these identical actions by the two countries, they were markedly

Photograph courtesy of Ralph K. White.
Reprinted by permission.

Box 15–1   RALPH K. WHITE, *Authority on International Relations*

Ralph White spent more than 50 years studying the psychological aspects of international affairs, especially the causes and prevention of war. He took his Ph.D. with Kurt Lewin at the University of Iowa and later spent 17 years of service in the U.S. government, particularly the U.S. Information Agency, with first-hand experience in Berlin, Saigon, and Moscow. Subsequently he taught for many years at George Washington University, where he is Professor Emeritus of Psychology.

Much of White's research and writing dealt with attitudes concerning the East–West conflict, the Vietnam War, and the Arab–Israeli conflict. His books include Nobody Wanted War: Misperception in Vietnam and Other Wars, Fearful Warriors: A Psychological Profile of U.S.-Soviet Relations, *and* Psychology and the Prevention of Nuclear War. *He has been honored by election as president of Psychologists for Social Responsibility and of the International Society of Political Psychology.*

more favorable toward almost every one of the U.S. actions than to the comparable Russian action. Some of the differences were as large as 4 points on a 6-point scale; for instance, the students felt quite favorable to the U.S. blockading a nearby area but quite unfavorable toward Russia blockading an area near her.

This double standard in evaluating international events made possible the mirror-image phenomenon. People generally see any action by their own country, whether warlike or peaceful, in a much more favorable light than similar actions taken by an opposing country (Oskamp & Hartry, 1968; Burn & Oskamp, 1989; Tobin & Eagles, 1992). This view is maintained by attributions in which the actions of one's own country are ascribed to altruistic motives whereas the similar actions of an enemy are attributed to self-serving motives (Sande et al., 1989).

Changes in Images of the USSR

Representative national samples of Americans have displayed changing attitudes toward the Soviet Union. From the peak of Cold War hostility in the early 1950s until about 1975, there was a gradual decline in Americans' negative views, but three subsequent events were each followed by successively higher levels of unfavorability to the USSR: namely, the North Vietnamese takeover of Saigon and South Vietnam in 1975, the Soviet invasion of Afghanistan at the end of 1979, and the Russian shooting down of a Korean airliner in 1983. However, despite President Reagan's March 1983 speech describing the Soviet Union as an "evil empire," a substantial *decrease* in American antipathy occurred from 1984 to 1988 (Yatani & Bramel, 1989).

A major factor in the increasing general favorability toward the USSR was the policies and statements of Mikhail Gorbachev after he became the Soviet leader in 1985. In late 1987, following his signing of a treaty with the U.S. banning intermediate-range nuclear missiles, he became the first Soviet leader ever to be named by Americans to their list of the ten most-admired men (*Gallup Report*, 1987, No. 267). The key basis of Gorbachev's popularity was the perceived degree of his efforts to stop the arms race (Church, 1987), but relatively positive American attitudes toward Russia have continued under subsequent Russian leaders, as shown earlier in Table 15–2.

INTERNATIONALISM VERSUS ISOLATIONISM

Internationalism means a national policy of active involvement in foreign relations, including international trade, treaties, and cooperation. In contrast, **isolationism** is a national policy of withdrawing from and avoiding treaties and commitments with foreign nations (Foster, 1983). The continuum between these two extreme viewpoints is a crucial dimension of foreign-policy attitudes, and its internationalist end includes two possible options: unilateral activism or a preference for multilateral government actions. Another key dimension is willingness to use military force, which we discuss a little later (Hinckley, 1992).

There were immense changes in American public opinion about foreign relations during the twentieth century. Public revulsion over World War I, which was supposed to be "a war to end all wars," led to an extreme degree of American isolationism in the 1930s. For instance, a Gallup Poll in 1937 asked, "If another war like World War I developed in Europe, should America take part again?" and 95% of Americans said "No"! As late as 1939, 66% of Americans said the United States should not help either side if Germany and Italy went to war against England and France (Free & Cantril, 1967, p. 63). Congress shared this revulsion toward war and "foreign entanglements"; consequently it had defeated President Wilson's efforts to have the U.S. join the League of Nations, and it had passed legislation prohibiting U.S. sales of military supplies to other countries. That restriction on military sales was the reason that, when aid to Britain became clearly necessary to prevent her defeat by Hitler, it took the form of "lend-lease" supplies. It was only after Hitler's conquest of Holland, Belgium, and France in the spring of 1940 that a majority of Americans became convinced that the U.S. might have to become involved in the European war and should aid Britain despite that risk (Foster, 1983). Even in late 1941, shortly before the Japanese attack on Pearl Harbor, only 32% of Americans said they would vote to enter the war against Germany (Erikson & Tedin, 2001).

With that background of pre-World War II isolationism, the extent of U.S. internationalism after the war is nothing short of amazing. Large majorities of the public approved of joining the United Nations and of the Marshall Plan for aid to European countries, the founding of NATO for mutual national defense, the airlifts sending supplies to Berlin when it was blockaded by Soviet troops, U.S. entry into the Korean War as the major component of the United Nations forces opposing the North Korean invasion of South Korea, and many other activist measures. Despite some setbacks stemming from public discouragement over the long-protracted Korean War and from Senator Joseph McCarthy's investigations in the early 1950s of alleged Communist Party subversion of our government, U.S. internationalism not only persisted but reached a high point about 1965 (Page & Shapiro, 1982)—see Figure 15–1.

In 1964 a landmark study of internationalism found 65% of a national probability sample of respondents to be internationalistic, 27% mixed, and only 8% isolationistic (Free & Cantril, 1967). This very high level of internationalism was a dramatic and important finding, particularly in comparison with the extreme levels of isolationism in America before

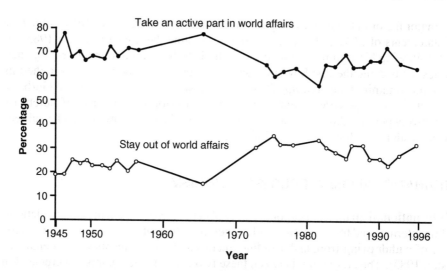

FIGURE 15–1 U.S. levels of internationalism over 50 years (percent of responses to "Do you think it would be best for the future of this country if we take an active part in world affairs, or if we stayed out of world affairs?").

Source: Erikson & Tedin (2001, p. 92). Reprinted with permission from Pearson Education.

World War II. However, by 1968, public protest over the Vietnam War had diminished the U.S. level of internationalism, and by 1974 the picture was substantially different, though not reversed (41% on the internationalistic side, 38% mixed, and 21% on the isolationistic side—Watts & Free, 1974). Another item showed a massive 87% agreement that "The U.S. should continue to play a major role internationally, but cut down on some of its responsibilities abroad" (Watts & Free, 1973, p. 204). Thus the legacy of the Vietnam War seemed to be a modified internationalism—less willingness to send American troops abroad, but even more willingness to send economic aid and to invest in national defense (Foster, 1983).

By 1980 another change occurred, involving reactions to the Iranian capture of U.S. hostages and American opposition to the Soviet occupation of Afghanistan. At this point American internationalism climbed markedly again (Free & Watts, 1980), though this increase was skipped over by the data in Figure 15–1. The general public approval of U.S. activism in foreign affairs but disapproval of military intervention continued with little change in the 1980s (Benson, 1982; *Public Opinion*, 1989, No. 6). U.S. internationalism rose still higher during the Persian Gulf War of 1991 and then persisted at a relatively high level throughout the 1990s (*Public Perspective*, 2001, No. 1), but support for military involvement again diminished (Richman, 1993).

The American public's activist stance developed a distinctly multilateral character in the 1990s (Richman, 1993). For example, despite some strident criticisms of the United Nations, in 1997 85% of Americans said it played a necessary role in the world, and 88% favored our continued membership compared with 9% who said we should give up our membership (*Gallup Poll Monthly*, 1997, No. 387). In 1999–2000 82% of Americans said that "In deciding on its foreign policies, the U.S. should take into account the views of its major allies," and only 36% said that it "should take action even if its allies disagree with its decision" (*Public Perspective*, 2001, No. 1, p. 28). This public multilateralist preference was challenged by the Bush administration's initial unilateralist approach to many foreign policy issues in 2001 and subsequently in the Iraq War of 2003.

Nationalism Versus Patriotism

A concept that is often contrasted with the viewpoint of internationalism is the attitude of nationalism, or predominant devotion to the interests of one's own country. However, these two viewpoints are not diametrically opposed, for the best interests of one's country may often demand international trade or cooperation, as in the World War II alliance against the Axis powers. A useful empirical analysis of nationalism was made by Kosterman and Feshbach (1989), who differentiated between **nationalism** (belief that one's nation is superior and should be dominant) and **patriotism** (positive attachment to one's nation). They developed scales to measure these two attitudes as well as internationalism, and results showed that the three concepts were in fact quite distinct. That is, one can have strong feelings of love for one's country (patriotism) without believing that it is necessarily right or best (nationalism), and neither of these viewpoints is necessarily connected with isolationism (the opposite of internationalism). The fact that these three attitudes are empirically distinct and hardly correlated with each other illustrates the multidimensionality of attitudes in the international arena.

ATTITUDES CONCERNING WAR

Nuclear War Attitudes

During the Cold War, Americans' attitudes about war were heavily influenced by the perceived dangers of an all-out nuclear conflict. These feelings peaked in 1983, midway in Reagan's first term as president. In 1983–1984, 86% of U.S. adults were worried about the prospect of a future nuclear war; 83% believed that "if either superpower were to use nuclear weapons, it would turn into all-out nuclear war"; 89% agreed that "there can be no winner in an all-out nuclear war; both the U.S. and the Soviet Union would be completely destroyed"; and 83% said that "we cannot be certain that life on earth will continue after a nuclear war" (Public Agenda Foundation, 1984; Plous, 1985).

Americans' beliefs about the devastating consequences of a nuclear war were supported by reports such as the following (summarized by Oskamp, 1985, pp. 9–10):

> If a full-scale nuclear war should occur, the estimated number of deaths in the United States within the first 30 days ranges from 75 million to 145 million (that is, from one-third to two-thirds of the population), even in the highly unlikely case of the population being sheltered as fully as possible. "However, deaths from burns, injuries, and radiation sickness can be expected to continue far beyond this particular [30-day] interval" (U.S. Congress, 1979, p. 97). In fact, even in the most limited nuclear war, in which "only one city is attacked, and the remaining resources of the nation are available to help, medical facilities would be inadequate to care for the injured" (U.S. Congress, 1979, p. 6). Even in such a limited attack, the entire amount of U.S. blood supplies for a year might be needed within the first 24 hours (Chivian et al., 1982).

A 1983 national poll found that 67% of American adults believed that there was a likelihood of a "third world war breaking out in the next 20 years" (Plous, 1985). In research comparing nationwide samples in many countries, U.S. beliefs in the likelihood of a major war in the next 5 or 10 years were much higher than in any of 28 other countries (*Gallup Report*, 1986, No. 255; Listhaug, 1986). A pioneering study in 1987, comparing the beliefs of Americans with those of a sample of Moscow residents, found that nearly five times as many Americans as Russians predicted a high chance of a world war, and only about half as many Americans were optimistic about the possibility of totally eliminating all nuclear weapons (*Gallup Report*, 1987, No. 258; 1987, No. 266).

These widespread fears, together with the increased danger of war accompanying the installation of American Pershing II nuclear missiles in Europe, and the belligerent rhetoric of President Reagan's first term, led to an unprecedented upsurge of international support for a "nuclear freeze" in the early 1980s (de Boer, 1985; Rochon, 1988). Many psychologists made important research and theoretical contributions to this peace movement (e.g., Deutsch, 1983; Janis, 1985; White, 1985). In 1982, huge majorities of Americans supported arms control: 73% favored banning the production, storage, and use of nuclear weapons; 86% wanted the U.S. and the USSR to negotiate a nuclear arms reduction agreement; and 81% favored an agreement not to produce any new nuclear weapons as long as the two superpowers had a rough nuclear equivalence (Klineberg, 1984). The U.S. experienced a number of enormous antinuclear rallies, and nuclear-freeze resolutions were adopted by hundreds of town meetings and some city councils and state legislatures; but the movement was even stronger in several European countries, where it led to the rise of antinuclear political parties and the election of a number of antinuclear members of various parliaments.

After 1983, the nuclear-freeze movement declined in public prominence, though Americans' attitudes on nuclear issues remained much the same (Gilbert, 1988). The U.S. House of Representatives responded to the movement by passing a nuclear-freeze resolution, and in his second term, President Reagan began to espouse arms control proposals and eventually negotiated and signed a treaty with the USSR banning intermediate-range nuclear missiles. Thus, in the U.S. as well as in Europe, many of the goals of the nuclear-freeze movement were accepted by more mainstream groups, indicating that in some cases such grass-roots movements can have an effect on public policy.

Attitudes Toward Limited Military Interventions

Since the end of the Cold War, Americans' fears of nuclear war have receded, and public attention has sporadically turned to other types of military action, such as limited, nonnuclear wars (Persian Gulf, Afghanistan, Iraq), "peacekeeping" missions (Somalia, Bosnia, Kosovo), and combating terrorism. There are many complex conditions that affect Americans' willingness to approve of a specific war, including the nature and source of the threat to our interests, the anticipated costs and likelihood of success, and the possibility of alternative means for countering the threat, particularly multilateral actions (Richman, 1995). Sometimes presidents have been able to persuade the public to support limited military actions such as Reagan's invasion of the Caribbean island of Grenada in 1983 or Bush's use of troops to depose the Panamanian dictator Noriega in 1989.

In recent decades, Americans have generally been strongly reluctant to go to war to protect weak nations from aggression, but more willing to do so if they feel convinced that they are curbing the spread of communism, preventing proliferation of nuclear weapons (or other "weapons of mass destruction"), or stopping the flow of drugs or the rise of terrorist groups (Mueller, 2002). Even when those goals are clearly involved, American public opinion has generally been negative toward potential wars if as many as 1,000 U.S. troops were expected to die.

Another fairly common foreign-policy intervention has been to send American military "advisors" or instructors and military aid, rather than American combatants, to other countries that were involved in civil wars, such as Colombia or The Philippines. This approach has usually met little public resistance because American lives were not being put at risk. However, in Nicaragua, the Reagan administration and, at times, Congress reversed the usual recipients of support by sending massive amounts of military aid to the "Contras," guerrilla warriors who were fighting against the Sandinista government. During the mid-1980s this policy was regularly opposed by a majority of Americans (as many as 63% at times). However, the administration ignored this opposition and organized clandestine arms sales to Iran in order to obtain funds, which were then funneled illegally to the Contras. This secret activity eventually gained public attention as the Iran-Contra scandal, and it led to a 20-point drop in President Reagan's approval rating (Brody & Shapiro, 1989; Sobel, 1993).

In humanitarian peacekeeping missions, Americans have been willing to commit troops for periods of years, as long as no or very few casualties occurred. However, attitudes have turned strongly negative when even a few Americans were killed or taken hostage, such as the deaths of 18 U.S. soldiers in Somalia in 1993: "It seems clear that policing efforts will be tolerated only as long as the costs in lives for the policing forces remain extremely low" (Mueller, 2002, p. 161). Attitudes about military action to combat terrorist groups are discussed in a later section.

Public Opinion About the Korean and Vietnam Wars

A notable instance in which public opinion eventually affected U.S. government policy was during the Vietnam War, which has been called the most divisive and bitter American experience since the Civil War. To investigate that claim scientifically, Mueller (1971, 1973) summarized national poll data about attitudes toward the war from start to finish, and compared them with the progression of similar attitudes during the course of American involvement in the Korean War of 1950–1953. His findings will probably surprise you.

Many times during the Vietnam and Korean Wars citizens were asked, "Do you think the U.S. made a mistake sending troops to fight in Vietnam (Korea)?" The changing patterns of support over time for the Korean War and the Vietnam War are plotted graphically in Figure 15–2. In reading this graph, note that the figures shown can be below 50% and still be pluralities, for usually 10%–18% of respondents were undecided. Because the Vietnam War had no clear starting point, and was initially given little attention by U.S. public opinion, Mueller chose as its beginning date mid-1965, when American troops and bombers were being committed to the war in large numbers.

These data demonstrate several points. First, both wars began with high public support (over 60% pro and less than 25% con)—what Mueller called a "rally-round-the-flag phenomenon." Then, fairly quickly, there was a marked drop in public enthusiasm, followed by a slow decline in support over a period of years. There were also fluctuations in attitudes related to a few highly dramatic events—particularly in the Korean War, when the Chinese entry into the war caused a huge early drop in support, and President Eisenhower's visit to Korea to speed up the truce talks produced a clear increase in public support. However, in general, most events do not seem to have had much effect on the underlying trend of public support for the wars.

When support for the two wars is compared, it is clear that the Korean War was lower in public support for almost its whole course. This finding is sharply contrary to the many claims that the Vietnam War was "the most unpopular war in [U.S.] history" (Wise, 1968). However, Mueller (1971) pointed out that the Korean War started abruptly and involved much higher early casualties than the Vietnam War. Using the statistical technique of regression analysis, he was able to demonstrate that:

> In each war, support . . . started at much the same level and then every time American casualties increased by a factor of 10 (i.e., from 100 to 1,000 or from 10,000 to 100,000) support for the war dropped by about 15 percentage points. (p. 366)

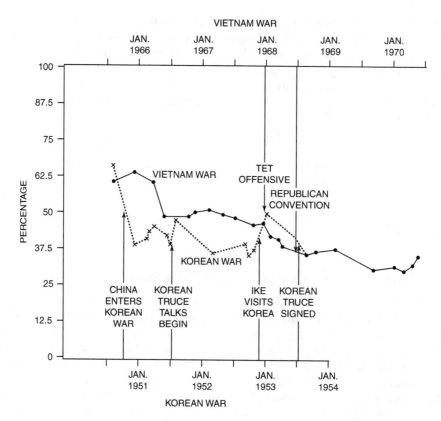

FIGURE 15–2 Public support for the Vietnam and Korean Wars.
Source: Adapted from Mueller (1971, pp. 362, 364).

Thus Mueller concluded that patterns of public support for the two wars were very similar. It is true, of course, that approval of the Vietnam War eventually dropped lower than the Korean War levels, but it only did so after the war had gone on longer and American casualties had climbed much higher than in Korea.

ATTITUDES TOWARD TERRORISM

Terrorism can be defined as the use of clandestine violence or the threat of violence by individuals or groups to create fear and accomplish some desired political goals (cf. Ruby, 2002a). There is a wide spectrum of possible terrorist acts, and there are various categories of potential terrorist groups. Post (2002a) proposed a classification of types of terrorist groups that includes (a) left-wing social revolutionary groups aiming to overthrow the economic and social order, (b) ethnic or nationalist separatists aiming to establish a new ethnic state or nation, (c) right-wing groups or ideological individuals opposed to government actions or power, and (d) religious fundamentalist groups that are "killing in the name of God." "Most nonstate terrorists see themselves as revolutionaries or freedom fighters" (McCauley, 2002, p. 4).

Post (2002a) also differentiated terrorist acts into the following categories: large-scale conventional attacks (e.g., truck bombs), chemical or biological (CB) hoaxes (sham anthrax attacks), small-scale CB attacks (the actual anthrax-laden letters that killed a few people in 2001), large-scale attacks (killing from 20 to hundreds), and catastrophic attacks (e.g., poisoning a city's air or water supply). To this classification scheme, Montiel and Anuar (2002) added global structural violence, and government-legitimized acts of terror—a category that is much more prevalent and deadly than nonstate terrorism (McCauley, 2002; Pilisuk & Wong, 2002).

Following these definitions, in this section we describe the nature of international terrorism and some of the motivations behind it. Then we briefly summarize American public opinion about how great a threat it is, what actions should be taken to combat it, how successful such actions have been, and expectations and worries for the future. Finally, we present some psychologically informed proposals about desirable ways of reducing or preventing terrorism.

Terrorism has existed for thousands of years in international affairs, but it rarely affected the U.S. directly until the 1980s. In late 1979, 66 American diplomats were taken hostage from the U.S. embassy in Tehran, Iran, and held there for over a year; and later occasional incidents of plane or ship hijacking, hostage-taking, bombing of buildings, and airliner destruction occurred in other countries (Hinckley, 1992). In the 1990s, terrorist attacks became more destructive and some were launched against targets in the United States. For instance, in 1993 a truck bomb seriously damaged the basement garage of the World Trade Center in New York City; in 1995 a huge blast outside the Federal Building in Oklahoma City claimed 168 lives; in 1998 U.S. embassies in two African countries were destroyed by bombs, leaving 300 dead and over 5,000 injured; and in 1995 a poisonous sarin gas attack in the Tokyo subway killed 12 people and injured over 5,000 (Post, 2002a). However, it was not until the September 2001 attacks on the WTC and the Pentagon that international terrorism became a continuing, urgent worry for Americans (Jones, 2002b).

Motivations Behind Terrorism.   "Why do they hate us?" was an often-asked question following the September 2001 destruction of the World Trade Center. The last two categories of terrorism listed above—government-sponsored terrorism and global structural violence—help greatly in answering that question, for people in foreign countries often see U.S. actions as utilizing state-sponsored terrorist violence or as being partially responsible for repressive actions by their own government. Examples that occurred in 2001 include "aerial carpet bombings in Afghanistan, formal or informal support of Israel's armed offensives against Palestine, and U.S. troop deployment on the Philippine island of Mindanao" (Montiel & Anuar, 2002, p. 203). These actions involved *direct* violence, but **structural violence** can be just as insidious in provoking international hatred. It is "indirect political, economic, and social injustice arising from the structure of society: poverty, dictatorship, and racial discrimination are examples" (Wagner, 2002b, p. 185; cf. Galtung, 1996). Such structural conditions, and particularly direct violence by U.S. organizations or governments that we support, can convert "legitimate complaints about political systems" into terrorist acts that target American citizens, organizations, or interests (Ruby, 2002b, p. 217). A volume that is useful in understanding the roots of terrorism is Moghaddam and Marsella (2004).

American Public Opinion About Terrorism

Throughout the 1980s and 1990s, the *salience* of terrorism in American minds usually depended on the length of time since the last terrorist incident—the closer in time, the greater was the salience and perceived importance. Historically, on national polls with open-ended questions, less than 1% of respondents mentioned terrorism as the nation's most important problem. On two occasions in the mid-1980s, however, just after a plane hijacking and an airport massacre, terrorism was the most-mentioned national problem, but even then by only 13%–15% of the respondents. Thus it was hardly ever a highly salient worry to Americans. However, when they were asked specifically about terrorism—for example, how serious a threat it was to U.S. national security—typically 70% to 80% of respondents said it was an "extremely" or "very" serious problem (Hinckley, 1992; Kuzma, 2000).

In the 1980s, a majority of Americans did not blame terrorism on structural, social conditions of poverty or injustice, but rather on "irrational fanatics seeking to aggrandize their own political power who were supported and financially backed by some states that are equally radical and ambitious," particularly Libya, Syria, and Iran (Hinckley, 1992, p. 93). When asked about ways to prevent terrorism, Americans rarely mentioned ameliorating the sources of injustice cited by the terrorists. Instead, they gave three types of answers. A first group, comprising anywhere from 20% to 40% of respondents, generally said that nothing could be done to foil the terrorists. Another large group focused on increasing security measures at likely targets, such as better screening of airline passengers and baggage, restricting movement of immigrants and foreigners, and better coordination of information and police personnel.

A third group of Americans suggested *retaliatory* actions against terrorists—diplomatic or economic sanctions, or military strikes. During a series of terrorist attacks in 1985–1986, this latter view grew from a minority to a majority of about 60%, and in April 1986 the U.S. did send air force bombers to attack Libya for its alleged support of terrorists who had bombed nightclubs and blown up airliners. Subsequently, less than 10% of the U.S. public advocated "no action" against terrorists, about 30% still favored diplomatic or economic sanctions, 40% favored military attacks on terrorist facilities in a country that supported terrorists, and 20% advocated even broader military action against any economic or military target in such a country. Two-thirds of Americans viewed such military actions against a nation as retaliation, whereas only about 30% favored making *preemptive* attacks designed to prevent future terrorist acts (Hinckley, 1992). Surprisingly, the public was not optimistic in the 1980s and 1990s about the success of military attacks in preventing terrorism (Kuzma, 2000). Only about one-fourth of respondents expected them to reduce terrorism, whereas usually a majority said that they would probably lead to even more terrorist acts. Only about one-third saw such attacks as the beginning of a process of repeated military attacks to combat terrorism (Hinckley, 1992).

Crimes or Warfare?   There are two basic ways that terrorist attacks can be treated by society—as crimes, which require a response through the criminal and legal systems, or as warlike acts, which warrant a military response (M. Smith, 2002; Sarbin, 2003). In the 1980s and 1990s, almost all terrorist attacks against U.S. interests were treated as crimes, whose perpetrators should be captured and punished legally—except for our 1986 bombing attack on Libya. Then in 1991 the U.S. led a large coalition of nations into war against Iraq, but the chief rationale for the war was that Iraq had conquered and occupied a neighboring country, Kuwait. This occupation by Iraq was not considered a terrorist action, but was clearly a military campaign, which could be seen as justifying a military response. The three major terrorist attacks against the U.S. in the 1990s that were previously mentioned—the truck bomb in the World Trade Center garage, the Federal Building bombing in Oklahoma City, and the destruction of U.S. embassies in Africa—were all dealt with through the criminal and legal systems rather than by military means or even diplomatic or economic sanctions.

Retaliation as a Response.   Following the destruction of the World Trade Center in September, 2001, the U.S. response was very different. President George W. Bush proclaimed that this was an act of war, and that the U.S. would now launch both a *retaliatory* and *preemptive* "war on terrorism." However, this war was different than any our nation had ever fought, because the enemy was not a nation but rather a nebulous group of individuals from many nations with many different grievances, and because the U.S. would initiate preemptive military strikes. The Afghanistan military campaign of late 2001 and the Iraq War of 2003 both followed this new model.

Most of the American public appeared to be favorable toward this new American policy. On the very day of the September 11 attacks, several telephone surveys were conducted, which asked about military responses to the attacks and did not mention possible diplomatic, economic, or legal measures (Solop & Hagen, 2002). In response, 86% of Americans agreed when they were asked if the attacks were "an act of war." In another survey, which offered the alternative that the attacks were an isolated terrorist incident, only about 20% chose that option, whereas about 70% answered that they were an act of war (Saad, 2001e). About 20% of those surveyed on September 11 agreed with the response alternative of immediate military strikes against known terrorist organizations "*even if it is unclear who caused today's attacks,*" whereas about 70% said they favored military strikes only after the responsible terrorist organizations were clearly identified, and only about 5% opposed military strikes (Moore, 2001e). About three-fourths of Americans responded that the terrorist attack represented a permanent turning point for the U.S., whereas only about 20% said that things would eventually return to normal (Saad, 2001a).

Encouraged by President Bush's postattack rhetoric, these belligerent attitudes of Americans continued at a very high level. Later in September, public support for retaliatory military action remained at about 90%, with no more than 10% opposing military strikes (Newport, 2001c). Intelligence reports identified the attackers as members of al Qaeda, a far-flung organization headed by Osama bin Laden, with terrorist training camps in Afghanistan under the protection of its Taliban government. By early October the U.S. began bombing raids against some of these training camps and against Taliban military forces, and by December the Taliban government had been defeated by a combination of western troops and Afghan resistance forces.

Public support for the attacks on al Qaeda and the Taliban remained at 90% throughout the Afghan fighting, though initial public approval of using American ground troops was only about 75%, and support for the attacks was only 65% when respondents were reminded that Afghan civilians could be killed in the process (Moore, 2001f; Jones, 2002a). More than half of Americans said they had a favorable opinion of the Afghan people, and also of Arabs in general, whereas nearly two-thirds said they felt favorable to people of the Islamic faith; but over 90% felt *un*favorable to the Taliban government (Jones, 2001a). At the start of military action in October, the average American expected the fighting in Afghanistan to last a year or more (Moore, 2001f), but by December the Taliban government had collapsed and over half of respondents expected the fighting to be over within a few months (Newport, 2001g). Six months after the WTC attack, there was only sporadic fighting in Afghanistan, but the percent of Americans who believed it was at least somewhat likely that Osama bin Laden would be killed or captured had dropped sharply to 55%. Looking to the future, a bare majority of respondents (52%) favored mounting a long-term war to defeat global terrorism (Jones, 2002a).

Other Dimensions of Opinions About Terrorism

Public Worries.   A key aspect of terrorism is how serious a problem it is in people's minds. Survey data on the nation's "most important problem" show that terrorism zoomed

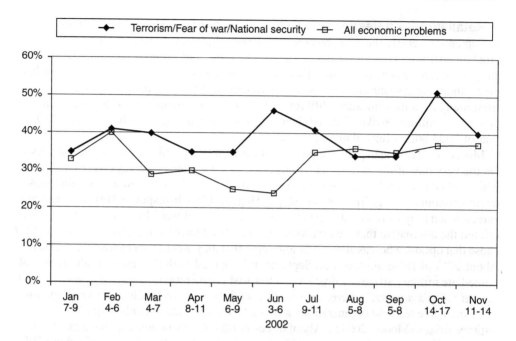

FIGURE 15–3 Americans' worries in 2002 (percent saying that international concerns versus economic concerns were the nation's most important problem).

Source: Data are from the Gallup Poll (Jones, 2002b).

from zero to top place in the month after the September 11 attacks, with 46% of Americans listing it as most important and 18% more mentioning national security or fears of war (64% total). For a brief period, this level of international concern was about as high as had been reached during the Korean and Vietnam Wars. The total for international concerns decreased to 59% in November 2001, and then leveled off around 40%, continuing to vacillate around the 40% level throughout 2002. For most months of 2002 they exceeded the total of all economic concerns (Jones, 2001b, 2002b)—see Figure 15–3.

Earlier, following the 1995 bombing of the Federal Building in Oklahoma City, over 85% of Americans had said that it was at least somewhat likely that similar acts of violence would occur in the U.S. in the future. In 1995, despite the minuscule proportion of terrorist victims in the U.S., slightly over 40% of respondents had expressed worry that "you or someone in your family" would become a victim of such an attack, but that figure had dropped to about 25% in 2000 (*Gallup Poll Monthly*, 2001, No. 432). After the September 11 attacks, the worry figure approached 60% for 2 months and then decreased to around 35% and stayed near there for the next 1 1/2 years (Moore, 2003b). The percentage of people saying that future terrorist attacks on the U.S. were at least somewhat likely peaked at 85% in October, 2001, declined to about 60% by December, and remained roughly at that level before and after the Iraq War, which officially ended in May 2003 (Moore, 2003b).

Success in Combating Terrorism? Americans' beliefs that the U.S. and its allies were "winning the war on terrorism" peaked at 66% in January 2002 following victory in Afghanistan, decreased to about 35% for the latter part of 2002, and briefly spurted again to 65% as the Iraq War was winding down in April 2003 (Moore, 2003b). However, a year after the attacks, 60% of the public believed that "the terrorists will always find a way to launch major attacks no matter what the U.S. government does" (Newport, 2002a). Accordingly, about 90% of the public expected the war on terrorism to be a long one in the first months after the attacks (in comparison, only half of Americans expected a long war in the days after Japan's attack on Pearl Harbor in 1941—Newport, 2001f).

Concern for Civil Liberties.   A major result of terrorism may be political consequences stemming from overconcern with national security: "Among these are the compromise of civil liberties, group scapegoating, muting of political opposition, and extremist political movements" (Smelser & Mitchell, 2002, p. 4). During the 1 1/2 years after the September 11 attacks, public concern for civil liberties in the U.S. grew stronger, rising from 49% up to 64% of people who said that steps to prevent additional terrorist acts should be taken "only if those steps would not violate basic civil rights" (Moore, 2003b). As examples, support for government surveillance policies was only 26% when monitoring of the respondent's own phone line or e-mail was mentioned, and support for trying suspected terrorists in military tribunals dropped substantially when the question mentioned that evidence might be withheld or that a less-than-unanimous verdict might be accepted (Huddy, Khatib, & Capelos, 2002).

Ways of Reducing or Preventing Terrorism.   The preceding paragraphs give a strong indication of how difficult it will be to overcome the threats of terrorism in the modern world. Galtung (2002) has pointed out how common is the vicious cycle in which violence and counterviolence—terrorism and government-sponsored terrorism— each respond to and provoke the other. A particularly clear example of this is the long-standing and bitter Israeli–Palestinian conflict, but it also applies to many U.S. international actions. Galtung's prescription is "To end terrorism, end state terrorism" (p. 10). Because that goal will be extremely difficult to accomplish, what other steps can be taken? Several edited volumes and journal issues are good sources of wisdom in this area (Stout, 2002; Unger, 2002; Wagner, 2002a; Moghaddam & Marsella, 2004); and the National Academies of Science and the American Psychological Association have both established committees to suggest behavioral science approaches to addressing the threat of violence (Smelser & Mitchell, 2002; Pyszczynski, Solomon, & Greenberg, 2002; Levant, 2003).

The topic of how to reduce or prevent terrorism is much too complex to discuss at length here. However, some psychologically informed suggestions may be briefly mentioned. One important pathway is to work toward reducing the levels of structural violence in the world, for instance by helping other countries to "improve their economic conditions, advance greater equality, and reduce repression." Another is to reduce "us–them differentiation" and devaluation of outgroups, whether national, ethnic, religious, or cultural (Staub, 2002, p. 211). Post (2002b) suggested the necessity of winning the hearts and minds of third-world peoples by cooperating with their national and religious leaders to reduce the attractiveness of and support for terrorist groups. Wessells (2002) proposed four other policy changes for the U.S.: stop supporting repressive national regimes, stop supplying military arms all over the world, give leadership and financial support to providing education as a basic right for all children, and encourage inclusive political participation and democratization in countries overseas.

All of these proposed steps go beyond the simple retaliatory cycle of violence leading to counterviolence, for they aim to address the many root causes of violence. In this process, a vital skill for Westerners to develop is practicing "realistic empathy," the process of carefully imagining oneself in the situation of other cultural groups and coming to understand their thoughts and feelings (McNamara & Blight, 2001; M. B. Smith, 2002).

It is important for U.S. citizens to realize that our typical views of the righteousness of U.S. international actions are disputed by many people in many other nations. Indeed,

> Although the United States regularly denounces various countries as "rogue states," in the eyes of many countries it is becoming the rogue superpower. . . . They view the United States as intrusive, interventionist, exploitative, hegemonic, hypocritical, and applying double standards, engaging in what they call "financial imperialism" and "intellectual colonialism". . . . (Huntington, 1999, pp. 42–43)

Public Opinion About the Iraq War

Americans had a history of enmity toward Saddam Hussein, going back to the Persian Gulf War of 1991—one so strong that in 1997 about 75% said we should have continued fighting until he was removed from power and about 40% still favored a covert assassination plan against him (*Gallup Poll Monthly*, 1997, No. 387). After the defeat of the Taliban government in Afghanistan, President Bush did not rest on that achievement, but began a publicity campaign to convince the American people and the United Nations that a war against Iraq was required to eliminate the danger of Saddam Hussein's using weapons of mass destruction (WMD) against other nations. In October, he succeeded in persuading Congress to vote to authorize him to use military force to accomplish "regime change" in Iraq; but throughout late 2002 public support for using American ground troops to invade Iraq remained only about 55% (Newport, 2002b).

In late 2002, as the United Nations and other countries debated about U.S. plans to pressure Iraq, key issues in the U.S. became the adequacy of our diplomatic efforts and the support we would have from other countries. In October less than half of the U.S. public said that we had done all we could diplomatically. Similarly, if the UN and other nations supported military action, then about 80% of Americans said they would favor it, but without UN or allied support, less than 40% favored unilateral military action by the U.S. In a surprising finding, a majority of the public stated opposition to a preemptive (first-strike) U.S. military attack against an unspecified other nation, but they made an exception in the case of Iraq, with about two-thirds saying that "the U.S. should be able to attack Iraq if it thinks that Iraq might attack the U.S." (Saad, 2002e, p. 46).

In November 2002, the UN required Iraq to readmit UN weapons inspectors to search for WMD, and thereafter central issues became whether the inspectors had searched fully enough, whether they had found anything incriminating, and whether they should continue their searches or give way to preemptive military action. No clear evidence of Iraq having chemical or biological WMD was ever found, but 66% of Americans believed it had them and 27% more thought it was trying to develop them. Nevertheless, 63% of the public said a war would not be justified if such weapons were found *and* Iraq agreed to destroy them, and 64% said the U.S. should not attack Iraq without getting a further authorization from the UN. However, as early as November, nearly 60% of the population thought President Bush had already decided to go to war against Iraq (Moore, 2002d). In December, about two-thirds of Americans opposed going to war until the inspectors found evidence of WMD, and over 60% said that, to justify an invasion, the U.S. should publicly release its information that Iraq had WMD (Moore, 2002e).

In January 2003, over three-fourths of the U.S. public said that the UN weapons inspectors in Iraq had been doing a good job (Carlson, 2003a). Only 55% of Americans said they were somewhat or very satisfied with the role that America plays in world affairs, down from 66% a year previously (McComb, 2003). In February 2003, about 60% of the public in both Great Britain and Canada were opposed to the U.S. taking military action against Iraq (Burkholder, 2003). Yet, in mid-March, when Bush gave Saddam Hussein just

48 hours to leave Iraq or else face an invasion, about two-thirds of the U.S. respondents approved of the ultimatum and thought that the U.S. had done all it could to resolve the crisis diplomatically. This poll also showed that 44% approved because they were convinced that going to war was the right thing to do, 21% were unsure but approved because they supported the president, and 30% disapproved of Bush's decision. A bare majority of the public thought that the war would make the U.S. more safe, and 70% were worried about going to war. Only 25% thought that the number of people killed in the war would be "low" (Moore, 2003a).

In the week after U.S. and British forces invaded Iraq, 72% of the U.S. public expressed approval for the war, and Bush's job approval rating jumped 13%, from 58% to 71% (Newport, 2003). Despite the lack of clear evidence, almost 90% of the U.S. public said they thought Saddam Hussein supported terrorist groups that planned to attack the U.S., and half of respondents thought he was personally involved in the September 11 terrorist attacks (Carlson, 2003b). In mid-April, as the Iraqi army was mostly defeated, two thirds of Americans said they were somewhat or very satisfied with the position of the U.S. in the world (up from before the war). Although the U.S. invasion had had little international backing, 61% of respondents said they thought the U.S. rated somewhat or very favorably in the eyes of the world (Jones, 2003b). However, a bare majority of Americans said they thought that the war had had a positive effect on life in the United States, whereas after the 1991 Persian Gulf War, 78% of Americans had answered that question positively (Carlson, 2003c).

Although the Iraq War was officially concluded on May 1, 2003, Saddam Hussein and his sons were not confirmed as killed or captured for several months, and the country remained in chaos for some time. Continuing guerrilla attacks on U.S. and British soldiers and on Iraqi police and other personnel assisting the occupation forces disrupted supply and security operations for many months and made administration of the country very difficult. A continuing danger is that the war, occupation, and disruption will generate a new and larger group of anti-West terrorists than those who launched attacks before the war. By June, 2004, 13 months after the official conclusion of the war, 53% of U.S. registered voters said that going to war in Iraq had not been worth it, and 57% said that Bush's policies in Iraq had "given countries around the world a more negative opinion of the U.S." (Brownstein, 2004, p. A31).

WHO HOLDS WHICH INTERNATIONAL ATTITUDES?

In this section we discuss the **correlates** of isolationist versus internationalist attitudes and attitudes toward war. That is, we ask this question: What subgroups of people tend to hold specific types of international attitudes? Although there is considerable agreement among research studies in this area, an important caution to keep in mind here is that significant differences that are reported usually represent at most a moderate degree of relationship—that is, one that would allow for many exceptions in individual cases.

Isolationism

Three early national survey studies of isolationist versus internationalist attitudes reported findings that were largely complementary (Free & Cantril, 1967; McClosky, 1967; Free & Watts, 1980). McClosky's study was unique in studying a national cross section of about 1,500 people as well as over 3,000 political leaders who had been delegates and alternates to national political conventions. More recent data come mainly from repeated national surveys, both commercial and academic.

Demographic Correlates of Isolationism. All three early studies agreed that poorly-informed individuals and those with little education were more likely to be isolationists, as were rural residents. Persons aged 60 and over and non-labor-force members (mostly retired people) tended toward isolationism, as did women in general. Protestants were more likely to be isolationistic than Catholics, and Jews were least so. The southern states that first shifted to voting Republican were most isolationistic, whereas the East and the Midwest were more internationalist. The poor and blue-collar workers were much more likely to be isolationistic than were those better off financially, including white-collar workers and professional and business people.

Recent data confirm the continuation of most of these patterns, but with added complexity because isolationists now often favor greater defense spending and warlike actions. People's educational level is generally positively correlated with internationalist attitudes, but much less so with support for wars. Younger individuals (below age 30) tend to be more internationalist, though on some particular wars they have registered a more dovish stance. Women, too, are typically more dovish on issues of war or the use of force. On some policy issues, Protestants are less internationalistic than Catholics, and Jews are more internationalistic, but these differences reverse on support for war. The South is markedly conservative on foreign policy, including support for defense spending and wars, whereas the East and West are somewhat more internationalistic (Erikson & Tedin, 2001).

Personality Correlates of Isolationism. McClosky's (1967) study utilized over 70 different scales, most of them measures of personality characteristics. His results can be briefly summarized as follows: Isolationists showed many of the characteristics of authoritarianism, such as ethnocentric and anti-Semitic beliefs, and tendencies to acquiesce to authority. They also exhibited intolerance of ambiguity, obsessive tendencies, rigidity, and inflexibility. They tended to be low in democratic convictions and commitment, and high in political alienation (cynicism, suspiciousness, and a sense of political futility).

Another prime characteristic of isolationists, according to McClosky's findings, was misanthropy. They tended toward hostile and paranoid views of the world, including lack of faith in people, contempt for weakness, and intolerance of human frailty. Yet at the same time they were low in ego strength themselves, suffering from anxiety, guilt feelings, frustrations, and lack of satisfaction in life.

In an important distinction, McClosky divided isolationists empirically into two subtypes: peaceful, and aggressive (or jingoistic). The peaceful isolationist wanted the nation to withdraw into its shell and avoid most contacts with other nations, including any threats or use of force. The jingoistic isolationist, on the other hand, relied on power and the threat of force to ensure the nation's safety behind its impregnable defenses. McClosky showed that peaceful isolationists were less driven by aversive psychological needs like hostility and alienation, and therefore were more like nonisolationists than were jingoistic isolationists.

Attitudes Concerning War

Reviews of studies on hard-line Cold War attitudes versus conciliatory viewpoints have reported findings closely resembling those for isolationism (Scott, 1965; Rosenberg, 1967). That is, militaristic hard-liners share many characteristics of isolationists.

Bringing these findings up to date, let's examine attitudes toward recent wars. During the Iraq War of 2003, the largest group difference in support for the war was between Republicans and Democrats—93% versus 53% favorable. The groups least supportive of the war were African Americans (29% favorable) and liberals (44%), whereas people with household incomes below $30,000 (58% favorable), individuals with postgraduate levels of education (60%), and urban residents (62%) were also well below average in support for the war. Women were 12% less favorable than men. The East was the least-supportive area, and the West was the most-supportive (Jones, 2003a). Among other differences, Americans who were more religious, particularly white, born-again Protestants, were more favorable to the war than were less-religious respondents (Newport et al., 2003). Group differences were very similar during the Afghanistan fighting except that college-educated respondents were considerably more favorable than those with a high school education to the use of U.S. ground troops (Newport, 2001e).

In fears of terrorism, similar to the preceding findings, women were more worried than men in November 2001 (45% to 24%), high-school-educated respondents were more worried than college-educated ones (41% to 31%), and low-income Americans were more worried than those with incomes above $50,000 (48% to 28%)—(Saad, 2001f). Immediately after the September 11 attacks, Americans aged 18–29 were considerably more worried about future terrorism than were older Americans, particularly those 65 and older (Saad & Carroll, 2001).

Although government policymakers are much better informed than the average citizen about foreign-policy issues, they too are subject to attitudinal influences. Two opposing images of international conflict tend to predominate among policy officials: the *deterrence* image is typical among "hard-liners," who criticize appeasement and cite the pre-World War II Munich agreement as their key analogy; whereas the *conflict-spiral* image is typical among "conciliators," who cite the pre-World War I buildup of world tensions as their most pertinent example (Tetlock, 1983b, 1998). These two types of policymakers have been shown to have personality differences similar to those previously described for isolationists versus internationalists (Etheredge, 1978). For example, content analysis of speeches in the U.S. Senate showed that isolationistic Senators presented foreign-policy issues in more simple, rigid, and emotionally-charged terms than did their nonisolationistic colleagues (Tetlock, 1981).

Attitudes of the Mass Public Versus Elites

Several studies of international attitudes have contrasted average citizens with elite groups (e.g., Oldendick & Bardes, 1982; Schneider, 1983; Public Agenda Foundation, 1984). Elites have generally been defined as being senior leaders in fields relevant to the topic under consideration, including government, business, labor, education, religion, journalism, and civic service. Although such elites agree with the mass public on many issues, there are moderate-to-extreme differences between them on other issues.

In Oldendick and Bardes's (1982) study, the most striking of these differences was that much higher percentages of the elites were internationalistic (e.g., 38% higher on the U.S. taking an active role in world affairs). On the dimension of militarism, the elites were 33% higher in favor of selling military equipment and giving military aid to other countries. There were somewhat smaller differences on desirable American goals (e.g., elites were 14% lower on bringing democracy to other nations) and on moving toward detente with the USSR (elites were 22% higher on favoring joint energy efforts). There were mixed differences on international diplomacy (e.g., elites were 26% *lower* on the goal of strengthening the UN, but 22% higher in favoring more active opposition to apartheid—Oldendick & Bardes, 1982; Foster, 1983).

These major differences between the public and elites have continued to the present. In the 1980s, elites were 40% higher than the public in favoring diplomatic negotiations with Cuba, and 21% higher in favoring a mutual nuclear freeze with the USSR (Schneider,

1983). In 1998, elites were higher than the public in beliefs that the U.S. had a vital interest in many foreign countries (e.g., 42% higher re Brazil, 31% higher re China, 27% higher re Mexico, 17% higher re Russia—*Public Perspective*, 2001). In addition to these substantive differences, political elites' views on policy issues are usually much more internally consistent and more stable over time than average citizens' opinions (Jennings, 1992).

HOW DO INTERNATIONAL ATTITUDES CHANGE?

Although views about foreigners and other nations are typically developed without any direct contact with the attitude object, once formed, international attitudes are usually quite resistant to major changes, even through relevant personal experience (Tetlock, 1998). Given that resistance, what factors can produce changes in people's international attitudes?

Contact with Foreigners.   Foreign travel is often thought to influence attitudes of both the traveler and those host-country citizens with whom the visitor comes in contact. For instance, foreign student programs and cultural exchanges have often assumed that getting to know foreigners will lead to greater liking for them and increase international goodwill. However, review of empirical studies of such programs shows that these assumptions are much too simple and are frequently in error (Pool, 1965). The purpose of the travel (study, tourism, business trip, military assignment, etc.) must be considered, as well as the social and cultural situation that travelers meet in relation to their backgrounds and expectations. Foreign contact will usually increase detail and differentiation in attitudes, but it may cause either favorable or unfavorable changes, no change at all, or a change from either extreme toward a more moderate view. A common finding is a U-shaped curve of favorability toward the host country over the time period of the visit—a low point in the middle when initial enthusiasm has worn off and everyday complications and annoyances are salient, followed by increasing favorability as the time to leave approaches. Some research has shown a second U-shaped pattern of favorability to one's own country after one's return (Selltiz & Cook, 1962; Gullahorn & Gullahorn, 1963).

Personal Experiences.   In addition to contact with foreigners, personal experiences of other sorts can sometimes affect international attitudes. A prime example is Rappoport and Cvetkovich's (1968) report on attitude changes in a group of Vietnam veterans. Although hardly any of them had felt negative toward the war before their own overseas duty, most of the veterans who had been in intense combat had become much more critical of the war; by contrast, a majority of the light-combat and rear-echelon non-combat groups had become more positive toward the war while in Vietnam. These findings are particularly interesting because they run counter to predictions that would be made from the dissonance-theory principle that one comes to like what one has suffered for.

Impact of Events.   Helpful reviews of this topic by Deutsch and Merritt (1965) and Page and Shapiro (1982) have stated the following principles. Attitude change can result from spectacular events, which receive much media coverage, or from "cumulative events," which take place gradually over a long time (e.g., increasing industrialization of a country). However, often even spectacular events have no effect on attitudes, or they may cause only a brief fluctuation followed by a return to the preexisting attitude. For instance, following the failure of the Cuban Bay of Pigs invasion attempt, the events of the Cuban missile crisis in 1962 did not change the level of U.S. public opposition to an American invasion of Cuba (about 65% opposed).

When rapid attitude shifts occur, they are usually related to major events in international affairs or in the economy, such as the improvement in U.S.–Soviet relations that took place under Gorbachev, and particularly the fall of the Berlin Wall, which signaled the end of the Cold War. As a contrasting example, after the Chinese army's massacre of student protesters in Tiananmen Square in 1989, the percentage of Americans who expressed favorable opinions of China plunged briefly from 72% to 31% (*Gallup Report, 1989,* No. 287). However, even the most dramatic changes in political alignments usually involve attitude changes by only 20% to 30% of the population, and such changes almost always involve a combination of spectacular events and cumulative events. Either type of event alone is apt to produce attitude changes of no more than 10%.

Education and Persuasion. A review of research on education and persuasion attempts to influence international attitudes (Janis & Smith, 1965) indicates that there are many sources of resistance to such approaches. For instance, both group affiliations and personality needs are likely to reinforce people for maintaining their current attitudes. For this reason, intended audiences often do not receive adequate exposure to the message, let alone take the further steps of attention, comprehension, and acceptance (e.g., Star & Hughes, 1950). Little research has been done specifically on persuasion regarding international attitudes, but a few studies have shown that significant attitude changes can be achieved under the right conditions (e.g., Putney & Middleton, 1962; Nelson, 1988). A particularly powerful intervention, which combines intergroup contact with educational and persuasive communication, is unofficial international problem-solving workshops. A series of these meetings have been held between politically-influential Israelis and Palestinians for over 20 years, organized and facilitated by Kelman (1997).

Government or Media Programs. Governments and the mass media manage much of the public presentation of information relevant to international attitudes. By giving special attention to (or withholding it from) certain events, developments, or policies— that is, agenda-setting—they are in a position of potential influence over public attitudes (Deutsch & Merritt, 1965). For instance, some commercial public relations campaigns in the U.S. media have been successful in improving the image of various foreign countries in Americans' minds (Manheim & Albritton, 1984). Conversely, the U.S. news media have usually ignored developments in major areas of the world, such as the Arab world of the Middle East and North Africa, except for events which threaten U.S. or Israeli interests (Adams, 1982). The way in which the emphasis of news programs can determine the topics that influence American public opinion has been convincingly demonstrated by Iyengar and Kinder (1986—see Chapter 8).

In the era of the Cold War between the United States and the USSR, some proposals were advanced for ways to break the vicious circle of mutual distrust, suspicion, and hostility. For instance, Osgood (1962, 1986) proposed what he called the GRIT strategy (the initials stand for Graduated and Reciprocated Initiatives in Tension-reduction). In this strategy one of the two superpowers would begin a preannounced program of small unilateral steps to reduce world tensions, such as dismantling some missiles, which the other major power would be urged to reciprocate in ways that it felt would further reduce tension. This approach would reverse the upward spiral of the arms race and break the typical logjam of intransigence in negotiations that allowed each nation to prevent any beneficial movement by the other. Experimental tests of the GRIT strategy have shown that it works well in laboratory situations (Lindskold, 1978). Moreover, Etzioni (1967) described the actions and statements of the Kennedy administration between June and November, 1963, as a partial test of this gradualist approach to detente, which he called the "Kennedy experiment." He concluded that these actions did lead to a reduction of world tensions and to less-hostile international attitudes. In the late 1980s, Soviet leader Gorbachev appears to have followed parts of this strategy in his arms reduction initiatives, which had a dramatic effect on U.S. public opinion and on actions of the Reagan and the Bush administrations (Tetlock, 1998).

RESEARCH ON INTERNATIONAL ATTITUDES

Most research on international attitudes has been unsophisticated and descriptive in nature. Many studies have only presented item responses for a whole sample of respondents, and most studies provide data for only one point in time and one nation (or, frequently, for one subgroup within a nation, such as students). Such descriptive surveys are valuable in aiding communication of public viewpoints and letting decision-makers know in some detail about public beliefs and feelings. However, there is a need for more sophisticated studies comparing attitudes across several periods of time, and in several countries, and using statistical analyses to show the significance and stability of trends (Etzioni, 1969; Tetlock, 1998). The *Eurobarometer* surveys of European countries provide some of the best examples of comparative research across countries and years.

To achieve a causal understanding of factors in attitude change, experimental and quasi-experimental research designs are needed to test and verify hypotheses developed from anecdotal and descriptive studies. In the field of international attitudes, relatively little experimental research on attitude change has been done, but testable hypotheses have been offered—for example, about factors that have inhibited arms control activism on the part of American citizens (Gilbert, 1988). In quasi-experimental, time-series research, Tetlock (1985) demonstrated how the level of complexity of official U.S. and Soviet foreign-policy rhetoric responded to the other country's behavior and to important current events. Good experimental research has been done by Lindskold (1978) on effects of Osgood's GRIT strategy on conflict and cooperation, and by Iyengar and Kinder (1986) on the way that TV network newscasts can prime public responses to international issues. Similarly, an experimental study of international simulations, in which American citizens take the roles of policy-makers from other nations, revealed factors that prevented their goal of improved international attitudes from occurring (Trost, Cialdini, & Maass, 1989). There is a wide-open field for more experimental research of this sort on international attitudes.

SUMMARY

Our images of foreign nations and peoples are often incomplete and distorted. Particularly in the area of world affairs, public information is sharply limited. Children begin to form their views of foreign peoples as early as age 6, basing them largely on ingroup–outgroup relationships and on shaping by parents and teachers. Adults' stereotypes of other nations also seem to be based largely on national alliances or competition.

Other nations' attitudes toward the U.S. have varied considerably with events, being highly favorable during our post–World War II aid to Europe, but much less positive during the Vietnam War, the first part of the Reagan administration, and after 2000 when the Bush administration's foreign policy was seen as unilateral and militaristic. America's culture and way of life are also viewed with ambivalence and disfavor in many countries, particularly Muslim ones.

The Cold War competition between the United States and Russia generated mirror-image perceptions of world affairs in which each side saw itself as peace loving and virtuous and saw the other side as aggressive and reckless. However, after Gorbachev became the Soviet leader, and since the dissolution of the USSR, American attitudes toward Russia have become quite favorable.

After World War II Americans became strongly internationalistic, in stark contrast to their views before World War II, but both the Korean War and the Vietnam War were markedly unpopular in the U.S. by the time they were concluded. U.S. internationalism was reduced by the Vietnam War, but it recovered by 1980 and stayed high through the 1990s despite the Persian Gulf War of 1991. Since the end of the Cold War, Americans have become more willing to support both "peacekeeping" missions and limited wars. In general, much higher percentages of elite groups than of the mass public tend to be internationalistic.

International terrorism has increased since the 1980s, and it jumped to a position as the nation's most important problem after the September 2001 destruction of the World Trade Center. Terrorist acts are often a reaction to government-sponsored terrorism and/or global structural violence that creates poverty and injustice. However, these causes are rarely recognized, and recent American reactions to terrorism have treated it as an act of war rather than a crime, focusing largely on retaliation as in the Afghanistan and Iraq Wars. Americans are not optimistic about the likelihood of completely preventing future terrorist acts, and they are becoming more concerned about potential damage to civil liberties in the war on terrorism. Preventing terrorism will require breaking out of the vicious cycle of violence provoking counterviolence.

Although international attitudes are often formed without any direct contact with the attitude object, these attitudes are usually quite resistant to major changes, even through personal experience. The main factors that (on occasion) are effective in influencing international attitudes are these: contact with foreigners, personal experiences such as combat participation, spectacular or cumulative world events, education and persuasion campaigns, and government or media programs combining international actions and public statements.

16

Racism and Prejudice

There is no more evil thing in this present world than race prejudice, none at all. . . . It justifies and holds together more baseness, cruelty, and abomination than any other sort of error in the world.—H. G. Wells.

No State shall make or enforce any law which shall abridge the privileges or immunities of citizens of the United States; nor shall any State deprive any person of life, liberty, or property, without due process of law; nor deny to any person within its jurisdiction the equal protection of the laws.—The Fourteenth Amendment to the U.S. Constitution.

The status of black Americans today can be characterized as a glass that is half full—if measured by progress since 1939—or as a glass that is half empty—if measured by the persisting disparities between black and white Americans since the early 1970s.—Gerald D. Jaynes & Robin M. Williams, Jr., 1989.

Americans like to think of the U.S. as "one nation . . . with liberty and justice for all." However, despite these high ideals, our nation has a long history of intolerance, injustice, and violence—first toward the Native Americans, and then toward a succession of immigrant groups, each of which had to struggle to gain the freedom, equality, and justice guaranteed to them by the Constitution. To cite just one example, anti-Catholicism was rampant in all of the American colonies settled by Protestants, even leading to the execution of priests. It grew even stronger when large numbers of Catholic immigrants began arriving in the nineteenth century. Powerful groups formed the violently anti-Catholic Know-Nothing Party, and later the Ku Klux Klan persecuted Catholics as well as blacks and Jews. Although the Irish, Italians, Poles, and other immigrant groups gradually gained local political power, on the national scene New York Governor Alfred Smith's Catholicism doomed his presidential bid in 1928 and stirred up more anti-Catholic violence. Even in 1960, John F. Kennedy nearly lost the presidential election because of anti-Catholic sentiment and votes. Since then, those passions have mostly evaporated, but it was 1979 before a Pope could be entertained in the White House and welcomed as a visitor by Americans of all religious persuasions (Morrow, 1979).

BACKGROUND OF RACE RELATIONS IN THE U.S.

This chapter on prejudice and discrimination focuses mostly on race relations involving black Americans, the group that was stigmatized most severely by slavery in America and later by legalized "Jim Crow" segregation. However, it is important to realize that fairly similar accounts could be written about *religious* persecution, not only against Catholics but also against Jews, Muslims, and others, and about *ethnic, racial, and national* prejudice against Hispanics, Asians, Native Americans, Irish, Italians, and many other groups (e.g., Winston, 1996; Acuna, 2000). To provide a context for recent developments, we recap here a few of the key events of black history in America. Former Secretary of Health, Education, and Welfare John Gardner (1984) has written about the black struggle for civil rights as follows:

> In 1776 we proclaimed to the world that "all men are created equal." Eighty-seven years elapsed before Lincoln issued his Emancipation Proclamation. That's a long time to wait.
>
> We fought a tragic and bloody war to free the slaves, and their rights as free citizens were embedded in the Thirteenth, Fourteenth, and Fifteenth Amendments to the Constitution. After the Civil War, Congress passed rudimentary civil rights legislation, but the Supreme Court invalidated much of it, and it left no mark whatever after the period of Reconstruction. Worse yet, the Court chose to interpret the post-Civil War amendments in such a way as to minimize their impact on civil rights. More than three quarters of a century passed before the Court faced up to the post-Civil War amendments. That's a long time too. (p. 38)

After the end of Reconstruction, most southern states passed laws prohibiting most Negroes[1] from voting, and segregation soon spread to public transportation, education, hospitals, government employment, hotels and restaurants, and other public facilities. In its *Plessy v. Ferguson* ruling of 1896, the Supreme Court for the first time interpreted the Fourteenth Amendment as allowing "separate but equal" facilities. Before and during the Depression years of the 1930s there were many lynchings of blacks in the South, and the Ku Klux Klan held considerable political power. With the urgent need for national unity in World War II, there was a beginning of racial integration in some parts of the armed forces and industry, but full integration of the armed forces did not occur until President Truman's order in 1948 (Oskamp & Schultz, 1998).

Soon afterward, the cause of integrated education was pressed in many communities. For instance, Topeka, Kansas, had a separate school system for black children even though Kansas had been a free state ever since its admission to the Union. Black parents there and elsewhere filed lawsuits demanding integrated education on the grounds that separate schools were inherently unequal (Smith, 1988). The Supreme Court agreed and ordered desegregation of education in its 1954 *Brown v. Board of Education of Topeka, Kansas* decision. However, practically no action followed until 1964, when 99% of black children were still attending segregated schools (Edelman, 1973).

Thus in the 1960s "Jim Crow" segregation still persisted, with separate restrooms, separate water fountains, and separate facilities of all kinds for blacks throughout the South. The civil rights movement in the South sprouted when local black people refused any longer to sit only in the back of buses and demanded to be served at formerly segregated lunch counters in drugstores and variety stores. When black protest marchers were beaten by local gangs and by police, the national publicity drew thousands of whites to the South to aid the civil rights movement, but there were also protest riots with huge fires, many deaths, and much destruction of property in a number of northern cities. In 1964, Congress passed the first civil rights act since Reconstruction, and since then other laws have guaranteed access to public accommodations, voting rights, nondiscrimination in housing, and equal employment opportunity for all Americans. Since the 1970s blacks and other racial minorities have been voting in larger and larger numbers and have gained correspondingly greater political power. Concomitantly, their rights to equal treatment

---

[1]In this chapter, and elsewhere in the book, we will use the terms "black" and "African American" interchangeably, and occasionally also the earlier term "Negro" when it was used by the original reports to which we refer (cf. Smith, 1992).

have been recognized in most U.S. localities and establishments (Schuman, Steeh, & Bobo, 1985).

However, there is a dark underside of opposition to this progress, challenging and circumscribing it by resistance and retrenchment (Schuman et al., 1997). Since the 1980s the courts have sharply limited the scope of government programs aimed at increasing equality and remedying discrimination. Poverty and unemployment among ethnic minorities have continued at devastating levels. In the 1990s the median income of black families was only 58% of that of white families, and their median net worth was less than 10% of whites' (Feagin, Vera, & Batur, 2001). Rates of blacks entering college declined, and levels of segregation in residential areas and in public school systems remained extremely high. There were increased incidents of hate speech and hate crimes such as racial harassment, violence, and even dozens of hate killings—mostly of blacks. Programs of affirmative action to assist disadvantaged citizens came under widespread attack, and research showed evidence of continuing racial discrimination in job hiring, bank lending, and housing rentals and purchases (Turner, Fix, & Struyk, 1991; Jackson, 1995; Yinger, 1996), as well as in restaurants and stores (Feagin, 1991). Patterns of police harassment and brutality against minorities were pervasive and led to riots and huge destruction in several cities, most notably Miami and Los Angeles.

In summary, the progress in American race relations during recent decades has been extensive, and a source of justifiable pride. American black leaders have served in Congress, in the Cabinet, and in the United Nations, have been elected mayors of many American cities, and have run for the presidency of the U.S. Blacks have also made great progress in business as well as in sports and entertainment. Yet, "the glass is still half-empty," for evidence shows that racism is still a fact of American life, so much more progress is needed: This chapter summarizes some of the past progress and the present remaining problems in race relations.

WHAT IS RACISM?

The term **racism** is a broader one than "racial prejudice," and it is generally used to include not only prejudice, but also "hostility, discrimination, segregation, and other negative *action* expressed toward an ethnic group" (Marx, 1970, p. 101; italics added). **Prejudice**, in turn, can be defined as an intolerant, unfair, or irrational unfavorable *attitude* toward another group of people (Harding et al., 1969). Although prejudice is usually used to mean unfavorable attitudes against another group, it can also include unfounded *favorable* attitudes toward a group, as we will see in a later section (cf. Jones, 1997).

Authorities agree that racism can be found at both the individual level and the institutional level. An individual would be considered a racist if prejudiced attitudes *and* discriminatory behavior against another racial group were important and central parts of his or her life—shown, for instance, by frequently talking about them, acting upon them, or trying to persuade other people to share the same attitudes and behavior patterns. Individual racism makes the basic assumption that one's own ethnic group is superior, and therefore it entails "strong in-group preference and solidarity" and rejection of people who have other ethnic backgrounds or behavioral customs (Jones, 1997, p. 12).

Institutional racism is a relatively new term in our language, but it describes an age-old pattern of behavior. It refers to formal and explicit laws and regulations that discriminate against certain ethnic groups, as well as to informal, but powerful, social norms limiting the opportunities and choices available to certain ethnic groups. In pointed contrast, members of the majority group have a dominant hierarchical position in social settings, which confers on them an often-unspoken sense of entitlement and privilege (Feagin et al., 2001).

Examples of formal institutional racism include the dual school systems in the South before 1964, housing covenants that formerly prohibited the sale of homes in certain areas to "undesirable" minority groups, and laws prohibiting interracial marriages. On the informal level, colleges and universities have had quotas to admit only a small percentage of minority applicants no matter how good their qualifications. Similarly, many business firms have hired only the "right" sort of person—one who would be acceptable at the club. Real estate agents and lending institutions still often "steer" minority group members away from purchasing homes in certain areas. On a subtler level, the use of certain standardized procedures like aptitude testing for job selection or college admission can be a form of institutional racism if it unfairly or invalidly discriminates against minority-group members who could actually succeed on the job or in the college if given a chance (Jones, 1997). With examples like these in mind, racism has also been defined as "a system of oppression of . . . people of color by white Europeans and white Americans" (Feagin et al., 2001, p. 3).

Individual racism and institutional racism are mutually reinforcing. It is doubtful that institutional racism could develop or survive without support from many individual racists, nor is it likely that individual racism would thrive without strong social support. Underlying both forms of racism is a strong conviction that social groups' access to societal power and privileges should be structured in a hierarchical manner, with one's own group on top—a viewpoint that Sidanius and his colleagues have termed **social dominance orientation** (Pratto et al., 1994). This chapter concentrates on *individual* racism and particularly on racial attitudes regarding black people. However, keep in mind that the focus of the civil rights movement was on combating institutional racism, which was seen as the most important factor in the oppression of ethnic minorities.

CHILDREN'S RACIAL ATTITUDES

Bigots are made, not born. As described in Chapter 8, children learn about the world not only through personal experience, but also through social interaction with parents, teachers, and peers, and through the influence of the media. As Allport (1954) pointed out in his classic volume on prejudice, many of our attitudes and opinions toward groups of people are *adopted*—that is, learned from our family and culture—rather than *developed*—that is, learned through life experiences that lead us to fear or dislike minority groups (Aboud & Levy, 2000).

Attitudes cannot exist without awareness of the attitude object, and racial awareness has been found to develop quite early. Children as young as 3 years old can identify their own race and the race of others. By 7 years of age, almost 100% can accurately discriminate between their own and other racial groups and they also display clear affective reactions to them (Clark & Clark, 1947; Goodman, 1964; Aboud, 1987).

A number of ingenious methods have been used to elicit racial preferences and attitudes from very young children. The best-known is the doll technique developed by Kenneth and Mamie Clark (1947). Children are shown two dolls (or sometimes more), one representing a black child, the other a white child, and asked to respond to a number of questions by choosing one of the dolls. The questions include these: Which doll is most like you? Which is the black (white, Negro, colored) doll? Which is the good (bad) doll? Which is the doll you would like to play with? On the basis of such doll choices, it was established that white children had a strong preference for the white dolls. Further, white children

Photograph courtesy of Kenneth B. Clark.
Reprinted by permission.

Box 16–1   KENNETH B. CLARK, *Pioneer Racial Attitude Researcher*

Kenneth B. Clark, Distinguished Professor of Psychology Emeritus at the City College of New York, had a noteworthy impact on the position of minority groups in the United States. Born in Panama in 1914, he grew up in Harlem, attended Howard University, and earned a Ph.D. at Columbia University in 1940. After brief periods of teaching and research during World War II, he joined the faculty at City College of New York, where he remained for the rest of his career. In later years, he also served as president of the Metropolitan Applied Research Center and, on retirement in 1975, he founded a consulting firm dealing with human relations and affirmative action issues.

The early research of Clark and his wife on the self-images of Negro children was cited in the 1954 U.S. Supreme Court decision regarding school desegregation, Brown v. Board of Education. *Subsequently he served as consultant to many organizations and wrote books such as* Prejudice and Your Child, Dark Ghetto, The Negro American, A Relevant War Against Poverty, *and* Pathos of Power. *He was a member of the New York State Board of Regents for 20 years, and he was elected to serve as president of the American Psychological Association in 1971.*

tended to attribute good qualities to the white dolls and bad qualities to the black dolls (e.g., Clark & Clark, 1947; Asher & Allen, 1969). There has been little disagreement in the interpretation of the results of these studies for white children. White children appear to learn racial discrimination early in life. They generally have strong positive attitudes toward themselves and other members of their race, and they have negative reactions to blacks.

Until the late 1960s, the results for black children seemed equally unambiguous. They too preferred and identified with *white* dolls and rejected black dolls. These data, from the studies just cited and many others, were interpreted to mean that black children developed the same racial attitudes as white children (prowhite, antiblack). The result was a diminished self-concept coupled with an unrealistic and self-defeating wish to be white (Chethick et al., 1967; Coles, 1968).

In the late 1960s, new studies began to challenge the earlier findings. Greenwald and Oppenheim (1968) argued that black children may have misidentified themselves as white in earlier studies because experimenters failed to take account of the range of skin color of black Americans. From the light-skinned black child's point of view, the white doll may in fact have looked more like himself or herself than did the black doll. It was found that, in earlier studies, the percentage of "misidentification" was much higher among light-skinned than dark-skinned blacks (80% versus 23% in the Clarks' study). There were also data-based arguments about whether black children's apparent preferences for white dolls were statistically different from a chance distribution (Banks, 1976; Williams & Morland, 1979).

In addition to these possible experimental artifacts, two developments in U.S. society seemed to have had an impact on black children's self-images. Both the "black pride" movement, with its emphasis on positive cultural traditions and values, and the sharply increased amount of racial integration in public schools were expected to improve black children's self-concepts. Findings consistent with these expectations were reported by Hraba and Grant (1970), who discovered that black children in integrated schools in Lincoln, Nebraska, were as problack in their doll choices as white children were prowhite. Similarly, Crooks (1970) reported that black children in Halifax, Nova Scotia, who had just completed an enriched, integrated, preschool program, identified themselves as black and chose black dolls as the ones they preferred more frequently than a control group of black children who had not experienced the program. These results suggested that for some black children under some conditions racial preferences were changing.

However, in spite of these societal trends, later research findings seem to have reverted to the earlier picture of prowhite doll preference among most black children (Toufexis, 1987). Also, school desegregation has too often been carried out under unfortunate conditions, which decreased rather than increased black pupils' self-esteem and led to increased prejudice by whites toward blacks and vice versa (Stephan, 1978; Cook, 1979, 1984; Gerard, 1983). In sum, it is clear that both black children and white children can and do learn racial prejudice early. Although some children of both races may have profited from the black pride movement and from increased cross-racial contact in desegregated schools, the majority of black and white children still remain both the holders and the targets of racial prejudice.

RACIAL AND ETHNIC STEREOTYPES

What are "they" like, anyway? Most of us, whether we care to admit it or not, hold many ethnic stereotypes: the "crafty" Jew, the "lazy" black, the "gentlemanly" Briton, the "drunken" Irishman, the "stupid" Pole. A **stereotype** is the beliefs we hold about most members of a group of people. Even if we reject the accuracy or appropriateness of stereotypes, we can laugh when a TV comedian uses them, for we have learned that many other people in our society believe them (Vidmar & Rokeach, 1974). In Chapters 2 and 8 we have described the nature and development of stereotypes in general. See Hilton and von Hippel (1996) or Schneider (2003) for reviews of recent research on the nature of stereotypes and factors affecting their formation, occurrence, maintenance, application, and change.

In the racial area, as with international attitudes (see Chapter 15), the degree of stereotyping has usually been measured in terms of the amount of consensus in people's choice of traits as typical of members of an ethnic group—for instance, by having them check pertinent adjectives from an offered list. If the percentage of agreement is high, a stereotype is said to exist. A classic study of this sort done by Katz and Braly in 1933 found that Princeton undergraduates showed very high agreement (above 75%) in describing Negroes as superstitious and lazy, and more than 25% agreement in viewing them as happy-go-lucky, ignorant, ostentatious, and musical.

Over the next 35 years, the specific adjective *content* of students' stereotypes of blacks remained quite similar, but the amount of *consensus* on these terms declined quite markedly. Thus in the late 1960s more than 25% of Princeton students agreed that blacks were musical, happy-go-lucky, pleasure-loving, lazy, and ostentatious (Karlins, Coffman, & Walters, 1969), and a 1976 sample of California college students agreed more than 25% *only* on the traits of "musical" and "aggressive" (Borden, 1977). This fading of social stereotypes has been accompanied by greater reluctance on the part of many raters to attribute traits to whole racial groups. However, there still are much higher levels of agreement when raters are asked what traits *others* attribute to blacks than when they are asked about their *own* perceptions—that is, people have a clear awareness of the social stereotype of blacks. For example, Devine and Elliot (1995) found that over 25% of white University of Wisconsin students reported that blacks were generally considered to be athletic, rhythmic, lazy, low in intelligence, poor, loud, hostile, and criminal. They also showed that low-prejudice and high-prejudice white respondents were equally knowledgeable about the cultural stereotype of blacks. However, high-prejudice whites were much more likely to believe that the stereotype was true than were low-prejudice white participants (see also Lepore & Brown, 1997; Rush, 1997).

Although stereotype research is often done in college classes, college students are probably less likely than older and less-educated citizens to make such stereotypic attributions. A 1936 report written by high-ranking officers at the Army War College illustrates that invidious stereotypes of blacks were common throughout American society:

> The Negro is docile, tractable, light-hearted, care-free, and good-natured.... He is careless, shiftless, irresponsible, and secretive. He resents censure and is best handled with praise and ridicule. He is unmoral, untruthful, and his sense of right doing is relatively inferior. (National Science Foundation, 1969, p. 18)

In a 1991 survey of a representative national sample, 60% of white Americans said that most blacks lack discipline, 50% said they were aggressive or violent, and 31% said they were lazy (Peffley & Hurwitz, 1998). It is obvious that awareness of such negative stereotypes can damage the self-concept of their target groups, and that they can be invoked to rationalize all sorts of harmful discrimination and injustice (cf. Porter & Washington, 1979; Crocker & Major, 1989). However, stereotyping in its milder forms is apparently a universal cognitive tendency that helps people to simplify environmental complexity (Macrae & Bodenhausen, 2000), and therefore an important issue is whether cognitive stereotypes are necessarily carried over into discriminatory behavior. The mere availability of stereotypes may often contribute to prejudice and discrimination, but it is also possible that people can possess stereotypes of groups without letting them affect their behavior and attitudes toward *individuals* (Brewer & Kramer, 1985; Devine, Plant, & Buswell, 2000). This issue is discussed further toward the end of this chapter.

Racial Stereotypes in the Mass Media

The mass media not only reflect a society's stereotypes but greatly contribute to them as well. Since the heyday of radio and the later advent of television, there have been dramatic changes in the depiction of ethnic minorities in the media. Three major stages have been described: first, nonrecognition of their existence, then a period of ridicule which highlighted the most extreme stereotypes (as in *Amos and Andy*'s eye-rolling, shuffling, and fractured English), and later a modicum of inclusion (Clark, 1969).

In the 1950s less than 1% of all TV prime-time characters were black and only 2% were Hispanic. With the civil rights movement of the 1960s, pressure on the networks increased and the percentage of black roles rose to 7%, including a few starring roles (as on *Mission: Impossible*) and notably excluding the old dim-witted, servile stereotypes. In the 1970s

TV adopted the "black pride" theme by pioneering some all-black sitcoms such as *The Jeffersons* and *Sanford and Son*, often in ghetto settings. The characters in these shows were presented as having strengths, but also flaws and foibles that highlighted some other stereotypes: "The shows substituted jivin' and struttin' for grinnin' and shufflin'. This was seen by many as no great improvement" (Lichter et al., 1987, p. 14). Concurrently the range of parts for blacks expanded to include a much wider variety of occupations, including a greater number of negative roles and some criminals and villains, whereas almost all of the few Hispanics on TV were still portrayed as hustlers, criminals, or drug lords.

In the 1980s blacks comprised nearly 10% of television prime-time characters (still well below their percentage of the population), whereas the number of Hispanics had not advanced from the 2% level, with characters spanning "a narrow spectrum from villains to second bananas" (Lichter et al., 1987, p. 16). Subsequently, Bill Cosby's two successive comedy shows became highly popular programs for many years, and depicted blacks as having positive roles and values similar to those of the white middle class. However, the news media continued to portray blacks disproportionately in the roles of criminals, athletes, or entertainers (Martindale, 1986; Entman, 1997). Even today, in both the news and entertainment media, "African Americans are often portrayed as poor or as criminals, and demanding of additional rights and social resources" (Ruscher, 2001, p. 157). A clear example comes from pictures of poor people in U.S. news magazines such as *Time*. In the 1990s, when 29% of Americans at the poverty level were black, fully 62% of the news magazine pictures of poor people were of African Americans; similarly, though 42% of the African American poor were employed, the magazine pictures showed only 12% who were working (Gilens, 1996; see also Signorielli & Kahlenberg, 2001). Such images can subtly reinforce negative stereotypes without the awareness of audience members.

Despite the progress in combating old stereotypes of blacks on prime-time TV, other racial groups, particularly Hispanics and Asians, remained underrepresented and portrayed much less realistically. Also, the many video rentals and reruns of old movies and former TV serials continue to present the derogatory racial images of past decades: the drunken or bloodthirsty Indian, the sinister, inscrutable Oriental, and the shuffling, happy-go-lucky "darkie" (Ruscher, 2001).

The *effects* of these stereotypic media presentations are hard to measure because they are confounded with so many other factors. Some experimental research has shown that unfavorable video portrayals of ethnic groups can increase prejudiced attitudes toward them (e.g., Garrett, Treanor, & Roffey, 2003). However, studies of single programs, even one as phenomenally popular as *Roots*, have generally found relatively minor effects, if any, on the racial attitudes of viewers (Ball-Rokeach, Grube, & Rokeach, 1981). Yet research suggests that the *cumulative* effects of many repeated media presentations of stereotypic information may be very powerful in establishing and maintaining racial attitudes—an example of the media's *enculturation function* (see Chapter 9). Moreover, a meta-analysis of all available research on television effects has concluded that the effects of stereotyping in single programs are consistently larger than those of programs that feature *anti*stereotyping content (Hearold, 1986). Although unfortunate, this is not surprising, for the stereotyping messages are consistent with the overall cultural impact, whereas the antistereotyping programs have to combat it.

THE NATURE OF ETHNIC PREJUDICE

For many people, racial and ethnic attitudes are learned early in life and become relatively important and central in their belief systems (Converse, 1964; Sears, 1975). In addition to the beliefs and stereotypes that they include, they may also have a strong emotional aspect (Sears, 1988b). In many cases, they are likely to remain stable over time and persist into adulthood. On the other hand, research has also shown that they can be malleable during adulthood in reaction to major societal events, mass media influences, and changes in individual life situations such as moving to a different region of the country (Sigel, 1989). In such changing contexts, racial policy preferences often change quite strongly, whereas prejudiced attitudes change more modestly. Thus, research has provided evidence both for temporal persistence of racial and ethnic attitudes and for their modification through the process of adult socialization (Glaser & Gilens, 1997).

We have defined **prejudice** as an intolerant, unfair, or irrational unfavorable attitude toward another group of people, and also an unfounded *favorable* attitude toward a group. Research has shown that ethnic prejudice is usually a *generalized* attitude. That is, people who are prejudiced against one racial or ethnic group are apt to be prejudiced against other outgroups, such as other ethnic groups, homosexuals, foreigners, poor people, and the elderly (e.g., Agnew, Thompson, & Gaines, 2000; McFarland & Mattern, 2003).

Intergroup Biases

The evaluative biases that are found in much research on intergroup attitudes are *ingroup favoritism*—the favorable side of prejudice—rather than strong outgroup derogation or antagonism (Hewstone, Rubin, & Willis, 2002). For example, research in the minimal group situation has shown that individuals tend to hold favorable attitudes toward any group that they are associated with, and that these attitudes arise automatically and without awareness (Otten & Wentura, 1999). Brewer (1999) has attributed this ingroup favoritism to features such as expecting to have common values, common goals, and feelings of moral superiority. As another example, the subtle forms of prejudice that are common today are largely prowhite rather than antiblack in nature (Dovidio, Kawakami, & Gaertner, 2000)— see the later section on aversive racism for fuller discussion. In contrast, situations in which ingroup favoritism gives way to outgroup derogation or hostility are apt to be ones in which strong emotions are aroused or threats to the ingroup are felt (Brewer, 2001).

The overview of research on intergroup bias by Hewstone et al. (2002) summarized five theoretical approaches, each of which proposes somewhat different motivational bases for prejudice. It also specified a number of moderator variables that have been found to increase the level of intergroup bias. They include collectivist cultural patterns, lower educational levels, and greater positive feelings about and identification with one's group (Mullen, Brown, & Smith, 1992). Other variables increasing bias are high-status and high-power groups, groups that are numerical minorities, the task of allocating benefits (as contrasted with allocating harm), personality characteristics such as authoritarianism, and perception of threats to one's group. The threats may be realistic ones, or symbolic (e.g., to one's values), or feelings of intergroup anxiety in interacting with an outgroup, or strong negative stereotypes of the outgroup (Stephan & Stephan, 2000).

WHITE RACIAL ATTITUDES ABOUT BLACKS

"This is our basic conclusion: Our nation is moving toward two societies, one black, one white—separate and unequal" (*Report of the National Advisory Commission on Civil Disorders*, 1968, p. 1). This prophetic statement, made in the wake of the racial disorders of the mid-1960s, summarized the despair of many Americans about the future of race relations in the United States. The same theme of a chasm between black and white

Americans grew in the 1980s and 1990s and persists today (e.g., Kinder & Sanders, 1996; Eberhardt & Fiske, 1998). A highly respected black journalist has even written a book predicting *The Coming Race War in America* (Rowan, 1996). Is there good reason for such despair, or were all of these authors exaggerating the problem? There is no simple answer to this question.

It has become popular among white liberals and black militants to describe the United States as a racist society. Yet the status of race relations in the United States is so complex that no simple summary statement, no catch phrase such as "white racism," can do justice to the complexity. The past 50 years have been marked by both progress and backsliding in U.S. race relations. In fact, even within a given individual, there are very often conflicting and inconsistent racial attitudes on different aspects of the topic. Moreover, this has been true since the founding of our nation, as shown in the lives of two of our most famous Presidents, Jefferson and Lincoln. Jefferson wrote that "all men are created equal" and avowed that he ardently wished for the abolition of slavery, yet he owned many slaves and did not free them. Although Lincoln opposed slavery for many years, he did not believe that blacks and whites could live as equals, and he hesitated long before initiating the Emancipation Proclamation. Even then, he restricted it only to the rebellious southern states, not applying it to the slave-holding border states fighting on the Union side (Bobo, 1988).

Four Aspects of Racial Attitudes

Social Distance.   One important aspect of racial attitudes is the first area that was measured scientifically, the amount of social distance that people desire to maintain from any given ethnic group (Bogardus, 1925). Later research by Triandis (1964) showed that there were five relatively separate dimensions of social distance: exclusion, respect, friendship acceptance, marital acceptance, and superordination (supervising or commanding). Various activities in our lives involve different degrees of intimacy, and it has been common for members of a particular racial group to be accepted for some of these activities but not for others.

In general, white Americans have resisted interracial relationships most strongly in situations where intimacy is greatest (as in dating or marriage) and least in situations where interaction is limited and formal (as in many job situations or customer–salesperson relationships). For instance, in a major study of white racial attitudes in the 1970s, only 12% of the respondents said they would mind a lot or a little if they had a qualified black supervisor on their job, whereas 44% said they would mind a lot or a little if a black family of the same income and education moved next door (A. Campbell, 1971). In the same era 73% of Americans said they disapproved of "marriage between whites and nonwhites" (Schuman et al., 1997). Thus, as the intimacy of relationships increases, prejudice also increases. However, most people are willing to accept equality in some spheres of their lives, if not in all of them.

Most importantly, white Americans' social distance measures have changed markedly toward greater interracial acceptance over the decades since systematic survey studies began. This is shown most dramatically in questions about racial intermarriage, the most intimate level of relationship (see Figure 16–1). As recently as 1958, only 4% of respondents expressed approval of intermarriage "between whites and nonwhites," but by 1997, 67% approved of intermarriage even though it was described more specifically as "between blacks and whites" (Schuman et al., 1997). The same steep increase in acceptance is seen in other social distance items, several of which have topped out at close to 100% acceptance. For instance, this is true of sending one's children to a school in which a

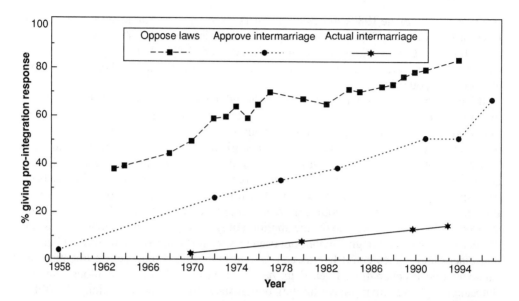

FIGURE 16–1 Comparison of attitudes opposing laws against racial intermarriage, attitudes approving of intermarriage, and actual intermarriage rates, over five decades.

Source: Reprinted by permission of the publisher from *Racial Attitudes in America: Trends and Interpretations* (p. 313), by Howard Schuman, Charlotte Steeh, and Lawrence Bobo, Cambridge, Mass.: Harvard University Press, Copyright © 1985, 1997 by the President and Fellows of Harvard College.

few children are black, and also of having a black family live next door, whereas in 1942 only 36% of respondents were accepting of having "a Negro with the same income and education as you move into your block." Similarly, when the item was last asked in 1985, acceptance of having a family member bring a black friend home to dinner had risen to about 80% of the white population (Schuman et al., 1997). Thus social distance items have shown huge increases in white acceptance of blacks in the past 60 years or so.

Principles of Equal Treatment.   Another racial attitude area involves support for general principles of equal treatment, nondiscrimination, and integration of the races. Survey questions concerning these principles have been asked on topics of school integration, residential integration, equal treatment in employment, public accommodations and public transportation, and willingness to vote for a well-qualified black man for President of the U.S. Just as with the area of social distance, white attitudes on all of these topics have shown very large, parallel increases in favorability over the past several decades. For example, Americans' stated willingness to vote for "a generally well-qualified person for president who happened to be black" reached near-unanimity by 1999 (95%, compared with 66% in 1969 and only 37% in 1958—Newport, 1999). Schuman et al. (1997) summarized the general findings as follows:

> [M]ost questions…about broad principles of equal treatment and integration show much the same almost inexorable upward movement. A revolution in what the white American population took for granted about the relation of blacks and whites occurred between the 1940s and today. (p. 108)

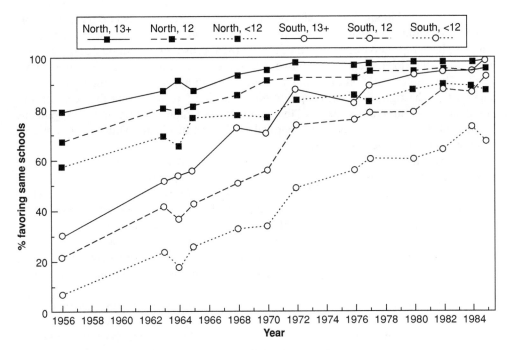

FIGURE 16–2 Percent of white respondents favoring integrated schools over time, by region of the country and educational level.

Source: Reprinted by permission of the publisher from *Racial Attitudes in America: Trends and Interpretations* (p. 110), by Howard Schuman, Charlotte Steeh, and Lawrence Bobo, Cambridge, Mass.: Harvard University Press, Copyright © 1985, 1997 by the President and Fellows of Harvard College.

Figure 16–2 gives a dramatic example of this trend over time, showing results from a question about preference for whites and blacks to attend the same schools rather than separate schools (Schuman et al., 1997). It displays results separately for residents of northern and southern states, and for respondents having three different educational levels (less than high school, high school, and at least some college). The lines for all six subgroups show steep increases from 1956 to 1985, and moreover they converge on a very high level of support for attending the same schools (93% overall in 1985). The responses from the South start out dramatically below those from the North and remain so until the 1970s or 1980s. (In 1942, not shown on the graph, the average level of support for all Southerners was only 2%, and that for all Northerners was 42%, whereas by 1985 the figures were 86% and 96%, respectively.) Finally, the lines for the three educational levels, in both North and South, display systematic differences, with the higher educational levels consistently stating more support for same schools. By 1985, only the least-educated Southerners remained below the national norm of overwhelming support for same schools, but even they showed strong majority support (about 66%).

Certainly data such as these do *not* support the conclusion of the presidential Commission on Civil Disorders quoted at the beginning of this section that American society was becoming more separate and unequal. However, two other aspects of racial attitudes must still be considered, and they present quite a different picture.

Implementation of Principles of Equality. This attitude area deals with steps that the government (federal or local) might take to combat segregation or discrimination or to reduce racial inequality in status or income. In this area, the general picture is more complex and confusing than in the two previous areas. On the six poll questions of this sort that have been repeated frequently since the 1960s, approval of government activism went up in three questions, went down in two, and stayed unchanged in one (Schuman et al., 1997). The implementation questions that increased in approval concerned government support for "the right of black people to go to any hotel or restaurant they can afford," approval of a community-wide law "that a homeowner cannot refuse to sell to someone because of their race or color," and approval of "busing black and white school children from one school district to another."

In contrast to those increases, two items showed somewhat decreasing public support of government implementation actions. They concerned approval of government action to "see to it that black people get fair treatment in jobs" (38% approval in 1964, down to 28% in 1996), and to "see to it that white and black children go to the same schools" (42% approval in 1964, down to 25% in 1994). Unfortunately, the wording of these questions presents some interpretive problems because they both included third alternatives of "no interest" in the question, which was chosen by over one-third of respondents in the 1990s versus about 12% in the 1960s, making the balance of "approve" versus "disapprove" answers more equal than it first appears.

However, some clear patterns do emerge from the implementation questions. First, all of them—both those on which public approval increased and those on which it decreased— show levels of approval much lower than 100%. On their last presentation in the 1990s, the highest level of approval was on the item about a local open-housing law (67%), the next highest was on supporting access to any hotel or restaurant (56%), and the item on busing children between school districts registered only 33% approval. Second, public support for government implementation of equal treatment is far lower than is support for the questions on principles of equal treatment that we discussed just before them. The difference in support for the principles of equality and implementation of them may reflect a differing level of commitment to combating discrimination (Schuman et al., 1997), much like the concept of situational difficulty involved in the pseudo inconsistency between attitude and behavioral measures that we discussed in Chapter 12. Third, different approval levels by region of the country and educational level occur again in these items, with Northerners and more-educated respondents expressing more approval. Fourth, various national events may help to account for some of the confusing patterns in these implementation items.

These conclusions about principles of equality and their implementation show up particularly clearly in Figure 16–3, which depicts responses to items about school integration. There you can see final points showing support for the principle of school integration ending about 50% higher than support for federal implementation measures, which leveled off after 1978 at about 40%. Also, in the 1960s there were very large North–South differences on both topics. As we saw in Figure 16–2, those differences on the principle item diminished greatly, with both regions becoming very strongly positive. On the implementation item, the differences also diminished to near-identity by 1978, but they changed in the opposite direction—the Northerners decreased their approval from 1972 onward. Schuman et al. (1997) suggest that this was largely due to a change in the focus of school desegregation efforts from the South to de facto segregation in the North, which was accompanied by more busing of children. Interdistrict school busing has always had a low nationwide approval rating by Americans, but it has gradually gained in acceptance, first achieving 20% approval in 1983 and 30% approval in 1990.

Thus, in the area of government implementation of programs to promote racial equality, some of these programs are favored by only a minority of Americans, and the size of their supportive group has been increasing only slowly or even decreasing. What are we

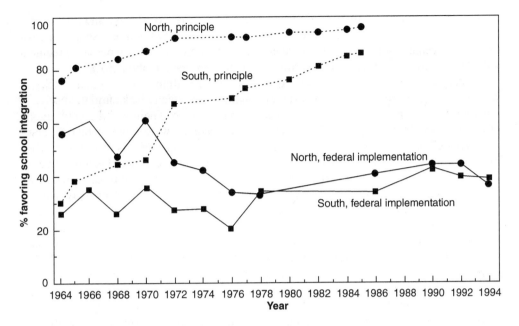

FIGURE 16–3 Attitudes of white respondents toward the principle of school integration and toward federal implementation of school integration, by region of the country.

Source: Reprinted by permission of the publisher from *Racial Attitudes in America: Trends and Interpretations* (p. 126), by Howard Schuman, Charlotte Steeh, and Lawrence Bobo, Cambridge, Mass.: Harvard University Press, Copyright © 1985, 1997 by the President and Fellows of Harvard College.

to make of this paradox of massive and increasing endorsement of principles of racial equality, but slow or no increase in support for implementation of those principles? Is this an indication of vast American hypocrisy and racism? Or are there other explanations? After the next brief section, we will discuss several of the viewpoints on this issue that different researchers have advanced.

Beliefs About Inequality. Why are blacks disadvantaged in American society? Survey questions on this topic have usually stated that black Americans "have worse jobs, income, and housing than white people," and then asked whether that is mainly due to less inborn ability, to discrimination, to a poor chance for education, or to low motivation or willpower. These four alternative explanations were asked separately, so respondents could answer that more than one was mainly responsible. The time series here only began in 1977, more than a decade after the peak of the civil rights movement (Schuman et al., 1997). In that year, the percentage of white respondents' endorsements for the four explanations showed a clear stepwise pattern: inborn ability 27%, discrimination 41%, poor chance for education 50%, and low motivation 66%. In all surveys since then, the order has stayed the same, with low motivation being the most popular explanation and a poor chance for education being second. Interestingly, however, the percentage of agreement with each explanation has decreased over the years up to 1996 by about 10%—which may show a decreasing tendency for whites to give any single answer as *the* explanation for racial inequality.

A similar question asked "if blacks would only try harder, they could be just as well off as whites"—blaming blacks' disadvantages largely on their low motivation. In contrast, a parallel question asked if their plight was due to "generations of slavery and discrimination." In 1972, both questions received about 70% agreement by white respondents, but by 1994 agreement with "not trying hard enough" had increased a bit, whereas agreement with "generations of slavery and discrimination" had dropped to about 50%.

A sharp choice was presented in a question by the Gallup Poll: whether blacks or whites were "more to blame for the present conditions in which blacks find themselves." Although 20%–30% of respondents typically said "both" or "neither," the split among other respondents in 1963 was 70% saying "white people" were more to blame versus 30% saying "blacks." That year, 1963, was the peak of the civil rights movement, when black and white "freedom marchers" in the South were being clubbed, beaten, and even killed by southern police and vigilantes. As a result, whites throughout most of the nation were appalled by the viciousness of the southern forces and sympathized strongly with the plight of blacks. However, by 1968, federal civil rights laws had been passed, black crowds had rioted destructively in many major cities, and many whites were becoming frightened by the "black power" slogan, which proclaimed black militancy and even separatist goals. As a result, the survey responses reversed, with 70% of white respondents saying "blacks" were more to blame for their plight and only 30% saying "whites." Since then, up through 1996, the answers have become even more extreme, with 80% saying "blacks" and only 20% saying "whites" (Schuman et al., 1997).

Another key issue is how much racial discrimination exists in American society. The years from 1963 to 1978 saw a sharp drop in the percentage of whites who thought blacks didn't have as good a chance as whites to get a job in their community—from about 50% to only about 20%. The 20% figure who perceived antiblack job discrimination has remained roughly the same up through 1997. Similarly, in the 1980s and 1990s, the percentage of whites who thought blacks were discriminated against in "getting decent housing" and in "getting managerial jobs" has remained close to 20%. The only area in which whites' perception of antiblack discrimination has increased notably is in police treating blacks unfairly—from about 40% agreement in 1981 to nearly 50% during the 1990s (Schuman et al., 1997). Thus, in most respects, whites' recognition of discrimination against blacks in America has decreased sharply since the 1960s.

THEORIES OF WHITE RACIAL ATTITUDES

The preceding sections portray a complex picture of differing findings for the several aspects of white racial attitudes—increasing social acceptance of blacks over the past 60 years, markedly increasing public endorsement of principles of racial equality, but much lower support for implementation of those principles, decreasing recognition of the widespread occurrence of discrimination in the U.S., and a prevalent tendency to blame blacks' problems on their own low motivation. These paradoxical findings have given rise to several theoretical viewpoints, which the next sections summarize.

Modern Racism

One persuasive explanation of these findings is that the nature of racism and prejudice has changed markedly during the last century (McConahay, Hardee, & Batts, 1981). Examples of "old-fashioned" racist attitudes include support for segregation laws and beliefs in the intellectual and moral inferiority of blacks. Since the civil rights movement of the 1960s, such blatant prejudice has been abandoned, first by elite, trend-setting groups in society and then by most other citizens, except for a few die-hard segregationists such as members of the KKK or White Citizens Party. However, the concept of **modern racism** emphasizes that the *affective* aspects of racial attitudes are usually acquired in childhood and are harder to change than the cognitive belief aspects. Thus, many people who have given up the old-fashioned racist beliefs and attitudes nevertheless still harbor negative, aversive feelings toward blacks (for related evidence, see Crosby, Bromley, & Saxe, 1980).

The result of these contrasting tendencies is that, for many people, their negative racial feelings come to influence new issues of the era, including ones that are not overtly racial on their face. However, whites generally do not perceive their attitudes on these new issues as racist, and they tend to justify their positions on nonracial grounds. Examples of such new issues include attitudes toward busing of school children, and support for various government programs to aid the poor. McConahay (1986) outlined four key beliefs that are central to modern racism: racial discrimination is no longer common in the U.S.; blacks are pushing their goals too hard and too fast; their tactics and demands are unfair; and the recent gains and attention they have received are undeserved.

McConahay and his colleagues (1981) developed scales to measure both old-fashioned and modern racism in order to study their relationship. Some of their old-fashioned racism items (with the racist answer in parentheses) are

- Black people are generally not as smart as whites. (agree)
- Generally speaking, I favor full racial integration. (disagree)

Examples of more subtle, modern racism items are

- The streets are not safe these days without a policeman around. (agree)
- It is easy to understand the anger of black people in America. (disagree)
- Over the past few years the government and news media have shown more respect to blacks than they deserve. (agree)

Research findings showed that respondents recognized the old-fashioned items as being more indicative of prejudice than the modern racism items, though the latter were not perceived as racially neutral. Also, in a situation where faking lack of prejudice was socially desirable, respondents moderated their answers only on the obvious, old-fashioned racism items. Other findings have shown that the modern racism scale predicts antiblack voting and degree of preferred racial social distance, and that it correlates with other measures of negative feelings toward blacks (McConahay et al., 1981). Thus it provides a measure for the extent of subtle racial prejudice, which may not be uncovered by the more-obvious, old-fashioned racism items.

Symbolic Racism

Rather closely akin to the modern racism viewpoint, this concept adds another element. **Symbolic racism** is defined as a blend of antiblack affect and belief in traditional American values related to the Protestant Ethic:

> a form of resistance to change in the racial status quo based on moral feelings that blacks violate such traditional American values as individualism and self-reliance, the work ethic, obedience, and discipline. (Kinder & Sears, 1981, p. 416)

Measurement of this concept has generally used items very similar to those in the modern racism scale. However, its proponents emphasize that these items have an abstract, symbolic character that is quite unrelated to respondents' personal lives, but closely connected to their moral code and social ideals (Sears, 1988b; Sears & Henry, 2003).

As a result of this conceptualization, research has often contrasted symbolic racism (and more broadly, symbolic politics) with behavior based on threats to respondents' personal *self-interest* (see the related discussion in Chapter 14). For instance, studies have shown that symbolic racism was a stronger predictor of voting against a black political candidate than were realistic personal racial threats stemming from crime in the community, local school or neighborhood integration, or job competition (Kinder & Sears, 1981). Similarly, several studies have found opposition to busing of school children more closely related to symbolic racism scores than to self-interest variables, such as living in impacted neighborhoods or having children who would be affected by such busing (Sears & Allen, 1984).

However, you can see that these research findings use a narrow definition of self-interest in terms of individual impact on the respondent. If individuals who have no young children vote against busing, based on what they feel is best for their community, they will not be classified as following self-interest by this definition. Indeed, Kinder and Kiewiet (1981) have suggested the term **sociotropic voting** for this kind of broader community or national focus in voting. Clearly, citizens' general values and ideological commitments will be important in such voting, which is why Sears and his colleagues have stressed the importance of traditional American values in their concept of symbolic racism. However, traditional values are not enough to predict or explain voters' rejection of a black candidate or a school busing plan; empirical findings of several studies have shown that an important predictor is the kind of antiblack feeling that is tapped by items measuring modern racist beliefs and affect.

Recent extensive empirical research on symbolic racist attitudes has demonstrated that (a) they make a dominant contribution to explaining whites' opposition to race-targeted government policies, as well as to evaluations of black political candidates and ethnocentric white candidates; (b) their contribution to whites' decisions about these political issues and candidates is much stronger than that of old-fashioned racism or of racial stereotypes; and (c) their contribution on these topics is different from and greater than that of ideological conservatism or of authoritarianism (Sears et al., 1997; Sears, Henry, & Tarman, 2003).

Although people differ in the strength of their symbolic racist feelings, Sears (1988) has suggested that in our society it is probably almost impossible for anyone of any race to escape some degree of antiblack feeling based on centuries-long cultural patterns of deeply ingrained racist assumptions. Thus it is common for people to believe that blacks deserve to have all the rights of citizenship, but also to agree that they "should not push themselves where they're not wanted" or that "white people have a right to keep blacks out of their neighborhoods" (*Public Opinion*, 1987, No. 2).

Aversive Racism

The theory of **aversive racism** stresses several principles. First, in agreement with the preceding paragraph, most people have some degree of negative feelings toward blacks and other disadvantaged groups. These negative feelings are derived from normal processes of cognitive categorization of other people, as well as from motivational factors such as desires for power and status, and from social experiences with members of other groups and with cultural values. Second, powerful norms of fairness and equality are also widespread in modern societies. Third, consequently, many people who have internalized these norms, and who believe themselves to be unprejudiced, nevertheless hold conscious and/or unconscious negative feelings and stereotypes about ethnic minority groups. Fourth, the internal struggle and ambivalence stemming from these conflicting forces create an *aversive* tendency to avoid interaction with minority-group members when possible (Gaertner & Dovidio, 1986; Dovidio et al., 2000).

One result of this theory is that, because aversive racists consciously want to be fair and equalitarian, they generally do not discriminate against blacks in clear-cut situations where discrimination would be obvious to themselves and others. For instance, in an experimental emergency situation in which a black person needed help and no other helpers were available, whites offered help even more readily than they did to a white person (95% vs. 83%)—so old-fashioned racism was not operating there. But when other potential helpers were available, so that they could rationalize their lack of helping on a basis other than race, whites were only half as likely to help black victims as they were to help white victims (38% vs. 75%)—clear evidence for the aversive racism position (Gaertner & Dovidio, 1977).

Another corollary of the theory is that aversive racism is subtle rather than obvious, and this makes it prototypic of modern or subtle prejudice toward ethnic minorities, which is found in many European nations as well as in the U.S. (Meertens & Pettigrew, 1997). Indeed, a Dutch study suggested that aversive racism is more subtle than symbolic racism because aversive racists are consciously trying to be nonprejudiced (Kleinpenning & Hagendoorn, 1993). Thus most aversive racist attributions and actions tend to be "prowhite"—ones that favor whites, rather than openly derogating blacks—for instance, giving positive ratings to well-qualified job applicants who are black, but rating equivalent whites even higher (cf. Brewer's, 1999, discussion of ingroup favoritism). However, though this prejudice is subtle, its *results* are painfully obvious to a well-qualified black person who is not hired. Moreover, the cumulative effect of millions of such actions contributes to blacks' drastic underrepresentation in higher-status jobs and their lower incomes than those of equally educated whites (Federal Glass Ceiling Commission, 1995; Dovidio & Gaertner, 1998).

Because aversive racism has been conceptualized as largely unconscious, it has also been studied as an implicit attitude, by use of response latency measures (see Chapter 4). Research has shown that implicit prejudice is typically not highly correlated with explicit prejudice, and valuable applied findings have flowed from studies on implicit aversive racism (see the subsequent section on implicit racial attitudes).

Realistic Group Conflict

Another possible basis for antiblack feelings is the idea that different racial groups are in realistic conflict over the distribution of limited economic and political resources (Bobo, 1983, 1988). This view deemphasizes the symbolic aspects of prejudice and racism, though it does not deny them entirely, and it gives more attention to *group* struggles to gain political power, educational and job opportunities, and so on. Supporting this viewpoint are findings that racial attitudes have several distinguishable dimensions, and that the dimension that best predicts opposition to school busing is a person's attitude toward black political activism (Bobo, 1983). In fact, group interests are clearly reflected in both whites' and blacks' responses to a poll question about whether blacks are pushing for change "at about the right speed" or not. In the civil rights era of 1964, 74% of whites said blacks were moving "too fast," compared with only 9% of blacks. However, in 1980, a period of much less civil rights activism, the number of whites saying "at about the right speed" had doubled from 25% to 51%, whereas blacks giving that response had dropped from 63% to 49% (Bobo, 1988). Thus the group conflict viewpoint interprets whites' limited support for implementing equalitarian principles and the mixed record of changes over the past several decades as being based in group self-interest—a "go-slow" philosophy that aims to hold on to group privilege as long as possible within the bounds of the law and political reality. Recently, Bobo (1999) has rephrased this viewpoint in terms of the importance of *group position*. In this view, prejudice involves a sense of one's own ethnic group as having a deserved relative position in a social hierarchy, and resistance to ameliorating racist social conditions is rooted in a sense of threat of losing that position and its accompanying privileges.

Opposition to Government Intervention

A final possible explanation of why responses to implementation items have changed little in recent decades is that such items confound attitudes toward integration with more general attitudes toward government intervention (Kuklinski & Parent, 1981; Sniderman & Piazza, 1993). During the 1980s, the theme of "getting government off our backs" was a popular one with many voters, so opposition to government intrusion or activism might cause such people to oppose concrete steps toward implementing racial equality even though they sincerely believed in the principles of integration and equality. There may be some truth to this claim, but there is also some contradictory evidence. For example, on three implementation items, particularly the ones about local open-housing laws and about federal intervention to desegregate public accommodations such as hotels and restaurants, there have been clear positive trends in public opinion over time. Thus, in some circumstances, there is increasing white support for government intervention. However, over roughly the same time period, there was a marked drop in public support for federal intervention to enforce school integration. Therefore these opposing trends do not seem logically related to concern over government intervention per se, but rather to the more threatening nature of integration in neighborhood schools than in less-personal spheres of interaction.

These findings seem quite consistent with the discussion of social distance earlier in this chapter: People are more opposed to government intrusion in areas that involve greater intimacy of contact than in areas where social interaction is more limited and formal (Schuman et al., 1985, 1997). Also, people are less inclined to act on the basis of abstract principles that they believe in if their support for those principles is lukewarm, or if those principles conflict with other valued principles (such as individualism) or goals (such as a high-quality school for one's children). Of course, one result of this widespread opposition to government action in enforcing equality is that minority groups are largely forced to rely on their own meager resources in trying to assert their rights to equal treatment and opportunity, and this happens most often in exactly those areas where they need the most help because of general public resistance.

Affirmative Action, a Controversial Policy Issue

Affirmative action is a policy that was designed to help ethnic minorities, women, and other groups that had formerly been discriminated against in employment and educational settings. As we have discussed, black Americans have had the most extensive history of subjugation, abuse, and discrimination, starting with over 240 years of slavery in the U.S., and still today experiencing unfair and unequal treatment in employment, education, the courts, and other areas of social relations. Throughout this whole period white males have benefited hugely from favoritism in all spheres of life. Consequently, affirmative action policies were developed to begin to compensate for this long history of discrimination, beginning after passage of the Civil Rights Act in 1964. Even before that, since 1941, federal **equal-opportunity** laws and regulations had been developed to give all individuals an equal chance for employment, based on their qualifications, not their race or sex.

However, they did nothing to remedy the deleterious effects of past discrimination, such as poverty, poor education, and undeveloped skills.

To overcome this history of past discrimination, affirmative action (AA) programs implement remedial measures, which may be court-ordered, or required by laws or regulations, or voluntarily adopted by employers and educational institutions. Examples include special efforts to recruit underrepresented groups as applicants, special career and skills training, careful validation of selection criteria and measures, monitoring the success of efforts to achieve diversity, and setting goals for eventual future representation of target groups. As a result of the Supreme Court's ruling in the *Bakke* case, AA programs *cannot* involve fixed numerical quotas for hiring or selection—a point that is not understood by many Americans who have criticized these programs (Taylor, 1991). There is no question that AA programs have been very effective in increasing access to employment and education for both women and ethnic minorities in the U.S. (Clayton & Crosby, 1992). Research showing the need for and the effectiveness of AA programs has been summarized by the American Psychological Association (1996), Dovidio and Gaertner (1996), and Crosby et al. (2003).

Despite their success, AA programs have remained publicly controversial, and since 1989 the courts have increasingly limited the conditions for their application. In 1995 and 1996 the university systems in both California and Texas eliminated all AA measures in student admissions (Gwynne, 1996), but in 2003, the Supreme Court approved a carefully specified use of AA to ensure diversity in law school admissions at the University of Michigan (Bailey, 2003).

Photograph courtesy of James M. Jones.
Reprinted by permission.

Box 16–2   JAMES M. JONES, *Authority on Racism and Prejudice*

James M. Jones is a professor of psychology at the University of Delaware, having earned his B.A. from Oberlin College in 1963, an M.A. from Temple University, and a Ph.D. in social psychology from Yale in 1970. He then taught at Harvard and later at Howard University before moving to Delaware in 1981. He has also served for many years as a senior staff member at the American Psychological Association, directing the Minority Fellowship Program since 1977 and being chosen as the first head of the Public Interest Directorate in 1987.

Jones is author of a classic book, Prejudice and Racism *(1972, 1997), and his current research interests focus on black personality, and racism and culture. His honors include election as president of the Society of Experimental Social Psychology and of the Society for the Psychological Study of Social Issues, as well as appointment to the editorial boards of numerous scientific journals. This chapter cites his analyses of prejudice and racism in America.*

Public attitudes toward AA show a mixed pattern of support for some methods and rejection of others. In 1995, about three-fourths or more of a national sample approved of three AA aspects: special recruitment efforts to find qualified applicants, special college-preparatory classes, and job-training programs to increase skills. However, large majorities disapproved of hiring a minority applicant instead of a better qualified white applicant and of setting aside scholarships for specific minority groups (Norman, 1995). Trends over the years on questions about AA have only been available since the 1970s. On questions about government spending, they show a continuing level of about 50% of white respondents who say the amount of spending to "improve the condition of blacks" is about right, plus about 25% who say it is too little. However, typically, only about 20% or less of respondents say that the government should give "special treatment" to help blacks, or that the government should "make every possible effort to improve the social and economic position of blacks." Responses to these questions changed very little between 1970 and 1996. On questions involving preferential treatment, less than 30% of white respondents have favored universities' setting quotas "to reserve openings for black students," and less than 15% have favored giving blacks "preference in hiring and promotion" because of past discrimination. These questions, also, did not show any consistent changes in responses through the 1980s and 1990s (Schuman et al., 1997).

The lack of enthusiasm of white respondents for any programs of preferential treatment for blacks to compensate for past discrimination against them is consistent with the public attitudes we previously discussed—that is, many whites' skepticism about the occurrence and importance of discrimination, and their strong tendency to blame blacks' disadvantages on low motivation. Psychological research on affirmative action has shown that it is very poorly understood by the public and also that it has been implemented in an immense variety of ways (Turner & Pratkanis, 1994). Some of the resistance to AA is due to inadequacies in the ways that it has been publicly presented and justified, but research has indicated that a substantial part of the resistance is also due to aversive racism (Murrell et al., 1994). White respondents who perceive that there is racial discrimination in the workplace are more favorable toward preferential AA programs designed to compensate for past inequities (Hing, Bobocel, & Zanna, 2000; Iyer & Crosby, 2000).

IMPLICIT RACIAL ATTITUDES

As we previously mentioned, recent research on prejudice and racism has begun to examine the nonconscious (i.e., implicit) aspects of racial stereotypes and attitudes, using response latency measures. Importantly, much research has shown that implicit prejudice is usually only modestly correlated with explicit prejudice—typical correlations are about 0.2 (e.g., Karpinski & Hilton, 2001; Nosek et al., 2002b; Ottaway et al., 2001). However, as with measures of explicit prejudice, implicit prejudice measures toward various outgroups (e.g., blacks, women, poor people, homosexuals, etc.) correlate more strongly and form a single general factor (McFarland & Mattern, 2003). Frequently, the Implicit Association Test (IAT) has been used with race-indicative stimuli (e.g., words or pictures related to African Americans) to provide a measure of implicit racial prejudice. Alternatively, a race-relevant priming stimulus can be exposed very briefly before each trial of a decision task, and the amount of facilitation of response times on the task (i.e., faster responses to negative words after a black prime) can be used as a measure of implicit bias (e.g., Gaertner & McLaughlin, 1983).

Using the latter approach, Dovidio et al. (2002) studied the interactions and perceptions of two people in a black–white dyad. The two were told to conduct a brief "getting acquainted" conversation, but the black in each dyad was a confederate of the experimenter and played a relatively standard role. The data showed that whites' self-reported (explicit) prejudice scores were significantly correlated with their perceptions of their own degree of bias (lack of friendliness) in the interaction and to bias in their *verbal* behavior, as rated by outside observers. However, whites' implicit prejudice scores were significantly correlated with their *nonverbal* behavior, and also with their partner's perception of bias in their interaction and the outside observers' ratings of bias in their interaction. Thus, blacks' perceptions of their white partner's bias were related to the white participants' *nonverbal* behavior and to their *implicit* prejudice score, not to their explicit prejudice score. These results suggest that the black participants may have been paying more attention to the white person's nonconscious behaviors, such as eye-blinking, limited eye contact, and other nonverbal indications of discomfort, which the white participants were unaware of.

Continuing this line of research, Dovidio (2003) had whites with varying degrees of implicit prejudice interact in a dyad with a black person, working on a problem-solving task. He studied how the participants' implicit prejudice could cause difficulties in the dyadic working relationship, as measured by the efficiency and speed of the dyad's problem-solving. Dyads with a white member who was low in both explicit and implicit prejudice were the fastest—apparently their members felt comfortable enough with each other to focus quickly and successfully on the task at hand. Much the slowest were dyads containing whites who were aversive racists (low in explicit prejudice but high in implicit prejudice). The researchers suggested that their efficiency in problem-solving was decreased by having to work through "mixed messages" contained in their nonverbal and verbal behavior, stemming from the white participant's differing levels of implicit and explicit prejudice. Perhaps surprisingly, the dyads containing whites who were *high* in both implicit and explicit prejudice were considerably faster—suggesting that there was consistency in the white member's nonverbal and verbal behavior that allowed the dyad to function fairly efficiently without dealing with "mixed messages"—that is, "what you see is what you get."

WHICH WHITES HOLD WHICH ATTITUDES?

Personality

The book titled *The Authoritarian Personality* (Adorno et al., 1950) provided an influential explanation of prejudice based on psychoanalytic theory (see Chapter 12). Its authors concluded that prejudiced individuals were the product of authoritarian childrearing practices (strict physical punishment, reverence for parents and other authority figures, denial of sexuality, and so on). Among the consequences of these childrearing practices was an inability to accept negative feelings about oneself or one's own group. Denial of self-blame led to the attribution of blame for bad thoughts and deeds to "scapegoats"— usually minority groups, who could not defend themselves and who occupied a low status in the community. Everything that could not be accepted in oneself was "projected" onto a weaker target. Thus prejudice was seen in effect, as a personality disorder—a viewpoint termed the **scapegoat theory of prejudice**. In this theoretical view, people use prejudice as a crutch to hold up their low self-esteem, and they blame minority groups as scapegoats for poor economic or social conditions. Research based on this viewpoint has also found prejudice to be related to dogmatic opposition to women's liberation, opposition to civil liberties in general, a rigidly punitive attitude about law enforcement, and a conservative ideological position (Maykovich, 1975).

Although *The Authoritarian Personality* provided some important insights into the dynamics of prejudice, later research has produced several other explanations of prejudice. In Chapter 12 we discussed Altemeyer's social-learning perspective on authoritarianism, and also research on threat and motivated social cognition. The motivated social cognition approach suggests that social attitudes are linked to both dispositional and situational bases (Jost et al., 2003). Similarly, Pettigrew (1971) summarized findings that prejudice stemmed from both conformity to social norms and limited education. Thus, in understanding prejudice, it is important to consider the social context, as well as the personality characteristics of individuals. Let us briefly summarize some of these demographic and group factors.

Demography

Generally, there are four important correlates of racial prejudice for whites: region of the country, education, gender, and age (Schuman et al., 1997). First, women are more favorable than men in their racial attitudes on almost all items. Second, Southerners hold generally less-favorable attitudes toward blacks than do Northerners. It is now agreed that the regional difference is not a function of differences in personality between people in the North and South, but rather a difference in social norms (Pettigrew, 1959). In the South, important social institutions like the churches and schools were (and still are) more likely to support segregation than are similar institutions in the North. Therefore, racial prejudice in the South was a sign that a person was well-integrated into his or her community—conforming to its social norms—whereas in a more equalitarian social system, racial prejudice might be a sign of personality disturbance, as proposed by Adorno et al. (1950).

Some of the specific changes in racial attitudes over the past several decades have been parallel in the North and the South, with both regions becoming more favorable toward the principle of integration and its implementation, but the gap between the regions remaining about the same. However, on several specific topics, people in the South changed faster so that the gap decreased, and, as we saw in Figure 16–2, on some items the two regions became almost identical as early as the 1980s (Schuman et al., 1997). On some of the questions about implementation, however, there was little or no favorable change, and regional convergence came through the northerners becoming less favorable, as Figure 16–3 illustrated.

White Americans with more education, particularly those who have attended college, are less prejudiced on the average than those who have less education. The difference is largest on items describing general principles of equality and is usually smaller on items involving implementation of principles, social distance preferences, or explanations for blacks' inequality (Schuman et al., 1997). Campbell (1971) suggested that it is primarily an individual's *personal* experience with college in recent years that results in a more liberal racial attitude. Because parents' education does not seem to matter, it is not the child's background that is responsible for the difference.

Younger white Americans hold more positive racial attitudes than older people do, and each age cohort of Americans is more liberal in its racial attitudes than the next-older cohort. Since the 1960s each cohort has changed in a positive direction at roughly the same rate on the items about social distance and principles of equal treatment. On the questions about implementation also, the age cohorts maintained the same relative position, though overall population attitudes on some of these items became more negative over the years, whereas others became more positive. On the items about explanations for inequality, the cohort differences have been smaller, and most of the changes over the past decades have been similar for the several cohorts (Schuman et al., 1997). A portion of the relationship between youth and positive racial attitudes seems to be due to the steady increase in the proportion of young people who attend college (Taylor, Sheatsley, & Greeley, 1978). There are fewer differences in racial attitudes between young and old for those who have not attended college.

RACIAL ATTITUDES OF BLACK AMERICANS

Early surveys of racial attitudes did not usually include black respondents for several reasons. Often survey sampling guidelines excluded racial minorities and, even if they were included, there were usually too few respondents of a given minority group to yield reliable estimates of their attitudes. Also, race relations was seen as basically a white issue that whites would have to solve. Thus it was not until the early 1960s that large samples of blacks were interviewed about their racial attitudes, so the available data on their time trends cover a shorter period than for whites, and they are sparser because the same survey questions have not been repeated as often with large black samples. In addition, most survey interviewers are white, and blacks often present more conciliatory or favorable attitudes when interviewed by a white person than by a black person, so this well-established race-of-interviewer effect must be remembered when findings are interpreted (Schuman et al., 1997). We will discuss the data that are available on black attitudes after presenting a brief sketch of black demographic conditions.

The Circumstances and Goals of Blacks

It is widely recognized that blacks have been at the bottom of the U.S. economic and social hierarchy ever since they were first brought to this country as slaves. Their disadvantage still exists at the beginning of the twenty-first century, despite many important social changes (Sidanius, Levin, & Pratto, 1998; Sears et al., 2000). To put this picture in perspective, it is important to realize that major improvements in some of the conditions of black Americans occurred in the 1960s and 1970s as a result of the civil rights movement. For instance, the median amount of education completed by blacks rose from 9 years in 1968 to 12 years in 1985, and the proportion of black adults who had completed high school doubled from 30% to 60%. By the 1980s, half of all black American families owned their own homes, and the number of blacks in high-status jobs had risen sharply. Yet at that same time, only 56% of black men were employed, *down* 14% from 1968 (Zinsmeister, 1988). Moreover, these indicators of progress were still well below the levels for whites, and since the 1980s most of them have stalled or even reversed (Farley, 1996; Feagin et al., 2001).

Thus the problems of poverty and deprivation remain acute for much of the black populace. As an amazing example, *32%* of African American males in their twenties are either in prison or jail or on probation or parole. Research has shown the huge degree of bias that produces these figures—for instance, only 13% of monthly drug users in the U.S. are blacks, but blacks comprise 35% of drug possession arrests, 55% of drug possession convictions, and 74% of prison sentences for drug possession (Mauer & Huling, 1995). A key reason for these disproportionate figures is that Congress passed a 1986 law setting a mandatory prison term for possession of *5 grams* or more (less than 1/5 of an ounce) of crack cocaine and the same term for possession of *500 grams* or more (over one pound) of powder cocaine. Although there is no difference in the criminality associated with the two forms, crack cocaine is much more readily available than powder cocaine in black urban areas, and young black males who are unemployed or make too little to live on frequently supplement their income by selling drugs (Sidanius et al., 1998).

Across the U.S., the average black family earns only 58% as much as the average white family; and even for doing the same job, blacks earn only 76% of what whites earn (Abdel-Ghany & Sharpe, 1994; Feagin et al., 2001). In the work force, the unemployment rate for blacks is more than twice as high as for whites, and nearly twice as many employed blacks as whites are in low-paying service jobs and blue-collar labor jobs (Russell, 1995). In education, twice as high a percentage of whites as of blacks complete college, and blacks' rate of college graduation has been decreasing (Farley, 1996). In politics, though blacks comprise 11% of the American electorate, only 2% of elected officials are black (Sears et al., 2000). In health, the average life expectancy for U.S. blacks was under 72 years in 2000, whereas for whites it was over 77 years (U.S. Census Bureau, 2000). In housing, black isolation from whites is so great that it has been termed "hypersegregation" (Massey & Denton, 1993), and careful research has shown high levels of discrimination against blacks by realtors and landlords (Yinger, 1996). Thus, even middle-class blacks are constantly exposed to discrimination in areas of employment, education, housing, health care, financial services, retail sales, and the criminal justice system (Feagin & Sykes, 1994; Jones, 1997). As a result, most blacks are intimately aware of the lack of equality in America.

In general, blacks and whites in America share many of the same aspirations. They want the same things for themselves and for their children—a good income (and the comforts that brings), good schools, freedom from fear of repression and crime, opportunities to get ahead, and so on. However, blacks and whites disagree considerably on how blacks might best achieve the goals of middle America. In the 1980s, many more blacks than whites (58% to 17%) scored high on the value of social justice, which stresses the role of government in providing for the needy, whereas more whites than blacks (28% to 11%) scored high on a belief in America's boundless ability to solve its problems (Colasanto, 1988). At the beginning of the 2000s, 74% of whites said that blacks were treated the same way as whites in their local community, whereas only 36% of blacks agreed (Ludwig, 2000). Similarly, 60% of blacks were dissatisfied with the way society treated their group, whereas only 34% of whites were dissatisfied with the way blacks were treated. The areas of life in which blacks were most dissatisfied were their financial situation and safety from physical harm or violence (Saad & Newport, 2001).

Principles of Equality, and Social Distance

On some principles of equal treatment, blacks are practically unanimous in their views. Very close to 100% of nationwide black samples agree that "white students and black students should go to the same schools" rather than to separate schools, and that "black people have a right to live wherever they can afford to, just like anybody else" rather than that "white people have a right to keep black people out of their neighborhoods if they want to." Moreover, the unanimity on these items has not changed at all over many years. In contrast, 90% or more of whites agree with these items, and that figure has increased by 30–40 percentage points since the 1960s (Schuman et al., 1997). Similarly, nearly 100% of blacks say that they would have no objection to a member of their family bringing a white guest home to dinner, whereas less than 80% of whites are that accepting of having a black dinner guest (about 25 percentage points more than in the early 1960s).[2]

On other principles, blacks are more divided. Over 80% approve of marriage between whites and nonwhites, and that figure has increased only about 5% (compared with 67%

---

[2]Here and throughout, we report the change in percentage points, and not the proportionate change in percentage. Thus, a change from 50% to 75% is called an increase of 25%.

of whites who approved in 1997). The general question about approval of desegregation was last asked in 1978. At that time only 56% of blacks said they favored desegregation rather than "strict segregation, or something in between," and that figure had dropped 22% since 1964, whereas those favoring "something in between" increased 21%, to 38%. In comparison, whites have increased about 10% on each of these options to 34% for desegregation and 60% for something in between (Schuman et al., 1997).

Implementation of Principles of Equality

On implementation items, blacks, like whites, are less favorable than they are on the corresponding general principles. For blacks, the gap between support of principles and of their implementation is smaller than for whites, but in recent years their percentage of approval for government intervention has declined substantially on some issues (Schuman et al., 1997). For instance, blacks expressed 72% support for federal actions to keep hotels and restaurants open to blacks (down almost 20% from 1964); 64% support for federal action to ensure fair treatment on jobs (down almost 30%); 57% support for federal action to ensure school desegregation (down 25%); and 45% support for federal help to improve the social and economic position of blacks (down about 30%). For most of these items, the decreased level of endorsement was mainly due to an increase of 20%–25% in those who responded that lately they hadn't had an interest in the question or "hadn't thought much about it"—suggesting that these issues had receded from the national civil rights agenda.

Blacks' highest level of support on implementation items in recent years was 84% who favored local laws to ensure open housing (up 13% since it was first asked in 1978); 70% favored increased government spending to improve the condition of blacks; 59% favored busing to achieve school integration; and neither of these latter items had changed much since they were first asked. On questions about preferential treatment, 76% of blacks favored quotas to reserve college admissions for blacks, and 59% favored preference in hiring and promotion (both slightly down over time), whereas white respondents were about 50% lower on each of these items (very slightly down over time—see Figure 16–4) (Schuman et al., 1997).

Explanations for Inequality

In explaining why "African Americans have worse jobs, income, and housing than white people," blacks' endorsement of several reasons has changed some over the years (Schuman et al., 1997). Discrimination as a reason has decreased 13% to 66%; a poor chance for education has decreased 20% to 54%, but low motivation or willpower has increased 6% to 41%. In comparison, whites' agreement with discrimination as a reason was much lower (34%), their agreement with a poor chance for education was lower (45%), but their agreement that blacks had low motivation was higher (52%). Blacks have been 40%–50% higher than whites in perceiving discrimination against them in housing (54%), in getting managerial jobs (68%), and in police behavior (91%). Finally, 29% of blacks said that most white people "want to keep blacks down" while 27% said they "want to see blacks get a better break"; the comparable figures for white respondents were 11% saying that whites want to keep blacks down whereas 53% said that whites want blacks to get a better break (Schuman et al., 1997).

In judging civil rights efforts, whites and blacks have shown opposing opinion trends about whether "civil rights leaders are trying to push too fast, are going too slowly, or are moving at about the right speed." Over the years since the heyday of the civil rights movement in 1964, greatly increasing proportions of whites have been saying "about

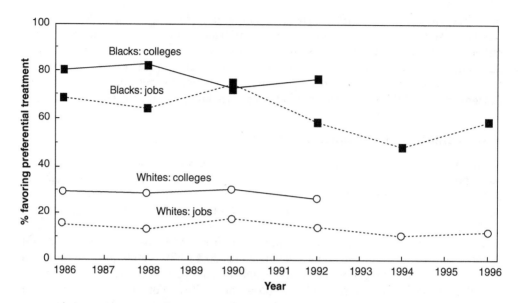

FIGURE 16–4 Comparison of black and white respondents' approval of preferential treatment for blacks in college admissions and job hiring and promotion.

Source: Reprinted by permission of the publisher from *Racial Attitudes in America: Trends and Interpretations* (p. 271), by Howard Schuman, Charlotte Steeh, and Lawrence Bobo, Cambridge, Mass.: Harvard University Press, Copyright © 1985, 1997 by the President and Fellows of Harvard College.

right," and far fewer have been saying "too fast." In contrast, increasing proportions of blacks have been saying "too slow" and fewer saying "about right." Over 40% of blacks say civil rights leaders are pushing "too slowly," compared with about 10% of whites (Schuman et al., 1997). These conflicting views are a good illustration of how realistic group conflict can lead to contrasting perceptions of the same events.

In summary, there are some parallels between the racial attitudes of blacks and those of whites. Although blacks' approval of both general principles of equality and actions to implement those principles is generally higher than whites' approval—sometimes much higher—both racial groups are less enthusiastic about the implementation actions than about the principles. Also, the drop in support since the 1960s was quite parallel for both groups on the issue of federal intervention to ensure school integration, and black decreases in support for several other implementation actions have brought them somewhat closer to average white attitudes on those issues. The minority of blacks who oppose busing for integration mention reasons including school quality, safety, inconvenience, freedom of choice, and preference for neighborhood schools; and the overlap of these reasons with those of white busing opponents provides further evidence that opposition to busing is not merely a smokescreen for white racism (Schuman et al., 1997).

The Distribution of Black Racial Attitudes

Because of small sample sizes for black respondents, data on demographic differences in blacks' attitudes are sketchy. The best large samples in recent years are provided by Gurin, Hatchett, and Jackson (1989), Tate (1993), and Dawson (1994). Like the racial attitudes of whites, black racial attitudes can be related to region of the country, education, and age. However, the findings are often less clear than they are for whites. In general, southern blacks have been slightly more conservative than northern blacks, but that does not mean that they were more passive or docile (Goldman, 1970). In northern urban centers that had race-related riots, self-reported black participants in the riots were more often long-term residents of the city, relatively better educated than nonrioters, higher in their job aspirations, more likely to have voted, and more favorable in their self-perceptions and perceptions of their race. In short, these data sharply disputed the "riff-raff theory" of rioting and protest (Caplan, 1970).

For whites, a college education is apt to be linked to more-favorable racial attitudes, but for blacks the opposite result is found. If education helps to create a critical awareness of our society, it is not surprising to find that, during college, blacks become more alienated toward white society, whereas whites become more sympathetic toward black protest. For instance, the most-educated blacks perceive more discrimination against blacks in jobs, housing, and by police—90% of those with some graduate education say that the police treat blacks unfairly, compared with only 54% of those with a grade school education. Perhaps as a result, more-educated blacks are more intent on reaching the goals of integration and equality, and are more likely to say that civil rights leaders are pushing "too slowly." They also more strongly reject low motivation as an explanation of black disadvantage, favor open-housing laws, and are more supportive of racial intermarriage (as young blacks are also). The least-educated blacks are more opposed to open-housing laws and willing to accept constraints on free residential choice. Surprisingly, however, blacks with high income and education are more *opposed* to preferential treatment in employment—a position they share with highly-educated whites (Dawson, 1994; Schuman et al., 1997).

CHANGING RACIAL ATTITUDES

Over the past 60 years, whites' racial attitudes have generally become much more positive. The many civil rights marches, sit-ins, and protests dramatized the issues of discrimination and led to laws mandating racial equality. In turn, it is clear that the changes in laws and regulations affecting segregation practices often led to more favorable racial attitudes, *rather than* more favorable attitudes preceding the changes in laws and practices. Thus, though whites often complain about civil rights changes being too rapid, when a new law is passed or a new desegregation step is taken, people's attitudes soon adjust, and more and more people express favorable opinions toward the new practice. One clear example, discussed previously, is the positive change in attitudes concerning school integration, which followed the Supreme Court decision ordering school desegregation, and which continued into the late 1990s. Another example is favorable racial attitude changes that often occur in suburban neighborhoods some months after the first black family moves into the neighborhood (Hamilton, Carpenter, & Bishop, 1984).

Of course there have been occasional local setbacks, as in the violence and protest over school busing that erupted in Boston in 1975 and 1976. Usually these violent episodes have occurred when important community leaders publicly opposed the changes, as happened in Boston, thus making it easier for firebrands to whip up disorder and violence. On the other hand, when community leaders (whatever their private feelings) unite in advocating orderly and nonviolent procedures, even major social changes have usually been made with little public disturbance (U.S. Commission on Civil Rights, 1977). These findings again show the greater importance of social norms, compared with the impact of private attitudes, in the area of race relations (Pettigrew, 1969).

Black racial attitudes have also shown changes, both up and down, in the course of the past 40 years. Since the early 1960s, blacks have become somewhat more optimistic about progress toward racial equality and about whites' willingness to assist in that progress, despite their increased feeling that civil rights leaders are pushing for equality "too slowly" (Schuman et al., 1997). However, a disturbing trend has been evident in surveys of high school seniors since about 1986, when both black and white young people began expressing increasing pessimism and worry about the state of race relations in the U.S. (Tuch, Sigelman, & MacDonald, 1999). In general, it has been shown that U.S. attitudes toward integration, among both whites and blacks, are most positive in people who have experienced integration and much less favorable in people who have not had close and personalized interracial contact (Brewer & Miller, 1984; Pettigrew, 1998; N. Miller, 2002). Thus any societal trends or events that encourage greater separation of the races are likely to lead to less-favorable racial attitudes among both blacks and whites.

Of course, not all contact has led to reduced interracial hostility. Just as in the area of international contact (see Chapter 15), a number of conditions must be met before contact with other races will improve racial attitudes (see the following sections). Having one or a few black friends or acquaintances, especially if they are of lower social status, is not enough to overcome prejudice (Jackman & Crane, 1986). However, with the transformation of racial practices in the U.S., friendly and respectful types of contact that were impossible in the past have become commonplace today. Americans of all ethnic origins share public accommodations, work together, and, in many places, go to the same schools in relative peace and harmony. If this trend continues, the fear of many white Americans about interracial neighborhoods and even interracial marriage will also become a thing of the past.

Levels and Variables in Combating Prejudice

Organized attempts to reduce prejudice and discrimination can operate at three main levels (cf. Duckitt, 1992). The most powerful level, as mentioned above, is laws and regulations, as well as social norms that are so widespread that they carry the same force as law (e.g., the incest taboo). Next in strength are society-wide structures of social influence, such as the mass media and the educational system. The third level, which is the focus of most social psychologists, is group and interpersonal methods of influence, such as interventions in specific organizations or groups.

Because the causes of prejudice and discrimination are multiple and elaborately intertwined, programs aimed at reducing prejudice also need to consider and combat its multiple causes. However, such programs can be categorized in terms of their primary emphases, with the following dimensions:

- Behavioral, cognitive, or motivational approaches,
- Normative or informational influence methods,
- Active or passive participation (active usually has stronger effects—see Chapter 11).

The following section includes examples of programs that use each of these emphases, and detailed discussions of prejudice-reduction approaches can be found in Oskamp (2000b).

Experimental Studies of Racial Attitude Change

This section briefly examines some of the methods social scientists have tried in experimental attempts to change prejudiced racial attitudes. There are many paths by which prejudice and discrimination can be reduced (Oskamp, 2000a). Examples in the following pages all involve attempts to change explicit racial attitudes. A complementary approach of changing *implicit* racial attitudes has also been suggested by various authors (e.g., Banaji & Greenwald, 1994), but research efforts of that sort are very recent. One approach to implicit attitude change by Kawakami and her colleagues (2000) involved an extensive retraining period (480 trials), in which participants practiced *negating* stereotypically associated words (e.g., "aggressive") in response to pictures of individuals belonging to a particular category (e.g., skinheads)—in other words, they were taught to "just say no." A similar training technique was used by Plant and Peruche (2003) to inhibit negative behavioral responses in reaction to pictures of blacks. In both of these studies, differential implicit associations to the target category of persons were successfully eliminated.

Interracial Contact. One of the most prominent hypotheses about race relations is that contact between groups who dislike each other, under favorable conditions, will lead to increased liking and decreased prejudice. This is an interactive and behavioral approach. Research findings suggest that the following conditions must be met: (a) the members of each group must be of equal status *or* the members of the minority group of a higher status than the majority-group members, (b) there must be a favorable climate for intergroup contact, (c) the contact must be of an intimate rather than casual nature, (d) the contact must be rewarding and pleasant, and (e) the two groups should have a mutual goal that requires interdependent and cooperative action (Amir, 1969).

Unfortunately, all of these conditions are seldom met completely in "real life," so evidence of their importance has to come primarily from experiments in which some or all of them can be created or controlled. Many experimental studies have demonstrated that induced cooperation can weaken hostility between rival groups (e.g., Sherif et al., 1961), and several groups of researchers have applied this principle to reduction of interracial animosity. For example, in newly desegregated junior and senior high schools, Weigel, Wiser, and Cook (1975) established some experimental classrooms where small groups of students of mixed ethnic composition (black, Hispanic, and white) worked interdependently. They found that these students were more likely to engage in cross-ethnic helping behavior and to have greater relative respect for each other than students taught in regular classrooms where individual competition was stressed.

To provide a quantitative summary of the findings of all the available studies on intergroup contact, Pettigrew and Tropp (2000) conducted an exhaustive meta-analysis of 203 such studies, which included 313 independent samples. The results demonstrated that intergroup contact (of varying sorts) was moderately negatively related to subsequent intergroup prejudice (contact led to less prejudice). For the 313 samples, Cohen's *d* was -0.39, equivalent to a correlation of -0.19. The more detailed findings displayed interesting results for various moderator variables. For instance, in studies where the participants had no choice (i.e., they could not opt out and avoid the contact), the *d* for samples was -0.69, quite a large effect. Studies that used structured programs that maximized most of the conditions considered optimal for reducing prejudice were found to have a *d* of -0.60. Other variables that produced larger-than-average effects were situations with observed contact (rather than reported or assumed contact), studies in work or organizational settings (rather than labs, schools, housing, or recreational settings), and studies in which outgroups were based on sexual orientation or race (rather than on physical disability, nationality, age, etc.). Importantly, reduction in prejudice was found to generalize to other members of the pertinent outgroup, and even to *other outgroups* not involved in the contact.

All of these results support the conclusion that administrative arrangements involving properly structured intergroup contact can affect racial attitudes favorably. The question of exactly how the intergroup contact should be established and explained has been the topic of great scientific debate and research. Brewer (2000) proposed that contact situations should be analyzed in terms of social identity theory principles (Tajfel, 1978), which posit that people categorize social situations in terms of ingroups and outgroups. Specifically, people view ingroup members as more similar to themselves, feel more positive toward them, and expect outgroups to be competitive toward their ingroup. These principles lead to three possible models by which intergroup contact situations can be organized in attempts to reduce prejudice:

- **Decategorization**, in which initial ingroup–outgroup categorizations are weakened and superseded by other cross-cutting similarities between ingroup and outgroup members, which are learned about through personalized interactions (e.g., "that outgroup member is like me in. . . ."—Brewer & Miller, 1984).
- **Recategorization**, in which the initial ingroup–outgroup categorization is weakened by uniting both groups in a common superordinate identity (e.g., "we're all Americans"—Gaertner et al., 1994).
- **Mutual differentiation**, which maintains the initial social category distinctions but explicitly emphasizes that the groups are mutually interdependent (e.g., "our groups are different, but we need to work together to reach our goals"—Brown, 1995).

The first two of these models are more compatible with an assimilationist view of majority–minority relationships, whereas the third model is closer to a pluralistic view. However, the three models are not completely in opposition, and Brewer (2000) suggested that their elements can be combined in interventions that aim to maintain minority groups' social identity while still achieving the goal of social integration for the broader society. Dovidio et al. (2000) have termed this approach a "dual-identity" model—like "different groups on the same team"—an image that avoids the "melting pot" image's liability of minority groups losing their group identity. There is evidence that this model is beneficial to intergroup relations in societal contexts (Huo et al., 1996; Smith & Tyler, 1996), not just in laboratory experiments. Thus research is converging on the principle that the intergroup contact situation should not completely obscure the minority participants' membership in a social outgroup.

Cooperative Learning.   Going beyond the contact hypothesis, the most widespread approach to improving intergroup relations in school settings is cooperative learning programs—another active, behavioral approach. These programs also aim to improve learning outcomes, and they typically use carefully developed procedures in which small groups of mixed ethnic composition work together cooperatively on assigned lessons. Some methods add the element of intergroup competition between the small cooperative groups.

An influential example of cooperative learning approaches was the **jigsaw classroom** technique, developed by Aronson et al. (1978). Small, cooperative, mixed-race learning groups were established for part of the school day in elementary schools. The researchers reported increased cross-racial liking, as well as improved self-esteem and liking for school, higher school performance by the minority students, decreased competitiveness, and more willingness to learn from other students. In other states and nations, several other research teams have demonstrated favorable results for equal-status, cooperative-learning methods (Sharan, 1980; Slavin, 1980; Johnson, Johnson, & Maruyama, 1983; Johnson & Johnson, 2000). These methods have generally been found to be successful in reducing prejudice and negative intergroup stereotypes.

Publicity About Positive Role Models.   Fears based on symbolic threats from an outgroup can often be countered by publicity about or exposure to role models who contradict the symbolic area of threat—usually a passive, cognitive approach. For instance, Michael Jordan is admired by black and white youngsters alike, and the widely publicized achievements of Colin Powell have contradicted many of the stereotypes and symbolic fears that whites have about blacks in U.S. society. In addition to such effects on explicit racial attitudes, recent research has shown that exposure to positive role models from minority ethnic groups can reduce (nonconscious) implicit prejudice (Dasgupta & Greenwald, 2001).

This approach to combating prejudice can be one of the strengths of affirmative action programs, if they successfully select exemplary individuals who demonstrate the falsity of prevalent fears and stereotypes about a particular outgroup (Pratkanis & Turner, 1994). However, this process is made more difficult by the fact that presenting one or two exceptional members of a minority group may allow them to be considered as *subtypes* who are not prototypic of their group, and thus be largely discounted as prejudice-reduction influences (Johnston & Hewstone, 1992).

Reducing Realistic Conflict.   In cases where prejudice is partially due to realistic threats from an outgroup, a helpful approach would be to reduce the bases of realistic conflict. This might be done by sharing power with the outgroup more equally, or ceding the outgroup specific areas of responsibility or authority, or "enlarging the pie" of resources available to the contending groups. These kinds of solutions are often proposed and sometimes accomplished in research on intergroup negotiations (e.g., Fisher & Ury, 1981; Thompson, 1990). Suggested methods have been called "integrative bargaining" or "interactive problem-solving." However, a major obstacle to this approach is that it conflicts with the dominant group's usual strong motivation to maintain power over subordinate groups (cf. Sidanius & Veniegas, 2000).

Planned, Personal Experience of Discrimination.   This is an interactive, experiential method, in which majority-group members are exposed to prejudice and discrimination, such as those that minority-group individuals undergo every day. The expectation is that this experience should make them more empathetic and understanding of the problems of minorities. Although this method has seldom been carefully evaluated, there are numerous anecdotal reports of its success in elementary school classes. An example is the teacher-initiated "blue eyes vs. brown eyes" exercise, which is depicted in the film *The Eye of the Storm* (1970).

Research by Weiner and Wright (1973) demonstrated that white children who were given a planned experience of arbitrary discrimination in their classrooms were more willing to interact with black children and showed decreased prejudice as compared to a control group who had not undergone the experience. Role-playing the part of a minority group member has become a regular part of many human relations training programs that attempt to increase the sensitivity of public officials (particularly police officers) to minority problems (e.g., Pfister, 1975; Sata, 1975).

Spotlighting Value Conflicts.   This is a technique that combines cognitive and motivational bases for reducing prejudice, using normative influence attempts, usually with passive participation. It usually aims to motivate people to change their beliefs and behavior in the direction of consistency with key underlying values, such as fairness and equality. By demonstrating inconsistencies among each participant's values, it engages their self-concept, and it often develops guilt motivation (cf. Devine et al., 2000). Rokeach

*Photograph courtesy of
Sandra J. Ball-Rokeach.
Reprinted by permission.*

Box 16–3 MILTON ROKEACH, *Crusader for Equality*

One of the most creative contributors to social psychology, Milton Rokeach was born in 1918 in Poland and emigrated to the U.S. at age 7. He grew up in Brooklyn and graduated from Brooklyn College in 1941. Following service in the Army Air Force in World War II, he earned his Ph.D. at the University of California at Berkeley, working as an assistant on the Authoritarian Personality *project and writing his dissertation on ethnocentrism. He taught at Michigan State University for 23 years and spent 14 years as Professor of Sociology and Psychology at Washington State University, before a final move to the Annenberg School of Communications at the University of Southern California, where he died in 1988.*

Rokeach was outstanding both as a conceptualizer and a researcher. He introduced the concept of dogmatism in his book The Open and Closed Mind, *and he conducted the most extensive social science study of values in three successive volumes, culminating in* Understanding Human Values *(1979). These contributions converged in his research on prejudice, racial attitudes and behavior, experiments on value change, and advocacy of equality as a key value, all of which are discussed in this chapter. Among his many honors were election as president of the Society for the Psychological Study of Social Issues and receipt of the Kurt Lewin Memorial Award.*

and his colleagues demonstrated that long-lasting attitude and behavioral changes could be produced with this relatively simple technique—a method they termed *value self-confrontation* (e.g., Rokeach, 1971; Ball-Rokeach, Rokeach, & Grube, 1984). Rokeach's typical experimental procedure pointed out individual participants' inconsistencies between their ratings of the importance of two values (freedom and equality), and described the relationship of these values to civil rights attitudes and behavior.

Grube, Mayton, and Ball-Rokeach (1994) have summarized the results of 27 such studies. They reported that 96% of them demonstrated changes in the values that were targeted, and that large but lower percentages also showed changes in relevant attitudes (73%) and behaviors (56%). For instance, Rokeach (1971) found behavioral changes that lasted as long as 21 months—specifically, increased enrollment in ethnic relations courses, and membership in civil rights organizations such as the National Association for the Advancement of Colored People (NAACP). These results are very impressive for such a simple and straightforward procedure, and this method of value confrontation seems a promising intervention to use in attempts to reduce prejudice and discrimination. However, some recent research has suggested that Rokeach's method may only work well with a subset of high-prejudice individuals (Monteith & Walters, 1998).

In sum, all of the methods described in the preceding sections provide promising demonstrations of ways to make attitude-change research relevant to socially important issues. They suggest possible approaches toward resolving the "new American dilemma"—the conflict between Americans' beliefs in justice and equality and their resistance to implementing them fully (Taylor & Katz, 1988).

SUMMARY

Many commentators have declared that racism is pervasive in the United States, as demonstrated by the necessity for sweeping court decisions and civil rights laws. At the individual level, *racism* means a pattern of prejudiced attitudes and discriminatory behavior that is important and central in a person's life. *Institutional racism* refers to formal, explicit laws and regulations discriminating against certain ethnic groups, and also to informal social norms that limit the opportunities and choices available to certain ethnic groups. Individual racism and institutional racism operate so as to support and bolster each other.

Children learn racial discriminations and preferences early in life from key socializers (parents, school, church) more often than from personal experience. The specific content of racial stereotypes in the U.S. has remained fairly similar over the past 70 years, but the degree of consensus about stereotypes and the willingness to stereotype have decreased substantially. Yet stereotyped images of minorities are still very common in our mass media. Recent research on racism has begun to include implicit measures of racial stereotypes and attitudes, using response latency measures, and these studies have shown that implicit prejudice is usually only modestly correlated with explicit prejudice.

Whites' explicit racial attitudes depend in part on social distance. Most are willing to grant equality to blacks and other minority groups in areas of interaction (such as employment) that do not require close personal contact, but many whites still resist more intimate contact such as mixed neighborhoods, dating, and marriage. Since the civil rights movement of the 1960s, the proportion of whites supporting principles of equal treatment has increased to very large majorities, but the number favoring various government actions toward implementation of those principles has risen little and is far lower than the support for principles of equal treatment. Among the theoretical viewpoints proposed to explain this contrast are the concepts of modern racism or symbolic racism, aversive racism, realistic group conflict, and opposition to government activism. Although affirmative action programs are designed to "level the playing field" by helping to compensate for centuries of antiblack discrimination and oppression, they have become controversial among many U.S. whites. More white Americans explain blacks' disadvantage as due to low motivation than as due to poor chances for education or a pattern of discrimination.

Overall, African Americans have made much economic and social progress in the past 40 years, but the problems of poverty and deprivation remain acute for much of the black populace. In general, huge majorities of blacks support principles of equality and desegregation, largely because they believe that whites control access to the good things in life rather than because they are eager for social integration. Like whites, blacks are somewhat less favorable toward specific programs to implement racial equality than they are toward principles of equality, and in recent years their approval of some government intervention programs has declined substantially. Yet increasing proportions of blacks have been stating that civil rights progress is too slow. The better-educated and younger groups of blacks perceive more antiblack discrimination in jobs, housing, and by police; are more likely to see civil rights progress as too slow; and more strongly reject low motivation as an explanation of black disadvantage.

Positive changes in racial attitudes since the 1950s have been caused largely by changes in the law and in public practices brought about through peaceful protest. Although whites often complain about civil rights changes being too rapid, they have adjusted and become increasingly favorable to new laws or practices. People who have experienced racial integration, both whites and blacks, are more favorable to it than those who have not.

Experimental studies of racial attitude change have been carried out by social scientists in attempts to pinpoint the conditions that will facilitate positive attitude change. The types of programs that have been studied include interracial contact with equal-status, cooperative activities; cooperative-learning programs in schools; favorable publicity about black role models; methods of reducing realistic group conflict; planned, personal experiences of discrimination; and spotlighting personal value inconsistencies. This attitude-change research offers promising approaches toward improving race relations and resolving the centuries-old "American dilemma."

17

Gender-Role Attitudes

Women are our property. . . . They belong to us, just as a tree that bears fruit belongs to a gardener.—Napoleon Bonaparte.

God put both sexes on earth and each has its own purpose. I'd hate like hell to wake up next to a pipefitter.—Barry Goldwater.

The only position for women in SNCC is prone.—Stokeley Carmichael, head of Student Nonviolent Coordinating Committee (SNCC).

Both men and women have one main role—that of a human being.—Edmund Dahlstrom.

The disparaging quotes above could be paralleled scores of times, but positive ones are rare. A predominant theme in reference to women throughout history is that women are different from, less than, and subordinate to men. A German proverb states, "A woman has the form of an angel, the heart of a serpent, and the mind of an ass." Because women have been viewed in these stereotyped ways, their place in society has been prescribed on the basis of their sex rather than individual characteristics. At the same time, the range of allowable behavior for men has also been limited by related stereotypes of appropriate masculine conduct.

Research and writing related to sex and gender have been expanding at a rapid pace since the late 1960s (Deaux & LaFrance, 1998; Swann, Langlois, & Gilbert, 1999; Unger, 2001). Questions about sex and gender differences have attracted much research in recent years, with an estimated 2,000 new publications on the topic per year (Kimball, 2001). Two journals specifically covering these topics were founded in the mid-1970s, *Sex Roles* and *Psychology of Women Quarterly*. Women's studies curricula have been established on many college and university campuses, and interdisciplinary contributions to understanding of women's roles have been published in countless popular books and magazine articles. Subsequently, a parallel but much smaller resurgence of interest in men's roles also developed (e.g., Good & Sherrod, 2001; Addis & Mahalik, 2003). In 1997, the Society for the Psychological Study of Men and Masculinity (Division 51 of the American Psychological Association) was created, and several scientific journals devoted to the psychology of men have also been established. Social science findings about changing male and female roles have influenced public policy debates and decisions in our government and judicial systems (Russo & Denmark, 1984; Schreiber, 2002).

Usage of the terms *sex* and *gender* has also changed over the years, and there is still variability in different authors' use of the terms (Unger, 1998; Ruble & Martin, 1998; Eckes & Trautner, 2000). For our purposes, we will use the term **sex** to refer to genetically based biological differences between males and females. We will use the term **gender** to refer to the *socially determined* psychological and behavioral characteristics that are typical of males and females, and we will consider **gender roles** as social expectations—learned cultural prescriptions for sex-appropriate personality and behavior.

Research shows that men and women differ in many ways—not just in physical char-acteristics, but also in personality traits, role behaviors, and cognitive abilities (see the 104 chapters in the *Encyclopedia of Women and Gender* for a review of topics—Worell, 2001). But this raises two important questions: What are the sources of these various dif-ferences? And what attitudes do people hold about gender characteristics? Following a bit of historical background, this chapter considers the origins of gender roles, their typical patterns in our society, the various sources from which people's gender-role attitudes are learned, and the ways that these attitudes have been changing in recent decades.

SEXISM AND RACISM

The 1970s added a new word to the language of prejudice: **sexism**, a prejudiced attitude or discriminatory behavior based on the presumed inferiority or difference of women as a group. It is no semantic accident that this word is a first cousin to "racism." In the United States the link between the struggle, on the part of blacks and women, for equality and self-determination is historically rooted. In the nineteenth century, the abolitionist and feminist movements were closely interrelated; many suffragist leaders, both men and women, had honed their political skills in the slavery abolition movement (Myrdal, 1944).

The women's movement of the twentieth century is also linked to black equality. In 1964, Title VII of the Civil Rights Act was passed, prohibiting discrimination on the basis of race or sex. The "sex" provision was added as an intended stumbling block to the bill's passage (Bird, 1968). Subsequent neglect of that provision by the Equal Employment Opportunities Commission led to the 1966 formation of the National Organization for Women, which has since spearheaded the moderate wing of the women's movement (Freeman, 1973).

The parallel between the struggle of blacks and that of women is not only historical, but based on a similar ideology and experience of subordination. This point was made nearly 100 years ago in a penetrating analysis titled "The mind of woman and the lower races" (Thomas, 1907). Myrdal (1944) pointed out the paternalism basic to our society, which provides a rationale and arguments favoring inequality. Kirkpatrick (1963) discussed the analogous situations of blacks and women, listing 36 parallel items. These ranged from rationales for subordination (biological inferiority and religious prescriptions), to discrim-inatory practices in education, sexuality, and occupations, to the minimizing of individual-ity through stereotyping (as being emotional, infantile, and sly). Similarly, Hacker (1951) described various accommodating attitudes (such as deference, concealment of feelings, and subtlety in getting one's way) that are defense mechanisms employed by both groups. Finally, there were great personal and political advantages to white males in keeping both blacks and women in the subordinate status of servants.

However, several major differences can be traced in the subordination of women and that of blacks. First, blacks were a numerically small minority in most places outside the South, and thus many whites might never see or contact them and might have only an abstract conception of the realities of racism. In contrast, because women comprise over half the population, it would be impossible for a male to grow up without contact with them and without personal experience of the differential treatment of women (Reid, 1988). Second, blacks were separated out as a group, whereas women's lives have been individually and intimately intertwined with members of the dominant male group. Women have gained far greater informal power through liaison with individual men, but had little strength as a group.

Third, blacks were literally owned and sold as property on the auction block, whereas women were "wards" by law. The influence of British common law in American history gave husbands custody of the wife's person, property, earnings, and children; yet, ironically, one of the ways of "keeping woman in her place" was to put her on a pedestal (Lewin, 1984). A Madonna view of womanhood—at its height in the nineteenth century—contrasted with a coarser image of men, supported the sexual double standard, and restricted women's activities. Man's "better half" was kept in the kitchen or nursery, unsullied by the evils of the labor market and the sordidness of politics. The "weaker sex" was protected from the physical strain of employment and the mental and emotional stress of higher education. Women found it harder to object to subjugation when it was combined with veneration! Yet, ironically, though black men who had once been slaves received the right to vote after the Civil War in 1865, American women had to wait until 1920 to win that badge of full citizenship.

A final difference between the subordination of blacks and women is that the type of racism directed at blacks in the U.S. is a unique result of American historical, political, and social conditions—differing in important details from racism in other nations and times—whereas the characteristics of sexism in America are very like the practices and beliefs of many other nations (Rogers, 1981; Apparala, Reifman, & Munsch, 2003; Inglehart & Norris, 2003). In fact, sexism may be the most deeply rooted prejudice of the human race, for it is founded on the fundamental dichotomization of the human race into male and female, with "Adam's Rib" as the second sex. Like all prejudice, it cuts two ways, and men's behavior is limited by the reverse of the stereotypes evolved for women. The study of gender roles will be incomplete until equal attention has been given to the problems involved for men.

The facts of discrimination against women in many realms of life have been very thoroughly documented by statistical data, gathered by sources such as the U.S. Department of Labor (e.g., 2003b; Hecker, 1998). Also, the literature of the feminist movement is now prolific and readily available, though its thrust tends to be more polemical than empirical. To complement these well-established bodies of literature, this chapter focuses on research into gender role attitudes and their origins.

ORIGINS OF GENDER ROLES—BIOLOGICAL OR CULTURAL?

The extent to which men and women differ with respect to social behavior has been a subject of much research (Kimball, 2001). Beginning in the 1990s, researchers have assessed these differences by using meta-analytic techniques, which quantitatively combine the results of many studies concerning the characteristics of men and women. Varying interpretations of the meta-analytic findings have sparked considerable debate (Halpern, 1994; Eagly, 1995; Unger, 1998; Eagly & Wood, 2003). Yet the research seems clear in showing that there are clear-cut differences in the social behavior of men and women (Eagly, 1995; Halpern, 1997; Kling et al., 1999), and that many of these differences tend to be quite large. Consequently, we next consider their origin, highlighting two prominent theories about the origin of male–female differences: an evolutionary theory and a social-role theory (Eagly & Wood, 2003).

An Evolutionary Explanation.   From an evolutionary perspective, sex differences are adaptive. That is, sex differences that exist today are the result of natural selection, and their presence helped humans to survive (Buss, 1995; Buss & Kenrick, 1998). Survival of the human species requires reproduction of viable offspring, and those behaviors that enhanced reproductive success were passed on, whereas those behaviors that decreased reproductive success were selected out.

Because women are restricted in the number of children they can bear during their lives, they were more invested than men were in the success of each individual child. They were willing to devote greater care and nurturing to each child, and were motivated to seek out mates who would provide for them during the 9-month pregnancy, and who would protect them while they nursed and cared for their young children. Men were not so restricted in their number of offspring and therefore were less invested in each individual child. For men, the quantity of their mates was more important than quality, whereas for women quality was more important. Many of the sex differences that are observed in the social behavior of men and women (aggressiveness, nurturing, interdependence, and so on) are considered to be the direct result of these contrasting sexual strategies: "Men and women differ in domains where they faced different adaptive problems over human evolutionary history" (Buss & Kenrick, 1998, p. 994).

There are many studies that are consistent with the evolutionary explanation. In terms of mate selection, for instance, numerous studies show that women tend to be attracted to men who are more able to provide and care for them—for instance, men who are older, more established in their careers, and wealthier. In contrast, men tend to be attracted to women who are more likely to provide viable offspring—for instance, women who are young, healthy, and fertile. Buss et al. (1990) have provided evidence that these mate preferences exist across cultures. Similar evidence for the evolutionary explanation has been presented for other male–female differences, including aggression, sexuality, and child care (Kenrick & Luce, 2000).

Social-Role Theory.   From the perspective of social-role theory, male–female differences in social behavior are the result of the typical activities in which men and women engage. As previously stated, **gender roles** are learned cultural prescriptions for sex-appropriate personality and behavior—expectations about what is appropriate behavior for men and women. Historically, women have had less status and power than men; they controlled fewer resources and had less social mobility. In this patriarchal social structure, women were engaged in more domestic work than men (e.g., cooking, cleaning, and child rearing) whereas men tended to work outside the home (hunting, foraging, and, more recently, in paid employment). Although social-role theorists acknowledge that this division of labor may be partly based on biological differences (e.g., men tend to be larger and physically stronger), they emphasize that it is the socialization of boys and girls in preparation for a life in these roles that produces differences between men and women.

There is considerable evidence to suggest that social roles can substantially influence behavior, and that these roles are not biologically determined. For example, Margaret Mead (1935) startled the world with her early study of three New Guinea tribes that showed marked variation in role differentiation and expression. Mead found that Arapesh men and women were both typically "feminine" in western terms: considerate, gentle, and cooperative. Mundugumor men and women both displayed "masculine" traits of aggressiveness and the absence of tenderness. The Tchambuli displayed differential personality traits, but they reversed the western patterns: Men were dependent and nurturant, whereas the women were impersonal and managerial. Although there have been critiques of Mead's research procedures (Freeman, 1983), her underlying conclusion of wide cultural variability is well established. A thorough study of ethnographic reports on 110 primitive societies found many varying patterns of gender roles; some matched, others reversed, and still others blurred our typical dichotomous patterns (Barry, Bacon, & Child, 1957).

Photograph courtesy of Margaret Mead.
Reprinted by permission.

Box 17–1   MARGARET MEAD, *Pioneer Researcher on Gender Roles*

Both by her research and her example, Margaret Mead has been uniquely influential in expanding the role of women in our society. Retired as Curator Emeritus of Ethnology at the American Museum of Natural History in New York after 43 years of continuous service, she continued to lecture, go on anthropological expeditions, and work for causes she believed in until her death in 1978.

Born in 1901 in Philadelphia, Mead attended Barnard College and earned her Ph.D. in anthropology at Columbia in 1929. By then she had already been on an expedition and written her first famous book, Coming of Age in Samoa. *It was quickly followed by* Growing Up in New Guinea, Sex and Temperament in Three Primitive Societies, *and eventually by 40 other books.*

In addition to her curator duties, Mead held over 20 short-term lectureships at universities in five different countries, made 24 anthropological expeditions, accepted over 20 honorary degrees and 30 special awards, and served on innumerable boards, committees, and councils. Notable among her honors were membership in the National Academy of Sciences and election as president of the American Anthropological Association, and the American Association for the Advancement of Science.

More recent research has elaborated on this variability in gender roles across cultures, and suggested that it is these roles—not biology—that are responsible for gender differences. In their cross-cultural analysis of the behavior of men and women in 187 countries, Wood and Eagly (2002) argued that "To the extent that women more than men occupy roles that involve domestic activities (e.g., cooking, provision of emotional support), the associated skills, values, and motives become stereotypic of women and are incorporated into the female gender role" (p. 701). These social roles have been further elaborated throughout history—for instance, maternal child care, which was essential during lactation, was extended beyond the mandatory period; and those who hunted became the "obvious" persons to make weapons and tools (D'Andrade, 1966). Their original rationale now long forgotten, these gender roles became normative patterns, and strong attitudes supporting them were perpetuated in succeeding generations by culturally prescribed customs and child-rearing patterns. Moreover, the activities prescribed for males in any given society, whatever they might be, were virtually always valued more than the prescribed female activities (Rosaldo, 1974).

Now, however, as the roles that men and women occupy in a society change, so too should the size of the differences between men's and women's characteristics. Developments during the twenty-first century should help untangle issues of biological versus cultural causation, at least for women in industrialized nations. They have been freed by the population boom and the pill from the mandate of motherhood, and they can now choose whether or not to enter an automated work world where physical strength is no longer a prerequisite. Their handling of these options will powerfully affect gender-role attitudes in the future.

TRADITIONAL GENDER ROLES AND STEREOTYPES

Let us briefly sketch the traditional stereotypes of gender roles. In doing so we must recognize that any brief description has to be a caricature of the full detail of gender expectations and behavior. We should also realize that there have been variations of these themes in different historical eras as well as in different nations and subcultures. However, a number of cross-cultural studies have indicated that stereotypes about men and women are surprisingly similar across countries. Williams and Best (1982, 1990) found that gender stereotypes in 30 nations, ranging from Peru to Malaysia, were highly similar. In summarizing their cross-cultural findings, Best and Williams (1998) stated, "In sum, in the area of gender stereotypes the evidence for pancultural similarities greatly outweighs the evidence of cultural differences" (p. 110).

Gender stereotypes have at least four main aspects: personality traits, role behaviors, physical characteristics, and cognitive abilities that are expected of women or of men (Deaux & Lewis, 1984; Deaux & LaFrance, 1998; Kite, 2001). One major theme that appears over and over again in descriptions of gender roles is that women tend to have more **expressive** traits (e.g., being more emotional or sentimental) whereas men have more **instrumental** traits (e.g., acting to reach a goal—Parsons, 1955). A closely related theme is that women are more **communal** (selfless and concerned with others), whereas men display more **agency** (being self-interested, self-assertive, and motivated toward mastery—Block, 1973). Thus, among the trait terms that are stereotypically feminine are affectionate, gentle, appreciative, and sensitive, but also complaining, weak, and nagging. In contrast, stereotypically masculine traits are forceful, aggressive, independent, and ambitious, but also boastful, coarse, and disorderly (Williams & Bennett, 1975; Diekman & Eagly, 2000). A selection of gender-stereotypic traits is shown in Table 17–1.

You might think that these gender stereotypes have been changing rapidly in recent years, because of much higher numbers of women being employed and the general effects of the women's movement. However, the research on this topic has yielded mixed results. On one hand, there has been a general shift toward more egalitarian beliefs concerning

TABLE 17–1 Traits Associated with Men and Women

Associated with men	Associated with women
Can make decisions easily	Able to devote self to others
Competitive	Aware of others' feelings
Feels superior	Emotional
Independent	Gentle
Never gives up easily	Kind
Self-confident	Understanding
Stands up well under pressure	Warm

Source: Items from the Personal Attributes Questionnaire. Spence, J. T., & Helmreich, R. L. (1978). *Masculinity and femininity: Their psychological dimensions, correlates, and antecedents.* Austin, TX: University of Texas Press.

the roles of women and men (Spence & Hahn, 1997; Twenge, 1997a; Eagly, Wood, & Diekman, 2000). We discuss these data later in the chapter. However, there still remains a basic gender stereotype about personality traits in which men are seen as more agentic and women as more communal. Research has shown that the specific characteristics which are seen as typically female or male in our society have remained quite stable since the 1970s (e.g., Spence, Helmreich, & Stapp, 1974; Ruble, 1983). This does not mean, though, that people uniformly endorse these beliefs, for there is evidence that women have been coming to view themselves as increasingly agentic (Twenge, 1997b).

To illustrate the difference in perceived characteristics, a study by Powell, Butterfield, and Parent (2002) examined gender stereotypes in a business context. Business students were asked to rate a series of characteristics as the qualities of "a good manager." Of the characteristics, 10 were traditionally masculine and 10 were traditionally feminine, similar to those shown in Table 17–1. Results were compared with similar data collected in 1976 and 1984. Overwhelmingly (and consistently across the three decades), a good manager was described as masculine, but the discrepancy between masculinity and femininity ratings was lower in the 1999 sample than in the two previous decades. Interestingly, although "good managers" were described as less masculine over the years, there was no change in the femininity ratings for good managers, and only a small percentage of the respondents identified good managers as possessing primarily feminine qualities (less than 10% at all three time points).

The Female Role

A detailed description of the traditional American female gender role of the twentieth century was presented in a book entitled *Fascinating Womanhood* (Andelin, 1980). The description sounds as if it might be a parody, but it is actually the foundation of an organization aimed at teaching women how to live out this pattern. Its portrayal of desirable "feminine dependency" included the following description:

- Dispense with any air of strength and ability, of competence and fearlessness, and acquire instead an attitude of frail dependency. . . .
- Be submissive: . . . To be feminine, a woman must be yielding to her husband's rule. . . .
- Don't try to excel him: . . . Don't compete with men in anything which requires masculine ability. . . .
- Need his care and protection: Let him open doors for you, help you on with your coat, pull up your chair. . . . (pp. 241–244)

The Male Role

A central aspect of the American male role is a man's work. His job and his role as breadwinner typically take precedence over other aspects of the husband and father roles, such as caring for children, helping with housework, and sharing intimacy with his wife. Good and Sherrod (2001) have suggested the following six elements as core prescriptions for the stereotypical male role:

- Strong and silent—men are generally stoic and unemotional.
- Toughness and violence—men should be tough and "give 'em hell."
- Self-sufficiency—men are uncomfortable "attaching" to others or "needing" assistance.

- Being a stud—nonrelational sex is valued, but in the context of a committed relationship, sex is devalued.
- No sissy stuff—men do not display any behaviors associated with femininity or homosexuality.
- Be powerful and successful—men should be competitive and successful.

Influences of Gender Stereotypes on Behavior

Believing in such gender stereotypes, even in part, or interacting with other people who do, can have far-reaching effects on the behavior of men and women. A very typical effect has been termed the **self-fulfilling prophecy** (Merton, 1957). Many studies have demonstrated that people tend to behave in ways that confirm other people's expectations of them (e.g., Berger, Rosenholtz, & Zelditch, 1980; Darley & Fazio, 1980; Klein & Snyder, 2003). In one study, undergraduate women applying for a part-time job were led to believe that the interviewer had a concept of the ideal job applicant that either closely matched or markedly differed from the traditional feminine gender stereotype. The women in the traditional condition presented themselves in a substantially more "feminine" manner. For instance, they dressed more conservatively and talked much less than the women in the nontraditional condition (von Baeyer, Sherk, & Zanna, 1981).

However, despite the pervasiveness and power of gender roles on people's behavior, research has also shown that their influence can be overcome in some situations. In laboratory experiments on social cognition, in which participants are given a file of information about several people and asked to make decisions about them (e.g., which one to hire as a kindergarten teacher), the influence of information about their gender may be greatly outweighed by other information that is logically related to the decision (e.g., their performance as a practice teacher, or their love of young children—Locksley et al., 1980). However, in the actual world such characteristics are apt to be positively correlated and, even when they are not, judges making decisions *expect* them to be. Hence the relative influence of gender labels and other characteristics cannot normally be teased apart in real-world situations, and gender stereotypes are apt to play a major role in such decisions as job hiring and evaluation (Deaux, 1985).

SOURCES OF GENDER-ROLE ATTITUDES

How do gender roles originate and develop? A great deal of research has examined influences that may be responsible for current gender-role views (cf. Powlishta et al., 2001). These socializing pressures are the "attitudes behind our attitudes." Among these sources of influence are all of the socializing agents that we discussed in Chapter 7—parents, teachers, peers, and the mass media—plus some others that are particularly relevant to transmission of gender attitudes. These include clinicians who treat our minds and bodies, social scientists who describe our place in society, writers of children's literature who shape early attitudes, and even the everyday language that we speak and hear. Here are some brief examples of each of these types of influence on gender-role attitudes.

Parents, Teachers, and Peers

Parents treat infant boys and girls differently, starting from the very day of their birth. American mothers and fathers tend to describe their day-old girls as tiny, soft, delicate, and the like, whereas they describe their newborn boys as strong, alert, firm, and bigger—despite the fact that the infants in the research were not objectively different in size or muscle tone (Rubin, Provenzano, & Luria, 1974). In the first 6 months of life, boys in our society receive more physical contact (being touched, held, nursed, etc.), whereas girls get more nonphysical attention (being looked at, talked to, etc.—Lewis, 1972; Maccoby & Jacklin, 1974). These differences in treatment set the stage for the children's expected gender-role behavior. Lest you think that the treatment differences are elicited by different characteristics of the infants, some studies have found these differential patterns of treatment toward the *same infant*, when it was dressed and introduced to adults as a boy versus as a girl (e.g., Smith & Lloyd, 1978; Sidorowicz & Lunney, 1980). Adults talked quietly to a 6-month-old "girl" and offered "her" a doll to play with, whereas the same child dressed as a boy was typically given a toy hammer and encouraged to engage in large-scale vigorous play.

Parents make more demands on boys in their first few years than on girls, and they reprimand boys more severely than girls for acting in gender-inappropriate ways (Hartley, 1974; Hort, Leinbach, & Fagot, 1990). Although American parents often deny that they pick baby clothes according to the child's sex, the clothing usually identifies the infant as a boy or a girl (Shakin, Sternglanz, & Shakin, 1985). Most clothing for infants designates their sex not only by its color and direction of fastening, but also by style of collars, type of trim, patterns and embroidery, and so forth. Boys' clothes tend to be durable and give more freedom of movement, whereas girls' garments usually have more delicate prints and dainty fabrics (Richardson, 1988).

Toys, too, are highly gender-typed, as demonstrated by an analysis of a Sears toy catalog. Toys on a page section illustrated with a boy's figure were almost entirely manipulatory (e.g., blocks, Lego assembly units, or vehicles), whereas those grouped with a girl's picture were mostly related to marriage and child rearing (e.g., dolls, kitchen toys). Cultural and educational toys were more equitably illustrated—most often with no models or with mixed genders (Richardson, 1988). As a result of parental and societal conditioning, children as young as 2 years old tend to show preferences for gender-appropriate toys (Blakemore, LaRue, & Olejnik, 1979; Blakemore, 2003), as do older children in their requests to Santa Claus (Richardson & Simpson, 1982). As early as age 3, boys and girls are extremely accurate in identifying which toys, hairstyles, games, and activities are more appropriate for boys or for girls (Edwards, Knoche, & Kumru, 2001).

The impact of teachers and the school environment on gender socialization is an issue of some dispute (Fagot, Rodgers, & Leinbach, 2000). There is evidence, however, that teachers, just like parents, often display gender-role stereotyping. Teachers hold expectations for children, based at least in part on gender, and they interact with them in ways that reinforce these expectations. For instance, in one study, nursery school teachers were found to reward boys more for aggressive behavior and girls more for dependency. They also tended to help girls perform tasks, whereas they more often gave boys verbal instructions for carrying out tasks on their own. Such interactions encourage boys to be capable and independent and girls to feel helpless and dependent (Serbin & O'Leary, 1975; Fagot et al., 1985, 2000).

In nursery school and elementary school, children's peers become increasingly strict monitors and enforcers of gender-role norms in activities, toy preferences, friendships, and so on (Langlois & Downs, 1980; Pitcher & Schultz, 1983; Carter & McCloskey, 1983–1984). Even in college, when gender-role options become broader and less restrictive, peers still remain major influences on students' gender-role attitudes and behaviors (Komarovsky, 1985).

Psychotherapists

The writings of psychotherapists have had a profound impact on social attitudes toward the personality and role of women. Clinicians are frequently called on to distinguish between behavior that is normal and behavior that is "pathological" (Gilbert & Rader, 2001). Freud's view of woman—that her anatomy was her destiny—assigned her firmly to her place in the home. Freud defined woman biologically and psychologically as an incomplete male, who envied the man's penis and superior creative capacities.

In addition to Freud, other leaders in the psychiatric field (e.g., Bettelheim, Erikson, and Rheingold) have described the well-adjusted woman as defining herself in terms of men—in the roles of wife, mother, and homemaker (Weisstein, 1971). Chesler (1972) asserted that this kind of viewpoint among "healing" professionals has contributed greatly to pathological diagnoses of women who do not fit the mold, and to the fact that about twice as many women as men are hospitalized for emotional disturbance in the U.S.

A frequently cited study suggested that many clinicians continued to view women patients much as Freud did (Broverman et al., 1970). In it, male and female psychiatrists, psychologists, and social workers were asked to describe mentally healthy men, women, and "adults" (no gender specified) on a list of behavioral and personality traits. Results showed that a double standard of mental health was held by both male and female practitioners. Trait ratings of the healthy man and the healthy adult were highly similar, but ratings of the healthy woman differed from both. She was described as more dependent, submissive, easily influenced, emotional, and subjective, and less competitive, aggressive, and adventuresome—all characteristics that were otherwise attributed to *un*healthy adults.

Results of this study imply that, if these clinicians practice what they preach, they may encourage women patients to adjust to norms that are opposed to increasing maturity and individuality. However, it is well to note that the dichotomous way that ratings were reported in this study tended to exaggerate the relatively small differences that the therapists saw between the healthy man and the healthy woman. Also, when rating the "healthy adult," the judges may have thought of that person as a man, and if so, the results would be very logical and not a sign of an invidious view of women as less mentally healthy than men. It is encouraging that later studies of a similar sort have found little or no stereotypic bias in therapists' ratings of the mental health of men and women (e.g., M. L. Smith, 1980; Hare-Mustin, 1983; Beckwith, 1993).

Nevertheless, in response to reports and concerns about sexist practices in psychotherapy, the American Psychological Association established a Task Force on Sex Bias and Sex-Role Stereotyping in Psychotherapeutic Practice. Its report (APA, 1975) warned of the potential dangers of sexism in four aspects of psychotherapy: fostering of traditional gender roles, bias in expectations and devaluation of women, sexist use of psychoanalytic concepts, and responding to women in treatment as sex objects. Going beyond these proscriptions, new groups of feminist therapists have begun to offer clients nonsexist, individualized treatment approaches aimed at equality between men and women and that seek to change society in that direction.

History, Sociology, and Marriage and Family Textbooks

The writings of social scientists may influence public opinion because of people's faith in the objectivity and factuality of scientific findings. However, attitudes toward gender roles revealed by writers in sociology and other social sciences are characterized by androcentrism (a focus on men), stereotyping, and a bipolar view of gender roles. Research into history books has illustrated these biases (Rosen, 1971):

> Sexism in historical writing is much like sexism in daily life. For the most part women are made invisible. When discussed at all, women... appear as part of the domestic scenery behind the real actors and action of national life. (p. 541)

Even writers who have tried to focus on women have found it difficult to examine their activities in history without reference to domestic roles. One author, for example, called the work and friends of suffragists "spouse surrogates," as if women were incomplete in themselves.

The textbooks used in marriage and family classes, above all sources, would be expected to present a realistic picture of gender roles as they are and as they may develop. However, as late as the 1960s, they were shot through with unsubstantiated "facts" and prescriptive judgments. Ehrlich (1971) analyzed the content of six leading marriage and family texts on several important dimensions, and her findings were a serious indictment of family writers' scientific objectivity. Examining sexual attitudes, she found women typically described as asexual. The active, aggressive male was depicted as normal; the woman with a high sexual drive was a "nymphomaniac," needed "psychiatric attention," and/or "endangered her marriage" with her demands. Traditional homemaker/breadwinner roles were upheld as natural, proper, and expedient. The textbooks suggested that a woman might take a job (preferably part-time) to add to family income, *provided that her husband agreed and her work did not interfere with her household obligations.*

Examination of more recent marriage and family textbooks shows encouraging efforts to avoid these past deficiencies. Many of them now emphasize the recent changes in expected roles for American men and women and highlight the resulting greater latitude in occupational choices, personality traits, sexual behavior, and everyday social interactions. However, there are other texts that still do not mention the concept of gender roles, give relatively little space to "sex roles," and tend to discuss them as if they were biologically or ethically mandated rather than broadly variable and produced by social expectations and pressures. Recent research has shown that images in marriage and family textbooks in the 1990s were more egalitarian, but that the basic pattern of traditional gender role images still persists (Low & Sherrard, 1999).

Children's Literature

An important critique of books for children was contained in a small paperback called *Dick and Jane as Victims* (Women on Words and Images, 1975). This carefully documented content analysis of 134 elementary school readers revealed a consistent pattern of stereotypic messages to the nation's children. The differential treatment accorded boys and girls in the 2,760 stories that were studied illustrates some assumptions underlying gender-role attitudes that may be learned in school. Boys in these school readers were more clever than girls by a four-to-one ratio. They were more heroic (ratio 4:1)—for example, saving others from fires, stampedes, storms, and rampaging buffaloes. They had far-flung adventures (ratio 3:1) such as panning for gold, weathering tornadoes, and catching cattle rustlers. By contrast, girls stood passively, hands behind their backs, admiring the feats of their brothers. They carried out domestic work (ratio 3:1 compared with boys) and did so cheerfully whereas boys more grudgingly helped Mother with "her" chores. In the stories, father was the fun person, the problem-solver and adventure-promoter. Mother was colorless and unimaginative as she obsessively cleaned, cooked, and scolded.

*Photograph courtesy of
University of Texas
News and Information Service.
Reprinted by permission.*

Box 17–2   JANET T. SPENCE, *Authority on Gender Roles*

After earning her B.A. from Oberlin College and her Ph.D. in psychology from the University of Iowa, Janet Spence joined the faculty at Northwestern University. She subsequently spent several years as a research psychologist at Iowa City Veterans Administration Hospital because the nepotism rules of that time prevented her and her husband from both being on the university psychology faculty. In 1964 she moved to the University of Texas at Austin, where she remains as Professor Emeritus of Psychology and Educational Psychology.

A central theme in Spence's research is how motivation, personality, and attitudes are related to observable behavior. In her early research she became famous as author of the Taylor Manifest Anxiety Scale. More recently she has focused on gender-role attitudes and behavior, where she is noted for developing the Attitudes towards Women Scale and other objective measures which are discussed in this chapter. Among her many scientific and professional honors, she has been elected president of both the American Psychological Society and the American Psychological Association, from which she also received the Award for Outstanding Lifetime Contribution to Psychology.

Another early research project (Weitzman et al., 1972) examined the socialization of preschool children through prize-winning picture books. The Caldecott Medal is given yearly by the American Library Association to the best preschool book; it may mean 60,000 sales for the book, and it is influential in setting standards for other children's literature. The study analyzed 18 Caldecott winners and runners-up for the period 1967–1971. The gender roles portrayed were similar to those described in the previous study. There was an active/passive, outdoor/indoor, task-oriented/person-oriented dichotomy between males and females.

A prototypical example from an earlier preschool book titled *The Very Little Girl* is an illustration showing a fragile little girl being dragged along by a tiny dachshund on a leash. A companion book called *The Very Little Boy*, by the same author and illustrator, contains a parallel drawing of a boy of the same age successfully giving commands to and caring for a dog twice his size (Weitzman et al., 1972). Perhaps the most flagrant fallacy in the Caldecott Award books concerned the occupational picture presented. During a period when close to half of American women worked, the only occupational roles portrayed for women were wife and mother, *fairy, fairy godmother, and underwater maiden!* Hardly a realistic set of options!

Some subsequent studies of children's books have reported similar patterns of lopsided concentration on male characters, with active, adventurous, problem-solving roles for males versus passive, fantasy, or home-centered activities for females (e.g., Stockard & Johnson, 1980). More recent studies of children's books have shown a shift toward greater visibility of women and girls as characters, and a greater range of personality traits and behavioral activities being depicted for females (e.g., Williams et al., 1987; Oskamp, Kaufman, & Wolterbeek, 1996; Gooden & Gooden, 2001; Clark et al., 2003). For example, an analysis of award-winning children's books found that the percentage without female characters decreased from 33% in the 1960s, to 25% in the 1980s, and to 15% in the 1990s. Although some gender-stereotypic patterns are still evident in recent preschool books and school readers, they are usually less blatant. Also encouraging is the number of children's novels that have begun to reflect the goals of the women's movement and to show greater male–female equality, less dominance for males, and a much wider range of roles for girls and women (Trites, 1997).

Everyday Language

Just like children's literature, our everyday speech often expresses and reinforces gender-role stereotypes. As Henley (1989) has summarized, our use of language treats men and women unequally:

1. Language deprecates women. For instance, there are from 6 to 10 times more feminine terms than masculine terms for various negative concepts (e.g., a sexually promiscuous person) and, conversely, many more masculine terms for prestigious concepts. As another example, the common use of "girl" to refer to a mature woman is infantilizing, in the same way that using "boy" to address a mature black man is insulting.

2. Language use reflects gender stereotypes. For instance, phrases like "woman doctor" or "male nurse" show our society's normal expectations about the sex of individuals in those occupations. Similarly, the differentiation of marital status in our traditional terms of address for women (*Miss, Mrs.*) but not for men (*Mr.*) indicates that marriage is considered more crucial to women's status.

3. Language treats the male as normative and ignores women. The most widespread example of this is use of the masculine as a generic form, as in *chairman, layman, workman's compensation*, or *he* or *him* used to include persons of both sexes.

Some defenders of the linguistic status quo have argued that these common usages are just a matter of convenience and do not matter in terms of women's treatment in society. However, in recent years, much research contradicting that view has accumulated. For instance, a story about a woman political candidate using sexist terms such as "lady candidate" and "girl" made readers more negative to the candidate's seriousness and competence than did reading the same story purged of sexist language (Dayhoff, 1983). All of the many studies on the generic masculine form have shown that it introduces a bias in people's thinking because it does not call to mind females as readily as it does males (e.g., Martyna, 1980; Henley, 1989; McConnell & Fazio, 1996). Furthermore, information written in the generic masculine form gives males an advantage, for research has shown that men remember such material better than gender-neutral material, whereas women remember it less well (Crawford & English, 1984). Moreover, job descriptions written in the generic masculine (e.g., "The professor is expected to. . . . He also must. . . .") cause females to be less interested in considering such jobs, and cause readers to deprecate females' ability to perform the jobs (Bem & Bem, 1973; Briere & Lanktree, 1983; Hyde, 1984). Thus the linguistic form may influence highly consequential social and behavioral choices, and use of the generic *he* is a subtle way of brainwashing women (and men) about their place in society.

In view of these detrimental effects of sexism in language, the efforts to eliminate it should be applauded and extended. The American Psychological Association (1977) has published guidelines for nonsexist use of language and incorporated them in its *Publication Manual*, which applies to articles in all APA journals and most other psychological journals. However, many undergraduates are still unconvinced that sexist language is offensive or that it has damaging consequences. Parks and Roberton (1998) found that 53% of college students opposed some aspects of nonsexist language, and 21% opposed all forms. Therefore a demonstration by Adamsky (1981) can be a useful classroom device. In some of her classes she made a point of using the generic *feminine* form for a few days (always using "she" as the generic pronoun), and she found that it not only raised everyone's awareness of the issue, but also made some of the women students feel proud and powerful, and motivated them to continue that usage in their written papers. Although it is difficult to get people to change their linguistic habits, our society's general adoption of the terms "black" or "African American" to replace "Negro" shows that it can be done.

The Mass Media

The mass media, which pervade modern life, generally present consistent stereotyped messages about gender roles. The extensiveness of bias may be demonstrated by analysis of popular songs, television, and commercials.

You might think that popular music, which is predominantly created and consumed by young people, would be the medium most likely to challenge traditional gender roles. Indeed, in recent decades, popular songs have prominently protested against war, pollution, racism, and restrictive middle-class lifestyles. However, in most respects, they still reflect traditional gender-role stereotypes (Chafetz, 1974; Hyden & McCandless, 1983). A majority of popular songs are about males, and a large majority are sung by males. Characteristics that typify men but not women in these songs include being aggressive, rational, demanding, a breadwinner, sexually aggressive, nonconformist, rigid, egotistical, adventuresome, and using drugs. By contrast, women are depicted as domestic, passive, flirtatious, idealistic, dependent, and childlike. The only ways that these songs depart from traditional gender stereotypes are in portraying a large minority of women as secure and depicting many men as sensitive, emotional, loving, and gentle. Analyses of music videos show a more extreme pattern, in which women tend to be underrepresented and portrayed in a manner that emphasizes physical appearance and sexuality (Signorielli, McLeod, & Healy, 1994; Gow, 1996).

In television entertainment programs, gender-role stereotypes have been very pervasive (e.g., Butler & Paisley, 1980). Historically, men have been depicted as smarter, more powerful, rational, and stable, but also as more violent and evil. Women characters are generally shown as younger, more attractive, warmer, and happier than men (Tedesco, 1974). A similar pattern has been found on children's television shows: aggressive and constructive men, ineffective and deferential women (Sternglanz & Serbin, 1974; Williams, LaRose, & Frost, 1981). Although this high degree of gender-stereotyped portrayals of men and women lasted through the 1980s, more recent data suggest that the pattern is beginning to erode.

Several studies of prime-time television broadcasts in the 1990s showed reductions in stereotypic portrayals (although still not an accurate reflection of reality). Analysis of the jobs in which male and female characters were cast found that 76% of men were portrayed as employed, compared with 60% of women characters. Although men were shown in a wider array of jobs, women and men were equally likely to be cast as professionals (Signorielli & Kahlenberg, 2001). In a more detailed analysis of prime-time television occupational roles, Signorielli and Bacue (1999) found that women were portrayed in traditionally female occupations (secretary, nurse, teacher, etc.) 17% of the time, in gender-neutral jobs 39%, and in traditionally male jobs 25% (e.g., doctor, lawyer). For men, the pattern was more stereotypic: 50% of male characters were in traditionally male jobs, 33% were in gender-neutral jobs (artist, journalist), and only 4% were in traditionally female jobs. Signorielli and Kahlenberg (2001) concluded that

> television has improved in the way the occupations of women and people of color are portrayed in prime-time programs. . . . Nevertheless, . . . the world of work still contains several stereotypic portrayals in relation to gender, race, marital status, and work. On television, more women than men still cannot be classified by occupation or are portrayed as not working outside of the home. . . . (p. 19)

A summary of the occupational portrayals of men and women in prime-time television broadcasts from the 1970s through the 1990s is shown in Table 17–2.

Although prime-time television has shown some change toward egalitarian gender presentations since the 1980s, this is not the case in the world of advertising (Kaufman, 1999). In television commercials, women are usually subordinate. They appear much less frequently than men, and are most often shown as housewives being advised or persuaded to use a household product, whereas the advice-giver is usually a man, and the authoritative off-screen voice summarizing the product's benefits is almost always a man (Women's Action Alliance, 1981; Courtney & Whipple, 1983). Women in commercials are less likely to be shown in a work environment, and when they are it tends to be in a clerical or service position (Coltrane & Adams, 1997). Unlike other areas of media, there is no evidence that gender portrayals in television commercials have changed in the past 30 years. In their research report, Ganahl, Prinsen, and Netzley (2003) concluded that "gender stereotypes still pervade the advertising industry" (p. 550). Similarly, Coltrane and Messineo (2000) described television commercials as perpetuating subtle prejudice and concluded that since the 1960s "there has been no fundamental change in the ways that television marketing tends to essentialize gender and race/ethnic differences" (p. 386).

TABLE 17–2 Prime-Time Television Depictions of Women and Men Across Three Decades

Variable	1970s	1980s	1990s
Percent of characters who are female	28%	34%	40%
Chronological age (estimated by viewers)			
Men	37	38	35
Women	32	34	32
Occupations for men and women			
Men who are working	85%	84%	76%
Women who are working	55	61	60
Professional men	21	23	32
Professional women	21	22	30
Gender-typed occupations			
Men in traditionally male jobs	64%	54%	50%
Women in traditionally male jobs	20	26	25
Men in traditionally female jobs	4	6	4
Women in traditionally female jobs	24	11	17

Source: Signorielli, N., & Bacue, A. (1999). Recognition and respect: A content analysis of prime-time characters across three decades. *Sex Roles, 40,* 527–544. Data are extracted from Tables 1, 2, 5, and 6.

Despite the slow pace of change in gender stereotypes in the mass media, we believe that there is room for optimism. In recent years a number of shows have cast women in positions of authority (e.g., *Judging Amy*, *ER*). Laboratory studies that have exposed women to a few vivid television shows or commercials showing nontraditional gender-role activities have found that they can have clear short-term effects on career aspirations and social behavior (e.g., Geis et al., 1984). For example, studies of a children's TV series called *Freestyle*, which highlighted nontraditional occupational possibilities for girls and boys, found that viewers displayed a broadened set of career viewpoints and gender-role beliefs (Johnston & Ettema, 1982). Given results such as these, it seems certain that American children must be powerfully influenced by the cumulative impact of gender role portrayals in the 20,000 hours of television programs and 350,000 commercials that they see, on the average, as they are growing up (Adler et al., 1980; Kunkel, 2001). If media gender portrayals are changing, people's gender-role attitudes may also change.

Enculturation.   As discussed in Chapter 9, the most widespread effect of the mass media is **enculturation** (or **cultivation**)—the process of instilling and reinforcing the attitudes and views of reality that are held by most members of a given culture. The studies cited in the preceding sections show that this process has begun to receive the research attention that its importance merits. A major review of mass communication effects (Roberts & Bachen, 1981) concluded that:

> Work on sex-role socialization supports a cultivation effect interpretation. The media appear to contribute to the continuance of sex-stereotyped perceptions, but are capable of establishing new perceptual sets when nonstereotypic content is introduced. (p. 346)

TRENDS OVER TIME IN GENDER-ROLE ATTITUDES

We have examined the major influences that help to shape current gender-role attitudes. Now let's look back more than half a century and trace the historical pattern of attitudinal shifts on certain key topics: attitudes about women's rights and equality, the idea of a woman President for the U.S. (as reflected in opinion-poll data), views of women and work, and attitudes toward women's roles.

Women's Rights and Equality

The unsuccessful struggle to ratify the Equal Rights Amendment (ERA) to the U.S. Constitution was the symbolic peak of the modern American women's movement. The amendment was passed by an overwhelming majority in Congress in 1972, and it merely said: "Equality of rights under the law shall not be denied or abridged by the United States or by any state on account of sex." Initially, this was a very popular position, but a small group of vociferous opponents of the amendment led by Phyllis Schlafly raised issues such as the likelihood that unisex bathrooms would be required, that husbands would no longer have to support their wives, and that women would be drafted for military combat duty.

Opposition to the ERA was based very largely on beliefs that traditional gender roles were biologically determined and should not be tampered with, and many opposing legislators were outspoken in stating their antifeminist sentiments, calling ERA supporters "bra-less brainless broads" and declaring that women would "rather be loved than liberated" (Mansbridge, 1986). Thus, the opposition had a strong symbolic, value-laden character, similar to the symbolic racism discussed in Chapter 16, but the openly sexist nature of the opposing arguments was more extreme than the public reactions to blacks that are heard in this era of modern, subtle racism.

Over the next 10 years, legislatures in most of the states voted approval of the amendment, but after bitter battles in the remaining states, the final total of support fell a few states short of the three-fourths needed for its ratification. As a result, the amendment died in 1982, though there have been continued attempts to reintroduce it in Congress and begin the ratification process all over again (cf. http://www.equalrightsamendment.org).

What did the public think about the ERA? There was a substantial majority support for it ever since it was passed by Congress. The lowest percentage of support that it received in Gallup Polls was 57% in 1976, with only 24% opposed and 19% expressing no opinion. Also noteworthy is the fact that up until 1980 women were about 7% *less* in favor of the ERA than men were. Ironically, in 1981, less than a year before the amendment's demise, and despite President Reagan's opposition to it, nationwide public support rose to 63% (32% opposed, and 5% no opinion), with women and men equally favorable, and even conservatives supporting it 58% to 38% (*Gallup Report*, 1981, No. 190). Finally, by 1988, long after the ERA was a dead letter, public support for it had increased to 73% (16% opposed, 11% no opinion), and by this time women were 7% *more* favorable than men (*Gallup Report*, 1988, No. 274). These fascinating changes are statistically significant, and the history of the ERA demonstrates once again that heavy public support for a policy does not ensure its governmental adoption (cf. Chapter 12).

A Woman for President?

Public attitudes toward the employment capabilities of women are perhaps most stringently tested by this question: "If your party nominated a woman for President, would you vote for her if she were qualified for the job?" The Gallup Poll and other survey organizations have posed this question, with slight variations in wording, to citizens since 1937 (Erskine, 1971). Combining data for both sexes, public opinion has changed dramatically since 1937, when only 33% of survey respondents said they would vote for a qualified woman for president. Over seven decades, the percentage climbed steadily and strongly, peaking at 92% in 1999 (Jones & Moore, 2003). Some of the increase was due to mass media attention to the issues of the women's liberation movement and the status of women, which burgeoned in the 1970s. Despite this apparent strong public support for women political candidates, women hold only 14% of elected offices in the federal government, and only once, 20 years ago, has a woman been nominated on a major party's national ticket (Geraldine Ferraro was the Democratic vice-presidential nominee on the ticket with Walter Mondale in 1984).

Women and Work

The past 60 years have brought profound changes in American women's roles, particularly in employment. Between 1940 and 1981, the number of women employed outside the home more than tripled, and the number of working *mothers* increased more than tenfold. Since the early 1980s, well over 50% of adult women have been employed in the American labor force. In 2002, 72% of women who had children under 18 years of age were employed, and even among women with preschool-age children, 64% were employed. In the United States, 99% of women will work for pay at some point in their lives (U.S. Department of Labor, 2003a).

With passage of the Equal Pay Act in 1963 and Title VII of the Civil Rights Act in 1964, equal opportunity in employment for men and women of all races became the national

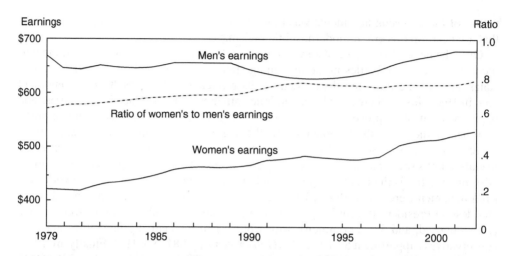

FIGURE 17–1 The gender wage gap: Comparison of men's and women's median usual weekly earnings, for full-time wage and salary workers in constant (2002) dollars, 1979–2002.

Source: U.S. Department of Labor (2003b, p. 3).

policy. However, in the subsequent years a consistent, albeit narrowing, **wage gap** has continued. In the early 2000s, the pay of full-time working women averaged only about 76% of what employed men made, up from 63% in 1979. Overall, in their median weekly earnings, women earned $530, whereas men earned $680 (see Figure 17–1). Even for men and women with a college education, the difference persisted: The median weekly earnings for women with a bachelor's degree were $809, compared with $1,089 for men with a bachelor's degree (U.S. Department of Labor, 2003a).

Part of the wage gap differential is due to occupation, because women are more likely to work in lower-paying professional occupations, such as teacher or nurse, whereas men are more likely to work in higher-paying occupations, such as engineer or computer scientist. However, even when matched for occupation, men outearn women (Hecker, 1998). In managerial and professional positions (48% of which are held by women), women earned only 68% of a man's salary in 2002, up from 64% in 1983. A similar but less-extreme pattern holds for traditionally female occupations—as elementary school teachers, where women outnumber men 5-to-1, they earn 90% of a man's salary (U.S. Department of Labor, 2003b). A careful analysis of earnings for male and female college graduates, at the same level of education, in the same major field, and in the same age group, found that on average across all positions women earned 87% as much as men (Hecker, 1998).

The interpretations and arguments surrounding these wage differentials have been complex, but the pattern seems a clear reflection of the stereotyped values of American culture, in which women's work is valued less than men's work (Lips, 2003). As a result of this and many other types of gender discrimination, the women's movement has vigorously supported laws and court rulings requiring affirmative action in hiring and promotion, equal pay for equal work, and, more recently, comparable worth as a basis for computing appropriate pay for women (for background information, see Clayton & Crosby, 1992; Crosby et al., 2003).

How have Americans' attitudes about working women changed during recent decades? There has been a "fundamental and profound shift in public expectations of women's roles at work and at home" (Huddy, Neely, & Lafay, 2000, p. 310). The first available survey data from the 1930s showed a high level of disapproval for women in the work force (Spitze & Huber, 1980). For example, when asked if a married woman should work "if she has a husband capable of supporting her," only 18% of respondents approved in 1936. By 1998, the approval level had risen to 82% (Gallup, 1972; Caplow, Hicks, & Wattenberg, 2000; General Social Survey, 2004). Despite this growing support for women in the work force, and despite the marked shift in the number of women who are employed, there is still strong support for the notion that, when financially possible, it is best for women to stay home with their children. A large majority (70%) of respondents to a nationwide survey conducted in 2000 indicated that "the best child care arrangement during a child's earliest years is to have one parent stay home." Furthermore, nearly 70% believed that it would be better if mothers stayed home with their young children, though a large majority (75% of women and 66% of men) said that women can have a successful career *and* be a good mother (Public Agenda, 2000).

Gender stereotypes about traits relevant to employment have also been changing. Shortly after World War II, men were credited with more ability than women by both sexes, and as late as 1970, 49% of men and 40% of women believed that women could not run businesses as well as men (Erskine, 1971). However, these stereotypic gender-role attitudes have been declining. For example, in a cross-sectional sample, Agassi (1982) found that over 90% of both men and women said that women can manage or supervise just as well as men, and even higher numbers said that women can do mathematics just as well as men. Despite such favorable reports, there is still evidence of more subtle unfavorable attitudes toward women on the part of supervisors and managers (e.g., Martin, Harrison, & Dinitto, 1983). Women are typically viewed as possessing less leadership ability than men, and their performance can often be undermined when their characteristics and their role are perceived to be incongruent (Carli & Eagly, 1999; Eagly & Karau, 2002).

Although the data reported in this section generally show dramatic changes in the favorability of attitudes toward women workers, there still remains a great deal of behavioral discrimination against them. This is evident in their substantially higher unemployment rates, occupational segregation into jobs and work groups that are mostly female, lower pay even for identical jobs and responsibilities, and widespread exposure to sexual harassment on the job (Kahn & Crosby, 1985). A majority of Americans are aware of the widespread discrimination against women workers, but a surprisingly large percentage of women deny being aware of any individual disadvantage in their personal job situation (Crosby et al., 1989). Survey data show that a majority of men (59%) and women (70%) believe that men get paid more for "doing the same work." However, when women were asked "if you personally feel that because you are a woman, you get paid less," 70% believed that this was not case (*Publicagenda.org*, 2003).

The contrast between generally favorable attitudes and frequent discriminatory behavior against women workers parallels the findings in Chapter 16 about the more subtle, modern forms of racism. The discriminatory behavior that occurs is often not the result of individual prejudice against women workers, but rather of situational and organizational norms that perpetuate unequal treatment (e.g., paying men higher starting wages, favoring them for management training, or evaluating them more favorably for promotion). Both unfavorable individual attitudes and inequitable institutional norms are likely to operate as self-fulfilling prophecies that hinder the advancement of women (e.g., Rice, Bender, & Vitters, 1980). Kahn and Crosby (1985) summarized this process:

> Most people do not make it a point to exclude or oppress working women. People may, at the same time, continue in their work-force behaviors to favor this man or that in one situation

or another. . . . Many discrete individual actions, each perpetuating a seemingly insignificant male advantage in one place or another, accumulate and the aggregate effect becomes one of keeping women severely at a disadvantage. (p. 228)

This subtle form of sexism is reflected in studies using *implicit* measures of gender attitudes. You will recall from Chapter 4 that implicit attitudes are measured in ways that do not require self-report, and therefore are not subject to the social desirability effects inherent in self-report measures. One of the first, and most consistent, findings from studies using the IAT procedure, was that both men and women show a strong tendency to associate males with science and females with liberal arts (Nosek, Banaji, & Greenwald, 2002a, 2002b). In addition, there are clear differences in associations of gender with career and family: Women are strongly associated with family, whereas men are associated with careers. Interestingly, IAT data also show an association of women with positive characteristics, a pattern that has also been found in studies that use explicit measures (Eagly, Mladinic, & Otto, 1991; Carpenter, 2001; Skowronski & Lawrence, 2001).

Questionnaire Studies of Women's Roles

Most of the survey studies cited in previous sections have used interview methods and representative samples of men and women to collect their data. An alternative approach is to use written questionnaires, and these are usually given to local samples (e.g., of workers in a particular company or city), who are apt to be less representative of the whole population. However, carefully developed questionnaires have the advantages of reliability and repeatability, which are important in tracking trends in gender-role attitudes.

As far back as the 1930s, Kirkpatrick (1963) developed his Belief-Pattern Scale, containing 40 feminist and 40 antifeminist statements. Giving it to college students and their parents, he found the students to be more liberal, especially the girls. A gradual ensuing trend toward liberality in gender-role attitudes was interrupted by a sharp drop in the 1960s, similar to one that occurred for women respondents during the 1960s on the woman-for-President question.

Spence and Helmreich (1972) took up where Kirkpatrick left off, using similar questionnaire categories with updated content. They administered an Attitudes towards Women Scale to large samples of college students and their parents. Like Kirkpatrick, they found students significantly more liberal than the older generation and women significantly more liberal than men for both generations. By 1980, both the students and their parents had become markedly more egalitarian than in 1972 (Helmreich, Spence, & Gibson, 1982). In the ensuing years, both men and women have become increasingly liberal and egalitarian in their attitudes toward women's roles. However, women still tend to be more egalitarian, whereas on average men hold more sexist attitudes about the appropriate roles for men and women (Loo & Thorpe, 1998; Frieze et al., 2003). Other measures of gender-role attitudes and stereotypes include the Personal Attributes Questionnaire (Spence et al., 1974), the Bem Sex-Role Inventory (Bem, 1974), the Modern Sexism Scale (Swim et al., 1995; Swim & Cohen, 1997), and the Ambivalent Sexism Inventory (Glick & Fiske, 1996, 2001), which are discussed in a later section.

In summary, both poll data and questionnaire studies have indicated a trend over time toward liberalization of U.S. gender-role attitudes. However, because of persisting subtle prejudice and opposing institutional norms and pressures, there has been less change in widespread societal patterns of discrimination against women in various realms of life.

Attitudes Toward the Women's Movement

Since the 1960s, the women's movement has fought against personality and behavioral stereotyping and has spearheaded the campaign for changes in women's roles. In examining attitudes toward gender roles, therefore, it is especially informative to look at people's opinions of this movement, which is also referred to as the women's liberation movement.

Although the women's movement gained prominence only in the late 1960s, it quickly made a notable impact on American society. By 1973, approximately half of a very large sample of *Redbook* magazine's women readers credited the women's movement with having made them aware of society's discrimination against women. However, research in the 1980s suggested that most women had not become personally aggrieved by their lack of power in society, and consequently they had not become dedicated to group organizing and collective action to remedy their grievances. Then and now, more women favored an individual approach to social change—working separately for their own benefit—rather than a collective approach (Institute for Social Research, 1982; Huddy et al., 2000).

In the past three decades, there have been great increases in public approval of the goals of the women's movement. In 1970, when a representative nationwide sample was asked, "Do you favor or oppose most of the efforts to strengthen and change women's status in society today?", only 40% of women and 44% of men stated approval. Throughout the 1970s more men than women continued to state their support, but by 1985 women had overtaken men, and the overall approval level had reached 70% (Wilkins & Miller, 1985). The public support for strengthening women's status in society continued to increase through the 1990s and then leveled off at 78% for women and 71% for men. However, when the phrase "women's liberation" is included in the question, approval tends to be markedly reduced (Huddy et al., 2000).

The meaning of the word "feminist" has also changed over the years. Nationwide surveys in the late 1990s, asking "would you consider yourself to be a feminist or not?", found that only 33% of women and only 14% of men considered themselves feminists (Huddy et al., 2000). Since 1970, a number of public opinion polls have asked about the meaning of the terms "women's liberation," "women's movement," and "feminist." The most frequently mentioned aspects across all three terms are support for equal rights, equal pay, and fairness in the workplace. In a 1998 survey, the highest rated descriptions for the term "feminist" were supporting equal pay (85%), equal rights (85%), working against sexual harassment (81%), supporting abortion rights (72%), and working for affordable day care (65%). However, also associated with the label "feminist" were "don't respect women who stay home and take care of families" (44%), "don't like most men" (37%), and "are often lesbians" (22%) (Huddy et al., 2000).

It is clear that the women's movement has had a broad impact on the American public. A majority of respondents (59% in a 1994 survey) agreed that the women's movement had had "a good influence on the way things are going in this country," and 69% of women affirmed that the women's movement had made things better for women. However, as we have seen, the descriptive terms associated with "feminist" and "women's movement" are both positive and negative, and many men and women have distanced themselves from the movement, as reflected in the low rate of self-identification as "feminists" (Huddy et al., 2000).

Changes in Gender Attitudes Around the World

What kinds of changes have occurred in gender attitudes in other countries around the world? The World Values Surveys are an ongoing set of studies designed to measure basic values and beliefs in representative samples of people in many countries. Beginning in 1981 with surveys in 22 European countries, the project has expanded to 55 nations and 250,000 participants in the most recent survey (Inglehart & Norris, 2003). Among the project's many measures, we focus here on a gender-equality scale. Its five items ask respondents whether men or women make better political leaders, should have more rights to scarce jobs, and have more important needs for a university education; whether a woman has to have children in order to be fulfilled; and "if a women wants to have a child as a single parent but she doesn't want to have a stable relationship with a man, do you approve or disapprove?" Responses to the five items were summed to create an equality scale, and then standardized to a 100-point scale for ease of interpretation.

Two findings from a detailed book by Inglehart and Norris (2003) are especially relevant here. The first finding is the large cross-national differences in attitudes about gender equality. Figure 17–2 shows the gender-equality scale scores for 61 nations obtained between

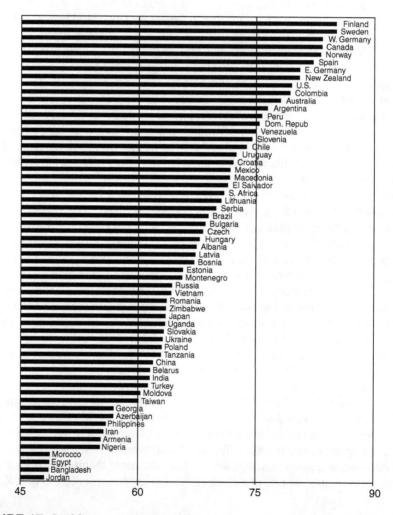

FIGURE 17–2 Mean gender-equality scale scores for many nations (data collected 1995–2001).

Source: Inglehart, R., & Norris, P. (2003, p. 33). *Rising tide: Gender equality and cultural change around the world.* New York: Cambridge University Press. Reprinted with the permission of Cambridge University Press.

1995 and 2001. At the highest level of gender equality were many Western European countries (Finland, Sweden, Germany, Norway, Spain), Canada, New Zealand, and the United States. At the lowest levels of gender equality were various countries in the Middle East (Jordan, Egypt, Iran), Africa (Morocco, Nigeria), and Southern Asia (Bangladesh, Philippines). Across the nations, attitudes of gender equality were strongly and positively correlated with per capita gross domestic product ($r = 0.73$). That is, favorable attitudes about gender equality are more common among residents of wealthier nations.

The second pertinent finding is changes in gender-equality attitudes over generations. Although the World Values Surveys contain only 20 years of data, indirect evidence for change can be obtained through a cohort analysis, examining attitudes among different generations of respondents (i.e., groups with different birth years). Overall, the data show substantial changes since 1900. Although the changes were substantial across the entire sample, they were particularly evident in postindustrial societies (Norway, Sweden, Canada, Germany, United States), followed by industrial societies (Brazil, Mexico, Bulgaria), whereas little change was evident in agrarian societies. This pattern of results is shown in Figure 17–3. An additional finding, not shown in the figure, was that greater change has occurred for women than for men, and this gender difference in egalitarian attitudes was found consistently across postindustrial, industrial, and agrarian societies.

The recent trend in gender roles is clearly in the direction of broader possibilities and loosening of past constraints. Worldwide changes in technology and work, expanding life opportunities, and novel personal experiences are alerting both women and men to previously unavailable options. Yet societies in general, and men in particular, have a

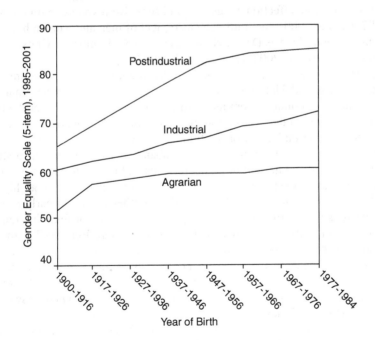

FIGURE 17–3 Mean gender-equality scale scores for different birth-year cohorts in three types of societies.

Source: Inglehart, R., & Norris, P. (2003, p. 39). *Rising tide: Gender equality and cultural change around the world.* New York: Cambridge University Press. Reprinted with the permission of Cambridge University Press.

major stake in maintaining the past traditions of family and work life. It remains to be seen how far the current open attitudes will be carried into far-reaching social changes.

ASPECTS OF CURRENT GENDER-ROLE ATTITUDES

Because gender roles are social prescriptions for sex-appropriate personality and behavior, they involve expectations about other people. A famous early sociologist, Thomas (1923), recognized that what we expect often influences our view of "reality" more than objective facts do. If we define women as illogical and men as insensitive, we will "see" these traits in individual women or men, whether or not they are there. Furthermore, gender-role stereotypes provide a rationale for rigidly prescribing role behavior without allowing for individuality. They restrict societal options as well as personal flexibility. However, beginning in the late 1960s, the impact of the American women's movement began to change many formerly fixed expectations and norms about women's and men's behavior, and we have seen that similar changes also occurred in many other countries (Steinmann, 1975; Inglehart & Norris, 2003).

Sex-Typed Personality Traits

Psychological gender-role stereotypes have most often been studied through the use of adjective check lists. As described earlier in this chapter, typical findings are that men are viewed as more aggressive, independent, and ambitious (instrumental traits), whereas women are seen as more affectionate, gentle, and sensitive (expressive traits). Moreover, from the 1970s to the 2000s, the traits seen as typical of men and women have remained essentially unchanged (Spence, Deaux, & Helmreich, 1985; Lombardo, Cretser, & Roesch, 2001; Prentice & Carranza, 2002; Krueger et al., 2003).

However, changes have occurred in the way that masculinity and femininity are conceptualized and measured. Until the 1970s, most measures used a bipolar organization of items along a single continuum from masculine at one end to feminine at the other end. This approach is rooted in the assumption that femininity is the opposite, the absence, or even the negative of masculinity (Constantinople, 1973).

Beginning in the 1970s, several researchers abandoned this approach to stereotypes and instead conceptualized masculine characteristics and feminine characteristics as two relatively independent dimensions. Thus it is possible for a person to score high on both or low on both. In addition these authors avoided another fallacy of early research, the labeling of persons not scoring in the "appropriate" masculine or feminine range on the scale as confused or ambivalent about their sexuality. Sandra Bem (1974) and Berzins, Welling, and Wetter (1978) developed rather similar approaches for measuring psychological **androgyny**, meaning the balanced possession of both typically masculine and typically feminine characteristics. Within their systems, an individual who scores high on just the masculine or feminine scale can be referred to as **sex-typed** or **sex-reversed**, depending on the person's sex. An individual who scores high on both scales is called **androgynous**, whereas one who scores low on both is often referred to as undifferentiated.

This alternative approach encouraged improved research into the relationship between personality types and gender-role behavior. For instance, Bem (1975) compared the comfort and flexibility of sex-typed, sex-reversed, and androgynous individuals on some experimental tasks which required independence of judgment and other tasks which required nurturance and expressive behavior (such as interacting with a young baby). A number of early studies indicated that sex-typed persons are typically somewhat less flexible, creative, intellectual, and socially poised, and have greater anxiety and lower self-esteem than androgynous individuals. These findings confirmed that psychological masculinity and femininity can be measured as relatively separate traits rather than as opposite ends of one continuum, and they suggested that gender-stereotypic personalities are not as socially functional for men and women as our society has assumed.

However, more recent research findings have introduced complications (Cook, 1985; Lenny, 1991). For one thing, the content and scoring methods of the various scales, such as those of Bem, Berzins et al., and Spence et al., are different, and as a result they agree only about 50% of the time in their classification of individuals into the four gender-role categories. Second, the research findings have not convincingly demonstrated the hypothesized greater flexibility of androgynous individuals in both masculine and feminine tasks. In her later writings, Bem (1981) deemphasized the behavioral flexibility interpretation of androgyny in favor of a cognitive gender-schema theory, which posits that sex-typed individuals are particularly likely to process incoming information in terms of culturally based definitions of masculinity and femininity, and to shape their self-concepts and behavior accordingly.

The stereotypically masculine traits are valued in American society, but many of the stereotypically feminine traits are also valued in both men and women (Spence et al., 1974). Accordingly, androgynous individuals have generally been found to be high in self-esteem, adjustment, sociability, leadership, and many other positive characteristics. However, high masculinity alone (for men *or* for women) may be as socially important as androgyny, for many studies have found it also to be predictive of self-esteem, adjustment, emotional stability, and assertiveness. Persons scoring high on femininity typically are lower on those characteristics but, as expected, higher on nurturance, empathy, friendliness, and conformity. Undifferentiated individuals (those scoring low on both dimensions) have the worst personality picture; they report more psychological problems, poor social interactions, and few positive characteristics (Cook, 1985).

Criticisms have also been raised about the measurement characteristics and scoring methods of masculinity-femininity scales, particularly the Bem Sex-Role Inventory (BSRI). Its 60 adjectives were chosen on the basis of Stanford University undergraduates' judgments that they were more desirable in American society for men or for women. Several studies replicating its construction or testing its validity have concluded that many of the BSRI adjectives are not differentially desirable for American men and women (Edwards & Ashworth, 1977; Myers & Gonda, 1982; Konrad & Harris, 2002; Choi & Fuqua, 2003). Consequently, it seems possible either that Bem's undergraduate judges were different in their gender norms from judges elsewhere, or that American standards of gender-role behavior have been changing rapidly enough to partially outdate the BSRI. A revised 30-item form of the scale was developed later in response to some critiques (Bem, 1979), but questions about its item content and validity have continued.

Traditional, Modern, and Benevolent Sexism

Throughout this chapter, we have seen that attitudes toward women have become considerably more egalitarian over the past 100 years. People today are less likely than in the past to state traditional beliefs about the roles of men and women, and even less likely to admit negative or sexist attitudes. **Old-fashioned sexism** involves endorsement of traditional gender roles, beliefs that women are less competent than men, and expectations that women and men should be treated differently. Although these old-fashioned sexist attitudes have been on the decline, there is evidence that sexism continues to pervade modern society, though in a more subtle form (Swim et al., 2001). **Modern sexism** is characterized by antagonism toward women's demands for equality, continued discrimination and differential treatment of men and women, and lack of support for policies intended to help women (Swim et al., 1995). Swim and her colleagues have argued that the early measures of gender-role attitudes, like the Attitudes towards Women Scale discussed previously in this chapter, measure overt sexism rather than modern sexism, and research has provided evidence for the distinction between modern and old-fashioned sexism (Conn et al., 1999).

An alternative approach to understanding sexism was proposed by Glick and Fiske (1996, 2001). They argued that not all sexist attitudes are negative, as would be suggested by old-fashioned sexist beliefs. Rather, some traditional beliefs about women's roles can be quite positive, and therefore it is important to distinguish between hostile sexism and benevolent sexism. Illustrative **benevolent sexism** items are "A good woman should be set on a pedestal," "Women have a more refined sense of culture and taste," and "Every man ought to have a woman he adores." Despite its positive elements, benevolent sexism still entails a limiting and prejudicial set of beliefs. For example, believing that women should be loved and cherished is paternalistic and implies a power differential for men and women. Most of the **hostile sexism** items are more subtle than old-fashioned sexist beliefs in women's inferiority, focusing instead on gender competition and women's unreasonable behavior in various interaction situations (e.g., "Women are too easily offended").

Scores on the hostile and benevolent sexism scales are quite highly and positively correlated, meaning that many people score about equally high or low on both (Glick & Fiske, 1996). However, they can be interpreted independently, and it is possible to score high on one and low on the other, and thus to be primarily a hostile or a benevolent sexist. A person scoring low on both is nonsexist, whereas scoring high on both scales is interpreted as **ambivalent sexism**—i.e., the person holds simultaneously benevolent and hostile sexist attitudes. Research findings show that hostile sexism scores correlate positively with overt sexist behaviors, like sexual harassment by men (Begany & Milburn, 2002). In contrast, benevolent sexism scores are stronger predictors of more subtle, less overtly sexist beliefs and behaviors, like negative attitudes toward women who breast-feed (Forbes et al., 2003). In another study, benevolent and hostile sexist attitudes were found to be associated with different reactions toward rape victims. Research participants who were classified as benevolent sexists were more likely than hostile sexists to blame the woman victim in a case of acquaintance rape, whereas those classified as hostile sexists reported a greater proclivity to commit acquaintance rape (Abrams et al., 2003).

Marital Roles

How do you feel about a traditional marriage in which the "husband assumes responsibility for providing for the family and the wife runs the house and takes care of the children" versus a marriage in which husband and wife "both work and share housekeeping and child care responsibilities" (Simon & Landis, 1989, p. 273)? In a 1974 national study, almost exactly 50% of both men and women preferred the traditional marriage, but by 1985 only 37% of women and 43% of men stated that preference, whereas 57% of women and 50% of men preferred the marriage of shared responsibilities (a few percent expressed no opinion). A similar, but more extreme, trend can be seen in beliefs that "a woman's place is in the home." When asked in 1972, 29% of Americans endorsed this position, but the percentage steadily decreased to only 8% in 2000 (NES, 2003).

Although these data show a clear shift in a liberal direction (that is, away from traditional marital roles), there are still large minorities of both men and women who prefer the traditional marriage arrangement. That point is highlighted by national poll responses to this item: "It is much better for everyone involved if the man is the achiever outside the home and the woman takes care of the home and family" (Simon & Landis, 1989, p. 275). In 1977 the percentage of respondents saying "strongly agree" or "agree" was 62% of women and 68% of men; by 1986 these figures had decreased significantly to 47% of both men and women—still a high figure. Similarly, there are still pockets of support for the NES item that "a woman's place is in the home," despite the general population's rejection of that opinion. In 2000, that traditional viewpoint was endorsed by 42% of farmers, 38% of respondents who did not have a high school diploma, 20% of unskilled laborers, 14% of housewives, and 12% of southern respondents (NES, 2003).

The gender-role characteristics of two marital partners can influence their marital happiness, in a rather complex pattern (Brooks, 2000). Given the rapid change in Americans' beliefs about appropriate marital roles over the past 50 years, and the concurrent increase in divorce rates, you might speculate that more liberal attitudes have led to a decrease in marital satisfaction. Similarly, it could be the case that ambiguity in marital roles has led to unrealistic expectations, and thus to reduced marital satisfaction. Research findings indicate that women who have more egalitarian attitudes do tend to report more dissatisfaction with their marriages and higher rates of divorce (Whyte, 1990), and this is especially true if their partners have more traditional role attitudes (Antill, Cotton, & Tindale, 1983; Veroff et al., 1998). In addition, traditional sex-role attitudes are positively and strongly correlated with marital satisfaction among men (Hill & Peplau, 1998), but husbands who have traditional role attitudes express *less* marital satisfaction if their wives have egalitarian attitudes (Antill et al., 1983). For women, the pattern is different—whatever a wife's own gender-role attitudes may be, her marital happiness tends to be greater if her husband has egalitarian gender-role attitudes. Overall, the research literature suggests that both egalitarian and traditional attitudes about sex roles can lead to marital satisfaction, depending on the life circumstances of the couple and the match in their attitudes. Across a broad range of psychological variables, including attitudes about gender roles, similarity between husbands and wives is generally an important predictor of marital satisfaction (Kurdek, 1998).

Another aspect of marital roles that has been studied is the division of household duties and the amount of time that each spouse spends doing housework (Brooks & Gilbert, 1997). Traditionally in America, the division of household duties has been highly sextyped—husbands typically do repairs, auto maintenance, and yard care, whereas wives do cooking, cleaning, shopping, and child care (Blood & Wolfe, 1960). Of course some families disregard this pattern altogether, and many minor variations occur within families. However, the massive influx of women into the paid work force during the 1960s would have been impossible without a reduction in the amount of time women devoted to household chores. An interesting comparison of women living in Muncie, Indiana, illustrates this change. In 1924, 87% of married women there spent 4 or more hours each day doing housework. By 1977, the comparable figure was 43%, and by 1999 it was only 14% (Caplow et al., 2000).

Despite the dramatic reduction in the number of hours women spend engaged in housework, there is still a sizable discrepancy between husbands and wives in the amount of time that they spend doing housework. Between 1965 and 1985, women's average time devoted to housework decreased nearly 8 hours per week (from 27 to less than 20), while men's housework time increased about 5 hours per week (from less than 5 to almost 10). Very little further change occurred in the division of housework through the early 2000s, and women typically spend about twice as many hours as men in housework, compared with six times as many hours as men in 1965 (Robinson, 1988; Robinson & Godbey, 1997). However, these totals do not include child care, which is largely done by women. Husbands of working wives do *proportionally* more of the household duties traditionally assigned to women than do husbands of full-time homemakers. However, the reason for this is *not* that the husband spends more time, but rather that the working wife spends *less* time doing housework (Pleck, 1985; Robinson & Godbey, 1997).

There is a striking contrast between the current gender attitudes expressed by many Americans and their behavior concerning housework. A majority of married couples believe that household tasks should be shared responsibilities, but very few couples share them equally (Hiller & Philliber, 1986; Amato et al., 2003). Similarly, in a national sample of high school seniors, a majority stated that child care and housework should be shared equally by both spouses, but at the same time they expected men to be the primary family breadwinners and women not to work full-time when their children were preschoolers (Herzog, Bachman, & Johnston, 1983). Behaviorally, women as well as men conform to the traditional gender norms concerning housework more than they do in their expressed attitudes, and equality in family and household activities is far from being attained by most couples. More housework is typically done by husbands who are younger, have children, work in jobs without long hours, or do not work a day shift (Staines & Pleck, 1984; Coverman, 1985). Analyses of marital satisfaction indicate that increased rates of housework by husbands are associated with less marital satisfaction for them, but greater satisfaction for their wives (Amato et al., 2003; Frisco & Williams, 2003).

Dual-Career Couples.   As recently as 1920, only 12% of women with professional careers ever married (Chafe, 1976). Today, in contrast, couples both of whom have professional careers (not just routine jobs) are common and have been widely studied (Gilbert, 1993). More than half of all people in the work force are married to an employed spouse (Waite & Neilson, 2001). Dual-career marriages face extra problems in integrating work and family life because of the heavy work commitments of both partners (Moen & Yu, 2000). They undergo especial stress in cases where the wife's career success outpaces the husband's, and such marriages rarely survive unless both partners are egalitarian in their role attitudes (Hiller & Philliber, 1982). Maintaining the relationship often requires sacrifices in both spouses' careers, but in most cases the woman's career is affected more, for even egalitarian couples often end up making traditional role choices (e.g., Foster, Wallston, & Berger, 1980). In fact, dual-career couples do not share household tasks any more equally than other dual-worker couples, though their higher incomes do allow many of them to hire outside help for some household responsibilities (Gilbert, 1985; Brooks & Gilbert, 1997).

Changes in the Male Role

As the women's movement has transformed the situation for women in this country, men's expected roles have also been changing, but there has not been the same kind of an organized movement to help men adapt to the new reality. The result of these changes for men has been called **role strain** (Pleck, 1981, 1995). The traditional male gender role and the modern one are partially contradictory, and some aspects of the traditional one are maladaptive in today's world. For instance, aggressiveness and hostility are counterproductive in modern society, and physical strength and dominance are often irrelevant to the tasks that men perform in their work or home lives. Also, some of the expressive aspects that are expected in the modern male role—being a warm, sensitive, loving husband and father—are hard to learn and to perform if one has been socialized in opposite patterns. Therefore many men are confused about what is expected of them, and their plight is made worse because, traditionally, violations of gender roles are frowned on and punished more for males than for females (Kite, 2001). These confusions and contradictions concerning the modern male role may be one reason for the gap between men's expressions of support for egalitarian role behavior and their frequent failure to carry it into action.

SUMMARY

In the United States, there has been a continuing link since the nineteenth century between the struggles against racism and sexism. Women, like blacks, have faced some parallel forms of stereotyping and discrimination have prevented fulfillment of their individual potential. Gender roles are largely culturally determined, and traditional gender stereotypes in most modern societies picture women's personalities and behavior as being mainly expressive and communal, whereas men are expected to display more instrumentality and agency.

Among the early influences on children's gender-role development are parents' behavior toward the child and their choice of clothing and toys, as well as teachers' and peers' monitoring of gender-role norms. Other important influences that help to enculturate society's dominant gender-role attitudes include biased presentations by psychotherapists, textbooks discussing marriage and the family, and authors of children's literature. Even our everyday language often deprecates and/or ignores women and reflects biased gender stereotypes, and the mass media also feature the predominant presence, authority, and positive presentation of men as compared to women.

Over the past 60 years in the U.S., a strong trend toward more liberal gender-role attitudes has been evident, both in poll data and in detailed questionnaire studies. Similar changes toward more gender equality have occurred in most countries of the world, though most strongly in postindustrial nations and relatively little in agrarian nations. However, despite these changes toward greater gender equality, large pay differentials and subtle discrimination directed at employed women still remain common in the U.S. and other nations.

In the 1970s new approaches to measuring the gender-related personality traits of men and women were proposed, leading to a burst of research on "androgynous" individuals— ones who are high on both masculine (instrumental) and feminine (expressive) characteristics. More recently, measures of subtle sexism have been developed, such as scales of hostile and benevolent sexism, and researchers using implicit measures have added further evidence of stereotypic patterns of gender-role associations.

Research on attitudes toward the women's movement since 1970 has demonstrated large increases toward strong public approval of its goals, which most Americans view as equal rights, equal pay, and fairness in the workplace. However, only a small minority of people consider themselves to be feminists. Many people (especially men but also women) who express liberal gender-role attitudes do not carry them into more egalitarian behavior in their everyday lives. This is particularly clear in marital roles, for many Americans still prefer traditional patterns, and even the majority who express egalitarian attitudes rarely share household responsibilities equally. It is unclear whether the past century's widespread liberal changes in gender-role attitudes and the accompanying loosening of constraints on people's social behavior will be carried into further-reaching societal transformations.

18

Environmental Attitudes

We travel together, passengers in a little space ship, dependent upon its vulnerable resources of air and soil...preserved from annihilation only by the care, the work and, I will say, the love we give our fragile craft.—Adlai Stevenson, 1965.

Mankind's true moral test, its fundamental test (which lies deeply buried from view), consists of its attitude towards those who are at its mercy: animals. And in this respect mankind has suffered a fundamental debacle, a debacle so fundamental that all others stem from it.—Milan Kundera, 1929.

The goal of life is living in agreement with nature.—Zeno, circa 300 B.C.

Consider the quote from Kundera above. What is your attitude about animals? Or more broadly, what is your attitude about the natural environment? When you think about "nature" or "the environment," do you picture a pristine forest, or perhaps a quiet meadow with deer grazing? For many people, these are the images that come to mind. But these are romantic images, and unrealistic. Such views emerged only during the latter half of the twentieth century, whereas before that time, the natural environment was generally viewed as something to be avoided, or as a frontier to be conquered and tamed. It was dangerous, dirty, uncomfortable, and an obstacle to be overcome.

A HISTORICAL OVERVIEW

Before the 1950s, environmental problems were nonissues. Although public polls have been widely used since the 1920s, national polls that asked respondents to name the most important problems facing the country rarely turned up an environmental concern before about 1968 (Ladd & Bowman, 1995). For example, in a 1970 Gallup Poll, the Vietnam War was named as the most important problem facing the country. It was followed by a host of other social issues involving education and the economy, but fewer than 3% of respondents mentioned the environment. Yet only a few years later, environmental issues, particularly pollution and energy production, but also overpopulation and depletion of natural resources, regularly appeared among the top 10 problems cited by the public (Ladd & Bowman, 1995). Although levels of concern have fluctuated over the years, problems of the environment, pollution, and natural resources have often ranked close to other major issues like inflation, crime, and government corruption as central national problems for Americans (Erskine, 1972a; Dunlap & Saad, 2001; Saad, 2001a).

The time focus of the question can sharply influence how much concern is expressed for the environment. For example, the 2001 U.S. national survey that was summarized previously in Table 13–2 asked an open-ended question: "What do you think is the most important problem facing this country today?" The top responses were education (16%), ethical and moral issues involving family and childrearing (11%), the economy (10%), crime (8%), and health care (7%). Environmental issues ranked sixteenth, mentioned by only 2%. However, when respondents were asked to look ahead and identify "the most important problem facing our nation 25 years from now," the environment jumped to the top of the list with 11%, followed in second place by energy issues (7%). Relegated to lower places were education (6%), ethical issues (6%), crime (6%), and the economy (5%) (Dunlap & Saad, 2001; see also Saad, 2003).

Recent studies of environmental attitudes in many countries have consistently found a high degree of support for environmental protection (Dunlap, Gallup, & Gallup, 1992, 1993; Lee & Norris, 2000). In a 1992 "Health of the Planet" survey, the Gallup International Institute conducted interviews with representative samples of approximately 1,000 people from each of 24 countries (Dunlap et al., 1992). These in-depth interviews included a wide range of questions about environmental problems, including the seriousness of many problems and support for environmental protection. Half of the countries were industrialized nations (e.g., Denmark, Ireland, Japan, Portugal), and half were developing nations (e.g., Mexico, Korea, Philippines, Poland, Russia, India, Nigeria). The first question in the survey asked "What do you think is the most important problem facing our nation?" At this point, respondents did not know anything about the survey, and they were not prompted to think about environmental issues. Yet in 16 of the 24 countries, environmental issues were among the top three problems identified; only economic issues were mentioned more often. When asked about their "personal concern about the environment," more than 50% of respondents in all but three of the countries (Switzerland, Turkey, and Poland) stated it as "a great deal" or a "fair amount." Comparisons across the countries showed no significant differences between the samples from industrialized and those from developing nations.

Since the late 1960s, when public opinion surveys systematically began to include questions about environmental issues, responses have shown a slow but steady increase in recognition of, and concern about, environmental issues. Sparked by the first Earth Day in 1970, environmental problems emerged as one of the most pressing social issues. Although shadowed by the threat of global nuclear war that dominated public concern throughout the Cold War period before 1990, U.S. citizens' recognition of the importance and severity of environmental problems continued to grow steadily into the 1990s. Key environmental events during this period included the embargo of oil shipments to the U.S. by some of the OPEC oil-producing countries during Mideast conflicts in 1973 and 1979, which led to huge price increases for gasoline and long lines of cars at gas stations, desperately hoping to get some of the limited supplies of gas.

Public concern for environmental problems reached an all-time peak in the early 1990s and has declined somewhat since then (Dunlap & Scarce, 1991; Kempton, Boster, & Hartley, 1995; Dunlap & Saad, 2001; Dunlap, 2002; Saad, 2003). One example of this decline can be found in answers to this question: "Do you consider yourself to be an environmentalist, or not?" When asked in a 1989 nationwide survey conducted by the Yankelovich Partners, 76% of respondents said "Yes." In 1991, the percentage had risen to 78%, but by 1999 it had dropped to only 50% (*Pollingreport.com*, 2003). Similarly, concerned responses to the question "Are we spending too much, too little, or about the right amount on improving and protecting the environment" peaked in 1990 with 71% saying "too little." Since then the figure has steadily declined to 62% in 2000 (Dunlap, 2002). However, not all measures of environmental concern have shown this decrease; some have shown continued high levels up to 2000 or later.

Why Did the Environmental Movement Arise?

Environmental issues emerged in the early 1960s as a result of the apparent harm being caused by industrial production and consumption. The consumer-driven American society

Photograph courtesy of Riley Dunlap.
Reprinted by permission.

Box 18–1   RILEY DUNLAP, *Pioneer in Environmental Research*

Riley Dunlap has been studying environmental issues for more than 30 years. He is best-known for developing the New Environmental Paradigm scale, his research on the demographic and ideological correlates of environmental attitudes and activism, and his public opinion studies on environmental issues, all of which are discussed in this chapter. He was the project director for the 24-nation Health of the Planet survey conducted by the Gallup Institute in 1992.

Dunlap earned his Ph.D. in sociology from the University of Oregon in 1973. He taught nearly 30 years in the department of sociology and rural sociology at Washington State University, eventually being named the Boeing Distinguished Professor of Environmental Sociology. In 2001 he moved to Finland, where he currently holds the position of Donner Professor at Åbo Akademi University. Dunlap has been a leader in developing and defining the field of environmental sociology, both within the American Sociological Association and internationally. In 2002 he capped this work by editing The Handbook of Environmental Sociology.

had experienced an unprecedented level of growth and personal wealth. Following the end of World War II, the U.S. economy soared. The level of production and consumption grew dramatically, and the appetite of the American consumer for new products spurred innovation and new technologies. It became possible for nearly all households to own a television, telephone, automobile, and many other luxuries previously unavailable or unaffordable.

But with this new-found wealth came problems. First, manufacturing these products required huge amounts of natural resources, and it gradually became clear that the level of production and consumption was not sustainable—we would soon exhaust the Earth's capacity to renew itself. Second, the production process resulted in pollution and contamination. The air in many of the major cities around the world became increasingly polluted. Evidence of pollution in the groundwater and food supply began to come from all parts of the world—toxic chemicals were found even in remote, unpopulated areas. Moreover, the issue of population growth emerged as an important social problem—especially for developing countries, but also for the United States. More people mean a greater demand for natural resources, greater consumption, and more pollution.

WHAT ARE THE MAIN ENVIRONMENTAL PROBLEMS?

Following is a brief list of some of the environmental problems we face today. Much of the data for this summary comes from the *State of the World* series of annual volumes produced by the Worldwatch Institute (e.g., Flavin, 2001; Gardner et al., 2003). For other summaries, see Oskamp (2000c), McKenzie-Mohr (2002), or World Resources Institute (2002).

Overconsumption

- **Deforestation.** Between 1960 and 1990, logging and destruction of forests increased dramatically around the world. It is estimated that only 22% of the world's original (old-growth) forests remain today (Bryant, Nielsen, & Tangley, 1997; Abramovitz, 1998).
- **Species Extinction.** Within the past 50 years, the rate at which species are becoming extinct has accelerated greatly. One recent forecast suggested that if the current rate of destruction continues, half of all plant and animal species will be extinct by the end of the twenty-first century (Rensberger, 1999; Tuxill, 1999). Although much of the loss of biodiversity is associated with logging and deforestation of the tropical rainforests of the world, the United States has the largest number of plant species that are threatened of any country in the world (Walter & Gillett, 1997).
- **Exhaustion of Fisheries.** Overfishing has led to substantial reductions in the number of fish in the oceans, and in the catches available for consumption. Since about 1970, the catch levels of most of the world's major fish species have shown a drop-off, and some species have declined as much as 70% to 80% (McGinn, 1998).
- **Depletion of Freshwater Supplies.** The amount of freshwater available for consumption and for agriculture has been decreasing steadily over the past 30 years in every continent in the world. Many water tables have dropped as much as 5 to 10 feet per year (Brown, 1999).

Pollution

- **Global Warming and Greenhouse Gases.** The release of carbon dioxide (CO_2) and other gases into the atmosphere has led to a gradual increase in the earth's temperature. Greenhouse gases (primarily CO_2, but also methane and nitrous oxide) result primarily from burning wood and fossil fuels (e.g., gasoline in cars, natural gas to generate electricity, deforestation in tropical nations). During the twentieth century, the average global temperature increased 0.6° Celsius (about 1° Fahrenheit), and projections for the twenty-first century predict increases ranging from 1.4° to 5.8° C (2.5–10.5° F). These increases are potentially catastrophic, with consequences such as a rise in sea levels, melting of glacial and polar ice sheets, disruption of agriculture, destruction of habitats, and changes in global weather patterns, according to the Intergovernmental Panel on Climate Change (IPCC, 2001).
- **Loss of the Ozone Layer.** The release of chemicals into the atmosphere has also led to a reduction in the ozone layer, which protects the Earth's surface from ultraviolet radiation. Chlorofluorocarbons (CFCs), commonly used as coolants in air conditioners and refrigerators, have caused a sharp drop in stratospheric ozone (the so-called "ozone hole"). The resulting increase in ultraviolet radiation reaching the Earth's surface has been linked to increases in skin cancer, cataracts, and crop damage.
- **Acid Rain.** Acid rain is caused by the release of oxides of sulfur and nitrogen into the air, primarily resulting from the burning of coal. These acids then return to the Earth's surface through rain, which damages forests and crops and also kills fish, plants, and other organisms in lakes and rivers.
- **Exposure to Toxic Chemicals.** As a result of manufacturing and agriculture, people are exposed to many toxic chemicals in their daily lives. For example, dioxin, a chemical

resulting from manufacturing processes involving chlorine (e.g., pesticides, paper products, plastics) has been shown to cause cancer, to disrupt female reproductive systems, and to reduce male sperm count. Studies in the United States and internationally have shown alarming levels of dioxin in body tissue (Schecter, 1994). Other dangerous substances to which people are exposed include pesticides, mercury, and lead.

Population Growth

Aggravating the problems of overconsumption and pollution just outlined is the rapidly growing number of humans living on the planet. More people means more consumption, a greater demand for resources, and more pollution and waste. Population growth over the past 100 years has been staggering. For several million years of human existence on this planet, there were fewer than 10 million people on the planet. In 1830, less than 200 years ago, the human population first reached 1 billion; in 1930 it reached 2 billion, and since then the growth has continued exponentially. As of 2000, there were slightly over 6 billion people on the planet, and this number was growing by 80 million every year. Projections about the number of people the earth can support vary, but it is absolutely clear that it cannot support 6 billion people living the consumptive lifestyle that is widespread in industrialized nations like the United States, Western Europe, or Japan—that is not a sustainable possibility (Meadows, Meadows, & Randers, 1992; Brown & Flavin, 1999).

When these problems are considered in combination, their seriousness is obvious. At the very least, they threaten the quality of life for the current and future generations of all living things. At the extreme, they threaten the long-term survival of human life on this planet.

ATTITUDES ABOUT POLLUTION AND ENERGY

Given these numerous environmental issues, which ones are people most concerned about, and why? And what types of attitudes do people hold about these issues, and why? In the following sections, we examine several topics: public opinion data about some of the key environmental issues people care about, worldviews and values that underlie these concerns, theoretical perspectives on the bases for environmental attitudes, and demographic and experiential factors that influence group differences in environmental concern. Finally, we discuss evidence about the link between environmental attitudes and behaviors.

First, some definitions. The term **environmental concern** is used to refer to affect, or worry, associated with specific or general environmental problems. In a sense it is an attitude, because it includes not only affect, but also cognitive beliefs and behavioral intentions regarding an environmental issue. However, environmental concerns are typically not measured in terms of favorability, as attitudes are. A common approach to measuring environmental concern asks, "How much does each of the following environmental problems worry you?" In contrast, attitudes about environmental issues are typically measured by asking about degrees of agreement with statements such as "I favor opening the Alaskan Arctic Wildlife Refuge for oil exploration," or "I support spending more government money for environmental protection." The broad construct of **environmental attitudes** can refer to any of the evaluative beliefs, affect, and/or behavioral intentions a person holds regarding environmentally related activities or issues. In practice, the terms "environmental concern" and "environmental attitudes" are often used interchangeably. As Fransson and Gärling (1999, p. 370) put it, "environmental concern has been treated as an evaluation or attitude towards facts, one's own behaviour, or others' behaviour with consequences for the environment."

TABLE 18–1   Specific Environmental Concerns of the U.S. Public in 2002 (Percent of Respondents Worrying About Each One)

Q: I'm going to read you a list of environmental problems. As I read each one, please tell me if you personally worry about this problem a great deal, a fair amount, only a little, or not at all.

Survey item	A great deal	A fair amount	Only a little	Not at all	No opinion
Pollution of drinking water	57	25	13	5	
Pollution of rivers, lakes, and reservoirs	53	32	12	3	
Contamination of soil and water by toxic waste	53	29	15	3	
Maintenance of the nation's supply of fresh water for household needs	50	28	17	5	
Air pollution	45	33	18	4	
Damage to the Earth's ozone layer	38	29	21	11	1
Loss of tropical rain forests	38	27	21	12	2
Extinction of plant and animal species	35	30	22	12	1
The "greenhouse effect" or global warming	29	29	23	17	2
Acid rain	25	23	31	19	2

Source: Data from Gallup Poll (Saad, 2002c).

Concern About Pollution

In terms of specific environmental concerns, pollution has historically been at the top of the list of environmental problems about which Americans are concerned. A 2002 telephone survey of 1,006 U.S. households conducted by the Gallup Organization examined specific concerns, including many of those listed in the preceding section (pollution of drinking water, contamination of soil and water by toxic waste, maintenance of the nation's supply of fresh water, damage to the Earth's ozone layer, extinction of plant and animal species, global warming, and so on). The results are displayed in Table 18–1, which shows that the public's top concerns were those involving pollution, and more specifically pollution of drinking water. Note also that global warming, potentially the most serious problem of all, was almost the lowest on the public's list of concerns. Similar data have been obtained in several other polls (*Publicagenda.org*, 2002; Saad, 2002c).

Public Opinion About Energy

Energy is a specific environmental issue that has attracted a great deal of research attention, because the availability of affordable energy is crucial for the world economy. Over the past 30 years, worldwide energy consumption has nearly doubled, from 207 quadrillion Btu in 1970, to 382 quads in 1999 (U.S. Department of Energy, 2002a). The United States is by far the world's largest consumer of energy, and approximately 40% of our energy comes from petroleum. The remainder comes from natural gas (24%), coal (23%), nuclear (4%), wood (4%), and hydroelectricity (4%), with less than 1% from solar, wind, and geothermal sources (E. Smith, 2002).

After the end of World War II, the U.S. demand for energy increased dramatically. The price of energy dropped steadily through the 1950s and 1960s, and personal and industrial consumption climbed steeply. Energy was cheap, and people could afford more modern conveniences that made use of this energy. Although there were several political crises during this period that involved oil (the 1956 Suez Crisis, and the 1967 Six-Day War in the Mideast), these events did not directly affect the American public because there was an excess of petroleum on the world market. However, things changed dramatically in the early 1970s. The U.S. demand for oil continued to grow, but world supply did not keep pace, and the cost began to increase.

A huge price shock occurred during the 1973 Arab–Israeli war, in which the U.S. openly backed Israel. This U.S. stand led to an embargo of oil to the U.S. by several oil-producing countries. As a result, the price of oil skyrocketed, from $3 per barrel to nearly $12 per barrel in only 3 months, and limited supplies of gas led to long lines of cars at gas stations competing for the few available gallons. A second energy crisis started in 1978, again because of political turmoil in the Middle East. The result was the same: greatly increased costs of oil, escalating gasoline prices, long lines at gas stations, and gasoline shortages. By the end of the 1970s, the price of oil had leaped to more than $30 per barrel—over 10 times its cost 10 years before (U.S. Department of Energy, 2002c), and in late 2004 its price climbed to over $50 per barrel.

In the 30 years since the 1973 energy crisis, many other energy events have occurred:

* the Three Mile Island nuclear plant disaster in 1978
* the 1986 meltdown of the Chernobyl nuclear reactor in the USSR
* the 1989 Exxon Valdez accident that spilled 11,000,000 gallons of crude oil off the coast of Alaska
* the 2000–2001 "electricity crisis" in California

Clearly, problems concerning power and energy have been, and will continue to be, fundamental political as well as environmental issues. See E. Smith (2002) for an excellent summary and overview of these issues.

Given the turmoil surrounding energy issues, one might think that they would be at the forefront of the American political agenda. If so, we might have seen rebates and incentives for the development and purchase of energy-efficient products, reductions in the per capita consumption of energy, and conservation becoming a daily activity as a result of widespread attitudes that were easily accessible and influential in people's everyday decisions. However, this has not been the case. Although energy consumption per capita did drop following the two energy crises of the 1970s (because of a combination of more efficient technologies and personal and corporate conservation actions), the trend quickly reversed, and consumption has climbed steadily since 1982 (U.S. Department of Energy, 2002b). Although today's energy technologies are considerably more efficient, Americans also have higher expectations for energy consumption (e.g., air-conditioned homes, air travel, personal computers, gas-powered lawn mowers, and high-horsepower cars). A prime example is the current popularity of sport utility vehicles (SUVs), which are extremely inefficient in their use of gasoline. Such expectations and gas-guzzling vehicles would probably not have been developed if energy costs had remained high (either through political conflict or through government taxation).

The general attitude of the American public can be characterized as follows: We want cheap energy, produced somewhere else, with no pollution (E. Smith, 2002). We want to have affordable gasoline and inexpensive electricity, and not to think about the pollution or environmental problems associated with energy use. At the heart of the issue is our reliance on oil (much of which is imported from foreign countries), making us dependent on Mideast nations for an absolutely essential input to our economy.

Valuable survey data on the attitudes and opinions of the American public regarding energy production date back to the first energy crisis of 1973. These surveys show that attitudes about various energy sources are directly affected by the price of energy. The main focus has been on three energy options: expanding U.S. production of coal, nuclear power, and oil (both by offshore drilling and drilling on public lands). National opinion polls show that support for each of these sources of energy increases during times when energy costs are high (i.e., 1973, 1978, 2000), and then falls off steadily whenever the cost of energy decreases. E. Smith (2002) analyzed the changes in attitudes toward oil drilling over a 20-year time span up through the late 1990s, and showed that aggregate public attitudes about offshore drilling remained fairly stable from one year to the next. However, as the cost of oil went up, as measured by the Consumer Price Index or the price of gasoline, so did public favorability toward offshore drilling. Similar results were found for attitudes toward strip mining for coal.

A recent example of this issue is the proposal to drill for oil in the Arctic National Wildlife Refuge, and a national survey in 2002 found that only 40% of respondents favored such oil exploration (Moore, 2002b). A related issue is the ongoing exploration and drilling for oil along the coasts of California, Oregon, and Washington, for which attitudinal data are available since the early 1970s. Recent surveys of California residents indicate that their attitudes are heavily negative toward offshore drilling—fewer than 20% support the activity. However, in nationwide samples, the percentage who support the activity is considerably higher (generally more than 60%—E. Smith, 2002). We examine this discrepancy in a later section of this chapter.

Solving Energy Problems.   Given the long-running issues surrounding energy in the U.S., what do people think should be done? We have seen that demand for energy has increased steadily over the past 30 years, while supply has increased more slowly (Roberts, 2004). In the case of petroleum, the crossover of demand exceeding supplies is estimated to occur by 2010 (Ivanhoe, 1997). What will happen when the world's supply of oil begins to run out (and it will)? Will we reduce our use of energy (conserve) to make supplies last longer, or will we try to produce more to meet the demand? When this question was asked in a national poll, 60% of respondents sided with conservation and 30% with more production (Saad, 2001a).

So at the abstract level, Americans believe in the importance of conservation. However, when it comes to specific actions and decisions, personal sacrifice is less popular. When asked about specific energy-related proposals, large majorities of the respondents in a national poll favored higher pollution standards for energy producers (83%), stronger enforcement of environmental regulations (78%), and more government money spent on solar and wind power (76%) (Moore, 2002b). But when asked about setting limits on consumer energy use, only 35% were supportive (see Figure 18–1).

WHY DO PEOPLE CARE? WORLDVIEWS AND VALUES

Because most environmental problems result from the production or consumption of natural resources, the issue is often presented as a trade-off—preserving forests or loggers' jobs; clean air or cheap gasoline; protection of wetlands or a new housing development.

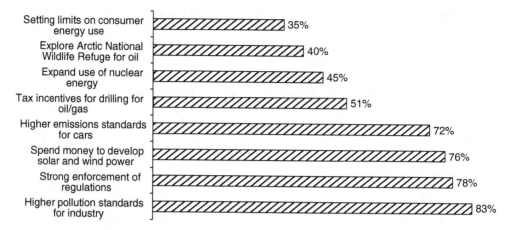

FIGURE 18–1 Percent of Americans who favor various environmental policy proposals.

Source: Data are from the Gallup Poll (Moore, 2002b).

On a broader level, these issues are framed as a conflict between growth and environmental protection. At the individual level, they also may be framed as convenience versus sacrifice. Protecting the environment may involve giving up some convenience or comfort in exchange for less environmental impact.

The issue of growth versus environmental protection has been included in several public opinion polls. The Gallup Organization has asked this question:

> With which one of these statements about the environment and the economy do you most agree? [Rotate] Protection of the environment should be given priority, even at the risk of curbing economic growth. OR, Economic growth should be given priority, even if the environment suffers to some extent.

The order of asking about growth versus environment was rotated to control for order effects in responding. The results from nearly 20 years of public opinion polling are shown in Figure 18–2. In 2003 (the most recent data available at the time of this writing), 47% of respondents favored environmental protection over economic growth, whereas 42% favored economic growth (4% had no opinion about the issue, and 7% assigned equal priority). The 2003 measure is the lowest level of support for environmental protection recorded in the 20 years of survey research on the topic. However, it is important to note that public opinion during that time period was strongly influenced by an economic recession, increased threats of terrorism, and the Iraq war. Yet even in such tumultuous times, a plurality of U.S. respondents *still* favored environmental protection over economic growth (Saad, 2003).

The high level of support for environmental protection in the United States may not be surprising given that the U.S. is a relatively wealthy country. It is easier to worry about environmental quality and protection when you have enough to eat and are generally financially secure. Indeed, some scholars have argued that concern for environmental issues is a **postmaterialist value**—a concern that emerges only after the material needs of individuals have been met (cf. Inglehart, 1977, 1990; Muller-Rommel, 1989). So, would people in poorer countries express a similar set of concerns? Would they be willing to trade

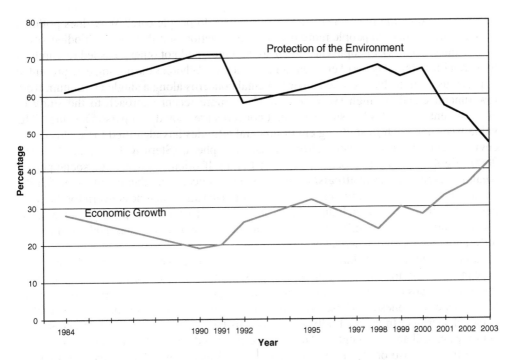

FIGURE 18–2 Percent of the U.S. public favoring environmental protection versus economic growth, 1984–2003. Years when the question was asked are shown on the baseline. Responses of "no opinion" (ranging from 3% to 11%) and "equal priority" (ranging from 2% to 8%) are omitted from the graph.

Source: Data are from the Gallup Poll (Saad, 2003).

economic growth for environmental protection? Data from Gallup's Health of the Planet project discussed early in this chapter are useful for addressing this issue. Recall that interviews with approximately 1,000 people were conducted in each of 24 countries. The results from the study showed that a majority of people in 17 of the 24 countries (including many developing countries like India, Chile, and Mexico) expressed a willingness to pay more for products to improve environmental quality. When asked which should be given priority—economic growth or environment—more than 50% chose environment in 21 of the 24 countries. Only India (43%), Turkey (43%), and Nigeria (30%) subordinated environmental protection to economic growth (Dunlap et al., 1992). So, even in most of the poor, developing countries that have been studied, levels of concern for environmental protection are high.

Types of Environmental Values

The polling data presented thus far have all been based on single-item questions about general concern for environmental issues, or attitudes about specific environmental problems, or economic growth versus environmental protection. In the study summarized in Table 18–1, for instance, we found that pollution was the environmental problem that concerned people the most (Saad, 2002c). But *why* do people care? Why does polluted drinking water concern people more than ozone depletion or reductions in biodiversity?

The question of *why* people care about some issues, and not others, has led researchers to search for different types of environmental concerns. Whereas the polling data presented in previous sections have studied environmental concerns along a single continuum from low (unconcerned) to high (very concerned), a more recent approach to the study of environmental attitudes has suggested that concerns are rooted in a person's values. The value-basis approach to studying environmental attitudes has identified three clusters of environmental values: egoistic, altruistic, and biospheric (Stern & Dietz, 1994; Stern, 2000). **Egoistic** values are focused on oneself and self-oriented goals (e.g., social power, wealth, personal success); **altruistic** values indicate concern for other people (e.g., family, community, friends, humanity in general); **biospheric** values include concern for the well-being of all living things (including plants, animals, and trees). Conceptually, each of these sets of values can lead to different attitudes about environmental issues, and ultimately to different behaviors when activated.

Going a step further, Schultz (2000, 2001, 2002) argued that these types of value bases vary in the extent to which they are related to self-interest. Egoistic concerns are narrow, specific to issues that affect the individual, and are driven primarily by avoiding harmful consequences to oneself. These types of concerns tend to focus on personal health, or personal sacrifice. In contrast, altruistic concerns take in a broader group of people, but yet they are still anthropocentric. These concerns include oneself, but are more *inclusive* in that they are also oriented toward other people. Finally, biospheric concerns are even broader, oriented toward all living things, but they are still inclusive of other people, and still inclusive of oneself.

Several recent studies have examined egoistic, altruistic, and biospheric concerns in the United States and internationally. Schultz (2000, 2001) asked respondents to "...rate each of the following items from 1 (not important) to 7 (supreme importance)" in response to the question, "I am concerned about environmental problems because of the consequences for____." Participants then rated a series of items, which were either egoistic (my health, my prosperity, my lifestyle), altruistic (future generations, humanity, children), or biospheric (plants, animals, birds). To date, groups of respondents from over 20 countries have answered this question. The results from this research have provided two clear findings. First, the three-part classification system captures the way in which most people from all of these countries think about environmental problems. Yet within countries, there are differences in the attitudes of respondents—it is not the case that all people from one country or one culture hold the same set of attitudes or concerns.

Second, the findings show clear differences across countries in the levels of egoistic, altruistic, and biospheric attitudes. For ease of presentation and interpretation, let's examine just the egoistic and biospheric scores, based on published data from 7 countries (Schultz, 2001) and unpublished data from 5 additional countries. A sample of results is shown in Figure 18–3, which demonstrates that the U.S. respondents (university students in California) scored substantially lower on both the egoistic and biospheric concerns than did the college student samples from Latin American countries, but much higher than those from Germany. Also, the U.S. and Russian samples scored higher on egoistic concerns than on biospheric concerns, whereas most of the other countries showed the opposite pattern, with biospheric concerns higher than egoistic ones.

Value Paradigms.   Despite the recent attention given to environmental issues, human activity has always affected the natural environment in which it occurred (Ponting, 1991). However, the magnitude and seriousness of this impact has been exacerbated by our

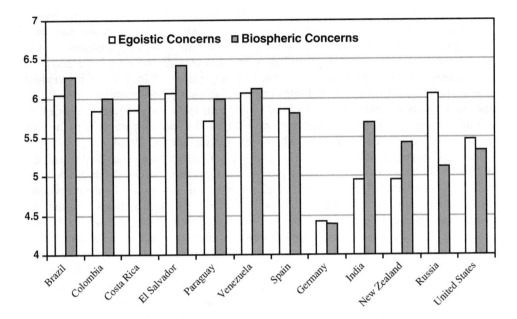

FIGURE 18–3 Average levels of egoistic and biospheric environmental concerns for selected countries.

Source: Schultz (2001) plus unpublished data from Brazil, Germany, India, New Zealand, and Russia.

industrial power and capitalistic economic system. Many of the environmental problems we listed earlier in this chapter have resulted from the values and traditions of western culture. These traditional values have been referred to as the **dominant social paradigm** (Pirages & Ehrlich, 1974; Milbrath, 1984; Dunlap & Van Liere, 1984). The values emphasized within the dominant social paradigm include individualism, materialism, limited government, economic growth, and the importance of progress. This worldview forms the core of the western cultural heritage and is transmitted from generation to generation.

The environmental movement that began in the 1960s, and was officially christened at the first Earth Day in 1970, challenged many of the fundamental values of western culture. Dunlap and Van Liere (1978) referred to this emerging worldview as a **new environmental paradigm**. This new paradigm emphasizes beliefs about the delicate balance of nature, the limits of growth, and humanity's need to live in balance with nature rather than to "rule" it. At the core of the new emerging worldview is the concept of a human–nature relationship— that people must live in balance with the natural environment. Dunlap and Van Liere (1978) developed a 12-item New Environmental Paradigm (NEP) scale to measure endorsement of these emerging values, and they recently published a revised version (Dunlap et al., 2000). Although the NEP scale measure is made up of attitudinal items, it is conceptualized as measuring a "primitive" set of beliefs. That is, endorsement of the new environmental paradigm is conceived of as a precursor to attitudes about more specific environmental issues and to proenvironmental behavior (Stern, Dietz, & Guagnano, 1995; Dunlap et al., 2000; Stern, 2000).

In their research on the new environmental paradigm in the 1970s, Dunlap and Van Liere (1978) surveyed a sample of Washington State residents. The results showed a high degree of endorsement of the items. For example, 73% of respondents agreed with the statement that "We are approaching the limit of the number of people the earth can support." In a follow-up study 14 years later, Dunlap et al. (2000) obtained a similar sample of Washington State residents. These results showed a modest increase in endorsement of the new environmental paradigm, with the largest changes coming on items that asked about the likelihood of an ecological catastrophe. For example, in 1976, 60% of respondents agreed with the statement that "If things continue on their present course, we will soon experience a major ecological catastrophe," whereas in 1990, 78% of respondents agreed with this statement (the 1990 percentages were adjusted to be comparable with the 1976 data by omitting "unsure" responses, which were not included in 1976).

The 1990 survey showed a high level of endorsement for the new ecological worldview, but like the public opinion data reported previously, more recent data indicate a substantial decline. Illustrative results come from telephone and mail surveys of Michigan residents, which although not exactly comparable to the Washington State samples, did measure a broad and diverse group of respondents (Mertig & Koval, 2002). Across the 10 NEP scale items used, the level of endorsement was considerably lower than that found in the 1990 Washington data. For example, only 53% of the Michigan sample agreed (either "strongly" or "mildly") with the statement, "We are approaching the limit of the number of people the earth can support" (again the percentages were adjusted to omit the "unsure" responses). This figure was lower than in the Washington sample, for which the percentage was 73% in 1976 and 67% in 1990. Similarly, in response to the item, "If things continue on their present course, we will soon experience a major ecological disaster," 64% agreed, compared with 60% in Washington in 1976 and 78% in 1990. These findings are consistent with other public opinion data in indicating a rather broad decline in environmental concerns since 1990.

DETERMINANTS OF ENVIRONMENTAL ATTITUDES

What are the psychological reasons or experiences that lead one person to care more than another about the environment? There are several theoretical models that have been developed to explain people's environmental attitudes and behaviors. Our focus here is largely on attitudes, but interested readers can explore Stern's value–belief–norm theory of environmental behavior, and research using the norm-activation model to understand and promote proenvironmental behavior (Stern & Dietz, 1994; Stern, 2000).

Rational Choice Models

One of the earliest perspectives on environmental attitudes and behavior, and one that is still strongly defended, is **rational choice theory**. The central element of this theory is that individuals care about (and act on) issues that directly affect them. That is, people are reasoning animals who are primarily motivated to choose a course of action that has a beneficial outcome for themselves. This theory has been used, largely by economists, to support development of incentive-based programs to promote environmental behavior. Consequently, the theory is sometime referred to as *homo economicus*—the economic man. It emphasizes that, in thinking about an issue or in choosing a behavior, people weigh the costs and benefits associated with it. Costs might include financial costs, effort, pain, social ridicule, and so on. Benefits might include money, praise from friends, pleasure, and so on. The theory posits that a person weights the anticipated results by his or her own values and preferences and chooses the behavioral option that will have the greatest likelihood of a rewarding outcome.

As an example, let's look at a specific environmental behavior: What is your attitude about riding your bike to work (or school)? I (PWS) hold a favorable attitude toward this behavior. I live close to work so the effort required is minimal, it's faster to park my bike than to park my car, I get a sense of personal accomplishment from riding my bike, and my family praises me when I do it. So the benefits outweigh the costs (and indeed I often ride my bike to work). However, someone else might have a negative attitude toward riding their bike: It's potentially dangerous, it requires physical exertion, it exposes you to dirt and bugs, and it's an unusual behavior (at least in Southern California).

Research on the rational choice model has been generally encouraging. There are many studies showing that, as the costs associated with a behavior increase, the frequency of the action decreases (and similarly actions increase when the incentives are increased—Gardner & Stern, 2002). However, if we focus solely on attitudes, the evidence is less clear. In essence, rational choice attitudes are egoistic—that is, they are based on the relation of the attitude object to oneself. One example of such an attitude is the **NIMBY** viewpoint—an acronym standing for "not in my back yard." This term describes people who are opposed, for instance, to new construction projects in their neighborhood, such as a new housing development nearby. The NIMBY attitude characterizes someone who opposes such a development only because of its proximity to his or her residence, but who does not have a negative attitude toward housing developments in general. A related term for the development itself is **LULU**—"locally unwanted land uses." For example, a LULU might be a new landfill in one's city. Many people are not opposed to landfills in general (because their trash is buried there along with other people's), but they may oppose one nearby, based solely on its proximity to them.

Despite use of these terms in everyday parlance, there is little research evidence showing that people are more concerned about issues that directly affect them. For instance, data on the relationship between proximity (to, say, a nuclear power plant) and attitudes are mixed. The data we saw earlier on attitudes toward offshore oil drilling are consistent with a NIMBY attitude—fewer than 20% of Californians supported offshore drilling, whereas 60% of a national sample did so (E. Smith, 2002). There is also some evidence from national studies that people are more favorable toward nuclear power in the abstract than they are if a plant is going to be built in their community (Rankin, Nealy, & Melber, 1984; Rosa & Dunlap, 1994).

However, in situations where an environmental hazard is already present, there is little evidence to suggest that people who live closer to such a hazardous site hold more negative attitudes toward it. In a rigorous analysis of several decades of data from California surveys, E. Smith (2002) found no relationship between proximity to a nuclear power plant or oil development site and attitudes toward them. He concluded, "In sum, no NIMBY effects appeared in any of these data" (p. 159). Moreover, there is some evidence that, over time, attitudes among people who live in a community near a nuclear power plant become more favorable—a long-tem adaptation effect (van der Pligt, Eiser, & Spears, 1986, 1987).

Another factor supporting more favorable attitudes toward a polluting plant or industry in one's community is that many community residents are apt to be employed there, and so their economic well-being is linked to the presence of the plant. This is another side of rational choice influences on attitudes.

Postmaterialist Values

Another theoretical approach is the **postmaterialist values** perspective, which suggests that concern for quality-of-life issues, like free speech, liberty, and environmental protection, occur only after individuals have met their more basic needs for food, shelter, and safety. This approach stems from the work of Maslow (1970) on the hierarchy of human needs. Inglehart (1990, 1995) and others have argued that the emergence of environmental concern in the past 30 years was due to a shift from materialist values, which were widespread in the early part of the century, toward postmaterialist values in recent decades. That is, people who grew up with the backdrop of World War I, the Depression, and World War II, worried more about basic material needs, whereas people who grew up during the prosperous years following World War II are more focused on broader social values like freedom, self-expression, and quality of life.

Although this postmaterialist viewpoint fits with our notions of human values and functioning, there is little supporting empirical evidence for it (Dunlap & Mertig, 1995; Davis, 1996; Kemmelmeier, Krol, & Young, 2002; E. Smith, 2002). Inglehart's (1990) approach to measuring values is to ask people to prioritize the importance of four goals:

- fighting rising prices
- maintaining order in the nation
- giving people more say in government decisions
- protecting freedom of speech

In what order would you rank these four goals? Which is most important? The first two are materialist values, and the last two are postmaterialist values. Research using this technique (and similar ones with an expanded number of materialist and postmaterialist goals) has tended to find no relationship between postmaterialist values and attitudes about a range of environmental issues, such as use of nuclear power, or drilling for oil. In analyzing data from 20 countries, Kemmelmeier et al. (2002) found that, although the wealth of a country was positively correlated with its average level of environmental concern, this relationship was not mediated by postmaterialist values. They concluded that "Apparently, post-materialism cannot account for how economic prosperity . . . influences environmentalism" (p. 278).

One possible explanation for the lack of relationship between postmaterialist values and attitudes could be the breadth with which attitudes are measured. In the preceding section, we distinguished among the egoistic, altruistic, and biospheric bases for environmental concern. In testing the postmaterialist values hypothesis, researchers have used broad measures of attitudes that ignore these distinctions. As an example, take the issue of nuclear power. Three people could hold the same negative attitude toward nuclear power, but for fundamentally different reasons: nuclear power poses a risk to my health (egoistic), nuclear power poses a risk to the people who live near the reactors (altruistic), or nuclear power poses a risk to many living organisms (biospheric). From the postmaterialist values perspective, materialists should be more likely to hold egoistic attitudes, whereas postmaterialists should be more likely to hold biospheric attitudes.

A recent study by Göksen, Adaman, and Zenginobuz (2002) provides some evidence for a link between postmaterialist values and specific types of attitudes. The sample consisted of 1,565 households drawn at random from metropolitan Istanbul, Turkey. Environmental attitudes were measured with 15 different items, divided into local issues (e.g., pollution, solid waste, soil pollution) and global issues (e.g., deforestation, ozone depletion, global warming). Results showed that higher levels of education, and being born in an urban location, were positively related to both local and global environmental attitudes. However, as hypothesized, postmaterialist values were negatively related to attitudes about local environmental problems. That is, respondents with more materialist values were more concerned about issues that directly affected their daily lives—what we have referred to above as egoistic concerns.

Other Values

Going beyond the mixed evidence for the postmaterialist explanation of environmental concern, a broader approach is to examine the relationship between other human values (not just postmaterialist values) and attitudes about environmental issues. Several studies have utilized Schwartz's theory and measures about the structure of human values (Schwartz, 1992, 1994; Schwartz & Sagie, 2000). The value dimensions from Schwartz's model that are relevant here are values of self-enhancement and self-transcendence. Self-enhancement values, as the name implies, emphasize life goals that focus on the individual—for example, valuing wealth, personal achievement, ambition, success, and social recognition. In contrast are values of self-transcendence, which emphasize broader life goals like wisdom, equality, honesty, and meaning in life.

In recent years, several large-scale studies have examined the relationship between values and environmental attitudes in a range of different countries (e.g., Gouveia, 2002). In samples from many Latin American countries, Schultz (2001) found egoistic environmental concerns to be positively correlated with self-enhancement and negatively correlated with self-transcendence. In contrast, biospheric environmental concerns were negatively correlated with self-enhancement and positively correlated with self-transcendence. Other studies on values have reported similar findings (Stern, Dietz, & Kalof, 1993; Karp, 1996; Schultz & Zelezny, 1999; Nordlund & Garvill, 2002).

Photograph courtesy of Paul Stern.
Reprinted by permission.

Box 18–2   PAUL STERN, *Analyst of Human Impacts on Environmental Problems*

Paul Stern is a study director of the Committee on the Human Dimensions of Global Change at the U.S. National Research Council in Washington, D.C. He is also a Research Professor of Sociology at George Mason University and president of the Social and Environmental Research Institute. He earned a Ph.D. in social psychology at Clark University in 1975 and taught for several years at Elmira College before moving to his present position as a staff officer at the National Academy of Sciences in 1980.

Stern's research has focused primarily on the study of environmental values, beliefs, and behavior, and the development of deliberative approaches to environmental decision-making. Since 1990, he has coauthored or coedited eight volumes, including Environmental Problems and Human Behavior, Global Environmental Change: Understanding the Human Dimensions, Understanding Risk: Informing Decisions in a Democratic Society, Environmentally Significant Consumption, Making Climate Forecasts Matter, *and* New Tools for Environmental Protection. *He is known for his theorizing and research using a norm-activation model to understand and promote proenvironmental behavior.*

GROUP DIFFERENCES IN ENVIRONMENTAL ATTITUDES

Let us now examine the factors, other than values, that lead some people to be more concerned than others about environmental issues. Among the variables that have been most studied are demographic variables and instigating life experiences.

Demographic Variables Associated with Environmental Concern

Education is one of the most important demographic variables that distinguish people highly concerned about environmental quality from those less concerned (Dillman & Christenson, 1972; McEvoy, 1972; Van Liere & Dunlap, 1980; Mertig & Koval, 2001; Weakliem, 2002). Across many studies, people with more formal education typically express higher levels of concern for environmental issues. This basic effect has been found for both general environmental attitudes and for specific attitudes. For example, McEvoy (1972) reported that 62% of respondents who had never finished high school favored offshore oil drilling, compared with 39% of those with a post-college education. About 30 years later, among Californians, both figures were lower but the difference was still present—35% of those who never completed high school favored more drilling, compared with only 22% of those with a post-college education (E. Smith, 2002).

Age. As a general rule, studies have found that younger respondents are more concerned about environmental issues than are older respondents (Van Liere & Dunlap, 1980; Howell & Laska, 1992; Mertig & Koval, 2001). However, the effects tend to be inconsistent across studies and attitude domains. In Smith's analysis of survey data of Californians regarding offshore oil drilling, 21% of those aged 18–31 years supported more drilling, whereas 26% of those over age 61 did so. Van Liere and Dunlap (1980) suggested that younger people are less integrated into the social order and are therefore less likely to endorse the dominant social paradigm. Another possible explanation for the effect is that, as people age, they become less open to new ideas and less flexible in their thinking (see Chapter 8).

Income. Research on the relationship between income and environmental attitudes has tended to find that wealthier respondents are more concerned than are poorer respondents (Dillman & Christenson, 1972; McEvoy, 1972; Van Liere & Dunlap, 1980). However, the results tend to be small and very inconsistent across studies. In Smith's (2002) analysis of offshore oil drilling, there was no significant relationship between income and attitudes toward drilling. Respondents' occupation often helps to explain the relationship between income and environmental attitudes. For instance, Hine and Gerlach (1970) found that business owners and executives were less concerned than working professionals or government officials.

Gender. In recent years, gender has been the most studied of the demographic correlates of environmental attitudes. In general, the findings show that women are more environmentally concerned than men, especially regarding local health-related issues, whereas men are more inclined to favor economic growth (Borden & Francis, 1978; McStay & Dunlap, 1983; Schahn & Holzer, 1990; Mohai, 1992; Zelezny, Chua, & Aldrich, 2000). These gender differences in attitudes also appear in cross-cultural samples (Zelezny et al., 2000; Eisler, Eisler, & Yoshida, 2003).

Although the gender difference in environmental attitudes is well-documented, research has failed to identify a clear explanation for *why* women are more concerned (Dietz, Kalof, & Stern, 2002). There are several relevant theoretical arguments that have been made for the gender difference (for an overview, see Winter, 2002). One of the most widely discussed explanations for the gender difference has to do with gender socialization. Gilligan (1982, 1986) has argued that girls are socialized to value caring, relationships, and affection, whereas boys are socialized to value objectivity, emotional distance, and autonomy. **Ecofeminists** have used this theoretical perspective to explain why women are more concerned about environmental issues—in essence, because they are more other-oriented. However, studies measuring degrees of femininity in personality patterns or endorsement of traditional gender roles have failed to find persuasive evidence that these socialization patterns are indeed the reason for the gender difference. Although there is considerable evidence that men and women differ in gender-role socialization and values, it is unclear whether these are the sources of the gender difference in environmental concern (cf. Dietz et al., 2002; D. Smith, 2001).

Ethnicity. Over the 30-plus years of environmental research, a few studies have specifically examined differences in environmental attitudes across ethnic groups. Some early studies indicated that white Americans were more concerned about environmental issues than were nonwhites, but more recent studies have failed to find these differences (Parker & McDonough, 1999). In fact, some studies have found that Latinos and other immigrants to the United States tend to be *more* concerned about environmental issues when they first arrive, but the disparity in attitudes quickly fades over time (Hunter, 2000; Schultz, Unipan, & Gamba, 2000).

Religion. Studies of the relationship between religious beliefs and environmental attitudes date back to White's (1967) argument that Judeo–Christian doctrine was inherently anthropocentric and antienvironmental. Subsequent research over the years has tended to find substantial differences in environmental concern between religious denominations, with Catholics least concerned and those with no formal religious affiliation most concerned. The clearest finding is for studies that ask about belief in the Bible. Respondents who believe that the Bible is the literal word of God tend to be less concerned about environmental issues than do people who believe that the Bible is the "inspired word of God" or that the Bible is a "collection of stories and legends, God had nothing to do with it" (Eckberg & Blocker, 1989; Guth et al., 1995; Schultz et al., 2000).

Political Affiliation. One of the strongest correlates of environmental attitudes is political party identification (Van Liere & Dunlap, 1980). When political identification is classified from strong Democratic to strong Republican, research has consistently found Democrats to be more concerned than Republicans about environmental issues (Weigel, 1977; Samdahl & Robertson, 1989; Dunlap, Xiao, & McCright, 2001). At a more general level, analyses of ideological stance (from strong liberal to strong conservative) have found that liberals are much more concerned about environmental issues and more likely to support environmental conservation policies than are conservatives (Schultz & Stone, 1994). In E. Smith's (2002) analysis of survey data from Californians about offshore oil drilling, only 11% of strong liberals supported drilling, whereas 30% of conservatives did. This difference is on the low end of those found in studies of ideology. For example, when asked about drilling for oil in state parklands, only 9% of strong liberals expressed support, whereas 51% of conservatives did (Moore, 2001c).

Rural Versus Urban Residence.   Place of residence has also been examined as a correlate of environmental concern (Guagnano & Markee, 1995; Kaiser & Keller, 2001), but the expected direction of the relationship is unclear—should rural residents be more or less concerned than urban residents? On one hand, people who live in rural settings often make their living from the land (e.g., farming, ranching, mining, logging, fishing) and therefore may be more willing to sacrifice environmental quality for economic gain. On the other hand, rural communities are typically less affected by salient environmental problems, like pollution, smog, litter, and overcrowding, so their residents might be more disturbed by such environmental despoliation.

As one might expect, given these two arguments, the research findings on environmental attitudes of people living in rural and urban communities are mixed (Tremblay & Dunlap, 1978; Freudenburg, 1991; Bogner & Wiseman, 1997; E. Smith, 2002). The initial research suggested that urban residents were more concerned about environmental problems and quality than were rural residents. However, more recent studies have indicated that the issue is more complex than a simple rural–urban dichotomy. For example, Lutz, Simpson-Housley, and De Man (1999) found that rural and urban residents did not differ in their attitudes toward wilderness environmental protection, but there were differences in what they considered to be wilderness—urban residents had a much broader definition of "wilderness" and were more likely to include such areas as a hydroelectric dam, an agricultural field, and a sparsely populated sea coast. To summarize the findings with regard to place of residence, the differences are typically small (when found at all), and can generally be explained by other variables, like income differences (urban residents tend to be higher than rural), occupation, and personal familiarity with the environmental problem being considered.

Significant Life Experiences

An emerging perspective on the study of environmental attitudes is an emphasis on the personal experiences that lead a person to care about environmental problems and to adopt proenvironmental behaviors and lifestyles. Much of this research can be traced back to Tanner's (1980) study of **significant life experiences**, which tried to identify the key experiences that lead individuals to work actively toward "the maintenance of a varied, beautiful, and resource-rich planet for future generations" (p. 20). This quotation typifies much of the research on instigating experiences: Most of the studies have been conducted with the goal of creating effective environmental education programs. The reasoning is that, if we can identify the experiences in a person's life history that led to proenvironmental attitudes and behavior, then we can integrate these experiences into future environmental education curricula. One of the primary goals of environmental education is to "help social groups and individuals acquire an awareness of and sensitivity to the total environment and its allied problems" (UNESCO, 1980, p. 71).

Studies of instigating experiences are primarily retrospective. That is, they begin by identifying individuals who have proenvironmental attitudes or lifestyles, and then they work backwards to identify the key experiences that these individuals identify as the source of those attitudes or behaviors (Peterson & Hungerford, 1982; Palmer, 1993; Chawla, 1999; Degenhardt, 2002). Although such an approach can lead only to tentative conclusions because it is not a longitudinal study of personal changes over time, there are a number of interesting findings from this area of research. In a review of research on significant life experiences, Chawla (1998) summarized the results from seven such retrospective studies. Across a wide range of conservationists—including staff and officers at organizations like the National Wildlife Federation or the Sierra Club, interpreters at national parks, and college students majoring in environmental studies—the findings were amazingly consistent. In all the studies, exposure to natural outdoor areas during childhood emerged as the most significant experience. Consistent with the research on attitude formation discussed in Chapter 8, these experiences occurred primarily in the context of family—on vacations, camping, hunting, or fishing trips. Tanner (1980) summarized the recurring theme as "many childhood hours spent alone or with a few friends in a more or less pristine environment" (p. 21). Two other experiences that emerged as important instigators were encouragement and support for environmental concerns by parents and family, and the loss of a valued natural area to development (see Chawla, 1998, Tables 1–7).

Environmental Identity. A possible explanation for the finding that early periods of time spent in natural environments lead to attitudes of concern for environmental issues comes from some recent studies of environmental identity. Recall that research on the "new environmental paradigm" has suggested that a new set of values and beliefs are emerging, centered on the fundamental belief that humans are an integral part of nature and must live in harmony with the natural environment (Dunlap et al., 2000). Several recent articles have applied this concept to an individual's self-identity—that is, the extent to which the individual believes that he or she is part of nature. Such a belief can form an important component of an individual's sense of self, and of identity (cf. Clayton & Opotow, 2003).

This notion of **environmental identity** and of an individual's relationship with the natural environment has been a recurrent theme in recent research on environmental attitudes (Bragg, 1996; Weigert, 1997; Kahn, 1999; Kidner, 2001). Several studies have demonstrated a significant correlation between an individual's belief that he or she is part of nature, and the types of attitudes that the person holds (Schultz, 2001, 2002; Clayton, 2003). Schultz (2002) used an implicit measure of self-concept to assess the extent to which an individual associated himself or herself with the natural environment. Specifically, the Implicit Association Test assessed the strength of the association between "self" words (I, me, my, mine) and natural words (trees, animals, birds). This association was termed "connectedness." The findings showed that there was a general tendency for respondents to associate themselves with nature—that is, people generally had a greater association between self and nature, than between self and "built" words (street, building, computer). Furthermore, as predicted, the measure of implicit connectedness correlated positively with biospheric environmental concerns, and negatively with egoistic environmental concerns.

FROM ATTITUDES TO ACTIONS

Let's examine one final issue here—the relationship between environmental attitudes and behaviors. Do concerns for environmental issues translate into action? The issue of attitude–behavior correspondence has been a continuing theme throughout this book, and it is particularly relevant to programs and interventions designed to promote sustainable behaviors. On one hand, researchers have argued that environmental concern is the first step toward proenvironmental behavior (e.g., Kals & Maes, 2002):

> Awareness about the extent of the ecological crisis and its various problems is a basic prerequisite for personal renunciations for the sake of the natural environment. . . . . A considerable amount of research has shown that this general ecological awareness has a stable impact on behavioral decisions to promote sustainable development. (p. 103)

Such a conclusion highlights the importance of environmental concern in understanding and encouraging environmental behavior. But other researchers have reached rather different conclusions. For example, in their review, Vining and Ebreo (2002) stated:

> Many studies of the relations between environmental attitudes and pro-environmental behavior have focused on the prediction of behavior from general attitudes about the environment, that is, from environmental concern. However, measures of environmental concern have generally been found to be only weakly related to the performance of pro-environmental behaviors. (p. 545)

We agree with this conclusion. Overall, environmental attitudes tend to be positively correlated with a range of specific environmental behaviors (e.g., recycling, energy conservation, buying "green" products). However, reviews of research in this area have been unanimous in concluding that the relationship is a weak one (Hines, Hungerford, & Tomera, 1986–1987; Tarrant & Cordell, 1997; Fransson & Gärling, 1999; Bamberg, 2003).

As we have seen in Chapter 12, there are several factors that can produce a weak relationship between attitudes and behaviors, and these findings apply to studies of environmental attitudes. Two of these moderators deserve reiteration here. First is *measurement specificity*. The construct of environmental attitudes is a broad one, and studies have tended to find a moderate positive relationship between general environmental concern and general environmental behavior (cf. Tarrant & Cordell, 1997). However, in trying to explain *specific* environmental actions (like recycling), studies that have utilized measures of *specific* attitudes (like attitudes toward recycling) have found stronger relationships than studies that measured general environmental attitudes (Gamba & Oskamp, 1994; Bamberg, 2003). Second, *contextual factors* like convenience, availability of environmental programs, or incentives influence environmental behavior and consequently reduce the strength of the relationship between attitudes and actions (Schultz & Oskamp, 1996). As Stern (2000) noted, "the attitude–behavior association is strongest when contextual factors are neutral and [it] approaches zero when contextual factors are strongly positive or negative" (p. 415).

In recent years, there have been several advances toward developing a broad model for understanding the link between values, environmental attitudes, and environmental behavior (Stern & Oskamp, 1987; Dahlstrand & Biel, 1997; Stern, 2000). One line of research has applied the theory of planned behavior (TPB) to the study of proenvironmental behavior (Ajzen, 1991). Recall from Chapter 12 that the TPB and its predecessor, the theory of reasoned action, view intention as the immediate precursor to action. Intention, in turn, is determined by a person's attitude toward the behavior, subjective norms, and perceived control. The attitudinal variable in the TPB is specific—that is, it's not a general concern about environmental issues, but rather a specific attitude about a particular behavior (for example, saving energy by reducing air conditioner use, or recycling, or carpooling). In contrast with the results of studies that used general environmental concern as a predictor, studies using the TPB to predict environmental behaviors have generally found attitudes to be significantly (and positively) correlated with intentions and with environmental behavior (Taylor & Todd, 1997; Harland, Staats, & Wilke, 1999; Lam, 1999; Kaiser & Gutscher, 2003).

A second line of research has applied models of altruistic behavior to understanding both environmental attitudes and environmental behavior. Building on Schwartz's (1977) model of norm-activation, Stern and his colleagues have developed a value–belief–norm theory to explain a variety of environmental attitudes and actions (Stern et al., 1995, 1999; Stern, 2000). Their model postulates a specific causal chain of five variables that leads to environmental behavior. Values (egoistic, altruistic, and biospheric) lead to an individual's ecological worldview (as represented in the new ecological paradigm), and become *activated* when the person perceives adverse consequences for valued objects and perceives an ability to mitigate the threat. Once activated, these values lead to a *sense of obligation* to take action, which ultimately leads to behavior. Stern (2000) has summarized a number of studies showing the usefulness of this model in explaining a range of environmental actions. The essence of the value–belief–norm model is the *interaction* of person and environment. The various types of environmental attitudes can lead to differing patterns of behavior when they are activated by the contextual situation.

Research examining the link between environmental attitudes and behaviors can be a useful tool for promoting proenvironmental behavior and fostering sustainable development (Gardner & Stern, 2002). If we can understand the psychological factors that lead people to care about environmental issues, and the variables that lead to action, we can use this knowledge to develop effective environmental programs. Potential applications range from environmental education programs, to energy conservation, to recycling, to responsible consumer choices. Psychological models of environmental attitudes and behaviors offer hope in combating the burgeoning threats of environmental problems.

SUMMARY

Research on attitudes and concerns about environmental issues is a relatively new phenomenon. Before the 1950s, environmental problems were nonissues, and it was only in the early 1970s that systematic research on environmental attitudes began. Since that time, environmental problems have often appeared on lists of the most important national issues identified in U.S. public opinion polls, and they have been named as the top social issue to be addressed in the next 25 years. Trends in concern about environmental problems showed a steady increase throughout the 1970s and 1980s, peaking in the 1990s, and then decreasing somewhat into the 2000s. High levels of concern for environmental issues are also found in many countries throughout the world.

Environmental issues are often characterized as involving a trade-off between production and conservation, or between development and environmental protection. Survey research in the United States has consistently found that a majority of respondents favor environmental protection over development. However, these attitudes are related to the cost of energy—as the cost of energy increases, attitudes toward increased production and development become more favorable.

One important research topic is the "new environmental paradigm"—a set of attitudes and beliefs that view humans as part of nature, and emphasize limits to growth and the need for humans to live in balance with nature. Another approach has examined the value basis for environmental concern, distinguishing between egoistic, altruistic, and biospheric attitudes. Egoistic environmental concerns are oriented around oneself; altruistic concerns are oriented around other people; and biospheric concerns are oriented around all living things.

Several psychological theories have attempted to explain environmental attitudes and behavior. Rational choice theory holds that people will be concerned (and act) mainly when it is in their self-interest. Postmaterialist theory proposes that conservationist attitudes about environmental issues will occur only when a person's more fundamental needs for food, safety, and shelter are met. Other values, such as self-transcendence, have also been proposed as explanations of environmental concern, but the evidence for all of these approaches is mixed. The demographic variables of higher education and income, younger age, feminine gender, nonfundamentalist religious views, and Democratic political affiliation have all been found to predict proenvironmental attitudes.

Research on significant life experiences has concluded that exposure to natural environments during childhood (for example, in family vacations or outdoor play) is quite strongly associated with proenvironmental attitudes. Environmental identity—associating one's sense of self with nature—is also predictive of forming proenvironmental attitudes. Much research in this tradition is aimed at encouraging patterns of environmental attitudes and behavior that will preserve the life-sustaining environmental properties of the Earth and thus allow a desirable quality of life for all future generations of human beings.

References

ABC/Washington Post Poll. (2002, December 17). Need more evidence. Retrieved June, 2003, from http://abcnews.go.com/sections/world/DailyNews/iraqpoll021217.html

Abdel-Ghany, M., & Sharpe, D. L. (1994). Racial wage differentials among young adults. Evidence from the 1990s. *Journal of Family and Economic Issues, 15*, 279–294.

Abelson, R. P. (1959). Modes of resolution of belief dilemmas. *Journal of Conflict Resolution, 3*, 343–352.

Abelson, R. P. (1968). Computers, polls and public opinion—Some puzzles and paradoxes. *Trans-action, 5*(9), 20–27.

Abelson, R. P. (1976). A script theory of understanding, attitude, and behavior. In J. Carroll & T. Payne (Eds.), *Cognition and social behavior*. Potomac, MD: Lawrence Erlbaum Associates.

Abelson, R. P. (1981). The psychological status of the script concept. *American Psychologist, 36*, 715–729.

Abelson, R. P. (1986). Beliefs are like possessions. *Journal for the Theory of Social Behaviour, 16*, 223–250.

Abelson, R. P., Kinder, D. R., Peters, M. D., & Fiske, S. T. (1982). Affective and semantic components in political person perception. *Journal of Personality and Social Psychology, 42*, 619–630.

Abelson, R. P., & Rosenberg, M. J. (1958). Symbolic psycho-logic: A model of attitudinal cognition. *Behavioral Science, 3*, 1–13.

Aboud, F. E. (1987). The development of ethnic self-identification and attitudes. In J. S. Phinney & M. J. Rotheram (Eds.), *Children's ethnic socialization: Pluralism and development* (pp. 32–55). Newbury Park, CA: Sage.

Aboud, F. E., & Levy, S. R. (2000). Interventions to reduce prejudice and discrimination in children and adolescents. In S. Oskamp (Ed.), *Reducing prejudice and discrimination* (pp. 269–293). Mahwah, NJ: Lawrence Erlbaum Associates.

Aboud, F. E., & Taylor, D. M. (1971). Ethnic and role stereotypes: Their relative importance in person perception. *Journal of Social Psychology, 85*, 17–27.

Abramovitz, J. N. (1998). Sustaining the world's forests. In L. R. Brown et al. (Eds.), *State of the world 1998* (pp. 21–40). New York: Norton.

Abramowitz, A. I., & Saunders, K. L. (2002). Ideological realignment and U.S. congressional elections. In B. Norrander & C. Wilcox (Eds.), *Understanding public opinion* (2nd ed., pp. 203–218). Washington, DC: CQ Press.

Abrams, D., Viki, G. T., Masser, B., & Bohner G. (2003). Perceptions of stranger and acquaintance rape: The role of benevolent and hostile sexism in victim blame and rape proclivity. *Journal of Personality and Social Psychology, 84*, 111–125.

Abrams, M. (1970). The opinion polls and the 1970 British general election. *Public Opinion Quarterly, 34*, 317–324.

Abramson, L. Y., & Martin, D. J. (1981). Depression and the causal inference process. In J. H. Harvey, W. J. Ickes, & R. F. Kidd (Eds.), *New directions in attribution research* (Vol. 3, pp. 117–168). Hillsdale, NJ: Lawrence Erlbaum Associates.

Abramson, P. R. (1983). *Political attitudes in America: Formation and change*. San Francisco: Freeman.

Abramson, P. R., Aldrich, J. H., & Rohde, D. W. (1982). *Change and continuity in the 1980 elections*. Washington, DC: Congressional Quarterly.

Abramson, P. R., Aldrich, J. H., & Rohde, D. W. (2003). *Change and continuity in the 2000 and 2002 elections*. Washington, DC: CQ Press.

Abramson, P. R., & Finifter, A. W. (1981). On the meaning of political trust: New evidence from items introduced in 1978. *American Journal of Political Science, 25*, 297–307.

Abt, C. C. (1980). Social science in the contract research firm. In R. F. Kidd & M. J. Saks (Eds.), *Advances in applied social psychology* (Vol. 1). Hillsdale, NJ: Lawrence Erlbaum Associates.

Achen, C. H. (1975). Mass political attitudes and the survey response. *American Political Science Review, 69*, 1218–1231.

Ackerman, B., & Ayres, I. (2002). *Voting with dollars: A new paradigm for campaign finance*. New Haven, CT: Yale University Press.

Acuna, R. (2000). *Occupied America: A history of Chicanos* (4th ed.). New York: Longman.

Adage.com. (2003). 100 leading national advertisers, 2001. Retrieved June, 2003, from www.adage.com/datacenter.cms?dataCenterid=1

Adair, J. G. (1988). Research on research ethics. *American Psychologist, 43*, 825–826.

Adair, J. G., Dushenko, D. W., & Lindsay, R. C. L. (1985). Ethical regulations and their impact on research practice. *American Psychologist, 40*, 59–72.

Adams, W. C. (1982). Middle East meets West: Surveying American attitudes. *Public Opinion, 5*(2), 51–55.

Adams, W. C. (1984). Media coverage of campaign '84: A preliminary report. *Public Opinion, 7*(2), 9–13.

Adams, W. C. (1986). Whose lives count? TV coverage of natural disasters. *Journal of Communication, 36*, 113–122.

Adams, W. C., & Smith, D. J. (1980). Effects of telephone canvassing on turnout and preferences: A field experiment. *Public Opinion Quarterly, 44*, 389–395.

Adamsky, C. (1981). Changes in pronominal usage in a classroom situation. *Psychology of Women Quarterly, 5*, 773–779.

Addis, M. E., & Mahalik, J. R. (2003). Men, masculinity, and the context of help seeking. *American Psychologist, 58*, 5–14.

Adler, R. P., Lesser, G. S., Meringoff, L. K., Robertson, T. S., & Ward, S. (1980). *The effects of television advertising on children*. Lexington, MA: Heath.

Adorno, T. W., Frenkel-Brunswik, E., Levinson, D. J., & Sanford, R. N. (1950). *The authoritarian personality*. New York: Harper.

Agassi, J. B. (1982). *Comparing the work attitudes of women and men*. Lexington, MA: Lexington.

Agnew, C. R., Thompson, V. D., & Gaines, S. O., Jr. (2000). Incorporating proximal and distal influences on prejudice: Testing a general model across outgroups. *Personality and Social Psychology Bulletin, 26*, 403–418.

Aguinis, H., & Henle, C. (2001). Empirical assessment of the ethics of the bogus pipeline. *Journal of Applied Social Psychology, 31*, 352–375.

Ahammer, I. M., & Murray, J. P. (1979). Kindness in the kindergarten: The relative influence of role playing and prosocial television in facilitating altruism. *International Journal of Behavioral Development, 2*, 133–157.

Ajzen, I. (1988). *Attitudes, personality, and behavior*. Chicago: Dorsey.

Ajzen, I. (1991). The theory of planned behavior. *Organizational Behavior and Human Decision Processes, 50*, 179–211.

Ajzen, I. (2001). Nature and operation of attitudes. *Annual Review of Psychology, 52*, 27–58.

Ajzen, I. (2002). Residual effects of past on later behavior: Habituation and reasoned action perspectives. *Personality and Social Psychology Review, 6*, 107–122.

Ajzen, I., & Fishbein, M. (1970). The prediction of behavior from attitudinal and normative variables. *Journal of Experimental Social Psychology, 6*, 466–487.

Ajzen, I., & Fishbein, M. (1977). Attitude–behavior relations: A theoretical analysis and review of empirical research. *Psychological Bulletin, 84*, 888–918.

Ajzen, I., & Fishbein, M. (1980). *Understanding attitudes and predicting social behavior*. Englewood Cliffs, NJ: Prentice-Hall.

Ajzen, I., & Fishbein, M. (2000). Attitudes and the attitude–behavior relation: Reasoned and automatic processes. In W. Stroebe & M. Hewstone (Eds.), *European review of social psychology* (Vol. 11, pp. 1–33). Chichester, England: Wiley.

Ajzen, I., & Madden, T. J. (1986). Prediction of goal-directed behavior: Attitudes, intentions, and perceived behavioral control. *Journal of Experimental Social Psychology, 22*, 453–474.

Ajzen, I., & Sexton, J. (1999). Depth of processing, belief congruence, and attitude–behavior correspondence. In S. Chaiken & Y. Trope (Eds.), *Dual-process theories in social psychology* (pp. 117–140). New York: Guilford.

Aldrich, J. H., Sullivan, J. L., & Borgida, E. (1989). Foreign affairs and issue voting: Do presidential candidates "waltz before a blind audience"? *American Political Science Review, 83*, 123–141.

Alford, J. R. (2001). We're all in this together: The decline of trust in government, 1958–1996. In J. R. Hibbing & E. Theiss-Morse (Eds.), *What is it about government that Americans dislike?* (pp. 28–46). Cambridge, England: Cambridge University Press.

Allen, C. L. (1965). Photographing the TV audience. *Journal of Advertising Research, 5*, 2–8.

Alley, T. R. (1981). Head shape and the perception of cuteness. *Developmental Psychology, 17*, 650–654.

Allport, G. W. (1935). Attitudes. In C. Murchison (Ed.), *A handbook of social psychology* (pp. 798–844). Worcester, MA: Clark University Press.

Allport, G. W. (1954). *The nature of prejudice*. Reading, MA: Addison-Wesley.

Allport, G. W. (1985). The historical background of social psychology. In G. Lindzey & E. Aronson (Eds.), *The handbook of social psychology* (3rd ed., Vol. 1, pp. 1–46). New York: Random House.

Altemeyer, B. (1988). *Enemies of freedom: Understanding right-wing authoritarianism.* San Francisco: Jossey-Bass.

Altemeyer, B. (1996). *The authoritarian specter.* Cambridge, MA: Harvard University Press.

Altemeyer, B. (1998). The other "authoritarian personality." In M. P. Zanna (Ed.), *Advances in experimental social psychology* (Vol. 30, pp. 48–92). San Diego, CA: Academic Press.

Altheide, D. L. (1976). *Creating reality: How TV news distorts news events.* Beverly Hills, CA: Sage.

Altschuler, B. E. (1982). *Keeping a finger on the public pulse: Private polling and presidential elections.* Westport, CT: Greenwood.

Altschuler, B. E. (1986). Lyndon Johnson and the public polls. *Public Opinion Quarterly, 50,* 285–299.

Alvarez, R. M., & Brehm, J. (2002). *Hard choices, easy answers: Values, information, and American public opinion.* Princeton, NJ: Princeton University Press.

Amato, P., Johnson, D., Booth, A., & Rogers, S. (2003). Continuity and change in marital quality between 1980 and 2000. *Journal of Marriage and the Family, 65,* 1–22.

American Enterprise. (1994, November/December). How much do we know? pp. 114–119.

American Psychological Association. (1953). *Ethical standards of psychologists.* Washington, DC: Author.

American Psychological Association. (1967). *Casebook on ethical standards of psychologists.* Washington, DC: Author.

American Psychological Association. (1973). *Ethical principles in the conduct of research with human participants.* Washington, DC: Author.

American Psychological Association. (1975). Report of the task force on sex bias and sex-role stereotyping in psychotherapeutic practice. *American Psychologist, 30,* 1169–1175.

American Psychological Association. (1977). Guidelines for nonsexist language in APA journals. *American Psychologist, 32,* 487–494.

American Psychological Association. (1981). Ethical principles of psychologists. *American Psychologist, 36,* 633–638.

American Psychological Association. (1982). *Ethical principles in the conduct of research with human participants* (rev. ed.). Washington, DC: Author.

American Psychological Association. (1992). Ethical principles of psychologists and code of conduct. *American Psychologist, 47,* 1597–1611.

American Psychological Association. (1993). *Violence and youth: Psychology's response.* Washington, DC: Author.

American Psychological Association. (1996). *Affirmative action: Who benefits?* Washington, DC: Author.

American Psychological Association. (2002). Ethical principles of psychologists and code of conduct. Retrieved September, 2003, from http://www.apa.org/ethics/

Amidon, A., & Boldry, J. (2002, June 28). *Revisiting outgroup homogeneity and its moderating variables.* Paper presented at Society for the Psychological Study of Social Issues meeting, Toronto.

Amir, Y. (1969). Contact hypothesis in ethnic relations. *Psychological Bulletin, 71,* 319–342.

Anastasi, A., & Urbina, S. (1997). *Psychological testing* (7th ed.). Upper Saddle River, NJ: Prentice-Hall.

Andelin, H. B. (1980). *Fascinating womanhood* (rev. ed.). New York: Bantam.

Anderson, B. A., Silver, B. D., & Abramson, P. R. (1988). The effects of the race of the interviewer on race-related attitudes of black respondents in SRC/CPS national election studies. *Public Opinion Quarterly, 52,* 289–324.

Anderson, C. A., Lepper, M. R., & Ross, L. (1980). Perseverance of social theories: The role of explanation in the persistence of discredited information. *Journal of Personality and Social Psychology, 39,* 1037–1049.

Anderson, D. R., & Collins, P. A. (1988). *The impact on children's education: Television's influence on cognitive development* (Office of Research Working Paper No. 2). Washington, DC: U.S. Department of Education.

Anderson, N. H. (1971). Integration theory and attitude change. *Psychological Review, 78,* 171–206.

Anderson, N. H. (1981). *Foundations of information integration theory.* New York: Academic Press.

Anderson, N. H., & Farkas, A. J. (1973). New light on order effects in attitude change. *Journal of Personality and Social Psychology, 28,* 88–93.

Andreasen, M. (1994). Patterns of family life and television consumption from 1945 to the 1990s. In D. Zillmann, J. Bryant, & A. Huston (Eds.), *Media, children, and the family: Social scientific, psychodynamic, and clinical perspectives* (pp. 19–36). Hillsdale, NJ: Lawrence Erlbaum Associates.

Ansolabehere, S., & Iyengar, S. (1995). *Going negative: How attack ads shrink and polarize the electorate.* New York: Free Press.

Antill, J. K., Cotton, S., & Tindale, S. (1983). Egalitarian or traditional: Correlates of the perception of an ideal marriage. *Australian Journal of Psychology, 35,* 245–257.

Antonak, R. F., & Livneh, H. (1995). Randomized response technique: A review and proposed extension to disability attitude research. *Genetic, Social, and General Psychology Monographs, 121*, 97–145.

Apparala, M., Reifman, A., & Munsch, J. (2003). Cross-national comparison of attitudes toward fathers' and mothers' participation in household tasks and childcare. *Sex Roles, 48*, 189–203.

Aquilino, W. S. (1994). Interview mode effects in surveys of drug and alcohol use: A field experiment. *Public Opinion Quarterly, 58*, 210–240.

Arkin, R. M., Appelman, A. J., & Burger, J. M. (1980). Social anxiety, self-presentation, and the self-serving bias in causal attributions. *Journal of Personality and Social Psychology, 38*, 23–35.

Armitage, C. J., & Conner, M. (2000). Attitude ambivalence: A test of three key hypotheses. *Personality and Social Psychology Bulletin, 26*, 1421–1432.

Armitage, C., & Conner, M. (2001). Efficacy of the theory of planned behaviour: A meta-analytic review. *British Journal of Social Psychology, 40*, 471–499.

Aronson, E. (1968). Dissonance theory: Progress and problems. In R. P. Abelson, E. Aronson, W. J. McGuire, T. M. Newcomb, M. J. Rosenberg, & P. H. Tannenbaum (Eds.), *Theories of cognitive consistency: A sourcebook* (pp. 5–27). Chicago: Rand McNally.

Aronson, E. (1969). The theory of cognitive dissonance: A current perspective. In L. Berkowitz (Ed.), *Advances in experimental social psychology* (Vol. 4, pp. 1–34). New York: Academic Press.

Aronson, E. (1992). The return of the repressed: Dissonance theory makes a comeback. *Psychological Inquiry, 3*, 303–311.

Aronson, E. (1999). Dissonance, hypocrisy, and the self-concept. In E. Harmon-Jones & J. Mills (Eds.), *Cognitive dissonance: Progress on a pivotal theory in social psychology* (pp. 103–126). Washington, DC: American Psychological Association.

Aronson, E., Blaney, N., Stephan, C., Sikes, J., & Snapp, M. (1978). *The jigsaw classroom.* Beverly Hills, CA: Sage.

Aronson, E., Brewer, M., & Carlsmith, J. M. (1985). Experimentation in social psychology. In G. Lindzey & E. Aronson (Eds.), *The handbook of social psychology* (3rd ed., Vol. 1, pp. 441–486). New York: Random House.

Aronson, E., Fried, C., & Stone, J. (1991). Overcoming denial and increasing the intention to use condoms through the induction of hypocrisy. *American Journal of Public Health, 81*, 1636–1638.

Aronson, E., & Golden, B. W. (1962). The effect of relevant and irrelevant aspects of communicator credibility on attitude change. *Journal of Personality, 30*, 135–146.

Aronson, E., & Linder, D. (1965). Gain and loss of esteem as determinants of interpersonal attraction. *Journal of Experimental Social Psychology, 1*, 156–171.

Arterton, R. C. (1984). *Media politics: The news strategies of presidential campaigns.* Lexington, MA: Heath.

Arvey, R. D., Bouchard, T. J., Segal, N. L., & Abraham, L. M. (1989). Job satisfaction: Environmental and genetic components. *Journal of Applied Psychology, 74*, 187–192.

Asch, S. E. (1946). Forming impressions of personality. *Journal of Abnormal and Social Psychology, 41*, 258–290.

Asch, S. E. (1956). Studies of independence and conformities. *Psychological Monographs, 70*(9, Whole No. 416).

Asher, S. R., & Allen, V. L. (1969). Racial preference and social comparison processes. *Journal of Social Issues, 25*(1), 157–166.

Ashmore, R. D., & Del Boca, E. K. (1976). Psychological approaches to understanding intergroup conflicts. In P. A. Katz (Ed.), *Towards the elimination of racism.* Elmsford, NY: Pergamon.

Assmus, G., Farley, J. U., & Lehmann, D. R. (1984). How advertising affects sales: Meta-analysis of econometric results. *Journal of Marketing Research, 21*, 65–74.

Atkin, C. K., Bowen, L., Nayman, O. B., & Sheinkopf, K. G. (1973). Quality versus quantity in televised political ads. *Public Opinion Quarterly, 37*, 209–224.

Atkin, C. K., Galloway, J., & Nayman, O. B. (1973). Mass communication and political socialization among college students. *Public Opinion Quarterly, 37*, 443–444.

Atkin, C. K., & Heald, G. (1976). Effects of political advertising. *Public Opinion Quarterly, 40*, 216–228.

Augoustinos, M., & Rosewarne, D. (2001). Stereotype knowledge and prejudice in children. *British Journal of Developmental Psychology, 19*, 143–156.

Axelrod, R. (1967). The structure of public opinion on policy issues. *Public Opinion Quarterly, 31*, 51–60.

Axelrod, R. (1986). Presidential election coalitions in 1984. *American Political Science Review, 80*, 281–284.

Axelrod, S., & Apsche, J. (1982). *The effects of punishment on human behavior.* New York: Academic Press.

Babbie, E. (1990). *Survey research methods* (2nd ed.). Belmont, CA: Wadsworth.

Bachman, J. G., & O'Malley, P. M. (1984). Yea-saying, nay-saying, and going to extremes: Black-white differences in response styles. *Public Opinion Quarterly, 48*, 491–509.

Backstrom, C. H. (1972). Congress and public: How representative is the one of the other? *Public Opinion Quarterly, 36,* 420–421.

Baer, R., Hinkle, S., Smith, K., & Fenton, M. (1980). Reactance as a function of actual versus projected autonomy. *Journal of Personality and Social Psychology, 38,* 416–422.

Bagdikian, B. H. (1962). Bias in the weekly newsmagazines. In R. M. Christenson & R. O. McWilliams (Eds.), *Voice of the people: Readings in public opinion and propaganda* (pp. 148–164). New York: McGraw-Hill.

Bagozzi, R. E. (1981). Attitudes, intentions, and behavior: A test of some key hypotheses. *Journal of Personality and Social Psychology, 41,* 607–627.

Bagozzi, R. P., Tybout, A. M., Craig, C. S., & Sternthal, B. (1979). The construct validity of the tripartite classification of attitudes. *Journal of Marketing Research, 16,* 88–95.

Bailey, D. S. (2003, October). Affirmative action in focus. *Monitor on Psychology, 34*(9), 48–49.

Bain, R. (1928). An attitude on attitude research. *American Journal of Sociology, 33,* 940–957.

Baker, W. D., & Oneal, J. R. (2001). Patriotism or opinion leadership?: The nature and origins of the "rally 'round the flag" effect. *Journal of Conflict Resolution, 45,* 661–687.

Ball-Rokeach, S. J., Grube, J. W., & Rokeach, M. (1981). "Roots: The Next Generation": Who watched and with what effect? *Public Opinion Quarterly, 45,* 58–68.

Ball-Rokeach, S. J., Rokeach, M., & Grube, J. W. (1984). *The great American values test: Influencing behavior and belief through television.* New York: Free Press.

Bamberg, S. (2003). How does environmental concern influence specific environmentally related behaviors?: A new answer to an old question. *Journal of Environmental Psychology, 23,* 21–32.

Banaji, M. R., & Bhaskar, R. (2000). Implicit stereotypes and memory: The bounded rationality of social beliefs. In D. L. Schacter & E. Scarry (Eds.), *Memory, brain, and belief* (pp. 139–175). Cambridge, MA: Harvard University Press.

Banaji, M. R., & Greenwald, A. G. (1994). Implicit stereotyping and prejudice. In M. P. Zanna & J. M. Olson (Eds.), *The psychology of prejudice: The Ontario Symposium* (Vol. 7, pp. 55–76). Hillsdale, NJ: Lawrence Erlbaum Associates.

Banaji, M. R., & Greenwald, A. G. (1995). Implicit gender stereotyping in judgments of fame. *Journal of Personality and Social Psychology, 68,* 181–198.

Bancroft, G., & Welch, E. H. (1946). Recent experience with problems of labor force measurement. *Journal of the American Statistical Association, 41,* 303–312.

Bandura, A. (1977). *Social learning theory.* Englewood Cliffs, NJ: Prentice-Hall.

Banks, W. C. (1976). White preference in blacks: A paradigm in search of a phenomenon. *Psychological Bulletin, 83,* 1179–1186.

Banse, R., Seise, J., & Zerbes, N. (2001). Implicit attitudes towards homosexuality: Reliability, validity, and controllability of the IAT. *Zeitschrift fuer Experimentelle Psychologie, 48,* 145–160.

Barber, T. X., & Silver, M. J. (1968). Fact, fiction, and the experimenter bias effect. *Psychological Bulletin Monograph Supplement, 70* (6, Pt. 2), 1–29.

Bargh, J. A. (1989). Conditional automaticity: Varieties of automatic influence in social perception and cognition. In J. S. Uleman & J. A. Bargh (Eds.), *Unintended thought* (pp. 3–51). New York: Guilford.

Bargh, J. A. (1994). The four horsemen of automaticity: Awareness, intention, efficiency, and control in social cognition. In R. Wyer & T. Srull (Eds.), *Handbook of social cognition* (Vol. 1, pp. 1–40). Hillsdale, NJ: Lawrence Erlbaum Associates.

Bargh, J. A. (1999). The cognitive monster: The case against the controllability of automatic stereotype effects. In S. Chaiken & Y. Trope (Eds.), *Dual-process theories in social psychology* (pp. 361–382). New York: Guilford.

Bargh, J. A. (2001). The psychology of the mere. In J. A. Bargh & D. Apsley (Eds.), *Unraveling the complexities of social life: A festschrift in honor of Robert B. Zajonc* (pp. 25–38). Washington, DC: American Psychological Association.

Bargh, J. A., Chaiken, S., Govender, R., & Pratto, F. (1992). The generality of the automatic attitude activation effect. *Journal of Personality and Social Psychology, 62,* 893–912.

Barone, M. (1997, April/May). Polls are part of the air politicians breathe. *Public Perspective, 8*(3), 1–2.

Barron, R. (1959). Review of the Edwards Personal Preference Schedule. In O. K. Buros (Ed.), *The fifth mental measurements yearbook* (pp. 114–117). Highland Park, NJ: Gryphon.

Barry, H., Bacon, M. K., & Child, I. L. (1957). A cross-cultural survey of some sex differences in socialization. *Journal of Abnormal and Social Psychology, 55,* 327–332.

Bartels, L. (2000). Partisanship and voting behavior, 1952–1996. *American Journal of Political Science, 44,* 35–51.

Bartsch, R. A., & Judd, C. M. (1993). Majority–minority status and perceived ingroup variability revisited. *European Journal of Social Psychology, 23,* 471–483.

Bass, B. M. (1955). Authoritarianism or acquiescence? *Journal of Abnormal and Social Psychology, 51*, 616–623.

Bassili, J. N., & Fletcher, J. F. (1991). Response-time measurement in survey research: A method for CATI and a new look at nonattitudes. *Public Opinion Quarterly, 55*, 331–346.

Bauer, R. A. (1964). The obstinate audience: The influence process from the point of view of social communication. *American Psychologist, 19*, 319–328.

Bauer, R. A. (1966). *Social indicators*. Cambridge, MA: MIT Press.

Bauer, R. A., & Greyser, S. A. (1968). *Advertising in America: The consumer view*. Boston: Graduate School of Business Administration, Harvard University.

Bauman, K. E., & Dent, C. W. (1982). Influence of an objective measure on self-reports of behavior. *Journal of Applied Psychology, 67*, 623–628.

Baumeister, R. F. (1982). A self-presentational view of social phenomena. *Psychological Bulletin, 91*, 3–26.

Baumrind, D. (1985). Research using intentional deception: Ethical issues revisited. *American Psychologist, 40*, 165–174.

Beal, R. S., & Hinckley, R. H. (1984). Presidential decision making and opinion polls. *The Annals of the American Academy of Political and Social Science, 47*, 72–84.

Beaman, A. L., Cole, C. M., Preston, M., Klentz, B., & Steblay, N. M. (1983). Fifteen years of foot-in-the-door research: A meta-analysis. *Personality and Social Psychology Bulletin, 9*, 181–196.

Beasley, R., & Joslyn, M. (2001). Cognitive dissonance and post-decision attitude change in six presidential elections. *Political Psychology, 22*, 521–540.

Beauchamp, T. L., Faden, R. R., Wallace, R. J., Jr., & Walters, I. R. (Eds.). (1982). *Ethical issues in social science research*. Baltimore: Johns Hopkins University Press.

Beckwith, J. B. (1993). Gender stereotypes and mental health revisited. *Social Behavior and Personality, 21*, 85–88.

Begany, J. J., & Milburn, M. (2002). Psychological predictors of sexual harassment: Authoritarianism, hostile sexism, and rape myths. *Psychology of Men and Masculinity, 3*, 119–126.

Behr, R. L., & Iyengar, S. (1985). Television news, real-world cues, and changes in the public agenda. *Public Opinion Quarterly, 49*, 38–57.

Bem, D. J. (1965). An experimental analysis of self-persuasion. *Journal of Experimental Social Psychology, 1*, 199–218.

Bem, D. J. (1967). Self-perception: An alternative interpretation of cognitive dissonance phenomena. *Psychological Review, 74*, 183–200.

Bem, D. J. (1970). *Beliefs, attitudes, and human affairs*. Belmont, CA: Brooks/Cole.

Bem, D. J. (1972). Self-perception theory. In L. Berkowitz (Ed.), *Advances in experimental social psychology* (Vol. 6, pp. 1–62). New York: Academic Press.

Bem, D. J., & McConnell, H. K. (1970). Testing the self-perception explanation of dissonance phenomena: On the salience of premanipulation attitudes. *Journal of Personality and Social Psychology, 14*, 23–31.

Bem, S. L. (1974). The measurement of psychological androgyny. *Journal of Consulting and Clinical Psychology, 42*, 155–162.

Bem, S. L. (1975). Sex role adaptability: One consequence of psychology androgyny. *Journal of Personality and Social Psychology, 31*, 634–643.

Bem, S. L. (1979). Theory and measurement of androgyny: A reply to the Pedhazur-Tetenbaum and Locksley-Colten critiques. *Journal of Personality and Social Psychology, 37*, 1047–1054.

Bem, S. L. (1981). Gender schema theory: A cognitive account of sex typing. *Psychological Review, 88*, 354–364.

Bem, S. L., & Bem, D. J. (1973). Does sex-biased job advertising "aid and abet" sex discrimination? *Journal of Applied Social Psychology, 3*, 6–18.

Benham, T. W. (1965). Polling for a presidential candidate: Some observations on the 1964 campaign. *Public Opinion Quarterly, 29*, 185–199.

Beniger, J. R. (1983). The popular symbolic repertoire and mass communication. *Public Opinion Quarterly, 47*, 479–484.

Bennett, E. (1955). Discussion, decision, commitment and consensus in "group decisions." *Human Relations, 8*, 251–274.

Bennett, S. (1998). Young Americans' indifference to media coverage of public affairs. *PS: Political Science and Politics, 31*, 535–541.

Bennett, W. L. (1975). *The political mind and the political environment*. Lexington, MA: Heath.

Bennett, W. L. (1980). *Public opinion in American politics*. New York: Harcourt Brace Jovanovich.

Bennett, W. L. (1989). Marginalizing the majority: Conditioning public opinion to accept managerial democracy. In M. Margolis & G. A. Mauser (Eds.), *Manipulating public opinion: Essays on public opinion as a dependent variable*. Pacific Grove, CA: Brooks/Cole.

Ben-Shakhar, G., Bar-Hillel, M., & Kremnitzer, M. (2002). Trial by polygraph: Reconsidering the use of the guilty knowledge technique in court. *Law and Human Behavior, 26*, 527–541.

Benson, J. M. (1982). The polls: U.S. military intervention. *Public Opinion Quarterly, 46*, 592–598.

Bentler, P. M., & Speckart, G. (1981). Attitudes "cause" behaviors: A structural equation analysis. *Journal of Personality and Social Psychology, 40*, 226–238.

Berelson, B. R., Lazarsfeld, P. F., & McPhee, W. N. (1954). *Voting: A study of opinion formation in a presidential election*. Chicago: University of Chicago Press.

Berger, J., Rosenholtz, S. J., & Zelditch, M., Jr. (1980). Status organizing processes. *Annual Review of Sociology, 6*, 479–508.

Berkowitz, L. (1972). Social norms, feelings, and other factors affecting helping and altruism. In L. Berkowitz (Ed.), *Advances in experimental social psychology* (Vol. 6, pp. 63–108). New York: Academic Press.

Berkowitz, L., & Donnerstein, E. (1982). External validity is more than skin deep: Some answers to criticisms of laboratory experiments. *American Psychologist, 37*, 245–257.

Berkun, M. M., Bialek, H. M., Kern, R. P., & Yagi, K. (1962). Experimental studies of psychological stress in man. *Psychological Monographs, 76*(15, Whole No. 534).

Berman, D. R., & Stookey, J. (1980). Adolescents, television, and support for government. *Public Opinion Quarterly, 44*, 330–340.

Bermant, G., Kelman, H. C., & Warwick, D. P. (Eds.). (1978). *The ethics of social intervention*. Washington, DC: Hemisphere.

Berzins, J. L., Welling, M. A., & Wetter, R. E. (1978). A new measure of psychological androgyny based on the Personality Research Form. *Journal of Consulting and Clinical Psychology, 46*, 126–138.

Best, D., & Williams, J. (1998). Masculinity and femininity in the self and ideal self descriptions of university students in 14 countries. In G. Hofstede (Ed.), *Masculinity and femininity: The taboo dimension of national cultures* (pp. 106–116).Thousand Oaks, CA: Sage.

Bettman, J. R., & Weitz, B. A. (1983). Attributions in the boardroom: Causal reasoning in corporate annual reports. *Administrative Science Quarterly, 28*, 165–183.

Bickman, L. (Ed.). (2000). *Validity and social experimentation: Donald Campbell's legacy*. Thousand Oaks, CA: Sage.

Bierbrauer, G. (1973). *Effect of set, perspective, and temporal factors in attribution research*. Unpublished doctoral dissertation, Stanford University, Stanford, CA.

Billiet, J., & Loosveldt, G. (1988). Improvement of the quality of responses to factual survey questions by interviewer training. *Public Opinion Quarterly, 52*, 190–211.

Bird, C. (1968). *Born female: The high cost of keeping women down*. New York: McKay.

Bishop, G. F. (1976). The effect of education on ideological consistency. *Public Opinion Quarterly, 40*, 337–348.

Bishop, G. F., & Fisher, B. S. (1995). "Secret ballots" and self-reports in an exit-poll experiment. *Public Opinion Quarterly, 59*, 568–588.

Bishop, G. F., & Frankovic, K. A. (1981). Ideological consensus and constraint among party leaders and followers in the 1978 election. *Micropolitics, 1*, 87–111.

Bishop, G. F., Oldendick, R. W., & Tuchfarber, A. J. (1982). Effects of presenting one versus two sides of an issue in survey questions. *Public Opinion Quarterly, 46*, 69–85.

Bishop, G. F., Oldendick, R. W., Tuchfarber, A. J., & Bennett, S. E. (1978). The changing structure of mass belief systems: Fact or artifact? *Journal of Politics, 40*, 781–787.

Bishop, G. F., & Smith, A. (1991). Gallup split ballot experiments. *Public Perspective, 2*(5), 25–27.

Bishop, G. F., Tuchfarber, A. J., & Oldendick, R. W. (1986). Opinions on fictitious issues: The pressure to answer survey questions. *Public Opinion Quarterly, 50*, 240–250.

Blair, S. (1992). The sex-typing of children's household labor. Parental influence on daughters' and sons' housework. *Youth and Society, 24*, 178–203.

Blakemore, J. E. (2003). Children's beliefs about violating gender norms: Boys shouldn't look like girls, and girls shouldn't act like boys. *Sex Roles, 48*, 411–419.

Blakemore, J. E., LaRue, A. A., & Olejnik, A. B. (1979). Sex-appropriate toy preference and the ability to conceptualize toys as sex-role related. *Developmental Psychology, 15*, 339–340.

Blanchflower, D. G., & Oswald, A. J. (2000). *Well-being over time in Britain and the USA* (Working Paper 7487). Cambridge, MA: National Bureau of Economic Research.

Blanton, S. L. (1996). Images in conflict: The case of Ronald Reagan and El Salvador. *International Studies Quarterly, 40*, 23–44.

Blee, K. M., & Tickamyer, A. (1995). Racial differences in men's attitudes about women's gender roles. *Journal of Marriage and the Family, 57*, 21–30.

Blendon, R. J., Benson, J. M., Morin, R., Altman, D. E., Brodie, M., Brossard, M., & James, M. (1997). Changing attitudes in America. In J. S. Nye, Jr., P. D. Zelikow, & D. C. King (Eds.), *Why people don't trust government* (pp. 205–216). Cambridge, MA: Harvard University Press.

Blendon, R. J., Young, J. T., & Hemenway, D. (1996). The American public and the gun control debate. *Journal of the American Medical Association, 275*, 1719–1722.

Block, J. H. (1973). Conceptions of sex role: Some cross-cultural and longitudinal perspectives. *American Psychologist, 28*, 512–526.

Block, J. H., & Funder, D. (1986). Social roles and social perception: Individual differences in attribution and error. *Journal of Personality and Social Psychology, 51*, 1200–1207.

Blood, R. O., Jr., & Wolfe, D. M. (1960). *Husbands and wives: The dynamics of married living.* New York: Free Press.

Blumenthal, S. (1982). *The permanent campaign.* New York: Simon & Schuster.

Blumler, J. G., & McQuail, D. (1969). *Television in politics: Its uses and influence.* Chicago: University of Chicago Press.

Bobo, L. (1983). Whites' opposition to busing: Symbolic racism or realistic group conflict? *Journal of Personality and Social Psychology, 45*, 1196–1210.

Bobo, L. (1988). Group conflict, prejudice, and the paradox of contemporary racial attitudes. In P. A. Katz & D. A. Taylor (Eds.), *Eliminating racism: Profiles in controversy* (pp. 85–114). New York: Plenum.

Bobo, L. D. (1999). Prejudice as group position: Microfoundations of a sociological approach to racism and race relations. *Journal of Social Issues, 55*, 445–472.

Bochner, S. (Ed.). (1982). *Cultures in contact: Studies in cross-cultural interaction.* Elmsford, NY: Pergamon.

Bochner, S., & Insko, C. A. (1966). Communicator discrepancy, source credibility, and opinion change. *Journal of Personality and Social Psychology, 4*, 614–621.

Bogardus, E. S. (1925). Measuring social distance. *Journal of Applied Sociology, 9*, 299–308.

Bogardus, E. S. (1928). *Immigration and race attitudes.* Boston: Heath.

Bogart, L. (1972a). *Silent politics: Polls and the awareness of public opinion.* New York: Wiley-Interscience.

Bogart, L. (1972b). Warning: The Surgeon General has determined that TV violence is moderately dangerous to your child's mental health. *Public Opinion Quarterly, 36*, 491–521.

Bogart, L. (1998). Politics, polls, and poltergeists. *Society, 35*(4), 8–16.

Bogner, F. X., & Wiseman, M. (1997). Environmental perception of rural and urban pupils. *Journal of Environmental Psychology, 17*, 111–122.

Boniecki, K., & Jacks, J. Z. (2002). The elusive relationship between measures of implicit and explicit prejudice. *Representative Research in Social Psychology, 26*, 1–14.

Borden, B. (1977, April). *Social stereotypes among college undergraduates.* Paper presented at Western Psychological Association meeting, Seattle, WA.

Borden, R., & Francis, J. (1978). Who cares about ecology? Personality and sex differences in environmental concern. *Journal of Personality, 46*, 190–203.

Borgida, E., & Brekke, N. (1981). The base rate fallacy in attribution and prediction. In J. H. Harvey, W. J. Ickes, & R. F. Kidd (Eds.), *New directions in attribution research* (Vol. 3). Hillsdale, NJ: Lawrence Erlbaum Associates.

Borgida, E., & Campbell, B. (1982). Belief relevance and attitude–behavior consistency: The moderating role of personal experience. *Journal of Personality and Social Psychology, 42*, 239–247.

Borgida, E., & Nisbett, R. E. (1977). The differential impact of abstract vs. concrete information on decisions. *Journal of Applied Social Psychology, 7*, 258–271.

Boster, F. J., & Mongeau, P. (1984). Fear-arousing persuasive messages. In R. N. Bostrom (Ed.), *Communication yearbook* (Vol. 8, pp. 330–375). Beverly Hills, CA: Sage.

Bradburn, N. M., & Sudman, S. (1979). *Improving interviewing method and questionnaire design.* San Francisco: Jossey-Bass.

Bradburn, N. M., & Sudman, S. (1988). *Polls & surveys: Understanding what they tell us.* San Francisco: Jossey-Bass.

Brady, H. E., Herron, M. C., Mebane, W. R., Jr., Sekhon, J. S., Shotts, K. W., & Wand, J. (2001). Law and data: The butterfly ballot episode. *PS: Political Science and Politics, 34*, 59–69.

Brady, H. E., & Johnston, R. (1987). What's the primary message: Horse race or issue journalism? In G. R. Orren & N. W. Polsby (Eds.), *Media and momentum: The New Hampshire primary and nomination politics.* Chatham, NJ: Chatham House.

Brady, H. E., & Orren, G. R. (1992). Sources of error in public opinion surveys. In T. E. Mann & G. R. Orren (Eds.), *Media polls in American politics.* Washington, DC: Brookings Institute.

Brady, H. E., & Sniderman, P. M. (1985). Attitude attribution: A group basis for political reasoning. *American Political Science Review, 79*, 1061–1078.

Bragg, E. A. (1996). Towards ecological self: Deep ecology meets constructionist self-theory. *Journal of Environmental Psychology, 16*, 93–108.

Bramel, D. (1963). Selection of a target for defensive projection. *Journal of Abnormal and Social Psychology, 66*, 318–324.

Breckler, S. I. (1984). Empirical validation of affect, behavior, and cognition as distinct components of attitude. *Journal of Personality and Social Psychology, 47*, 1191–1205.

Brehm, J. (1993). *The phantom respondents: Opinion surveys and political representation.* Ann Arbor: University of Michigan Press.

Brehm, J. W. (1966). *A theory of psychological reactance.* New York: Academic Press.

Brehm, J. W., & Cohen, A. R. (1962). *Explorations in cognitive dissonance.* New York: Wiley.

Brehm, S. S., & Brehm, J. W. (1981). *Psychological reactance: A theory of freedom and control.* New York: Academic Press.

Brent, E., & Granberg, D. (1982). Subjective agreement with the presidential candidates of 1976 and 1980. *Journal of Personality and Social Psychology, 42*, 393–403.

Brewer, M. B. (1999). The psychology of prejudice: Ingroup love or outgroup hate? *Journal of Social Issues, 55*, 429–444.

Brewer, M. B. (2000). Reducing prejudice through cross-categorization: Effects of multiple social identities. In S. Oskamp (Ed.), *Reducing prejudice and discrimination* (pp. 165–183). Mahwah, NJ: Lawrence Erlbaum Associates.

Brewer, M. B. (2001). Ingroup identification and intergroup conflict: When does ingroup love become outgroup hate? In R. Ashmore, L. Jussim, & D. Wilder (Eds.), *Social identity, intergroup conflict, and conflict reduction* (pp. 17–41). New York: Oxford University Press.

Brewer, M. B., & Kramer, R. M. (1985). The psychology of intergroup attitudes and behavior. *Annual Review of Psychology, 36*, 219–243.

Brewer, M. B., & Miller, N. (1984). Beyond the contact hypothesis: Theoretical perspectives on desegregation. In N. Miller & M. B. Brewer (Eds.), *Groups in contact: The psychology of desegregation* (pp. 281–302). Orlando, FL: Academic Press.

Brewer, P. R. (2002). Public opinion, economic issues, and the vote: Are presidential elections "all about the Benjamins"? In B. Norrander & C. Wilcox (Eds.), *Understanding public opinion* (2nd ed., pp. 243–262). Washington, DC: Congressional Quarterly.

Brians, C. L., & Wattenberg, M. P. (1996). Campaign issue knowledge and salience: Comparing reception from TV commercials, TV news, and newspapers. *American Journal of Political Science, 40*, 172–193.

Bridges, S., & Rodriguez, W. (2000). Gay-friendly affiliation, community size, and color of address in return of lost letters. *North American Journal of Psychology, 2*, 39–45.

Briere, J., & Lanktree, C. (1983). Sex-role related effects of sex bias in language. *Sex Roles, 9*, 625–632.

Brigham, J. C., & Cook, S. W. (1970). The influence of attitude and judgments of plausibility: A replication and extension. *Educational and Psychological Measurement, 30*, 283–292.

Briñol, P., & Petty, R. (2003). Overt head movements and persuasion: A self-validation analysis. *Journal of Personality and Social Psychology, 84*, 1123–1139.

Brock, T. C., & Shavitt, S. (1983). Cognitive-response analysis in advertising. In L. Percy & A. Woodside (Eds.), *Advertising and consumer psychology.* Lexington, MA: Heath.

Brodt, S. E., & Zimbardo, E. G. (1981). Modifying shyness-related social behavior through symptom misattribution. *Journal of Personality and Social Psychology, 41*, 437–449.

Brody, R. A., & Shapiro, C. R. (1989). Policy failure and public support: The Iran-Contra affair and public assessment of President Reagan. *Political Behavior, 11*, 353–370.

Brody, R. A., & Sigelman, L. (1983). Presidential popularity and presidential elections: An update and extension. *Public Opinion Quarterly, 47*, 325–328.

Bronfenbrenner, U. (1961). The mirror image in Soviet–American relations: A social psychologist's report. *Journal of Social Issues, 17*(3), 45–56.

Brooks, G. R. (2000). The role of gender in marital dysfunction. In R. M. Eisler (Ed.), *Handbook of gender, culture, and health* (pp. 449–470). Mahwah, NJ: Lawrence Erlbaum Associates.

Brooks, G. R., & Gilbert, L. A. (1997). Men in families: Old constraints, new possibilities. In R. F. Levant & W. S. Pollack (Eds.), *A new psychology of men* (pp. 252–279). New York: Basic Books.

Broverman, I. K., Broverman, D. M., Clarkson, F. E., Rosenkrantz, E. S., & Vogel, S. R. (1970). Sex-role stereotypes and clinical judgments of mental health. *Journal of Consulting and Clinical Psychology, 34*, 1–7.

Brown, L. R. (1999). Feeding nine billion. In L. R. Brown et al., *State of the world 1999* (pp. 115–132). New York: Norton.

Brown, L. R., & Flavin, C. (1999). A new economy for a new century. In L. R. Brown et al., *State of the world 1999* (pp. 3–21). New York: Norton.

Brown, R. (1965). *Social psychology.* New York: Free Press.

Brown, R. (1995). *Prejudice: Its social psychology.* Oxford, England: Blackwell.

Brownstein, R. (2004, June 11). Going to war not worth it, more voters say. *Los Angeles Times*, pp. 1, 31.

Bryant, D., Nielsen, D., & Tangley, L. (1997). *The last frontier forests: Ecosystems and economies on the edge.* Washington, DC: World Resources Institute.

Bryant, J., & Miron, D. (2002). Entertainment as media effect. In J. Bryant & D. Zillmann (Eds.), *Media effects: Advances in theory and research* (pp. 549–582). Mahwah, NJ: Lawrence Erlbaum Associates.

Buchanan, W. (1986). Election predictions: An empirical assessment. *Public Opinion Quarterly, 50*, 222–227.

Buchanan, W., & Cantril, H. (1953). *How nations see each other: A study in public opinion.* Urbana: University of Illinois Press.

Buckingham, D. (2000). *The making of citizens: Young people, news, and politics.* London, England: Routledge.

Budd, R. I., & Spencer, C. (1984). Latitude of rejection, centrality and certainty: Variables affecting the relationship between attitudes, norms and behavioral intentions. *British Journal of Social Psychology, 23*, 1–8.

Burger, J. M., & Caldwell, D. F. (2003). The effects of monetary incentives and labeling on the foot-in-the-door effect: Evidence for a self-perception process. *Basic and Applied Social Psychology, 25*, 235–241.

Burger, J. M., & Guadagno, R. (2003). Self-concept clarity and the foot-in-the-door procedure. *Basic and Applied Social Psychology, 25*, 79–86.

Burgoon, M., & Klingle, R. (1998). Gender differences in being influential and/or influenced: A challenge to prior explanations. In D. Canary & K. Dindia (Eds.), *Sex differences and similarities in communication: Critical essays and empirical investigations of sex and gender in interaction* (pp. 257–285). Mahwah, NJ: Lawrence Erlbaum Associates.

Burkholder, R. (2003, February 14). Unwilling coalition? Majorities in Britain, Canada oppose military action in Iraq. *Gallup Poll Tuesday Briefing*, pp. 38–41.

Burn, S. M., & Oskamp, S. (1989). Ingroup biases and the U.S.–Soviet conflict. *Journal of Social Issues, 45*(2), 73–89.

Burnham, W. D. (1970). *Critical elections and the mainsprings of American politics.* New York: Norton.

Burnham, W. D. (1985). The 1984 election and the future of American politics. In E. Sandoz & C. V. Crabb, Jr. (Eds.), *Election 84: Landslide without a mandate?* (pp. 204–260). New York: New American Library.

Burnham, W. D. (1991). Critical realignment: Dead or alive? In B. E. Shafer (Ed.), *The end of realignment? Interpreting American electoral eras* (pp. 101–139). Madison: University of Wisconsin Press.

Busch, R. J., & Lieske, J. A. (1985). Does time of voting affect exit poll results? *Public Opinion Quarterly, 49*, 94–104.

Buss, D. M. (1995). Psychological sex differences: Origins through sexual selection. *American Psychologist, 50*, 164–168.

Buss, D. M., Abbott, M., Angleitner, A., Biaggio, A., Blanco-Villasenor, A., Bruchon-Schweitzer, M., et al. (1990). International preferences in selecting mates: A study of 37 cultures. *Journal of Cross-Cultural Psychology, 21*, 5–47.

Buss, D. M., & Kenrick, D. T. (1998). Evolutionary social psychology. In D. T. Gilbert, S. T. Fiske, & G. Lindzey (Eds.), *The handbook of social psychology* (4th ed., Vol. 2, pp. 982–1026). New York: McGraw-Hill.

Butler, D., & Stokes, D. (1974). *Political change in Britain.* New York: St. Martin's.

Butler, M., & Paisley, W. (Eds.). (1980). *Women and the mass media: Sourcebook for research and action.* New York: Human Sciences Press.

Byrne, D. (1971). *The attraction paradigm.* New York: Academic Press.

Cacioppo, J. T., Bush, L. K., & Tassinary, L. G. (1992). Microexpressive facial actions as a function of affective stimuli: Replication and extension. *Personality and Social Psychology Bulletin, 18*, 515–526.

Cacioppo, J. T., Crites, S. L., Berntson, G. G., & Coles, M. G. (1993). If attitudes affect how stimuli are processed, should they not affect the event-related brain potential? *Psychological Science, 4*, 108–112.

Cacioppo, J. T., Crites, S. L., & Gardner, W. L. (1996). Attitudes to the right: Evaluative processing is associated with lateralized late positive event-related brain potentials. *Personality and Social Psychology Bulletin, 22*, 1205–1219.

Cacioppo, J. T., Crites, S. L., Gardner, W. L., & Berntson, G. G. (1994). Bioelectrical echoes from evaluative categorization: I. A late positive brain potential that varies as a function of trait negativity and extremity. *Journal of Personality and Social Psychology, 67*, 115–125.

Cacioppo, J. T., Gardner, W. L., & Berntson, G. G. (1997). Beyond bipolar conceptualizations and measures: The case of attitudes and evaluative space. *Personality and Social Psychology Review, 1*, 3–25.

Cacioppo, J. T., Marshall-Goodell, B. S., Tassinary, L. G., & Petty, R. E. (1992). Rudimentary determinants of attitudes: Classical conditioning is more effective when prior knowledge about the attitude stimulus is low than high. *Journal of Experimental Social Psychology, 28*, 207–233.

Cacioppo, J. T., & Petty, R. E. (1979). Effects of message repetition and position on cognitive responses, recall, and persuasion. *Journal of Personality and Social Psychology, 37*, 97–109.

Cacioppo, J. T., & Petty, R. E. (1980). Sex differences in influenceability: Toward specifying the underlying processes. *Personality and Social Psychology Bulletin, 6*, 651–656.

Cacioppo, J. T., & Petty, R. E. (1981a). Effects of extent of thought on the pleasantness ratings of P-O-X triads: Evidence for three judgmental tendencies in evaluating social situations. *Journal of Personality and Social Psychology, 40*, 1000–1009.

Cacioppo, J. T., & Petty, R. E. (1981b). Social psychological procedures for cognitive response assessment: The thought-listing technique. In T. V. Merluzzi, C. R. Glass, & M. Genest (Eds.), *Cognitive assessment.* New York: Guilford.

Cacioppo, J. T., & Petty, R. E. (1983). *Social psychophysiology: A sourcebook.* New York: Guilford.

Cacioppo, J. T., Petty, R. E., Feinstein, J., & Jarvis, B. (1996). Dispositional differences in cognitive motivation: The life and times of individuals varying in need for cognition. *Psychological Bulletin, 119*, 197–253.

Cacioppo, J. T., Petty, R. E., Kao, C., & Rodriguez, A. (1986). Central and peripheral routes to persuasion: An individual differences perspective. *Journal of Personality and Social Psychology, 51*, 1032–1043.

Cacioppo, J. T., Petty, R. E., Losch, M., & Kim, H. S. (1986). Electromyographic activity over facial muscle regions can differentiate the valence and intensity of affective reactions. *Journal of Personality and Social Psychology, 50*, 260–268.

Cacioppo, J. T., Petty, R. E., & Marshall-Goodell, B. S. (1984). Electromyographic specificity during simple physical and attitudinal tasks: Location and topographical features of integrated EMG responses. *Biological Psychology, 18*, 85–121.

Cahalan, D. (1968). Correlates of respondent inaccuracy in the Denver validity study. *Public Opinion Quarterly, 32*, 607–621.

Cahalan, D. (1989). The *Digest* poll rides again! *Public Opinion Quarterly, 53*, 129–133.

Calder, I. J., Insko, C. A., & Yandell, B. (1974). The relation of cognitive and memorial processes to persuasion in a simulated jury trial. *Journal of Applied Social Psychology, 4*, 62–93.

Calvo, D., Jensen, E., & Simon, R. (2002, November 6). Networks, voters forced to wait for count as exit poll system collapses. *Los Angeles Times*, p. A14.

Campbell, A. (1962). Has television reshaped politics? *Columbia Journalism Review, 1*(2), 10–13.

Campbell, A. (1964). Voters and elections: Past and present. *Journal of Politics, 26*, 745–757.

Campbell, A. (1966). A classification of presidential elections. In A. Campbell, P. E. Converse, W. E. Miller, & D. E. Stokes, *Elections and the political order* (pp. 66–77). New York: Wiley.

Campbell, A. (1971). *White attitudes toward black people.* Ann Arbor: Institute for Social Research, University of Michigan.

Campbell, A. (1981). *The sense of well-being in America: Recent patterns and trends.* New York: McGraw-Hill.

Campbell, A., Converse, P. E., Miller, W. E., & Stokes, D. E. (1960). *The American voter.* New York: Wiley.

Campbell, A., Converse, P. E., & Rodgers, W. L. (1976). *The quality of American life: Perceptions, evaluations, and satisfactions.* New York: Russell Sage Foundation.

Campbell, A., Gurin, G., & Miller, W. E. (1954). *The voter decides.* New York: Harper & Row.

Campbell, A., & Stokes, D. E. (1959). Partisan attitudes and the presidential vote. In E. Burdick & A. J. Brodbeck (Eds.), *American voting behavior* (pp. 353–371). Glencoe, IL: Free Press.

Campbell, D. T. (1947). *The generality of social attitudes.* Unpublished doctoral dissertation, University of California, Berkeley.

Campbell, D. T. (1963). Social attitudes and other acquired behavioral dispositions. In S. Koch (Ed.), *Psychology: A study of a science* (Vol. 6, pp. 94–172). New York: McGraw-Hill.

Campbell, D. T. (1967). Stereotypes and the perception of group differences. *American Psychologist, 22*, 817–829.

Campbell, D. T. (1988). The experimenting society. In D. T. Campbell & S. Overman (Eds.), *Methodology and epistemology for social science: Selected papers* (pp. 290–314). Chicago: University of Chicago Press.

Campbell, D. T., & Stanley, J. C. (1966). *Experimental and quasi-experimental designs for research.* Chicago: Rand McNally.

Canary, D. J., & Seibold, D. R. (1984). *Attitude and behavior: An annotated bibliography.* New York: Praeger.

Cannell, C. F., Groves, R. M., Magilavy, L. J., Mathiowetz, N. A., Miller, P. V., & Thornberry, O. T. (1987). *An experimental comparison of telephone and personal health interview surveys* (Vital and health statistics, ser. 2, no. 106. DHHS pub. no. (PHS)87-1380). Washington, DC: U.S. Government Printing Office.

Cannell, C. F., Miller, P. V., & Oksenberg, L. (1981). Research on interviewing techniques. In S. Leinhardt (Ed.), *Sociological methodology*. San Francisco: Jossey-Bass.

Canon, L. K., & Mathews, K. E., Jr. (1972). Concern over personal health and smoking-relevant beliefs and behavior. *Proceedings of the 80th Annual Convention of the American Psychological Association, 7*, 271–272.

Cantril, A. H., & Cantril, S. D. (1991). *The opinion connection: Polling, politics, and the press*. Washington, DC: Congressional Quarterly.

Cantril, A. H., & Cantril, S. D. (1999). *Reading mixed signals: Ambivalence in American public opinion about government*. Washington, DC: Woodrow Wilson Center Press.

Cantril, H. (1940). *The invasion from Mars*. Princeton, NJ: Princeton University Press.

Cantril, H. (1967). *The human dimension: Experiences in policy research*. New Brunswick, NJ: Rutgers University Press.

Cantril, H., & Allport, G. W. (1935). *The psychology of radio*. New York: Harper.

Caplan, N. (1970). The new ghetto man: A review of recent empirical studies. *Journal of Social Issues, 26*(1), 59–73.

Caplan, N., Morrison, A., & Stambaugh, R. J. (1975). *The use of social science knowledge in policy decisions at the national level: A report to respondents*. Ann Arbor: Institute for Social Research, University of Michigan.

Caplow, T. (1982). Decades of public opinion: Comparing NORC and Middletown data. *Public Opinion, 5*(5), 30–31.

Caplow, T., Hicks, L., & Wattenberg, B. (2000). *The first measured century: An illustrated guide to trends in America: 1900–2000*. Washington, DC: Institute Press.

Cappella, J. N., Turow, J., & Jamieson, K. H. (1996). *Call-in political talk radio: Background, content, audiences, portrayal in mainstream media*. Philadelphia: University of Pennsylvania, Annenberg Public Policy Center.

Carli, L., & Eagly, A. H. (1999). Gender effects on social influence and emergent leadership. In G. Powell (Ed.), *Handbook of gender and work* (pp. 203–222). Thousand Oaks, CA: Sage.

Carlsmith, J. M., Collins, B. E., & Helmreich, R. L. (1966). Studies on forced compliance: I. The effect of pressure for compliance on attitude change produced by face-to-face role-playing and anonymous essay writing. *Journal of Personality and Social Psychology, 4*, 1–13.

Carlson, D. K. (2000, January). Who's who? Gallup polls the public on prominent public figures. *Gallup Poll Monthly*, No. 412, pp. 63–65.

Carlson, D. K. (2002, September 10). One year later, concern for civil liberty rising. *Gallup Poll Tuesday Briefing*, p. 40.

Carlson, D. K. (2003a, March 11). Inspecting the inspectors: Public rates U.N. *Gallup Poll Tuesday Briefing*, pp. 12–13.

Carlson, D. K. (2003b, March 25). Public convinced Saddam is a terrorist. *Gallup Poll Tuesday Briefing*, pp. 38–39.

Carlson, D. K. (2003c, May 6). Iraq War: Did Americans take it personally? *Gallup Poll Tuesday Briefing*, pp. 9–10.

Carlson, E. R. (1956). Attitude change through modification of attitude structure. *Journal of Abnormal and Social Psychology, 52*, 256–261.

Carlston, D. E., & Cohen, J. L. (1980). A closer examination of subject roles. *Journal of Personality and Social Psychology, 38*, 857–870.

Carpenter, S. J. (2001). *Implicit gender attitudes*. Unpublished doctoral dissertation, Yale University, New Haven, CT.

Carter, D. B., & McCloskey, L. A. (1983–1984). Peers and the maintenance of sex-typed behavior: The development of children's conceptions of cross-gender behavior in their peers. *Social Cognition, 2*, 294–314.

Cartwright, D., & Harary, E. (1956). Structural balance: A generalization of Heider's theory. *Psychological Review, 63*, 277–293.

CDC AIDS Community Demonstration Projects Research Group. (1999). The CDC AIDS Community Demonstration Projects: A multi-site community-level intervention to promote HIV risk reduction. *American Journal of Public Health, 89*, 336–345.

Cervone, D., & Peake, E. K. (1986). Anchoring, efficacy, and action: The influence of judgmental heuristics on self-efficacy judgments and behavior. *Journal of Personality and Social Psychology, 50*, 492–501.

Chafe, W. H. (1976). Looking backward in order to look forward: Women, work and social values in America. In J. M. Kreps (Ed.), *Women and the American economy: A look to the 1980's*. Englewood Cliffs, NJ: Prentice-Hall.

Chafetz, J. S. (1974). *Masculine, feminine or human? An overview of the sociology of sex roles*. Itasca, IL: Peacock.

Chaffee, S. H., & Yang, S. M. (1990). Communication and political socialization. In O. Ichilov (Ed.), *Political socialization, citizenship education, and democracy* (pp. 137–157). New York: Teachers College Press.

Chaiken, S. (1980). Heuristic versus systematic information processing and the use of source versus message cues in persuasion. *Journal of Personality and Social Psychology, 39*, 752–766.

Chaiken, S., & Baldwin, M. W. (1981). Affective-cognitive consistency and the effect of salient behavioral information on the self-perception of attitudes. *Journal of Personality and Social Psychology, 41*, 1–12.

Chaiken, S., & Eagly, A. H. (1976). Communication modality as a determinant of message persuasiveness and message comprehensibility. *Journal of Personality and Social Psychology, 34*, 605–614.

Chaiken, S., Giner-Sorolla, R., & Chen, S. (1996). Beyond accuracy: Defense and impression motives in heuristic and systematic information processing. In P. M. Gollwitzer & J. A. Bargh (Eds.), *The psychology of action: Linking cognition and motivation to behavior* (pp. 553–578). New York: Guilford.

Chaiken, S., Pomerantz, E. M., & Giner-Sorolla, R. (1995). Structural consistency and attitude strength. In R. E. Petty & J. A. Krosnick (Eds.), *Attitude strength: Antecedents and consequences* (pp. 387–412). Hillsdale, NJ: Lawrence Erlbaum Associates.

Chaiken, S., & Stangor, C. (1987). Attitudes and attitude change. *Annual Review of Psychology, 38*, 575–630.

Chaiken, S., & Trope, Y. (Eds.). (1999). *Dual-process theories in social psychology*. New York: Guilford.

Chaiken, S., Wood, W., & Eagly, A. H. (1996). Principles of persuasion. In E. Higgins & A. Kruglanski (Eds.), *Social psychology: Handbook of basic principles* (pp. 702–742). New York: Guilford.

Chanley, V. A., Rudolph, T. J., & Rahn, W. M. (2000). The origins and consequences of public trust in government: A time series analysis. *Public Opinion Quarterly, 64*, 239–256.

Chapanis, N. E., & Chapanis, A. (1964). Cognitive dissonance: Five years later. *Psychological Bulletin, 61*, 1–22.

Chawla, L. (1998). Significant life experiences revisited: A review of research. *Journal of Environmental Education, 29*, 11–22.

Chawla, L. (1999). Life paths into effective environmental action. *Journal of Environmental Education, 31*, 15–26.

Chen, H., Reardon, R., Rea, C., & Moore, D. (1992). Forewarning of content and involvement: Consequences for persuasion and resistance to persuasion. *Journal of Experimental Social Psychology, 28*, 523–541.

Chen, S., & Chaiken, S. (1999). The heuristic-systematic model in its broader context. In S. Chaiken & Y. Trope (Eds.), *Dual-process theories in social psychology* (pp. 73–96). New York: Guilford.

Chesler, P. (1972). *Women and madness*. Garden City, NY: Doubleday.

Chethick, M., Fleming, E., Meyer, M. F., & McCoy, J. N. (1967). Quest for identity. *American Journal of Orthopsychiatry, 37*, 71–77.

Cheung, G., & Rensvold, R. (2000). Assessing extreme and acquiescence response sets in cross-cultural research using structural equations modeling. *Journal of Cross-Cultural Psychology, 31*, 187–212.

Childs, H. L. (1965). *Public opinion: Nature, formation, and role*. Princeton, NJ: Van Nostrand.

Chivian, E., Chivian, S., Lifton, R. J., & Mack, J. E. (Eds.). (1982). *Last aid: The medical dimensions of nuclear war*. San Francisco: Freeman.

Choi, I., & Nisbett, R. E. (2000). Cultural psychology of surprise: Holistic theories and recognition of contradiction. *Journal of Personality and Social Psychology, 79*, 890–905.

Choi, N., & Fuqua, D. (2003). The structure of the Bem Sex Role Inventory: A summary report of 23 validation studies. *Educational and Psychological Measurement, 63*, 872–887.

Christensen, L. (1988). Deception in psychological research: When is its use justified? *Personality and Social Psychology Bulletin, 14*, 664–675.

Christenson, P. G., & Roberts, D. F. (1983). The role of television in the formation of children's social attitudes. In M. J. A. Howe (Ed.), *Learning from television: Psychological and educational research* (pp. 79–99). London, England: Academic Press.

Christie, R., & Jahoda, M. (Eds.). (1954). *Studies in the scope and method of the authoritarian personality*. New York: Free Press.

Christie, R., Havel, J., & Seidenberg, B. (1958). Is the F scale irreversible? *Journal of Abnormal and Social Psychology, 56*, 143–159.

Church, G. J. (1987, June 22). Back to the wall: Reagan rallies with a strong speech. *Time*, pp. 18–20.

Cialdini, R. B. (2000). *Influence: Science and practice* (4th ed.). Boston: Allyn & Bacon.

Cialdini, R. B., Levy, A., Herman, P., Kozlowski, L., & Petty, R. E. (1976). Elastic shifts of opinion: Determinants of direction and durability. *Journal of Personality and Social Psychology, 34*, 663–672.

Cialdini, R. B., & Petty, R. E. (1981). Anticipatory opinion effects. In R. E. Petty, T. M. Ostrom, & T. C. Brock (Eds.), *Cognitive responses in persuasion* (pp. 217–235). Hillsdale, NJ: Lawrence Erlbaum Associates.

Cialdini, R. B., Petty, R. E., & Cacioppo, J. T. (1981). Attitude and attitude change. *Annual Review of Psychology, 32*, 357–404.

Cialdini, R. B., & Trost, M. R. (1998). Social influence: Social norms, conformity, and compliance. In D. T. Gilbert, S. T. Fiske, & G. Lindzey (Eds.), *The handbook of social psychology* (4th ed., Vol. 2, pp. 151–192). Boston: McGraw-Hill.

Cialdini, R. B., Trost, M. R., & Newsom, J. T. (1995). Preference for consistency: The development of a valid measure and the discovery of surprising behavioral implications. *Journal of Personality and Social Psychology, 69*, 318–328.

Citrin, J., & Luks, S. (2001). Political trust revisited: *Deja vu* all over again? In J. R. Hibbing & E. Theiss-Morse (Eds.), *What is it about government that Americans dislike?* (pp. 9–27). Cambridge, England: Cambridge University Press.

Clark, C. C. (1969). Television and social controls: Some observations on the portrayal of ethnic minorities. *Television Quarterly, 8*, 18–22.

Clark, K. B., & Clark, M. P. (1947). Racial identification and preference in Negro children. In T. M. Newcomb & E. L. Hartley (Eds.), *Readings in social psychology* (pp. 169–178). New York: Holt, Rinehart & Winston.

Clark, R., Almeida, M., Gurka, T., & Middleton, L. (2003). Engendering tots with Caldecotts: An updated update. In E. S. Adler & R. Clark (Eds.), *How it's done: An invitation to social research* (2nd ed., pp. 379–385). Belmont, CA: Wadsworth.

Clary, E. G., Snyder, M., Ridge, R. D., Miene, P. K., & Haugen, J. A. (1994). Matching messages to motives in persuasion: A functional approach to promoting volunteerism. *Journal of Applied Social Psychology, 24*, 1129–1149.

Clayton, S. D. (2003). Environmental identity: A conceptual and an operational definition. In S. D. Clayton & S. V. Opotow (Eds.), *Identity and the natural environment: The psychological significance of nature* (pp. 45–65). Cambridge, MA: MIT Press.

Clayton, S. D., & Crosby, F. J. (1992). *Justice, gender, and affirmative action.* Ann Arbor: University of Michigan Press.

Clayton, S. D., & Opotow, S. V. (Eds.). (2003). *Identity and the natural environment.* Cambridge, MA: MIT Press.

CNN.com. (2002, November 22). Global goofs: U.S. youth can't find Iraq. Retrieved July 9, 2003, from http://edition.cnn.com/2002/EDUCATION/11/20/geography.quiz/index.html

Cnudde, C. F., & McCrone, D. J. (1966). The linkage between constituency attitudes and Congressional voting behavior: A causal model. *American Political Science Review, 60*, 66–72.

Cohen, B. C. (1963). *The press and foreign policy.* Princeton, NJ: Princeton University Press.

Cohen, R., & Alwin, D. (1993). Bennington women of the 1930s: Political attitudes over the life course. In K. D. Hurlbert & D. T. Schuster (Ed.), *Women's lives through time: Educated American women of the twentieth century* (pp. 117–139). San Francisco: Jossey-Bass.

Colasanto, D. (1988). Black attitudes. *Public Opinion, 10*(5), 45–49.

Coles, R. (1968). *Children of crisis.* Boston: Faber.

Coles, R. (1986). *The political life of children.* Boston: Atlantic Monthly Press.

Collins, B. E. (1969). The effect of monetary inducements on the amount of attitude change produced by forced compliance. In A. C. Elms (Ed.), *Role playing, reward, and attitude change* (pp. 209–223). New York: Van Nostrand Reinhold.

Collins, B. E., & Hoyt, M. F. (1972). Personal responsibility-for-consequences: An integration and extension of the forced compliance literature. *Journal of Experimental Social Psychology, 8*, 558–593.

Coltrane, S., & Adams, M. (1997). Work-family imagery and gender stereotypes: Television and the reproduction of difference. *Journal of Vocational Behavior, 50*, 323–347.

Coltrane, S., & Messineo, M. (2000). The perpetuation of subtle prejudice: Race and gender imagery in 1990s television advertising. *Sex Roles, 42*, 363–389.

Committee on Community Reactions to the Concorde. (1977). *Community reactions to the Concorde: An assessment of the trial period at Dulles Airport.* Washington, DC: National Academy of Sciences.

Comstock, G. (1985). Television and film violence. In S. J. Apter & A. P. Goldstein (Eds.), *Youth violence: Programs and prospects.* New York: Pergamon.

Comstock, G. (1988). Today's audiences, tomorrow's media. In S. Oskamp (Ed.), *Television as a social issue: Applied social psychology annual* (Vol. 8, pp. 324–345). Newbury Park, CA: Sage.

Comstock, G., Chaffee, S., Katzman, N., McCombs, M., & Roberts, D. (1978). *Television and human behavior.* New York: Columbia University Press.

Comstock, G., & Scharrer, E. (1999). *Television: What's on, who's watching, and what it means.* San Diego, CA: Academic Press.

Conger, J. J. (1981). Freedom and commitment: Families, youth and social change. *American Psychologist, 36*, 1475–1484.

Conn, A. B., Hanges, P., Sipe, W., & Salvaggio, A. (1999). The search for ambivalent sexism: A comparison of two measures. *Educational and Psychological Measurement, 59*, 898–909.

Constantinople, A. (1973). Masculinity–femininity: An exception to the famous dictum'? *Psychological Bulletin, 80*, 389–405.

Converse, J. M. (1984). Strong arguments and weak evidence: The open/closed questioning controversy of the 1940s. *Public Opinion Quarterly, 48*, 267–282.

Converse, J. M. (1987). *Survey research in the United States: Roots and emergence, 1890–1960.* Berkeley: University of California Press.

Converse, P. E. (1964). The nature of belief systems in mass publics. In D. Apter (Ed.), *Ideology and discontent* (pp. 206–261). New York: Free Press.

Converse, P. E. (1974). Comment: The status of nonattitudes. *American Political Science Review, 68*, 650–660.

Converse, P. E. (1975). Public opinion and voting behavior. In F. Greenstein & N. Polsby (Eds.), *Handbook of political science* (Vol. 4, pp. 75–169). Reading, MA: Addison-Wesley.

Converse, P. E. (1976). *The dynamics of party support: Cohort analyzing party identification.* Beverly Hills, CA: Sage.

Converse, P. E. (1980). Comment: Rejoinder to Judd and Milburn. *American Sociological Review, 45*, 644–646.

Converse, P. E. (1996). The advent of polling and political representation. *PS: Political Science and Politics, 29*, 649–657.

Converse, P. E., Dotson, J. D., Hoag, W. J., & McGee, W. H., III. (Eds.). (1980). *American social attitudes data sourcebook 1947–1978.* Cambridge, MA: Harvard University Press.

Converse, P. E., & Markus, G. B. (1979). The new CPS election study panel. *American Political Science Review, 73*, 32–49.

Converse, P. E., Miller, W. E., Rusk, J. G., & Wolfe, A. C. (1969). Continuity and change in American politics: Parties and issues in the 1968 election. *American Political Science Review, 63*, 1083–1105.

Converse, P. E., & Pierce, R. (1985). *Political representation in France.* Cambridge, MA: Harvard University Press.

Conway, M. M., Wyckoff, M., Feldbaum, E., & Ahern, I. (1981). The news media in children's political socialization. *Public Opinion Quarterly, 45*, 164–178.

Cook, E. P. (1985). *Psychological androgyny.* New York: Pergamon.

Cook, S. W. (1979). Social science and school desegregation: Did we mislead the Supreme Court? *Personality and Social Psychology Bulletin, 5*, 420–437.

Cook, S. W. (1984). The 1954 Social Science Statement and school desegregation: A reply to Gerard. *American Psychologist, 39*, 819–832.

Cook, S. W., & Selltiz, C. (1964). A multiple-indicator approach to attitude measurement. *Psychological Bulletin, 62*, 36–55.

Cook, T. D., Appleton, H., Conner, R. E., Shaffer, A., Tamkin, G., & Weber, S. J. (1975). *Sesame Street revisited.* New York: Russell Sage Foundation.

Cook, T. D., Bean, J. R., Calder, B. J., Frey, R., Krovetz, M. L., & Reisman, S. R. (1970). Demand characteristics and three conceptions of the frequently deceived subject. *Journal of Personality and Social Psychology, 14*, 185–194.

Cook, T. D., & Campbell, D. T. (1979). *Quasi-experimentation: Design & analysis issues for field settings.* Chicago: Rand McNally.

Cook, T. D., Campbell, D. T., & Peracchio, L. (1990). Quasi-experimentation. In M. D. Dunnette & L. M. Hough (Eds.), *Handbook of industrial and organizational psychology* (2nd ed., Vol. 1, pp. 491–576). Palo Alto, CA: Consulting Psychologists Press.

Cook, T. D., & Flay, B. R. (1978). The persistence of experimentally induced attitude change. In L. Berkowitz (Ed.), *Advances in experimental social psychology* (Vol. 11, pp. 1–57). New York: Academic Press.

Cook, T. D., Gruder, C. L., Hennigan, K. M., & Flay, B. R. (1979). History of the sleeper effect: Some logical pitfalls in accepting the null hypothesis. *Psychological Bulletin, 86*, 662–679.

Cook, T. D., & Insko, C. (1968). Persistence of attitude change as a function of conclusion re-exposure: A laboratory field experiment. *Journal of Personality and Social Psychology, 9*, 322–328.

Cooks, L. M., & Orbe, M. P. (1993). Beyond the satire: Selective exposure and selective perception in "In Living Color." *Howard Journal of Communications, 4*, 217–233.

Coombs, C. H. (1950). Psychological scaling without a unit of measurement. *Psychological Review, 57*, 145–158.

Coombs, S. L. (1981). Editorial endorsements and electoral outcomes. In M. B. MacKuen & S. L. Coombs (Eds.), *More than news* (pp. 145–230). Beverly Hills, CA: Sage.

Cooper, J., & Croyle, R. T. (1984). Attitudes and attitude change. *Annual Review of Psychology, 35*, 395–426.

Cooper, J., & Fazio, R. H. (1984). A new look at dissonance theory. In L. Berkowitz (Ed.), *Advances in experimental social psychology* (Vol. 17, pp. 229–264). New York: Academic Press.

Cordes, C. (1982). NAS gives behavioral research a boost: Study calls the benefits "significant and lasting." *APA Monitor, 13*(8), 40–41.

Corson, K. (1996). *A genetic and environmental analysis of right-wing authoritarianism in twins reared apart and together.* Unpublished doctoral dissertation: University of Minnesota.

Cotter, P. R., Cohen, J., & Coulter, P. B. (1982). Race-of-interviewer effects in telephone interviews. *Public Opinion Quarterly, 46,* 278–284.

Cottrell, N. B. (1975). Heider's structural balance principle as a conceptual rule. *Journal of Personality and Social Psychology, 31,* 713–720.

Couch, A., & Keniston, K. (1960). Yeasayers and naysayers: Agreeing response set as a personality variable. *Journal of Abnormal and Social Psychology, 60,* 151–174.

Couper, M. P. (2000). Web surveys: A review of issues and approaches. *Public Opinion Quarterly, 64,* 464–494.

Couper, M. P., Traugott, M. W., & Lamias, M. J. (2001). Web survey design and administration. *Public Opinion Quarterly, 65,* 230–253.

Courtney, A. E., & Whipple, T. W. (1983). *Sex stereotyping in advertising.* Lexington, MA: Lexington.

Coverman, S. (1985). Explaining husbands' participation in domestic labor. *Sociological Quarterly, 26,* 81–97.

Cox, A. (1983, October). The business of attitudes. *United,* p. 11.

Cramer, P. (2000). Defense mechanisms in psychology today. *American Psychologist, 55,* 637–646.

Crano, W. (2000). Social influence: Effects of leniency on majority- and minority-induced focal and indirect attitude change. *Revue Internationale de Psychologie Sociale, 13,* 89–121.

Crano, W. D. (1995). Attitude strength and vested interest. In R. E. Petty & J. A. Krosnick (Eds.), *Attitude strength: Antecedents and consequences* (pp. 131–157). Hillsdale, NJ: Lawrence Erlbaum Associates.

Crano, W. D., & Chen, X. (1998). The leniency contract and persistence of majority and minority influence. *Journal of Personality and Social Psychology, 74,* 1437–1450.

Crawford, M., & English, L. (1984). Generic versus specific inclusion of women in language: Effects on recall. *Journal of Psycholinguistic Research, 13,* 373–381.

Crespi, I. (1971). What kinds of attitude measures are predictive of behavior? *Public Opinion Quarterly, 35,* 327–334.

Crespi, I. (1980). Polls as journalism. *Public Opinion Quarterly, 44,* 462–476.

Crespi, I. (1988). *Pre-election polling: Sources of accuracy and error.* New York: Russell Sage Foundation.

Crespi, I. (1997). *The public opinion process: How the people speak.* Mahwah, NJ: Lawrence Erlbaum Associates.

Crewe, I. (1987). Why the British don't like us anymore. *Public Opinion, 9*(6), 51–56.

Crispell, D. (2001, January/February). McWorld? America, from outside looking in. *Public Perspective, 12*(1), 18–21.

Crites, S. L., Cacioppo, J. T., Gardner, W. L., & Berntson, G. G. (1995). Bioelectrical echoes from evaluative categorization: II. A late positive brain potential that varies as a function of attitude registration rather than attitude report. *Journal of Personality and Social Psychology, 68,* 997–1013.

Crittenden, J. (1962). Aging and party affiliation. *Public Opinion Quarterly, 26,* 648–657.

Crittenden, K. S. (1983). Sociological aspects of attribution. *Annual Review of Sociology, 9,* 425–446.

Crocker, J., & Major, B. (1989). Social stigma and self-esteem: The self-protective properties of stigma. *Psychological Review, 96,* 608–630.

Cronbach, L. J. (1984). *Essentials of psychological testing* (4th ed.). New York: Harper & Row.

Cronbach, L. J., & Furby, L. (1970). How should we measure "change"—or should we? *Psychological Bulletin, 74,* 68–80.

Cronin, T. E. (1985). The presidential election of 1984. In E. Sandoz & C. V. Crabb, Jr. (Eds.), *Election 84: Landslide without a mandate?* (pp. 28–65). New York: New American Library.

Crooks, R. C. (1970). The effects of an interracial preschool program upon racial preference, knowledge of racial differences, and racial identification. *Journal of Social Issues, 26*(4), 137–144.

Crosby, F. J., Bromley, S., & Saxe, L. (1980). Recent unobtrusive studies of black and white discrimination and prejudice: A literature review. *Psychological Bulletin, 87,* 546–563.

Crosby, F. J., Iyer, A., Clayton, S., & Downing, R. A. (2003). Affirmative action: Psychological data and the policy debates. *American Psychologist, 58,* 93–115.

Crosby, F. J., Pufall, A., Snyder, R. C., O'Connell, M., & Whalen, P. (1989). The denial of personal disadvantage among you, me, and all the other ostriches. In M. Crawford & M. Gentry (Eds.), *Gender and thought: Psychological perspectives* (pp. 79–99). New York: Springer-Verlag.

Crossley, H. M. (1971). Honesty with respondents and interviewers. *Public Opinion Quarterly, 35,* 476–478.

Crowne, D. P., & Marlowe, D. (1964). *The approval motive.* New York: Wiley.

Culbertson, E. M. (1957). Modification of an emotionally held attitude through role playing. *Journal of Abnormal and Social Psychology, 54,* 230–234.

Cunningham, M. (2001). The influence of parental attitudes and behaviors on children's attitudes toward gender and household labor in early childhood. *Journal of Marriage and the Family, 63*, 111–122.

Cunningham, W. A., Preacher, K. J., & Banaji, M. R. (2001). Implicit attitude measures: Consistency, stability, and convergent validity. *Psychological Science, 12*, 163–170.

Cutlip, S. C. (1954). Content and flow of AP news—From trunk to TTS to reader. *Journalism Quarterly, 31*, 434–446.

Dahlstrand, U., & Biel, A. (1997). Pro-environmental habits: Propensity levels in behavioural change. *Journal of Applied Social Psychology, 27*, 588–601.

D'Andrade, R. G. (1966). Sex differences and cultural institutions. In E. E. Maccoby (Ed.), *The development of sex differences* (pp. 174–204). Stanford, CA: Stanford University Press.

Darley, J. M., & Fazio, R. H. (1980). Expectancy confirmation processes arising in the social interaction sequence. *American Psychologist, 35*, 867–881.

Darley, J. M., & Gross, P. H. (1983). A hypothesis-confirming bias in labeling effects. *Journal of Personality and Social Psychology, 44*, 20–33.

Dasgupta, N., & Greenwald, A. G. (2001). On the malleability of automatic attitudes: Combating automatic prejudice with images of admired and disliked individuals. *Journal of Personality and Social Psychology, 81*, 800–814.

Davidson, A. R., & Jaccard, J. (1979). Variables that moderate the attitude-behavior relation: Results of a longitudinal survey. *Journal of Personality and Social Psychology, 37*, 1364–1376.

Davis, D. W. (1997). Nonrandom measurement error and race of interviewer effects among African Americans. *Public Opinion Quarterly, 61*, 183–207.

Davis, J. (1975). Communism, conformity, cohorts, and categories: American tolerance in 1954 and 1972–73. *American Journal of Sociology, 81*, 491–513.

Davis, J. (1992). Changeable weather in a cooling climate atop the liberal plateau. *Public Opinion Quarterly, 56*, 261–306.

Davis, J. (1996). Review essay on Paul R. Abramson and Ronald Inglehart, "Value change in global perspective." *Public Opinion Quarterly, 60*, 322–332.

Davison, W. P. (1983). The third-person effect in communication. *Public Opinion Quarterly, 47*, 1–15.

Dawes, R. M., & Smith, T. L. (1985). Attitude and opinion measurement. In G. Lindzey & E. Aronson (Eds.), *The handbook of social psychology* (3rd ed., Vol. 1, pp. 509–566). New York: Random House.

Dawson, M. C. (1994). *Behind the mule: Race and class in African-American politics*. Princeton, NJ: Princeton University Press.

Dayhoff, S. A. (1983). Sexist language and person perceptions: Evaluation of candidates from newspaper articles. *Sex Roles, 9*, 543–555.

de Boer, C. (1985). The polls: The European peace movement and deployment of nuclear missiles. *Public Opinion Quarterly, 49*, 119–132.

De Houwer, J., Hermans, D., & Eelen, P. (1998). Affect and identity priming with episodically associated stimuli. *Cognition and Emotion, 12*, 145–169.

De Houwer, J., Thomas, S., & Baeyens, F. (2001). Associative learning of likes and dislikes: A review of 25 years of research on human evaluative conditioning. *Psychological Bulletin, 127*, 853–869.

De Vries, N. K., De Dreu, C. K., Gordijn, E. H., & Schuurman, M. (1996). Majority and minority influence: A dual role interpretation. *European Review of Social Psychology, 36*, 33–48.

Dearing, J., & Rogers, E. (1996). *Agenda setting*. Thousand Oaks, CA: Sage.

Deaux, K. (1985). Sex and gender. *Annual Review of Psychology, 36*, 49–81.

Deaux, K., & LaFrance, M. (1998). Gender. In D. T. Gilbert, S. T. Fiske, & G. Lindzey (Eds.), *The handbook of social psychology* (4th ed., Vol. 1, pp. 788–827). New York: McGraw-Hill.

Deaux, K., & Lewis, L. L. (1984). The structure of gender stereotypes: Interrelationships among components and gender label. *Journal of Personality and Social Psychology, 46*, 991–1004.

Deaux, K., Winton, W., Crowley, M., & Lewis, L. L. (1985). Levels of social categorization and content of gender stereotypes. *Social Cognition, 3*, 145–167.

Deci, E. L., Koestner, R., & Ryan, R. M. (1999). A meta-analytic review of experiments examining the effects of extrinsic rewards on intrinsic motivation. *Psychological Bulletin, 125*, 627–668.

Deci, E. L., Koestner, R., & Ryan, R. M. (2001). Extrinsic rewards and intrinsic motivation in education: Reconsidered once again. *Review of Educational Research, 71*, 1–27.

Deci, E. L., & Ryan, R. M. (1985). *Intrinsic motivation and self-determination in human behavior*. New York: Plenum.

Declercq, E., Hurley, T. L., & Luttbeg, N. R. (1975). Voting in American presidential elections: 1956–1972. In S. A. Kirkpatrick (Ed.), *American electoral behavior: Change and stability* (pp. 9–33). Beverly Hills, CA: Sage.

DeFleur, M. L., & Westie, F. R. (1958). Verbal attitudes and overt acts: An experiment on the salience of attitudes. *American Sociological Review, 23*, 667–673.

DeFleur, M. L., & Westie, F. R. (1963). Attitude as a scientific concept. *Social Forces, 42*, 17–31.

Degenhardt, L. (2002). Why do people act in sustainable ways? Results of an empirical survey of lifestyle pioneers. In P. Schmuck & P. W. Schultz (Eds.), *Psychology of sustainable development* (pp. 123–148). Boston: Kluwer Academic.

DeJong, W. (1979). An examination of self-perception mediation of the foot-in-the-door effect. *Journal of Personality and Social Psychology, 37*, 2221–2239.

Delli Carpini, M. X., & Keeter, S. (1991). Stability and change in the U.S. public's knowledge of politics. *Public Opinion Quarterly, 55*, 583–612.

Delli Carpini, M. X., & Keeter, S. (1992, January 14). *An analysis of information items on the 1990 and 1991 NES surveys: A report to the board of overseers for the National Election Studies.* New York: Columbia University Press.

Delli Carpini, M. X., & Keeter, S. (1996). *What Americans know about politics and why it matters.* New Haven, CT: Yale University Press.

Derzon, J., & Lipsey, M. (2002). A meta-analysis of the effectiveness of mass-media communication for changing substance-use knowledge, attitudes, and behavior. In W. Crano & M. Burgoon (Eds.), *Mass media and drug prevention: Classical and contemporary theories and research* (pp. 231–258). Mahwah, NJ: Lawrence Erlbaum Associates.

Deutsch, E. M. (1989). The false consensus effect: Is the self-justification hypothesis justified? *Basic and Applied Social Psychology, 10*, 83–99.

Deutsch, K. W., & Merritt, R. L. (1965). Effects of events on national and international images. In H. C. Kelman (Ed.), *International behavior: A social-psychological analysis* (pp. 132–187). New York: Holt, Rinehart & Winston.

Deutsch, M. (1983). The prevention of World War III: A psychological perspective. *Political Psychology, 4*, 3–31.

Deutsch, M., & Krauss, R. M. (1965). *Theories in social psychology.* New York: Basic Books.

Deutscher, I. (1965). Words and deeds: Social science and social policy. *Social Problems, 13*, 235–254.

Deutscher, I. (1973). *What we say/what we do: Sentiments and acts.* Glenview, IL: Scott, Foresman.

Deutschmann, E. J. (1962). Viewing, conversation, and voting intentions. In S. Kraus (Ed.), *The great debates* (pp. 232–252). Bloomington: Indiana University Press.

Devine, P. G. (1989). Stereotypes and prejudice: Their automatic and controlled components. *Journal of Personality and Social Psychology, 56*, 5–18.

Devine, P. G., & Elliot, A. J. (1995). Are racial stereotypes really fading? The Princeton trilogy revisited. *Personality and Social Psychology Bulletin, 21*, 1139–1150.

Devine, P. G., Plant, E. A., & Buswell, B. N. (2000). Breaking the prejudice habit: Progress and obstacles. In S. Oskamp (Ed.), *Reducing prejudice and discrimination* (pp. 185–208). Mahwah, NJ: Lawrence Erlbaum Associates.

Diekman, A., & Eagly, A. H. (2000). Stereotypes as dynamic constructs: Women and men of the past, present, and future. *Personality and Social Psychology Bulletin, 26*, 1171–1188.

Dietz, T., Kalof, L., & Stern, P. (2002). Gender, values, and environmentalism. *Social Science Quarterly, 83*, 353–364.

Dillehay, R. C. (1973). On the irrelevance of the classical negative evidence concerning the effect of attitudes on behavior. *American Psychologist, 28*, 887–891.

Dillman, D. A. (2000). *Mail and internet surveys: The tailored design method.* New York: Wiley.

Dillman, D. A. (2002). Navigating the rapids of change: Some observations on survey methodology in the early twenty-first century. *Public Opinion Quarterly, 66*, 473–494.

Dillman, D. A., & Christenson, J. A. (1972). The public value for pollution control. In W. R. Burch, N. Cheek, & L. Taylor (Eds.), *Social behavior, natural resources, and the environment* (pp. 237–256). New York: Harper & Row.

Donaldson, S. (2002). High-potential mediators of drug-abuse prevention program effects. In W. Crano & M. Burgoon (Eds.), *Mass media and drug prevention: Classic and contemporary theories and research* (pp. 215–230). Mahwah, NJ: Lawrence Erlbaum Associates.

Donohue, G. A., Tichenor, P. J., & Olien, C. N. (1975). Mass media and the knowledge gap: A hypothesis reconsidered. *Communication Research, 2*, 3–23.

Doob, A. N. (1982). The role of the mass media in creating exaggerated levels of fear of being the victim of a violent crime. In P. Stringer (Ed.), *Confronting social issues: Some applications of social psychology* (Vol. 1). London, England: Academic Press.

Doob, L. W. (1947). The behavior of attitudes. *Psychological Review, 54*, 135–156.

Doob, L. W. (1950). Goebbels' principles of propaganda. *Public Opinion Quarterly, 14*, 419–442.

Doty, R. M., Peterson, B. E., & Winter, D. G. (1991). Threat and authoritarianism in the United States, 1978–1987. *Journal of Personality and Social Psychology, 61*, 629–640.

Dovidio, J. F. (2003, February). *Insights from attitude research: Dual attitudes and racial ambivalence.* Paper presented at Society of Personality and Social Psychology meeting, Los Angeles.

Dovidio, J. F., & Gaertner, S. L. (1996). Affirmative action, unintentional racial biases, and intergroup relations. *Journal of Social Issues, 52*, 51–75.

Dovidio, J. F., & Gaertner, S. L. (1998). On the nature of contemporary prejudice: The causes, consequences, and challenges of aversive racism. In J. L. Eberhardt & S. T. Fiske (Eds.), *Confronting racism: The problem and the response* (pp. 3–32). Thousand Oaks, CA: Sage.

Dovidio, J. F., Kawakami, K., & Gaertner, S. L. (2000). Reducing contemporary prejudice: Combating explicit and implicit bias at the individual and intergroup level. In S. Oskamp (Ed.), *Reducing prejudice and discrimination* (pp. 137–163). Mahwah, NJ: Lawrence Erlbaum Associates.

Dovidio, J. F., Kawakami, K., & Gaertner, S. L. (2002). Implicit and explicit prejudice and interracial interaction. *Journal of Personality and Social Psychology, 82*, 62–68.

Dovidio, J. F., Kawakami, K., Johnson, C., Johnson, B., & Howard, A. (1997). On the nature of prejudice: Automatic and controlled processes. *Journal of Experimental Social Psychology, 33*, 510–540.

Dreyer, E. C. (1971). Media use and electoral choices: Some political consequences of information exposure. *Public Opinion Quarterly, 35*, 544–553.

Duckitt, J. (1992). *The social psychology of prejudice.* New York: Praeger.

Duckitt, J., & Fisher, K. (2003). The impact of social threat on world view and ideological attitudes. *Political Psychology, 24*, 199–222.

Duckitt, J., Wagner, C., du Plessis, I., & Birum, I. (2002). The psychological bases of ideology and prejudice: Testing a dual process model. *Journal of Personality and Social Psychology, 83*, 75–93.

Duffy, M., Carney, J., Dickerson, J. F., Tumulty, K., & Edwards, T. M. (2000, November 20). Reversal of... fortune. *Time*, pp. 28–41.

Dunlap, R. E. (2002). An enduring concern: Light stays green for environmental protection. *Public Perspective, 13*, 10–14.

Dunlap, R. E., Gallup, G., & Gallup, A. (1992). *Health of the planet: Results of a 1992 international environmental opinion survey of citizens in 24 countries.* Princeton, NJ: Gallup Institute.

Dunlap, R. E., Gallup, G., & Gallup, A. (1993). Global environmental concern: Results from an international public opinion survey. *Environment, 35*, 7–15, 33–39.

Dunlap, R. E., & Mertig, A. G. (1995). Global concern for the environment: Is affluence a prerequisite? *Journal of Social Issues, 51*(4), 121–137.

Dunlap, R. E., & Saad, L. (2001). Only one in four Americans are anxious about the environment: Most favor moderate approach to environmental protection. *Gallup Poll Monthly*, No. 427, pp. 6–16.

Dunlap, R. E., & Scarce, R. (1991). The polls and poll trends: Environmental problems and protection. *Public Opinion Quarterly, 55*, 651–672.

Dunlap, R. E., & Van Liere, K. D. (1978). The "new environmental paradigm": A proposed measuring instrument and preliminary results. *Journal of Environmental Education, 9*, 10–19.

Dunlap, R. E., & Van Liere, K. D. (1984). Commitment to the dominant social paradigm and concern for environmental quality. *Social Science Quarterly, 65*, 1013–1028.

Dunlap, R. E., Van Liere, K. D., Mertig, A. G., & Jones, R. E. (2000). Measuring endorsement of the New Ecological Paradigm: A revised NEP scale. *Journal of Social Issues, 56*, 425–442.

Dunlap, R. E., Xiao, C., & McCright, A. (2001). Politics and environment in America: Partisan and ideological cleavages in public support for environmentalism. *Environmental Politics, 10*, 23–48.

Dutton, D. G. (1971). Reactions of restaurateurs to blacks and whites violating restaurant dress requirements. *Canadian Journal of Behavioral Science, 3*, 298–302.

Eagly, A. H. (1967). Involvement as a determinant of response to favorable and unfavorable information. *Journal of Personality and Social Psychology Monograph Supplement, 7*, No. 643, 1–15.

Eagly, A. H. (1981). Recipient characteristics as determinants of responses to persuasion. In R. E. Petty, T. M. Ostrom, & T. C. Brock (Eds.), *Cognitive responses in persuasion* (pp. 173–195). Hillsdale, NJ: Lawrence Erlbaum Associates.

Eagly, A. H. (1995). The science and politics of comparing women and men. *American Psychologist, 50*, 145–158.

Eagly, A. H., & Carli, L. L. (1981). Sex of researchers and sex-typed communication as determinants of sex differences in influenceability. *Psychological Bulletin, 90*, 1–20.

Eagly, A. H., & Chaiken, S. (1984). Cognitive theories of persuasion. In L. Berkowitz (Ed.), *Advances in experimental social psychology* (Vol. 17, pp. 268–359). New York: Academic Press.

Eagly, A. H., & Chaiken, S. (1993). *The psychology of attitudes*. Fort Worth, TX: Harcourt Brace Jovanovich.

Eagly, A. H., & Chaiken, S. (1998). Attitude structure and function. In D. T. Gilbert, S. T. Fiske, & G. Lindzey (Eds.), *The handbook of social psychology* (4th ed., Vol. 1, pp. 269–322). New York: McGraw-Hill.

Eagly, A. H., Chaiken, S., & Wood, W. (1981). An attributional analysis of persuasion. In J. H. Harvey, W. J. Ickes, & R. F. Kidd (Eds.), *New directions in attribution research* (Vol. 3, pp. 37–62). Hillsdale, NJ: Lawrence Erlbaum Associates.

Eagly, A. H., Chen, S., Chaiken, S., & Shaw-Barnes, K. (1999). The impact of attitudes on memory: An affair to remember. *Psychological Bulletin, 125*, 64–89.

Eagly, A. H., & Karau, S. (2002). Role congruity theory of prejudice toward female leaders. *Psychological Review, 109*, 573–598.

Eagly, A. H., Kulesa, P., Brannon, L. A., Shaw, K., & Hutson-Comeaux, S. (2000). Why counterattitudinal messages are as memorable as proattitudinal messages: The importance of active defense against attack. *Personality and Social Psychology Bulletin, 26*, 1392–1408.

Eagly, A. H., Kulesa, P., Chen, S., & Chaiken, S. (2001). Do attitudes affect memory? Tests of the congeniality hypothesis. *Current Directions in Psychological Science, 10*, 5–9.

Eagly, A. H., Mladinic, A., & Otto, S. (1991). Are women evaluated more favorably than men? An analysis of attitudes, beliefs, and emotions. *Psychology of Women Quarterly, 15*, 203–216.

Eagly, A. H., Mladinic, A., & Otto, S. (1994). Cognitive and affective bases of attitudes toward social groups and social policies. *Journal of Experimental Social Psychology, 30*, 113–137.

Eagly, A. H., & Wood, W. (2003). The origins of sex differences in human behavior: Evolved dispositions versus social roles. In C. B. Travis (Ed.), *Evolution, gender, and rape* (pp. 265–304). Cambridge, MA: MIT Press.

Eagly, A. H., Wood, W., & Chaiken, S. (1978). Causal inferences about communicators and their effect on opinion change. *Journal of Personality and Social Psychology, 36*, 424–435.

Eagly, A. H., Wood, W., & Diekman, A. (2000). Social role theory of sex differences and similarities: A current appraisal. In T. Eckes & H. Trautner (Eds.), *The developmental social psychology of gender* (pp. 123–174). Mahwah, NJ: Lawrence Erlbaum Associates.

Easton, D., & Dennis, J. (1965). The child's image of government. *Annals of the American Academy of Political and Social Science, 361*, 40–57.

Eaves, L. J., Eysenck, H. J., & Martin, N. G. (1989). *Genes, culture, and personality: An empirical approach*. London, England: Academic Press.

Eberhardt, J. L., & Fiske, S. T. (Eds.). (1998). *Confronting racism: The problem and the response*. Thousand Oaks, CA: Sage.

Eckberg, D. L., & Blocker, T. J. (1989). Variations in religious involvements and environmental concerns: Testing the Lynn White thesis. *Journal for the Scientific Study of Religion, 28*, 509–517.

Eckes, T., & Trautner, H. (2000). Developmental social psychology of gender: An integrative framework. In T. Eckes & H. Trautner (Eds.), *The developmental social psychology of gender* (pp. 3–32). Mahwah, NJ: Lawrence Erlbaum Associates.

Edelman, M. W. (1973). Southern school desegregation, 1954–1973: A judicial-political overview. *Annals of the American Academy of Political and Social Science, 407*, 32–42.

Edgell, S. E., Himmelfarb, S., & Duchan, K. L. (1982). Validity of forced responses in a randomized response model. *Sociological Methods and Research, 11*, 89–100.

Edwards, A. L. (1964). The assessment of human motives by means of personality scales. In D. Levine (Ed.), *Nebraska symposium on motivation* (Vol. 12, pp. 135–162). Lincoln: University of Nebraska Press.

Edwards, A. L., & Ashworth, C. D. (1977). A replication study of item selection for the Bem Sex-Role Inventory. *Applied Psychological Measurement, 1*, 501–508.

Edwards, A. L., & Kilpatrick, F. P. (1948). A technique for the construction of attitude scales. *Journal of Applied Psychology, 32*, 374–384.

Edwards, C. D., & Williams, J. E. (1970). Generalization between evaluative words associated with racial figures in preschool children. *Journal of Experimental Research in Personality, 4*, 144–155.

Edwards, C. P., Knoche, L., & Kumru, A. (2001). Play patterns and gender. In J. Worell (Ed.), *Encyclopedia of women and gender: Sex similarities and differences and the impact of society on gender* (Vol. 2, pp. 809–815). San Diego: Academic Press.

Egan, L. M. (1978). Children's viewing patterns for television news. *Journalism Quarterly, 55*, 347–352.

Ehrlich, C. (1971). The male sociologist's burden: The place of women in marriage and family texts. *Journal of Marriage and the Family, 33*, 421–430.

Ehrlich, J. S., & Riesman, D. (1961). Age and authority in the interview. *Public Opinion Quarterly, 25*, 39–56.

Eiser, J. R., & Stroebe, W. (1972). *Categorization and social judgment*. London, England: Academic Press.

Eisler, A. D., Eisler, H., & Yoshida, M. (2003). Perception in human ecology: Cross-cultural and gender comparisons. *Journal of Environmental Psychology, 23*, 89–101.

Ekman, P. (1971). Universals and cultural differences in facial expressions of emotion. In J. K. Cole (Ed.), *Nebraska symposium on motivation* (Vol. 19, pp. 207–283). Lincoln: University of Nebraska Press.

Ekman, P. (1999). Facial expressions. In T. Dagleish & M. Power (Eds.), *Handbook of cognition and emotion* (pp. 301–320). New York: Wiley.

Ekman, P. (2001). *Telling lies: Clues to deceit in the marketplace, politics, and marriage.* New York: Norton.

Ekman, P., Friesen, W. V., & Ancoli, S. (1980). Facial signs of emotional experience. *Journal of Personality and Social Psychology, 39*, 1125–1134.

Elaad, E. (1990). Detection of guilty knowledge in real-life criminal investigations. *Journal of Applied Psychology, 75*, 521–529.

Elliot, A. J., & Devine, P. G. (1994). On the motivational nature of cognitive dissonance: Dissonance and psychological discomfort. *Journal of Personality and Social Psychology, 67*, 382–394.

Elms, A. C. (1967). Role playing, incentive, and dissonance. *Psychological Bulletin, 68*, 132–148.

Embretson, S., & Reise, S. (2000). *Item response theory for psychologists.* Mahwah, NJ: Lawrence Erlbaum Associates.

Entman, R. (1997). African Americans according to TV news. In E. E. Dennis & E. C. Pease (Eds.), *The media in black and white.* New Brunswick, NJ: Transaction.

Epstein, E. J. (1973). *News from nowhere: Television and the news.* New York: Random House.

Epstein, L., & Strom, G. (1984). Survey research and election night predictions. *Public Opinion, 7*(1), 48–50.

Erber, M. W., Hodges, S. D., & Wilson, T. D. (1995). Attitude strength, attitude stability, and the effects of analyzing reasons. In R. E. Petty & J. A. Krosnick (Eds.), *Attitude strength: Antecedents and consequences* (pp. 433–454). Hillsdale, NJ: Lawrence Erlbaum Associates.

Erber, R., & Lau, R. R. (1990). Political cynicism revisited: An information-processing reconciliation of policy-based and incumbency-based interpretations of changes in trust in government. *American Journal of Political Science, 34*, 236–253.

Erikson, R. S. (1976). The influence of newspaper endorsements in presidential elections: The case of 1964. *American Journal of Political Science, 20*, 207–233.

Erikson, R. S. (1979). The SRC panel data and mass political attitudes. *British Journal of Political Science, 9*, 89–114.

Erikson, R. S., & Tedin, K. L. (2001). *American public opinion: Its origins, content, and impact* (6th ed.). New York: Longman.

Erikson, R. S., & Wlezien, C. (1999). Presidential polls as a time series: The case of 1996. *Public Opinion Quarterly, 63*, 163–177.

Erskine, H. G. (1962). The polls: The informed public. *Public Opinion Quarterly, 26*, 669–677.

Erskine, H. G. (1963a). The polls: Textbook knowledge. *Public Opinion Quarterly, 27*, 133–141.

Erskine, H. G. (1963b). The polls: Exposure to international information. *Public Opinion Quarterly, 27*, 658–662.

Erskine, H. G. (1971). The polls: Women's role. *Public Opinion Quarterly, 35*, 275–290.

Erskine, H. G. (1972a). The polls: Pollution and its costs. *Public Opinion Quarterly, 36*, 120–135.

Erskine, H. G. (1972b). The polls: Gun control. *Public Opinion Quarterly, 36*, 455–469.

Etheredge, L. S. (1978). *A world of men.* Cambridge, MA: MIT Press.

Etzioni, A. (1967). The Kennedy experiment. *Western Political Quarterly, 20*, 361–380.

Etzioni, A. (1969). Social-psychological aspects of international relations. In G. Lindzey & E. Aronson (Eds.), *The handbook of social psychology* (2nd ed., Vol. 5, pp. 538–601). Reading, MA: Addison-Wesley.

Eurobarometer 59. (2003, June). Early results: United States has a somewhat tarnished image. Retrieved July 9, 2003, from http://europa.eu.int/en/comm/dg10/infcom/epo/eb.htm

Evans, R. I., Rozelle, R. M., Maxwell, S. E., Raines, B. E., Dill, C. A., Guthrie, I. J., Henderson, A. H., & Hill, P. C. (1981). Social modeling films to deter smoking in adolescents: Results of a three-year field investigation. *Journal of Applied Psychology, 66*, 399–414.

The Eye of the Storm. (1970). ABC News documentary film. Available from Guidance Associates, The Center for Humanities, Communications Park, Box 3000, Mount Kisco, NY 10549.

Fagot, B. I., Hagan, R., Leinbach, M. D., & Kronsberg, S. (1985). Different reactions to assertive and communicative acts of toddler boys and girls. *Child Development, 56*, 1499–1505.

Fagot, B. I., Rodgers, C., & Leinbach, M. D. (2000). Theories of gender socialization. In T. Eckes & H. Trautner (Eds.), *The developmental social psychology of gender* (pp. 65–89). Mahwah, NJ: Lawrence Erlbaum Associates.

Fairchild, H. H. (1988). Creating positive television images. In S. Oskamp (Ed.), *Television as a social issue: Applied social psychology annual* (Vol. 8, pp. 270–279). Newbury Park, CA: Sage.

Farley, R. (1996). *The new American reality: Who we are, how we got here, where we are going.* New York: Russell Sage Foundation.

Farnsley, C. P. (1965). Polls as a tool of government. *Public Opinion Quarterly, 29*, 463–464.

Fazio, R. H. (1986). How do attitudes guide behavior? In R. M. Sorrentino & E. T. Higgins (Eds.), *The handbook of motivation and cognition: Foundations of social behavior.* New York: Guilford.

Fazio, R. H. (1987). Self-perception theory: A current perspective. In M. P. Zanna, J. M. Olson, & C. P. Herman (Eds.), *Social influence: The Ontario Symposium* (Vol. 5, pp. 129–150). Hillsdale, NJ: Lawrence Erlbaum Associates.

Fazio, R. H. (1988). On the power and functionality of attitudes: The role of attitude accessibility. In A. R. Pratkanis, S. J., Breckler, & A. G. Greenwald (Eds.), *Attitude structure and function* (pp. 153–179). Hillsdale, NJ: Lawrence Erlbaum Associates.

Fazio, R. H. (1990). Multiple processes by which attitudes guide behavior. The MODE model as an integrative framework. In L. Berkowitz (Ed.), *Advances in experimental social psychology* (Vol. 23, pp. 75–109). Orlando, FL: Academic Press.

Fazio, R. H. (1993). Variability in the likelihood of automatic attitude activation: Data reanalysis and commentary on Bargh, Chaiken, Govender, and Pratto (1992). *Journal of Personality and Social Psychology, 64*, 753–758; Addendum, 764–765.

Fazio, R. H. (1995). Attitudes as object-evaluation associations: Determinants, consequences, and correlates of attitude accessibility. In R. E. Petty & J. A. Krosnick (Eds.), *Attitude strength: Antecedents and consequences* (pp. 247–282). Hillsdale, NJ: Lawrence Erlbaum Associates.

Fazio, R. H. (2000). Accessible attitudes as tools for object appraisal: Their costs and benefits. In G. R. Maio & J. M. Olson (Eds.), *Why we evaluate: Functions of attitudes* (pp. 1–36). Mahwah, NJ: Lawrence Erlbaum Associates.

Fazio, R. H. (2001). On the automatic activation of associated evaluations: An overview. *Cognition and Emotion, 15*, 115–141.

Fazio, R. H. (2004, February). *On the nature of the associations assessed by the IAT.* Paper presented at the annual meeting of the Society for Personality and Social Psychology, Austin, TX.

Fazio, R. H., Chen, J., McDonel, E. C., & Sherman, S. J. (1982). Attitude accessibility, attitude-behavior consistency, and the strength of the object-evaluation association. *Journal of Experimental Social Psychology, 18*, 339–357.

Fazio, R. H., Jackson, J. R., Dunton, B. C., & Williams, C. J. (1995). Variability in automatic activation as an unobtrusive measure of racial attitudes: A bona fide pipeline? *Journal of Personality and Social Psychology, 69*, 1013–1027.

Fazio, R. H., & Olson, M. A. (2003). Implicit measures in social cognition research: Their meaning and use. *Annual Review of Psychology, 54*, 297–327.

Fazio, R. H., & Towles-Schwen, T. (1999). The MODE model of attitude-behavior processes. In S. Chaiken & Y. Trope (Eds.), *Dual-process theories in social psychology* (pp. 97–116). New York: Guilford.

Fazio, R. H., & Williams, C. J. (1986). Attitude accessibility as a moderator of the attitude–perception and attitude–behavior relations: An investigation of the 1984 presidential election. *Journal of Personality and Social Psychology, 51*, 505–514.

Fazio, R. H., & Zanna, M. P. (1981). Direct experience and attitude-behavior consistency. In L. Berkowitz (Ed.), *Advances in experimental social psychology* (Vol. 14, pp. 161–202). New York: Academic Press.

Fazio, R. H., Zanna, M. P., & Cooper, J. (1977). Dissonance and self-perception: An integrative view of each theory's proper domain of application. *Journal of Experimental Social Psychology, 13*, 464–479.

Feagin, J. R. (1991). The continuing significance of race: Antiblack discrimination in public places. *American Sociological Review, 56*, 101–116.

Feagin, J. R., & Sykes, M. (1994). *Living with racism: The black middle-class experience.* Boston: Beacon.

Feagin, J. R., Vera, H., & Batur, P. (2001). *White racism* (2nd ed.). New York: Routledge.

Feather, N. T. (1962). Cigarette smoking and lung cancer: A study of cognitive dissonance. *Australian Journal of Psychology, 14*, 55–64.

Feather, N. T. (1967). A structural balance approach to the analysis of communication effects. In L. Berkowitz (Ed.), *Advances in experimental social psychology* (Vol. 3, pp. 100–166). New York: Academic Press.

Federal Glass Ceiling Commission. (1995). *Good for business: Making full use of the nation's human capital.* Washington, DC: U.S. Government Printing Office.

Feldman, S. (2003). Enforcing social conformity: A theory of authoritarianism. *Political Psychology, 24*, 41–74.

Feldman, S., & Zaller, J. R. (1992). The political culture of ambivalence: Ideological responses to the welfare state. *American Journal of Political Science, 36*, 268–307.

Felson, M., & Sudman, S. (1975). The accuracy of presidential-preference primary polls. *Public Opinion Quarterly, 39*, 232–236.

Festinger, L. (1953). Laboratory experiments. In L. Festinger & D. Katz (Eds.), *Research methods in the behavioral sciences* (pp. 136–172). New York: Dryden.

Festinger, L. (1954). A theory of social comparison processes. *Human Relations, 7*, 117–140.

Festinger, L. (1957). *A theory of cognitive dissonance.* Stanford, CA: Stanford University Press.

Festinger, L. (Ed.). (1964). *Conflict, decision, and dissonance.* Stanford, CA: Stanford University Press.

Festinger, L., & Carlsmith, J. M. (1959). Cognitive consequences of forced compliance. *Journal of Abnormal and Social Psychology, 58*, 203–210.

Festinger, L., Riecken, H. W., & Schachter, S. (1956). *When prophecy fails: A social and psychological study of a modern group that predicted the destruction of the world.* New York: Harper.

Fiedler, K., Schmid, J., & Stahl, T. (2002). What is the current truth about polygraph lie detection? *Basic and Applied Social Psychology, 24*, 313–324.

Field, C. G. (1980). Social testing for United States housing policy: The Experimental Housing Allowance Program. In Organization for Economic Co-operation and Development, *The utilisation of the social sciences in policy making in the United States: Case studies.* Paris, France: Author.

Field, J. O., & Anderson, R. E. (1969). Ideology in the public's conceptualization of the 1964 election. *Public Opinion Quarterly, 33*, 380–398.

Field, M. D. (1971). The researcher's view. *Public Opinion Quarterly, 35*, 342–346.

Fields, C. M. (1981, February 2). Much research with human subjects freed from close scrutiny by panels. *Chronicle of Higher Education*, pp. 1, 16.

Fields, I. M., & Schuman, H. (1976). Public beliefs about the beliefs of the public. *Public Opinion Quarterly, 40*, 427–448.

Fillenbaum, S., & Frey, R. (1970). More on the "faithful" behavior of suspicious subjects. *Journal of Personality, 38*, 43–51.

Fink, A. (Ed.). (2003). *The survey kit* (2nd ed., Vols. 1–10). Thousand Oaks, CA: Sage.

Finlay, W. M. L., & Lyons, E. (2002). Acquiescence in interviews with people who have mental retardation. *Mental Retardation, 40*, 14–29.

Fiorina, M. P. (1981). *Retrospective voting in American national elections.* New Haven, CT: Yale University Press.

Fiorina, M. P. (1992). *Divided government.* New York: Macmillan.

Fisch, S. (2002). Vast wasteland or vast opportunity? Effects of educational television on children's academic knowledge, skills, and attitudes. In J. Bryant & D. Zillmann (Eds.), *Media effects: Advances in theory and research* (2nd ed., pp. 397–426). Mahwah, NJ: Lawrence Erlbaum Associates.

Fischoff, S. (1979). "Recipe for a jury" revisited: A balance theory prediction. *Journal of Applied Social Psychology, 9*, 335–349.

Fishbein, M., & Ajzen, I. (1972). Attitudes and opinions. *Annual Review of Psychology, 23*, 487–544.

Fishbein, M., & Ajzen, I. (1974). Attitudes toward objects as predictors of single and multiple behavioral criteria. *Psychological Review, 81*, 59–74.

Fishbein, M., & Ajzen, I. (1975). *Belief, attitude, intention, and behavior: An introduction to theory and research.* Reading, MA: Addison-Wesley.

Fishbein, M., Ajzen, I., & Hinkle, R. (1980). Predicting and understanding voting in American elections: Effects of external variables. In I. Ajzen & M. Fishbein (Eds.), *Understanding attitudes and predicting social behavior* (pp. 173–195). Englewood Cliffs, NJ: Prentice-Hall.

Fishbein, M., Guenther-Grey, C., Johnson, W. D., Wolitski, R. J., McAlister, A., Rietmeijer, C. A., & O'Reilly, K. (1996). Using a theory-based community intervention to reduce AIDS risk behaviors: The CDC's AIDS Community Demonstration Projects. In S. Oskamp & S. C. Thompson (Eds.), *Understanding and preventing HIV risk behavior: Safer sex and drug use* (pp. 177–206). Thousand Oaks, CA: Sage.

Fishbein, M., Hall-Jamieson, K., Zimmer, E., von Haeften, I., & Nabi, R. (2002). Avoiding the boomerang: Testing the relative effectiveness of antidrug public service announcements before a national campaign. *American Journal of Public Health, 92*, 238–245.

Fisher, M., Kupferman, L. B., & Lesser, M. (1992). Substance use in a school-based clinic population: Use of the randomized response technique to estimate prevalence. *Journal of Adolescent Health, 13*, 281–285.

Fisher, R., & Ury, W. (1981). *Getting to yes.* New York: Penguin.

Fiske, A. P., Kitayama, S., Markus, H., & Nisbett, R. (1998). The cultural matrix of social psychology. In G. Lindzey & E. Aronson (Eds.), *The handbook of social psychology* (3rd ed., Vol. 2, pp. 915–981). New York: Random House.

Fiske, S. T. (1993). Social cognition and social perception. *Annual Review of Psychology, 44*, 155–194.

Fiske, S. T., & Taylor, S. E. (1984). *Social cognition.* Reading, MA: Addison-Wesley.

Fiske, S. T., & Taylor, S. E. (1991). *Social cognition* (2nd ed.). New York: McGraw-Hill.

Fitzsimmons, S. J., & Osburn, H. G. (1968). The impact of social issues and public affairs television documentaries. *Public Opinion Quarterly, 32*, 379–397.

Flanagan, T. J., & Longmire, D. R. (1996). *Americans view crime and justice: A national public opinion survey.* Thousand Oaks, CA: Sage.

Flavin, C. (2001). Rich planet, poor planet. In L. R. Brown et al., *State of the world 2001* (pp. 3–20). New York: Norton.

Fleisher, R., & Bond, J. R. (2002). Evidence of increasing polarization among ordinary citizens. In J. E. Cohen, R. Fleisher, & P. Kantor (Eds.), *American political parties: Decline or resurgence?* (pp. 55–77). Washington, DC: CQ Press.

Fleishman, J. A. (1986). Types of political attitude structure: Results of a cluster analysis. *Public Opinion Quarterly, 50,* 371–386.

Fletcher, G. J. O., & Ward, C. (1988). Attribution theory and processes: A cross-cultural perspective. In M. H. Bond (Ed.), *The cross-cultural challenge to social psychology* (pp. 230–244). Newbury Park, CA: Sage.

Forbes, G., Adams-Curtis, L., Hamm, N., & White, K. (2003). Perceptions of the woman who breastfeeds: The role of erotophobia, sexism, and attitudinal variables. *Sex Roles, 49,* 379–388.

Foster, H. S. (1983). *Activism replaces isolationism: U.S. public attitudes 1940–1975.* Washington, DC: Foxhall.

Foster, M. A., Wallston, B. S., & Berger, M. (1980). Feminist orientation and job-seeking behavior among dual-career couples. *Sex Roles, 6,* 59–66.

Fowler, F. J. (1992). How unclear terms affect survey data. *Public Opinion Quarterly, 56,* 218–231.

Fox, J. A., & Tracy, E. E. (1986). *Randomized response: A method for sensitive surveys.* Beverly Hills, CA: Sage.

Fox, R. J., Crask, M. R., & Kim, J. (1988). Mail survey response rate: A meta-analysis of selected techniques for inducing response. *Public Opinion Quarterly, 52,* 467–491.

Fox, R. L., & Smith, E. R. (1998). The role of candidate sex in voter decision-making. *Political Psychology, 19,* 405–419.

Frank, R. E., & Greenberg, M. G. (1980). *The public's use of television: Who watches and why.* Beverly Hills, CA: Sage.

Fransson, N., & Gärling, T. (1999). Environmental concern: Conceptual definitions, measurement methods, and research findings. *Journal of Environmental Psychology, 19,* 369–382.

Franz, M., & Goldstein, K. (2002). Following the (soft) money: Party advertisements in American elections. In L. S. Maisel (Ed.), *The parties respond: Changes in American parties and campaigns* (4th ed., pp. 139–162). Boulder, CO: Westview.

Fredricks, A. J., & Dossett, D. L. (1983). Attitude–behavior relations: A comparison of the Fishbein–Ajzen and the Bentler–Speckart models. *Journal of Personality and Social Psychology, 45,* 501–512.

Free, L. A., & Cantril, H. (1967). *The political beliefs of Americans: A study of public opinion.* New Brunswick, NJ: Rutgers University Press.

Free, L. A., & Watts, W. (1980). Internationalism comes of age . . . Again. *Public Opinion, 3*(2), 46–50.

Freedman, J. L. (1963). Attitudinal effects of inadequate justification. *Journal of Personality, 31,* 371–385.

Freedman, J. L. (1964). Involvement, discrepancy, and change. *Journal of Abnormal and Social Psychology, 69,* 290–295.

Freedman, J. L. (1984). Effect of television violence on aggressiveness. *Psychological Bulletin, 96,* 227–246.

Freedman, J. L., & Fraser, S. C. (1966). Compliance without pressure: The foot-in-the-door technique. *Journal of Personality and Social Psychology, 4,* 195–202.

Freedman, P., & Goldstein, K. (1999). Measuring media exposure and the effects of negative campaign ads. *American Journal of Political Science, 43,* 1189–1208.

Freeman, D. (1983). *Margaret Mead and Samoa: The making and unmaking of an anthropological myth.* Cambridge, MA: Harvard University Press.

Freeman, J. (1973). The origins of the women's liberation movement. In I. Huber (Ed.), *Changing women in a changing society* (pp. 30–49). Chicago: University of Chicago Press.

Frenkel-Brunswik, E., & Havel, J. (1953). Prejudice in the interviews of children: Attitudes toward minority groups. *Journal of Genetic Psychology, 82,* 91–136.

Freud, S. (1949). *The origins and development of psychoanalysis.* Chicago: Regnery. (Original work published 1910)

Freudenburg, W. (1991). Rural-urban differences in environmental concern: A closer look. *Rural Sociology, 61,* 167–198.

Frey, D. (1982). Different levels of cognitive dissonance, information seeking, and information avoidance. *Journal of Personality and Social Psychology, 43,* 1175–1183.

Frey, D. (1986). Recent research on selective exposure to information. In L. Berkowitz (Ed.), *Advances in experimental social psychology* (Vol. 19, pp. 41–80). Orlando, FL: Academic Press.

Frey, D., Schulz-Hardt, S., & Stahlberg, D. (1996). Information seeking among individuals and groups and possible consequences for decision-making in business and politics. In E. Witte & J. Davis (Eds.),

Understanding group behavior: Small group processes and interpersonal relations (Vol. 2, pp. 211–225). Mahwah, NJ: Lawrence Erlbaum Associates.

Fried, S. B., Gumpper, D. C., & Allen, J. C. (1973). Ten years of social psychology: Is there a growing commitment to field research? *American Psychologist, 28*, 155–156.

Friedman, H. S., DiMatteo, M. R., & Mertz, T. I. (1980). Nonverbal communication on television news: The facial expressions of broadcasters during coverage of a presidential election campaign. *Personality and Social Psychology Bulletin, 6*, 427–435.

Friedman, J., & Weinberg, D. H. (Eds.). (1983). *The great housing experiment.* Beverly Hills, CA: Sage.

Friedrich, L. K., & Stein, A. H. (1975). Pro-social television and young children: The effects of verbal labeling and role playing on learning and behavior. *Child Development, 46*, 27–38.

Frieze, I., Ferligoj, A., Kogovsek, T., Rener, T., Horvat, J., & Sarlija, N. (2003). Gender-role attitudes in university students in the United States, Slovenia, and Croatia. *Psychology of Women Quarterly, 27*, 256–261.

Frisco, M., & Williams, K. (2003). Perceived housework equity, marital happiness, and divorce in dual-earner households. *Journal of Family Issues, 24*, 51–73.

Funkhouser, G. R. (1973). The issues of the sixties: An exploratory study in the dynamics of public opinion. *Public Opinion Quarterly, 37*, 62–75.

Gaddy, G. D. (1986). Television's impact on high school achievement. *Public Opinion Quarterly, 50*, 340–359.

Gaertner, S. L., & Dovidio, J. F. (1977). The subtlety of white racism, arousal, and helping behavior. *Journal of Personality and Social Psychology, 35*, 691–707.

Gaertner, S. L., & Dovidio, J. F. (1986). The aversive form of racism. In J. F. Dovidio & S. L. Gaertner (Eds.), *Prejudice, discrimination, and racism* (pp. 61–89). Orlando, FL: Academic Press.

Gaertner, S. L., & McLaughlin, J. (1983). Racial stereotypes: Associations and ascriptions of positive and negative characteristics. *Social Psychology Quarterly, 46*, 23–30.

Gaertner, S. L., Rust, M. C., Dovidio, J. F., Bachman, B. A., & Anastasio, P. A. (1994). The contact hypothesis: The role of a common ingroup identity on reducing intergroup bias. *Small Group Research, 25*, 224–249.

Gaes, G. G., Kalle, R. J., & Tedeschi, J. T. (1978). Impression management in the forced compliance situation. *Journal of Experimental Social Psychology, 14*, 493–510.

Gallup, G. H. (1948). *A guide to public opinion polls* (2nd ed.). Princeton, NJ: Princeton University Press.

Gallup, G. H. (1965). Polls and the political process—Past, present, and future. *Public Opinion Quarterly, 29*, 544–549.

Gallup, G. H. (1972). *The Gallup Poll: Public opinion 1935–1971.* New York: Random House.

Gallup, G. H. (1976). *The sophisticated poll watcher's guide* (rev. ed.). Princeton, NJ: Princeton Opinion Press.

Gallup, G. H. (1978). *The Gallup Poll: Public opinion 1972–77* (Vol. 2). Wilmington, DE: Scholarly Resources.

Gallup Opinion Index. (1978, April). Panama Canal treaties gaining more support as awareness grows. No. 153, pp. 15–24.

Gallup Opinion Index. (1979, April). Awareness of Three Mile Island incident. No. 165, p. 3.

Gallup Opinion Index. (1980, March). Ratings of nations—Trends. No. 176, p. 32.

Gallup Opinion Index. (1980, December). 1980 election one of most unusual. No. 183, pp. 29–30.

Gallup Poll Monthly. (1990, March). Americans ignorant of basic census facts. No. 294, pp. 2–4.

Gallup Poll Monthly. (1990, October). Location of United Nations. No. 301, p. 19.

Gallup Poll Monthly. (1991, May). Most important problem—Recent trends. No. 308, p. 35.

Gallup Poll Monthly. (1994, November). Gallup Poll accuracy record. No. 350, p. 53.

Gallup Poll Monthly. (1995, July). Long term national trend—Major issues. No. 358, p. 49.

Gallup Poll Monthly. (1996, February). Split sample experiments: How worried are people about maintaining their standard of living? No. 365, pp. 22–24.

Gallup Poll Monthly. (1996, November). Gallup Poll accuracy record. No. 374, p. 15.

Gallup Poll Monthly. (1997, February). Questionnaire experiments: "Ideal number of children" influenced by question wording. No. 377, pp. 24–26.

Gallup Poll Monthly. (1997, December). Gallup short subjects. No. 387, pp. 28–56.

Gallup Poll Monthly. (1999, January). Most important problems—Recent trend. No. 400, pp. 50–51.

Gallup Poll Monthly. (2000). The most important events of the century from the viewpoint of the people. In *Year 2000 review*, pp. 8–19.

Gallup Poll Monthly. (2001, March). Most important problem. No. 426, pp. 22–23.

Gallup Poll Monthly. (2001, September). Terrorist attacks: Public opinion from April 1995–January 2001. No. 432, pp. 35–47.

Gallup Poll Tuesday Briefing. (2002, June 28). Americans' confidence in military, presidency up; big business, organized religion drop. pp. 98–100.

Gallup Report. (1981, July). Public support for ERA reaches new high. No. 190, pp. 23–25.

Gallup Report. (1983, December). Most important problem, 1981–1983. No. 219, p. 6.

Gallup Report. (1985, March). Aware of "Star Wars" proposal. No. 234, p. 13.

Gallup Report. (1985, June). United Nations slowly grows in Americans' esteem. No. 237, pp. 26–27.

Gallup Report. (1985, October). Gallup Poll anniversary: Public's views and behavior have changed greatly since 1935. No. 241, pp. 5–6.

Gallup Report. (1986, March). Awareness of Halley's Comet. No. 246, pp. 34–35.

Gallup Report. (1986, April). Awareness of AIDS. No. 247, p. 20.

Gallup Report. (1986, December). Gallup international: Americans more fearful of world war than are people of other nations. No. 255, p. 6.

Gallup Report. (1987, March). U.S./Soviet relations: Americans more cynical than Soviets about eliminating nuclear weapons. No. 258, p. 34.

Gallup Report. (1987, May). Most important problem. No. 260, pp. 6–7.

Gallup Report. (1987, November). Gallup international: Soviets more likely than Americans to predict a peaceful 1988. No. 266, p. 35.

Gallup Report. (1987, December). Gorbachev is first Soviet leader chosen among "most admired" in U.S. No. 267, pp. 26–27.

Gallup Report. (1988, July). Equal Rights Amendment. No. 274, p. 15.

Gallup Report. (1988, September). Poverty: Most Americans reject notion that U.S. is divided into "haves," "have-nots." No. 276, pp. 8–12.

Gallup Report. (1988, October). Geographic knowledge deemed vital, but many lack basic skills. No. 277, p. 35.

Gallup Report. (1988, November). The economy: Bush campaign seen gaining from low "misery index." No. 278, p. 28.

Gallup Report. (1988, December). Confidence in institutions. No. 279, pp. 29–30.

Gallup Report. (1989, March/April). Social values. No. 282/283, pp. 35–44.

Gallup Report. (1989, August). Ratings of foreign countries. No. 287, pp. 13–14.

Galtung, J. (1996). *Peace by peaceful means.* London, England: Sage.

Galtung, J. (2002, Fall). To end terrorism, end state terrorism. *Peace Psychology Newsletter,* pp. 10–11.

Gamba, R., & Oskamp, S. (1994). Factors influencing community residents' participation in commingled curbside recycling programs. *Environment and Behavior, 26,* 587–612.

Ganahl, D., Prinsen, T., & Netzley, S. B. (2003). A content analysis of prime time commercials: A contextual framework of gender representation. *Sex Roles, 49,* 545–551.

Gans, H. J. (1979). *Deciding what's news: A study of CBS Evening News, NBC Nightly News, Newsweek, and Time.* New York: Pantheon.

Garcia, F. C. (1973). *Political socialization of Chicano children.* New York: Praeger.

Garcia-Marques, L., Maddox, K., & Hamilton, D. L. (2002). Exhaustive and heuristic retrieval processes in person cognition: Further tests of the TRAP model. *Journal of Personality and Social Psychology, 82,* 193–207.

Gardner, G., et al. (2003). *State of the world 2003.* New York: Norton.

Gardner, G. T., & Stern, P. C. (2002). *Environmental problems and human behavior* (2nd edition). Boston: Pearson.

Gardner, J. W. (1984). *Excellence* (rev. ed.). New York: Norton.

Garramone, G. M. (1985). Effects of negative political advertising: The roles of sponsor and rebuttal. *Journal of Broadcasting & Electronic Media, 32,* 415–427.

Garramone, G. M., & Atkin, C. K. (1986). Mass communication and political socialization: Specifying the effects. *Public Opinion Quarterly, 50,* 76–86.

Garrett, A., Treanor, M., & Roffey, P. A. (2003, May). *Effect of the media's portrayal of ethnic groups on prejudicial attitudes.* Paper presented at Western Psychological Association meeting, Vancouver, BC, Canada.

Geis, E. L., Brown, V., Jennings (Walstedt), J., & Porter, N. (1984). TV commercials as achievement scripts for women. *Sex Roles, 10,* 513–525.

Geller, D. M. (1982). Alternatives to deception: Why, what, and how? In J. E. Sieber (Ed.), *NIH readings on the protection of human subjects in behavioral and social science research: Conference proceedings and background papers* (pp. 39–55). Frederick, MD: University Publications of America.

General Social Survey. (2004). *1972–2002 General Social Survey cumulative file.* Berkeley, CA: University of California. Retrieved January, 2004, from http://sda.berkeley.edu

Gerard, H. B. (1983). School desegregation: The social science role. *American Psychologist, 38,* 869–877.

Gerard, H. B., & Orive, R. (1987). The dynamics of opinion formation. In L. Berkowitz (Ed.), *Advances in experimental social psychology* (Vol. 20, pp. 171–202). San Diego: Academic Press.

Gerber, A. S., & Green, D. P. (2001). Do phone calls increase voter turnout? A field experiment. *Public Opinion Quarterly, 65,* 75–85.

Gerbner, G. (Ed.). (1977). *Mass media policies in changing cultures.* New York: Wiley.

Gerbner, G. (1993). *Women and minorities in television: A study in casting fate.* Philadelphia: Annenberg School for Communication, University of Pennsylvania.

Gerbner, G., Gross, L., Morgan, M., & Signorielli, N. (1980). The "mainstreaming" of America: Violence profile no. 11. *Journal of Communication, 30*(3), 10–29.

Gerbner, G., Gross, L., Morgan, M., Signorielli, N., & Shanahan, J. (2002). Growing up with television: Cultivation processes. In J. Bryant & D. Zillmann (Eds.), *Media effects: Advances in theory and research* (pp. 43–67). Mahwah, NJ: Lawrence Erlbaum Associates.

Gibbons, F. X. (1978). Sexual standards and reactions to pornography: Enhancing behavioral consistency through self-focused attention. *Journal of Personality and Social Psychology, 36,* 976–987.

Gilbert, L. A. (1985). *Men in dual-career families: Current realities and future prospects.* Hillsdale, NJ: Lawrence Erlbaum Associates.

Gilbert, L. A. (1993). *Two careers/one family: The promise of gender equality.* Newbury Park, CA: Sage.

Gilbert, L. A., & Rader, J. (2001). Counseling and psychotherapy: Gender, race/ethnicity, and sexuality. In J. Worell (Ed.), *Encyclopedia of women and gender: Sex similarities and differences and the impact of society on gender* (Vol. 1, pp. 265–277). San Diego: Academic Press.

Gilbert, R. K. (1988). The dynamics of inaction: Psychological factors inhibiting arms control activism. *American Psychologist, 43,* 755–764.

Gilbert, W. S. (1932). *The best known works of W. S. Gilbert.* New York: Illustrated Editions.

Gilens, M. (1996). Race and poverty in America: Public misperceptions and the American news media. *Public Opinion Quarterly, 60,* 515–541.

Gillig, P. M., & Greenwald, A. G. (1974). Is it time to lay the sleeper effect to rest? *Journal of Personality and Social Psychology, 29,* 132–139.

Gilligan, C. (1982). *In a different voice: Psychological theory and women's development.* Cambridge, MA: Harvard University Press.

Gilligan, C. (1986). Reply by Carol Gilligan. *Moral Development, 6,* 325–333.

Ginzel, L. E., Jones, E. E., & Swann, W. B., Jr. (1987). How "naive" is the naive attributer?: Discounting and augmentation in attitude attribution. *Social Cognition, 5,* 108–130.

Glaser, J. M., & Gilens, M. (1997). Interregional migration and political resocialization: A study of racial attitudes under pressure. *Public Opinion Quarterly, 61,* 72–86.

Glass, D. P. (1985). Evaluating presidential candidates: Who focuses on their personal attributes? *Public Opinion Quarterly, 49,* 517–534.

Glazer, A., & Robbins, M. (1985). Congressional responsiveness to constituency change. *American Journal of Political Science, 29,* 259–273.

Glenn, N. D. (1973). Class and party support in the United States: Recent and emerging trends. *Public Opinion Quarterly, 37,* 1–20.

Glenn, N. D. (1987). Social trends in the United States: Evidence from sample surveys. *Public Opinion Quarterly, 51,* s109–s126.

Glenn, N. D., & Weaver, C. N. (1982). Enjoyment of work by full-time workers in the U.S., 1955 and 1980. *Public Opinion Quarterly, 46,* 459–470.

Glick, P., & Fiske, S. T. (1996). The Ambivalent Sexism Inventory: Differentiating hostile and benevolent sexism. *Journal of Personality and Social Psychology, 70,* 491–512.

Glick, P., & Fiske, S. T. (2001). Ambivalent sexism. In M. P. Zanna (Ed.), *Advances in experimental social psychology* (Vol. 33, pp. 115–188). San Diego, CA: Academic Press.

Glynn, C. J., Herbst, S., O'Keefe, G. J., & Shapiro, R. Y. (1999). *Public opinion.* Boulder, CO: Westview.

Goethals, G. R., Cooper, J., & Naficy, A. (1979). Role of foreseen, foreseeable, and unforeseeable behavioral consequences in the arousal of cognitive dissonance. *Journal of Personality and Social Psychology, 37,* 1179–1185.

Göksen, F., Adaman, F., & Zenginobuz, E. U. (2002). On environmental concern, willingness to pay, and post-materialist values: Evidence from Istanbul. *Environment and Behavior, 34,* 616–633.

Goldberg, L. R. (1981). Unconfounding situational attributions from uncertain, neutral, and ambiguous ones: A psychometric analysis of descriptions of oneself and various types of others. *Journal of Personality and Social Psychology, 41,* 517–552.

Goldberg, M. E., & Gorn, G. J. (1974). Children's reactions to television advertising: An experimental approach. *Journal of Consumer Research, 1,* 69–75.

Goldhaber, G. M. (1984). A pollsters' sampler. *Public Opinion, 7*(3), 47–53.

Goldman, P. (1970). *Report from black America.* New York: Simon & Schuster.

Goldner, F. H. (1971). Public opinion and survey research: A poor mix. *Public Opinion Quarterly, 35,* 447–448.

Good, G. E., & Sherrod, N. (2001). The psychology of men and masculinity: Research status and future directions. In R. K. Unger (Ed.), *Handbook of the psychology of women and gender* (pp. 201–214). New York: Wiley.

Gooden, A. M., & Gooden, M. A. (2001). Gender representation in notable children's picture books: 1995–1999. *Sex Roles, 45*, 89–101.

Goodman, M. E. (1964). *Race awareness in young children* (rev. ed.). New York: Crowell Collier.

Gorassini, D. R., & Olson, J. M. (1995). Does self-perception change explain the foot-in-the-door effect? *Journal of Personality and Social Psychology, 69*, 91–105.

Gordijn, E., De Vries, N., & De Dreu, C. (2002). Minority influence on focal and related attitudes: Change in size, attributions and information processing. *Personality and Social Psychology Bulletin, 28*, 1315–1326.

Gordon, C. (1987). Fresh eggs and APA meet on Madison Ave. *APA Monitor, 18*(5), 25.

Gordon, R. A. (2000). *Eating disorders: Anatomy of a social epidemic* (2nd ed.). Malden, MA: Blackwell.

Gore, A. (1960). Political public opinion polls. *Congressional Record, 106*, 16958–16965.

Gorn, G. J., & Goldberg, M. E. (1982). Behavioral evidence of the effects of televised food messages on children. *Journal of Consumer Research, 9*, 200–205.

Gorsuch, R. L., & Ortberg, J. (1983). Moral obligation and attitudes: Their relation to behavioral intentions. *Journal of Personality and Social Psychology, 44*, 1025–1028.

Gouveia, V. (2002). Self, culture, and sustainable development. In P. Schmuck & P. W. Schultz (Eds.), *Psychology of sustainable development* (pp. 151–174). Boston: Kluwer Academic.

Gow, J. (1996). Reconsidering gender roles on MTV: Depictions in the most popular music videos of the early 1990s. *Communication Reports, 9*, 151–161.

Graber, D. A. (1987). Kind pictures and harsh words: How television presents the candidates. In K. L. Schlozman (Ed.), *Elections in America* (pp. 115–141). Boston: Allen & Unwin.

Graber, D. A. (1997). *Mass media and American politics*. Washington, DC: Congressional Quarterly.

Graham, S., & Folkes, V. S. (Eds.). (1990). *Attribution theory: Applications to achievement, mental health, and interpersonal conflict*. Hillsdale, NJ: Lawrence Erlbaum Associates.

Granberg, D. (1982). Family size preferences and sexual permissiveness as factors differentiating abortion activists. *Social Psychology Quarterly, 45*, 15–23.

Granberg, D. (1984). Attributing attitudes to members of groups. In J. R. Eiser (Ed.), *Attitudinal judgement* (pp. 85–108). New York: Springer-Verlag.

Granberg, D., & Brent, E. E. (1980). Perceptions of issue positions of presidential candidates. *American Scientist, 68*, 617–646.

Granberg, D., & Robertson, C. (1982). Contrast effects in estimating the policies of the federal government. *Public Opinion Quarterly, 46*, 43–53.

Greeley, A. M. (1981). The state of the nation's happiness. *Psychology Today, 15*(1), 14–16.

Greenberg, B. S. (1964). Diffusion of news of the Kennedy assassination. *Public Opinion Quarterly, 28*, 225–232.

Greenberg, E. (1970). Black children and the political system. *Public Opinion Quarterly, 34*, 335–348.

Greenberg, J., Arndt, J., Schimel, J., Pyszczynski, T., & Solomon, S. (2001). Clarifying the function of mortality salience-induced worldview defense: Renewed suppression or reduced accessibility of death-related thoughts. *Journal of Experimental Social Psychology, 37*, 70–76.

Greenberg, J., Pyszczynski, T., & Solomon, S. (1982). The self-serving attributional bias: Beyond self-presentation. *Journal of Experimental Social Psychology, 18*, 56–67.

Greenleaf, E. A. (1992). Measuring extreme response style. *Public Opinion Quarterly, 56*, 328–351.

Greenwald, A. G. (1980). The totalitarian ego: Fabrication and revision of personal history. *American Psychologist, 35*, 603–618.

Greenwald, A. G. (2004, January). *Revised top ten list of things wrong with the IAT*. Paper presented at Society for Personality and Social Psychology Meeting, Austin, Texas.

Greenwald, A. G., & Albert, R. D. (1968). Acceptance and recall of improvised arguments. *Journal of Personality and Social Psychology, 8*, 31–34.

Greenwald, A. G., & Banaji, M. R. (1995). Implicit social cognition: Attitudes, self-esteem, and stereotypes. *Psychological Review, 102*, 4–27.

Greenwald, A. G., Banaji, M. R., Rudman, L. A., Farnham, S. D., Nosek, B. A., & Mellott, D. S. (2002). A unified theory of implicit attitudes, stereotypes, self-esteem, and self-concept. *Psychological Review, 109*, 3–25.

Greenwald, A. G., Brock, T. C., & Ostrom, T. M. (Eds.). (1968). *Psychological foundations of attitudes*. New York: Academic Press.

Greenwald, A. G., Klinger, M. R., & Liu, T. J. (1989). Unconscious processing of dichoptically masked words. *Memory and Cognition, 17*, 35–47.

Greenwald, A. G., McGhee, D. E., & Schwartz, J. L. K. (1998). Measuring individual differences in implicit cognition. *Journal of Personality and Social Psychology, 74*, 1464–1480.

Greenwald, A. G., Pratkanis, A. R., Leippe, M. R., & Baumgardner, M. H. (1986). Under what conditions does theory obstruct research progress? *Psychological Review, 93*, 216–229.

Greenwald, A. G., & Ronis, D. L. (1978). Twenty years of cognitive dissonance: A case study of the evolution of a theory. *Psychological Review, 85*, 53–57.

Greenwald, H. J., & Oppenheim, D. B. (1968). Reported magnitude of self-misidentification among Negro children—Artifact? *Journal of Personality and Social Psychology, 8*, 49–52.

Grofman, B. (1980). Jury decision making models and the Supreme Court: The jury cases from *Williams v. Florida* to *Ballew v. Georgia. Policy Studies Journal, 8*, 749–772

Gross, A. E., & Fleming, I. (1982). Twenty years of deception in social psychology. *Personality and Social Psychology Bulletin, 8*, 402–408.

Groves, R. M., & Kahn, R. L. (1979). *Surveys by telephone: A national comparison with personal interviews.* New York: Academic Press.

Groves, R. M., & Mathiowetz, N. A. (1984). Computer assisted telephone interviewing: Effects on interviewers and respondents. *Public Opinion Quarterly, 48*, 356–369.

Grube, J. W., Mayton, D. M., II, & Ball-Rokeach, S. J. (1994). Inducing change in values, attitudes, and behaviors: Belief system theory and the method of value self-confrontation. *Journal of Social Issues, 50*(4), 153–173.

Gruder, C. L., Cook, T. D., Hennigan, K. M., Flay, B. R., Alessi, C., & Halamaj, J. (1978). Empirical tests of the absolute sleeper effect predicted from the discounting cue hypothesis. *Journal of Personality and Social Psychology, 36*, 1061–1074.

Grush, J. E. (1976). Attitude formation and mere exposure phenomena: A nonartifactual explanation of empirical findings. *Journal of Personality and Social Psychology, 33*, 281–290.

Grush, J. E. (1979). A summary review of mediating explanations of exposure phenomena. *Personality and Social Psychology Bulletin, 5*, 154–159.

Grush, J. E. (1980). Impact of candidate expenditures, regionality, and prior outcomes on the 1976 Democratic presidential primaries. *Journal of Personality and Social Psychology, 38*, 337–347.

Guadagno, R. E., Asher, T., Demaine, L., & Cialdini, R. (2001). When saying yes leads to saying no: Preference for consistency and the reverse foot-in-the-door effect. *Personality and Social Psychology Bulletin, 27*, 859–867.

Guagnano, G., & Markee, N. (1995). Regional differences in the sociodemographic determinants of environmental concern. *Population and Environment, 17*, 135–150.

Gullahorn, J. T., & Gullahorn, J. E. (1963). An extension of the U-curve hypothesis. *Journal of Social Issues, 19*(3), 33–47.

Gurevitch, M., & Blumler, J. G. (1982). The construction of election news: An observation study at the BBC. In J. S. Ettema & D. C. Whitney (Eds.), *Individuals in mass media organizations: Creativity and constraint* (pp. 179–204). Beverly Hills, CA: Sage.

Gurin, P., Hatchett, S., & Jackson, J. S. (1989). *Hope and independence: Black response to electoral and party politics.* New York: Russell Sage Foundation.

Guth, J., Green, J., Kellstedt, L., & Smidt, C. (1995). Faith and the environment: Religious beliefs and attitudes on environmental policy. *American Journal of Political Science, 39*, 364–382.

Guttman, L. (1944). A basis for scaling qualitative data. *American Sociological Review, 9*, 139–150.

Gwynne, S. C. (1996, April 1). Undoing diversity: A bombshell court ruling curtails affirmative action. *Time*, p. 54.

Hacker, H. M. (1951). Women as a minority group. *Social Forces, 30*, 60–69.

Haemmerlie, E. M., & Montgomery, R. L. (1984). Purposefully biased interactions: Reducing heterosocial anxiety through self-perception theory. *Journal of Personality and Social Psychology, 47*, 900–908.

Hafer, C., Reynolds, K., & Obertynski, M. (1996). Message comprehensibility and persuasion: Effects of complex language in counterattitudinal appeals to laypeople. *Social Cognition, 14*, 317–337.

Halpern, D. (1994). Stereotypes, science, censorship, and the study of sex differences. *Feminism and Psychology, 4*, 523–530.

Halpern, D. (1997). Sex differences in intelligence: Implications for education. *American Psychologist, 52*, 1091–1102.

Hambleton, R. K. (1989). Principles and selected applications of item response theory. In R. Linn (Ed.), *Educational measurement* (3rd ed., pp. 147–200). New York: Macmillan.

Hambleton, R. K., Swaminathan, H., & Rogers, H. J. (1991). *Fundamentals of item response theory.* Newbury Park, CA: Sage.

Hamill, R., Wilson, T. D., & Nisbett, R. E. (1980). Insensitivity to sample bias: Generalizing from atypical cases. *Journal of Personality and Social Psychology, 39*, 578–589.

Hamilton, D. L. (Ed.). (1981a). *Cognitive processes in stereotyping and intergroup behavior*. Hillsdale, NJ: Lawrence Erlbaum Associates.

Hamilton, D. L. (1981b). Illusory correlation as a basis for stereotyping. In D. L. Hamilton (Ed.), *Cognitive processes in stereotyping and intergroup behavior* (pp. 115–144). Hillsdale, NJ: Lawrence Erlbaum Associates.

Hamilton, D. L., Carpenter, S., & Bishop, G. D. (1984). Desegregation of urban neighborhoods. In N. Miller & M. B. Brewer (Eds.), *Groups in contact: The psychology of desegregation* (pp. 97–121). Orlando, FL: Academic Press.

Hamilton, D. L., Devine, P. G., & Ostrom, T. M. (1994). Social cognition and classic issues in social psychology. In P. G. Devine, D. L. Hamilton, & T. M. Ostrom (Eds.), *Social cognition: Impact on social psychology* (pp. 1–13). San Diego, CA: Academic Press.

Hamilton, D. L., & Rose, T. L. (1980). Illusory correlation and the maintenance of stereotypic beliefs. *Journal of Personality and Social Psychology, 39*, 832–845.

Hamilton, D. L., Stroessner, S. J., & Mackie, D. M. (1993). The influence of affect on stereotyping: The case of illusory correlations. In D. M. Mackie & D. L. Hamilton (Eds.), *Affect, cognition, and stereotyping: Interactive processes in group perception*. San Diego, CA: Academic Press.

Hammond, J. L. (1986). Yuppies. *Public Opinion Quarterly, 50*, 487–501.

Hammond, K. R. (1948). Measuring attitudes by error-choice: An indirect method. *Journal of Abnormal and Social Psychology, 43*, 38–48.

Hansemark, O. (2000). Predictive validity of TAT and CMPS on the entrepreneurial activity, "start of a new business": A longitudinal study. *Journal of Managerial Psychology, 15*, 634–650.

Harding, J., Proshansky, H., Kutner, B., & Chein, I. (1969). Prejudice and ethnic relations. In G. Lindzey & E. Aronson (Eds.), *The handbook of social psychology* (2nd ed., Vol. 5, pp. 1–76). Reading, MA: Addison-Wesley.

Hardyck, J. A., & Braden, M. (1962). Prophecy fails again: A report of a failure to replicate. *Journal of Abnormal and Social Psychology, 65*, 136–141.

Hare-Mustin, R. T. (1983). An appraisal of the relationship between women and psychotherapy: 80 years after the case of Dora. *American Psychologist, 38*, 593–601.

Harkins, S. G., & Petty, R. E. (1981). Effects of source magnification of cognitive effort on attitudes: An information processing view. *Journal of Personality and Social Psychology, 40*, 401–413.

Harland, P., Staats, H., & Wilke, H. A. M. (1999). Explaining proenvironmental intention and behavior by personal norms and the theory of planned behavior. *Journal of Applied Social Psychology, 29*, 2505–2528.

Harmon, R. R., & Coney, K. A. (1982). The persuasive effects of source credibility in buy and lease situations. *Journal of Marketing Research, 19*, 255–260.

Harmon-Jones, E. (1999). Toward an understanding of the motivation underlying dissonance effects: Is the production of aversive consequences necessary? In E. Harmon-Jones & J. Mills (Eds.), *Cognitive dissonance: Progress on a pivotal theory in social psychology* (pp. 71–99). Washington, DC: American Psychological Association.

Harmon-Jones, E. (2000a). A cognitive dissonance theory perspective on the role of emotion in the maintenance and change of beliefs and attitudes. In N. Frijda, A. Manstead, & S. Bem (Eds.), *Emotions and beliefs: How feelings influence thoughts* (pp. 185–211). Paris, France: Cambridge University Press.

Harmon-Jones, E. (2001). The role of affect in cognitive-dissonance processes. In J. Forgas (Ed.), *Handbook of affect and social cognition* (pp. 237–255). Mahwah, NJ: Lawrence Erlbaum Associates.

Harmon-Jones, E., Brehm, J. W., Greenberg, J., Simon, L., & Nelson, D. E. (1996). Evidence that the production of aversive consequences is not necessary to create cognitive dissonance. *Journal of Personality and Social Psychology, 70*, 5–16.

Harmon-Jones, E., & Mills, J. (Eds.). (1999). *Cognitive dissonance: Progress on a pivotal theory in social psychology*. Washington, DC: American Psychological Association.

Harris, R. J. (1969). Dissonance or sour grapes? Post-"decision" changes in ratings and choice frequencies. *Journal of Personality and Social Psychology, 11*, 334–344.

Harter, S., & Pike, R. (1984). The Pictorial Scale of Perceived Competence and Social Acceptance for Young Children. *Child Development, 55*, 1969–1982.

Hartley, R. E. (1974). Sex-role pressures and the socialization of the male child. In J. Pleck & J. Sawyer (Eds.), *Men and masculinity* (pp. 7–13). Englewood Cliffs, NJ: Prentice-Hall.

Hass, R. G. (1981). Effects of source characteristics on cognitive responses and persuasion. In R. E. Petty, T. M. Ostrom, & T. C. Brock (Eds.), *Cognitive responses in persuasion* (pp. 141–172). Hillsdale, NJ: Lawrence Erlbaum Associates.

Hass, R. G., & Grady, K. (1975). Temporal delay, type of forewarning and resistance to influence. *Journal of Experimental Social Psychology, 11*, 459–469.

Hastie, R., Penrod, S. D., & Pennington, N. (1984). *Inside the jury*. Cambridge, MA: Harvard University Press.

Hatchett, S., & Schuman, H. (1975). White respondents and race-of-interviewer effects. *Public Opinion Quarterly, 39*, 523–528.

Haugtvedt, C. P., & Petty, R. E. (1992). Personality and persuasion: Need for cognition moderates the persistence and resistance of attitude changes. *Journal of Personality and Social Psychology, 63*, 308–319.

Haugtvedt, C. P., & Wegener, D. T. (1994). Message order effects in persuasion: An attitude strength perspective. *Journal of Consumer Research, 21*, 205–218.

Hawkins, R. P., & Pingree, S. (1982). TV influence on social reality and conceptions of the world. In D. Pearl, L. Bouthilet, & J. Lazar (Eds.), *Television and behavior: Ten years of scientific progress and implications for the eighties* (Vol. 2, pp. 224–247). Washington, DC: U.S. Government Printing Office.

Hearold, S. (1986). A synthesis of 1043 effects of television on social behavior. In G. Comstock (Ed.), *Public communication and behavior* (Vol. 1, pp. 65–133). Orlando, FL: Academic Press.

Hechinger, E. M. (1979, March 13). About education: Council to fight U.S. students' parochial views. *New York Times*, p. C-5.

Hecker, D. E. (1998, March). Earnings of college graduates: Women compared with men. *Monthly Labor Review, 121*, 62–71.

Heclo, H., & Rein, M. (1980). Social science and negative income taxation. In Organisation for Economic Cooperation and Development, *The utilisation of the social sciences in policy making in the United States: Case studies*. Paris, France: Author.

Hedges, C. (1999, November 12). 35% of high school seniors fail national civics test. *New York Times*, Sec. 1, p. 17.

Heesacker, M. (1985). Applying attitude change theory to counseling. *Contemporary Social Psychology, 11*, 209–213.

Heider, F. (1944). Social perception and phenomenal causality. *Psychological Review, 51*, 358–374.

Heider, F. (1946). Attitudes and cognitive organization. *Journal of Psychology, 21*, 107–112.

Heider, F. (1958). *The psychology of interpersonal relations*. New York: Wiley.

Heine, S., & Lehman, D. (1997). Culture, dissonance, and self-affirmation. *Personality and Social Psychology Bulletin, 23*, 389–400.

Heller, J. E., Pallak, M. S., & Picek, J. M. (1973). The interactive effects of intent and threat on boomerang attitude change. *Journal of Personality and Social Psychology, 26*, 273–279.

Helmreich, R. L., Spence, J. T., & Gibson, R. H. (1982). Sex-role attitudes: 1972–1980. *Personality and Social Psychology Bulletin, 8*, 656–663.

Helson, H. (1964). *Adaptation level theory: An experimental and systematic approach to behavior*. New York: Harper & Row.

Helwig, C. (1998). Children's conceptions of fair government and freedom of speech. *Child Development, 69*, 518–531.

Henley, N. M. (1989). Molehill or mountain? What we know and don't know about sex bias in language. In M. Crawford & M. Gentry (Eds.), *Gender and thought: Psychological perspectives* (pp. 59–78). New York: Springer-Verlag.

Hennessy, B. C. (1970). A headnote on the existence and study of political attitudes. *Social Science Quarterly, 51*, 463–476.

Hennessy, B. C. (1975). *Public opinion* (3rd ed.). North Scituate, MA: Duxbury.

Hense, R., Penner, L., & Nelson, D. (1995). Implicit memory for age stereotypes. *Social Cognition, 13*, 399–415.

Herek, G. M. (1986). The instrumentality of attitudes: Toward a neofunctional theory. *Journal of Social Issues, 42*(2), 99–114.

Herek, G. M. (1987). Can functions be measured? A new perspective on the functional approach to attitudes. *Social Psychology Quarterly, 50*, 285–303.

Herek, G. M. (2000). The social construction of attitudes: Functional consensus and divergence in the U.S. public's reactions to AIDS. In G. R. Maio & J. M. Olson (Eds.), *Why we evaluate: Functions of attitudes* (pp. 325–364). Mahwah, NJ: Lawrence Erlbaum Associates.

Hermans, D., De Houwer, J., & Eelen, P. (1994). The affective priming effect: Automatic activation of evaluative information in memory. *Cognition and Emotion, 8*, 515–533.

Herrnson, P. S. (2000). *Congressional elections: Campaigning at home and in Washington* (3rd ed.). Washington, DC: CQ Press.

Herz, M. E. (1949). Some psychological lessons from leaflet propaganda in World War II. *Public Opinion Quarterly, 13*, 471–486.

Herzog, A. R., Bachman, J. G., & Johnston, L. D. (1983). Paid work, child care and housework: A national survey of high school seniors' preferences for sharing responsibilities between husband and wife. *Sex Roles, 9*, 109–135.

Hess, R. D. (1963). The socialization of attitudes toward political authority: Some cross-national comparisons. *International Social Science Journal, 25*, 542–559.

Hess, R. D., & Torney, J. V. (1967). *The development of political attitudes in children*. Chicago: Aldine.

Hetherington, M. J. (1998). The political relevance of political trust. *American Political Science Review, 92*, 791–808.

Hewstone, M. (1989). *Causal attribution: From cognitive processes to collective beliefs*. Oxford, England: Blackwell.

Hewstone, M., Rubin, M., & Willis, H. (2002). Intergroup bias. *Annual Review of Psychology, 53*, 575–604.

Hiatt, F., & Atkinson, R. (1985, December 1). Arms and America's fortunes; Is the trillion-dollar buildup exacting a hidden cost? *Washington Post*, p. A1.

Higgins, E. T., & Bargh, J. A. (1987). Social cognition and social perception. *Annual Review of Psychology, 38*, 369–425.

Hill, C., & Peplau, A. (1998). Premarital predictors of relationship outcomes: A 15-year follow-up of the Boston Couples Study. In T. Bradbury (Ed.), *The developmental course of marital dysfunction* (pp. 237–278). New York: Cambridge University Press.

Hill, P., Dill, C., & Davenport, E. (1988). A reexamination of the bogus pipeline. *Educational and Psychological Measurement, 48*, 587–601.

Hiller, D. V., & Philliber, W. W. (1982). Predicting marital and career success among dual-worker couples. *Journal of Marriage and the Family, 44*, 53–62.

Hiller, D. V., & Philliber, W. W. (1986). The division of labor in contemporary marriage: Expectations, perceptions, and performance. *Social Problems, 33*, 191–201.

Hilton, J. L., & von Hippel, W. (1996). Stereotypes. *Annual Review of Psychology, 47*, 237–271.

Himmelweit, H. T., Humphreys, E., Jaegers, M., & Katz, M. (1981). *How voters decide: A longitudinal study of political attitudes and voting extending over fifteen years*. London, England: Academic Press.

Himmelweit, H. T., Oppenheim, A. N., & Vince, E. (1958). *Television and the child*. London, England: Oxford University Press.

Hinckley, R. H. (1992). *People, polls, and policy makers: American public opinion and national security*. New York: Lexington.

Hine, V., & Gerlach, L. P. (1970). Many concerned, few committed. *Natural History, 79*(10), 16–17&ff.

Hines, J. M., Hungerford, H. R., & Tomera, A. N. (1986–1987). Analysis and synthesis of research on responsible pro-environmental behavior: A meta-analysis. *Journal of Environmental Education, 18*(2), 1–8.

Hing, L. S. S., Bobocel, D. R., & Zanna, M. P. (2000, June). *Discrimination perceptions mitigate justice-based opposition to affirmative action*. Paper presented at Society for the Psychological Study of Social Issues meeting, Minneapolis, MN.

Hippler, H. J., & Schwarz, N. (1986). Not forbidding isn't allowing: The cognitive basis of the forbid-allow asymmetry. *Public Opinion Quarterly, 50*, 87–96.

Hirsch, E. M. (1990). The "scary world" of the nonviewer and other anomalies. *Communication Research, 7*, 403–456.

Hodson, G., Maio, G. R., & Esses, V. M. (2001). The role of attitudinal ambivalence in susceptibility to consensus information. *Basic and Applied Social Psychology, 23*, 197–205.

Hoffman, L. W. (1977). Changes in family roles, socialization and sex differences. *American Psychologist, 32*, 644–657.

Hogarth, R. M. (1981). Beyond discrete biases: Functional and dysfunctional aspects of judgmental heuristics. *Psychological Bulletin, 90*, 197–217.

Holland, R., Meertens, R., & Van Vugt, M. (2002). Dissonance on the road: Self esteem as a moderator of internal and external self-justification strategies. *Personality and Social Psychology Bulletin, 28*, 1713–1724.

Holleman, B. (2000). *The forbid/allow asymmetry: On the cognitive mechanisms underlying wording effects in surveys*. Amsterdam, Netherlands: Rodopi.

Holmes, D. S., & Bennett, D. H. (1974). Experiments to answer questions raised by the use of deception in psychological research: I. Role playing as an alternative to deception; II. Effectiveness of debriefing after a deception; III. Effect of informed consent on deception. *Journal of Personality and Social Psychology, 29*, 358–367.

Holt, R. R., (1999). Empiricism and the Thematic Apperception Test: Validity is the payoff. In L. Gieser & M. Stein (Eds.), *Evocative images: The Thematic Apperception Test and the art of projection* (pp. 99–106). Washington, DC: American Psychological Association.

Holt, R. R., & Silverstein, B. (1989). The image of the enemy: U.S. views of the Soviet Union. *Journal of Social Issues, 45*(2), 1–175.

Hornik, R. C. (Ed.). (2002). *Public health communication: Evidence for behavior change*. Mahwah, NJ: Lawrence Erlbaum Associates.

Hort, B. E., Leinbach, M. D., & Fagot, B. I. (1990). Are people's notions of maleness more stereotypically framed than their notions of femaleness? *Sex Roles, 23*, 197–212.

Houston, D. A., Doan, K., & Roskos-Ewoldsen, D. R. (1999). Negative political advertising and choice conflict. *Journal of Experimental Psychology: Applied, 5*, 3–16.

Houston, D. A., & Fazio, R. H. (1989). Biased processing as a function of attitude accessibility: Making objective judgments subjectively. *Social Cognition, 7*, 51–66.

Hovland, C. I. (1959). Reconciling conflicting results derived from experimental and survey studies of attitude change. *American Psychologist, 14*, 8–17.

Hovland, C. I., Harvey, O. J., & Sherif, M. (1957). Assimilation and contrast effects in communication and attitude change. *Journal of Abnormal and Social Psychology, 55*, 244–252.

Hovland, C. I., Janis, I. L., & Kelley, H. H. (1953). *Communication and persuasion.* New Haven, CT: Yale University Press.

Hovland, C. I., Lumsdaine, A. A., & Sheffield, F. D. (1949). *Experiments on mass communication.* Princeton, NJ: Princeton University Press.

Hovland, C. I., Mandell, W., Campbell, E. H., Brock, T., Luchins, A. S., Cohen, A. E., McGuire, W. J., Janis, I. L., Feierabend, R. L., & Anderson, N. H. (1957). *The order of presentation in persuasion.* New Haven, CT: Yale University Press.

Hovland, C. I., & Sherif, M. (1952). Judgmental phenomena and scales of attitude measurement: Item displacement in Thurstone scales. *Journal of Abnormal and Social Psychology, 47*, 822–832.

Howard, J., & Rothbart, M. (1980). Social categorization and memory for ingroup and outgroup behavior. *Journal of Personality and Social Psychology, 38*, 301–310.

Howard-Pitney, B., Borgida, E., & Omoto, A. M. (1986). Personal involvement: An examination of processing differences. *Social Cognition, 4*, 39–57.

Howell, S. E., & Fagan, D. (1988). Race and trust in government: Testing the political reality model. *Public Opinion Quarterly, 52*, 343–350.

Howell, S. E., & Laska, S. B. (1992). The changing face of the environmental coalition: A research note. *Environment and Behavior, 24*, 134–144.

Hraba, J., & Grant, G. (1970). Black is beautiful: A reexamination of racial preference and identification. *Journal of Personality and Social Psychology, 16*, 398–402.

Huckfeldt, R., & Sprague, J. (1993). Citizens, contexts, and politics. In A. Finifter (Ed.), *Political science: The state of the discipline II* (pp. 281–303). Washington, DC: American Political Science Association.

Huckfeldt, R., & Sprague, J. (1995). *Citizens, politics, and social communication: Information and influence in an election campaign.* Cambridge, England: Cambridge University Press.

Huddy, L., Khatib, N., & Capelos, T. (2002). The polls—Trends: Reactions to the terrorist attacks of September 11, 2001. *Public Opinion Quarterly, 66*, 418–450.

Huddy, L., Neely, F., & Lafay, M. (2000). Support for the women's movement. *Public Opinion Quarterly, 64*, 309–350.

Hugick, L. (1992, March). Satisfaction with U.S. at a ten-year low: But eight in ten are satisfied with their personal life. *Gallup Poll Monthly,* No. 318, pp. 47–50.

Hugick, L., & Gallup, A. M. (1991). "Rally events" and presidential approval. *Gallup Poll Monthly,* No. 309, pp. 15–27.

Hunter, L. (2000). A comparison of the environmental attitudes, concern, and behaviors of native-born and foreign-born U.S. residents. *Population and Environment, 21*, 565–580.

Huntington, S. P. (1999). The lonely superpower. *Foreign Affairs, 78*(2), 35–49.

Huo, Y. J., Smith, H., Tyler, T. R., & Lind, A. E. (1996). Superordinate identification, subgroup identification, and justice concerns: Is separatism the problem? Is assimilation the answer? *Psychological Science, 7*, 40–45.

Hurwitz, J., & Peffley, M. (1987). How are foreign policy attitudes structured? A hierarchical model. *American Political Science Review, 81*, 1099–1120.

Huskinson, T., & Haddock, G. (2004). Individual differences in attitude structure: Variance in the chronic reliance on affective and cognitive information. *Journal of Experimental Social Psychology, 40*, 82–90.

Huston, A. C., Anderson, D. R., Wright, J. C., Linebarger, D. L., & Schmitt, K. L. (2001). *Sesame Street* viewers as adolescents: The recontact study. In S. M. Fisch & R. T. Truglio (Eds.), *"G" is for growing: Thirty years of research on children and Sesame Street* (pp. 131–144). Mahwah, NJ: Lawrence Erlbaum Associates.

Hyde, J. S. (1984). Children's understanding of sexist language. *Developmental Psychology, 20*, 697–706.

Hyden, E., & McCandless, N. J. (1983). Men and women as portrayed in the lyrics of contemporary music. *Popular Music and Society, 9*(2), 10–26.

Hyman, H. H. (1972). *Secondary analysis of sample surveys: Principles, procedures, and potentialities.* New York: Wiley.

Hyman, H. H., & Sheatsley, P. B. (1947). Some reasons why information campaigns fail. *Public Opinion Quarterly, 11*, 412–423.

Inglehart, R. (1977). *The silent revolution: Changing values and political styles among Western publics.* Princeton, NJ: Princeton University Press.

Inglehart, R. (1985). Aggregate stability and individual-level flux in mass belief systems: The level of analysis paradox. *American Political Science Review, 79,* 97–116.

Inglehart, R. (1990). *Culture shift in advanced industrial society.* Princeton, NJ: Princeton University Press.

Inglehart, R. (1995). Public support for environmental protection: The impact of objective problems and subjective values in 43 societies. *PS: Political Science and Politics, 28,* 57–71.

Inglehart, R., & Norris, P. (2003). *Rising tide: Gender equality and cultural change around the world.* New York: Cambridge University Press.

Insko, C. A. (1965). Verbal reinforcement of attitude. *Journal of Personality and Social Psychology, 2,* 621–623.

Insko, C. A. (1967). *Theories of attitude change.* New York: Appleton-Century-Crofts.

Insko, C. A., Nacoste, R. W., & Moe, J. L. (1983). Belief congruence and racial discrimination: Review of the evidence and critical evaluation. *European Journal of Social Psychology, 13,* 153–174.

Institute for Social Research. (1982, Spring/Summer). Group consciousness. *ISR Newsletter, 10*(1&2), 4–5.

Intergovernmental Panel on Climate Change. (2001). *Climate change 2001: Impacts, adaptation, and vulnerability.* Geneva, Switzerland: Author.

Ito, T., Larsen, J., Smith, N. K., & Cacioppo, J. T. (2002). Negative information weighs more heavily on the brain: The negativity bias in evaluative categorizations. In J. T. Cacioppo et al. (Eds.), *Foundations in social neuroscience* (pp. 575–597). Cambridge, MA: MIT Press.

Ivanhoe, L. F. (1997). Get ready for another oil shock. *Futurist, 31,* 20–35.

Iyengar, S. (1991). *Is anyone responsible? How television frames political issues.* Chicago: University of Chicago Press.

Iyengar, S., & Kinder, D. R. (1986). More than meets the eye: TV news, priming, and public evaluations of the president. In G. Comstock (Ed.), *Public communication and behavior* (Vol. 1, pp. 135–171). Orlando, FL: Academic Press.

Iyengar, S., & Kinder, D. R. (1987). *News that matters: Television and American opinion.* Chicago: University of Chicago Press.

Iyengar, S., Kinder, D. R., Peters, M. D., & Krosnick, J. A. (1984). The evening news and presidential evaluations. *Journal of Personality and Social Psychology, 46,* 778–787.

Iyengar, S., & Simon, A. F. (2000). New perspectives and evidence on political communication and campaign effects. *Annual Review of Psychology, 51,* 149–169.

Iyer, A., & Crosby, F. J. (2000, June). *Beliefs about inequality and attitudes toward affirmative action: The mediating role of white guilt.* Paper presented at Society for the Psychological Study of Social Issues meeting, Minneapolis, MN.

Jaccard, J. (1979). Personality and behavioral prediction: An analysis of behavioral criterion measures. In L. Kahle & D. Fiske (Eds.), *Methods for studying person-situation interactions.* San Francisco: Jossey-Bass.

Jaccard, J., Knox, R., & Brinberg, D. (1980). Designing political campaigns to elect a candidate: Toward a social psychological theory of voting behavior. *Journal of Applied Social Psychology, 10,* 367–383.

Jackman, M. (1973). Education and prejudice or education and response sets? *American Sociological Review, 38,* 327–339.

Jackman, M. R., & Crane, M. (1986). "Some of my best friends are black. . .": Interracial friendship and whites' racial attitudes. *Public Opinion Quarterly, 50,* 459–486.

Jackson, J. E. (1983). Election night reporting and voter turnout. *American Journal of Political Science, 27,* 613–635.

Jackson, W. E. (1995). Discrimination in mortgage lending markets as rational economic behavior: Theory, evidence, and public policy. In M. E. Lashley & M. N. Jackson (Eds.), *African Americans and the new policy consensus: Retreat of the liberal state?* (pp. 157–178). Westport, CT: Greenwood.

Jacobs, L. (1993). *The health of nations: Public opinion in the making of American and British health policy.* Ithaca, NY: Cornell University Press.

Jacobson, G. C. (2001). *The politics of congressional elections* (5th ed.). New York: Addison-Wesley.

Jacoby, J. (1974). The construct validity of opinion leadership. *Public Opinion Quarterly, 38,* 81–89.

Jamieson, D. W., & Zanna, M. P. (1988). Need for structure in attitude formation and expression. In A. R. Pratkanis, S. J. Breckler, & A. G. Greenwald (Eds.), *Attitude structure and function.* Hillsdale, NJ: Lawrence Erlbaum Associates.

Jamieson, K. H., & Cappella, J. N. (1996, July). News frames, political cynicism, and media cynicism. *Annals of the American Academy of Political and Social Science, 546,* 71–84.

Jamner, M. S., Wolitski, R. J., Corby, N. H., & Fishbein, M. (1998). Using the theory of planned behavior to predict intention to use condoms among female sex workers. *Psychology and Health, 13,* 187–205.

Janis, I. L. (1983). The role of social support in adherence to stressful decisions. *American Psychologist, 38,* 143–160.

Janis, I. L. (1985). International crisis management in the nuclear age. In S. Oskamp (Ed.), *International conflict and national public policy issues: Applied social psychology annual 6* (pp. 63–86). Beverly Hills, CA: Sage.

Janis, I. L., & Feshbach, S. (1953). Effects of fear-arousing communications. *Journal of Abnormal and Social Psychology, 48*, 78–92.

Janis, I. L., & Field, P. B. (1959). Sex differences and personality factors related to persuasibility. In I. L. Janis, C. I. Hovland, et al., *Personality and persuasibility* (pp. 55–68). New Haven, CT: Yale University Press.

Janis, I. L., Hovland, C. I., Field, E. B., Linton, H., Graham, E., Cohen, A. R., Rife, D., Abelson, R. P., Lesser, G. S., & King, B. T. (1959). *Personality and persuasibility.* New Haven, CT: Yale University Press.

Janis, I. L., & Mann, L. (1977). *Decision making.* New York: Free Press.

Janis, I. L., & Smith, M. B. (1965). Effects of education and persuasion on national and international images. In H. C. Kelman (Ed.), *International behavior: A social-psychological analysis* (pp. 190–235). New York: Holt, Rinehart & Winston.

Jänke, L. (1994). An EMG investigation of the coactivation of facial muscles during the presentation of affect-laden stimuli. *Journal of Psychophysiology, 8*, 1–10.

Jarman, B. J. (1997, April). The prevalence and precedence of socially condoned sexual aggression within a dating context as measured by direct questioning and the randomized response technique. *Dissertation Abstracts International* (Section B, Vol. 57, 10-B, p. 6651). Ann Arbor, MI: University Microfilms International.

Jaspars, J., Fincham, F., & Hewstone, M. (Eds.). (1983). *Attribution theory research: Conceptual, developmental and social dimensions.* London, England: Academic Press.

Jaynes, G. D., & Williams, R. M., Jr. (Eds.). (1989). *A common destiny: Blacks and American society.* Washington, DC: National Academy Press.

Jellison, W., McConnell, A., & Gabriel, S. (2004). Implicit and explicit measures of sexual orientation attitudes. *Personality and Social Psychology Bulletin, 30*, 629–642.

Jennings, M. K. (1992). Ideological thinking among mass publics and political elites. *Public Opinion Quarterly, 56*, 419–441.

Jennings, M. K., & Niemi, R. G. (1968). The transmission of political values from parent to child. *Political Science Review, 62*, 169–184.

Jennings, M. K., & Niemi, R. G. (1974). *The political character of adolescence.* Princeton, NJ: Princeton University Press.

Jervis, R. (1970). *The logic of images in international relations.* Princeton, NJ: Princeton University Press.

Jervis, R. (1986). Cognition and political behavior. In R. R. Lau & D. O. Sears (Eds.), *Political cognition: The 19th Annual Carnegie Symposium on Cognition* (pp. 319–336). Hillsdale, NJ: Lawrence Erlbaum Associates.

Johnson, B. T., & Eagly, A. H. (1989). The effects of involvement on persuasion: A meta-analysis. *Psychological Bulletin, 106*, 290–314.

Johnson, B. T., & Eagly, A. H. (1990). Involvement and persuasion: Types, traditions, and the evidence. *Psychological Bulletin, 107*, 375–384.

Johnson, B. T., Lin, H., Symons, C. S., Campbell, L. A., & Ekstein, G. (1995). Initial beliefs and attitudinal latitudes as factors in persuasion. *Personality and Social Psychology Bulletin, 21*, 502–511.

Johnson, D. W., & Johnson, R. T. (2000). The three Cs of reducing prejudice and discrimination. In S. Oskamp (Ed.), *Reducing prejudice and discrimination* (pp. 239–268). Mahwah, NJ: Lawrence Erlbaum Associates.

Johnson, D. W., Johnson, R. T., & Maruyama, G. (1983). Interdependence and interpersonal attraction among heterogeneous and homogeneous individuals: A theoretical formulation and a meta-analysis of the research. *Review of Educational Research, 53*, 5–54.

Johnson, H. H., & Scileppi, J. A. (1969). Effects of ego-involvement conditions on attitude change to high and low credibility communicators. *Journal of Personality and Social Psychology, 13*, 31–36.

Johnson, J. T., Cain, L. M., Falke, T. L., Hayman, J., & Perillo, E. (1985). The "Barnum effect" revisited: Cognitive and motivational factors in the acceptance of personality descriptions. *Journal of Personality and Social Psychology, 49*, 1378–1391.

Johnston, J., & Ettema, J. S. (1982). *Positive images: Breaking stereotypes with children's television.* Beverly Hills, CA: Sage.

Johnston, J., Ettema, J. S., & Davidson, T. (1980). *An evaluation of "Freestyle": A television series to reduce sex role stereotypes.* Ann Arbor, MI: Institute for Social Research.

Johnston, L., & Hewstone, M. (1992). Cognitive models of stereotype change: (3) Subtyping and the perceived typicality of disconfirming group members. *Journal of Experimental Social Psychology, 28*, 360–386.

Johnstone, D. C. (1999, September 5). Gap between rich and poor found substantially wider. *New York Times*, p. A14.

Jonas, E., Schulz-Hardt, S., Frey, D., & Thelen, N. (2001). Confirmation bias in sequential information search after preliminary decisions: An expansion of dissonance theoretical research on selective exposure to information. *Journal of Personality and Social Psychology, 80*, 557–571.

Jones, E. E. (1985). Major developments in social psychology during the past five decades. In G. Lindzey & E. Aronson (Eds.), *The handbook of social psychology* (3rd ed., Vol. 1, pp. 47–107). New York: Random House.

Jones, E. E., & Davis, K. E. (1965). From acts to dispositions: The attribution process in person perception. In L. Berkowitz (Ed.), *Advances in experimental social psychology* (Vol. 2, pp. 219–266). New York: Academic Press.

Jones, E. E., & Gerard, H. B. (1967). *Foundations of social psychology*. New York: Wiley.

Jones, E. E., & Harris, V. A. (1967). The attribution of attitudes. *Journal of Experimental Social Psychology, 3*, 1–24.

Jones, E. E., Kanouse, D. E., Kelley, H. H., Nisbett, R. E., Valins, S., & Weiner, B. (1972). *Attribution: Perceiving the causes of behavior.* Morristown, NJ: General Learning Press.

Jones, E. E., & McGillis, D. (1976). Correspondent inferences and the attribution cube: A comparative reappraisal. In J. H. Harvey, W. J. Ickes, & R. F. Kidd (Eds.), *New directions in attribution research* (Vol. 1, pp. 389–420). Hillsdale, NJ: Lawrence Erlbaum Associates.

Jones, E. E., & Nisbett, R. E. (1972). The actor and the observer: Divergent perceptions of the causes of behavior. In E. E. Jones, D. E. Kanouse, H. H. Kelley, R. E. Nisbett, S. Valins, & B. Weiner (Eds.), *Attribution: Perceiving the causes of behavior* (pp. 79–94). Morristown, NJ: General Learning Press.

Jones, E. E., & Pittman, T. S. (1982). Toward a general theory of strategic self-presentation. In J. Suls (Ed.), *Psychological perspectives on the self* (pp. 231–262). Hillsdale, NJ: Lawrence Erlbaum Associates.

Jones, E. E., & Sigall, H. (1971). The bogus pipeline: A new paradigm for measuring affect and attitude. *Psychological Bulletin, 76*, 349–364.

Jones, J. M. (1997). *Prejudice and racism* (2nd ed.). New York: McGraw-Hill.

Jones, J. M. (2001a, October). Americans view Afghans favorably, but not Taliban government. *Gallup Poll Monthly*, No. 433, pp. 41–43.

Jones, J. M. (2001b, November). Terrorism reaches status of Korean and Vietnam Wars as most important problem. *Gallup Poll Monthly*, No. 434, pp. 13–15.

Jones, J. M. (2002a, March). Support for military effort remains high. *Gallup Poll Monthly*, No. 438, pp. 16–20.

Jones, J. M. (2002b, November 18). Economy, terrorism continue to top list of most important problems. *Gallup Poll Tuesday Briefing*, pp. 64–65.

Jones, J. M. (2003a, March 28). Blacks showing decided opposition to war. *Gallup Poll Tuesday Briefing*, pp. 40–42.

Jones, J. M. (2003b, April 24). Americans' views of U.S. standing in world remain positive. *Gallup Poll Tuesday Briefing*, pp. 36–37.

Jones, J. M. (2004, June 4). Bush ratings show historical levels of polarization. *Gallup Poll News Service.* Retrieved June 9, 2004, from http://www.gallup.com/content/?ci=11884

Jones, J. M., & Moore, D. (2003, June 17). Generational differences in support for a woman president. *Gallup Poll Tuesday Briefing*, pp. 26–27.

Jones, R. A., Linder, D. E., Kiesler, C. A., Zanna, M. P., & Brehm, J. W. (1968). Internal states or external stimuli: Observers' attitude judgments and the dissonance-theory–self-persuasion controversy. *Journal of Experimental Social Psychology, 4*, 247–269.

Jost, J. T., Glaser, J., Kruglanski, A. W., & Sulloway, F. J. (2003). Political conservatism as motivated social cognition. *Psychological Bulletin, 129*, 339–375.

Jowell, R., Hedges, B., Lynn, P., Farrant, G., & Heath, A. (1993). The polls—A review: The 1992 British election: The failure of the polls. *Public Opinion Quarterly, 57*, 238–263.

Judd, C. M., Kenny, D. A., & Krosnick, J. A. (1983). Judging the positions of political candidates: Models of assimilation and contrast. *Journal of Personality and Social Psychology, 44*, 952–963.

Judd, C. M., Krosnick, J. A., & Milburn, M. A. (1981). Political involvement and attitude structure in the general public. *American Sociological Review, 46*, 660–669.

Judd, C. M., & Milburn, M. A. (1980). The structure of attitude systems in the general public: Comparisons of a structural equation model. *American Sociological Review, 45*, 627–643.

Judd, C. M., & Park, B. (1993). Definition and assessment of accuracy in social stereotypes. *Psychological Review, 100*, 109–128.

Kahle, L. R. (Ed.). (1983). *Social values and social change: Adaptation to life in America*. New York: Praeger.

Kahn, K. F., & Kenny, P. J. (1997). A model of candidate evaluations in senate elections: The impact of campaign intensity. *Journal of Politics, 59*, 1173–1206.

Kahn, K. F., & Kenny, P. J. (1999). Do negative campaigns mobilize or suppress turnout? Clarifying the relationship between negativity and participation. *American Political Science Review, 93*, 877–890.

Kahn, P. (1999). *The human relationship with nature: Development and culture*. Cambridge, MA: MIT Press.

Kahn, W. A., & Crosby, F. J. (1985). Discriminating between attitudes and discriminatory behaviors: Change and stasis. In L. Larwood, A. H. Stromberg, & B. A. Gutek (Eds.), *Women and work: An annual review* (Vol. 1, pp. 215–238). Beverly Hills, CA: Sage.

Kahneman, D., & Tversky, A. (1979). Prospect theory: An analysis of decision under risk. *Econometrica, 47*, 263–291.

Kahneman, D., & Tversky, A. (1982). The simulation heuristic. In D. Kahneman, P. Slovic, & A. Tversky (Eds.), *Judgment under uncertainty: Heuristics and biases* (pp. 201–208). Cambridge, England: Cambridge University Press.

Kaid, L. L. (1981). Political advertising. In D. D. Nimmo & K. R. Sanders (Eds.), *Handbook of political communication* (pp. 249–271). Beverly Hills, CA: Sage.

Kaiser, F. G., & Gutscher, H. (2003). The proposition of a general version of the theory of planned behavior: Predicting ecological behavior. *Journal of Applied Social Psychology, 33*, 586–603.

Kaiser, F. G., & Keller, C. (2001). Disclosing situational constraints to ecological behavior: A confirmatory application of the mixed Rasch model. *European Journal of Psychological Assessment, 17*, 212–221.

Kaiser, F. G., & Schultz, P. W. (2004). *The attitude–behavior relationship: A test of three models of the moderating role of behavioral difficulty.* Unpublished manuscript, Eindhoven, Netherlands.

Kals, E., & Maes, J. (2002). Sustainable development and emotions. In P. Schmuck & P. W. Schultz (Eds.), *Psychology of sustainable development* (pp. 97–122). Boston: Kluwer.

Kane, E. W., & Macaulay, L. J. (1993). Interviewer gender and gender attitudes. *Public Opinion Quarterly, 57*, 1–28.

Kaplan, K. J. (1972). On the ambivalence-indifference problem in attitude theory and measurement: A suggested modification of the semantic differential technique. *Psychological Bulletin, 77*, 361–372.

Karabenick, S. A. (1983). Sex-relevance of content and influenceability: Sistrunk and McDavid revisited. *Personality and Social Psychology Bulletin, 9*, 243–252.

Karlins, M., Coffman, T. L., & Walters, G. (1969). On the fading of social stereotypes: Studies in three generations of college students. *Journal of Personality and Social Psychology, 13*, 1–16.

Karp, D. G. (1996). Values and their effect on pro-environmental behavior. *Environment and Behavior, 28*, 111–133.

Karpinski, A., & Hilton, J. L. (2001). Attitudes and the Implicit Association Test. *Journal of Personality and Social Psychology, 81*, 774–788.

Kashima, Y., Siegel, M., Tanaka, K., & Kashima, E. S. (1992). Do people believe behaviors are consistent with attitudes? Toward a cultural psychology of attributional processes. *British Journal of Social Psychology, 31*, 111–124.

Kassin, S. M. (1979). Consensus information, prediction, and causal attribution: A review of the literature and issues. *Journal of Personality and Social Psychology, 37*, 1966–1981.

Kassin, S. M., Reddy, M. E., & Tulloch, W. F. (1990). Juror interpretation of ambiguous evidence: The need for cognition, presentation order, and persuasion. *Law and Human Behavior, 14*, 43–55.

Katosh, J. P., & Traugott, M. W. (1981). The consequences of validated and self-reported voting measures. *Public Opinion Quarterly, 45*, 519–535.

Katz, D. (1960). The functional approach to the study of attitudes. *Public Opinion Quarterly, 24*, 163–204.

Katz, D., & Braly, K. (1933). Racial stereotypes of 100 college students. *Journal of Abnormal and Social Psychology, 28*, 280–290.

Katz, E. (1957). The two-step flow of communications: An up-to-date report on an hypothesis. *Public Opinion Quarterly, 21*, 61–78.

Katz, E., & Feldman, J. J. (1962). The debates in the light of research: A survey of surveys. In S. Kraus (Ed.), *The great debates* (pp. 173–223). Bloomington: Indiana University Press.

Katz, E., & Lazarsfeld, P. F. (1955). *Personal influence.* Glencoe, IL: Free Press.

Kaufman, G. (1999). The portrayal of men's family roles in television commercials. *Sex Roles, 41*, 439–458.

Kawakami, K., Dion, K. L., & Dovidio, J. F. (1998). Racial prejudice and stereotype activation. *Personality and Social Psychology Bulletin, 24*, 407–416.

Kawakami, K., Dovidio, J. F., Moll, J., Hermsen, S., & Russin, A. (2000). Just say no (to stereotyping): Effects of training in the negation of stereotypic associations on stereotype activation. *Journal of Personality and Social Psychology, 78*, 871–888.

Kawakami, K., Young, H., & Dovidio, J. F. (2002). Automatic stereotyping: Category, trait, and behavioral activation. *Personality and Social Psychology Bulletin, 28*, 3–15.

Keeter, S. (1987). The illusion of intimacy: Television and the role of candidate personal qualities in voter choice. *Public Opinion Quarterly, 51*, 344–358.

Keeter, S. (1995). Estimating telephone noncoverage bias with a telephone survey. *Public Opinion Quarterly, 59*, 196–217.

Keeter, S., Miller, C., Kohut, A., Groves, R. M., & Presser, S. (2000). Consequences of reducing nonresponse in a national telephone survey. *Public Opinion Quarterly, 64*, 125–148.

Keith, B. E., Magleby, D. B., Nelson, C. J., Orr, E., Westlye, M. C., & Wolfinger, R. E. (1992). *The myth of the independent voter.* Berkeley: University of California Press.

Keller, L. M., Bouchard, T. J., Avery, R. D., & Segal, N. L. (1992). Work values: Genetic and environmental influences. *Journal of Applied Psychology, 77*, 79–88.

Kelley, H. H. (1967). Attribution theory in social psychology. In D. Levine (Ed.), *Nebraska symposium on motivation* (Vol. 15, pp. 192–238). Lincoln: University of Nebraska Press.

Kelley, H. H. (1972a). Attribution in social interaction. In E. E. Jones, D. E. Kanouse, H. H. Kelley, R. E. Nisbett, S. Valins, & B. Weiner (Eds.), *Attribution: Perceiving the causes of behavior* (pp. 1–26). Morristown, NJ: General Learning Press.

Kelley, H. H. (1972b). Causal schemata and the attribution process. In E. E. Jones, D. E. Kanouse, H. H. Kelley, R. E. Nisbett, S. Valins, & B. Weiner (Eds.), *Attribution: Perceiving the causes of behavior* (pp. 151–174). Morristown, NJ: General Learning Press.

Kelley, H. H., & Michela, J. L. (1980). Attribution theory and research. *Annual Review of Psychology, 31*, 457–501.

Kelley, J., & McAllister, I. (1984). Ballot paper cues and the vote in Australia and Britain: Alphabetic voting, sex, and title. *Public Opinion Quarterly, 48*, 452–466.

Kelly, E. L. (1955). Consistency of the adult personality. *American Psychologist, 10*, 659–681.

Kelman, H. C. (1958). Compliance, identification, and internationalization: Three processes of attitude change. *Journal of Conflict Resolution, 2*, 51–60.

Kelman, H. C. (1967). Human use of human subjects: The problem of deception in social psychological experiments. *Psychological Bulletin, 67*, 1–11.

Kelman, H. C. (1972). The rights of the subject in social research: An analysis in terms of relative power and legitimacy. *American Psychologist, 27*, 989–1016.

Kelman, H. C. (1974). Attitudes are alive and well and gainfully employed in the sphere of action. *American Psychologist, 29*, 310–324.

Kelman, H. C. (1982). Ethical issues in different social science methods. In T. L. Beauchamp, R. R. Faden, R. J. Wallace, Jr., & L. R. Walters (Eds.), *Ethical issues in social science research* (pp. 40–98). Baltimore: Johns Hopkins University Press.

Kelman, H. C. (1997). Group processes in the resolution of international conflicts: Experiences from the Israeli–Palestinian case. *American Psychologist, 52*, 212–220.

Kelman, H. C., & Hovland, C. I. (1953). "Reinstatement" of the communicator in delayed measurement of opinion change. *Journal of Abnormal and Social Psychology, 48*, 327–335.

Kemmelmeier, M., Krol, G., & Young, H. K. (2002). Values, economics, and proenvironmental attitudes in 22 societies. *Cross-Cultural Research, 36*, 256–285.

Kempton, W., Boster, J., & Hartley, J. (1995). *Environmental values in American culture.* Cambridge, MA: MIT Press.

Kennamer, J. D. (1985, May). *Debate viewing and debate discussion as predictors of campaign cognition.* Paper presented at American Association for Public Opinion Research Meeting, Great Gorge, NJ.

Kenny, D. A., & Judd, C. M. (1996). A general procedure for the estimation of independence. *Psychological Bulletin, 119*, 138–148.

Kenrick, D. T., & Gutierres, S. E. (1980). Contrast effects and judgments of physical attractiveness: When beauty becomes a social problem. *Journal of Personality and Social Psychology, 38*, 131–140.

Kenrick, D. T., & Luce, C. (2000). An evolutionary life-history model of gender differences and similarities. In T. Eckes & H. Trautner (Eds.), *The developmental social psychology of gender* (pp. 35–64). Mahwah, NJ: Lawrence Erlbaum Associates.

Kerlinger, E. N. (1984). *Liberalism and conservatism: The nature and structure of social attitudes.* Hillsdale, NJ: Lawrence Erlbaum Associates.

Kernell, S. (1978). Explaining presidential popularity. *American Political Science Review, 72*, 506–522.

Kerrick, J. S. (1958). The effect of relevant and non-relevant sources on attitude change. *Journal of Social Psychology, 47*, 15–20.

Kessel, J. H. (1965). Cognitive dimensions and political activity. *Public Opinion Quarterly, 29*, 377–389.

Kessel, J. H. (1968). *The Goldwater coalition.* Indianapolis: Bobbs-Merrill.

Key, V. O., Jr., & Cummings, M. C., Jr. (1966). *The responsible electorate: Rationality in presidential voting, 1936–1960.* Cambridge, MA: Harvard University Press.

Kidner, D. (2001). *Nature and psyche: Radical environmentalism and the politics of subjectivity.* New York: State University of New York Press.

Kiesler, C. A. (1968). Commitment. In R. E. Abelson et al. (Eds.), *Theories of cognitive consistency: A sourcebook.* Chicago: Rand McNally.

Kiesler, C. A. (1971). *The psychology of commitment: Experiments linking behavior to belief.* New York: Academic Press.

Kiesler, C. A. (1980). Psychology and public policy. In L. Bickman (Ed.), *Applied social psychology annual* (Vol. 1, pp. 49–67). Beverly Hills, CA: Sage.

Kiesler, C. A., Collins, B. E., & Miller, N. (1969). *Attitude change: A critical analysis of theoretical approaches.* New York: Wiley.

Kiesler, C. A., & Munson, P. A. (1975). Attitudes and opinions. *Annual Review of Psychology, 26,* 415–456.

Kihlstrom, J. F. (1987). The cognitive unconscious. *Science, 237,* 1445–1452.

Kihlstrom, J. F., Barnhardt, T. M., & Tataryn, D. J. (1992). The psychological unconscious: Found, lost, and regained. *American Psychologist, 47,* 788–791.

Killeya, L., & Johnson, B. T. (1998). Experimental induction of biased systematic processing: The directed-thought technique. *Personality and Social Psychology Bulletin, 24,* 17–33.

Kimball, M. (2001). Gender similarities and differences as feminist contradictions. In R. K. Unger (Ed.), *Handbook of the psychology of women and gender* (pp. 66–83). New York: Wiley.

Kinder, D. R. (1978). Political person perception: The asymmetrical influence of sentiment and choice on perceptions of presidential candidates. *Journal of Personality and Social Psychology, 36,* 859–871.

Kinder, D. R. (1981). Presidents, prosperity, and public opinion. *Public Opinion Quarterly, 45,* 1–21.

Kinder, D. R. (1994). Reason and emotion in American political life. In R. Schank & E. Langer (Eds.), *Beliefs, reasoning, and decision making* (pp. 277–314). Hillsdale, NJ: Lawrence Erlbaum Associates.

Kinder, D. R. (1998). Opinion and action in the realm of politics. In D. T. Gilbert, S. T. Fiske, & G. Lindzey (Eds.), *The handbook of social psychology* (4th ed., Vol. 1, pp. 778–867). Boston: McGraw-Hill.

Kinder, D. R., & Kiewiet, D. R. (1981). Sociotropic politics. *British Journal of Political Science, 11,* 129–161.

Kinder, D. R., & Sanders, L. M. (1996). *Divided by color: Racial politics and democratic ideals.* Chicago: University of Chicago Press.

Kinder, D. R., & Sears, D. O. (1981). Prejudice and politics: Symbolic racism versus racial threats to the good life. *Journal of Personality and Social Psychology, 40,* 414–431.

Kinder, D. R., & Sears, D. O. (1985). Public opinion and political action. In G. Lindzey & E. Aronson (Eds.), *The handbook of social psychology* (3rd ed., Vol. 2, pp. 659–741). New York: Random House.

King, B. T., & Janis, I. L. (1956). Comparison of the effectiveness of improvised vs. non-improvised role-playing in producing opinion changes. *Human Relations, 9,* 177–186.

King, M. (1977–1978). Assimilation and contrast of presidential candidates' issue positions, 1972. *Public Opinion Quarterly, 41,* 515–522.

King, R., & Schnitzer, M. (1968). Contemporary use of private political polling. *Public Opinion Quarterly, 32,* 431–536.

Kingdon, J. W. (1970). Opinion leaders in the electorate. *Public Opinion Quarterly, 34,* 256–261.

Kirkpatrick, C. (1963). *The family as process and institution* (2nd ed.). New York: Ronald.

Kirkpatrick, S. A. (1970a). Political attitude structure and component change. *Public Opinion Quarterly, 34,* 403–407.

Kirkpatrick, S. A. (1970b). Political attitudes and behavior: Some consequences of attitudinal ordering. *Midwest Journal of Political Science, 14,* 1–24.

Kirscht, J. E., & Dillehay, R. C. (1967). *Dimensions of authoritarianism: A review of research and theory.* Lexington: University of Kentucky Press.

Kite, M. (2001). Changing times, changing gender roles: Who do we want women and men to be? In R. Unger (Ed.), *Handbook of the psychology of women and gender* (pp. 215–227). New York: Wiley.

Kitt, A. S., & Gleicher, D. B. (1950). Determinants of voting behavior: A progress report on the Elmira election study. *Public Opinion Quarterly, 14,* 393–412.

Klapper, J. T. (1960). *The effects of mass communication.* New York: Free Press.

Klapper, J. T. (1963). The social effects of mass communication. In W. Schramm (Ed.), *The science of human communication* (pp. 65–76). New York: Basic Books.

Klatzky, R. L., Martin, G. L., & Kane, R. (1982). Influence of social-category activation on processing of visual information. *Social Cognition, 1,* 95–109.

Kleg, M., & Yamamoto, K. (1998). As the world turns: Ethno-racial distances after 70 years. *Social Science Journal, 35,* 183–191.

Klein, O., & Snyder, M. (2003). Stereotypes and behavioral confirmation: From interpersonal to intergroup perspectives. In M. P. Zanna (Ed.), *Advances in experimental social psychology* (Vol. 35, pp. 153–233). San Diego, CA: Academic Press.

Kleiner, M. (Ed.). (2002). *Handbook of polygraph testing.* San Diego, CA: Academic Press.

Kleinpenning, G., & Hagendoorn, L. (1993). Forms of racism and the cumulative dimension of ethnic attitudes. *Social Psychology Quarterly, 56,* 21–36.

Klineberg, O. (1984). Public opinion and nuclear war. *American Psychologist, 39,* 1245–1253.

Kling, K., Hyde, J., Showers, C., & Buswell, B. (1999). Gender differences in self-esteem: A meta-analysis. *Psychological Bulletin, 125,* 470–500.

Knack, S. (1992). Civic norms, social sanctions, and voter turnout. *Rationality and Society, 4,* 133–156.

Knowles, E. S., & Linn, J. A. (Eds.). (2004). *Resistance and persuasion*. Mahwah, NJ: Lawrence Erlbaum Associates.

Knowles, E. S., & Condon, C. A. (1999). Why people say "yes": A dual-process theory of acquiescence. *Journal of Personality and Social Psychology, 77*, 379–386.

Knox, R. E., & Inkster, J. A. (1968). Postdecision dissonance at post time. *Journal of Personality and Social Psychology, 8*, 319–323.

Kohut, A., & Ornstein, N. (1987). Constructing a winning coalition. *Public Opinion, 10*(4), 41–44.

Komarovsky, M. (1985). *Women in college*. New York: Basic Books.

Konrad, A., & Harris, C. (2002). Desirability of the Bem Sex Role Inventory items for women and men: A comparison between African Americans and European Americans. *Sex Roles, 47*, 259–271.

Korn, J. H. (1984). Research ethics needs careful scrutiny. *APA Monitor, 15*(12), 36.

Kosterman, R., & Feshbach, S. (1989). Toward a measure of patriotic and nationalistic attitudes. *Political Psychology, 10*, 257–274.

Kothandapani, V. (1971a). *A psychological approach to the prediction of contraceptive behavior*. Chapel Hill: University of North Carolina, Carolina Population Center.

Kothandapani, V. (1971b). Validation of feeling, belief, and intention to act as three components of attitude and their contribution to prediction of contraceptive behavior. *Journal of Personality and Social Psychology, 19*, 321–333.

Kraus, S. J. (1995). Attitudes and the prediction of behavior: A meta-analysis of the empirical literature. *Personality and Social Psychology Bulletin, 21*, 58–75.

Kraut, R. E., & McConahay, J. B. (1973). How being interviewed affects voting: An experiment. *Public Opinion Quarterly, 37*, 398–406.

Krech, D., Crutchfield, R., & Ballachey, E. (1962). *Individual in society*. New York: McGraw-Hill.

Krosnick, J. A. (1988). Attitude importance and attitude change. *Journal of Experimental Social Psychology, 24*, 240–255.

Krosnick, J. A. (1989). Question wording and reports of survey results: The case of Louis Harris and Associates and Aetna Life and Casualty. *Public Opinion Quarterly, 53*, 107–113.

Krosnick, J. A. (1999a). Maximizing questionnaire quality. In J. P. Robinson, P. Shaver, & L. Wrightsman (Eds.), *Measures of political attitudes* (pp. 37–58). San Diego, CA: Academic Press.

Krosnick, J. A. (1999b). Survey research. *Annual Review of Psychology, 50*, 537–567.

Krosnick, J. A., & Abelson, R. P. (1992). The case for measuring attitude strength. In J. M. Tanur (Ed.), *Questions about questions* (pp. 177–203). New York: Russell Sage Foundation.

Krosnick, J. A., & Berent, M. K. (1993). Comparisons of party identification and policy preferences: The impact of survey question format. *American Journal of Political Science, 37*, 941–964.

Krosnick, J. A., Boninger, D. S., Chuang, Y. C., Berent, M. K., & Carnot, C. G. (1993). Attitude strength: One construct or many related constructs? *Journal of Personality and Social Psychology, 65*, 1132–1151.

Krosnick, J. A., & Kinder, D. R. (1990). Altering the foundations of popular support for the president through priming: Reagan and the Iran–Contra affair. *American Political Science Review, 84*, 495–512.

Krosnick, J. A., Narayan, S., & Smith, W. R. (1996). Saisficing in surveys: Initial evidence. *New Directions for Evaluation, 70*, 29–44.

Krosnick, J. A., & Petty, R. E. (1995). Attitude strength: An overview. In J. A. Krosnick & R. E. Petty (Eds.), *Attitude strength: Antecedents and consequences* (pp. 1–24). Hillsdale, NJ: Lawrence Erlbaum Associates.

Krueger, J. H., Hasman, J., Acevedo, M., & Villano, P. (2003). Perceptions of trait typicality in gender stereotypes: Examining the role of attribution and categorization processes. *Personality and Social Psychology Bulletin, 29*, 108–116.

Kuklinski, J. H. (1978). Representatives and elections: A policy analysis. *American Political Science Review, 72*, 165–177.

Kuklinski, J. H., & Parent, W. (1981). Race and big government: Contamination in measuring racial attitudes. *Political Methodology, 7*, 131–159.

Kunda, Z. (1999). *Social cognition: Making sense of people*. Cambridge, MA: MIT Press.

Kunda, Z., & Oleson, K. C. (1995). Maintaining stereotypes in the face of disconfirmation: Constructing grounds for subtyping deviants. *Journal of Personality and Social Psychology, 68*, 565–579.

Kunkel, D. (2001). Children and television advertising. In D. G. Singer & J. L. Singer (Eds.), *Handbook of children and the media* (pp. 375–393). Thousand Oaks, CA: Sage.

Kurdek, L. (1998). Developmental changes in marital satisfaction: A 6-year prospective longitudinal study of newlywed couples. In T. Bradbury (Ed.), *The developmental course of marital dysfunction* (pp. 180–204). New York: Cambridge University Press.

Kutner, B., Wilkins, C., & Yarrow, E. R. (1952). Verbal attitudes and overt behavior involving racial prejudice. *Journal of Abnormal and Social Psychology, 47*, 649–652.

Kuzma, L. M. (2000). The polls—Trends: Terrorism in the United States. *Public Opinion Quarterly, 64*, 90–105.

La Raja, R. (2002). Political parties in the era of soft money. In L. S. Maisel (Ed.), *The parties respond: Changes in American parties and campaigns* (4th ed., pp. 163–188). Boulder, CO: Westview.

Ladd, E. C., Jr. (1981). Conservatism: A national review. *Public Opinion, 4*(1), 19–31.

Ladd, E. C., Jr. (1983). Politics in the 80's: An electorate at odds with itself. *Public Opinion, 5*(6), 2–5.

Ladd, E. C. (1991). Like waiting for Godot: The uselessness of "realignment" for understanding change in contemporary American politics. In B. E. Shafer (Ed.), *The end of realignment? Interpreting American electoral eras* (pp. 24–36). Madison: University of Wisconsin Press.

Ladd, E. C. (1998, June/July). States and regions in the US: How similar? Where different? *Public Perspective, 9*, 10–31.

Ladd, E. C., & Bowman, K. (1995). *Attitudes toward the environment*. Washington, DC: AEI Press.

Ladd, E. C., & Ferree, G. D. (1981). Were the pollsters really wrong? *Public Opinion, 3*(6), 13–20.

Lam, S. (1999). Predicting intentions to conserve water from the theory of planned behavior, perceived moral obligation, and perceived water right. *Journal of Applied Social Psychology, 29*, 1058–1071.

Lambert, W. E., & Klineberg, O. (1967). *Children's views of foreign peoples*. New York: Appleton-Century-Crofts.

Lammers, H. B., & Becker, L. A. (1980). Distraction effects on the perceived extremity of a communication and on cognitive responses. *Personality and Social Psychology Bulletin, 6*, 261–266.

Lane, R. E. (1962). *Political ideology: Why the American common man believes what he does*. New York: Free Press.

Lane, R. E. (1973). Patterns of political belief. In J. N. Knutson (Ed.), *Handbook of political psychology* (pp. 83–116). San Francisco: Jossey-Bass.

Lane, R. E. (2000). *The loss of happiness in market democracies*. New Haven, CT: Yale University Press.

Lang, K., & Lang, G. E. (1984). The impact of polls on public opinion. *The Annals of the American Academy of Political and Social Science, 472*, 129–142.

Lange, R., & Fishbein, M. (1983). Effects of category differences on belief change and agreement with the source of a persuasive communication. *Journal of Personality and Social Psychology, 44*, 933–941.

Langer, E. J. (1978). Rethinking the role of thought in social interaction. In J. H. Harvey, W. J. Ickes, & R. F. Kidd (Eds.), *New directions in attribution research* (Vol. 2, pp. 35–58). Hillsdale, NJ: Lawrence Erlbaum Associates.

Langer, E. J., Blank, A., & Chanowitz, B. (1978). The mindlessness of ostensibly thoughtful action. *Journal of Personality and Social Psychology, 36*, 635–642.

Langlois, J. H., & Downs, A. C. (1980). Mothers, fathers, and peers as socialization agents of sex-typed play behaviors in young children. *Child Development, 51*, 1217–1247.

Lanzetta, J. T., Sullivan, D. G., Masters, R. D., & McHugo, G. J. (1985). Emotional and cognitive responses to televised images of political leaders. In S. A. Kraus & R. M. Perloff (Eds.), *Mass media and political thought: An information-processing approach* (pp. 85–116). Beverly Hills, CA: Sage.

LaPiere, R. T. (1934). Attitudes vs. actions. *Social Forces, 13*, 230–237.

LaPiere, R. T. (1936). Type-rationalizations of group antipathy. *Social Forces, 15*, 232–237.

Lau, R. R., & Russell, D. (1980). Attributions in the sports pages. *Journal of Personality and Social Psychology, 39*, 29–38.

Lau, R. R., Sigelman, L., Heldman, C., & Babbitt, P. (1999). The effects of negative political advertisements: A meta-analytical assessment. *American Political Science Review, 93*, 851–875.

Lavine, H., & Snyder, M. (1996). Cognitive processing and the functional matching effect in persuasion: The mediating role of subjective perceptions of message quality. *Journal of Experimental Social Psychology, 32*, 580–604.

Lavine, H., Thomsen, C. J., & Gonzales, M. H. (1997). A shared consequences model of the development of inter-attitudinal consistency: The influence of values, attitude-relevant thought, and expertise. *Journal of Personality and Social Psychology, 72*, 735–749.

Lavrakas, P. J., & Traugott, M. W. (1995). News media's use of presidential polling in the 1990s: An introduction and overview. In P. J. Lavrakas, M. W. Traugott, & P. V. Miller (Eds.), *Presidential polls and the news media* (pp. 3–19). Boulder, CO: Westview.

Lawrence, D. G. (2001). On the resurgence of party identification in the 1990s. In J. E. Cohen, R. Fleisher, & P. Kantor (Eds.), *American political parties: Decline or resurgence?* (pp. 30–54). Washington, DC: CQ Press.

Lazarsfeld, P. F., Berelson, B., & Gaudet, H. (1948). *The people's choice*. New York: Columbia University Press.

Lazarsfeld, P. F., & Merton, R. K. (1948). Mass communication, popular taste and organized social action. In L. Bryson (Ed.), *The communication of ideas* (pp. 95–118). New York: Harper.

Lee, A., & Norris, J. (2000). Attitudes toward environmental issues in east Europe. *International Journal of Public Opinion Research, 12*, 372–397.

Lee, A. McC., & Lee, E. B. (1939). *The fine art of propaganda: A study of Father Coughlin's speeches*. New York: Harcourt, Brace.

Leff, D. R., Protess, D. L., & Brooks, S. C. (1986). Crusading journalism: Changing public attitudes and policymaking agendas. *Public Opinion Quarterly, 50*, 300–315.

Lehmann, S. (1970). Personality and compliance: A study of anxiety and self-esteem in opinion and behavior change. *Journal of Personality and Social Psychology, 15*, 76–86.

Leippe, M. R., & Elkin, R. A. (1987). When motives clash: Issue involvement and response involvement as determinants of persuasion. *Journal of Personality and Social Psychology, 52*, 269–278.

Lenart, S. (1994). *Shaping political attitudes: The impact of interpersonal communication and mass media.* Thousand Oaks, CA: Sage.

Lenny, E. (1991). Sex roles: The measurement of masculinity, femininity, and androgyny. In J. P. Robinson, P. R. Shaver, & L. Wrightsman (Eds.), *Measures of personality and social psychological attitudes* (pp. 573–649). San Diego: Academic Press.

Lepore, L., & Brown, R. (1997). Category and stereotype activation: Is prejudice inevitable? *Journal of Personality and Social Psychology, 72*, 275–287.

Lepore, L., & Brown, R. (1999). Exploring automatic stereotype activation: A challenge to the inevitability of prejudice. In D. Abrams & M. Hogg (Eds.), *Social identity and social cognition* (pp. 141–163). Malden, MA: Blackwell.

Lepper, M. R., & Greene, D. (1975). Turning play into work: Effects of adult surveillance and extrinsic rewards on children's intrinsic motivation. *Journal of Personality and Social Psychology, 31*, 479–486.

Levant, R. F. (2003, Summer). Psychology responds to terrorism. *Peace Psychology, 12*(1), 5.

Leventhal, H. (1970). Findings and theory in the study of fear communications. In L. Berkowitz (Ed.), *Advances in experimental social psychology* (Vol. 5, pp. 119–186). New York: Academic Press.

Leventhal, H., & Nerenz, D. (1983). Representations of threat and the control of stress. In D. Meichenbaum & M. Jaremko (Eds.), *Stress reduction and prevention: A cognitive behavioral approach.* New York: Plenum.

Levy, J. S. (1992). An introduction to prospect theory. *Political Psychology, 13*, 171–186.

Levy, M. R. (1983). The methodology and performance of election day polls. *Public Opinion Quarterly, 47*, 54–67.

Levy, M. R. (1984). Polling and the presidential election. *The Annals of the American Academy of Political and Social Science, 472*, 85–96.

Lewin, K. (1947). Group decision and social change. In T. M. Newcomb & E. L. Hartley (Eds.), *Readings in social psychology* (pp. 330–344). New York: Holt.

Lewin, M. (1984). The Victorians, the psychologists, and psychic birth control. In M. Lewin (Ed.), *In the shadow of the past: Psychology portrays the sexes* (pp. 39–76). New York: Columbia University Press.

Lewis, M. (1972). State as an infant–environment interaction: An analysis of mother-infant interactions as a function of sex. *Merrill-Palmer Quarterly, 18*, 95–121.

Lewis-Beck, M. S. (1987). A model performance. *Public Opinion, 9*(6), 57–58.

Lewis-Beck, M. S., & Rice, T. W. (1992). *Forecasting elections.* Washington, DC: Congressional Quarterly.

Lichter, S. R., Lichter, L. S., Rothman, S., & Amundson, D. (1987). Prime-time prejudice: TV's image of blacks and Hispanics. *Public Opinion, 10*(2), 13–16.

Lichter, S. R., & Noyes, R. E. (1995). *Good intentions make bad news: Why Americans hate campaign journalism.* Lanham, MD: Rowman & Littlefield.

Lichty, L. W. (1982). Video versus print. *Wilson Quarterly, 6*(5), 48–57.

Lieberman, S. (1956). The effects of changes in roles on the attitudes of role occupants. *Human Relations, 9*, 385–402.

Lifton, R. J. (1963). *Thought reform and the psychology of totalism.* New York: Norton.

Likert, R. (1932). A technique for the measurement of attitudes. *Archives of Psychology*, No. 140.

Linder, D. E., Cooper, J., & Jones, E. E. (1967). Decision freedom as a determinant of the role of incentive magnitude in attitude change. *Journal of Personality and Social Psychology, 6*, 245–254.

Lindskold, S. (1978). Trust development, the GRIT proposal, and the effects of conciliatory acts on conflict and cooperation. *Psychological Bulletin, 85*, 772–793.

Link, M. W., & Oldendick, R. W. (1999). Call screening: Is it really a problem for survey research? *Public Opinion Quarterly, 63*, 577–589.

Linville, E. W. (1982). The complexity-extremity effect and age-based stereotyping. *Journal of Personality and Social Psychology, 42*, 193–211.

Lippmann, W. (1922). *Public opinion.* New York: Harcourt, Brace & World.

Lips, H. M. (2003). The gender pay gap: Concrete indicator of women's progress toward equality. *Analyses of Social Issues and Public Policy, 3*, 87–109.

Lipset, S. M. (1966). The president, the polls, and Vietnam. *Trans-action, 3*(6), 19–24.

Lipset, S. M. (1982). No room for the ins: Elections around the world. *Public Opinion, 5*(5), 41–43.

Lipset, S. M. (2000, March/April). Socialism: Not in the United States. *Public Perspective, 11*(2), 31–33.

Lipset, S. M., & Schneider, W. (1983). *The confidence gap: Business, labor and government in the public mind*. New York: Free Press.

Listhaug, O. (1986). War and defence attitudes: A first look at survey data from 14 countries. *Journal of Peace Research, 23*, 69–76.

Litwak, E., Hooyman, N., & Warren, D. (1973). Ideological complexity and middle-American rationality. *Public Opinion Quarterly, 37*, 317–332.

Liu, J., & Latane, B. (1998). Extremitization of attitudes: Does thought- and discussion-induced polarization cumulate? *Basic and Applied Social Psychology, 20*, 103–110.

Locksley, A., Borgida, E., Brekke, N., & Hepburn, C. (1980). Sex stereotypes and social judgment. *Journal of Personality and Social Psychology, 39*, 821–831.

Lombardo, W., Cretser, G., & Roesch, S. (2001). For crying out loud—The differences persist into the '90s. *Sex Roles, 45*, 529–547.

London, P. (1970). The rescuers: Motivational hypotheses about Christians who saved Jews from the Nazis. In J. Macaulay & L. Berkowitz (Eds.), *Altruism and helping behavior: Social psychological studies of some antecedents and consequences* (pp. 241–250). New York: Academic Press.

Loo, R., & Thorpe, K. (1998). Attitudes toward women's roles in society: A replication after 20 years. *Sex Roles, 39*, 903–912.

Lord, C. G., Lepper, M. R., & Mackie, D. (1984). Attitude prototypes as determinants of attitude-behavior consistency. *Journal of Personality and Social Psychology, 46*, 1254–1266.

Lord, C. G., Ross, L., & Lepper, M. R. (1979). Biased assimilation and attitude polarization: The effects of prior theories on subsequently considered evidence. *Journal of Personality and Social Psychology, 37*, 2098–2109.

Los Angeles Times. (1970, October 16). Nixon repudiates U.S. commission's obscenity report.

Los Angeles Times. (1973, May 18). Public opinion polls—An interference or a help in the electoral process? Section II, p. 11.

Losch, M., & Cacioppo, J. T. (1990). Cognitive dissonance may enhance sympathetic tonus, but attitudes are changed to reduce negative affect rather than arousal. *Journal of Experimental Social Psychology, 26*, 289–304.

Love, R. E., & Greenwald, A. G. (1978). Cognitive responses to persuasion as mediators of opinion change. *Journal of Social Psychology, 104*, 231–241.

Low, J., & Sherrard, P. (1999). Portrayal of women in sexuality and marriage and family textbooks: A content analysis of photographs from the 1970s to the 1990s. *Sex Roles, 40*, 309–318.

Ludwig, J. (2000, February). Perceptions of black and white Americans continue to diverge on issue of race relations in the U.S. *Gallup Poll Monthly*, No. 413, pp. 53–63.

Lund, F. H. (1925). The psychology of belief: IV. The law of primacy in persuasion. *Journal of Abnormal and Social Psychology, 20*, 183–191.

Lundgren, S. R., & Prislin, R. (1998). Motivated cognitive processing and attitude change. *Personality and Social Psychology Bulletin, 24*, 715–726.

Luskin, R. C., McIver, J. P., & Carmines, E. G. (1989). Issues and the transmission of partisanship. *American Journal of Political Science, 33*, 440–458.

Luttbeg, N. E. (1968). The structure of beliefs among leaders and the public. *Public Opinion Quarterly, 32*, 398–409.

Lutz, A., Simpson-Housley, P., & De Man, A. (1999). Wilderness: Rural and urban attitudes and perceptions. *Environment and Behavior, 31*, 259–266.

Lynn, M., & Simons, T. (2000). Predictors of male and female servers' average tip earnings. *Journal of Applied Social Psychology, 30*, 241–252.

Maccoby, E., & Jacklin, C. N. (1974). *The psychology of sex differences*. Stanford, CA: Stanford University Press.

MacDonald, S. E., Rabinowitz, G., & Listhaug, O. (1995). Political sophistication and models of issue voting. *British Journal of Political Science, 25*, 453–483.

MacKuen, M. B. (1981). Social communication and the mass policy agenda. In M. B. MacKuen & S. L. Coombs (Eds.), *More than news: Media power in public affairs* (pp. 17–144). Beverly Hills, CA: Sage.

MacLeod, C., & Campbell, L. (1992). Memory accessibility and probability judgments: An experimental evaluation of the availability heuristic. *Journal of Personality and Social Psychology, 63*, 890–902.

Macrae, C. N., & Bodenhausen, G. V. (2000). Social cognition: Thinking categorically about others. *Annual Review of Psychology, 51*, 93–120.

Macrae, C. N., Hewstone, M., & Griffiths, R. J. (1993). Processing load and memory for stereotype-based information. *European Journal of Social Psychology, 23*, 77–87.

Madden, T., Ellen, P., & Ajzen, I. (1992). A comparison of the theory of planned behavior and the theory of reasoned action. *Personality and Social Psychology Bulletin, 18*, 3–9.

Maio, G. R., Bell, D. W., & Esses, V. M. (1996). Ambivalence in persuasion: The processing of messages about immigrant groups. *Journal of Experimental Social Psychology, 32,* 513–536.

Maio, G. R., & Olson, J. M. (1995). Relations between values, attitudes, and behavioral intentions: The moderating role of attitude function. *Journal of Experimental Social Psychology, 31,* 266–285.

Maio, G. R., & Olson, J. M. (2000a). What is a "value-expressive" attitude? In G. R. Maio & J. M. Olson (Eds.), *Why we evaluate: Functions of attitudes* (pp. 249–269). Mahwah, NJ: Lawrence Erlbaum Associates.

Maio, G. R., & Olson, J. M. (Eds.). (2000b). *Why we evaluate: Functions of attitudes.* Mahwah, NJ: Lawrence Erlbaum Associates.

Malvin, J. H., & Moskowitz, J. M. (1983). Anonymous versus identifiable self-reports of adolescent drug attitudes, intentions, and use. *Public Opinion Quarterly, 47,* 557–566.

Manheim, J. B., & Albritton, R. B. (1984). Changing national images: International public relations and media agenda setting. *American Political Science Review, 78,* 641–657.

Manis, M., Nelson, T. E., & Shedler, J. (1988). Stereotypes and social judgment: Extremity, assimilation, and contrast. *Journal of Personality and Social Psychology, 55,* 28–36.

Mann, L., & Janis, I. L. (1968). A follow-up study on the long-term effects of emotional role playing. *Journal of Personality and Social Psychology, 8,* 339–342.

Mansbridge, J. J. (1986). *Why we lost the ERA.* Chicago: University of Chicago Press.

Marcus, G. E., Sullivan, J. L., Theiss-Morse, E., & Wood, S. L. (1995). *With malice toward some: How people make civil liberties judgments.* Cambridge, UK: Cambridge University Press.

Marcus-Newhall, A., & Heindl, T. (1998). Coping with interracial stress in ethnically diverse classrooms: How important are Allport's contact conditions? *Journal of Social Issues, 54,* 813–830.

Marin, G., Gamba, R., & Marin, B. (1992). Extreme response style and acquiescence among Hispanics: The role of acculturation and education. *Journal of Cross-Cultural Psychology, 23,* 498–509.

Markey, C., Tinsley, B., Ericksen, A., Ozer, D., & Markey, P. (2002). Preadolescents' perceptions of females' body size and shape: Evolutionary and social learning perspectives. *Journal of Youth and Adolescence, 31,* 137–146.

Marks, G., & Miller, N. (1987). Ten years of research on the false-consensus effect: An empirical and theoretical review. *Psychological Bulletin, 102,* 72–90.

Marks, G., & Miller, N. (1988). Perceptions of attitude similarity: Effect of anchored versus unanchored positions. *Personality and Social Psychology Bulletin, 14,* 92–102.

Markus, G. B. (1988). The impact of personal and national conditions in the presidential vote: A pooled cross-sectional analysis. *American Journal of Political Science, 32,* 137–154.

Markus, H., & Zajonc, R. B. (1985). The cognitive perspective in social psychology. In G. Lindzey & E. Aronson (Eds.), *The handbook of social psychology* (3rd ed., Vol. 1, pp. 137–230). New York: Random House.

Marlin, J. T. (1992). *The livable cities almanac.* New York: HarperPerennial.

Marquis, K. H. (1978). *Record check validity of survey responses: A reassessment of bias in reports of hospitalization* (R-2319-HEW). Santa Monica, CA: Rand Corp.

Marquis, K. H., Duan, N., Marquis, M. S., & Polich, J. M. (1981). *Response errors in sensitive topic surveys* (R-1710-HHS). Santa Monica, CA: Rand Corp.

Martin, J. G., & Westie, E. R. (1959). The tolerant personality. *American Sociological Review, 24,* 521–528.

Martin, P. Y., Harrison, D., & Dinitto, D. (1983). Advancement for women in hierarchical organizations: A multilevel analysis of problems and prospects. *Journal of Applied Behavioral Science, 19,* 19–33.

Martin, R. (1998). Majority and minority influence using the afterimage paradigm: A series of attempted replications. *Journal of Experimental Social Psychology, 34,* 1–26.

Martindale, C. (1986). *The white press and black America.* Westport, CT: Greenwood.

Martindale, C. (1991). *Cognitive psychology: A neural-network approach.* Pacific Grove, CA: Brooks/Cole.

Martyna, W. (1980). Beyond the "he/man" approach: The case for nonsexist language. *Signs, 5,* 482–493.

Marx, G. T. (1970). Racism and race relations. In M. Wertheimer (Ed.), *Confrontation: Psychology and the problems of today* (pp. 100–102). Glenview, IL: Scott, Foresman.

Maslow, A. H. (1970). *Motivation and personality* (2nd ed.). New York: Harper.

Massey, D. S., & Denton, N. A. (1993). *American apartheid: Segregation and the making of the underclass.* Cambridge, MA: Harvard University Press.

Mastro, D., Eastin, M., & Tamborini, R. (2002). Internet search behaviors and mood alterations: A selective exposure approach. *Media Psychology, 4,* 157–172.

Mauer, M., & Huling, T. (1995, October). *Young black Americans and the criminal justice system: Five years later.* Washington, DC: The Sentencing Project.

Maykovich, M. K. (1975). Correlates of racial prejudice. *Journal of Personality and Social Psychology, 32,* 1014–1020.

Mazis, M. B. (1975). Antipollution measures and psychological reactance theory: A field experiment. *Journal of Personality and Social Psychology, 31*, 654–660.

McArdle, J. B. (1972). *Positive and negative communications and subsequent attitude and behavior change in alcoholics.* Unpublished doctoral dissertation, University of Illinois, Urbana.

McArthur, L. Z. (1972). The how and what of why: Some determinants and consequences of causal attribution. *Journal of Personality and Social Psychology, 22*, 171–193.

McCauley, C. (2002). Psychological issues in understanding terrorism and the response to terrorism. In C. E. Stout (Ed.), *The psychology of terrorism: Vol. 3. Theoretical understandings and perspectives* (pp. 3–29). Westport, CT: Praeger.

McClosky, H. (1958). Conservatism and personality. *American Political Science Review, 52*, 27–45.

McClosky, H. (1967). Personality and attitude correlates of foreign policy orientation. In J. N. Rosenau (Ed.), *Domestic sources of foreign policy* (pp. 51–109). New York: Free Press.

McClosky, H., & Brill, A. (1983). *Dimensions of tolerance: What Americans believe about civil liberties.* New York: Russell Sage Foundation.

McComb, C. (2003, January 28). Americans increasingly unsure about global role. *Gallup Poll Tuesday Briefing*, pp. 54–55.

McCombs, M. E. (1977). Newspapers versus television: Mass communication effects across time. In D. L. Shaw & M. E. McCombs (Eds.), *The emergence of American political issues: The agenda-setting function of the press* (pp. 89–105). St. Paul, MN: West.

McCombs, M. E., & Reynolds, A. (2002). News influence on our pictures of the world. In J. Bryant & D. Zillmann (Eds.), *Media effects: Advances in theory and research* (pp. 1–18). Mahwah, NJ: Lawrence Erlbaum Associates.

McConahay, J. B. (1986). Modern racism, ambivalence, and the modern racism scale. In J. F. Dovidio & S. L. Gaertner (Eds.), *Prejudice, discrimination and racism* (pp. 91–126). Orlando, FL: Academic Press.

McConahay, J. B., Hardee, B. B., & Batts, V. (1981). Has racism declined in America? It depends on who is asking and what is asked. *Journal of Conflict Resolution, 25*, 563–579.

McConnell, A. R., & Fazio, R. H. (1996). Women as men and people: Effects of gender-marked language. *Personality and Social Psychology Bulletin, 22*, 1004–1013.

McEvoy, J. (1972). The American concern with environment. In W. R. Burch, N. Cheek, & L. Taylor (Eds.), *Social behavior, natural resources, and the environment* (pp. 214–236). New York: Harper & Row.

McEwen, C. A. (1980). Continuities in the study of total and nontotal institutions. *Annual Review of Sociology, 6*, 143–185.

McFarland, S., & Mattern, K. (2003). *Generalized explicit and implicit prejudice.* Unpublished paper, Western Kentucky University, Bowling Green.

McGinn, A. P. (1998). Promoting sustainable fisheries. In L. R. Brown et al., *State of the world 1998* (pp. 59–78). New York: Norton.

McGinnies, E., & Ward, C. (1980). Better liked than right: Trustworthiness and expertise as factors in credibility. *Personality and Social Psychology Bulletin, 6*, 467–472.

McGraw, K. M. (2002). Manipulating public opinion. In B. Norrander & C. Wilcox (Eds.), *Understanding public opinion* (2nd ed., pp. 265–280). Washington, DC: CQ Press.

McGuire, W. J. (1960). A syllogistic analysis of cognitive relationships. In M. J. Rosenberg, C. I. Hovland, W. J. McGuire, R. P. Abelson, & J. W. Brehm, *Attitude organization and change: An analysis of consistency among attitude components* (pp. 65–111). New Haven, CT: Yale University Press.

McGuire, W. J. (1964). Inducing resistance to persuasion. In L. Berkowitz (Ed.), *Advances in experimental social psychology* (Vol. 1, pp. 191–229). New York: Academic Press.

McGuire, W. J. (1966). Attitudes and opinions. *Annual Review of Psychology, 17*, 475–514.

McGuire, W. J. (1968a). Personality and attitude change: An information-processing theory. In A. G. Greenwald, T. C. Brock, & T. M. Ostrom (Eds.), *Psychological foundations of attitudes* (pp.171–196). New York: Academic Press.

McGuire, W. J. (1968b). Personality and susceptibility to social influence. In E. F. Borgatta & W. W. Lambert (Eds.), *Handbook of personality theory and research* (pp. 1130–1187). Chicago: Rand McNally.

McGuire, W. J. (1969). The nature of attitudes and attitude change. In G. Lindzey & E. Aronson (Eds.), *The handbook of social psychology* (2nd ed., Vol. 3, pp. 136–314). Reading, MA: Addison-Wesley.

McGuire, W. J. (1973). The yin and yang of progress in social psychology: Seven koan. *Journal of Personality and Social Psychology, 26*, 446–456.

McGuire, W. J. (1983). A contextualist theory of knowledge: Its implications for innovations and reform in psychology research. In L. Berkowitz (Ed.), *Advances in experimental social psychology* (Vol. 16, pp. 1–47). New York: Academic Press.

McGuire, W. J. (1985). Attitudes and attitude change. In G. Lindzey & E. Aronson (Eds.), *The handbook of social psychology* (3rd ed., Vol. 2, pp. 233–346). New York: Random House.

McGuire, W. J. (1986). The myth of massive media impact: Savagings and salvagings. In G. Comstock (Ed.), *Public communication and behavior* (Vol. 1). Orlando, FL: Academic Press.

McIntosh, M. E., & Hinckley, R. H. (1992). Challenges to polling in eastern Europe. *Public Perspective, 3*(5), 32–34.

McKenzie-Mohr, D. (2002). The next revolution: Sustainability. In P. Schmuck & P. W. Schultz (Eds.), *Psychology of sustainable development* (pp. 19–36). Boston: Kluwer Academic.

McLeod, J. M., & Becker, L. B. (1981). The uses and gratifications approach. In D. D. Nimmo & K. R. Sanders (Eds.), *Handbook of political communication* (pp. 67–99). Beverly Hills, CA: Sage.

McLeod, J. M., Durall, J. A., Ziemke, D. A., & Bybee, C. R. (1979). Reactions of young and older voters: Expanding the context. In S. Kraus (Ed.), *The great debates: Carter vs. Ford, 1976* (pp. 348–367). Bloomington: Indiana University Press.

McLeod, J. M., & Reeves, B. (1980). On the nature of mass media effects. In S. B. Withey & R. P. Abeles (Eds.), *Television and social behavior: Beyond violence and children* (pp. 17–54). Hillsdale, NJ: Lawrence Erlbaum Associates.

McNamara, R. S., & Blight, J. G. (2001). *Wilson's ghost: Reducing the risk of conflict, killing, and catastrophe in the 21st century.* New York: Public Affairs.

McStay, J., & Dunlap, R. (1983). Male-female differences in concern for environmental quality. *International Journal of Women's Studies, 6*, 291–301.

Mead, M. (1935). *Sex and temperament in three primitive societies.* New York: Morrow.

Meadows, D. H., Meadows, D. L., & Randers, J. (1992). *Beyond the limits.* Post Mills, VT: Chelsea Green.

Meertens, R. W., & Pettigrew, T. F. (1997). Is subtle prejudice really prejudice? *Public Opinion Quarterly, 61*, 54–71.

Meloen, J. (1993). The F scale as a predictor of fascism: An overview of 40 years of authoritarian research. In W. F. Stone, G. Lederer, & R. Christie (Eds.), *Strength and weakness: The authoritarian personality today* (pp. 47–69). New York: Springer-Verlag.

Mendelsohn, H. (1973). Some reasons why information campaigns can succeed. *Public Opinion Quarterly, 37*, 50–61.

Mendelsohn, H., & O'Keefe, G. J. (1976). *The people choose a president: Influences on voter decision making.* New York: Praeger.

Mendelson, G., & Young, M. (1972). *Network children's programming: A content analysis of black and minority treatment on children's television.* Newtonville, MA: Action for Children's Television.

Merritt, S. (1984). Negative political advertising: Some empirical findings. *Journal of Advertising, 13*, 27–37.

Mertig, A., & Koval, M. (2001). *Attitudes toward natural resources and their management: A report on the "2000 Resource Attitudes in Michigan Survey."* East Lansing: Michigan Department of Natural Resources, Wildlife Division.

Mertig, A., & Koval, M. (2002). *Attitudes toward natural resources and their management: A report on the "2001 Resource Attitudes in Michigan Survey."* East Lansing: Michigan Department of Natural Resources, Wildlife Division.

Merton, R. (1957). *Social theory and social structure.* Glencoe, IL: Free Press.

Meyer, D. E., & Schvaneveldt, R. W. (1971). Facilitation in recognizing pairs of words: Evidence of dependence between retrieval operations. *Journal of Experimental Psychology, 90*, 227–234.

Midden, C. J., & Verplanken, B. (1990). The stability of nuclear attitudes after Chernobyl. *Journal of Environmental Psychology, 10*, 111–119.

Middleton, M. R., Tajfel, H., & Johnson, N. B. (1970). Cognitive and affective aspects of children's national attitudes. *British Journal of Social and Clinical Psychology, 9*, 122–134.

Milavsky, J. R., Kessler, R. C., Stipp, H. H., & Rubens, W. S. (1982). *Television and aggression: Results of a panel study.* New York: Academic Press.

Milavsky, J. R., Swift, A., Roper, B. W., Salant, R., & Abrams, F. (1985). Early calls of election results and exit polls: Pros, cons, and constitutional considerations. *Public Opinion Quarterly, 49*, 1–18.

Milbrath, L. W. (1962). Latent origins of liberalism-conservatism and party identification: A research note. *Journal of Politics, 24*, 679–688.

Milbrath, L. W. (1984). *Environmentalists: Vanguard for a new society.* Albany: State University of New York Press.

Milgram, S. (1963). Behavioral study of obedience. *Journal of Abnormal and Social Psychology, 67*, 371–378.

Miller, A., Engeman, M., Polulach, J., Sweet, D., & Ullman, R. (1980). Is positive or negative prior contact a determinant of the reinforcing function of approval? *Journal of Psychology, 106*, 265–276.

Miller, A. G. (1972). Role playing: An alternative to deception? A review of the evidence. *American Psychologist, 27*, 623–636.

Miller, A. H. (1974). Political issues and trust in government: 1964–1970. *American Political Science Review, 68*, 951–972.

Miller, A. H. (1979). Normal vote analysis? Sensitivity to change over time. *American Journal of Political Science, 23*, 406–420.

Miller, A. H. (1983). Is confidence rebounding? *Public Opinion, 6*(3), 16–20.

Miller, A. H., & Wattenberg, M. E. (1984). Politics from the pulpit: Religiosity and the 1980 elections. *Public Opinion Quarterly, 48*, 301–317.

Miller, A. H., Miller, W. E., Raine, A. S., & Brown, T. A. (1976). A majority party in disarray: Policy polarization in the 1972 election. *American Political Science Review, 70*, 753–778.

Miller, A. H., Wattenberg, M. P., & Malanchuk, O. (1986). Schematic assessments of presidential candidates. *American Political Science Review, 80*, 521–540.

Miller, C. E. (1980). Assessing the existence of "wishful thinking." *Personality and Social Psychology Bulletin, 6*, 282–286.

Miller, D. T., Norman, S. A., & Wright, E. (1978). Distortion in person perception as a consequence of the need for effective control. *Journal of Personality and Social Psychology, 36*, 598–602.

Miller, D. T., & Ross, M. (1975). Self-serving biases in the attribution of causality: Fact or fiction? *Psychological Bulletin, 82*, 213–225.

Miller, J. M., & Krosnick, J. A. (1998). The impact of candidate name order on election outcomes. *Public Opinion Quarterly, 62*, 291–330.

Miller, N. (2002). Personalization and the promise of contact theory. *Journal of Social Issues, 58*, 387–410.

Miller, N., & Campbell, D. T. (1959). Recency and primacy in persuasion as a function of the timing of speeches and measurements. *Journal of Abnormal and Social Psychology, 59*, 1–9.

Miller, R. S., & Schlenker, B. R. (1985). Egotism in group members: Public and private attributions of responsibility for group performance. *Social Psychology Quarterly, 48*, 85–89.

Miller, W. E. (1960). The political behavior of the electorate. In E. Latham et al. (Eds.), *American government annual, 1960–1961* (pp. 40–48). New York: Holt, Rinehart & Winston.

Miller, W. E. (1991). Party identification, realignment, and party voting: Back to the basics. *American Political Science Review, 85*, 557–568.

Miller, W. E. (2002). Party identification and the electorate at the start of the twenty-first century. In L. S. Maisel (Ed.), *The parties respond: Changes in American parties and campaigns* (4th ed., pp. 79–98). Boulder, CO: Westview.

Miller, W. E., & Shanks, J. M. (1996). *The new American voter: Conflict and consensus in American presidential elections.* Cambridge, MA: Harvard University Press.

Miller, W. E., & Stokes, D. E. (1963). Constituency influence in Congress. *American Political Science Review, 57*, 45–56.

Mills, J., & Harvey, J. (1972). Opinion change as a function of when information about the communicator is received and whether he is attractive or expert. *Journal of Personality and Social Psychology, 21*, 52–55.

Milne, S., Sheeran, P., & Orbell, S. (2000). Prediction and intervention in health related behavior: A meta analytic review of protection motivation theory. *Journal of Applied Social Psychology, 30*, 106–142.

Mirels, H. L. (1980). The avowal of responsibility for good and bad outcomes: The effects of generalized self-serving biases. *Personality and Social Psychology Bulletin, 69*, 299–306.

Mitchell, J. (1990). *An introduction to the logic of psychological measurement.* Hillsdale, NJ: Lawrence Erlbaum Associates.

Mitofsky, W. J. (1969). Who voted for Wallace? *Public Opinion Quarterly, 33*, 444–445.

Mitofsky, W. J. (1998). The polls—Review: Was 1996 a worse year for polls than 1948? *Public Opinion Quarterly, 62*, 230–249.

Mitofsky, W. J. (2001). Fool me twice: An election nightmare. *Public Perspective, 12*(3), 35–38.

Mitofsky, W. J., & Edelman, M. (1995). A review of the 1992 VRS exit polls. In P. J. Lavrakas, M. W. Traugott, & P. V. Miller (Eds.), *Presidential polls and the news media* (pp. 81–100). Boulder, CO: Westview.

Moen, P., & Yu, Y. (2000). Effective work/life strategies: Working couples, work conditions, gender, and life quality. *Social Problems, 47*, 291–327.

Moghaddam, F. M., & Marsella, A. J. (Eds.). (2004). *Understanding terrorism: Psychosocial roots, consequences, and interventions.* Washington, DC: American Psychological Association.

Mohai, P. (1992). Men, women, and the environment. *Society and Natural Resources, 5*, 1–19.

Monahan, J. L., Murphy, S. T., & Zajonc, R. B. (2000). Subliminal mere exposure: Specific, general, and diffuse effects. *Psychological Science, 11*, 462–466.

Mondak, J. J. (1995a). Media exposure and political discussion in U.S. elections. *Journal of Politics, 57*, 62–85.

Mondak, J. J. (1995b). Competence, integrity, and the electoral success of congressional incumbents. *Journal of Politics, 57*, 1043–1069.

Monroe, A. D. (1978). Public opinion as a factor in public policy formation. *Policy Studies Journal, 6*, 542–548.

Monroe, A. D. (1998). Public opinion and public policy, 1980–93. *Public Opinion Quarterly, 62*, 6–28.

Monteith, M. J., Sherman, J. W., & Devine, P. (1998). Supression as a stereotype control strategy. *Personality and Social Psychology Review, 2*, 63–82.

Monteith, M. J., & Walters, G. L. (1998). Egalitarianism, moral obligation, and prejudice-related personal standards. *Personality and Social Psychology Bulletin, 24*, 186–199.

Montiel, C. J., & Anuar, M. K. (2002). Other terrorisms, psychology, and media. *Peace and Conflict: Journal of Peace Psychology, 8*, 201–206.

Moore, D. W. (2001a, January). Clinton leaves office with mixed public reaction. *Gallup Poll Monthly*, No. 424, pp. 14–24.

Moore, D. W. (2001b, February). Americans most satisfied with living conditions in country, opportunities to get ahead. *Gallup Poll Monthly*, No. 425, pp. 2–5.

Moore, D. W. (2001c, May). Energy crisis: Americans lean toward conservation over production. *Gallup Poll Monthly*, No. 428, pp. 14–15.

Moore, D. W. (2001d, August). Most American workers satisfied with their jobs. *Gallup Poll Monthly*, No. 431, pp. 26–29.

Moore, D. W. (2001e, September). Americans see terrorist attacks as "act of war." *Gallup Poll Monthly*, No. 432, pp. 2–4.

Moore, D. W. (2001f, October). Public overwhelmingly backs Bush in attacks on Afghanistan. *Gallup Poll Monthly*, No. 433, pp. 16–18.

Moore, D. W. (2002a, March). Americans more unfavorable than favorable toward Muslim countries. *Gallup Poll Monthly*, No. 438, pp. 2–4.

Moore, D. W. (2002b, March). Public leans toward conservation approach to environmental policy. *Gallup Poll Monthly*, No. 438, pp. 35–38.

Moore, D. W. (2002c). Measuring new types of question-order effects: Additive and subtractive. *Public Opinion Quarterly, 66*, 80–91.

Moore, D. W. (2002d, November 26). Public: If Iraq fails inspections, second U.N. resolution needed for war. *Gallup Poll Tuesday Briefing*, pp. 117–119.

Moore, D. W. (2002e, December 12). Public taking wait-and-see attitude on U.N. inspections. *Gallup Poll Tuesday Briefing*, pp. 109–111.

Moore, D. W. (2003a, March 18). Public approves of Bush ultimatum by more than 2-to-1 margin. *Gallup Poll Tuesday Briefing*, pp. 21–22.

Moore, D. W. (2003b, May 6). Public more optimistic about progress in war on terrorism. *Gallup Poll Tuesday Briefing*, pp. 4–6.

Moore, M. (1979). Structural balance and international relations. *European Journal of Social Psychology, 9*, 323–326.

Morgan, M. (1982). Television and adolescents' sex role stereotypes: A longitudinal study. *Journal of Personality and Social Psychology, 43*, 947–955.

Morgan, M., & Shanahan, J. (1997). Two decades of cultivation research: An appraisal and meta-analysis. In B. Burleson (Ed.), *Communication yearbook* (Vol. 20, pp. 1–46). Thousand Oaks, CA: Sage.

Morrissette, J. O. (1958). An experimental study of the theory of structural balance. *Human Relations, 11*, 239–254.

Morrow, L. (1979, October 15). The rise and fall of anti-Catholicism. *Time*, pp. 36–38.

Moscovici, S. (1985). Social influence and conformity. In G. Lindzey & E. Aronson (Eds.), *The handbook of social psychology* (3rd ed., Vol. 2, pp. 347–412). New York: Random House.

Moscovici, S., & Nemeth, C. (1974). Social influence II: Minority influence. In C. Nemeth (Ed.), *Social psychology: Classic and contemporary integrations* (pp. 217–249). Chicago: Rand McNally.

Mosteller, E., Hyman, H., McCarthy, P. J., Marks, E. S., & Truman, D. B. (1949). *The pre-election polls of 1948*. New York: Social Science Research Council.

Mower-White, C. J. (1979). Factors affecting balance, agreement, and positivity biases in POQ and POX triads. *European Journal of Social Psychology, 9*, 129–148.

Mueller, J. E. (1970). Choosing among 133 candidates. *Public Opinion Quarterly, 34*, 395–402.

Mueller, J. E. (1971). Trends in popular support for the wars in Korea and Vietnam. *American Political Science Review, 65*, 358–375.

Mueller, J. E. (1973). *War, presidents and public opinion*. New York: Wiley.

Mueller, J. E. (1988). Trends in political tolerance. *Public Opinion Quarterly, 52*, 1–25.

Mueller, J. E. (1993). The polls—A review: American public opinion and the Gulf War: Some polling issues. *Public Opinion Quarterly, 57*, 80–91.

Mueller, J. E. (2002). American foreign policy and public opinion in a new era: Eleven propositions. In B. Norrander & C. Wilcox (Eds.), *Understanding public opinion* (2nd ed., pp. 149–172). Washington, DC: CQ Press.

Mullen, B., Brown, R., & Smith, C. (1992). Ingroup bias as a function of salience, relevance, and status: An integration. *European Journal of Social Psychology, 22*, 103–122.

Mullen, B., Futrell, D., Stairs, D., Tice, D. M., Baumeister, R. F., Dawson, K. E., et al. (1986). Newscasters' facial expressions and voting behavior of viewers: Can a smile elect a president? *Journal of Personality and Social Psychology, 51*, 291–295.

Mullen, B., & Hu, L. (1989). Perceptions of ingroup and outgroup variability: A meta-analytic integration. *Basic and Applied Social Psychology, 10*, 233–252.

Mullen, B., & Johnson, C. (1990). Distinctiveness-based illusory correlations and stereotyping: A meta-analytic integration. *British Journal of Social Psychology, 29*, 11–28.

Mullen, B., & Riordan, C. A. (1988). Self-serving attributions for performance in naturalistic settings: A meta-analytic review. *Journal of Applied Social Psychology, 18*, 3–22.

Muller-Rommel, F. (1989). *New politics in Western Europe: The rise and success of green parties and alternative lists.* Boulder, CO: Westview.

Murphy, S. T. (2001). Feeling without thinking: Affective primacy and the nonconscious processing of emotion. In J. Bargh & D. Apsley (Eds.), *Unraveling the complexities of social life: A festschrift in honor of Robert B. Zajonc* (pp. 39–54). Washington, DC: American Psychological Association.

Murray, J. P., & Kippax, S. (1979). From the early window to the late night show: International trends in the study of television's impact on children and adults. In L. Berkowitz (Ed.), *Advances in experimental social psychology* (Vol. 12, pp. 253–320). New York: Academic Press.

Murray, S. K., & Howard, P. (2002). Variation in White House polling operations: Carter to Clinton. *Public Opinion Quarterly, 66*, 527–558.

Murrell, A. J., Dietz-Uhler, B. L., Dovidio, J. F., Gaertner, S. L., & Drout, C. (1994). Aversive racism and resistance to affirmative action: Perceptions of justice are not necessarily color blind. *Basic and Applied Social Psychology, 15*, 71–86.

Mussweiler, T. (2001). Focus of comparison as a determinant of assimilation versus contrast in social comparison. *Personality and Social Psychology Bulletin, 27*, 38–47.

Mussweiler, T., & Strack, F. (2000). The use of category and exemplar knowledge in the solution of anchoring tasks. *Journal of Personality and Social Psychology, 78*, 1038–1052.

Mutz, D. C. (1995). Media, momentum and money: Horse race spin in the 1988 Republican primaries. In P. J. Lavrakas, M. W. Traugott, & P. V. Miller (Eds.), *Presidential polls and the news media* (pp. 229–254). Boulder, CO: Westview.

Myers, A. M., & Gonda, G. (1982). Empirical validation of the Bem Sex-Role Inventory. *Journal of Personality and Social Psychology, 43*, 304–318.

Myrdal, G. (1944). *An American dilemma: The Negro problem and modern democracy.* New York: Harper.

Narayan, S., & Krosnick, J. A. (1996). Education moderates some response effects in attitude measurement. *Public Opinion Quarterly, 60*, 58–88.

Nardulli, P. F. (1995). The concept of a critical realignment: Electoral behavior and political change. *American Political Science Review, 89*, 10–22.

National Academy of Science. (1993). *Understanding and preventing violence.* Washington, DC: National Academy Press.

National Commission on the Causes and Prevention of Violence. (1969). *To establish justice, to insure domestic tranquility.* New York: Award Books.

National Election Studies. (2001, August–September). *The NES guide to public opinion and electoral behavior.* Retrieved April, 2003, from http://www.umich.edu/~nes/nesguide/

National Election Studies. (2003). Equal role for women 1972–2000. Ann Arbor: University of Michigan. Retrieved April, 2003, from http://www.umich.edu/~nes/nesguide/toptable/tab4c_1.htm

National Geographic Education Foundation. (2002, November). *National Geographic-Roper 2002 global geographic literacy survey.* Washington, DC: Author.

National Science Foundation. (1969). *Knowledge into action: Improving the nation's use of the social sciences* (Report of the Special Commission on the Social Sciences of the National Science Board). Washington, DC: Author.

Nayakankuppam, D., & Priester, J. R. (2003). *The nature of evaluative judgments: Construction and retrieval processes as moderated by attitude strength.* Unpublished paper, University of Iowa.

Neely, J. H. (1977). Semantic priming and retrieval from lexical memory: Roles of inhibitionless spreading activation and limited-capacity attention. *Journal of Experimental Psychology: General, 106*, 226–254.

Neely, J. H. (1991). Semantic priming effects in visual word recognition: A selective review of current findings and theories. In D. Besner & G. W. Humphreys (Eds.), *Basic processes in reading: Visual word recognition* (pp. 264–336). Hillsdale, NJ: Lawrence Erlbaum Associates.

Nelson, L. (1988, August). *Influencing enemy perceptions and nuclear policy options with educational interventions.* Paper presented at American Psychological Association meeting, Atlanta, GA.

Nelson, T. E., & Kinder, D. R. (1996). Issue frames and group-centrism in American public opinion. *Journal of Politics, 58*, 1055–1078.

Netemeyer, R., & Burton, S. (1990). Examining the relationships between voting behavior, intention, perceived behavioral control, and expectation. *Journal of Applied Social Psychology, 20*, 661–680.

Neter, J., & Waksberg, J. (1964). A study of response errors in expenditures data from household interviews. *Journal of the American Statistical Association, 59*, 18–55.

Neuendorf, K. A. (2002). *The content analysis guidebook*. Thousand Oaks, CA: Sage.

Neuman, W. R. (1976). Patterns of recall among television news viewers. *Public Opinion Quarterly, 40*, 115–123.

Neuman, W. R. (1986). *The paradox of mass politics: Knowledge and opinion in the American electorate*. Cambridge, MA: Harvard University Press.

Newcomb, T. M. (1943). *Personality and social change*. New York: Dryden.

Newcomb, T. M., Koenig, K. E., Flacks, R., & Warwick, D. E. (1967). *Persistence and change: Bennington College and its students after 25 years*. New York: Wiley.

Newport, F. (1998, February). History shows presidential job approval ratings can plummet rapidly. *Gallup Poll Monthly*, No. 389, pp. 9–10.

Newport, F. (1999, March). Americans today much more accepting of a woman, black, Catholic, or Jew as President. *Gallup Poll Monthly*, No. 402, pp. 44–46.

Newport, F. (2001a, May). Satisfaction with way things are going in U.S. sinks to four-year low. *Gallup Poll Monthly*, No. 428, pp. 34–39.

Newport, F. (2001b, June). Military retains top position in Americans' confidence ratings. *Gallup Poll Monthly*, No. 429, pp. 52–55.

Newport, F. (2001c, September). Americans remain strongly in favor of military retaliation. *Gallup Poll Monthly*, No. 432, pp. 29–34.

Newport, F. (2001d, October). Trust in government increases sharply in wake of terrorist attacks. *Gallup Poll Monthly*, No. 433, pp. 25–29.

Newport, F. (2001e, October). Support for military action remains strong. *Gallup Poll Monthly*, No. 433, pp. 48–50.

Newport, F. (2001f, November). Overwhelming support for war continues. *Gallup Poll Monthly*, No. 434, pp. 16–19.

Newport, F. (2001g, December). Americans increasingly likely to say U.S. is winning war. *Gallup Poll Monthly*, No. 435, pp. 9–10.

Newport, F. (2002a, October 4). Public still positive about war on terrorism. *Gallup Poll Tuesday Briefing*, pp. 18–20.

Newport, F. (2002b, October 21). Pessimism about war on terrorism highest since Sept. 11. *Gallup Poll Tuesday Briefing*, pp. 73–75.

Newport, F. (2003, March 24). Seventy-two percent of Americans support war against Iraq. *Gallup Poll Tuesday Briefing*, pp. 36–37.

Newport, F., Moore, D. W., Jones, J. M., & Saad, L. (2003, March 21). Special release: American opinion on the war. *Gallup Poll Tuesday Briefing*, pp. 34–35.

Newport, F., & Saad, L. (2003, October 14). Bush job approval up despite Iraq, economy. *Gallup Poll Tuesday Briefing*, pp. 57–59.

Newton, N., & Newton, M. (1950). Relationship of ability to breast feed and maternal feeding. *Pediatrics, 5*, 869–875.

Nicholls, W., Baker, R., & Martin, J. (1997). The effect of new data collection technologies on survey data quality. In L. E. Lyberg et al. (Eds.), *Survey measurement and process quality* (pp. 221–248). New York: Wiley.

Nicks, S., Korn, J., & Mainieri, T. (1997). The rise and fall of deception in social psychology and personality research, 1921 to 1994. *Ethics and Behavior, 7*, 69–77.

Nie, N. H., & Andersen, K. (1974). Mass belief systems revisited: Political change and attitude structure. *Journal of Politics, 36*, 540–591.

Nie, N. H., Junn, J., & Stehlik-Barry, K. (1998). *Education and democratic citizenship in America*. Chicago: University of Chicago Press.

Nie, N. H., & Rabjohn, J. N. (1979). Revisiting mass belief systems revisited: Or, doing research is like watching a tennis match. *American Journal of Political Science, 23*, 139–175.

Nie, N. H., Verba, S., & Petrocik, J. R. (1979). *The changing American voter* (enlarged ed.). Cambridge, MA: Harvard University Press.

Nie, N. H., Verba, S., & Petrocik, J. R. (1981). Reply to Abramson and to Smith. *American Political Science Review, 75*, 149–152.

Niemi, R. G., & Jennings, M. K. (1991). Issues and inheritance in the formation of party identification. *American Journal of Political Science, 35,* 970–988.

Niemi, R. G., & Junn, J. (1998). *Civic education: What makes students learn?* New Haven, CT: Yale University Press.

Niemi, R. G., Ross, R. D., & Alexander, J. (1978). The similarity of political values of parents and of college-age youths. *Public Opinion Quarterly, 42,* 503–520.

Nisbett, R. E., Caputo, C., Legant, E., & Marecek, J. (1973). Behavior as seen by the actor and as seen by the observer. *Journal of Personality and Social Psychology, 27,* 154–164.

Nisbett, R. E., & Gordon, A. (1967). Self-esteem and susceptibility to social influence. *Journal of Personality and Social Psychology, 5,* 268–276.

Nisbett, R. E., & Ross, L. (1980). *Human inference: Strategies and shortcomings of social judgment.* Englewood Cliffs, NJ: Prentice-Hall.

Nisbett, R. E., & Valins, S. (1972). Perceiving the causes of one's own behavior. In E. E. Jones, D. E. Kanouse, H. H. Kelley, R. E. Nisbett, S. Valins, & B. Weiner, *Attribution: Perceiving the causes of behavior.* Morristown, NJ: General Learning Press.

Noel, J. G., Forsyth, D. R., & Kelley, K. N. (1987). Improving the performance of failing students by overcoming their self-serving attributional biases. *Basic and Applied Social Psychology, 8,* 151–162.

Nordlund, A., & Garvill, J. (2002). Value structures behind proenvironmental behavior. *Environment and Behavior, 34,* 740–756.

Norman, J. (1995). America's verdict on affirmative action is decidedly mixed. *The Public Perspective, 6*(4), 49–52.

Norpoth, H. (1987). Under way and here to stay: Party realignment in the 1980s? *Public Opinion Quarterly, 51,* 376–391.

Nosek, B. (2004, January). *The relationship between implicit and explicit attitudes.* Paper presented at Society for Personality and Social Psychology meeting, Austin, TX.

Nosek, B., Banaji, M., & Greenwald, A. (2002a). Math = male, me = female, therefore math not = me. *Journal of Personality and Social Psychology, 83,* 44–59.

Nosek, B., Banaji, M., & Greenwald, A. (2002b). Harvesting implicit group attitudes and beliefs from a demonstration web site. *Group Dynamics, 6,* 101–115.

Nunn, C. Z., Crockett, H. J., Jr., & Williams, J. A., Jr. (1978). *Tolerance for nonconformity.* San Francisco: Jossey-Bass.

Nuttin, J. M., Jr. (1975). *The illusion of attitude change: Towards a response contagion theory of persuasion.* London, England: Academic Press.

O'Keefe, G. J. (1973). A developmental analysis of political communication behavior in the young voter. *Public Opinion Quarterly, 37,* 442–443.

O'Keefe, G. J. (1985). "Taking a bite out of crime": The impact of a public information campaign. *Communication Research, 12,* 147–178.

O'Keefe, G. J., & Atwood, L. E. (1981). Communication and election campaigns. In D. D. Nimmo & K. R. Sanders (Eds.), *Handbook of political communication* (pp. 329–357). Beverly Hills, CA: Sage.

Oldendick, R. W., & Bardes, B. A. (1982). Mass and elite foreign policy options. *Public Opinion Quarterly, 46,* 368–382.

Oliver, M. B. (1999). Caucasian viewers' memory of black and white criminal suspects in the news. *Journal of Communication, 49,* 46–60.

Oliver, M. B. (2002). Individual differences in media effects. In J. Bryant & D. Zillmann (Eds.), *Media effects: Advances in theory and research* (pp. 507–524). Mahwah, NJ: Lawrence Erlbaum Associates.

Olson, J. M., & Maio, G. (2003). Attitudes in social behavior. In T. Millon & M. Lerner (Eds.), *Handbook of psychology: Personality and social psychology* (Vol. 5, pp. 299–325). New York: Wiley.

Olson, J. M., Vernon, P. A., Jang, K., & Harris, J. A. (2001). The heritability of attitudes: A study of twins. *Journal of Personality and Social Psychology, 80,* 845–860.

Olson, J. M., & Zanna, M. P. (1979). A new look at selective exposure. *Journal of Experimental Social Psychology, 15,* 1–15.

Olson, J. M., & Zanna, M. P. (1993). Attitudes and attitude change. *Annual Review of Psychology, 44,* 117–154.

Olson, M., & Fazio, R. (2001). Implicit attitude formation through classical conditioning. *Psychological Science, 12,* 413–417.

Olson, M., & Fazio, R. (2002). Implicit acquisition and manifestation of classically conditioned attitudes. *Social Cognition, 20,* 89–103.

Olson, M., & Fazio, R. (2003). Relations between implicit measures of prejudice: What are we measuring? *Psychological Science, 14,* 636–639.

O'Malley, M., & Thistlethwaite, D. L. (1980). Inference in inconsistency reduction: New evidence on the "Socratic effect." *Journal of Personality and Social Psychology, 39*, 1064–1071.

O'Neill, P., & Levings, D. E. (1979). Induced biased scanning in a group setting to change attitudes toward bilingualism and capital punishment. *Journal of Personality and Social Psychology, 37*, 1432–1438.

Orne, M. (2002). On the social psychology of the psychological experiment: With particular reference to demand characteristics and their implications. *Prevention and Treatment.* Retrieved September, 2004, from http://journals.apa.org/prevention/volume5/pre0050035a.html

Orne, M. T. (1969). Demand characteristics and the concept of quasi-controls. In R. Rosenthal & R. L. Rosnow (Eds.), *Artifact in behavioral research* (pp. 143–179). New York: Academic Press.

Ornstein, N. J., Mann, T. E., & Malbin, M. J. (1998). *Vital statistics on congress, 1997–1998.* Washington, DC: Congressional Quarterly.

Orton, B. (1982). Phony polls: The pollster's nemesis. *Public Opinion, 5*(3), 56–60.

Osgood, C. E. (1962). *An alternative to war or surrender.* Urbana: University of Illinois Press.

Osgood, C. E. (1965). Cross cultural comparability of attitude measurement via multi-lingual semantic differentials. In I. S. Steiner & M. Fishbein (Eds.), *Recent studies in social psychology* (pp. 95–107). New York: Holt, Rinehart & Winston.

Osgood, C. E. (1986). Graduated and reciprocated initiatives in tension-reduction: GRIT. In R. K. White (Ed.), *Psychology and the prevention of nuclear war* (pp. 194–207). New York: New York University Press.

Osgood, C. E., Suci, G. J., & Tannenbaum, P. H. (1957). *The measurement of meaning.* Urbana: University of Illinois Press.

Osgood, C. E., & Tannenbaum, P. H. (1955). The principle of congruity in the prediction of attitude change. *Psychological Review, 62*, 42–55.

Oskamp, S. (1965). Attitudes toward U.S. and Russian actions: A double standard. *Psychological Reports, 16*, 43–46.

Oskamp, S. (1985). Introduction: Social psychology, international affairs, and public policy. In S. Oskamp (Ed.), *International conflict and national public policy issues: Applied social psychology annual 6* (pp. 7–18). Beverly Hills, CA: Sage.

Oskamp, S. (2000a). Multiple paths to reducing prejudice and discrimination. In S. Oskamp (Ed.), *Reducing prejudice and discrimination* (pp. 1–19). Mahwah, NJ: Lawrence Erlbaum Associates.

Oskamp, S. (Ed.). (2000b). *Reducing prejudice and discrimination.* Mahwah, NJ: Lawrence Erlbaum Associates.

Oskamp, S. (2000c). A sustainable future for humanity? How can psychology help? *American Psychologist, 55*, 496–508.

Oskamp, S., & Hartry, A. (1968). A factor-analytic study of the double standard in attitudes toward U.S. and Russian actions. *Behavioral Science, 13*, 178–188.

Oskamp, S., Kaufman, K., & Wolterbeek, L. A. (1996). Gender role portrayals in preschool picture books. *Journal of Social Behavior and Personality, 11*(5), 27–39.

Oskamp, S., & Schultz, P. W. (1998). *Applied social psychology* (2nd ed.). Upper Saddle River, NJ: Prentice-Hall.

Ostlund, L. E. (1973). Interpersonal communication following McGovern's Eagleton decision. *Public Opinion Quarterly, 37*, 601–610.

Ostrom, C. W., & Simon, D. M. (1985). Promise and performance: A dynamic model of presidential popularity. *American Political Science Review, 79*, 334–358.

Ostrom, C. W., Jr., & Smith, R. M. (1992). Error correction, attitude persistence, and executive rewards and punishments: A behavioral theory of presidential approval. In J. R. Freeman (Ed.), *Political analysis: An annual publication* (Vol. 4, pp. 127–183). Ann Arbor: University of Michigan Press.

Ottaway, S. A., Hayden, D. C., & Oakes, M. A. (2001). Implicit attitudes and racism: Effects of word familiarity and frequency on the Implicit Association Test. *Social Cognition, 19*, 97–144.

Otten, S., & Wentura, D. (1999). About the impact of automaticity in the minimal group paradigm: Evidence from the affective priming tasks. *European Journal of Social Psychology, 29*, 1049–1071.

Ouellette, J. A., & Wood, W. (1998). Habit and intention in everyday life: The multiple processes by which past behavior predicts future behavior. *Psychological Bulletin, 124*, 54–74.

Owen, D., & Dennis, J. (1999, April/May). Kids and the presidency: Assessing Clinton's legacy. *Public Perspective, 10*, 41–44.

Page, B. I., & Shapiro, R. Y. (1982). Changes in Americans' policy preferences, 1935–1979. *Public Opinion Quarterly, 46*, 24–42.

Page, B. I., & Shapiro, R. Y. (1983). Effects of public opinion on policy. *American Political Science Review, 77*, 175–189.

Page, B. I., & Shapiro, R. Y. (1992). *The rational public: Fifty years of trends in Americans' policy preferences.* Chicago: University of Chicago Press.

Page, B. I., Shapiro, R. Y., & Dempsey, G. R. (1985, May). *The mass media do affect policy preferences.* Paper presented at American Association for Public Opinion Research meeting, McAfee, NJ.

Page, B. I., Shapiro, R. Y., & Dempsey, G. R. (1987). What moves public opinion? *American Political Science Review, 81,* 23–43.

Page, B. I., Shapiro, R. Y., Gronke, P. W., & Rosenberg, R. M. (1984). Constituency, party, and representation in congress. *Public Opinion Quarterly, 48,* 741–756.

Page, M. M. (1974). Demand characteristics and the classical conditioning of attitudes experiment. *Journal of Personality and Social Psychology, 30,* 468–476.

Pagel, M. D., & Davidson, A. R. (1984). A comparison of three social-psychological models of attitude and behavioral plan: Prediction of contraceptive behavior. *Journal of Personality and Social Psychology, 47,* 517–533.

Pallak, M. S., Cook, D. A., & Sullivan, J. J. (1980). Commitment and energy conservation. In L. Bickman (Ed.), *Applied social psychology annual* (Vol. 1, pp. 235–253). Beverly Hills, CA: Sage.

Palmer, J. (1993). Development of concern for the environment and formative experiences of educators. *Journal of Environmental Education, 24,* 26–30.

Palmgreen, P., & Clarke, P. (1977). Agenda-setting with local and national issues. *Communication Research, 4,* 435–452.

Paloutzian, R. F. (1981). Purpose in life and value changes following conversion. *Journal of Personality and Social Psychology, 41,* 1153–1160.

Parisot, L. (1988). Attitudes about the media: A five country comparison. *Public Opinion, 10*(5), 18–19, 60.

Park, B., & Rothbart, M. (1982). Perception of out-group homogeneity and levels of social categorization: Memory for the subordinate attributes of in-group and out-group members. *Journal of Personality and Social Psychology, 42,* 1051–1068.

Parker, J. D., & McDonough, M. (1999). Environmentalism of African Americans: An analysis of the subculture and barriers theories. *Environment and Behavior, 31,* 155–177.

Parks, J. B., & Roberton, M. A. (1998). Contemporary arguments against nonsexist language: Blaubergs (1980) revisited. *Sex Roles, 39,* 445–461.

Parry, H. J., & Crossley, H. M. (1950). Validity of responses to survey questions. *Public Opinion Quarterly, 14,* 61–80.

Parsons, T. (1955). Family structure and the socialization of the child. In T. Parsons & R. F. Bales (Eds.), *Family, socialization, and interaction process.* Glencoe, IL: The Free Press.

Patterson, T. E. (1980). *The mass media election: How Americans choose their president.* New York: Praeger.

Patterson, T. E. (2001, May 23). Party switching comes with political risks. *CNN: Inside Politics.* Retrieved September, 2003, from http://www.cnn.com/2001/ALLPOLITICS/05/23/party.switchers/

Patterson, T. E., & McClure, R. D. (1976). *The unseeing eye: The myth of television power in national elections.* New York: Putnam.

Pattullo, E. L. (1984). Institutional review boards and social research: A disruptive, subjective perspective, retrospective and prospective. In J. E. Sieber (Ed.), *NIH readings on the protection of human subjects in behavioral and social science research: Conference proceedings and background papers* (pp. 10–17). Frederick, MD: University Publications of America.

Paul, B., Salwen, M. P., & Dupagne, M. (2000). The third-person effect: A meta-analysis of the perceptual hypothesis. *Mass Communication and Society, 3,* 57–85.

Pavlidis, L., Eberhardt, N., & Levine, J. (2002). Seeing through the face of deception. *Nature (London), 415*(6867), 35.

Pavlos, A. J. (1982). *The cult experience.* Westport, CT: Greenwood.

Payne, S. L. (1951). *The art of asking questions.* Princeton, NJ: Princeton University Press.

Peake, E. K., & Cervone, D. (1989). Sequence anchoring and self-efficacy: Primacy effects in the consideration of possibilities. *Social Cognition, 7,* 31–50.

Peffley, M., & Hurwitz, J. (1998). Whites' stereotypes of blacks: Sources and political consequences. In J. Hurwitz & M. Peffley (Eds.), *Perception and prejudice: Race and politics in the United States* (pp. 58–99). New Haven, CT: Yale University Press.

Perlman, D., & Oskamp, S. (1971). The effects of picture content and exposure frequency on evaluations of Negroes and whites. *Journal of Experimental Social Psychology, 7,* 503–514.

Perloff, R. (2002). The third-person effect. In J. Bryant & D. Zillmann (Eds.), *Media effects: Advances in theory and research* (pp. 489–506). Mahwah, NJ: Lawrence Erlbaum Associates.

Perry, A. (1973). The effect of heredity on attitudes toward alcohol, cigarettes, and coffee. *Journal of Applied Psychology, 58,* 275–277.

Perry, P. K. (1960). Election survey procedures of the Gallup Poll. *Public Opinion Quarterly, 24,* 531–542.

Perry, P. K. (1979). Certain problems in election survey methodology. *Public Opinion Quarterly, 43,* 312–325.

Peterson, B. E., Doty, R. M., & Winter, D. G. (1993). Authoritarianism and attitudes toward contemporary social issues. *Personality and Social Psychology Bulletin, 19*, 174–184.

Peterson, B. E., & Duncan, L. E. (1999). Authoritarianism of parents and offspring: Intergenerational politics and adjustment to college. *Journal of Research in Personality, 33*, 494–513.

Peterson, B. E., & Lane, M. (2001). Implications of authoritarianism for young adulthood: Longitudinal analysis of college experiences and future goals. *Personality and Social Psychology Bulletin, 27*, 678–690.

Peterson, B. E., Smirles, K. A., & Wentworth, P. A. (1997). Generativity and authoritarianism: Implications for personality, political involvement, and parenting. *Journal of Personality and Social Psychology, 72*, 1202–1216.

Peterson, N., & Hungerford, H. R. (1982). Developmental variables affecting environmental sensitivity in professional environmental educators. *Current Issues in Environmental Education and Environmental Studies, 7*, 111–113.

Peterson, P. D., & Koulack, D. (1969). Attitude change as a function of latitudes of acceptance and rejection. *Journal of Personality and Social Psychology, 11*, 309–311.

Peterson, P. E., Jeffrey, D. B., Bridgwater, C. A., & Dawson, B. (1984). How pronutritional television programming affects children's dietary habits. *Developmental Psychology, 20*, 55–63.

Peterson, R. C., & Thurstone, L. L. (1933). *Motion pictures and the social attitudes of children.* New York: Macmillan.

Petrocik, J. R., & Steeper, F. T. (1987). The political landscape in 1987. *Public Opinion, 10*(3), 41–44.

Pettigrew, T. F. (1959). Regional differences in anti-Negro prejudice. *Journal of Abnormal and Social Psychology, 59*, 28–36.

Pettigrew, T. F. (1967). Social evaluation theory: Convergences and applications. In D. Levine (Ed.), *Nebraska symposium on motivation* (Vol. 15, pp. 241–311). Lincoln: University of Nebraska Press.

Pettigrew, T. F. (1969). Racially separate or together? *Journal of Social Issues, 25*(1), 43–69.

Pettigrew, T. F. (1971). Race relations. In R. Merton & R. Nisbet (Eds.), *Contemporary social problems* (pp. 407–466). New York: Harcourt Brace Jovanovich.

Pettigrew, T. F. (1979). The ultimate attribution error: Extending Allport's cognitive analysis of prejudice. *Personality and Social Psychology Bulletin, 5*, 461–476.

Pettigrew, T. F. (1998). Intergroup contact theory. *Annual Review of Psychology, 49*, 65–85.

Pettigrew, T. F., & Tropp, L. R. (2000). Does intergroup contact reduce prejudice? Recent meta-analytic findings. In S. Oskamp (Ed.), *Reducing prejudice and discrimination* (pp. 93–114). Mahwah, NJ: Lawrence Erlbaum Associates.

Petty, R. E., & Cacioppo, J. T. (1979a). Effects of forewarning of persuasive intent and involvement on cognitive responses and persuasion. *Personality and Social Psychology Bulletin, 5*, 173–176.

Petty, R. E., & Cacioppo, J. T. (1979b). Issue involvement can increase or decrease persuasion by enhancing message-relevant cognitive responses. *Journal of Personality and Social Psychology, 37*, 1915–1926.

Petty, R. E., & Cacioppo, J. T. (1981). *Attitudes and persuasion: Classic and contemporary approaches.* Dubuque, IA: Brown.

Petty, R. E., & Cacioppo, J. T. (1984). The effects of involvement on responses to argument quantity and quality: Central and peripheral routes to persuasion. *Journal of Personality and Social Psychology, 46*, 69–81.

Petty, R. E., & Cacioppo, J. T. (1986). *Communication and persuasion: Central and peripheral routes to attitude change.* New York: Springer-Verlag.

Petty, R. E., & Cacioppo, J. T. (1990). Involvement and persuasion: Tradition versus integration. *Psychological Bulletin, 107*, 367–374.

Petty, R. E., Cacioppo, J. T., & Goldman, R. (1981). Personal involvement as a determinant of argument-based persuasion. *Journal of Personality and Social Psychology, 41*, 847–855.

Petty, R. E., & Krosnick, J. A. (1995). *Attitude strength: Antecedents and consequences.* Hillsdale, NJ: Lawrence Erlbaum Associates.

Petty, R. E., Priester, J., & Briñol, P. (2002). Mass media attitude change: Implications of the elaboration likelihood model of persuasion. In J. Bryant & D. Zillmann (Eds.), *Media effects: Advances in theory and research* (2nd ed., pp. 155–198). Mahwah, NJ: Lawrence Erlbaum Associates.

Petty, R. E., Rucker, D., Bizer, G., & Cacioppo, J. T. (2004). The elaboration likelihood model. In J. S. Seiter & G. H. Gass (Eds.), *Perspectives on persuasion, influence, and compliance gaining.* Boston: Allyn & Bacon.

Petty, R. E., Tormala, Z. L., Hawkins, C., & Wegener, D. T. (2001). Motivation to think and order effects in persuasion: The moderating role of chunking. *Personality and Social Psychology Bulletin, 27*, 332–344.

Petty, R. E., & Wegener, D. T. (1998). Attitude change: Multiple roles for persuasion variables. In D. T. Gilbert, S. T. Fiske, & G. Lindzey (Eds.), *The handbook of social psychology* (4th ed., Vol. 1, pp. 323–390). Boston: McGraw-Hill.

Petty, R. E., & Wegener, D. T. (1999). The elaboration likelihood model: Current status and controversies. In S. Chaiken & Y. Trope (Eds.), *Dual-process theories in social psychology* (pp. 37–72). New York: Guilford.

Petty, R. E., Wegener, D. T., & Fabrigar, L. R. (1997). Attitudes and attitude change. *Annual Review of Psychology, 48*, 609–647.

Petty, R. E., Wells, G. L., & Brock, T. C. (1976). Distraction can enhance or reduce yielding to propaganda: Thought disruption versus effort justification. *Journal of Personality and Social Psychology, 34*, 874–884.

Petty, R. E., Wheeler, S. C., & Bizer, G. Y. (2000). Attitude functions and persuasion: An elaboration likelihood approach to matched versus mismatched messages. In G. R. Maio & J. M. Olson (Eds.), *Why we evaluate: Functions of attitudes* (pp. 133–162). Mahwah, NJ: Lawrence Erlbaum Associates.

Petty, R. E., Wheeler, S. C., & Tormala, Z. L. (2003). Persuasion and attitude change. In T. Millon, & M. Lerner (Eds.), *Handbook of psychology: Personality and social psychology* (Vol. 5, pp. 353–382). New York: Wiley.

Pfau, M., Tusing, K., Koerner, A., Lee, W., Godbold, L., Penaloza, L., Yang, V., & Hong, Y. (1997). Enriching the inoculation construct: The role of critical components in the process of resistance. *Human Communication Research, 24*, 187–215.

Pfister G. (1975). Outcomes of laboratory training for police officers. *Journal of Social Issues, 31*(1), 115–121.

Phillips, D. L., & Clancy, K. J. (1972). "Modeling effects" in survey research. *Public Opinion Quarterly, 36*, 246–253.

Pilisuk, M., & Wong, A. (2002). State terrorism: When the perpetrator is a government. In C. E. Stout (Ed.), *The psychology of terrorism. Vol. 2: Clinical aspects and responses* (pp. 105–132). Westport, CT: Praeger.

Pirages, D. C., & Ehrlich, P. R. (1974). *Ark II: Social response to environmental imperatives*. San Francisco, CA: Freeman.

Pitcher, E. G., & Schultz, L. H. (1983). *Boys and girls at play: The development of sex roles*. New York: Praeger.

Pittenger, D. (2002). Deception in research: Distinctions and solutions from the perspective of utilitarianism. *Ethics and Behavior, 12*, 117–142.

Plant, E. A., & Peruche, B. M. (2003, February). *Reducing implicit bias: Making race irrelevant*. Paper presented at Society of Personality and Social Psychology meeting, Los Angeles.

Pleck, J. H. (1981). *The myth of masculinity*. Cambridge, MA: MIT Press.

Pleck, J. H. (1985). *Working wives, working husbands*. Beverly Hills, CA: Sage.

Pleck, J. H. (1995). The gender role strain paradigm: An update. In R. Levant & W. Pollack (Eds.), *A new psychology of men* (pp. 11–32). New York: Basic Books.

Plissner, M. (2003). An * for 2002: Another bad election night for VNS. *Public Perspective, 14*(1), 4–6.

Plous, S. (1985). Psychological and strategic barriers in present attempts at nuclear disarmament: A new proposal. *Political Psychology, 6*, 109–133.

Pollingreport.com. (2003). Environment: Polling report. Retrieved March 19, 2003, from http://www.pollingreport.com/enviro.htm

Pomerantz, E. M., Chaiken, S., & Tordesillas, R. (1995). Attitude strength and resistance processes. *Journal of Personality and Social Psychology, 69*, 408–419.

Ponting, C. (1991). *A green history of the world: The environmental collapse of great civilizations*. New York: Penguin.

Pool, I. deS. (1965). Effects of cross-national contact on national and international images. In H. C. Kelman (Ed.), *International behavior: A social-psychological analysis* (pp. 106–129). New York: Holt, Rinehart & Winston.

Pool, I. deS., Abelson, R. P., & Popkin, S. L. (1964). *Candidates, issues, and strategies: A computer simulation of the 1960 presidential election*. Cambridge, MA: MIT Press.

Poole, D. A., & Lindsay, D. S. (2001). Children's eyewitness reports after exposure to misinformation from parents. *Journal of Experimental Psychology: Applied, 7*, 27–50.

Popkin, S. L. (1996). Voter learning in the 1992 presidential election. In S. Iyengar & R. Reeves (Eds.), *Do the media govern?* (pp. 171–180). Thousand Oaks, CA: Sage.

Poppleton, P. K., & Pilkington, G. W. (1964). A comparison of four methods of scoring an attitude scale in relation to its reliability and validity. *British Journal of Social and Clinical Psychology, 3*, 36–39.

Porter, J. R., & Washington, R. E. (1979). Black identity and self-esteem: A review of studies of black self-concept, 1968–1978. *Annual Review of Sociology, 5*, 53–74.

Posner, M. I., & Snyder, C. R. R. (1975). Attention and cognitive control. In R. L. Solso (Ed.), *Information processing and cognition: The Loyola Symposium* (pp. 55–85). Hillsdale, NJ: Lawrence Erlbaum Associates.

Post, J. M. (2002a). Differentiating the threat of chemical and biological terrorism: Motivations and constraints. *Peace and Conflict: Journal of Peace Psychology, 8*, 187–200.

Post, J. M. (2002b). Response. *Peace and Conflict: Journal of Peace Psychology, 8*, 223–227.

Powell, G., Butterfield, D. A., & Parent, J. D. (2002). Gender and managerial stereotypes: Have the times changed? *Journal of Management, 28*, 177–193.

Powlishta, K. K., Sen, M. G., Serbin, L. A., Poulin-Dubois, D., & Eichstedt, J. A. (2001). From infancy through middle childhood: The role of cognitive and social factors in becoming gendered. In R. K. Unger (Ed.), *Handbook of the psychology of women and gender* (pp. 116–132). New York: Wiley.

Pratkanis, A. R., Greenwald, A. G., Leippe, M. R., & Baumgardner, M. H. (1988). In search of reliable persuasion effects: III. The sleeper effect is dead. Long live the sleeper effect. *Journal of Personality and Social Psychology, 54*, 203–218.

Pratkanis, A. R., & Turner, M. E. (1994). Nine principles of successful affirmative action: Mr. Branch Rickey, Mr. Jackie Robinson, and the integration of baseball. *Nine: A Journal of Baseball History and Social Policy Perspectives, 3*, 36–65.

Pratto, F., Sidanius, J., Stallworth, L. M., & Malle, B. F. (1994). Social dominance orientation: A personality variable predicting social and political attitudes. *Journal of Personality and Social Psychology, 67*, 741–763.

Prentice, D. A., & Carranza, E. (2002). What women should be, shouldn't be, are allowed to be, and don't have to be: The content of prescriptive gender stereotypes. *Psychology of Women Quarterly, 26*, 269–281.

Prentice, D. A., & Miller, D. T. (2002). The emergence of homegrown stereotypes. *American Psychologist, 57*, 352–359.

Prescott-Allen, R. (2001). *The wellbeing of nations: A country-by-country index of quality of life and the environment*. Washington, DC: Island Press.

Price, K. O., Harburg, E., & Newcomb, T. M. (1966). Psychological balance in situations of negative interpersonal attitudes. *Journal of Personality and Social Psychology, 3*, 265–270.

Price, V., & Zaller, J. R. (1993). Who gets the news? *Public Opinion Quarterly, 57*, 133–164.

Priester, J., Wegener, D. T., Petty, R. E., & Fabrigar, L. R. (1999). Examining the psychological process underlying the sleeper effect: The elaboration likelihood model explanation. *Media Psychology, 1*, 27–48.

Public Agenda Foundation. (1984). *Voter options on nuclear arms policy: A briefing book for the 1984 elections*. New York: Author.

Public Agenda. (2000). Necessary compromises: How parents, employers and children's advocates view child care today. Retrieved August, 2003, from http://www.publicagenda.org/specials/childcare/childcare.htm

Public Agenda. (2001, September 13). Death toll still unknown in World Trade Center, Pentagon attacks. Retrieved January 23, 2003, from http://www.publicagenda.org/specials/terrorism/091301terror_pubopinion.htm

Publicagenda.org. (2002). People's chief concerns. Retrieved March 19, 2003, from http://www.publicagenda.org/issues/pcc.cfm?issue_type=environment.

Publicagenda.org. (2003). The economy: Quick takes. Retrieved November, 2003, from http://www.publicagenda.org/issues/angles.cfm?issue_type=economy

Public Opinion. (1980/1981, December/January). Opinion roundup: 1980 results. No. 6, pp. 21–44.

Public Opinion. (1985, October/November). Is it realignment? Surveying the evidence. No. 5, pp. 21–31.

Public Opinion. (1987, July/August). The state of intolerance in America. No. 2, pp. 21–31.

Public Opinion. (1987, November/December). Most important problems. No. 4, pp. 26–27.

Public Opinion. (1989, March/April). Attitudes today. No. 6, pp. 30–33.

Public Perspective. (1991, November/December). American values in comparative perspective. *3*(1), 5–8.

Public Perspective. (1997a, April/May). Six decades of Gallup polling: A Roper Center review. *8*(3), 12–60.

Public Perspective. (1997b, August/September). America in the world. *8*(5), 1–37.

Public Perspective. (1997c, October/November). Measuring American society and performance. *8*(6), 1–32.

Public Perspective. (2001, January/February). A Roper Center data review: An internationalist state of mind. *12*(1), 25–33.

Putney, S., & Middleton, R. (1962). Some factors associated with student acceptance or rejection of war. *American Sociological Review, 27*, 655–667.

Pyszczynski, T., Solomon, S., & Greenberg, J. (2002). *In the wake of 9/11: The psychology of terror*. Washington, DC: American Psychological Association.

Quigley-Fernandez, B., & Tedeschi, J. T. (1978). The bogus pipeline as lie detector: Two validity studies. *Journal of Personality and Social Psychology, 36*, 247–256.

Rademacher, E. W., & Smith, A. E. (2001). Poll call. *Public Perspective, 12*(2), 36–37.

Raden, D. (1977). Situational thresholds and attitude-behavior consistency. *Sociometry, 40*, 123–129.

Rainey, A. B., & Rust, J. O. (1999). Reducing gender stereotyping in kindergartners. *Early Child Development and Care, 150*, 33–42.

Raj, S. P. (1982). The effects of advertising on high and low loyalty consumer segments. *Journal of Consumer Research, 9*, 77–89.

Rankin, W. L., Nealy, S., & Melber, B. (1984). Overview of national attitudes toward nuclear energy: A longitudinal analysis. In W. Freudenburg & E. Rosa (Eds.), *Public reaction to nuclear power* (pp. 41–67). Boulder, CO: Westview.

Rappoport, L., & Cvetkovich, G. (1968). Opinion on Vietnam: Some findings from three studies. *Proceedings of the 76th Annual Convention of the American Psychological Association, 3*, 381–382.

Raskin, D. C., Honts, C. R., & Kircher, J. C. (1997). The scientific status of research on polygraph techniques: The case for polygraph tests. In D. L. Faigman, D. Kaye, M. J. Saks, & J. Sanders (Eds.), *Modern scientific evidence: The law and science of expert evidence* (pp. 565–582). St. Paul, MN: West.

Rathje, W. L., & Ritenbaugh, C. (Eds.). (1984). Household refuse analysis: Theory, methods, and applications in social science. *American Behavioral Scientist, 28*, 1–160.

Read, S. J. (1983). Once is enough: Causal reasoning from a single instance. *Journal of Personality and Social Psychology, 45*, 323–334.

Reese, S. D., Danielson, W. A., Shoemaker, P. J., Chang, T-K., & Hsu, H-L. (1986). Ethnicity-of-interviewer effects among Mexican-Americans and Anglos. *Public Opinion Quarterly, 50*, 563–572.

Regan, D. T., & Totten, J. (1975). Empathy and attribution: Turning observers into actors. *Journal of Personality and Social Psychology, 32*, 850–856.

Reich, J. W. (1982). *Experimenting in society: Issues and examples in applied social psychology.* Glenview, IL: Scott, Foresman.

Reid, E. T. (1988). Racism and sexism: Comparison and conflicts. In P. A. Katz & D. A. Taylor (Eds.), *Eliminating racism: Profiles in controversy* (pp. 203–221). New York: Plenum.

Reisenzein, R. (1983). The Schachter theory of emotion: Two decades later. *Psychological Bulletin, 94*, 239–264.

Reiter, H. L. (2003, March/April). Murdering the midterm myth. *Public Perspective, 14*(2), 42.

Rensberger, B. (1999). The final countdown. *Audubon, 101*, 64–68.

Renshon, S. A. (Ed.). (1977). *Handbook of political socialization: Theory and research.* New York: Free Press.

RePass, D. E. (1971). Issue salience and party choice. *American Political Science Review, 65*, 389–400.

Report of the National Advisory Commission on Civil Disorders. (1968). New York: Bantam.

Rettig, S. (1966). Relation of social systems to intergenerational changes in moral attitudes. *Journal of Personality and Social Psychology, 4*, 409–414.

Rhodes, N., & Wood, W. (1992). Self-esteem and intelligence affect influenceability: The mediating role of message reception. *Psychological Bulletin, 111*, 156–171.

Rice, R. W., Bender, L. R., & Vitters, A. G. (1980). Leader sex, follower attitudes toward women, and leadership effectiveness. *Organizational Behavior and Human Performance, 25*, 46–78.

Richardson L. (1988). *The dynamics of sex and gender: A sociological perspective* (3rd ed.). New York: Harper & Row.

Richardson, J. G., & Simpson, C. H. (1982). Children, gender, and social structure: An analysis of the contents of letters to Santa Claus. *Child Development, 53*, 429–436.

Richman, A. (1993). The polls—Poll trends: American support for international involvement. *Public Opinion Quarterly, 57*, 264–276.

Richman, A. (1995, April/May). When should we be prepared to fight? *Public Perspective, 6*(3), 44–47.

Riess, M., Rosenfeld, E., Melburg, V., & Tedeschi, J. T. (1981). Self-serving attributions: Biased private perceptions and distorted public descriptions. *Journal of Personality and Social Psychology, 41*, 224–251.

Riley, R. T., & Pettigrew, T. F. (1976). Dramatic events and attitude change. *Journal of Personality and Social Psychology, 34*, 1004–1015.

Ringold, D. J. (1988). Consumer response to product withdrawal: The reformulation of Coca-Cola. *Psychology and Marketing, 5*, 189–210.

Roberts, D. F., & Bachen, C. (1981). Mass communication effects. *Annual Review of Psychology, 32*, 307–356.

Roberts, D. F., & Maccoby, N. (1985). Effects of mass communication. In G. Lindzey & E. Aronson (Eds.), *The handbook of social psychology* (3rd ed., Vol. 2, pp. 539–598). New York: Random House.

Roberts, P. (2004). *The end of oil: On the edge of a perilous new world.* Boston: Houghton Mifflin.

Robinson, J. E., & Insko, C. A. (1969). Attributed belief similarity–dissimilarity versus race as determinants of prejudice: A further test of Rokeach's theory. *Journal of Experimental Research in Personality, 4*, 72–77.

Robinson, J. P. (1972). Perceived media bias and the 1968 vote: Can the media affect behavior after all? *Journalism Quarterly, 49*, 239–246.

Robinson, J. P. (1974). Public opinion during the Watergate crisis. *Communication Research, 1*, 391–405.

Robinson, J. P. (1976). Interpersonal influence in election campaigns: Two step-flow hypotheses. *Public Opinion Quarterly, 40*, 304–319.

Robinson, J. P. (1980). The changing reading habits of the American public. *Journal of Communication, 30*, 141–152.

Robinson, J. P. (1984). The ups and downs and ins and outs of ideology. *Public Opinion, 7*(1), 12–15.

Robinson, J. P. (1988). Who's doing the housework? *American Demographics, 10*(12), 24–28, 63.

Robinson, J. P., & Davis, D. K. (1990). Television news and the informed public: An information-processing approach. *Journal of Communication, 40*, 106–119.

Robinson, J. P., & Fleishman, J. A. (1988). The polls—A report: Ideological identification: Trends and interpretations of the liberal–conservative balance. *Public Opinion Quarterly, 52*, 134–145.

Robinson, J. P., & Godbey, G. (1997). *Time for life: The surprising ways Americans use their time.* University Park: Pennsylvania State University Press.

Robinson, J. P., & Levy, M. R. (1986a). Interpersonal communication and news comprehension. *Public Opinion Quarterly, 50*, 160–175.

Robinson, J. P., & Levy, M. R. (1986b). *The main source: Learning from television news.* Beverly Hills, CA: Sage.

Robinson, J. P., Shaver, P., & Wrightsman, L. (1999). *Measures of political attitudes.* San Diego: Academic Press.

Robison, J. (2002, July 16). Who smoked pot? You may be surprised. *Gallup Poll Tuesday Briefing*, p. 81.

Rochon, T. R. (1988). *Mobilizing for peace: The antinuclear movements in western Europe.* Princeton, NJ: Princeton University Press.

Roddy, B. L., & Garramone, G. M. (1988). Appeals and strategies of negative political advertising. *Journal of Broadcasting & Electronic Media, 32*, 415–427.

Rodin, J. (1985). The application of social psychology. In G. Lindzey & E. Aronson (Eds.), *The handbook of social psychology* (3rd ed., Vol. 2, pp. 805–881). New York: Random House.

Roese, N., & Jamieson, D. (1993). Twenty years of bogus pipeline research: A critical review and meta-analysis. *Psychological Bulletin, 114*, 363–375.

Rogers, E. R. (1982). *Diffusion of innovations* (3rd ed.). New York: Free Press.

Rogers, R. W. (1983). Cognitive and physiological processes in fear appeals and attitude change: A revised theory of protection motivation. In J. T. Cacioppo & R. E. Petty (Eds.), *Social psychophysiology* (pp. 153–177). New York: Guilford.

Rogers, R. W., & Prentice-Dunn, S. (1997). Protection motivation theory. In D. Gochman (Ed.), *Handbook of health behavior* (pp. 113–132). New York: Plenum.

Rogers, S. C. (1981). Woman's place: A critical review of anthropological theory. In S. Cox (Ed.), *Female psychology: The emerging self* (2nd ed.). New York: St. Martin's Press.

Rohan, M. J. (2000). A rose by any name? The values construct. *Personality and Social Psychology Review, 4*, 255–277.

Rokeach, M. (1968). *Beliefs, attitudes, and values: A theory of organization and change.* San Francisco: Jossey-Bass.

Rokeach, M. (1971). Long-range experimental modification of values, attitudes, and behavior. *American Psychologist, 26*, 453–459.

Rokeach, M. (1973). *The nature of human values.* New York: The Free Press.

Rokeach, M. (1979). Some unresolved issues in theories of beliefs, attitudes, and values. In H. E. Howe & M. M. Page (Eds.), *Nebraska symposium on motivation* (Vol. 27, pp. 261–304). Lincoln: University of Nebraska Press.

Rokeach, M., & Rothman, G. (1965). The principle of belief congruence and the congruity principle as models of cognitive interaction. *Psychological Review, 72*, 128–142.

Roll, C. W., Jr., & Cantril, A. H. (1980). *Polls: Their use and misuse in politics* (rev. ed.). Cabin John, MD: Seven Locks Press.

Romero, A., Agnew, C. R., & Insko, C. (1996). The cognitive mediation hypothesis revisited: An empirical response to methodological and theoretical criticism. *Personality and Social Psychology Bulletin, 22*, 651–665.

Roper, B. W. (1983). The polls' malfunction in 1982. *Public Opinion, 5*(6), 41–42.

Roper, B. W. (1984). Are polls accurate? *The Annals of the American Academy of Political and Social Science, 472*, 24–34.

Rosa, E., & Dunlap, R. (1994). Nuclear power: Three decades of public opinion. *Public Opinion Quarterly, 58*, 295–325.

Rosaldo, M. Z. (1974). Women, culture, and society: A theoretical overview. In M. Z. Rosaldo & L. Lamphere (Eds.), *Woman, culture, and society.* Stanford, CA: Stanford University Press.

Rosch, E. (1978). Principles of categorization. In E. Rosch & B. B. Lloyd (Eds.), *Cognition and categorization* (pp. 28–48). Hillsdale, NJ: Lawrence Erlbaum Associates.

Rosen, R. (1971). Sexism in history or, writing women's history is a tricky business. *Journal of Marriage and the Family, 33*, 541–544.

Rosenberg, M. J. (1960). An analysis of affective–cognitive consistency. In M. J. Rosenberg, C. I. Hovland, W. J. McGuire, R. P. Abelson, & J. W. Brehm (Eds.), *Attitude organization and change: An analysis of consistency among attitude components* (pp. 15–64). New Haven, CT: Yale University Press.

Rosenberg, M. J. (1967). Attitude change and foreign policy in the cold war era. In J. N. Rosenau (Ed.), *Domestic sources of foreign policy* (pp. 111–159). New York: Free Press.

Rosenberg, M. J. (1969). The conditions and consequences of evaluation apprehension. In R. Rosenthal & R. L. Rosnow (Eds.), *Artifact in behavioral research* (pp. 279–349). New York: Academic Press.

Rosenberg, M. J., & Abelson, R. P. (1960). An analysis of cognitive balancing. In M. J. Rosenberg, C. I. Hovland, W. J. McGuire, R. P. Abelson, & J. W. Brehm (Eds.), *Attitude organization and change: An analysis of consistency among attitude components* (pp. 112–163). New Haven, CT: Yale University Press.

Rosenberg, M. J., Hovland, C. I., McGuire, W. J., Abelson, R. P., & Brehm, J. W. (Eds.). (1960). *Attitude organization and change: An analysis of consistency among attitude components*. New Haven, CT: Yale University Press.

Rosenfeld, P., Giacalone, R. A., & Tedeschi, J. T. (1983). Cognitive dissonance vs. impression management. *Journal of Social Psychology, 120*, 203–211.

Rosenstone, S. J. (1983). *Forecasting presidential elections*. New Haven, CT: Yale University Press.

Rosenstone, S. J., & Hansen, J. M. (1993). *Mobilization, participation and democracy in America*. New York: Macmillan.

Rosenthal, R. (1976). *Experimenter effects in behavioral research*. New York: Irvington.

Rosenthal, R. (2002). Covert communication in classrooms, clinics, courtrooms, and cubicles. *American Psychologist, 57*, 839–849.

Rosenthal, R., & Rosnow, R. L. (1975). *The volunteer subject*. New York: Wiley.

Rosenthal, R., & Rosnow, R. L. (1991). *Essentials of behavioral research: Methods and data analysis* (2nd ed.). New York: McGraw-Hill.

Roshco, B., & Crespi, I. (1996). From alchemy to home-brewed chemistry—Polling transformed. *Public Perspective, 7*(3), 8–12.

Rosi, E. J. (1965). Mass and attentive opinion on nuclear weapons tests and fall out, 1954–1963. *Public Opinion Quarterly, 29*, 280–297.

Roskos-Ewoldsen, D. R., & Fazio, R. H. (1992). The accessibility of source likeability as a determinant of persuasion. *Personality and Social Psychology Bulletin, 18*, 19–25.

Rosnow, R. L., & Suls, J. M. (1970). Reactive effects of pretesting in attitude research. *Journal of Personality and Social Psychology, 15*, 338–343.

Ross, L. (1977). The intuitive psychologist and his shortcomings: Distortions in the attribution process. In L. Berkowitz (Ed.), *Advances in experimental social psychology* (Vol. 10, pp. 173–220). New York: Academic Press.

Ross, L., Amabile, T. M., & Steinmetz, J. L. (1977). Social roles, social control, and biases in social perception processes. *Journal of Personality and Social Psychology, 35*, 485–494.

Ross, L., Greene, D., & House, P. (1977). The "false consensus effect": An egocentric bias in social perception and attribution processes. *Journal of Experimental Social Psychology, 13*, 279–301.

Rosselli, F., Skelly, J., & Mackie, D. (1995). Processing rational and emotional messages: The cognitive and affective mediation of persuasion. *Journal of Experimental Social Psychology, 31*, 163–190.

Rossi, P. H., & Cutright, P. (1961). The impact of party organization in an industrial setting. In M. Janowitz (Ed.), *Community political systems* (pp. 81–116). Glencoe, IL: Free Press.

Rossi, P. H., & Lyall, K. C. (1976). *Reforming public welfare: A critique of the negative income tax experiment*. New York: Russell Sage Foundation.

Rossi, P. H., Wright, J. D., & Anderson, A. B. (Eds.). (1983). *Handbook of survey research*. New York: Academic Press.

Rothman, S., Lichter, S., & Lichter, L. (1992). Television's America. In S. Rothman (Ed.), *The mass media in liberal democratic societies* (pp. 221–266). New York: Paragon House.

Rotter, J. B. (1966). Generalized expectancies for internal versus external control of reinforcement. *Psychological Monographs, 80*(1, Whole No. 609).

Rowan, C. T. (1996). *The coming race war in America: A wake-up call*. Boston: Little, Brown.

Rubin, A. (2002). The uses-and-gratifications perspective of media effects. In J. Bryant & D. Zillmann (Eds.), *Media effects: Advances in theory and research* (2nd ed., pp. 525–548). Mahwah, NJ: Lawrence Erlbaum Associates.

Rubin, J., Provenzano, E., & Luria, Z. (1974). The eye of the beholder: Parents' views on sex of newborns. *American Journal of Orthopsychiatry, 44*, 512–519.

Ruble, D. N., & Martin, C. L. (1998). Gender development. In W. Damon (Ed.), *Handbook of child psychology* (5th ed., Vol. 3, pp. 933–1016). New York: Wiley.

Ruble, T. L. (1983). Sex stereotypes: Issues of change in the 1970s. *Sex Roles, 9*, 397–402.

Ruby, C. L. (2002a). The definition of terrorism. *Analyses of Social Issues and Public Policy, 2*(1), 9–14.

Ruby, C. L. (2002b). Response to Post: Can fundamentalist terrorists have political motivations? *Peace and Conflict: Journal of Peace Psychology, 8*, 215–218.

Rudman, L. A. (2004). Sources of implicit attitudes. *Current Directions in Psychological Science, 13*, 79–82.

Ruitter, R., Abraham, C., & Kok, G. (2001). Scaring warnings and rational precautions: A review of the psychology of fear appeals. *Psychology and Health, 16*, 613–660.

Rumelhart, D. E., Hinton, G., & McClelland, J. L. (1986). A general framework for parallel distributed processing. In D. E. Rumelhart & J. L. McClelland (Eds.), *Parallel distributed processing*. Cambridge, MA: MIT Press.

Ruscher, J. B. (2001). *Prejudiced communication: A social psychological perspective*. New York: Guilford.

Rush, L. L. (1997). *Stereotyping in black and white: Differences in stereotype knowledge and stereotype use*. Unpublished doctoral dissertation, University of Oklahoma, Norman.

Rushton, J. P. (1975). Generosity in children: Immediate and long-term effects of modeling, preaching and moral judgment. *Journal of Personality and Social Psychology, 31*, 459–466.

Rushton, J. P. (1982). Television and prosocial behavior. In D. Pearl, L. Bouthilet, & J. Lazar (Eds.), *Television and behavior: Ten years of scientific progress and implications for the eighties. Vol. 2: Technical reviews*. Washington, DC: U.S. Government Printing Office.

Russell, C. (1995). *The official guide to the American marketplace* (2nd ed.). Ithaca, NY: New Strategist.

Russo, E. D. (1971). A study of bias in TV coverage of the Vietnam War: 1969 and 1970. *Public Opinion Quarterly, 35*, 539–543.

Russo, N. E., & Denmark, F. L. (1984). Women, psychology, and public policy: Selected issues. *American Psychologist, 39*, 1161–1165.

Rutter, M., Maughan, B., Mortimore, P., & Ouston, J. (1979). *Fifteen thousand hours: Secondary schools and their effects on children*. Somerset, England: Open Books.

Saad, L. (1999, April). Independents rank as largest U.S. political group. *Gallup Poll Monthly*, No. 403, pp. 45–46.

Saad, L. (2001a, March). Americans mostly "green" in the energy vs. environment debate. *Gallup Poll Monthly*, No. 426, pp. 33–37.

Saad, L. (2001b, May). Majority considers sex before marriage morally okay. *Gallup Poll Monthly*, No. 428, pp. 46–48.

Saad, L. (2001c, June). Blacks less satisfied than Hispanics with their quality of life. *Gallup Poll Monthly*, No. 429, pp. 47–51.

Saad, L. (2001d, June). Women see room for improvement in job equity: But are generally satisfied with their lives. *Gallup Poll Monthly*, No. 429, pp. 56–63.

Saad, L. (2001e, September). Americans clearly support a military response to terrorist assault. *Gallup Poll Monthly*, No. 432, pp. 5–7.

Saad, L. (2001f, December). Fear of terrorism subsides despite persistent concerns about nation's security. *Gallup Poll Monthly*, No. 435, pp. 4–8.

Saad, L. (2002a, March). Americans believe Muslim antipathy toward United States based on misinformation. *Gallup Poll Monthly*, No. 438, pp. 5–10.

Saad, L. (2002b, March). Canada and Britain top Americans' country ratings once again. *Gallup Poll Monthly*, No. 438, pp. 24–27.

Saad, L. (2002c, March). Americans sharply divided on seriousness of global warming. *Gallup Poll Monthly*, No. 438, pp. 43–48.

Saad, L. (2002e, October 8). Top ten findings about public opinion and Iraq. *Gallup Poll Tuesday Briefing*, pp. 44–47.

Saad, L. (2003, April 17). Environmental concern down this Earth Day: Economic woes may be the cause. *Gallup Poll Tuesday Briefing*, pp. 26–28.

Saad, L., & Carroll, J. (2001). Even after attacks, majority of Americans not living in fear of terrorism. *Gallup Poll Monthly*, No. 432, pp. 8–11.

Saad, L., & Newport, F. (2001). Blacks and whites differ about treatment of blacks in America today. *Gallup Poll Monthly*, No. 430, pp. 58–63.

Sadler, O., & Tesser, A. (1973). Some effects of salience and time upon interpersonal hostility and attraction during social isolation. *Sociometry, 36*, 99–112.

Saks, M. J. (1974). Ignorance of science is no excuse. *Trial, 10*(6), 18–20.

Samdahl, D., & Robertson, R. (1989). Social determinants of environmental concern: Specification and test of the model. *Environment and Behavior, 21*, 57–81.

Sande, G. N., Goethals, G. R., Ferrari, L., & Worth, L. T. (1989). Value-guided attributions: Maintaining the moral self-image and the diabolical enemy-image. *Journal of Social Issues, 45*(2), 91–118.

Sarbin, T. R. (2003). The metaphor-to-myth transformation with special reference to the "war on terrorism." *Peace and Conflict: Journal of Peace Psychology, 9*, 149–157.

Sargant, W. (1957). *Battle for the mind: A physiology of conversion and brainwashing*. Garden City, NY: Doubleday.

Sarup, G., Suchner, R. W., & Gaylord, G. (1991). Contrast effects and attitude change: A test of the two-stage hypothesis of social judgment theory. *Social Psychology Quarterly, 54*, 364–372.

Sata, L. S. (1975). Laboratory training for police officers. *Journal of Social Issues, 31*(1), 107–114.

Saucier, G. (2000). Isms and the structure of social attitudes. *Journal of Personality and Social Psychology, 78*, 366–385.

Sawyer, E. (1988). Realities of television news programming. In S. Oskamp (Ed.), *Television as a social issue: Applied social psychology annual* (Vol. 8, pp. 30–43). Newbury Park, CA: Sage.

Sax, L. J., Astin, A. W., Korn, W. S., & Mahoney, K. M. (1998). *The American college freshman: National norms for fall of 1998.* Los Angeles: Higher Education Research Institute, University of California, Los Angeles.

Saxe, L. (1994). Detection of deception: Polygraph and integrity tests. *Current Directions in Psychological Science, 3*, 69–73.

Scammon, R. M., McGillivray, A. V., & Cook, R. (2001). *America votes 24: A handbook of contemporary election statistics.* Washington, DC: Congressional Quarterly Press.

Scarrow, H. A., & Borman, S. (1979). The effects of newspaper endorsements on election outcomes: A case study. *Public Opinion Quarterly, 43*, 388–393.

Schachter, S., & Singer, J. E. (1962). Cognitive, social, and physiological determinants of emotional state. *Psychological Review, 69*, 379–399.

Schaffner, P. E., Wandersman, A., & Stang, D. (1981). Candidate name exposure and voting: Two field studies. *Basic and Applied Social Psychology, 2*, 195–203.

Schahn, J., & Holzer, E. (1990). Studies of individual environmental concern: The role of knowledge, gender, and background variables. *Environment and Behavior, 22*, 767–786.

Schaie, K. W., & Willis, S. (1991). Adult personality and psychomotor performance: Cross-sectional and longitudinal analyses. *Journal of Gerontology: Psychological Sciences, 46*, 275–284.

Schecter, A. (Ed.). (1994). *Dioxins and health.* New York: Plenum.

Scheers, N. J., & Dayton, C. M. (1987). Improved estimation of academic cheating behavior using the randomized response technique. *Research in Higher Education, 26*, 61–69.

Schifter, D. E., & Ajzen, I. (1985). Intention, perceived control, and weight loss: An application of the theory of planned behavior. *Journal of Personality and Social Psychology, 49*, 843–851.

Schlegel, R. P., D'Avernas, J. R., Zanna, M. P., & DeCourville, N. H. (1992). Problem drinking: A problem for the theory of reasoned action? *Journal of Applied Social Psychology, 22*, 358–385.

Schlenker, B. R. (1980). *Impression management: The self-concept, social identity, and interpersonal relations.* Monterey, CA: Brooks/Cole.

Schlenker, B. R. (1982). Translating actions into attitudes: An identity-analytic approach to the explanation of social conduct. In L. Berkowitz (Ed.), *Advances in experimental social psychology* (Vol. 15, pp. 193–247). New York: Academic Press.

Schlenker, B. R., & Britt, T. (1999). Beneficial impression management: Strategically controlling information to help friends. *Journal of Personality and Social Psychology, 76*, 559–573.

Schlenker, B. R., Hallam, J. R., & McCown, N. E. (1983). Motives and social evaluation: Actor-observer differences in the delineation of motives for a beneficial act. *Journal of Experimental Social Psychology, 19*, 254–273.

Schlenker, B. R., Weigold, M. F., & Hallam, J. R. (1990). Self-serving attributions in social context: Effects of self-esteem and social pressure. *Journal of Personality and Social Psychology, 58*, 855–863.

Schneider, D. J. (2003). *The psychology of stereotyping.* New York: Guilford.

Schneider, D. J., Hastorf, A. H., & Ellsworth, P. C. (1979). *Person perception* (2nd ed.). Reading, MA: Addison-Wesley.

Schneider, W. (1983). Elite and public opinion: The alliance's new fissure? *Public Opinion, 6*(1), 5–8, 51.

Schonbach, P. (1981). *Education and intergroup attitudes.* London, England: Academic Press.

Schramm, W. (1964). *Mass media and national development.* Stanford, CA: Stanford University Press.

Schreiber, R. (2002). Injecting a woman's voice: Conservative women's organizations, gender consciousness, and the expression of women's policy preferences. *Sex Roles, 47*, 331–342.

Schuessler, K., Hittle, D., & Cardascia, J. (1978). Measuring responding desirably with attitude-opinion items. *Social Psychology, 41*, 224–235.

Schultz, P. W. (2000). Empathizing with nature: The effects of perspective taking on concern for environmental issues. *Journal of Social Issues, 56*, 391–406.

Schultz, P. W. (2001). The structure of environmental concern: Concern for self, other people, and the biosphere. *Journal of Environmental Psychology, 21*, 327–339.

Schultz, P. W. (2002). Inclusion with nature: The psychology of human–nature relations. In P. Schmuck & P. W. Schultz (Eds.), *Psychology of sustainable development* (pp. 61–78). Boston: Kluwer.

Schultz, P. W., & Oskamp, S. (1996). Effort as a moderator of the attitude–behavior relationship: General environmental concern and recycling. *Social Psychology Quarterly, 59*, 375–383.

Schultz, P. W., & Oskamp, S. (2000). *Social psychology: An applied perspective.* Upper Saddle River, NJ: Prentice-Hall.

Schultz, P. W., & Searleman, A. (2002). Rigidity of thought and behavior: 100 years of research. *Psychological Monographs, 128,* 165–207.

Schultz, P. W., Shriver, C., Tabanico, J., & Khazian, A. (2004). Implicit connections with nature. *Journal of Environmental Psychology, 24,* 31–42.

Schultz, P. W., & Stone, W. F. (1994). Authoritarianism and attitudes toward the environment. *Environment and Behavior, 26,* 25–37.

Schultz, P. W., Unipan, J. B., & Gamba, R. (2000). Acculturation and ecological worldview among Latino Americans. *Journal of Environmental Education, 31,* 22–27.

Schultz, P. W., & Zelezny, L. (1999). Values as predictors of environmental attitudes: Evidence for consistency across 14 countries. *Journal of Environmental Psychology, 19,* 255–265.

Schuman, H. (1972). Attitudes vs. actions versus attitudes vs. attitudes. *Public Opinion Quarterly, 36,* 347–354.

Schuman, H., & Johnson, M. P. (1976). Attitudes and behavior. *Annual Review of Sociology, 2,* 161–207.

Schuman, H., & Kalton, G. (1985). Survey methods. In G. Lindzey & E. Aronson (Eds.), *The handbook of social psychology* (3rd ed., Vol. 1, pp. 635–697). New York: Random House.

Schuman, H., & Presser, S. (1981a). The attitude-action connection and the issue of gun control. *The Annals of the American Academy of Political and Social Science, 455,* 40–47.

Schuman, H., & Presser, S. (1981b). *Questions and answers in attitude surveys: Experiments on question form, wording, and context.* New York: Academic Press.

Schuman, H., & Presser, S. (1996). *Questions and answers in attitude surveys: Experiments on question form, wording, and context.* Thousand Oaks, CA: Sage. (Original work published 1981)

Schuman, H., Steeh, C., & Bobo, L. (1985). *Racial attitudes in America: Trends and interpretations.* Cambridge, MA: Harvard University Press.

Schuman, H., Steeh, C., Bobo, L., & Krysan, M. (1997). *Racial attitudes in America: Trends and interpretations* (rev. ed.). Cambridge, MA: Harvard University Press.

Schwartz, S. H. (1977). Normative influences on altruism. In L. Berkowitz (Ed.), *Advances in experimental social psychology* (Vol. 10, pp. 221–279). New York: Academic Press.

Schwartz, S. H. (1978). Temporal instability as a moderator of the attitude–behavior relationship. *Journal of Personality and Social Psychology, 36,* 715–724.

Schwartz, S. H. (1992). Universals in the content and structure of values: Theoretical advances and empirical tests in 20 countries. In M. P. Zanna (Ed.), *Advances in experimental social psychology* (Vol. 25, pp. 1–65). San Diego: Academic Press.

Schwartz, S. H. (1994). Are there universal aspects in the structure and contents of human values? *Journal of Social Issues, 50*(4), 19–45.

Schwartz, S. H., & Sagie, G. (2000). Value consensus and importance: A cross-national study. *Journal of Cross-Cultural Psychology, 32,* 465–497.

Schwartz, S. H., & Tessler, R. C. (1972). A test of a model for reducing measured attitude-behavior discrepancies. *Journal of Personality and Social Psychology, 24,* 225–236.

Schwarz, N. (1999). Self-reports: How the questions shape the answers. *American Psychologist, 54,* 93–105.

Schwarz, N., Groves, R. M., & Schuman, H. (1998). Survey methods. In D. T. Gilbert, S. T. Fiske, & G. Lindzey (Eds.), *The handbook of social psychology* (4th ed., Vol. 1, pp. 143–179). Boston: McGraw-Hill.

Schwarz, N., & Hippler, H. J. (1991). Response alternatives: The impact of their choice and ordering. In P. Biemer, R. Groves, N. Mathiowetz, & S. Sudman (Eds.), *Measurement error in surveys* (pp. 41–56). Chichester, England: Wiley.

Scientific Advisory Committee on Television and Social Behavior. (1972). *Television and growing up: The impact of televised violence.* Report to the Surgeon General, USPHS. Washington, DC: U.S. Department of Health, Education, & Welfare.

Scott, J. E., & Fuller, J. R. (1965). *Genetics and social behavior of the dog.* Chicago: University of Chicago Press.

Scott, W. A. (1959). Attitude change by response reinforcement: Replication and extension. *Sociometry, 22,* 328–335.

Scott, W. A. (1965). Psychological and social correlates of international images. In H. C. Kelman (Ed.), *International behavior: A social-psychological analysis* (pp. 71–103). New York: Holt, Rinehart & Winston.

Scott, W. A. (1968). Attitude measurement. In G. Lindzey & E. Aronson (Eds.), *The handbook of social psychology* (2nd ed., Vol. 2, pp. 204–273). Reading, MA: Addison-Wesley.

Sears, D. O. (1975). Political socialization. In F. I. Greenstein & N. W. Polsby (Eds.), *Handbook of political science.* Reading, MA: Addison-Wesley.

Sears, D. O. (1986). College sophomores in the laboratory: Influences of a narrow data base on social psychology's view of human nature. *Journal of Personality and Social Psychology, 51,* 515–530.

Sears, D. O. (1988a). Review of *Communication and persuasion: Central and peripheral routes to attitude change. Public Opinion Quarterly, 52*, 262–265.

Sears, D. O. (1988b). Symbolic racism. In P. A. Katz & D. A. Taylor (Eds.), *Eliminating racism: Profiles in controversy* (pp. 53–84). New York: Plenum.

Sears, D. O. (1991). Whither political socialization research? The question of persistence. In O. Ichilov (Ed.), *Political socialization, citizenship and democracy.* New York: Teachers College Press.

Sears, D. O. (1997). The impact of self-interest on attitudes—a symbolic politics perspective on differences between survey and experimental findings: Comment on Crano (1997). *Journal of Personality and Social Psychology, 72*, 492–496.

Sears, D. O., & Abeles, R. P. (1969). Attitudes and opinions. *Annual Review of Psychology, 20*, 253–288.

Sears, D. O., & Allen, H. M., Jr. (1984). The trajectory of local desegregation controversies and whites' opposition to busing. In N. Miller & M. B. Brewer (Eds.), *Groups in contact: The psychology of desegregation* (pp. 123–151). New York: Academic Press.

Sears, D. O., & Citrin, J. (1985). *Tax revolt: Something for nothing in California* (enlarged ed.). Cambridge, MA: Harvard University Press.

Sears, D. O., & Freedman, J. L. (1967). Selective exposure to information: A critical review. *Public Opinion Quarterly, 31*, 194–213.

Sears, D. O., & Henry, P. J. (2003). The origins of symbolic racism. *Journal of Personality and Social Psychology, 85*, 259–275.

Sears, D. O., Henry, P. J., & Tarman, C. (2003, February). *Over thirty years later: A contemporary look at symbolic racism and its critics.* Paper presented at Society for Personality and Social Psychology meeting, Los Angeles.

Sears, D. O., Hetts, J. J., Sidanius, J., & Bobo, L. (2000). Race in American politics: Framing the debates. In D. O. Sears, J. Sidanius, & L. Bobo (Eds.), *Racialized politics: The debate about racism in America* (pp. 1–43). Chicago: University of Chicago Press.

Sears, D. O., Lau, R. R., Tyler, T. R., & Allen, H. M., Jr. (1980). Self-interest versus symbolic politics in policy attitudes and presidential voting. *American Political Science Review, 74*, 670–684.

Sears, D. O., van Laar, C., Carrillo, M., & Kosterman, R. (1997). Is it really racism? The origins of white Americans' opposition to race-targeted policies. *Public Opinion Quarterly, 61*, 16–53.

Sears, D. O., & Whitney, R. E. (1973). *Political persuasion.* Morristown, NJ: General Learning Press.

Seligman, C., Olson, J. M., & Zanna, M. P. (Eds.). (1996). *The psychology of values: The Ontario Symposium* (Vol. 8). Hillsdale, NJ: Lawrence Erlbaum Associates.

Sellers, C. (1965). The equilibrium cycle in two-party politics. *Public Opinion Quarterly, 29*, 16–38.

Selltiz, C., & Cook, S. W. (1962). Factors influencing attitudes of foreign students toward the host country. *Journal of Social Issues, 18*(1), 7–23.

Selznick, G. J., & Steinberg, S. (1969). *The tenacity of prejudice: Anti-Semitism in contemporary America.* New York: Harper & Row.

Serbin, L. A., & O'Leary, K. D. (1975, December). How nursery schools teach girls to shut up. *Psychology Today*, pp. 56–58.

Severy, L. J. (1974, December). *Procedures and issues in the measurement of attitudes* (TM Report 30). Princeton, NJ: ERIC Clearinghouse on Tests, Measurement, & Evaluation, Educational Testing Service.

Shadish, W. (2002). Revisiting field experiments: Field notes for the future. *Psychological Methods, 7*, 3–18.

Shakin, M., Sternglanz, S. H., & Shakin, D. (1985). Infant clothing: Sex labeling for strangers. *Sex Roles, 5*(2), 28–37.

Shamir, J. (1986). Preelection polls in Israel: Structural constraints on accuracy. *Public Opinion Quarterly, 50*, 62–75.

Shapiro, R. Y., & Jacobs, L. R. (2000). Who leads and who follows? U.S. presidents, public opinion, and foreign policy. In B. L. Nacos, R. Y. Shapiro, & P. Isernia (Eds.), *Decisionmaking in a glass house* (pp. 223–245). Lanham, MD: Rowman & Littlefield.

Sharan, S. (1980). Cooperative learning in small groups: Recent methods and effects on achievement, attitudes, and ethnic relations. *Review of Educational Research, 50*, 241–271.

Shavitt, S. (1989). Operationalizing functional theories of attitude. In A. R. Pratkanis, S. J. Breckler, & A. G. Greenwald (Eds.), *Attitude structure and function* (pp. 311–337). Hillsdale, NJ: Lawrence Erlbaum Associates.

Shavitt, S., & Nelson, M. R. (2000). The social-identity function in person perception: Communicated meanings of product preferences. In G. R. Maio & J. M. Olson (Eds.), *Why we evaluate: Functions of attitudes* (pp. 37–57). Mahwah, NJ: Lawrence Erlbaum Associates.

Shaw, M. E., & Costanzo, P. R. (1982), *Theories of social psychology* (2nd ed.). New York: McGraw-Hill.

Sheatsley, P. B. (1977). *Public Opinion*—A weekly journal. *Public Opinion Quarterly, 41*, 400–401.

Sheatsley, P. B., & Feldman, J. J. (1965). A national survey on public reactions and behavior. In B. S. Greenberg & E. B. Parker (Eds.), *The Kennedy assassination and the American public* (pp. 149–177). Stanford, CA: Stanford University Press.

Sheets, T., Radlinski, A., Kohne, J., & Brunner, G. A. (1974). Deceived respondents: Once bitten, twice shy. *Public Opinion Quarterly, 38*, 261–263.

Sheppard, B. H., Hartwick, J., & Warshaw, P. R. (1988). The theory of reasoned action: A meta-analysis of past research with recommendations for modifications and future research. *Journal of Consumer Research, 15*, 325–343.

Sherif, C. W., Sherif, M., & Nebergall, R. E. (1965). *Attitude and attitude change: The social judgment-involvement approach*. Philadelphia: Saunders.

Sherif, M., Harvey, O. J., White, B. J., Hood, W. E., & Sherif, C. W. (1961). *Intergroup conflict and cooperation: The Robber's Cave experiment*. Norman: University of Oklahoma Book Exchange.

Sherif, M., & Hovland, C. I. (1961). *Social judgment: Assimilation and contrast effects in communication and attitude change*. New Haven, CT: Yale University Press.

Sheth, J. N. (1974). A field study of attitude structure and the attitude-behavior relationship. In J. N. Sheth (Ed.), *Models of buyer behavior: Conceptual, quantitative, and empirical* (pp. 242–268). New York: Harper & Row.

Shively, W. P. (1992). From differential abstention to conversion: A change in electoral change, 1864–1988. *American Journal of Political Science, 36*, 309–330.

Shrum, L. J. (2002). Media consumption and perceptions of social reality: Effects and underlying processes. In J. Bryant & D. Zillmann (Eds.), *Media effects: Advances in theory and research* (pp. 69–96). Mahwah, NJ: Lawrence Erlbaum Associates.

Sidanius, J., Levin, S., & Pratto, F. (1998). Hierarchical group relations, institutional terror, and the dynamics of the criminal justice system. In J. L. Eberhardt & S. T. Fiske (Eds.), *Confronting racism: The problem and the response* (pp. 136–165). Thousand Oaks, CA: Sage.

Sidanius, J., & Pratto, F. (1993). The inevitability of oppression and the dynamics of social dominance. In P. Sniderman & P. Tetlock (Eds.), *Prejudice, politics, and race in America today* (pp. 173–211). Stanford, CA: Stanford University Press.

Sidanius, J., & Pratto, F. (1999). *Social dominance: An intergroup theory of social hierarchy and oppression*. Cambridge, England: Cambridge University Press.

Sidanius, J., & Veniegas, R. C. (2000). Gender and race discrimination: The interactive nature of disadvantage. In S. Oskamp (Ed.), *Reducing prejudice and discrimination* (pp. 47–69). Mahwah, NJ: Lawrence Erlbaum Associates.

Sidorowicz, L., & Lunney, G. S. (1980). Baby X revisited. *Sex Roles, 6*, 67–73.

Sieber, J. E. (Ed.). (1982). *The ethics of social research: Surveys and experiments*. New York: Springer-Verlag.

Sieber, J. E. (Ed.). (1984). *NIH readings on the protection of human subjects in behavioral and social science research: Conference proceedings and background papers*. Frederick, MD: University Publications of America.

Sieber, J. E. (1992). *Planning ethically responsible research: A guide for students and internal review boards*. Newbury Park, CA: Sage.

Sieber, J. E., Iannuzzo, R., & Rodriguez, B. (1995). Deception methods in psychology: Have they changed in 23 years? *Ethics and Behavior, 5*, 67–85.

Sigel, R. S. (Ed.). (1989). *Political learning in adulthood*. Chicago: University of Chicago Press.

Sigel, R. S., & Hoskin, M. B. (1981). *The political involvement of adolescents*. New Brunswick, NJ: Rutgers University Press.

Sigelman, L., & Sigelman, C. K. (1984). Judgments of the Carter–Reagan debate: The eyes of the beholders. *Public Opinion Quarterly, 48*, 624–628.

Signorielli, N., & Bacue, A. (1999). Recognition and respect: A content analysis of prime-time television characters across three decades. *Sex Roles, 40*, 527–544.

Signorielli, N., Gross, L., & Morgan, M. (1982). Violence in television programs: Ten years later. In D. Pearl, L. Bouthilet, & J. Lazar (Eds.), *Television and behavior: Ten years of scientific progress and implications for the eighties. Vol. 2: Technical reviews*. Washington, DC: U.S. Government Printing Office.

Signorielli, N., & Kahlenberg, S. (2001). Television's world of work in the nineties. *Journal of Broadcasting and Electronic Media, 45*, 4–23.

Signorielli, N., McLeod, D., & Healy, E. (1994). Gender stereotypes in MTV commercials: The beat goes on. *Journal of Broadcasting and Electronic Media, 38*, 91–101.

Silbey, J. H. (1991). Beyond realignment and realignment theory: American political eras, 1789–1989. In B. E. Shafer (Ed.), *The end of realignment? Interpreting American electoral eras* (pp. 3–23). Madison: University of Wisconsin Press.

Silver, B. D., Anderson, B. A., & Abramson, P. R. (1986). Who overreports voting? *American Political Science Review, 80*, 613–624.

Silverman, I. (1964). In defense of dissonance theory: Reply to Chapanis and Chapanis. *Psychological Bulletin, 62*, 205–209.

Silvia, P. J. (2002). Communicator similarity and persuasion: Exploring a balance model. *Dissertation Abstracts International, 62*(10), 4844B.

Simmons, C. H., & Zumpf, C. (1983). The lost letter technique revisited. *Journal of Applied Social Psychology, 13*, 510–514.

Simon, D. M., & Ostrom, C. W., Jr. (1989). The impact of televised speeches and foreign travel on presidential approval. *Public Opinion Quarterly, 53*, 58–82.

Simon, R. J., & Landis, J. M. (1989). The polls—A report: Women's and men's attitudes about a woman's place and role. *Public Opinion Quarterly, 53*, 265–276.

Simons, H. W., Berkowitz, N. N., & Moyer, R. J. (1970). Similarity, credibility, and attitude change: A review and a theory. *Psychological Bulletin, 73*, 1–16.

Singer, E., Frankel, M. R., & Glassman, M. B. (1983). The effect of interviewer characteristics and expectations on response. *Public Opinion Quarterly, 47*, 68–83.

Singh, D. (1993). Adaptive significance of female physical attractiveness: Role of waist-to-hip ratio. *Journal of Personality and Social Psychology, 65*, 293–307.

Singh, K., Leong, S. M., & Tan, C. T. (1995). A theory of reasoned action perspective of voting behavior: Model and empirical test. *Psychology and Marketing, 12*, 37–51.

Sistrunk, F., & McDavid, J. W. (1971). Sex variables in conforming behavior. *Journal of Personality and Social Psychology, 17*, 200–207.

Sivacek, J., & Crano, W. D. (1982). Vested interest as a moderator of attitude-behavior consistency. *Journal of Personality and Social Psychology, 43*, 210–221.

Skalaban, A. (1988). Do the polls affect elections? Some 1980 evidence. *Political Behavior, 10*, 136–150.

Skedgell, R. A. (1966). How computers pick an election winner. *Trans-action, 4*(1), 42–46.

Skinner, B. F. (1957). *Verbal behavior.* New York: Appleton-Century-Crofts.

Skowronski, J. J., & Carlston, D. E. (1989). Negativity and extremity biases in impression formation: A review of explanations. *Psychological Bulletin, 105*, 131–142.

Skowronski, J. J., & Lawrence, M. A. (2001). A comparative study of the implicit and explicit gender attitudes of children and college students. *Psychology of Women Quarterly, 25*, 155–165.

Slavin, R. E. (1980). Cooperative learning. *Review of Educational Research, 50*, 315–342.

Slovic, P., Fischhoff, B., & Lichtenstein, S. (1980). Facts vs. fears: Understanding perceived risk. In R. Schwing & W. A. Albers, Jr. (Eds.), *Societal risk assessment: How safe is safe enough?* New York: Plenum.

Smelser, N. J., & Mitchell, F. (Eds.). (2002). *Terrorism: Perspectives from the behavioral and social sciences.* Washington, DC: National Research Council.

Smith, C., & Lloyd, B. (1978). Maternal behavior and perceived sex of infant: Revisited. *Child Development, 49*, 1263–1265.

Smith, D. C. (2001). Environmentalism, feminism, and gender. *Sociological Inquiry, 71*, 314–334.

Smith, E. (2002). *Energy, the environment, and public opinion.* Lanham, MD: Rowman & Littlefield.

Smith, E. R. (1994). Social cognition contributions to attribution theory and research. In P. G. Devine, D. L. Hamilton, & T. M. Ostrom (Eds.), *Social cognition: Impact on social psychology* (pp. 77–108). San Diego: Academic Press.

Smith, E. R., & Manard, B. B. (1980). Causal attributions and medical school admissions. *Personality and Social Psychology Bulletin, 6*, 644–650.

Smith, H., & Tyler, T. R. (1996). Justice and power: When will justice concerns encourage the advantaged to support policies which redistribute economic resources and the disadvantaged to willingly obey the law? *European Journal of Social Psychology, 26*, 171–200.

Smith, J. F., & Kida, T. (1991). Heuristics and biases: Expertise and task realism in auditing. *Psychological Bulletin, 109*, 472–489.

Smith, L. B. (1988). Foreword. In P. A. Katz & D. A. Taylor (Eds.), *Eliminating racism: Profiles in controversy* (pp. xi–xiii). New York: Plenum.

Smith, M. B. (2002). The metaphor (and fact) of war. *Peace and Conflict: Journal of Peace Psychology, 8*, 249–258.

Smith, M. B., Bruner, J. S., & White, R. W. (1956). *Opinion and personality.* New York: Wiley.

Smith, M. L. (1980). Sex bias in counseling and psychotherapy. *Psychological Bulletin, 89*, 392–407.

Smith, T. W. (1985). The polls: America's most important problems. Part I: National and international. *Public Opinion Quarterly, 49*, 264–274.

Smith, T. W. (1987). That which we call welfare by any other name would smell sweeter: An analysis of the impact of question wording on response patterns. *Public Opinion Quarterly, 51*, 75–83.

Smith, T. W. (1990a). The first straw? A study of the origins of election polls. *Public Opinion Quarterly, 54*, 21–36.

Smith, T. W. (1990b). Liberal and conservative trends in the United States since World War II. *Public Opinion Quarterly, 54*, 479–507.

Smith, T. W. (1992). Changing racial labels: From "colored" to "Negro" to "Black" to "African American." *Public Opinion Quarterly, 56*, 496–514.

Smith, T. W. (1995a). The Holocaust denial controversy. *Public Opinion Quarterly, 59*, 269–295.

Smith, T. W. (1995b, August/September). World War II and the lessons of history. *Public Perspective, 6*(5), 51–53.

Sniderman, P. M., Brody, R. A., & Tetlock, P. E. (1991). *Reasoning and choice: Explorations in political psychology*. Cambridge, England: Cambridge University Press.

Sniderman, P. M., & Piazza, T. (1993). *The scar of race*. Cambridge, MA: Harvard University Press.

Snodgrass, S. E., & Rosenthal, R. (1982). Teacher suspiciousness of experimenter's intent and the mediation of teacher expectancy effects. *Basic and Applied Social Psychology, 3*, 219–230.

Snyder, J. M., Jr. (1996). Constituency preferences: California ballot propositions, 1974–1990. *Legislative Studies Quarterly, 21*, 463–488.

Snyder, M. (1987). *Public appearances, private realities*. New York: Freeman.

Snyder, M., & DeBono, K. G. (1987). A functional approach to attitudes and persuasion. In M. P. Zanna, J. M. Olson, & C. P. Herman (Eds.), *Social influence: The Ontario Symposium* (Vol. 5, pp. 107–125). Hillsdale, NJ: Lawrence Erlbaum Associates.

Snyder, M., & Kendzierski, D. (1982). Acting on one's attitudes: Procedures for linking attitudes and actions. *Journal of Experimental Social Psychology, 18*, 165–183.

Snyder, M., Tanke, E. D., & Berscheid, E. (1977). Social perception and interpersonal behavior: On the self-fulfilling nature of social stereotypes. *Journal of Personality and Social Psychology, 35*, 656–666.

Sobel, R. (Ed.). (1993). *Public opinion in U.S. foreign policy: The controversy over contra aid*. Lanham, MD: Rowman & Littlefield.

Sobel, R. (2001). *The impact of public opinion on U.S. foreign policy since Vietnam: Constraining the colossus*. New York: Oxford University Press.

Solomon, S., Greenberg, J., & Pyszczynski, T. (1991). A terror management theory of social behavior: The psychological functions of self-esteem and cultural worldviews. In M. P. Zanna (Ed.), *Advances in experimental social psychology* (Vol. 24, pp. 93–159). San Diego: Academic Press.

Solop, F. I., & Hagen, K. K. (2002, July/August). War or war? 9/11 surveys restricted the options. *Public Perspective, 13*(4), 36–37.

Sparks, G., & Sparks, C. (2002). Effects of media violence. In J. Bryant & D. Zillmann (Eds.), *Media effects: Advances in theory and research* (2nd ed., pp. 269–286). Mahwah, NJ: Lawrence Erlbaum Associates.

Spence, J. T., Deaux, K., & Helmreich, R. L. (1985). Sex roles in contemporary American society. In G. Lindzey & E. Aronson (Eds.), *The handbook of social psychology* (3rd ed., Vol. 2, pp. 149–178). New York: Random House.

Spence, J. T., & Hahn, E. D. (1997). The Attitudes towards Women Scale and attitude change in college students. *Psychology of Women Quarterly, 21*, 17–34.

Spence, J. T., & Helmreich, R. L. (1972). The Attitudes towards Women Scale: An objective instrument to measure attitudes toward the rights and roles of women in contemporary society. *JSAS Catalog of Selected Documents in Psychology, 2*, 66.

Spence, J. T., & Helmreich, R. L. (1978). *Masculinity and femininity: Their psychological dimensions, correlates, and antecedents*. Austin, TX: University of Texas Press.

Spence, J. T., Helmreich, R. L., & Stapp, J. (1974). The Personal Attributes Questionnaire: A measure of sex role stereotypes and masculinity-femininity. *JSAS Catalog of Selected Documents in Psychology, 4*, 43. (Ms. No. 617).

Spence, J. T., Helmreich, R. L., & Stapp, J. (1975). Ratings of self and peers on sex role attributes and their relation to self-esteem and conceptions of masculinity and femininity. *Journal of Personality and Social Psychology, 32*, 29–39.

Spinner, B., Adair, J. G., & Barnes, G. E. (1977). A reexamination of the faithful subject role. *Journal of Experimental Social Psychology, 13*, 543–551.

Spitze, G., & Huber, J. (1980). Changing attitudes toward women's nonfamily roles: 1938 to 1978. *Sociology of Work and Occupations, 7*, 317–335.

St. Pierre, R. G., & Puma, M. (2000). Toward the dream of the experimenting society. In L. Bickman (Ed.), *Validity and social experimentation: Donald Campbell's legacy* (Vol. 1, pp. 169–192). Thousand Oaks, CA: Sage.

Stagner, R. (1967). *Psychological aspects of international conflict*. Belmont, CA: Brooks/Cole.

Staines, G. L., & Pleck, J. H. (1984). Nonstandard work schedules and family life. *Journal of Applied Psychology, 69*, 515–523.

Stanley, B., Sieber, J., & Melton, G. (Eds.). (1996). *Research ethics: A psychological approach*. Lincoln: University of Nebraska Press.

Stanley, H. W., & Niemi, R. G. (2000). *Vital statistics of American politics, 1999–2000* (7th ed.). Washington, DC: Congressional Quarterly.

Stapp, J. (1978). What's new in measurement? *Society for the Advancement of Social Psychology Newsletter, 4*(4), 10–11.

Star, S. A., & Hughes, H. M. (1950). Report of an educational campaign: The Cincinnati plan for the United Nations. *American Journal of Sociology, 55,* 389–400.

Staub, E. (2002). Notes on terrorism: Origins and prevention. *Peace and Conflict: Journal of Peace Psychology, 8*(3), 207–214.

Steele, C. M. (1988). The psychology of self-affirmation: Sustaining the integrity of the self. In L. Berkowitz (Ed.), *Advances in experimental social psychology* (Vol. 21, pp. 261–302). Orlando, FL: Academic Press.

Steele, C. M., & Liu, T. J. (1983). Dissonance processes as self-affirmation. *Journal of Personality and Social Psychology, 45,* 5–19.

Steele, C. M., Spencer, S. J., & Lynch, M. (1993). Self-image resilience and dissonance: The role of affirmational resources. *Journal of Personality and Social Psychology, 64,* 885–896.

Steinmann, A. (1975). Female and male concepts of sex roles: An overview of twenty years of cross-cultural research. *Transnational Mental Health Research Newsletter, 17*(4), 2–4, 8–11.

Stephan, G. E., & McMullen, D. R. (1982). Tolerance of sexual nonconformity: City size as a situational and early learning determinant. *American Sociological Review, 47,* 411–415.

Stephan, W. G. (1978). School desegregation: An evaluation of predictions made in *Brown v. Board of Education. Psychological Bulletin, 85,* 217–238.

Stephan, W. G. (1985). Intergroup relations. In G. Lindzey & E. Aronson (Eds.), *The handbook of social psychology* (3rd ed., Vol. 2, pp. 599–658). New York: Random House.

Stephan, W. G., & Banks, J. (1999). *Reducing prejudice and stereotyping in schools.* New York: Teachers College Press.

Stephan, W. G., & Stephan, C. W. (2000). An integrated threat theory of prejudice. In S. Oskamp (Ed.), *Reducing prejudice and discrimination* (pp. 23–45). Mahwah, NJ: Lawrence Erlbaum Associates.

Stern, P. C. (2000). Toward a coherent theory of environmentally significant behavior. *Journal of Social Issues, 56,* 407–424.

Stern, P. C., & Dietz, T. (1994). The value basis of environmental concern. *Journal of Social Issues, 50*(3), 65–84.

Stern, P. C., Dietz, T., Abel, T., Guagnano, G. A., & Kalof, L. (1999). A value-belief-norm theory of support for social movements: The case of environmental concern. *Human Ecology Review, 6,* 81–97.

Stern, P. C., Dietz, T., & Guagnano, G. A. (1995). The new ecological paradigm in social-psychological context. *Environment and Behavior, 27,* 723–743.

Stern, P. C., Dietz, T., & Kalof, L. (1993). Value orientations, gender, and environmental concern. *Environment and Behavior, 25,* 322–348.

Stern, P. C., & Oskamp, S. (1987). Managing scarce environmental resources. In D. Stokols & I. Altman (Eds.), *Handbook of environmental psychology* (Vol. 2, pp. 1043–1088). New York: Wiley.

Stern, S., & Faber, J. (1997). The lost e-mail method: Milgram's lost letter technique in the age of the internet. *Behavior, Research Methods, Instruments, and Computers, 29,* 260–263.

Sternglanz, S., & Serbin, L. (1974). Sex role stereotyping on children's television programs. *Developmental Psychology, 10,* 710–715.

Sterngold, A., Warland, R. H., & Herrmann, R. O. (1994). Do surveys overstate public concerns? *Public Opinion Quarterly, 58,* 255–263.

Stockard, J., & Johnson, M. M. (1980). *Sex roles: Sex inequality and sex role development.* Englewood Cliffs, NJ: Prentice-Hall.

Stoker, L. (2001). Political value judgments. In J. Kuklinski (Ed.), *Citizens and politics: Perspectives from political psychology* (pp. 433–468). Cambridge, England: Cambridge University Press.

Stokes, D. E., & Miller W. E. (1962). Party government and the saliency of Congress. *Public Opinion Quarterly, 26,* 531–546.

Stone, J. (2003). Self-consistency for low self-esteem in dissonance processes: The role of self-standards. *Personality and Social Psychology Bulletin, 29,* 846–858.

Stone, J., Aronson, E., Crain, A. L., Winslow, M. P., & Fried, C. B. (1994). Inducing hypocrisy as a means of encouraging young adults to use condoms. *Personality and Social Psychology Bulletin, 20,* 116–128.

Stone, J., & Cooper, J. (2001). A self-standards model of cognitive dissonance. *Journal of Experimental Social Psychology, 37,* 228–243.

Stone, J., & Cooper, J. (2003). The effect of self-attribute relevance on how self-esteem moderates attitude change in dissonance processes. *Journal of Experimental Social Psychology, 39,* 508–515.

Stone, J., Cooper, J., Wiegand, A. W., & Aronson, E. (1997). When exemplification fails: Hypocrisy and the motive for self-integrity. *Journal of Personality and Social Psychology, 72,* 54–65.

Stone, W. F., Lederer, G., & Christie, R. (Eds.). (1993). *Strength and weakness: The authoritarian personality today*. New York: Springer-Verlag.

Stoneman, Z., & Brody, G. H. (1981). Peers as mediators of television food advertisements aimed at children. *Developmental Psychology, 17*, 853–858.

Storms, M. D. (1973). Videotape and the attribution process; Reversing actor's and observer's points of view. *Journal of Personality and Social Psychology, 27*, 165–175.

Stouffer, S. A. (1955). *Communism, conformity, and civil liberties*. New York: Doubleday.

Stout, C. E. (Ed.). (2002). *The psychology of terrorism* (Vols. 1–4). Westport, CT: Praeger.

Stovall, J. G., & Solomon, J. H. (1984). The poll as a news event in the 1980 presidential campaign. *Public Opinion Quarterly, 48*, 615–623.

Stricker, L. J., Messick, S., & Jackson, D. N. (1969). Evaluating deception in psychological research. *Psychological Bulletin, 71*, 343–351.

Stroebe, W., & Diehl, M. (1981). Conformity and counterattitudinal behavior: The effect of social support on attitude change. *Journal of Personality and Social Psychology, 41*, 876–899.

Stroebe, W., & Diehl, M. (1988). When social support fails: Supporter characteristics in compliance-induced attitude change. *Personality and Social Psychology Bulletin, 14*, 136–144.

Stults, D. M., Messe, L. A., & Kerr, N. L. (1984). Belief discrepant behavior and the bogus pipeline: Impression management or arousal attribution. *Journal of Experimental Social Psychology, 20*, 47–54.

Sudman, S. (1967). *Reducing the cost of surveys*. Chicago: Aldine.

Sudman, S. (1982). The presidents and the polls. *Public Opinion Quarterly, 46*, 301–310.

Sudman, S. (1983). The network polls: A critical review. *Public Opinion Quarterly, 47*, 490–496.

Sudman, S. (1986). Do exit polls influence voting behavior? *Public Opinion Quarterly, 50*, 331–339.

Sudman, S., & Bradburn, N. M. (1982). *Asking questions: A practical guide to questionnaire design*. San Francisco: Jossey-Bass.

Sudman, S., Bradburn, N. M., & Schwarz, N. (1996). *Thinking about answers: The application of cognitive processes to survey methodology*. San Francisco: Jossey-Bass.

Suedfeld, P. (1971). Models of attitude change: Theories that pass in the night. In P. Suedfeld (Ed.), *Attitude change: The competing views* (pp. 1–62). Chicago: Aldine-Atherton.

Sullivan, D. S., & Deiker, T. E. (1973). Subject-experimenter perceptions. *American Psychologist, 28*, 587–591.

Sullivan, J. L., Piereson, J. E., & Marcus, G. E. (1978). Ideological constraint in the mass public: A methodological critique and some new findings. *American Journal of Political Science, 228*, 233–249.

Sullivan, J. L., Piereson, J. E., & Marcus, G. E. (1979). An alternative conceptualization of political tolerance: Illusory increases 1950s–1970s. *American Political Science Review, 73*, 781–794.

Sullivan, J. L., & Transue, J. E. (1999). The psychological underpinnings of democracy: A selective review of research on political tolerance, interpersonal trust, and social capital. *Annual Review of Psychology, 50*, 625–650.

Sun Sentinel News. (2000). The virtual ballot. Available online at http://www.sun-sentinel.com/graphics/news/ballot.htm

Swann, W. B., Langlois, J. H., & Gilbert, L. A. (1999). Introduction. In W. B. Swann, J. H. Langlois, & L. A. Gilbert (Eds.), *Sexism and stereotypes in modern society: The gender science of Janet Taylor Spence* (pp. 3–7). Washington, DC: American Psychological Association.

Swim, J. K., Aikin, K. J., Hall, W. S., & Hunter, B. A. (1995). Sexism and racism: Old fashioned and modern prejudices. *Journal of Personality and Social Psychology, 68*, 199–214.

Swim, J. K., & Cohen, L. L. (1997). Overt, covert, and subtle sexism: A comparison between the Attitudes Toward Women and Modern Sexism scales. *Psychology of Women Quarterly, 21*, 103–118.

Swim, J. K., Hyers, L. L., Cohen, L. L., & Ferguson, M. J. (2001). Everyday sexism: Evidence for its incidence, nature, and psychological impact from three daily diary studies. *Journal of Social Issues, 57*, 31–53.

Swingle, E. G. (Ed.). (1973). *Social psychology in natural settings: A reader in field experimentation*. Chicago: Aldine.

Tajfel, H. (1978). Social categorization, social identity and social comparison. In H. Tajfel (Ed.), *Differentiation between social groups: Studies in the social psychology of intergroup relations* (pp. 61–76). London, England: Academic Press.

Tajfel, H. (1981). *Human groups and social categories: Studies in social psychology*. Cambridge, England: Cambridge University Press.

Tamm, M., & Prellwitz, M. (2001). "If I had a friend in a wheelchair": Children's thoughts on disabilities. *Child: Care, Health, and Development, 27*, 223–240.

Tang, S., & Hall, V. (1995). The overjustification effect: A meta-analysis. *Applied Cognitive Psychology, 9*, 365–404.

Tannenbaum, P. H. (1953). *Attitude toward source and concept as factors in attitude change through communications*. Unpublished doctoral dissertation, University of Illinois, Urbana.

Tannenbaum, P. H. (1967). The congruity principle revisited: Studies in the reduction, induction, and generalization of persuasion. In L. Berkowitz (Ed.), *Advances in experimental social psychology* (Vol. 3, pp. 270–320). New York: Academic Press.

Tannenbaum, P. H. (Ed.). (1980). *The entertainment functions of television.* Hillsdale, NJ: Lawrence Erlbaum Associates.

Tannenbaum, P. H., & Kostrich, L. J. (1983). *Turned-on TV/turned-off voters: Policy options for election projections.* Beverly Hills, CA: Sage.

Tanner, T. (1980). Significant life experiences. *Journal of Environmental Education, 11,* 20–24.

Tarrant, M., & Cordell, H. K. (1997). The effect of respondent characteristics on general environmental attitude-behavior correspondence. *Environment and Behavior, 29,* 618–637.

Tashakkori, A., & Insko, C. A. (1981). Interpersonal attraction and person perception: Two tests of three balance models. *Journal of Experimental Social Psychology, 17,* 266–285.

Tate, K. (1993). *From protest to politics: The new black voters in American elections.* Cambridge, MA: Harvard University Press.

Taylor, B. R. (1991). *Affirmative action at work: Law, politics, and ethics.* Pittsburgh, PA: University of Pittsburgh Press.

Taylor, D. A., & Katz, P. A. (1988). Conclusion. In P. A. Katz & D. A. Taylor (Eds.), *Eliminating racism: Profiles in controversy* (pp. 359–369). New York: Plenum.

Taylor, D. G. (1982). Pluralistic ignorance and the spiral of silence: A formal analysis. *Public Opinion Quarterly, 46,* 311–335.

Taylor, D. G., Sheatsley, P. B., & Greeley, A. M. (1978, June). Attitudes toward racial integration. *Scientific American, 238,* 42–51.

Taylor, D. M., & Jaggi, V. (1974). Ethnocentrism and causal attribution in a south Indian context. *Journal of Cross-Cultural Psychology, 5,* 162–171.

Taylor, S., & Todd, P. (1997). Understanding the determinants of consumer composting behavior. *Journal of Applied Social Psychology, 27,* 602–628.

Taylor, S. E. (1975). On inferring one's own attitudes from one's behavior: Some delimiting conditions. *Journal of Personality and Social Psychology, 31,* 126–131.

Taylor, S. E. (1998). The social being in social psychology. In D. T. Gilbert, S. T. Fiske, & G. Lindzey (Eds.), *The handbook of social psychology* (4th ed., Vol. 1, pp. 58–95). Boston: McGraw-Hill.

Taylor, S. E., & Koivumaki, J. H. (1976). The perception of self and others: Acquaintanceship, affect, and actor-observer differences. *Journal of Personality and Social Psychology, 33,* 403–408.

Tedeschi, J. T. (Ed.). (1981). *Impression management theory and social psychological research.* San Diego: Academic Press.

Tedeschi, J. T., & Rosenfeld, P. (1981). Impression management theory and the forced compliance situation. In J. T. Tedeschi (Ed.), *Impression management theory and social psychological research* (pp. 147–177). San Diego: Academic Press.

Tedeschi, J. T., Schlenker, B. R., & Bonoma, T. V. (1971). Cognitive dissonance: Private ratiocination or public spectacle? *American Psychologist, 26,* 685–695.

Tedesco, N. (1974). Patterns of prime time. *Journal of Communication, 24,* 119–124.

Teixeira, R. A. (1987). *Why Americans don't vote: Turnout decline in the United States, 1960–1984.* Westport, CT: Greenwood.

Tesser, A. (1978). Self-generated attitude change. In L. Berkowitz (Ed.), *Advances in experimental social psychology* (Vol. 11, pp. 289–338). San Diego: Academic Press.

Tesser, A. (1993). The importance of heritability in psychological research: The case of attitudes. *Psychological Review, 100,* 129–142.

Tesser, A., & Crelia, R. A. (1994). Attitude heritability and attitude reinforcement: A test of the niche building hypothesis. *Personality and Individual Differences, 16,* 571–577.

Tesser, A., & Leone, C. (1977). Cognitive schemas and thought as determinants of attitude change. *Journal of Experimental Social Psychology, 13,* 340–356.

Tesser, A., Martin, L., & Mendolia, M. (1995). The impact of thought on attitude extremity and attitude–behavior consistency. In R. E. Petty & J. A. Krosnick (Eds.), *Attitude strength: Antecedents and consequences* (pp. 73–92). Hillsdale, NJ: Lawrence Erlbaum Associates.

Tesser, A., & Shaffer, D. R. (1990). Attitudes and attitude change. *Annual Review of Psychology, 41,* 479–523.

Tetlock, P. E. (1981). Personality and isolationism: Content analysis of senatorial speeches. *Journal of Personality and Social Psychology, 41,* 737–743.

Tetlock, P. E. (1983a). Cognitive style and political ideology. *Journal of Personality and Social Psychology, 45,* 118–126.

Tetlock, P. E. (1983b). Policy-makers' images of international conflict. *Journal of Social Issues, 39*(1), 67–86.

Tetlock, P. E. (1985). Integrative complexity of American and Soviet foreign policy rhetoric: A time-series analysis. *Journal of Personality and Social Psychology, 49,* 1565–1585.

Tetlock, P. E. (1986). A value pluralism model of ideological reasoning. *Journal of Personality and Social Psychology, 50,* 819–827.

Tetlock, P. E. (1989). Structure and function in political belief systems. In A. R. Pratkanis, S. J. Breckler, & A. G. Greenwald (Eds.), *Attitude structure and function* (pp. 129–151). Hillsdale, NJ: Lawrence Erlbaum Associates.

Tetlock, P. E. (1998). Social psychology and world politics. In D. T. Gilbert, S. T. Fiske, & G. Lindzey (Eds.), *The handbook of social psychology* (4th ed., Vol. 2, pp. 868–912). Boston: McGraw-Hill.

Tetlock, P. E., Peterson, R. S., & Lerner, J. S. (1996). Revising the value pluralism model: Incorporating social content and context postulates. In C. Seligman, J. M. Olson, & M. P. Zanna (Eds.), *The psychology of values: The Ontario Symposium* (Vol. 8, pp. 25–51). Mahwah, NJ: Lawrence Erlbaum Associates.

Thomas, G. S. (1994). *The rating guide to life in America's fifty states.* Amherst, NY: Prometheus.

Thomas, M. (1985). Electoral proximity and senatorial roll call voting. *American Journal of Political Science, 29,* 96–111.

Thomas, W. I. (1907). The mind of woman and the lower races. *American Journal of Sociology, 12,* 435–569.

Thomas, W. I. (1923). *The unadjusted girl.* Boston: Little, Brown.

Thompson, B. (2002). *Score reliability: Contemporary thinking on reliability issues.* Thousand Oaks, CA: Sage.

Thompson, K. S., & Oskamp, S. (1974). Difficulties in replicating the proselyting effect in doomsday groups. *Psychological Reports, 35,* 971–978.

Thompson, L. (1990). Negotiation behavior and outcomes: Empirical evidence and theoretical issues. *Psychological Bulletin, 108,* 515–532.

Thornberry, O., & Massey, J. (1988). Trends in United States telephone coverage across time and subgroups. In R. Groves, P. Biemer, L. Lyberg, J. Massey, W. Nicholls, & J. Waksberg (Eds.), *Telephone survey methodology* (pp. 25–49). New York: Wiley.

Thornton, A., Alwin, D., & Camburn, D. (1983). Causes and consequences of sex-role attitudes and attitude change. *American Sociological Review, 48,* 211–227.

Thurstone, L. L. (1928). Attitudes can be measured. *American Journal of Sociology, 33,* 529–554.

Time. (2000, November 20). Numbers. p. 27.

Times Mirror. (1987). The people, the press and politics. Reading, MA: Addison-Wesley.

Timmer, S. G., Eccles, J., & O'Brien, K. (1985). How children use time. In F. T. Juster & F. P. Stafford (Eds.), *Time, goods, and well-being.* Ann Arbor, MI: Institute for Social Research.

Tittle, C. R., & Hill, R. J. (1967). Attitude measurement and prediction of behavior: An evaluation of conditions and measurement techniques. *Sociometry, 30,* 199–213.

Tobin, R. J., & Eagles, M. (1992). U.S. and Canadian attitudes toward international interactions: A cross-national test of the double-standard hypothesis. *Basic and Applied Social Psychology, 13,* 447–459.

Tolley, H., Jr. (1973). *Children and war: Political socialization to international conflict.* New York: Teachers College Press, Columbia University.

Tornatzky, L. G., Solomon, T., et al. (1982). Contributions of social science to innovation and productivity. *American Psychologist, 37,* 737–746.

Torney, J. V., Oppenheim, A. N., & Farnen, R. F. (1975). *Civic education in ten countries: An empirical study.* New York: Wiley.

Toufexis, A. (1987, September 14). A question of black pride. *Time,* p. 74.

Tourangeau, R., & Rasinski, K. A. (1988). Cognitive processes underlying context effects in attitude measurement. *Psychological Bulletin, 103,* 299–314.

Tourangeau, R., Rips, L., & Rasinski, K. (2000). *The psychology of survey response.* Cambridge, England: Cambridge University Press.

Tourangeau, R., Smith, T., & Rasinski, K. (1997). Motivation to report sensitive behaviors on surveys: Evidence from a bogus pipeline experiment. *Journal of Applied Social Psychology, 27,* 209–222.

Tourangeau, R., Steiger, D. M., & Wilson, D. (2002). Self-administered questions by telephone: Evaluating interactive voice responses. *Public Opinion Quarterly, 66,* 265–278.

Traugott, M. W. (1987). The importance of persistence in respondent selection for preelection surveys. *Public Opinion Quarterly, 51,* 48–57.

Traugott, M. W. (2001). Assessing poll performance in the 2000 campaign. *Public Opinion Quarterly, 65,* 389–419.

Traugott, M. W., & Katosh, J. P. (1979). Response validity in surveys of voting behavior. *Public Opinion Quarterly, 43,* 359–377.

Traugott, M. W., & Tucker, C. (1984). Strategies for predicting whether a citizen will vote and estimation of electoral outcomes. *Public Opinion Quarterly, 48,* 330–343.

Tremblay, K., & Dunlap. R. (1978). Rural–urban and concern with environmental quality: A replication and extension. *Rural Sociology, 43*, 474–491.

Triandis, H. C. (1964). Exploratory factor analyses of the behavioral component of social attitudes. *Journal of Abnormal and Social Psychology, 68*, 420–430.

Triandis, H. C. (1971). *Attitude and attitude change.* New York: Wiley.

Triandis, H. C. (1977). *Interpersonal behavior.* Monterey, CA: Brooks/Cole.

Triandis, H. C., & Triandis, L. M. (1962). A cross-cultural study of social distance. *Psychological Monographs, 76*(No. 21, Whole No. 540).

Trites, R. S. (1997). *Waking sleeping beauty: Feminist voices in children's novels.* Iowa City: University of Iowa Press.

Troldahl, V. C., & Van Dam, R. (1965). Face-to-face communication about major topics in the news. *Public Opinion Quarterly, 29*, 626–634.

Trost, M. R., Cialdini, R. B., & Maass, A. (1989). Effects of an international conflict simulation on perceptions of the Soviet Union: A FIREBREAKS backfire. *Journal of Social Issues, 45*(2), 139–158.

Tuch, S. A., Sigelman, L., & MacDonald, J. A. (1999). The polls—Trends: Race relations and American youth, 1976–1995. *Public Opinion Quarterly, 63*, 109–148.

Tuchman, G. (1978). *Making news: A study in the construction of reality.* New York: Free Press.

Tuckel, P. S., & Tejera, F. (1983). Changing patterns in American voting behavior, 1914–1980. *Public Opinion Quarterly, 47*, 230–246.

Turner, A. G. (1972). *The San Jose methods test of known crime victims.* Washington, DC: National Criminal Justice Information and Statistics Service, U.S. Department of Justice.

Turner, C. F., & Martin, E. (Eds.). (1981). *Surveys of subjective phenomena: Summary report.* Washington, DC: National Academy Press.

Turner, M. A., Fix, M., & Struyk, R. J. (1991). *Opportunities denied, opportunities diminished: Racial discrimination in hiring.* Washington, DC: Urban Institute Press.

Turner, M. E., & Pratkanis, A. R. (1994). Affirmative action: Insights from social psychological and organizational research. *Basic and Applied Social Psychology, 15*, 1–11.

Tuxill, J. (1999). Appreciating the benefits of plant diversity. In L. R. Brown et al., *State of the world 1999* (pp. 96–114). New York: Norton.

Tversky, A., & Kahneman, D. (1974). Judgment under uncertainty: Heuristics and biases. *Science, 185*, 1124–1131.

Tversky, A., & Kahneman, D. (1982). Judgments of and by representativeness. In D. Kahneman, P. Slovic, & A. Tversky (Eds.), *Judgement under uncertainty: Heuristics and biases* (pp. 84–98). Cambridge, England: Cambridge University Press.

Twenge, J. M. (1997a). Attitudes toward women, 1970–1995: A meta-analysis. *Psychology of Women Quarterly, 21*, 35–51.

Twenge, J. M. (1997b). Changes in masculine and feminine traits over time: A meta-analysis. *Sex Roles, 36*, 305–325.

Tybout, A. M., & Scott, C. A. (1983). Availability of well-defined internal knowledge and the attitude formation process: Information aggregation versus self-perception. *Journal of Personality and Social Psychology, 44*, 474–491.

UNESCO. (1960). *Rural television in Japan.* Paris, France: Author.

UNESCO. (1980). *Environmental education in the light of the Tbilisi conference.* Paris, France: Author.

Unger, R. K. (1998). *Resisting gender: Twenty-five years of feminist psychology.* London, England: Sage.

Unger, R. K. (2001). Women as subjects, actors, and agents in the history of psychology. In R. K. Unger (Ed.), *Handbook of the psychology of women and gender* (pp. 3–16). New York: Wiley.

Unger, R. K. (Ed.). (2002). Special feature: Terrorism and its consequences. *Analyses of Social Issues and Public Policy, 2*(1), 1–150

UNICEF. (1995). *State of the world's children.* New York: Author.

U.S. Census Bureau. (1997). *1997 economic census: Professional, scientific, and technical services—United States.* Retrieved September 27, 2002 from http://www.census.gov/epcd/ec97/us/US000_54.HTM

U.S. Census Bureau. (2000). *Statistical abstract of the United States: 2000.* Washington, DC: Author.

U.S. Census Bureau. (2001). *Statistical abstract of the United States: 2001* (121st ed.). Washington, DC, Author.

U.S. Census Bureau. (2002). Advertising estimated expenditures by medium. In *Statistical abstract of the U.S.: 2001* (p. 777). Washington, DC: Author.

U.S. Commission on Civil Rights. (1977). *Reviewing a decade of school desegregation, 1966–1975.* Washington, DC: U.S. Government Printing Office.

U.S. Congress, Office of Technology Assessment. (1979). *The effects of nuclear war.* Washington, DC: Author.

U.S. Department of Energy. (2002a). *Annual energy review, 2001*. Washington, DC: Author. Retrieved March 19, 2003, from http://www.eia.doe.gov/emeu/aer/enduse.html

U.S. Department of Energy. (2002b). *International energy outlook 2002*. Washington, DC: Author. Retrieved March 19, 2003, from http://www.eia.doe.gov/oiaf/ieo/index.html

U.S. Department of Energy. (2002c). *World oil market and oil price chronologies: 1970–2001*. Washington, DC: Author. Retrieved March 19, 2003, from http://www.eia.doe.gov/cabs/chron.html

U.S. Department of Health, Education, and Welfare. (1971). *The institutional guide to DHEW policy on protection of human subjects* (DHEW Publication No. (NIH) 72–102). Washington, DC: U.S. Government Printing Office.

U.S. Department of Labor. (2003a). *Employment characteristics of families in 2002*. Washington, DC: Bureau of Labor Statistics. Retrieved December, 2003, from www.bls.gov.cps

U.S. Department of Labor. (2003b, September). *Highlights of women's earnings in 2002*. Washington, DC: Bureau of Labor Statistics. Retrieved December, 2003, from http://www.bls.gov/cps/cpswom2002.pdf

Valins, S. (1966). Cognitive effects of false heart-rate feedback. *Journal of Personality and Social Psychology, 4*, 400–408.

Vallone, R. P., Ross, L., & Lepper, M. R. (1985). The hostile media phenomenon: Biased perception and perceptions of media bias in coverage of the Beirut massacre. *Journal of Personality and Social Psychology, 49*, 577–585.

Van der Pligt, J., Eiser, R., & Spears, R. (1986). Attitudes toward nuclear energy: Familiarity and salience. *Environment and Behavior, 18*, 75–93.

Van der Pligt, J., Eiser, R., & Spears, R. (1987). Nuclear waste: Facts, fears, and attitudes. *Journal of Applied Social Psychology, 17*, 453–470.

Van Liere, K. D., & Dunlap, R. E. (1980). The social bases of environmental concern: A review of hypotheses, explanations, and empirical evidence. *Public Opinion Quarterly, 44*, 181–197.

Varela, J. A. (1971). *Psychological solutions to social problems: An introduction to social technology.* New York: Academic Press.

Vargas, P. T., von Hippel, W., & Petty, R. E. (2004). Using partially structured attitude measures to enhance the attitude-behavior relationship. *Personality and Social Psychology Bulletin, 30*, 197–211.

Vavreck, L. (2000). How does it all "turnout"? Exposure to attack advertising, campaign interest, and participation in American presidential elections. In L. M. Bartels & L. Vavreck (Eds.), *Campaign reform: Insights and evidence.* Ann Arbor: University of Michigan Press.

Veroff, J., Douvan, E., Orbuch, T., & Acitelli, L. (1998). Happiness in stable marriages: The early years. In T. Bradbury (Ed.), *The developmental course of marital dysfunction* (pp. 152–179). New York: Cambridge University Press.

Vidmar, N., & Rokeach, M. (1974). Archie Bunker's bigotry: A study in selective perception and exposure. *Journal of Communication, 14*(1), 36–47.

Vining, J., & Ebreo, A. (2002). Emerging theoretical and methodological perspectives on conservation behavior. In R. Bechtel & A. Churchman (Eds.), *Handbook of environmental psychology* (pp. 541–558). New York: Wiley.

Viswanath, K., & Finnegan, J. R. (1996). The knowledge gap hypothesis: Twenty-five years later. In B. Burleson (Ed.), *Communication yearbook 19* (pp. 187–227). Thousand Oaks, CA: Sage.

Vitelli, R. (1988). The crisis issue assessed: An empirical analysis. *Basic and Applied Social Psychology, 9*, 301–309.

Vollebergh, W. (1996). The development of authoritarianism in adolescence: Longitudinal change and the impact of age, gender, and educational level. In K. Hurrelmann & S. Hamilton (Eds.), *Social problems and social contexts in adolescence: Perspectives across boundaries* (pp. 235–252). New York: DeGruyter.

von Baeyer, C. L., Sherk, D. L., & Zanna, M. P. (1981). Impression management in the job interview: When the female applicant meets the male "chauvinist" interviewer. *Personality and Social Psychology Bulletin, 7*, 45–51.

von Hippel, W., Sekaquaptewa, D., & Vargas, P. (1995). On the role of encoding processes in stereotype maintenance. In M. P. Zanna (Ed.), *Advances in experimental social psychology* (Vol. 27, pp. 177–254). Orlando, FL: Academic Press.

Voss, D. S., Gelman, A., & King, G. (1995). Pre-election survey methodology: Details from eight polling organizations, 1988 and 1992. *Public Opinion Quarterly, 59*, 98–132.

Wagner, R. V. (2002). September 11, 2001: How can peace psychologists be most helpful? *Peace and Conflict: Journal of Peace Psychology, 8*, 183–186.

Wagner, R. V. (Ed.). (2002a). *Peace and Conflict: Journal of Peace Psychology, 8*(3), 183–299.

Waite, L., & Neilson, M. (2001). The rise of the dual-career family 1963–1997. In R. Hertz & N. Marshall (Eds.), *Working families: The transformation of the American home.* Berkeley: University of California Press.

Walker Research. (1988). *Industry image study* (8th ed.). Indianapolis, IN: Author.

Waller, N. G., Kojetin, B. A., Bouchard, T. J., Lykken, D. T., & Tellegen, A. (1990). Genetic and environmental influences on religious interests, attitudes, and values: A study of twins reared apart and together. *Psychological Science, 1*, 138–142.

Walster, E. (1965). The effect of self-esteem on romantic liking. *Journal of Experimental Social Psychology, 1*, 184–197.

Walter, K. S., & Gillett, H. J. (1997). *IUCN red list of threatened plants*. Cambridge, England: World Conservation Union.

Walther, E. (2002). Guilty by mere association: Evaluative conditioning and the spreading attitude effect. *Journal of Personality and Social Psychology, 82*, 919–934.

Wand, J. N., Shotts, K. W., Sekhon, J. S., Mebane, W. R., Jr., Herron, M. C., & Brady, H. E. (2001). The butterfly did it: The aberrant vote for Buchanan in Palm Beach County, Florida. *American Political Science Review, 95*, 793–810.

Wang, C. K. A. (1932). Suggested criteria for writing attitude statements. *Journal of Social Psychology, 3*, 367–373.

Wanta, W., & Ghanem, S. (2003). Effects of agenda setting. In J. Bryant & R. Carveth (Eds.), *Meta-analyses of media effects*. Mahwah, NJ: Lawrence Erlbaum Associates.

Ware, J. E. (1978). Effects of acquiescent response set on patient satisfaction ratings. *Medical Care, 16*, 327–336.

Warwick, D. P. (1982). Types of harm in social research. In T. L. Beauchamp, R. R. Faden, R. J. Wallace, Jr., & L. R. Walters (Eds.), *Ethical issues in social science research* (pp. 101–124). Baltimore: Johns Hopkins University Press.

Watson, D. (1982). The actor and the observer: How are their perceptions of causality divergent? *Psychological Bulletin, 92*, 682–700.

Wattenberg, M. P. (1984). *The decline of American political parties, 1952–1980*. Cambridge, MA: Harvard University Press.

Wattenberg, M. P. (1987). The hollow realignment: Partisan change in a candidate-centered era. *Public Opinion Quarterly, 51*, 58–74.

Wattenberg, M. P. (2002). *Where have all the voters gone?* Cambridge, MA: Harvard University Press.

Watts, W. A. (1967). Relative persistence of opinion change induced by active compared to passive participation. *Journal of Personality and Social Psychology, 5*, 4–15.

Watts, W. A., & Free, L. A. (1973). *State of the nation*. New York: Universe Books.

Watts, W. A., & Free, L. A. (1974). *State of the nation 1974*. Washington, DC: Potomac Associates.

Watts, W. A., & McGuire, W. J. (1964). Persistence of induced opinion change and retention of inducing message content. *Journal of Abnormal and Social Psychology, 68*, 233–241.

Weakliem, D. (2002). The effects of education on political opinions: An international study. *International Journal of Public Opinion Research, 14*, 141–157.

Weary, G. (1980). Examination of affect and egotism as mediators of bias in causal attributions. *Journal of Personality and Social Psychology, 38*, 348–357.

Weary, G., Harvey, J. H., Schweiger, P., Olson, C. T., Perloff, R., & Pritchard, S., (1982). Self-presentation and the moderation of the self-serving bias. *Social Cognition, 1*, 140–159.

Weary, G., Stanley, M. A., & Harvey, J. H. (1989). *Attribution*. New York: Springer-Verlag.

Webb, E. J., Campbell, D. T., Schwartz, R. D., Sechrest, L., & Grove, J. (1981). *Nonreactive measures in the social sciences* (2nd ed.). Boston: Houghton Mifflin.

Webb, S. G. (1955). Scaling of attitudes by the method of equal-appearing intervals: A review. *Journal of Social Psychology, 42*, 215–239.

Weber, J. G. (1994). The nature of ethnocentric attribution bias: Ingroup protection or enhancement? *Journal of Experimental Social Psychology, 30*, 482–504.

Weber, S. J., & Cook, T. D. (1972). Subject effects in laboratory research: An examination of subject roles, demand characteristics, and valid inference. *Psychological Bulletin, 77*, 273–295.

Weeks, M. E., & Moore, R. E. (1981). Ethnicity-of-interviewer effects on ethnic respondents. *Public Opinion Quarterly, 45*, 245–249.

Wegner, D., & Bargh, J. (1998). Control and automaticity in social life. In D. T. Gilbert, S. T. Fiske, & G. Lindzey (Eds.), *The handbook of social psychology* (4th ed., Vol. 1, pp. 446–496). New York: McGraw-Hill.

Weigel, R. H. (1977). Ideological and demographic correlates of proecology behavior. *Journal of Social Psychology, 103*, 39–47.

Weigel, R. H., Wiser, P. L., & Cook, S. W. (1975). The impact of cooperative learning experiences on cross-ethnic relations and attitudes. *Journal of Social Issues, 31*(1), 219–244.

Weigert, A. J. (1997). *Self, interaction, and natural environment: Refocusing our eyesight*. Albany: State University of New York Press.

Weimann, G. (1994). *The influentials: People who influence people*. Albany: State University of New York Press.

Weiner, J. J., & Wright, F. E. (1973). Effects of undergoing arbitrary discrimination upon subsequent attitudes toward a minority group. *Journal of Applied Social Psychology, 3*, 94–102.

Weisberg, H. E. (1987). The demographics of a new voting gap: Marital differences in American voting. *Public Opinion Quarterly, 51*, 335–343.

Weisfeld, G. E., & Beresford, J. M. (1982). Erectness of posture as a mediator of dominance or success in humans. *Motivation and Emotion, 6*, 113–131.

Weiss, R. F. (1968). An extension of Hullian learning theory to persuasive communication. In A. G. Greenwald, T. C. Brock, & T. M. Ostrom (Eds.), *Psychological foundations of attitudes* (pp. 109–145). New York: Academic Press.

Weiss, W. (1969). Effects of the mass media of communication. In G. Lindzey & E. Aronson (Eds.), *The handbook of social psychology* (2nd ed., Vol. 5, pp. 77–195). Reading, MA: Addison-Wesley.

Weisstein, N. (1971). Psychology constructs the female. In V. Gomick & B. K. Moran (Eds.), *Woman in sexist society: Studies in power and powerlessness* (pp. 207–224). New York: Basic Books.

Weitzman, L. G., Eifler, D., Hokada, E., & Ross, C. (1972). Sex-role socialization in picture books for preschool children. *American Journal of Sociology, 77*, 1125–1149.

Wells, G. L., & Petty, R. E. (1980). The effects of overt head-movements on persuasion: Compatibility and incompatibility of responses. *Basic and Applied Social Psychology, 1*, 219–230.

Wessells, M. (2002). Terrorism, social injustice, and peace building. In C. E. Stout (Ed.), *The psychology of terrorism. Vol. 4: Programs and practices in response and prevention* (pp. 57–73). Westport, CT: Praeger.

Westie, F. R., & DeFleur, M. L. (1959). Autonomic responses and their relationship to race attitudes. *Journal of Abnormal and Social Psychology, 58*, 340–347.

Wheeler, M. (1976). *Lies, damn lies, and statistics: The manipulation of public opinion in America*. New York: Liveright.

White, G. L. (1980). Consensus and justification effects on attitude following counterattitudinal behavior. *Social Psychology Quarterly, 43*, 321–327.

White, J. E. (2000, November 27). The real winners: Black voters. *Time*, p. 60.

White, L. (1967). The historic roots of our ecological crisis. *Science, 55*, 1203–1207.

White, P. A., & Younger, D. P. (1988). Differences in the ascription of transient internal states to self and other. *Journal of Experimental Social Psychology, 24*, 292–309.

White, R. K. (1966). "Socialism" and "capitalism": An international misunderstanding. *Foreign Affairs, 44*, 216–228.

White, R. K. (1970). *Nobody wanted war: Misperception in Vietnam and other wars* (rev. ed.). Garden City, NY: Doubleday.

White, R. K. (1984). *Fearful warriors: A psychological profile of U.S.–Soviet relations*. New York: Free Press.

White, R. K. (1985). Ten psychological contributions to the prevention of nuclear war. In S. Oskamp (Ed.), *International conflict and national public policy issues: Applied social psychology annual 6* (pp. 45–61). Beverly Hills, CA: Sage.

Whyte, K. M. (1990). *Dating, mating, and marriage*. New York: Aldine de Gruyter.

Wicker, A. W. (1969). Attitudes versus actions: The relationship of verbal and overt behavioral responses to attitude objects. *Journal of Social Issues, 25*, 41–78.

Wicklund, R. A. (1974). *Freedom and reactance*. Potomac, MD: Lawrence Erlbaum Associates.

Wicklund, R. A., & Brehm, J. W. (1976). *Perspectives on cognitive dissonance*. Hillsdale, NJ: Lawrence Erlbaum Associates.

Wiest, W. M. (1965). A quantitative extension of Heider's theory of cognitive balance applied to interpersonal perception and self-esteem. *Psychological Monographs, 79*(1, Whole No. 607).

Wilcox, B. L. (1987). Pornography, social science, and politics: When research and ideology collide. *American Psychologist, 42*, 941–943.

Wilcox, L. D., Brooks, R. M., Beal, G. M., & Klonglan, G. E. (1972). *Social indicators and societal monitoring: An annotated bibliography*. San Francisco: Jossey-Bass.

Wilder, D. A., & Cooper, W. E. (1981). Categorization into groups: Consequences for social perception and attribution. In J. H. Harvey, W. J. Ickes, & R. F. Kidd (Eds.), *New directions in attribution research* (Vol. 3, pp. 247–277). Hillsdale, NJ: Lawrence Erlbaum Associates.

Wilker, H. R., & Milbrath, L. W. (1970). Political belief systems and political behavior. *Social Science Quarterly, 51*, 477–493.

Wilkins, S., & Miller, T. A. W. (1985). Working women: How it's working out. *Public Opinion, 8*(5), 44–48.

Williams, F., LaRose, R., & Frost, F. (1981). *Children, television, and sex-role stereotyping*. New York: Praeger.

Williams, J. A., Jr., Vernon, J. A., Williams, M. C., & Malecha, K. (1987). Sex role socialization in picture books: An update. *Social Science Quarterly, 68*, 148–156.

Williams, J. E., & Bennett, S. M. (1975). The definition of sex stereotypes via the adjective check list. *Sex Roles, 1*, 327–337.

Williams, J. E., & Best, D. L. (1982). *Measuring sex stereotypes: A thirty-nation study.* Beverly Hills, CA: Sage.

Williams, J. E., & Best, D. L. (1990). *Measuring sex stereotypes: A multinational study.* Newbury Park, CA: Sage.

Williams, J. E., & Morland, J. K. (1976). *Race, color, and the young child.* Chapel Hill: University of North Carolina Press.

Williams, J. E., & Morland, J. K. (1979). Comment on Banks's "White preference in blacks: A paradigm in search of a phenomenon." *Psychological Bulletin, 86*, 28–32.

Willimack, D. K., Schuman, H., Pennell, B-E., & Lepkowski, J. M. (1995). Effects of a prepaid nonmonetary incentive on response rates and response quality in a face-to-face survey. *Public Opinion Quarterly, 59*, 78–92.

Wilson, D. W., & Donnerstein, E. (1976). Legal and ethical aspects of nonreactive social psychological research: An excursion into the public mind. *American Psychologist, 31*, 765–773.

Wilson, E., & Sherrell, D. (1993). Source effects in communication and persuasion research: A meta-analysis of effect size. *Journal of the Academy of Marketing Science, 21*, 101–112.

Wilson, T. C. (1991). Urbanism, migration, and tolerance: A reassessment. *American Sociological Review, 56*, 117–123.

Wilson, T. C. (1994). Trends in tolerance toward rightist and leftist groups, 1976–1988. *Public Opinion Quarterly, 58*, 539–556.

Wilson, T. D., & Hodges, S. (1992). Attitudes as temporary constructions. In L. Martin & A. Tesser (Eds.), *The construction of social judgments* (pp. 37–66). New York: Springer-Verlag.

Wilson, T. D., & Linville, P. W. (1982). Improving the academic performance of college freshmen: Attribution therapy revisited. *Journal of Personality and Social Psychology, 42*, 367–376.

Wilson, W., & Miller, H. (1968). Repetition, order of presentation, and timing of arguments and measures as determinants of opinion change. *Journal of Personality and Social Psychology, 9*, 184–188.

Wilson, W. R. (1979). Feeling more than we can know: Exposure effects without learning. *Journal of Personality and Social Psychology, 37*, 811–821.

Winston, A. S. (1996). "As his name indicates": R. S. Woodworth's letters of reference and employment for Jewish psychologists in the 1930s. *Journal of the History of the Behavioral Sciences, 32*, 30–43.

Winter, D. (2002). (En)gendering sustainable development. In P. Schmuck & P. W. Schultz (Eds.), *Psychology of sustainable development* (pp. 79–96). Boston: Kluwer Academic.

Wise, D. (1968, November 3). The twilight of a president. *New York Times Magazine*, p. 27.

Witte, K., & Allen, M. (2000). A meta-analysis of fear appeals: Implications for effective public health campaigns. *Health Education and Behavior, 27*, 591–615.

Wittenbraker, J., Gibbs, B. L., & Kahle, L. R. (1983). Seat belt attitudes, habits, and behaviors: An adaptive amendment to the Fishbein model. *Journal of Applied Social Psychology, 13*, 406–421.

Wittenbrink, B., Judd, C. M., & Park, B. (1997). Evidence for racial prejudice at the implicit level and its relationship with questionnaire measures. *Journal of Personality and Social Psychology, 72*, 262–274.

Wittenbrink, B., Judd, C. M., & Park, B. (2001). Spontaneous prejudice in context: Variability in automatically activated attitudes. *Journal of Personality and Social Psychology, 81*, 815–827.

Wlezien, C. (1995). The public as thermostat: The dynamics of preferences for spending. *American Journal of Political Science, 39*, 981–1000.

Wlezien, C. (2001). On forecasting the presidential vote. *PS: Political Science and Politics, 34*, 25–31.

Wolfgang, M. E., & Weiner, N. A. (Eds.). (1982). *Criminal violence.* Beverly Hills, CA: Sage.

Wolfinger, R., & Linquiti, P. (1981). Tuning in and turning out. *Public Opinion, 4*(1), 56–60.

Women on Words and Images. (1975). *Dick and Jane as victims. Sex stereotyping in children's readers.* Princeton, NJ: Author.

Women's Action Alliance. (1981). *The radio and television commercial monitoring project: Summary report.* New York: Author.

Wood, B. D., & Anderson, A. H. (1998). The dynamics of senatorial representation, 1952–1991. *Journal of Politics, 60*, 705–736.

Wood, J. M., Nezworski, M. T., Lilienfeld, S., & Garb, H. (2003). *What's wrong with the Rorschach? Science confronts the controversial inkblot test.* San Francisco: Jossey-Bass.

Wood, W. (2000). Attitude change: Persuasion and social influence. *Annual Review of Psychology, 51*, 539–570.

Wood, W., & Eagly, A. H. (2002). A cross-cultural analysis of the behavior of women and men: Implications for the origins of sex differences. *Psychological Bulletin, 128*, 699–727.

Wood, W., Lundgren, S., Ouellette, J., Busceme, S., & Blackstone, T. (1994). Minority influence: A meta-analytic review of social influence processes. *Psychological Bulletin, 115*, 323–345.

Wood, W., Pool, G. J., Leck, K., & Purvis, D. (1996). Self-definition, defensive processing, and influence: The normative impact of majority and minority groups. *Journal of Personality and Social Psychology, 71*, 1181–1193.

Wood, W., & Quinn, J. (2003). Forewarned and forearmed? Two meta-analysis syntheses of forewarnings of influence appeals. *Psychological Bulletin, 129*, 119–138.

Worcester, R. M. (1980). Pollsters, the press, and political polling in Britain. *Public Opinion Quarterly, 44*, 548–566.

Worcester, R. M. (1984). The polls: Britain at the polls 1945–1983. *Public Opinion Quarterly, 48*, 824–833.

Worcester, R. M. (1987). The internationalization of public opinion research. *Public Opinion Quarterly, 51*, s79–s85.

Worell, J. (Ed.). (2001). *Encyclopedia of women and gender: Sex similarities and differences and the impact of society on gender.* San Diego: Academic Press.

World Resources Institute. (2002). *World resources 2000–2001.* Retrieved April, 2003, from http://www.wri.org/wri/wr2000/index.html

Wright, R. A., & Brehm, S. S. (1982). Reactance as impression management: A critical review. *Journal of Personality and Social Psychology, 42*, 608–618.

Wrightsman, L. S. (1969). Wallace supporters and adherence to "law and order." *Journal of Personality and Social Psychology, 13*, 17–22.

Wybrow, R. J. (1984, May). *A view from across the Atlantic: British attitudes towards America's world role.* Paper presented at American Association for Public Opinion Research meeting, Delavan, WI.

Wyer, R. S. (Ed.). (1997). *The automaticity of everyday life.* Mahwah, NJ: Lawrence Erlbaum Associates.

Wyer, R. S., Jr., & Gordon, S. E. (1982). The recall of information about persons and groups. *Journal of Experimental Social Psychology, 18*, 128–164.

Wyer, R. S., Jr., & Srull, T. K. (Eds.). (1994). *Handbook of social cognition* (2nd ed.). Hillsdale, NJ: Lawrence Erlbaum Associates.

Wyner, G. A. (1980). Response errors in self-reported number of arrests. *Sociological Methods and Research, 9*, 161–177.

Yalch, R. F. (1976). Interview effects on voter turnout. *Public Opinion Quarterly, 40*, 331–336.

Yang, S. J., & Alba, R. D. (1992). Urbanism and nontraditional opinion: A test of Fischer's subcultural theory. *Social Science Quarterly, 73*, 596–609.

Yankelovich, D. (1981). *New rules: Searching for self-fulfillment in a world turned upside down.* New York: Random House.

Yatani, C., & Bramel, D. (1989). Trends and patterns in Americans' attitudes toward the Soviet Union. *Journal of Social Issues, 45*(2), 13–32.

Yinger, J. (1996). *Closed doors, opportunities lost: The continuing costs of housing discrimination.* New York: Russell Sage Foundation.

Youniss, J. (1980). *Parents and peers in social development.* Chicago: University of Chicago Press.

Zajonc, R. B. (1968a). Attitudinal effects of mere exposure. *Journal of Personality and Social Psychology, 9*(2, Pt. 2), 1–27.

Zajonc, R. B. (1968b). Cognitive theories in social psychology. In G. Lindzey & E. Aronson (Eds.), *The handbook of social psychology* (2nd ed., Vol. 1, pp. 320–411). Reading, MA: Addison-Wesley.

Zajonc, R. B. (1980). Feeling and thinking: Preferences need no inferences. *American Psychologist, 35*, 151–175.

Zajonc, R. B. (2000). Feeling and thinking: Closing the debate over the independence of affect. In J. P. Forgas (Ed.), *Feeling and thinking: The role of affect in social cognition* (pp. 31–58). Cambridge, UK: Cambridge University Press.

Zajonc, R. B. (2001). Mere exposure: A gateway to the subliminal. *Current Directions in Psychological Science, 10*, 224–228.

Zaller, J. R. (1987). Diffusion of political attitudes. *Journal of Personality and Social Psychology, 53*, 821–833.

Zaller, J. R. (1992). *The nature and origins of mass opinion.* Cambridge, England: Cambridge University Press.

Zanna, M. P. (1990). On using a theory of knowledge acquisition to acquire knowledge. *Psychological Inquiry, 1*, 217–219.

Zanna, M. P., & Cooper, J. (1974). Dissonance and the pill: An attribution approach to studying the arousal properties of dissonance. *Journal of Personality and Social Psychology, 29*, 703–709.

Zanna, M. P., & Fazio, R. H. (1982). The attitude-behavior relation: Moving toward a third generation of research. In M. P. Zanna, E. T. Higgins, & C. P. Herman (Eds.), *Consistency in social behavior: The Ontario Symposium* (Vol. 2, pp. 283–301). Hillsdale, NJ: Lawrence Erlbaum Associates.

Zanna, M. P., Higgins, E. T., & Herman, C. P. (Eds.). (1982). *Consistency in social behavior: The Ontario Symposium* (Vol. 2). Hillsdale, NJ: Lawrence Erlbaum Associates.

Zanna, M. P., Kiesler, C. A., & Pilkonis, P. A. (1970). Positive and negative attitudinal affect established by classical conditioning. *Journal of Personality and Social Psychology, 14*, 321–328.

Zanna, M. P., & Rempel, J. K. (1988). Attitudes: A new look at an old concept. In D. Bar-Tal & A. W. Kruglanski (Eds.), *The social psychology of knowledge* (pp. 315–334). Cambridge, England: Cambridge University Press.

Zanna, M. P., & Sande, G. N. (1987). The effects of collective actions on the attitudes of individual group members: A dissonance analysis. In M. P. Zanna, J. M. Olson, & C. P. Herman (Eds.), *Social influence: The Ontario Symposium* (Vol. 5, pp. 151–163). Hillsdale, NJ: Lawrence Erlbaum Associates.

Zavalloni, M., & Cook, S. W. (1965). Influence of judges' attitudes on ratings of favorableness of statements about a social group. *Journal of Personality and Social Psychology, 1*, 43–54.

Zelezny, L., Chua, P. P., & Aldrich, C. (2000). Elaborating on gender differences in environmentalism. *Journal of Social Issues, 56*, 443–455.

Ziegler, R., Diehl, M., & Ruther, A. (2002). Multiple source characteristics and persuasion: Source inconsistency as a determinant of message scrutiny. *Personality and Social Psychology Bulletin, 28*, 496–508.

Zillmann, D. (1992). Pornography research, social advocacy, and public policy. In P. Suedfeld & P. Tetlock (Eds.), *Psychology and social policy* (pp. 165–189). New York: Hemisphere.

Zimbardo, P. G. (1960). Involvement and communication discrepancy as determinants of opinion conformity. *Journal of Abnormal and Social Psychology, 60*, 86–94.

Zimbardo, P. G., Weisenberg, M., Firestone, I., & Levy, B. (1965). Communicator effectiveness in producing public conformity and private attitude change. *Journal of Personality, 33*, 233–255.

Zinsmeister, K. (1988). Black demographics. *Public Opinion, 10*(5), 41–44.

Zuckerman, D. M., Singer, D. G., & Singer, J. L. (1980). Children's television viewing, racial and sex-role attitudes. *Journal of Applied Social Psychology, 10*, 281–294.

Zuckerman, M., Mann, R. W., & Bernieri, F. J. (1982). Determinants of consensus estimates: Attribution, salience, and representativeness. *Journal of Personality and Social Psychology, 42*, 839–852.

Name Index

Subject Index